Fodor's

BEST ROAD TRIPS IN THE USA

T0400847

TOP REASONS TO GO

★ **Iconic Drives:** From the Blue Ridge Parkway to the Pacific Coast Highway.

★ **Roadside Attractions:** The perfect places to stretch your legs along the way.

★ **Favorites Eats:** Eat at foodie destinations and diners only the locals know about.

★ **Getting There:** Take the fastest route or meander along the road less traveled.

★ **Where to Sleep:** Discover the best national park lodges or beachfront getaways.

★ **Shop Therapy:** Sample local delicacies and uncover one-of-a-kind artworks.

Welcome to the Road

Americans didn't invent the road trip—that honor goes to Germany's adventurous Bertha Benz, whose husband patented the first gas-powered carriage in 1886—but they did perfect it. They opened the first gas station (in Pittsburgh in 1905), paved the first modern highway (in New York in 1911), and pioneered a new kind of lodging called the "motor hotel" (in California's San Luis Obispo in 1925). Although today you might be searching for different amenities, such as a place to plug in your car, the lure of the open road still draws tens of millions of travelers every year.

The themes that can inspire a great road trip are as varied and alluring as the United States itself. Taking in unparalleled natural beauty has always called drivers to explore the narrow and winding routes of America's national parks, from Glacier's fabled Going-to-the-Sun Road to Acadia's rugged Park Loop Road.

But scenic roads can also deliver us back through time, showing us how momentous events in the past shaped the present. You can explore the backroads that link Revolutionary War battlefields in the Mid-Atlantic region and both Civil Rights and Civil War sites in the Southeast. Other adventures can fuel our passions for specific interests, such as driving among the historic blues and Cajun clubs of the Mississippi River Delta, the classic baseball stadiums and Frank Lloyd Wright architecture of the Midwest, and the International Dark Sky sites of the Southwest.

Sometimes the itinerary of a delightful road trip simply captures the eclectic charms of a particular corner of America, offering noteworthy local breakfast places, neighborhood bistros, and craft breweries along the way.

On that note, remember that the most satisfying road trips are a mix of stopping and going. It's when you step out of your car and interact with locals that you develop a truly authentic understanding of the region you're visiting.

As you plan your upcoming road trip, please reconfirm that places are still open and let us know when we need to make updates by writing to us at ✍ *corrections@fodors.com*.

Contents

MAPS

Chapter 1

EXPERIENCE THE BEST ROAD TRIPS IN THE USA

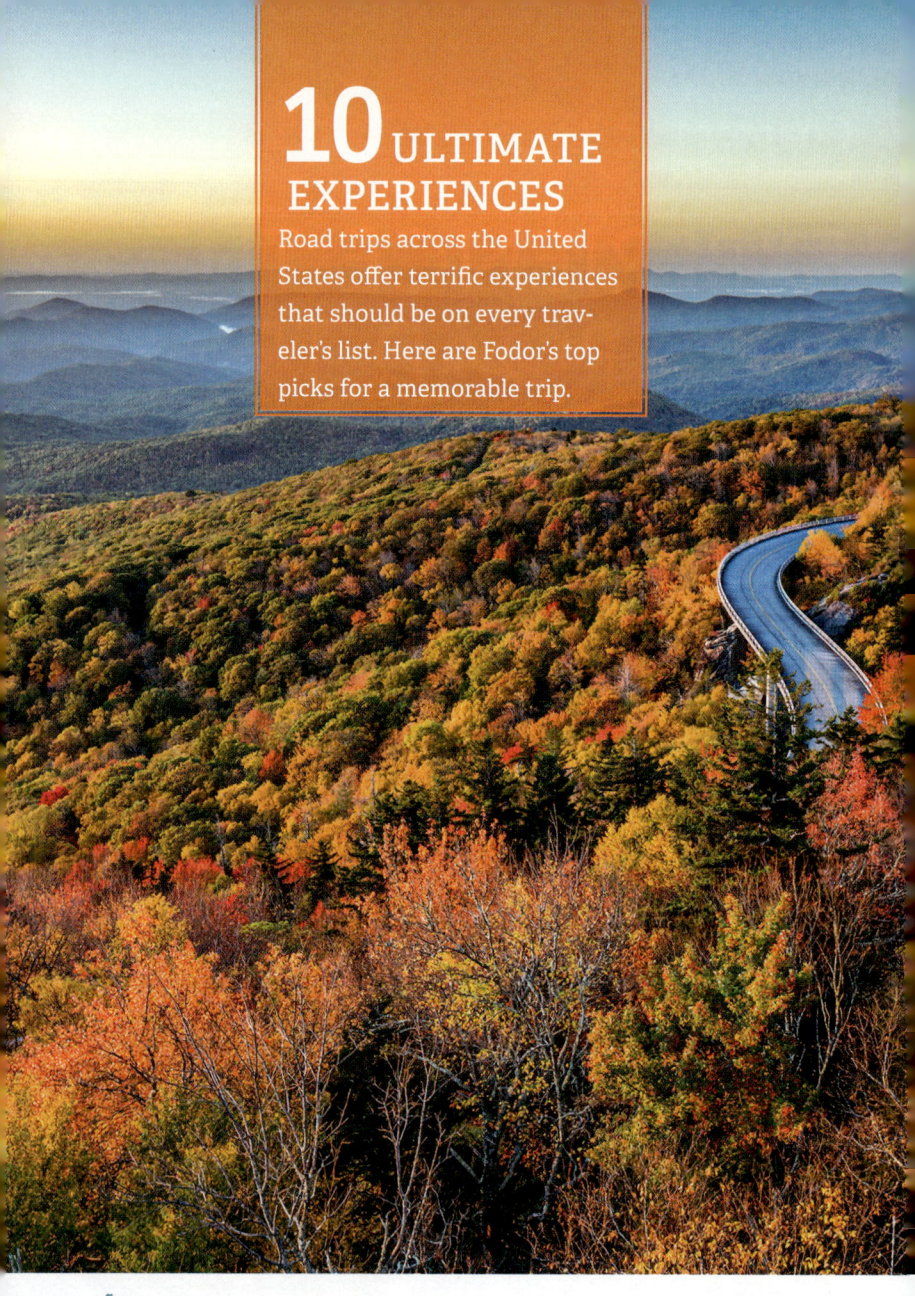

10 ULTIMATE EXPERIENCES

Road trips across the United States offer terrific experiences that should be on every traveler's list. Here are Fodor's top picks for a memorable trip.

1 The Blue Ridge Parkway

Running 469 miles through North Carolina and Virginia, this scenic mountain drive links Great Smoky Mountains and Shenandoah National Parks, taking you through stunning Appalachian vistas and charming small towns. *(Ch. 7)*

2 The Going-to-the-Sun Road

One of the West's most magnificent drives, this 50-mile-long road spans the width of Glacier National Park. *(Chs. 2, 4)*

3 Florida Keys Scenic Highway

Florida's "Overseas Highway" is a destination unto itself, one that crosses 42 bridges over water, including the Seven Mile Bridge. *(Ch. 7)*

4 The Road to Hana

One of the world's most famous drives, this precarious Maui road has more than 600 curves and crosses some 50 gulch-straddling bridges in just 52 coastline miles. *(Ch. 9)*

5 The Million Dollar Highway

Whether named for the cost of building it or the incredible views, this 25-mile highway in southwestern Colorado is a breathtaking journey through the San Juan Skyway. *(Ch. 4)*

6 Monument Valley

This remarkably remote region of Arizona and Utah is impossible to view in a single frame. A scenic 17-mile strip of Valley Drive will have you channeling Ansel Adams. *(Ch. 5)*

7 The High Road to Taos

For a scenic adventure, drive the 56 miles between Taos and Santa Fe via this breathtaking alpine route through quaint Spanish-colonial villages and past sweeping vistas. *(Ch. 5)*

8 Lake Champlain Byway

For classic New England vistas, travel along the 185-mile route that borders Vermont's Lake Champlain; it's especially scenic during peak fall foliage season. *(Ch. 8)*

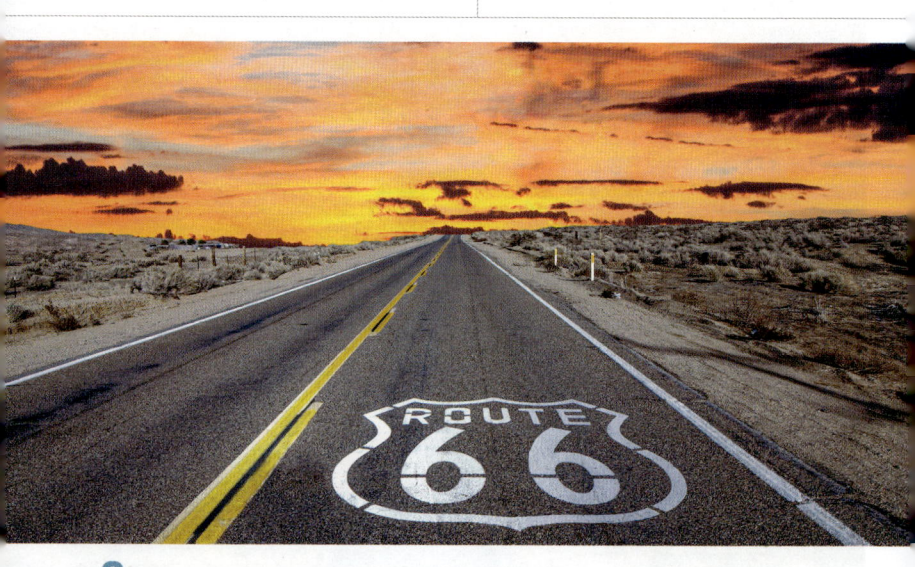

9 Historic Route 66

The Mother Road, spanning Chicago to Los Angeles, was one of America's first national highways and still provides travelers with a classic Americana experience. *(Ch. 2)*

10 The Pacific Coast Highway

One of the world's most spectacular coastal drives, Highway 1 winds around the Pacific Ocean and through jagged mountains and redwood trees. *(Ch. 3)*

Best Iconic Landmarks

GOLDEN GATE BRIDGE

Named for the mile-long strait at the mouth of San Francisco Bay that it crosses, this suspension bridge is known around the world for its graceful towers and rusty orange color. (It was originally intended to be blue and yellow, but the color of the primer stuck.)

MOUNT RUSHMORE

South Dakota's Black Hills would be famous without it, but this colossal sculpture of four presidents—Washington, Jefferson, Lincoln, and, slightly behind the other three, Theodore Roosevelt—makes them unforgettable. Created by artist Gutzon Borglum, Mount Rushmore's design changed several times before debuting in 1941.

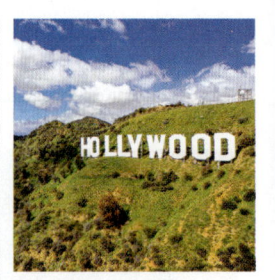

HOLLYWOOD SIGN

Fun fact: these 50-foot letters didn't originally spell "Hollywood." They advertised "Hollywood-land," an upscale real estate development. When they fell into disrepair, the city of Los Angeles came to the rescue with a new coat of paint, removing the last four letters in the process.

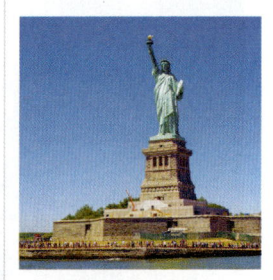

STATUE OF LIBERTY

People throw the word *iconic* around a lot these days, but New York's Statue of Liberty is perhaps the one landmark that truly represents the United States in the eyes of the world. You can visit the island, but the best way to enjoy the statue is standing on the deck of the (free) Staten Island Ferry.

SPACE NEEDLE
Built for the World's Fair in 1962, Seattle's 604-foot Space Needle is an unforgettable part of the Seattle skyline. The futuristic design was a compromise between two powerful men, one who wanted it to look like a balloon, the other like a flying saucer.

EDMUND PETTUS BRIDGE
The most potent symbol of America's Civil Rights struggle is this bridge outside Selma, Alabama. In 1965, state troopers brutally attacked 400 mostly African American demonstrators peacefully marching to Montgomery.

TAOS PUEBLO
One of the oldest continuously inhabited communities in the United States, Taos Pueblo is both a UNESCO World Heritage site and a National Historic Landmark. The adobe structures were originally home to the Ancestral Puebloan people.

Washington Monument

GATEWAY ARCH
The nation's tallest monument, the 630-foot St. Louis Gateway Arch provides sweeping views of the Mississippi River. (A futuristic tram whisks you to the top.) Don't miss the museum, which strives to weave in the stories of Native American people who lived in the region.

WASHINGTON MONUMENT
The world is full of similarly shaped obelisks, but there's something about the 1884 Washington Monument—maybe its location on top of a small hill, or the ring of flags surrounding its base—that inspires us. It's Washington, D.C.'s compass: east is the U.S. Capitol Building, north is the White House, and west is the Lincoln Memorial.

INDEPENDENCE HALL
A UNESCO World Heritage site, this 18th-century landmark is where the Declaration of Independence and the Constitution were adopted. It's the centerpiece of Philadelphia's Independence National Historical Park, home to the Liberty Bell, Congress Hall, and more.

Best National Parks

GRAND CANYON

You'll never forget your first visit to Arizona's Grand Canyon, gazing down at the seemingly endless expanse from the South Rim. Repeat visitors come for hiking, horseback riding, or whitewater rafting.

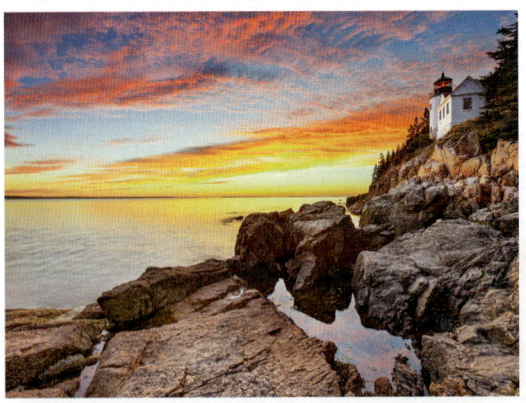

ACADIA

It includes 17 other islands and parts of the mainland, but most visitors to this coastal paradise in Maine stick to easily accessible Mount Desert Island. Bike the carriage roads, hike lofty Cadillac Mountain, or trek to Bass Harbor Head Lighthouse.

ARCHES

It took millions of years for erosion to form the sandstone arches that give this Utah park its name. Delicate Arch is the most famous and Landscape Arch is the longest, but there are more than 2,000 others to grab your attention, making this the largest collection of natural arches in the world.

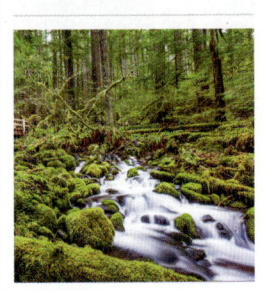

OLYMPIC

Covering 1 million acres, Washington State's jewel in the crown offers what is essentially three parks in one, with glacier-topped mountains, misty primeval forests filled with evergreens, and pristine beaches where you can set up camp and watch the waves roll in past sea stacks.

GREAT SMOKY MOUNTAINS
The country's most popular national park—partly because it sits close to large cities in Tennessee (Gatlinburg and Pigeon Forge) and North Carolina (Bryson City and Cherokee)—the Great Smoky Mountains are especially beautiful for hiking and camping in spring and fall.

YELLOWSTONE
Occupying the northwest corner of Wyoming and parts of Montana and Idaho, the country's first national park is known for the Old Faithful geyser, but it's dotted with steaming pools and bubbling mud pots, too.

DEATH VALLEY
Straddling the border of California and Nevada, Death Valley is the hottest place in the United States. It sets other records, being the driest (barely two inches of rain a year) and the lowest (282 feet below sea level) national park.

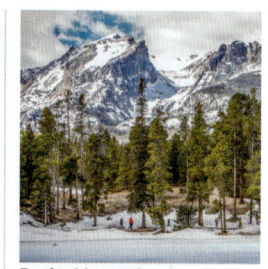

Rocky Mountain

YOSEMITE
The record-breaking granite peak of El Capitan gets star billing, but this 1,200-square-mile park in California's Sierra Nevada mountains has plenty of superlatives, including Yosemite Falls, the country's tallest waterfall.

ROCKY MOUNTAIN
Since it's split in two by the Continental Divide, the eastern half of this Colorado park is craggy mountains, while the western half is lush, green forests.

ZION
Other parks offer wide-open spaces, but Utah's Zion offers breathtaking spots like The Narrows, a slot canyon that is less than 20 feet wide in many places. Its soaring red cliffs attract casual hikers and serious rock climbers.

DENALI
With North America's highest mountain at its center, Denali showcases an untamed Alaskan landscape teeming with wildlife and stunning vistas.

Experience the Best Road Trips in the USA

1

BEST NATIONAL PARKS

Best Roadside Attractions

THE ENCHANTED HIGHWAY

If you're near Regent, North Dakota, locals will steer you to this 32-mile stretch of road north of town lined with metal sculptures. Massive pheasants dash across the plain, huge grasshoppers nibble on leaves, and trout leap from imaginary streams. The gift shop in Regent sells miniature versions of the larger-than-life sculptures.

CADILLAC RANCH

Outside the Texas town of Amarillo—mentioned prominently in the song "Route 66"—is this way-out art project. The brainchild of several San Francisco hippies, it's a series of 10 spray-painted Cadillacs buried grill-first in a pasture.

LUCY THE ELEPHANT

Built in 1881 just outside Atlantic City, New Jersey, to promote real estate sales and tourism, this six-story structure is now America's oldest-surviving roadside attraction; Lucy is now even a popular overnight rental on Airbnb.

HOLE N' THE ROCK

Within Utah's Canyonlands, Hole N' the Rock is a 5,000-square-foot home that was carved out of a huge sandstone rock in the early 1970s. You can take a guided tour of the home or visit its gift shop and trading post.

PRADA MARFA
Way out in the Texan desert, 26 miles northwest of the funky art town of Marfa, you'll find this art installation that captures a Prada storefront stuck in time in 2005.

CABAZON DINOSAURS
A frequent stop for anyone heading to Palm Springs and Joshua Tree from Los Angeles, the Cabazon Dinosaurs consist of two huge steel-and-concrete dinos; you can even go inside the brontosaurus to visit the small gift shop.

BLUE WHALE OF CATOOSA
Rising out of its own little lake near Catoosa, Oklahoma, the Blue Whale is one of the region's most whimsical sights. Built in the 1970s as an anniversary present, it's taken on a life of its own as a tourist attraction.

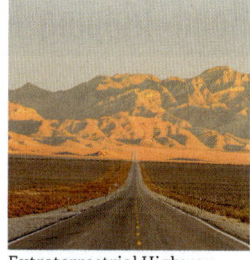
Extraterrestrial Highway

MYSTERY HOLE
This spot in Fayetteville, West Virginia, is the perfect example of the kitschy, side-show-esque roadside attractions of yore. The underground series of rooms are built at different angles to give the illusion of not following the laws of gravity.

EXTRATERRESTRIAL HIGHWAY
As Nevada Route 375 makes its way around mysterious Area 51 in the Nevada desert, it becomes the tourism-inspired Extraterrestrial Highway, where alien-inspired landmarks, restaurants, and shops abound.

Road-Tripping 101

USING THIS GUIDE

These trips are jam-packed with suggestions for making the most of your road trip and seeing the best of the regions they cover. They are designed for the road-tripper who actually enjoys being on the road and who believes the journey is really the biggest part of the adventure. Most of these trips suggest staying only one night at each destination, and while a two- or three-hour drive per day is typical, some days you'll see five or even more hours of driving. You can easily mix and match the destinations of our itineraries so they work for you and your optimal driving schedule.

Our trips were designed with the typical vacation schedule in mind, so if you have time to extend your trip and spend more time at certain destinations, feel free. Ultimately these trips are meant to act as inspiration for your road-trip travels, providing a framework for the best way to see these regions and the unmissable stops along the way.

WHEN TO GO

In a country as vast and diverse as the United States, there's no bad time to do a road trip, and you'll find trips in this book that work with any season. But it's still important to be smart as certain regions of the country can have more severe winters than others. It's a good idea to avoid a winter road trip in any place that regularly sees snow; indeed, many destinations have sights and hotels that close during this time. National parks can be particularly fraught to drive through during the winter, and some roads are closed seasonally. Depending on your destination, summer can also be a tricky time to hit the open road. Hurricanes and wildfires are big issues in the South and the West, and while you can't predict when they might hit, you can be prepared in case they happen while you're there. Beach and lake destinations tend to get booked up far in advance, so it's best to plan ahead if your summertime trip involves water. Generally, spring and fall are the best times to enjoy a road trip in the United States, no matter where you might be headed.

CAR RENTALS

All these trips begin and end at cities with major airports, with plenty of rental car companies to choose from. Not all the trips are round-trips, so be sure that your rental company also exists in your final destination and be prepared for potential extra fees to drop off at a different location.

Always reserve your rental car before arriving. To rent a car, you need a valid driver's license and to be at least 25 years old. Many companies will still rent to those younger than 25 for an additional fee. Note that there are also often fees for adding additional drivers. Always be sure you have insurance for your rental car; you can purchase it from the rental agency or if you already have your own insurance or have a credit card that provides this rental car coverage, confirm this before your trip.

BEFORE YOU GO

Be sure that your driver's license is up to date as is your vehicle registration and car insurance information if you're driving your own car. It's smart to take your car into a shop for a tune-up and oil change before you leave. Be sure to pack an emergency kit to keep in your car at all times; this should include a first aid kit, extra water, a blanket, a flashlight, and extra batteries; make sure your car also has a spare tire, flares, and jumper cables. If you're able, it's not a bad idea to splurge for a AAA membership for your trip just in case (or check to see if your car insurance policy has emergency roadside service). If you're planning on relying on your phone for directions, download the maps covering the areas you're headed to before you set out and make sure you have a workable setup to mount your phone on your car's dashboard (or a reliable copilot). Be sure to plan your route out in advance, and it's not a bad idea to do so on a physical road atlas in case you lose Wi-Fi or your phone dies. And, of course, make sure you bring the appropriate cables to keep your phone charged in your car and at your accommodations.

PACKING LIST

Aside from the essentials mentioned above, your packing list should reflect the destination you're traveling to. It's always good to bring layers for a car ride as well as a reusable water bottle. Make sure you also bring some cash and change for tolls or any cash-only businesses. And, of course, don't forget about your favorite road trip snacks.

RULES OF THE ROAD

Always be sure to obey traffic laws and speed limits and never text and drive. Some recommended stops include wineries or pubs, so be sure to drive responsibly. Remember to be aware of when you're crossing state lines, as laws (especially speed limits) can change. If you're entering California, be prepared to stop at an agricultural inspection station, designed to prevent nonnative species of plants and animals from interfering with the state's careful ecosystem. You're not allowed to bring certain foods and plants into the state, so be sure to check in advance if you're planning on picking up any snacks on a trip that ends in California.

TRAFFIC

Travel times in this book don't factor in possible traffic delays, which are an inevitable factor on any major road trip. Be sure to check travel times before you leave for the day, and if you have hotel reservations, leave early enough to avoid or account for traffic. It can be helpful to be flexible in terms of your stops, too. Make a list of the places you want to visit en route in order of importance to you; that way you know what to cut in case traffic hits. Coastal destinations in the summertime are notorious for traffic, so if you're on a summer road trip, be sure to factor traffic times into your planning.

TIME ZONES

Depending on your trip, it's quite possible you'll end up passing into one or more of the continental United States' four time zones. Be prepared for this in your travel plans and update your car's clock as needed.

SAFETY

Aside from having a good emergency kit in your car, the most important thing to keep in mind while setting off on a road trip is to know your limits. Long hours on the road can take their toll, so be sure to listen to your body if you're getting tired. Switch off driving with your travel companions regularly or don't hesitate to take a break if you need it. Make sure to book all your accommodations in advance so you aren't left without a place to stay. It's a good idea to fill your gas tank at the start of every travel day; if you know your day's route will be particularly remote, look up the nearest gas stations in advance so you can plan on them if you need it. And be sure to look at the weather forecast for all your destinations, especially if you're going to be traveling through different regions. The American landscape can vary drastically, even in the same season, so be prepared for what you might encounter weather-wise at each destination.

What to Read and Watch

BLUE HIGHWAYS BY WILLIAM LEAST HEAT-MOON

In this candid, evocative 1982 memoir, the author sets out from his home in Missouri in a ragged old van to traverse the Lower 48 states, meeting odd characters and encountering fascinating landscapes along the way.

CARS

This Pixar classic doesn't involve a road trip, but its cast of anthropomorphic cars will definitely give you a deeper appreciation for the many vehicles you'll pass on your journey. Most of the movie takes place in the fictional town of Radiator Springs, once a stop on Historic Route 66.

LITTLE MISS SUNSHINE

In this 2006 film, a dysfunctional family takes a cross-country trip in a yellow VW bus in order to help their daughter win the Little Miss Sunshine beauty pageant.

NOMADLAND

Moviegoers are fascinated with tales of people who leave everything behind and follow their dreams. This 2021 film features Oscar winner Frances McDormand as Fern, a down-on-her-luck woman who buys a van and joins a community of nomadic people who gather in temporary communities. It just happens to be filmed in some gorgeous spots: Nevada's Black Rock Desert, California's San Bernardino National Forest, and the austerely beautiful Badlands of South Dakota.

LOVECRAFT COUNTRY BY MATT RUFF

Now an HBO miniseries, this horror-esque book set in the Jim Crow era follows a young Black man and his uncle, a writer for a guidebook focusing on traveling while Black, as they travel from Chicago to New England to investigate his father's disappearance.

ON THE ROAD BY JACK KEROUAC

A seminal work of the Beat Generation, this 1957 novel tells the adventures of a group of friends (based on Kerouac and his own counterculture friends) as they set off on a cross-country adventure, enjoying drugs, poetry, and jazz along the way.

THE PRICE OF SALT BY PATRICIA HIGHSMITH

The basis for the movie Carol, this 1952 novel focuses on two women in the 1950s who drive across the country to escape their lives and defy society's expectations.

ROUTE 66

This classic early 1960s TV show, which is available for free on many streaming services, chronicles the adventures of two itinerant friends and was shot on location throughout the country.

TASTE THE NATION

Longtime Top Chef host Padma Lakshmi sets out on her own to discover the culinary traditions of various parts of the country, especially those whose roots here go back a generation at the most. The series is part cooking show, part travelogue, and part exploration of the immigrant experience. Most memorable is her conversation with a Thai woman whose high-end food was initially rejected by Las Vegas diners used to cheap and greasy fare. She triumphs, and so does the series.

THELMA AND LOUISE

The ultimate road trip buddy movie, 1991's Thelma and Louise features two best friends who set off on a road trip where chaos (and crime) ensues.

Chapter 2

TRIPS OF A LIFETIME

2

Updated by
Andrew Collins

WELCOME TO TRIPS OF A LIFETIME

TOP REASONS TO GO

★ **Yellowstone National Park:** The crowning jewel of the national park system is also an ultimate highlight of any northern cross-country trip.

★ **The Gulf Shores:** A southern cross-country trip takes you past some stunning landscapes, but also through the supremely underrated shores of the Gulf of Mexico.

★ **Route 66 Kitsch:** There's plenty to see along Route 66, but it might just be the many old-fashioned rest stops, diners, and motels that take you back to road trips past and keep the travelers coming.

★ **The Outer Banks:** As you hightail it up the East Coast, the Outer Banks of North Carolina give you some of the country's most stunning beach scenery.

★ **Gettysburg National Battlefield:** One of the country's most hallowed grounds, a visit to Gettysburg is a reminder of the history and horrors of the Civil War.

1 The Ultimate Cross-Country Road Trip: The Northern Route. From Seattle to Washington, D.C., travel through Yellowstone, the Badlands, and the Midwest.

2 The Ultimate Cross-Country Road Trip: The Southern Route. The drive from Jacksonville to San Diego takes you past the Gulf Shores, Texas, and the Southwest.

3 Route 66. The quintessential American road trip.

4 The East Coast's Best Beaches. A journey up the East Coast that gives you the best the Atlantic Ocean has to offer.

5 The Appalachian Trail. With this trip, nonhikers can still experience the beauty of America's epic hiking trail that takes you from Georgia to Maine.

6 Along the Mississippi River. Follow America's mightiest river from New Orleans to Minneapolis.

7 The Great American Baseball Road Trip. From famous stadiums to the Baseball Hall of Fame, this trip is the perfect way to embrace America's favorite pastime.

8 **Civil War Battlefields and History.** Delve deep into the history of America's bloodiest conflict by visiting its battlefields and historic sites.

9 **Retracing the American Revolution.** See the essential sites associated with America's Founding Fathers.

While any road trip can be considered epic, there are certain itineraries that truly define the word. These multiday journeys span regions and often coasts, exploring a multitude of different states, ecosystems, and time zones. Whether they're centered on a certain theme or a certain body of water, these are the once-in-a-lifetime adventures that should be on every road-tripper's bucket list.

The Ultimate Cross-Country Road Trip: The Northern Route

Written by Andrew Collins

Driving across the country's northern tier offers a bit of something for everyone: some of the world's most magnificent national parks, long stretches of sparsely populated open country, enormous and gorgeous lakes, youthful and artsy college towns, and a few bigger cities with grand architecture and superb museums. And although there's a span from western Wyoming to eastern South Dakota that's a bit of a food desert (unless you don't get tired of beer and burgers), this drive passes through some impressive culinary destinations, from Washington's wine country to vibrant farm-to-table scenes in Minneapolis and Madison and the diverse international fare of Cleveland, Pittsburgh, and Washington, D.C. From some of the country's most remote scenery to some of its most accessible, this coastal trip will leave you with a true sense of America's diversity and beauty.

At a Glance

Start: Seattle, WA

End: Washington, D.C.

Miles Traveled: 3,600 miles

Suggested Duration: 16 days

States Visited: Idaho, Illinois, Indiana, Maryland, Michigan, Minnesota, Montana, Ohio, Pennsylvania, South Dakota, Washington, Wyoming

Key Sights: Glacier National Park; Mount Rushmore; National Museum of African American History and Culture; Taliesin; Yellowstone National Park

Best Time to Go: It's best not to even consider this route between mid-November and April, as you're going to hit road closures in parts of Glacier and Yellowstone National Parks and pretty brutal, cold, windy, and potentially snowy weather across much of the route. The absolute best time weather-wise is July and August, but places can get crowded and expensive, so try to plan and reserve rooms well in advance if planning a summer adventure. Spring and fall are ideal for nice weather and fewer crowds.

Day 1: Seattle, WA, to Wenatchee, WA

140 miles (2 hours, 30 minutes without traffic and stops)

It's quickest to take I–90 east to U.S. 97, but you'll add only a little extra time to your adventure if you take the more scenic Highway 522 to U.S. 2, over gorgeous Stevens Pass in the Cascade Range, and by way of Leavenworth.

ALONG THE WAY

Shop: Just 20 miles northwest of Seattle, the town of Woodinville is entirely about selling one very specific product: wine. And we're talking about some of the greatest wine in North America, as nearly all of the town's 130 tasting rooms source grapes from the vaunted wine regions of eastern Washington, including Walla Walla, Yakima Valley, and the Columbia Valley. With limited time, make a visit to the granddaddy of all Washington wineries, **Chateau Ste. Michelle** (✉ 14111 N.E. 145th St. ☎ 425/488–1133 ⊕ www.ste-michelle.com).

Town: A favorite weekend getaway, Leavenworth is a charming (if a touch kitschy) Bavarian-style village that thrives with both old-fashioned and urbane restaurants and inns. It's also a hub for outdoor fun, including easily accessible hikes in the surrounding Okanogan-Wenatchee National Forest; the Icicle Ridge Trail is a favorite. The **Nutcracker Museum and Shop** (✉ 735 Front St. ☎ 509/548–4573 ⊕ www.nutcrackermuseum.com) contains nearly 7,000 modern and antique nutcrackers—some of them centuries

old, along with interesting exhibits on the region's Native American heritage.

Eat & Drink: Go full-on old-school Bavarian with a meal at **Andreas Keller Restaurant** (✉ 829 Front St. ☎ 509/548–6000 ⊕ www.andreaskellerrestaurant.com) in Leavenworth. Merry "oompah" music bubbles out from marching accordion players at this festive restaurant, where the theme is "Germany without the Passport." You can feast on a selection of wursts—bratwurst, knackwurst, and *weisswurst*—beef goulash, and schnitzel cordon bleu.

WENATCHEE

Do: Gaining popularity with an outdoorsy crowd and sophisticated wine lovers, Wenatchee is an attractive, fast-growing city located in a shallow valley at the confluence of the Wenatchee and Columbia Rivers. Stretch your legs with a stroll on the paved Apple Valley Recreation Loop Trail, which runs for 26 miles on both sides of the Columbia River, or by ambling through **Ohme Gardens** (✉ 3327 Ohme Rd. ☎ 509/662–5785 ⊕ www.ohmegardens.org), where you can commune with an artful arrangement of native rocks, ferns, mosses, pools, waterfalls, rock gardens, and conifers.

Eat & Drink: Set in a renovated warehouse along the Columbia River, Pybus Public Market is modeled loosely on Seattle's Pike Place Market and features vendors selling all manner of local farm goods, including locally made wines, and several excellent restaurants, including **Fire at Pybus Market** (✉ 7 N. Worthen St. ☎ 509/888–4347 ⊕ www.viscontis.com). **McGlinn's** (✉ 111 Orondo Ave. ☎ 509/663–9073 ⊕ www.mcglinns.com) is a beloved downtown gastropub with rustic brick walls, soaring woodbeam ceilings, and an extensive menu of elevated comfort fare.

Stay: One of the best lodgings in the area, the 1917 **Warm Springs Inn & Winery** (✉ 1611 Love La. ☎ 509/662–5683 ⊕ www.

Cross-Country:
The Northern Route

warmspringsinn.com) is set amid 10 acres of gardens and grapevines and offers elegant, well-appointed rooms filled with art and antiques.

Breakfast: Prodigious breakfast sandwiches with delicious fillings—such as the "monster biscuit"—are the specialty of **Sage Hills Bakery** (✉ *826 N. Wenatchee Ave.* ☎ *509/888–3912* ⊕ *www.facebook. com/sagehillsbakery*), a contemporary café that also serves decadent cookies and cinnamon rolls.

Day 2: Wenatchee, WA, to Sandpoint, ID

240 miles (4 hours, 30 minutes without traffic and stops)

Head north for a short but pretty drive along U.S. 97 bordering the Columbia River, then take U.S. 2 across the dramatic, windswept high desert of central and eastern Washington, passing through the attractive city of Spokane, and then cutting north up U.S. 2 to Newport and across the border to Sandpoint.

ALONG THE WAY

Town: Washington's second-largest city, Spokane is known for its beautiful public gardens and greenery as well as its wealth of well-preserved late-19th-century and early-20th-century buildings. The city's magnificent waterfalls form the heart of **Riverfront Park** (✉ *507 N. Howard St.* ☎ *509/625–6600* ⊕ *www.riverfront-spokane.org*), a 100-acre oasis that spans several islands and offers attractions like a 1909 hand-carved Looff carousel, a giant red slide shaped like a Radio Flyer wagon, and the Numerica SkyRide gondola, which whisks passengers directly over the dramatic falls.

Eat & Drink: Right off the Maple Street Bridge in Spokane, **Frank's Diner** (✉ *1516 W. 2nd Ave.* ☎ *509/747–8798* ⊕ *www. franksdiners.com*) is set in a 1906 railroad observation car with original

stained-glass windows. It's a colorful stop for generously portioned American fare, including salmon BLTs and turkey pot pie.

SANDPOINT

Do: A laid-back vacation community in rugged northern Idaho's panhandle, the pine-shaded town of Sandpoint sits along the northwest shore of the nation's fifth-deepest body of water, Lake Pend Oreille (pronounced pond-oh-ray). The area draws snow-sport enthusiasts to Schweitzer Mountain, the largest ski resort in the state, and in summer it's a hot spot for hiking (ride the chairlift up to the half-mile Summit View Loop). Other engaging pursuits include renting kayaks or taking a picturesque **Lake Pend Oreille Cruises** tour (☎ *208/255–5253* ⊕ *www. lakependoreillecruises.com*) of the lake along with browsing the galleries and specialty shops of **Cedar Street Bridge Public Market** (✉ *334 N. 1st Ave.* ☎ *208/946–9531* ⊕ *www.cedarstreetbridge.com*).

Eat & Drink: Serving up hefty prime steaks and classic cocktails, downtown's **Hydra Steakhouse** (✉ *115 Lake St.* ☎ *208/263–7123* ⊕ *www.hydrasteakhouse.net*) serves some of the region's most refined contemporary cuisine. Downtown's convivial **Idaho Pour Authority** (✉ *203 Cedar St.* ☎ *208/597–7096* ⊕ *www. idahopourauthority.com*) is a nice spot for craft sips and getting to know the locals.

Stay: You'll find cushy rooms with distinctive accents—colorful Talavera tiles in one, a 30-foot octagonal copper ceiling in another—at the **Talus Rock Retreat** (✉ *291 Syringa Heights Rd.* ☎ *208/255–8458* ⊕ *www.talusrockretreat.com*), a contemporary boutique lodge with a pool and hot tub that's close to downtown but set on 18 quiet woodland acres.

Breakfast: Get your morning caffeine fix—and a hearty organic breakfast burrito—at **Evans Brothers Coffee** (✉ *524 Church St.* ☎ *208/265–5553* ⊕ *www.evansbrotherscoffee.com*).

Day 3: Sandpoint, ID, to Whitefish, MT

200 miles (3 hours, 30 minutes without traffic and stops)

This scenic, sparsely populated route passes beneath the jagged peaks of the Cabinet and Purcell mountain ranges, from Idaho's panhandle into western Montana. From Sandpoint, follow U.S. 2 north through Bonners Ferry, and then east into Montana and through verdant evergreen forests to Kalispell, and then to picturesque Whitefish.

ALONG THE WAY

Eat & Drink: Roughly at the halfway point of today's drive, the **Cabinet Mountain Brewing Company** (✉ 206 Mineral Ave. ☎ 406/293–2739 ⊕ www.cabinetmountainbrewing.com) bills itself as the "living room" of Libby, an easygoing Montana town on the Kootenay River. Stop in for a plate of street tacos or a panini, along with a pint of the signature Yaak Attack IPA.

Town: The main drag of Kalispell, northwestern Montana's largest town, is lined with galleries, boutiques, and restaurants. An Andrew Carnegie library is now home to the **Hockaday Museum of Art** (✉ 302 2nd Ave. E ☎ 406/755–5268 ⊕ www.hockadaymuseum.com) and Kalispell's first school building has been turned into the **Northwest Montana History Museum** (✉ 124 2nd Ave. E ☎ 406/756–5381 ⊕ www.nwmhistory.org), but the highlight is visiting the **Conrad Mansion** (✉ 330 Woodland Ave. ☎ 406/755–2166 ⊕ www.conradmansion.com), a Norman-style mansion from the 1890s that sits on a ridge with dramatic mountain views.

Nature: From Kalispell, it's just a 10-mile drive south to explore the north shore of 370-foot-deep **Flathead Lake,** the largest natural freshwater lake in the western United States. It's a wonderful—and popular—place for sailing, fishing, and swimming.

WHITEFISH

Do: A hub for golfing, boating, hiking, mountain biking, and skiing, Whitefish sits at the base of Big Mountain Ski and Summer Resort, which provides outstanding views into Glacier National Park and the Canadian Rockies. In addition to offering plenty of outdoorsy diversions, this attractive and increasingly affluent town has a cute, shop-filled downtown.

Eat & Drink: The Louisiana-raised chef-owner of convivial **Tupelo Grille** (✉ 17 Central Ave. ☎ 406/862–6136 ⊕ www.tupelogrille.com) prepares excellent southern-inflected fare, such as Low Country shrimp and grits and fried green tomatoes remoulade. For a satisfying ending to any meal, be sure to check out **Sweet Peaks Ice Cream** (✉ 419 E. 3rd St. ☎ 406/862–4668 ⊕ www.sweetpeaksicecream.com), a minichain of artisan parlors that offers a slew of interesting flavors, like huckleberry-lemon pie and honey-cinnamon.

Stay: With a private beach and marina, the luxurious **Lodge at Whitefish Lake** (✉ 1380 Wisconsin Ave. ☎ 406/863–4000 ⊕ www.lodgeatwhitefishlake.com) has beautifully appointed rooms with rich wood tones, granite countertops, and slate bathrooms with large walk-in showers and deep soaking tubs—lovely for relaxing after a long day of driving or a strenuous hike.

Breakfast: In downtown Whitefish, **Loula's Cafe** (✉ 300 2nd St. E ☎ 406/862–5614 ⊕ www.loulaswhitefish.com) has become a favorite morning gathering spot for both locals and visitors. Regulars swear by the lemon-stuffed French toast and spicy-sausage breakfast enchiladas, but Loula's is also famous for homemade fruit pies, which are available in about 20 different flavors.

Did You Know?

Fishing is a popular activity on Flathead Lake—there's a wide variety of fish to be caught here, including trout, whitefish, and bass. Legend has it that the lake even has its own Nessie, a 7½-foot, 181-pound sturgeon caught in 1955 (sightings of other huge fish have been reported in the lake over the past century).

Extend Your Trip

From Seattle: The Pacific Coast Highway and Highway 101; the Best of the Pacific Northwest; Wine Countries of the Pacific Northwest (*Ch. 3*)

From Yellowstone and Cody: Big Sky Country; The Ultimate Wild West Road Trip (*Ch. 4*)

From Mount Rushmore: The Best of the Dakotas (*Ch. 5*)

From Minneapolis: Along the Mississippi (*Ch. 2*)

From Madison: The Best of the Heartland; Underrated Cities of the Midwest (*Ch. 6*)

From Cleveland: All the Great Lakes (*Ch. 6*)

From Pittsburgh: A Frank Lloyd Wright Tour (*Ch. 6*)

From Washington, D.C.: Retracing the American Revolution (*Ch. 2*)

Day 4: Whitefish, MT, to East Glacier Park Village, MT

105 miles (3 hours without traffic and stops)

One of the most spectacular drives of your cross-country adventure can happen on this day, assuming it's late June to mid-September, and the incredible Going-to-the-Sun Road through the heart of Glacier National Park is open. Take U.S. 2 east from Whitefish to West Glacier, and follow Going-to-the-Sun Road alongside the crystalline shore of Lake McDonald over Crystal Point and Logan Pass, along the north shore of St. Mary Lake, and south down U.S. 89 to East Glacier Park Village. If you're visiting when Going-to-the-Sun Road is closed, you can still explore the southern reaches of the park, and then take U.S. 2 around the southern end of the park to East Glacier (cutting about 20 miles off your trip).

ALONG THE WAY
Eat & Drink: In **Russell's Fireside Dining Room** at historic **Lake McDonald Lodge** (✉ *288 Lake McDonald Lodge*

Loop ☎ 855/733–4522 ⊕ www.glaciernationalparklodges.com), take in a great view while choosing between standards such as pasta and wild game, or local favorites, like the huckleberry elk burger or the Montana rainbow trout.

Nature: Although you currently need to make a reservation in order to drive the legendary Going-to-the-Sun Road, this is the **Glacier National Park** (☎ *406/888–7800 ⊕ www.nps.gov/glac*) experience that you absolutely shouldn't miss. Be sure to stop at Avalanche Creek Campground and make the 30-minute stroll along the fragrant Trail of the Cedars, and at the Jackson Glacier Overlook to view one of the park's largest glaciers.

EAST GLACIER VILLAGE
Do: A convenient, quiet base that's also home to the gorgeous Glacier Park Lodge, East Glacier also provides easy proximity to some notable attractions in the southeastern side of the park, such as Two Medicine Valley, a rugged, often windy, and always beautiful spot accessed via a stunning 9-mile drive from Highway 49, and Running Eagle Falls, a pair of cascades that originate from two different sources.

Eat & Drink: A unique natural log structure made from enormous trees, the **Great Northern Dining Room in Glacier Park Lodge** (✉ *499 MT-49* ☎ *844/868–7474* ⊕ *www. glaicerparkcollection.com*) provides a rustic environment for hearty comfort-food classics, from beef pot roast to butternut squash ravioli.

Stay: Just east of the park, the beautiful **Glacier Park Lodge,** dating to 1913, is supported by 500- to 800-year-old fir and 3-foot-thick cedar logs. Entertainers delight guests with storytelling and singing in the spectacular great hall. Rooms are sparsely decorated, but historic framed posters hang on the hallway walls.

Breakfast: Although Glacier Park Lodge is the most memorable place for breakfast, the friendly **Two Medicine Grill** (✉ *314 U.S. 2* ☎ *406/226–9227* ⊕ *www.seeglacier. com*) is a classic wood-paneled diner serving omelets, French toast, and the like.

Day 5: East Glacier Park Village, MT, to Bozeman, MT

280 miles (5 hours without traffic and stops)

Follow U.S. 2 east to Browning, and turn south on U.S. 89, following it through Choteau. Then pick up U.S. 287 south to Wolf Creek for a turn on I–15 to Helena, then U.S. 287 again south to I–90 for a final jog east to Bozeman.

ALONG THE WAY

Town: Montana's state capital, Helena is known for its numerous city parks, several museums, and thriving arts community. The southern part of town is hilly and thick with lush greenery in summer, and you'll find a trove of ornate brick-and-granite historic buildings along Last Chance Gulch. Be sure to at

least view the exterior of the imposing **Cathedral of St. Helena** (✉ *530 N. Ewing St.* ☎ *406/442–5825* ⊕ *www.sthelenas. org*)—modeled after a cathedral in Vienna, Austria, and known for its stained-glass windows and 230-foot-tall twin spires.

Eat & Drink: If it's serious sustenance you're craving, order a heaping plate of smoked chicken or Texas-style brisket at folksy **Bad Betty's Barbecue** (✉ *812 Front St.* ☎ *406/459–2303* ⊕ *www.badbettys-barbecue.com*)—saving room for the creamy banana pudding.

Nature: For a bird's-eye view of the city, scramble to the peak of Mount Helena, the crowning feature of 620-acre **Mount Helena City Park.** Several trails lead to the peak, with the 2.9-mile round-trip offering perhaps the best scenery. It's a moderately strenuous trek, but it only takes about 1½ to 2 hours.

BOZEMAN

Do: A mix of cowboys, professors, students, skiers, and celebrities makes Bozeman one of the more diverse communities in the northern Rockies as well as one of the fastest-growing towns in Montana. The boom has led to stylish new hotels and trendy eateries, but this recreation hub retains a decidedly easygoing, western vibe. The must-see here is the impressive **Museum of the Rockies** (✉ *600 W. Kagy Blvd.* ☎ *406/994–2251* ⊕ *www.museumoftherockies.org*), where you'll find a celebration of the history of the entire region, with exhibits ranging from prehistory to pioneers, plus a planetarium with laser shows.

Eat & Drink: Inside the cavernous former Northern Pacific Railroad depot, **Montana Ale Works** (✉ *611 E. Main St.* ☎ *406/587–7700* ⊕ *www.montanaaleworks.com*) offers a huge selection of Montana microbrews and a restaurant serving bison pot stickers, baked pasta dishes, and Caribbean and Spanish dishes. You'll find some fun bars downtown, including

Plonk Wine (✉ *29 E. Main St.* ☎ *406/587–2170* ⊕ *www.plonkwine.com*), a long narrow space that's as much fun for people-watching as it is for sipping vino from the extensive and impressive list.

Stay: With a striking art deco design, the gorgeous **Kimpton Armory Hotel** (✉ *24 W. Mendenhall St.* ☎ *406/551–7700* ⊕ *www. armoryhotelbzn.com*), located in Bozeman's former armory building, provides urbane accommodations and amenities in an appealing downtown location. There's a fantastic restaurant and bar, too.

Breakfast: Colorful murals, high ceilings, and exposed air ducts create a mod-industrial environment at **Jam!** (✉ *25 W. Main St.* ☎ *406/585–1761* ⊕ *www.jamon-main.com*), a bustling downtown café that serves breakfast all day as well as a selection of tasty lunch items. Specialties include the crab cake Benedict and challah bread French toast stuffed with jam-infused mascarpone cheese.

Day 6: Bozeman, MT, to Cody, WY

250 miles (7 hours without traffic and stops)

Of course, you could simply zoom along I-90 and U.S. 310 from Bozeman to Cody, for a straightforward 3½-hour drive. But by far the most rewarding route takes you through the heart of **Yellowstone National Park** (☎ *307/344–7381* ⊕ *www.nps.gov/yell*). If you don't have time for an extra night, you can make this drive in a long day—passing through the Mammoth Springs, Old Faithful, Canyon Village, and Yellowstone Lake section of the park, albeit perhaps having to rush a bit in places (get a very early start!).

ALONG THE WAY

Eat & Drink: An enjoyable stop for lunch just before you enter Yellowstone, the **Iron Horse Bar & Grille** (✉ *212 Spring St.* ☎ *406/848–7888* ⊕ *www.ironhorse-barandgrille.com*) in Gardiner is a rollicking roadhouse with a huge wooden deck overlooking the Yellowstone River and the mountains in the distance.

Nature: With limited time, concentrate on the two biggest attractions in Yellowstone: Old Faithful geyser and the Grand Canyon of the Yellowstone. After entering the park via the North Entrance, stop at Mammoth Hot Springs and walk the Lower Terrace Interpretive Trail past Liberty Cap and the other strange, brightly colored travertine formations. Then continue south to Old Faithful, where you should allow at least two hours to explore its eye-popping geothermal features. Eruptions occur approximately 90 minutes apart but can vary, so check with the visitor center for predicted times. As you backtrack north, it's well worth stopping to walk around Grand Prismatic Spring in Midway Geyser Basin. Next, make your way east through Madison and Norris to Canyon Village to see the Grand Canyon of the Yellowstone—the Artist Point overlook on the South Rim offers one of the best photo ops. Then continue south through sweeping Hayden Valley, keeping an eye out for buffalo roaming the prairies.

CODY

Do: Founded in 1896 and named for Pony Express rider, army scout, Freemason, and entertainer William F. "Buffalo Bill" Cody, this easygoing western town is best known as a base for visiting Yellowstone National Park but boasts its own impressive array of diversions. Part of the fun here is sauntering down Sheridan Avenue, stopping by the Irma Hotel for a refreshment, and attending the **Cody Nite Rodeo** (✉ *519 W. Yellowstone Ave.* ☎ *307/587–5155* ⊕ *www.codystam-pederodeo.com*), an intimate, family-friendly affair that takes place nightly all summer. Whatever you do, do not miss the **Buffalo Bill Center of the West** (✉ *720 Sheridan Ave.* ☎ *307/587–4771* ⊕ *www.*

centerofthewest.org), an extraordinary complex—and an affiliate of the Smithsonian Institution—that contains the Buffalo Bill Museum, the Whitney Western Art Museum, the Plains Indian Museum, the Cody Firearms Museum, and the Draper Natural History Museum.

Eat & Drink: The handsome **Cody Steakhouse** (✉ *1367 Sheridan Ave.* ☎ *307/586–2550* ⊕ *www.codysteakhouse.com*) is a favorite of red-meat eaters, but there's also a surprising variety of internationally inspired seafood and poultry dishes. A trip to Cody isn't complete without scooting your boots to live music, usually provided by the local group West the Band, at **Cassie's** (✉ *214 Yellowstone Ave.* ☎ *307/527–5500* ⊕ *www.cassiessteakhousecody.com*).

Stay: The quirkiest lodging in town is the **Irma Hotel** (✉ *1192 Sheridan Ave.* ☎ *307/587–4221* ⊕ *www.irmahotel.com*), built in 1902 by Buffalo Bill and named for his daughter. It's not fancy, but the Irma exudes character.

Breakfast: Set in an airy former Texaco garage, the **Station by Cody Coffee** (✉ *919 16th St.* ☎ *307/578–6661* ⊕ *www.codycoffee.com*) can fuel you with well-made lattes, nitro cold brews, and chai teas, while the kitchen serves an assortment of sweet and savory crepes as well as fresh-fruit smoothies.

Day 7: Cody, WY, to Deadwood, SD

370 miles (6 hours without traffic and stops)

This is a big day of driving, so try to set out early. Head east through the rugged mountains and grassy plains of eastern Wyoming, taking U.S. 14, Highway 30, and Highway 31 to the tiny and scenic village of Ten Sleep, continuing on U.S. 16—known along this stretch as the Cloud Peak Skyway Scenic Byway—over

the Bighorn Mountains and through Buffalo to I–90 and continuing east for Deadwood.

ALONG THE WAY

Eat & Drink: You won't encounter a ton of dining options on this journey, although the towns of Buffalo and Gillette offer some perfunctory options in a pinch. Nevertheless, in the incredibly scenic foothills of the Bighorn Mountains in the town of Ten Sleep, you will pass by one of the coolest little brewpubs in the state, **Ten Sleep Brewing Co.** (✉ *2549 U.S. 16* ☎ *307/366–2074* ⊕ *www.tensleepbrewingco.com*), which serves first-rate porters and golden ales to a friendly crowd. Most days, there's either a taco or pizza truck on hand by late in the afternoon, and live bands often perform too.

Detour: As you drive east from Gillette, the highways begin to rise into the forested slopes of the Black Hills. A detour north will take to **Devils Tower National Monument** (☎ *307/467–5283* ⊕ *www.nps.gov/deto*), a grooved butte that juts upward 1,280 feet above the plain of the Belle Fourche River. The tower was a tourist magnet long before a spaceship landed here in *Close Encounters of the Third Kind*—Teddy Roosevelt designated it the nation's first national monument in 1906. A stroll along the 1.3-mile paved trail around the base takes less than an hour and affords impressive views.

DEADWOOD

Do: You'll discover brick streets fronted by Victorian buildings—which house shops, restaurants, and gaming halls—in this relentlessly kitschy town that has boomed especially since the 2004–2006 run of its eponymous TV show. Highlights among the historic attractions include the **Adams Museum** (✉ *54 Sherman St.* ☎ *605/578–1714* ⊕ *www.deadwoodhistory.com*)—which showcases the region's first locomotive, photographs of the town's early days, and an exhibit featuring the largest gold nugget ever discovered in the Black Hills—and

Mount Moriah Cemetery (✉ *10 Mt. Moriah Dr.* ☎ *605/722–0837* ⊕ *www.cityofdead-wood.com*), also known as Boot Hill. It's the final resting place of Wild Bill Hickok, Calamity Jane, and other notable Deadwood residents. From the top of the cemetery, you'll have the best panoramic view of the town.

Eat & Drink: On the second floor of historic Saloon No. 10, **Deadwood Social Club** (✉ *657 Main St.* ☎ *605/578–1533* ⊕ *www.saloon10.com*) is filled with old-time photographs of Deadwood. And while the decor is western, the food is northern Italian, a juxtaposition that keeps patrons coming back.

Stay: One of the stateliest Victorian buildings in town, the **Martin Mason Hotel** (✉ *33 Deadwood St.* ☎ *605/722–3456* ⊕ *www.martinmasonhotel.com*) offers elegantly furnished rooms, a small casino with a pressed-tin ceiling, and a high-ceilinged café that serves reliably good comfort fare.

Breakfast: An active glass-blowing studio and gallery set in a former service station, **Pump House Coffee & Deli** (✉ *73 Sherman St.* ☎ *605/571–1071* ⊕ *www. mindblownstudio.com*) serves tasty egg sandwiches and espresso drinks.

Day 8: Deadwood, SD, to Wall, SD

150 miles (3 hours without traffic and stops)

Drive south along U.S. 385, stopping to view the Crazy Horse Memorial, then backtrack slightly and follow Highway 244 east via Mount Rushmore National Memorial, then U.S. 16A and U.S. 16 through Rapid City, and picking up I–90 east for the quickest route.

ALONG THE WAY

Attraction: Designed to be the world's largest work of art, **Crazy Horse Memorial** (☎ *605/673–4681* ⊕ *www.crazyhorseme-morial.org*) is a tribute to the spirit of the Lakota people. It depicts Crazy Horse, the legendary Lakota leader who helped defeat General Custer at Little Bighorn. A work in progress, thus far the warrior's head has been carved from the mountain, and the colossal head of his horse has begun to emerge.

Attraction: One of the nation's most recognized public art works in the country, **Mount Rushmore** (✉ *13000 SD-244* ☎ *605/574–2523* ⊕ *www.nps. gov/moru*) can be enjoyed in as little as 15 minutes, but you'll get more out of your visit if you stay a bit longer and walk through the excellent interpretive center and explore the network of easy trails.

Eat & Drink: Perfect for a bite to eat before or after visiting nearby Mount Rushmore, the **Powder House Restaurant** (✉ *24125 U.S. 16A* ☎ *605/666–4646* ⊕ *www.pow-derhouserestaurant.com*) in Keystone serves stick-to-your-ribs country fare, including local game dishes like elk burgers and buffalo stew.

WALL

Do: This tiny railroad hub—apart from being a gateway to Badlands National Park—is known for being home to one of the daffier roadside attractions in the country, **Wall Drug Store** (✉ *510 Main St.* ☎ *605/279–2175* ⊕ *www.walldrug. com*), which got its start in 1931 by offering free ice water to road-weary travelers. Today its four dining rooms can seat more than 520 customers at once, and a life-size mechanical Cowboy Orchestra and Chuckwagon Quartet greet curious customers as they enter. The attached Wall Drug Mall has more than a dozen shops selling all kinds of keepsakes, from cowboy hats, boots, and Black Hills gold jewelry to T-shirts and fudge.

Eat & Drink: With limited dining options in these parts, your best option is the **Badlands Saloon & Grille** (✉ *509 Main St.* ☎ *605/279–2210* ⊕ *www.visitbad-landssaloon.com*), which offers a lot more of what you've probably experienced over the past couple of days: cold beer, buffalo burgers, and plenty of local color.

Stay: Wall's best option is the pleasant, if functional, **Best Western Plains Motel** (✉ *712 Glenn St.* ☎ *605/279–2145* ⊕ *www.bestwestern.com*), which has a pool and a central location.

Breakfast: Stop by venerable Wall Drug for traditional American fare (and the store's famous homemade doughnuts).

Day 9: Wall, SD, to Sioux Falls, SD

330 miles (6 hours without traffic and stops)

The most interesting route today is by way of Highway 240 south from Wall to Badlands National Park to the town of Interior, exiting the park and following Highway 44 east across the prairie, then north on U.S. 81 and east on Highway 42.

ALONG THE WAY

Nature: So stark and forbidding are the chiseled spires, ragged ridgelines, and deep ravines of **Badlands National Park** (☎ *605/433–5361* ⊕ *www.nps.gov/badl*) that Lieutenant Colonel George Custer once described them as "hell with the fires burned out." Ruthlessly ravaged over the ages by wind and rain, the 380 square miles of wild terrain continue to erode and evolve, sometimes visibly changing shape in a few days. Prairie creatures thrive on the untamed territory, and animal fossils are in abundance. Badlands Loop Road circles through the park and accesses several overlooks along the way, including Pinnacles and Yellow Mounds, which are outstanding places to

examine the landscape's sandy pink- and brown-toned ridges and bizarre spires.

Eat & Drink: The pickings remain slim until you get to Sioux Falls, but laid-back **Shirley's Diner** (✉ *142 E. 2nd St.* ☎ *605/842–3903* ⊕ *shirleys-diner-winner.edan.io*) in Winner is handily situated about midway along your route and serves unfussy home cooking.

SIOUX FALLS

Do: South Dakota's largest city is also one of the fastest-growing communities in the upper Midwest, thanks to a high quality of life, a favorable business climate, and good balance of art, culture, and outdoor recreation. A highlight of any visit is strolling around the 128-acre **Falls Park** (✉ *131 E. Falls Park Dr.* ☎ *605/367–7430* ⊕ *www.siouxfalls.org*), where the Big Sioux River drops more than 100 feet over a series of rocky ledges. Throughout the city's downtown, you'll find dozens of appealing shops and eateries as well as the **Sioux Falls SculptureWalk** (✉ *300 S. Phillips Ave.* ☎ *605/838–8102* ⊕ *www.sculpturewalksiouxfalls.com*), an urban trail featuring more than 60 diverse works.

Eat & Drink: Close to Falls Park and just off the city's pleasing Sioux Falls Bike Trail, **Ode to Food and Drinks** (✉ *300 N. Cherapa Pl.* ☎ *605/275–6332* ⊕ *www.odetofoodanddrinks.com*) is smartly decorated—with curving stone walls and big windows overlooking the river—and serves an eclectic mix of American and international dishes. The classy tiki-inspired cocktail bar **Hello Hi** (✉ *120 S. Phillips Ave.* ☎ *605/275–4544* ⊕ *www.thehellohi.com*) is an inviting place to wind down your evening.

Stay: Occupying a stunningly restored 1918 bank tower, the **Hotel on Phillips** (✉ *100 N. Phillips Ave.* ☎ *605/274–7445* ⊕ *www.hotelonphillips.com*) has plush rooms that showcase the building's ornate design accents. Common spaces include a beautiful mezzanine overlooking the lobby, and the swish and clubby Treasury bar and restaurant.

Breakfast: Start the day with a blackened-salmon omelet or corned beef hash and eggs at hipster-favorite **Josiah's Coffeehouse and Café** (✉ *104 W. 12th St.* ☎ *605/759–8255* ⊕ *www.josiahscoffee.com*), an inviting space with a bakery serving delectable caramel rolls and scones.

Day 10: Sioux Falls, SD, to Minneapolis, MN

240 miles (4 hours without traffic and stops)

Start your drive from Sioux Falls along I–90 east to Worthington, turning northeast on Highway 60 to Mankato, then turning north on U.S. 169 to reach Minneapolis. It's a relaxing and mostly flat journey through wide-open prairies, with little traffic.

ALONG THE WAY

Town: Another fast-growing community with a high quality of life, Mankato is also home to Minnesota State University, which imbues it with a youthful, progressive personality. Set at the confluence of the Minnesota and Blue Earth Rivers, the city makes an especially pleasant stopover from late spring through early fall, when you can hike to a dramatic waterfall at **Minneopa State Park** (✉ *54497 Gadwall Rd.* ☎ *507/386–3910* ⊕ *www.dnr.state. mn.us*), or stroll along downtown's **Mankato Walking Sculpture Tour** (✉ *3 Civic Center Plaza* ☎ *507/388–1062* ⊕ *www. cityartmankato.com*).

Eat & Drink: A short walk from Mankato's pleasant Minnesota River Trail, **Coffee Hag** (✉ *329 N. Riverfront Dr.* ☎ *507/387–5533* ⊕ *www.facebook.com/thecoffeehag*) is an artsy, offbeat café that serves tasty vegetarian fare, chai lattes, and smoothies.

MINNEAPOLIS

Do: Whether you're looking for highbrow sophistication or a quiet picnic on the Chain of Lakes, Minneapolis offers a great mix of outdoor adventures and cultural attractions, plus a justly acclaimed, independent-spirited dining and retail scene. The gorgeously designed **Walker Art Center** (✉ *725 Vineland Pl.* ☎ *612/375–7600* ⊕ *www.walkerart.org*) contains an outstanding collection of 20th- and 21st-century American and European sculpture, prints, and photography, as well as acclaimed traveling exhibits. Set aside an extra half hour to walk through the adjacent and also excellent Minneapolis **Sculpture Garden** (✉ *725 Vineland Pl.* ☎ *612/375–7600* ⊕ *www.walkerart. org*). Take a walk to the Mill District, a patch of historic and stately old flour mill buildings and one very new, enthralling modern structure—the Guthrie Theater, with its 178-foot cantilevered bridge. The neighborhood is home to the excellent **Mill City Museum** (✉ *704 S. 2nd St.* ☎ *612/341–7555* ⊕ *www.mnhs. org/millcity*), whose interactive exhibits document the city's industrial history, and that overlooks Saint Anthony Falls. You can get an especially nice look at this series of cascades, locks, and dams on the Mississippi River by walking across the Stone Arch Bridge, which was built in 1883 for trains but is now used exclusively by pedestrians and bicycles.

Eat & Drink: A visit to Minneapolis presents the opportunity to experience the robustly flavored, beautifully plated dishes of Yia Vang, who's perhaps the most celebrated Hmong chef in the United States (the Twin Cities' vibrant Hmong community is the largest outside Asia). His food is served at the **Union Hmong Kitchen** (✉ *520 N. 4th St.* ☎ *612/431–5285* ⊕ *www.unionhmongkitchen.com*) and stylish **Vinai** (✉ *1300 N.E. 2nd St.* ⊕ *www.vinaimn.com*). Housed in a 1920s Ford auto garage, the beloved **Bryant Lake Bowl** (✉ *810 W. Lake St.* ☎ *612/825–3737* ⊕ *www.*

bryantlakebowl.com) is a lively bar, fun all-day restaurant, renowned cabaret theater, and very popular bowling alley, all rolled into one.

Stay: In the city's lively Warehouse District, the **Hewing Hotel** (✉ 300 N. Washington Ave. ☎ 651/468–0400 ⊕ www.hewinghotel.com) is an artfully executed boutique hotel. The stunning space occupies a late 1890s former lumber warehouse that's also home to acclaimed Tullibee restaurant as well as a sixth-floor rooftop bar with grand views of the neighborhood.

Breakfast: Head to the **Hi-Lo** (✉ 4020 E. Lake St. ☎ 612/353–6568 ⊕ www.hi-lo-diner.com), a landmark 1950s stainless-steel diner that offers a wide selection of breakfast greatest hits, from huevos rancheros with chorizo to lavender crème brûlée French toast.

Day 11: Minneapolis, MN, to Winona, MN

120 miles (2 hours, 30 minutes without traffic and stops)

This drive follows a picturesque stretch of the Mississippi River southeast, starting from St. Paul, then continuing on U.S. 10 along the east side of the river in Wisconsin, crossing back into Minnesota on U.S. 63 into Red Wing, and then following U.S. 61 along the west side of the river through Lake City and Wabasha to Winona.

ALONG THE WAY

Town: You might recognize the town of Red Wing because of its eponymous shoe manufacturer or for the beautiful glazed pottery that Red Wing Stoneware has been producing since 1877. But the town also stands out for its well-preserved 19th-century architecture and dramatic riverfront terrain, which you can fully appreciate from the top of Barn Bluff—it's an easy half-mile scramble

to the 340-foot summit of this rocky promontory that affords sweeping views of downtown and the countryside.

Eat & Drink: In Red Wing, the historic St. James Hotel's hip **Scarlet Kitchen & Bar** (✉ 406 Main St. ☎ 651/385–5544 ⊕ www.st-james-hotel.com) is a wonderfully atmospheric venue for brunch or dinner.

Nature: A fantastic place to learn about bald eagles, of which hundreds inhabit the Upper Mississippi River Valley, the **National Eagle Center** (✉ 50 Pembroke Ave. ☎ 651/565–4989 ⊕ www.nationaleaglecenter.org) sits on the banks of the river in downtown Wabasha, offering two floors of interactive exhibits, huge windows for glimpsing these birds in the wild, and the opportunity for up-close interactions with the rescued golden and bald eagles that reside here.

WINONA

Do: A little bigger than Red Wing but also with a historic downtown and a pleasing riverside location, Winona is notable for its superb **Minnesota Marine Art Museum** (✉ 800 Riverview Dr. ☎ 507/474–6626 ⊕ www.mmam.org), containing a remarkable permanent collection of nautical art and artifacts from around the world, including Emanuel Leutze's famous *Washington Crossing the Delaware* and works by J. M. W. Turner, Picasso, and several Hudson River School artists. If it's a nice day, climb to Winona's highest point, Sugar Loaf, a rocky butte reached via a 1.2-mile round-trip hike—be prepared for a pretty good workout.

Eat & Drink: The bright, fresh cuisine served at **Nosh Scratch Kitchen** (✉ 102 Walnut St. ☎ 507/474–7040 ⊕ www.noshrestaurant.com) showcases the seasonal bounty of the Upper Mississippi River valley and beyond. More casual fare and great ales are the specialty of **Island City Brewing** (✉ 65 E. Front St. ☎ 507/961–5015 ⊕ islandcitybrew.

com), which occupies a handsome old building with views of the levee and river.

Stay: Downtown Winona has a pair of charming bed-and-breakfasts within a few blocks of each other: the stately **Alexander Mansion** (✉ *274 E. Broadway St.* ☎ *507/474–4224* ⊕ *www.alexandermansionbb.com*), which was built for one of the town's early judges in 1886, and the white-clapboard **Carriage House** (✉ *420 Main St.* ☎ *507/452–8256* ⊕ *www.chbb.com*), an 1870 Victorian—both include sumptuous full breakfasts in the rates.

Breakfast: In a redbrick storefront near the riverfront, the **Acoustic Cafe** (✉ *77 Lafayette St.* ☎ *507/453–0394* ⊕ *www.acousticcafewinona.com*) serves house-roasted coffees and light sandwiches and pastries throughout the day.

Day 12: Winona, MN, to Madison, WI

160 miles (3 hours, 30 minutes without traffic and stops)

Drive a short way down U.S. 61 from Winona and cross the Mississippi River again on U.S. 14 into the city of La Crosse, and follow this hilly route through leafy southwestern Wisconsin through towns now famous for the architecture of Frank Lloyd Wright, before entering Madison from the west.

ALONG THE WAY
Town: The small town of Spring Green would make for a good stop even without its most famous attraction, **Taliesin** (✉ *5481 County Rd.* ☎ *608/588–7900* ⊕ *www.taliesinpreservation.org*), the 800-acre former estate, school, studio, and summer home of Frank Lloyd Wright; tours are an absolute must if you have even a slight interest in design and architecture.

Eat & Drink: Close to Taliesin, designed by Frank Lloyd Wright, and offering lovely views of the Wisconsin River, the **Riverview Terrace Cafe** (✉ *5607 County Rd.* ☎ *608/588–7900* ⊕ *www.taliesinpreservation.org*) serves farm-to-table fare, including aged-cheddar grilled-cheese sandwiches and homemade cookies.

MADISON
Do: This picturesque and progressive city—the center of which lies along an eight-block-wide isthmus—is known as much for being home to the lakefront campus of University of Wisconsin–Madison as for being the state's political center. Start your explorations at the regal **Wisconsin State Capitol** (✉ *2 E. Main St.* ☎ *608/266–0382* ⊕ *www.wisconsin.gov*), and also set aside time to tour the gorgeous, glass-walled **Madison Museum of Contemporary Art** (✉ *227 State St.* ☎ *608/257–0158* ⊕ *www.mmoca.org*), which contains a fantastic permanent collection by mostly 20th-century luminaries and a stunning rooftop sculpture garden. On the pretty campus of the University of Wisconsin–Madison, go for a stroll at Memorial Union, overlooking Lake Monona and home to beloved **Babcock Ice Cream** (✉ *1605 Linden Dr.* ☎ *608/262–3045* ⊕ *www.babcockdairystore.wisc.edu*).

Eat & Drink: One of the most renowned farm-to-table restaurants in the Upper Midwest, **L'Etoile** (✉ *1 S. Pinckney St.* ☎ *608/251–0500* ⊕ *www.letoile-restaurant.com*) has been an exemplar of the Slow Food movement since it opened in 1976—try to reserve in advance, and prepare to be blown away by the five-course tasting menu. Later in the evening, drop by **Up North** (✉ *150 S. Blair St.* ☎ *608/250–1730* ⊕ *www.upnorthbarmadison.com*), a popular cabin-in-the-woods-inspired haunt with eclectic live music.

Stay: For eye-popping water views and a great location near the University of Wisconsin, consider the historic **Edgewater** (✉ *1001 Wisconsin*

Pl. ☎ 608/535–8200 ⊕ www.theedge-water.com), which is home to a very nice full-service spa and the convivial Boathouse Bar & Grill.

Breakfast: Do as plenty of locals have been doing for years and grab a booth at retro-cool **Monty's Blue Plate Diner** (✉ 2089 Atwood Ave. ☎ 608/244–8505 ⊕ www.montysblueplatediner.com), where you can start your day off with meat loaf hash or eggs Mornay with poached eggs and smoked ham.

Day 13: Madison, WI, to Saugatuck, MI

315 miles (5 hours without traffic and stops)

With a lot of ground to cover today, it's best to stick with interstates. Take I–94 east to Milwaukee, and follow it south through Chicago, which, though amazing, isn't an ideal city for a stop when you're driving a long distance, as it can be congested and hard to find parking. Instead, continue around the south shore of Lake Michigan via I–90, through the northern end of Indiana, and then back up I–94 into Michigan, passing through Benton Harbor and picking up I–196 to Saugatuck.

ALONG THE WAY

Town: Wisconsin's largest city, Milwaukee is an international seaport with a handsome skyline of modern steel-and-glass high-rises and well-kept 19th-century buildings. If you have time for just one attraction, make it the singularly stunning **Milwaukee Art Museum** (✉ 700 N. Art Museum Dr. ☎ 414/224–3200 ⊕ www.mam.org), with its pleasing Lake Michigan location and spectacular curvilinear addition, designed by Santiago Calavatra.

Eat & Drink: The very traditional metropolis of Milwaukee, with deep central European roots, has long been famous for its old-world restaurants—casual **Von Trier** (✉ 2235 N. Farwell Ave. ☎ 414/272–1775 ⊕ www.vontriers.com) is a good lunch stop. Wherever you dine, save time for a trip to **Leon's Frozen Custard** (✉ 3131 S. 27th St. ☎ 414/383–1784 ⊕ leonsfrozencustardmke.com), a neon-lit landmark on your way south out of town that dispenses luscious cherry milkshakes and banana split sundaes.

SAUGATUCK

Do: This small, well-established art colony and LGBTQIA+-friendly vacation town at the mouth of the Kalamazoo River and along the Lake Michigan shoreline makes for a relaxing pause as you transition from the more sparsely populated western half of the country to the bigger cities of the Midwest. Saugatuck and its sister village Douglas sit along a wide section of river that's actually classified as Kalamazoo Lake, which is great for kayaking or taking a boat cruise around Lake Michigan. There are also plenty of cool art galleries, chic cafés, and stylish boutiques to explore. And there's **Oval Beach** (✉ 690 Perryman St. ☎ 269/857–2603 ⊕ www.saugatuck.com), one of the prettiest stretches of sand along Lake Michigan's shoreline, with its acres of protected sand dunes and blissful sunset views.

Eat & Drink: A 15-minute drive away in nearby Fennville, rustic yet sophisticated **Salt of the Earth** (✉ 114 E. Main St. ☎ 269/561–7258 ⊕ www.saltoftheearthfennville.com) sources as much of its menu as possible from within 50 miles and even offers some excellent Michigan wine, beer, and cider options.

Stay: Built in 1913 by a colleague of Frank Lloyd Wright in a loose interpretation of Prairie style, the grand **Belvedere Inn & Restaurant** (✉ 3656 63rd St. ☎ 269/857–5777 ⊕ www.thebelvedereinn.com) is now a sumptuous boutique hotel on 5 tranquil acres of gardens and lawns. The dining room is perfect for a leisurely romantic dinner, too.

Breakfast: In the heart of bustling Saugatuck village, **Uncommon Coffee Roasters** (✉ *127 Hoffman St.* ☎ *269/857–3333* ⊕ *www.uncommoncoffeeroasters. com*) offers sunny sidewalk seating as well as a cozy indoor space for enjoying yogurt parfaits and pesto-egg bagels.

Day 14: Saugatuck, MI, to Cleveland, OH

320 miles (5 hours without traffic and stops)

Follow I–196 and I–96 through Grand Rapids and Lansing, then head down U.S. 23 through the lively college town of Ann Arbor to Toledo, Ohio, where you'll pick up on I–90 to Cleveland. As this route passes through some urban areas, be prepared for more traffic, especially during the morning and evening rush hours.

ALONG THE WAY

Eat & Drink: If you're starting to feel a little peckish or thirsty when you pass through Grand Rapids, and especially if you're a fan of craft ale, pause in this attractive river town with an acclaimed beer scene for a bite to eat at **Founders Brewing** (✉ *235 Cesar E. Chavez Ave. SW* ☎ *616/776–1195* ⊕ *www.foundersbrewing.com*), a high-ceilinged taproom with hefty sandwiches and pub fare and lots of interesting sips on tap.

Town: Most famous as the location of the University of Michigan, Ann Arbor is roughly at the midway point between Saugatuck and Cleveland, and can be easily explored in a few hours. Ann Arbor's attractive downtown blends almost imperceptibly with the U. of M. campus, many of whose stately buildings were designed by architectural icons Albert Kahn and Eero Saarinen. East Liberty Street is lined with fun eateries and shops, and leads to the heart of campus and its picturesque "Diag," a huge green

where you're apt to find students sunbathing and studying on warm days.

Shop: Ann Arbor's distinctive **Kerrytown Market & Shops** (✉ *407 N. 5th Ave.* ☎ *734/662–5008* ⊕ *www.kerrytown. com*) anchors an eclectic neighborhood of redbrick lanes and dynamic cultural spaces. The market spreads across three carefully preserved late-Victorian industrial buildings and features vendors proffering all kinds of specialty foods, vintage clothiers, antiques shops, art spaces, several excellent restaurants, and both the Ann Arbor Farmers Market and the Sunday Artisan Market.

CLEVELAND

Do: Occupying a sweeping stretch of shoreline along Lake Erie, Cleveland was America's fifth-largest city a century ago, and its impressive wealth of early-20th-century landmarks is a testament to this fact. Its greatest draw is the striking I. M. Pei–designed **Rock & Roll Hall of Fame** (✉ *1100 E. 9th St.* ☎ *216/781–7625* ⊕ *www.rockhall.com*), which is enormously fun to explore. The crown jewel of the city's cultural hub, the **Cleveland Museum of Art** (✉ *11150 East Blvd.* ☎ *216/421–7350* ⊕ *www.clevelandart.org*) is another must-see, with 70 galleries spanning Mediterranean antiquity to the present.

Eat & Drink: Don't miss the legendary **West Side Market** (✉ *1979 W. 25th St.* ☎ *216/293–9830* ⊕ *www.westsidemarket.org*), which occupies a grand 1912 building with 44-foot-high vaulted ceilings and carries more than 75 vendors specializing in pierogi, Cambodian food, Middle Eastern specialties, and every other amazing cuisine under the sun.

Stay: The **Kimpton Schofield Hotel** (✉ *2000 E. 9th St.* ☎ *216/357–3250* ⊕ *www. theschofieldhotel.com*) occupies a dapper 14-story tower from the early 1900s in the heart of the city's theater district. Rooms have top-of-the-line bedding and bath amenities, and the restaurant, Betts, turns out artfully plated modern American fare.

Breakfast: Amid the striking bridges, viaducts, and beautifully restored warehouses and factory buildings in the city's formerly industrial and increasingly hip Flats district, **Lucky's Cafe** (✉ *777 Starkweather Ave.* ☎ *216/622–7773* ⊕ *www.luckyscafe. com*) works closely with Ohio farmers to source the ingredients for its gingerbread waffles topped with warm maple-roasted apples, and brûléed steel-cut oatmeal with dried-fruit compote.

Day 15: Cleveland, OH, to Pittsburgh, PA

135 miles (2 hours, 30 minutes without traffic and stops)

Follow I–77 south from Cleveland, allowing at least two hours to wander around Cuyahoga Valley National Park, then pick up I–80 east toward Youngstown, where you'll catch I–76 (the Pennsylvania Turnpike) southeast to Pittsburgh.

ALONG THE WAY

Photo Op: On your way out of Cleveland, we "triple-dog-dare ya" to stop in front of the **Christmas Story House** (✉ *3159 W. 11th St.* ☎ *216/298–4919* ⊕ *www.housefromachristmasstory.com*), which will forever be associated with the eponymous 1983 holiday movie.

Nature: One of the country's newer national parks, **Cuyahoga Valley National Park** (☎ *440/717–3890* ⊕ *www.nps.gov/ cuva*) is a 33,000-acre patch of greenery that extends for 22 meandering miles along the Cuyahoga River between Cleveland and Akron. There's fishing, biking, snowshoeing, and hiking throughout the park, which includes a 19.5-mile stretch of the historic Ohio and Erie Canal Towpath, and you can take a ride (especially nice in autumn) on the Cuyahoga Valley Scenic Railroad. Most of the park's top attractions are easily accessed

from major roads, including Brandywine Falls, which is the most photogenic of about 100 cascades throughout the park.

Eat & Drink: The best dining venue located within Cuyahoga Valley National Park, enchanting **Sarah's Vineyard** (✉ *1204 W. Steels Corners Rd.* ☎ *330/929– 8057* ⊕ *www.sarahsvineyardwinery.com*) is set amid several acres of grapevines and includes a winery and tasting room. You can walk through a butterfly garden, sip wine on a breezy deck, and order cheese plates, hummus, sandwiches, and pizzas to enjoy with your tasting.

PITTSBURGH

Do: Hilly and colorful Pittsburgh is one of the country's most distinctive urban environments. Once a center of steel manufacturing, today it's better known as a center of health care, finance, education, and technology. It's also home to some exceptional museums and lots of neighborhoods that, despite having gentrified to varying degrees, still maintain close-knit communities of various European, Asian, and Latin-American immigrants. One of the country's best museums devoted to a single artist, the **Andy Warhol Museum** (✉ *117 Sandusky St.* ☎ *412/237–8300* ⊕ *www.warhol. org*) devotes seven floors to the work of the native Pittsburgher and pop-art icon. From there, it's a short walk to the **Mattress Factory** (✉ *509 Jacksonia St.* ☎ *412/231–3169* ⊕ *www.mattress. org*), whose contemporary installations and experimental art exhibits often carry environmental themes; the rock garden outside is breathtaking.

Eat & Drink: Among the North Side's continuously evolving supply of restaurants, you'll find both old-school treasures—like **Max's Allegheny Tavern** (✉ *537 Suismon St.* ☎ *412/231–1899* ⊕ *www.maxsalleghenytavern.com*), with its Tiffany lamps, wooden booths, and hearty traditional German fare—and modern hot spots. Just over the river and back downtown, **Bridges & Bourbon** (✉ *930 Penn*

Ave. ☎ 412/586–4287 ⊕ www.bridge-sandbourbonpgh.com) is a chic cocktail lounge with tasty bar snacks.

Stay: A classic downtown hotel in a historic 1906 building just a stone's throw from PNC Park, the Andy Warhol Museum, and Pittsburgh's Cultural District, the **Renaissance Pittsburgh Hotel** (✉ 107 6th St. ☎ 412/562–1200 ⊕ www.marriott.com) is an elegant place to spend the night—many rooms have giant windows with river views.

Breakfast: Kick off your morning a couple of blocks from the Mattress Factory with an expertly prepared latte or Lapsang souchong tea at **Commonplace Coffee** (✉ 1501 Buena Vista St. ☎ 412/932–2433 ⊕ www.commonplacecoffee.com), which has several other inviting locations around the city.

Day 16: Pittsburgh, PA, to Washington, DC

240 miles (4 hours, 30 minutes without traffic and stops)

The most direct route to the nation's capital is entirely via interstates, but it's well worth taking a slightly more circuitous and quite scenic route, following I–76 east to Somerset, following Route 160 southeast to Cumberland, Maryland, and then heading east via I–68, I–70, I–270, I–495, and George Washington Memorial Parkway to Washington, D.C.

ALONG THE WAY

Detour: Just slightly off the main route an hour and a half southeast of Pittsburgh, you can tour **Fallingwater** (✉ 1491 Mill Run Rd., Mill Run, PA ☎ 724/329–8501 ⊕ www.fallingwater.org), Frank Lloyd Wright's residential masterwork—a stone, concrete, and glass house dramatically cantilevered over a waterfall. The only way to see this amazing house is on a guided tour, and it's best to book at least a couple of weeks ahead, especially in summer and on spring and fall weekends.

Town: Surrounded by the deep blue Allegheny Mountains, Cumberland, Maryland, developed as a major transportation hub where the Chesapeake & Ohio Canal, the Baltimore & Ohio Railroad, and the National Pike met. You can get a feel for the city's rich history at the **C&O Canal National Historical Park** (✉ 13 Canal St. ☎ 301/739–4200 ⊕ www.nps.gov/choh), which is the starting point for walking and biking the towpath, and taking tours on replica canal boats.

Eat & Drink: Set near a fountain on the brick pedestrian walkway, **City Lights** (✉ 59 Baltimore St. ☎ 301/722–9800 ⊕ www.citylightsamericangrill.com) brings urbane charm to downtown Cumberland. The menu of upscale American classics features seafood with a distinctively Chesapeake touch, hand-cut steaks, freshly made pies, and espresso drinks.

WASHINGTON, D.C.

Do: Having wrapped up your cross-country journey in the nation's capital, one of North America's truly remarkable museum cities, you could easily spend a week here without running out of memorable things to see and do. It can be tough to prioritize, as the 19 Smithsonian Museums—all of them offering free admission—focus on a wide range of subjects. But in keeping with this itinerary's themes of Americana and natural scenery, put these four at the top of your list: the **Smithsonian National Museum of Natural History** (✉ 10th St. and Constitution Ave. NW ☎ 202/633–1000 ⊕ www.naturalhistory.si.edu), the **Smithsonian National Museum of American History** (✉ 1300 Constitution Ave. NW ☎ 202/633–1000 ⊕ www.americanhistory.si.edu), the **National Museum of the American Indian** (✉ 4th St. SW ☎ 202/633–1000 ⊕ www.americanindian.si.edu), and the newest in the group, the **National Museum of African American History and Culture** (✉ 1400 Constitution Ave. NW ☎ 844/750–3012 ⊕ www.

nmaahc.si.edu). As these fantastic cultural draws put you squarely on the Capitol Mall, you'll also want to set aside time to explore the leafy rectangle's other sites, such as the Washington Monument and Lincoln Memorial.

Eat & Drink: In a city with no shortage of exceptional restaurants, the Logan Circle neighborhood—in particular 14th Street between Rhode Island Avenue and U Street—stands out for its variety of hip, inviting options. Enjoy a refined meal at **Le Diplomate** (⊠ *1601 14th St. NW* ☎ *202/332–3333* ⊕ *www.lediplomat-edc.com*), a hip spot for classic French bistro fare.

Stay: The snazzy **Kimpton Banneker** (⊠ *1315 16th St. NW* ☎ *202/234–6399* ⊕ *www.thebanneker.com*) has a cool rooftop bar for fair-weather socializing and roomy accommodations with colorful contemporary artwork and soft Frette linens.

Breakfast: Beloved breakfast restaurant **Ted's Bulletin** (⊠ *1818 14th St. NW* ☎ *202/265–8337* ⊕ *www.tedsbulletin.com*) has a few locations in the metro area, including one close to 14th and U Streets, and serves both traditional (breakfast burritos, French toast) and more creative (crab Benedicts, Pop Tarts–inspired blueberry-cheesecake pastries) breakfast dishes all day long.

The Ultimate Cross-Country Road Trip: The Southern Route

Written by Andrew Collins

Arguably the warmest route across the United States, this far-southern drive that skirts the Gulf of Mexico and the Mexico–U.S. border provides a compelling glimpse into the remarkably diverse heritage, folkways, and personality of the South and the Southwest. Starting in northern Florida, the itinerary passes through the Gulf South, connecting enchanting jewels of Spanish colonial, French, and Creole architecture with small, easygoing coastal communities. At the route's midpoint, in San Antonio, the verdant, humid landscape of the South gives way to the dry, sun-bleached, big-sky aspect of the American Southwest, with its vibrant though complicated mix of Indigenous, Hispanic, and Anglo culture.

This most southerly trans-U.S. route is relatively direct, especially if you stick to efficient if less interesting I–10 (switching to I–8 for the final stretch from Tucson to San Diego). For much of this adventure, however, try driving along the more engaging surface roads, U.S. 90 in particular, that pass directly along the shore of the Gulf of Mexico and through the vast prairies and high deserts of Texas, New Mexico, Arizona, and Southern California.

At a Glance

Start: Jacksonville, FL

End: San Diego, CA

Miles Traveled: 2,800 miles

Suggested Duration: 14 days

States Visited: Alabama, Arizona, California, Florida, Louisiana, Mississippi, New Mexico, Texas

Key Sights: The Alamo; Anza-Borrego State Park; Big Bend National Park; the French Quarter; Saguaro National Park

Best Time to Go: Although summer is quite popular for exploring this part of the country, it's also the one season that has some significant drawbacks: it's hot (humid on the Gulf Coast and arid but scorching in the Southwest), the beaches can get crowded, and traffic can get heavy in areas. Spring and fall offer the ideal balance, although beware the hordes of college students and families during spring break from the Florida Panhandle to Galveston. Winter is arguably the most rewarding time for this drive, with cool but sunny weather.

Day 1: Jacksonville, FL, to Pensacola, FL

360 miles (5 hours, 30 minutes without traffic and stops)

The most direct route is simply to follow I–10 west right across the top of Florida and across the Panhandle. But if you're up for seeing more of the scenery, U.S. 90 parallels the interstate and takes you right through a number of pleasant small towns. It's almost exactly the same number of miles, but it'll add two hours to your trip.

ALONG THE WAY

Town: Whichever route you take, you'll pass right through the heart of Tallahassee, a pleasant and relatively nontouristy city that looks and feels distinctly southern, with its looming live oak trees, fragrant flower gardens, and Greek revival and craftsman-style houses. Florida's capital is worth exploring for an hour or two, including downtown's historic 1845 Old Capitol building (now a museum) and, behind it, the "new" working capital. If you're the kind of road-tripper who's also an automobile buff, stop briefly to explore the **Tallahassee Antique Car Museum** (✉ 6800 Mahan Dr. ☎ 850/942–0137 ⊕ www.tacm.com), which contains about 130 vintage autos as well as actual Batmobiles used in several Hollywood films. Another easy stop north of town is **Alfred B. Maclay Gardens State Park** (✉ 3540 Thomasville Rd. ☎ 850/487–4556 ⊕ www.floridastateparks.org), whose 1,200 acres of gorgeous dogwoods, azaleas, and magnolias are laced with gracious pathways.

Eat & Drink: Go for a stroll around Tallahassee's lively All Saints District, which is close to Florida State University's campus and abounds with cool bars, food trucks, and beer gardens—be sure to check out the galleries around Railroad Square, too. **Fermentation Lounge** (✉ 416 All Saints St. ☎ 850/727–4033 ⊕ fermentationlounge.com) pours interesting ales from more than two dozen taps and serves tasty tacos, too.

PENSACOLA

Do: Take a stroll among the brick streets of the city's oldest neighborhood, Seville Square, which is centered on an attractive park shaded by live oak trees—it's also the site of one of the country's oldest European settlements, dating back to 1559. It includes **Historic Pensacola Village** (✉ 205 E. Zaragoza St. ☎ 850/595–5993 ⊕ www.historicpensacola.org), with its several history museums and restored homes. Then drive 10 miles southwest to see Pensacola's most renowned attraction, the mammoth **National Museum of Naval Aviation** (✉ 1750 Radford Blvd. ☎ 850/452–8450 ⊕ www.navalaviationmuseum.org), with its more than 140 aircraft, including the first plane to fly across the Atlantic (in 1919), the NC-4. The museum is next to Fort Barrancas, part of Gulf Islands National Seashore and a pleasant spot for a picnic or short hike along a nature trail.

Eat & Drink: For stellar, contemporary southern fare, book a table at **Restaurant Iron** (✉ 22 N. Palafox St. ☎ 850/476–7776 ⊕ www.restaurantiron.com). Whatever you order as a main dish, be sure to try a side of the jalapeño cornbread with sorghum butter. For a nightcap, stop nearby at **Old Hickory Whiskey Bar** (✉ 123 S. Palafox St. ☎ 850/332–5916 ⊕ www.oldhickorywhiskeybar.com), known for its encyclopedic menu of whiskies from around the world.

Stay: Steps from historic Seville Square, the smartly furnished **Oyster Bay Boutique Hotel** (✉ 400 Bayfront

Cross-Country:
The Southern Route

Pkwy. ☎ 850/912–8770 ⊕ www.
stayoysterbay.com) has roomy suites,
some of them with verandas overlooking
Pensacola Bay.

Breakfast: A few blocks from Seville
Square, **Cafe Single Fin** (✉ 380 N. 9th
Ave. ☎ 850/433–2929 ⊕ www.cafesing-
lefin.com) turns out delicious acai bowls,
smoothies, strawberry muffins, and
scrambled-egg wraps.

Day 2: Pensacola, FL, to Mobile, AL

*85 miles (2 hours without traffic and
stops)*

Forgo the interstate and stick to the scenic coastal route for this relatively easy
day on the road. Follow Routes 292 and
182 along the barrier islands overlooking
the Gulf, then zigzag north and west via
Route 59 and U.S. 98—through Foley and
Fairhope—to Mobile.

ALONG THE WAY

Nature: Here's hoping for sunny weather,
as today's drive on Alabama's Gulf Coast
is perfect for beachcombers. Southwest
of Pensacola, while still in Florida, the
first notable stop you'll come to is **Perdido
Key State Park** (✉ 15301 Perdido Key
Dr. ☎ 850/492–1595 ⊕ www.floridas-
tateparks.org), a beautiful, sweeping
stretch of sand that's a perfect place
to lounge on the beach for a bit. After
crossing the state border into Alabama,
continue west to **Gulf State Park** (✉ 20115
State Park Rd. ☎ 251/948–7275 ⊕ www.
alapark.com), where you can saunter
out along the longest pier on the Gulf
Coast—keep an eye out for nurse sharks
and dolphins.

Roadside Attraction: It's kitschy, often
overrun with spring breakers, and slightly
goofy, but the **Flora-Bama Lounge & Oyster
Bar** (✉ 17401 Perdido Key Dr., Perdido Key, FL ☎ 850/492–0611 ⊕ www.
florabama.com) has been party central

in these parts since it opened in 1964. It
contains an astounding 22 different bars
and hosts top country bands throughout
the year. It's a surprisingly good spot for
burgers, baked oysters, and bay shrimp
tacos.

Eat & Drink: Treat yourself to a sweet
snack at the **Yard Milkshake Bar** (✉ 3800
Gulf Shores Pkwy., Gulf Shores,
AL ☎ 251/948–0121 ⊕ www.theyardmilk-
shakebar.com) in Gulf Shores—the enormous shakes with names like the Peanut
Butter Finger Waffle are served in mono-
grammed Mason jars and festooned with
garishly colored toppings. The town of
Fairhope is a good place to be for dinner
(and to watch the sunset from the town
pier); art-filled **Tamara's Downtown** (✉ 104
N. Section St., Fairhope, AL ☎ 251/929–
2219 ⊕ www.tamarasdowntownfairhope.
com) specializes in local Gulf seafood,
such as crab cakes with remoulade
sauce and shrimp-and-grits with fried
green tomatoes.

MOBILE

Do: With tree-lined boulevards, French
and Spanish colonial architecture, and
a picturesque location on Mobile Bay,
Mobile bears some resemblance to
New Orleans—in fact, the celebration
of Mardi Gras began here, and you can
learn all about the festival's history at
the entertaining **Mobile Carnival Museum**
(✉ 355 Government St. ☎ 251/432–
3324 ⊕ www.mobilecarnivalmuseum.
com). Walk a few blocks northeast, past
the stunning 1927 Saenger Theater, to
bustling Dauphin Street and over to Bienville Square, the historic heart of the city.

Eat & Drink: Mobile's **Meat Boss**
(✉ 5401 Cottage Hill Rd. ☎ 251/591–
4842 ⊕ www.meatboss.com) is a perfect
opportunity to try Alabama-style white
(mayo-based) barbecue sauce, which
is great with chicken or pulled pork.
Steps from Bienville Square, dimly
lighted **Haberdasher** (✉ 113 Dauphin
St. ☎ 251/436–0989 ⊕ www.facebook.

Alabama's Gulf State Park is filled with white sand beaches.

com/thehabmobile) earns kudos for its superbly crafted cocktails.

Stay: Downtown Mobile's opulent **Battle House Renaissance Hotel** (✉ 26 N. Royal St. ☎ 251/338–2000 ⊕ www.marriott. com) has been popular with dignitaries and road-trippers alike since the mid-19th century—the on-site spa is exceptional as well.

Breakfast: A favorite breakfast and brunch venue along bustling Dauphin Street, cheerful **Spot of Tea** (✉ 310 Dauphin St. ☎ 251/433–9009 ⊕ www.spotoftea. com) serves decadent Belgian pecan waffles and Monte Cristo sandwiches.

Day 3: Mobile, AL, to Ocean Springs, MS

100 miles (2 hours, 30 minutes without traffic and stops)

Follow I–10 west from Mobile for about 10 miles, then sidetrack south along Route 193 to spend some time on Dauphin Island. From there, backtrack north, then take Route 188 west to U.S. 90, and continue across the border into Mississippi to Ocean Springs.

ALONG THE WAY

Nature: Although this outdoor romp through fabulous gardens is a decidedly curated form of nature, gracious **Bellingrath Gardens and Home** (✉ 12401 Bellingrath Gardens Rd. ☎ 251/973–2217 ⊕ www.bellingrath.org) in Theodore is a wonderful place to stroll amid the flowers and greenery.

Detour: A narrow barrier island with several notable attractions, Dauphin Island is a 165-square-mile swatch of picturesque beaches and pine groves that's worth the detour. The highlight is the **Alabama Aquarium at Dauphin Island Sea Lab** (✉ 102 Bienville Blvd. ☎ 251/861–7500 ⊕ www. disl.edu), a public aquarium and research institute where you can view more than 30 aquariums inhabited by myriad Gulf marine life and flora, including red snappers, octopus, sea turtles, and alligators (kids love the stingray touch pool). If you have an extra hour or so, consider stopping by the island's **Audubon Bird Sanctuary** (✉ *211 Bienville Blvd.* ☎ *251/861–3607* ⊕ *www.dauphinisland.org*), which has a 1,000-foot-long boardwalk and nature trail, and is a great place to view plovers, sandpipers, terns, and cormorants.

Eat & Drink: On Dauphin Island, laid-back **Lighthouse Bakery** (✉ *919 Chaumont Ave.* ☎ *251/861–2253* ⊕ *www.facebook.com/lighthousebakery*) is a good bet for sandwiches, pastries, and coffee, tea, and lemonade.

OCEAN SPRINGS

Do: Quiet, historic, and without the intense casino and resort development of nearby Biloxi and Gulfport, this artsy community makes an appealing overnight stop. The walkable downtown buzzes with cute eateries and galleries, and the beachfront is pretty but mellow, lined by homes rather than high-rises. On a live-oak-lined lane on the edge of downtown, the **Walter Anderson Museum of Art** (✉ *510 Washington Ave.* ☎ *228/872–3164* ⊕ *www.walterandersonmuseum.org*) contains more than 1,000 works by the eponymous local artist (1903–65) who became famous for his fanciful paintings and murals of coastal scenery, plants, and animals. The town is also home to the Mississippi District Headquarters of **Gulf Islands National Seashore** (✉ *3500 Park Rd.* ☎ *228/230–4100* ⊕ *www.nps.gov/guis*). You can learn about the region's natural history at the William M. Colmer Visitor Center, picnic, hike, and hang out on the fishing pier.

Eat & Drink: A romantic downtown bistro whose walls are lined with local artwork, **Vestige** (✉ *715 Washington Ave.* ☎ *228/818–9699* ⊕ *www.facebook.com/vestigerestaurant*) serves superb contemporary Asian-inspired southern fare. Whether you stay at the snazzy Roost hotel, do check out its stunning **Wilbur** speakeasy (✉ *604 Porter Ave.* ☎ *228/285–7989* ⊕ *www.wilburbar.*

com), designed with ancient reclaimed wood and decorated with Walter Anderson block prints.

Stay: With chic yet unfussy rooms, a cool grab-and-go market with tasty bites, and the aforementioned Wilbur speakeasy, **The Roost** (✉ *604 Porter Ave.* ☎ *228/285–7989* ⊕ *www.roostoceansprings.com*) is one of the most distinctive and inviting little hotels on the Gulf Coast.

Breakfast: Start the day with a hearty feast of inventive brunch fare at **Blue Dog Bistro** (✉ *1801 Government St.* ☎ *228/447–4023* ⊕ *www.bluedogbistro.com*), indulging in the signature house breakfast, which comes with three eggs, three slices of thick-cut bacon, pork hash, and a short stack of blueberry ricotta pancakes.

Day 4: Ocean Springs, MS, to New Orleans, LA

100 miles (2 hours without traffic and stops)

Although faster I–10 is an option, stick with U.S. 90 for the most enjoyable route, passing through the Mississippi coastal cities of Biloxi and Gulfport, and stopping in the more engaging smaller towns of Pass Christian and Bay St. Louis. From here, you have to bypass U.S. 90 (because the bridge at the state border is being rebuilt and won't open until at least 2028) and hop onto I–10 to travel through the wetlands of southeastern Louisiana and Bayou Sauvage National Wildlife Refuge to New Orleans.

ALONG THE WAY

Towns: Two small towns across the mouth of Bay St. Louis, Pass Christian and Bay St. Louis don't have much in the way of formal attractions, but have cute downtowns with a smattering of intriguing boutiques and eateries. In Pass Christian, walk the two or three blocks north on Davis Avenue from U.S. 90.

After crossing the Bay St. Louis Bridge, turn left on North Beach Boulevard and a few blocks later you'll be in the heart of little downtown Bay St. Louis, with its fishing pier, pretty beachfront, and easygoing bars and shops.

Eat & Drink: Shortly before you cross the Pearl River into Louisiana, you'll come to **Turtle Landing Bar & Grill** (✉ *16463 U.S. 90* ☎ *228/533–7000*) in Pearlington, famous for its views of alligators hanging around behind the restaurant in Cowan Bayou (note the "Beware, dock is weak, but the gators are hungry" sign out back). The burgers, po'boys, and fried seafood are all fine, but it's more about the location.

NEW ORLEANS

Do: The inimitable jewel of the Gulf Coast, New Orleans is the highlight of many a southern cross-country adventure. With limited time in this incredible city, try this strategy: spend half your time in the famous, or infamous, tourist heart, the French Quarter, and set aside the rest simply to amble around one of the city's many neighborhoods, like the historic Garden District or hip Faubourg Marigny and Bywater. No need to feel guilty if all you do is eat, drink, shop, and people-watch during your stay, but if you're up for getting a genuine sense of the city's rich history, check out the museums at **Jackson Square** (✉ *701 Decatur St.*) that make up part of the **Louisiana State Museum** (☎ *800/568–6968* ⊕ *www.louisianastatemuseum.org*), including the **Presbytère** (✉ *751 Chartres St.*), with its excellent exhibits on Mardi Gras and Hurricane Katrina; the **Cabildo** (✉ *701 Chartres St.*), where the Louisiana Purchase was finalized in 1803; and the **1850 House** (✉ *523 St. Ann St.*), a beautifully maintained townhouse and courtyard that's part of the fashionable Pontalba Buildings.

Eat & Drink: It's not so much that you can't go wrong in New Orleans (as the city does have its overpriced tourist traps), but you can eat incredibly well, every day,

for weeks, without dining at the same place twice. For an all-out, special-occasion, old-school experience, head to **Commander's Palace** (✉ *1403 Washington Ave.* ☎ *504/899–8221* ⊕ *www.commanderspalace.com*), setting aside time to stroll amid the gracious old homes of the surrounding Garden District. For a memorable meal in the less-touristy downriver neighborhoods, try **The Joint** (✉ *701 Mazant St.* ☎ *504/949–3232* ⊕ *www.alwayssmokin.com*) in Bywater for fantastic barbecue. For nightlife, drop by the **Spotted Cat** (✉ *623 Frenchmen St.* ⊕ *www.spottedcatmusicclub.com*) in Faubourg Marigny for old-time jazz and swing, and **Bacchanal Fine Wine & Spirits** (✉ *600 Poland Ave.* ☎ *504/948–9111* ⊕ *www.bacchanalwine.com*) in Bywater for stellar drinks and bar food, plus great music every night.

Stay: Due to potential traffic and parking issues in the French Quarter, consider staying in quieter but cool Bywater or Faubourg Marigny. The intimate and historic **Macarty House** (✉ *3820 Burgundy St.* ☎ *504/267–1564* ⊕ *www.macartyhouse.com*) has six lovely rooms and a cloistered pool.

Breakfast: In Bywater, funky **Elizabeth's Restaurant** (✉ *601 Gallier St.* ☎ *504/944–9272* ⊕ *www.elizabethsrestaurantnola.com*) lives up to its "real food, done real good" motto with its heavenly praline bacon and "redneck eggs" (fried green tomatoes with poached eggs and hollandaise).

Day 5: New Orleans, LA, to Lafayette, LA

190 miles (4 hours without traffic and stops)

Start out on I–10 and then I–310 to Luling, then follow the south bank of the Mississippi River along Highway 18 for a scenic riverside drive. At Donaldsonville,

The French Quarter in New Orleans comes alive at night.

turn south onto Highway 308, then southwest on Highway 70 to U.S. 90, and from there continue west through Morgan City to the heart of Louisiana's Cajun Country, centered around New Iberia and Lafayette.

ALONG THE WAY

Eat & Drink: Set in a handsome 1920s storefront building in downtown Donaldsonville, the dapper **Grapevine Cafe** (✉ *211 Railroad Ave.* ☎ *225/473–8463* ⊕ *www. grapevine.cafe*) serves superb crab cakes with roasted-garlic aioli and an extensive drinks menu.

Roadside Attraction: Sure, it's a bit silly, but for a spicy side trip, make the 10-mile drive southwest of New Iberia to Avery Island (not an island in the conventional sense but a salt dome) to visit the **Tabasco Factory** (✉ *32 Wisteria Rd.* ☎ *337/373–6129* ⊕ *www.tabasco. com*), where one of the world's favorite hot sauces has been distilled and bottled since the mid-19th-century.

LAFAYETTE

Do: Here you'll find exceptionally interesting opportunities to learn about Cajun Louisiana's rich history, starting with the **Acadian Cultural Center** (✉ *501 Fisher Rd.* ☎ *337/232–0789* ⊕ *www.nps.gov/ jela*), which is one of six units of the outstanding Jean Lafitte National Park and Preserve, of which three relate to Cajun heritage. At Acadian Village, you can watch a poignant film that dramatizes the Expulsion of the Acadians by the British from Canada's Maritime provinces and explore exhibits on Cajun folklore, food, and music. In spring and fall, ranger-guided boat tours along Bayou Vermilion are also offered. Right behind the center, you can tour the excellent Cajun living history museum, **Vermilionville** (✉ *300 Fisher Rd.* ☎ *337/233–4077* ⊕ *www.bayouvermiliondistrict.org*), which comprises about 20 historic structures, many with docents demonstrating various elements of early life in this part of the state.

Eat & Drink: The giant stuffed alligator that greets you at the door to **Prejean's** (✉ *3480 N.E. Evangeline Throughway* ☎ *337/896–3247* ⊕ *www.prejeans. com*) is a good indication of the Cajun aesthetic—and great food—inside this festive roadhouse that's been serving smoked duck–and–tasso ham gumbo, sautéed crab fingers, and shrimp and grits for decades. It's also a great spot to listen to live Cajun music. For a globally inspired and utterly sublime take on the region's cooking, snag a table at the intimately romantic **Vestal** (✉ *555 Jefferson St.* ☎ *337/534–0682* ⊕ *vestalrestaurant. com*). Then pop over to **Blue Moon Saloon** (✉ *215 E. Convent St.* ☎ *337/234–2422* ⊕ *www.bluemoonpresents.com*), an infectiously festive place to listen to great zydeco, Cajun, country, rockabilly, and other local and regional bands.

Stay: Most of the lodging options in town are major chains, with downtown's **Doubletree by Hilton Lafayette** (✉ *1521 W. Pinhook Rd.* ☎ *337/235–6111* ⊕ *www. hilton.com*) being one of the best.

Breakfast: Downtown's **Rêve Coffee Roasters** (✉ *200-A Jefferson St.* ☎ *337/534–8336* ⊕ *www.revecoffeeroasters.com*) is the best spot in this small city for expertly crafted coffee drinks, from nitro cold brews to single-origin pour overs.

Day 6: Lafayette, LA, to Galveston, TX

240 miles (5 hours without traffic and stops)

By far the fastest but least interesting route today is I–10 to I–45. It's better to take a leisurely drive along the Gulf, which takes about 90 minutes longer but offers rewarding scenery. When you reach the scenic Bolivar Peninsula, you'll have to catch a ferry across the mouth of Galveston Bay to Galveston Island. The 20-minute ride is free, but there can be

Essential Listening

There's something about the traditional music of Louisiana—zydeco, swamp pop, Afro-Caribbean, and other Cajun and Creole subgenres—that sounds inherently more enjoyable when you're actually here. You'll find great playlists on Spotify, and you can buy many of the top compilations from Louisiana Music Factory.

a long wait on busy weekends, so check the website for live updates. Your other option from Port Arthur, which is less scenic but often faster, is to follow Highway 73 to I–10, and take Highway 146 to I–45, which leads right onto the island.

ALONG THE WAY

Photo Op: As you head south toward the coast, take your time passing through the small town of Abbeville, a cute Cajun hamlet with two alluring and utterly photogenic squares surrounded by historic buildings, including the gorgeous 1915 St. Mary Magdalen Catholic Church.

Eat & Drink: In Abbeville, the famous **Dupuy's Oyster Shop** (✉ *108 S. Main St.* ☎ *337/893–2336* ⊕ *www.dupuys. com*) has been serving heaping platters of bivalves on the half shell or fried, along with other Cajun specialties, since 1869.

Nature: Pick up Highway 82 in Abbeville, which is a designated scenic byway known as the Creole Nature Trail. The road meanders through lush wetlands on its way toward Pecan Island and then through the 71,000-acre **Rockefeller Wildlife Refuge** (✉ *5476 Grand Chenier Hwy.* ☎ *337/491–2593* ⊕ *www.wlf. louisiana.gov/page/rockefeller-wildlife-refuge*), a pristine marshland flanking the Gulf of Mexico that's home to more than 400 species of birds as well as alligators, otters, nutria, and other critters. Just past the small hamlet of Cameron, take a short ferry (it crosses west every half hour) across the Calcasieu River/Ship Channel, and then you'll pass through Holly Beach, aka the "Cajun Riviera," which is a good spot to relax on the sand and take in views of the Gulf of Mexico. The Creole Nature Trail officially ends when you cross the Sabine River and enter Texas, but the scenery remains quite pretty as you drive through the small border city of Port Arthur and onto the Bolivar Peninsula.

GALVESTON

Do: Situated on a narrow barrier at the mouth of Galveston Bay, this picturesque city delights visitors with its long and broad beaches, ornate Victorian architecture, and friendly, free-spirited personality. Part of the fun here is simply milling around the beautiful **Historic Downtown Strand Seaport District** (✉ *502 20th St.* ☏ *409/795–7777* ⊕ *www.downtown-galveston.org*), ducking into galleries and boutiques, and marveling at the plaques on many older buildings that reveal the high-water lines during the several hurricanes that have inundated the island over the years (the most catastrophic was the Great Storm of 1900, during which at least 8,000 residents perished). You can learn about the storm and Galveston's storied naval and shipping history at the excellent **Texas Seaport Museum** (✉ *2200 Wharf Rd.* ☏ *409/763–1877* ⊕ *www. galvestonhistory.org*). A 20-minute drive west, be sure to visit the island's most impressive modern attraction, **Moody Gardens** (✉ *1 Hope Blvd.* ☏ *409/683–4200* ⊕ *www.moodygardens.org*), a complex of three glass pyramids that contain a science museum, aquarium, and—the highlight of the bunch—a tropical rain forest.

Eat & Drink: Steps from the beguiling Grand 1894 Opera House in the Strand district, **Rudy and Paco** (✉ *2028 Post-office St.* ☏ *409/762–3696* ⊕ *www.*

rudyandpaco.com) is a romantic venue for steaks and seafood prepared with Latin American recipes and ingredients. At sunset, the loveliest place in town to sip a margarita or glass of champagne is the Rooftop Bar, atop the **Tremont House** (✉ *2300 Ship Mechanic Row St.* ☏ *409/763–0300* ⊕ *www. thetremonthouse.com*), which offers dazzling panoramic views of downtown and the bay.

Stay: The most memorable of Galveston's many lodging options are its two sumptuous grand dames (they're sister properties), each of which has a different vibe. The turreted **Grand Galvez** (✉ *2024 Seawall Blvd.* ☏ *409/765–7721* ⊕ *www. grandgalvez.com*) dates to 1911 and is the best choice if you want one last beachside experience before cutting inland. If you would rather be close to the Strand's shops and restaurants, the stately Tremont House is a four-story Victorian-era gem whose rooms have soaring ceilings and windows.

Breakfast: Jumpstart your morning with a dirty chai latte or a fresh-fruit smoothie at funky **MOD Coffeehouse** (✉ *2126 Postoffice St.* ☏ *409/765–5659* ⊕ *www. modcoffeehouse.com*) in the Strand.

Day 7: Galveston, TX, to San Antonio, TX

250 miles (4 hours without traffic and stops)

Although it's possible to zigzag along back roads through Victoria and Karnes City, the scenery isn't especially memorable. The better option is sticking with I–45 and I–10, as the time you save driving you can spend with a stop in the underrated and thoroughly engaging city of Houston.

ALONG THE WAY

Town: It's understandable if trying to make a short visit to the nation's fourth-most populous city sounds a little daunting—greater Houston is more than 10,000 square miles (it's nearly the size of Massachusetts). If you have just a few hours at the most, your best strategy is to focus on one area or key attraction, like **Space Center Houston** (✉ 1601 E. NASA Pkwy. ☎ 281/244–2100 ⊕ www. spacecenter.org) or **Bayou Bend Collection and Gardens** (✉ 6003 Memorial Dr. ☎ 713/639–7750 ⊕ www.mfah.org). In the city's Museum District around Rice University, the must-see is the **Menil Collection** (✉ 1533 Sul Ross St. ☎ 713/525–9400 ⊕ www.menil.org), a peaceful campus of spectacular galleries and museum spaces. Although not officially part of the Menil, the neighborhood also includes the impressive **Rothko Chapel** (✉ 3900 Yupon St. ☎ 713/524–9839 ⊕ www. rothkochapel.org), which Philip Johnson designed, and whose walls house 14 large paintings by Mark Rothko.

Eat & Drink: Just a few blocks north of the Menil Collection, you'll find dozens of hip eateries and bars in the lively Montrose District, long a center of Houston's LGBTQIA+ community, and an all-around hot spot for shopping and dining. **Blacksmith Houston** (✉ 1018 Westheimer Rd. ☎ 832/360–7470 ⊕ www.instagram. com/bl4cksmith) is an airy, modern coffeehouse with tasty breakfast and lunch fare.

Roadside Attraction: On your way through Houston, stop to see the larger-than-life steel sculptures of animals—from a rust-colored armadillo to colorfully painted cows on a saucerlike pedestal—and small planes at the **Eclectic Menagerie Park** (☎ 715/598–9577 ⊕ www.texaspipe. com), a free, private collection of figures located on the grounds of a 108-acre pipe and supply company.

SAN ANTONIO

Do: San Antonio is the point in your cross-country journey when you truly transition from the lush, humid, and somewhat densely populated Gulf South to the sweeping, dry, and more sparsely inhabited Southwest. No visit to San Antonio is complete without at least a brief stroll along its famed **River Walk** (✉ 849 E. Commerce St. ☎ 210/227–4262 ⊕ www.thesanantonioriverwalk. com), a picturesque 15-mile pathway set below street level, the heart of which curves through downtown and is lined with bars and hotels. Many of San Antonio's top attractions, including the iconic **Alamo** (✉ 300 Alamo Plaza ☎ 210/225–1391 ⊕ www.thealamo.org), are within a block of this walkway, which in recent years has been extended several miles south to Mission Reach (where you can visit the excellent San Antonio Missions National Historical Park), north past the superb **San Antonio Art Museum** (✉ 200 W. Jones Ave. ☎ 210/978–8100 ⊕ www. samuseum.org), and up to the trendy Pearl Brewery District, a mixed-use development set around a historic brewery campus with cool boutiques, bars, and restaurants.

Eat & Drink: As you stroll up the River Walk from downtown, have a seat at the lushly landscaped **Elsewhere Garden Bar & Kitchen** (✉ 103 E. Jones Ave. ☎ 210/201–5595 ⊕ www.elsewheretexas.com), which offers a great selection of craft beer and other beverages along with addictively good deep-fried chicken with pickled jalapeños on a stick, double-cheese burgers, and Baja-style shrimp tacos. For drinks, **The Modernist** (✉ 516 E. Grayson St. ⊕ www.face-book.com/themodernistsa) is a swanky mid-century modern haunt with a festive patio and well-crafted cocktails.

Stay: The architectural centerpiece of the Pearl neighborhood, the elegant **Hotel Emma** (✉ 136 E. Grayson St. ☎ 210/448–8300 ⊕ www.thehotelemma.com)

showcases the historic opulence of its building while also reflecting a chic 21st-century design.

Breakfast: For old-school traditional Mexican breakfast fare, you can't beat **Pete's Tako House** (⊠ *502 Brooklyn Ave.* ☎ *210/224–2911* ⊕ *www.petestakohouse.com*), where a plate of chorizo-egg tacos or chilaquiles will fill you up for the day.

Day 8: San Antonio, TX, to Marathon, TX

330 miles (5 hours without traffic and stops)

It's a straight shot through the rocky and wide-open plains of southwestern Texas, along U.S. 90 to the small town of Marathon.

ALONG THE WAY

Eat & Drink: In Del Rio, **830 Kitchen** (⊠ *301 Ave. B* ☎ *830/308–3806* ⊕ *www.830kitchen.com*) is one of the best lunch stops along this route and a good spot to break up your journey. Expect big portions of chorizo burgers, avocado fries, carne asada fries, and other flavorful and filling, if not exactly healthy, comfort fare.

Town: Barely a blip along the otherwise largely uninhabited 185-mile stretch of U.S. 90 between Del Rio and Marathon, the hamlet of Langtry makes for a quirky pause, as does the dramatic 275-foot-high Pecos River Bridge, which you cross 17 miles before you get to Langtry. The town is closely associated with colorful, if notorious, saloonkeeper, justice of the peace, and self-proclaimed "only law west of the Pecos" Judge Roy Bean (portrayed famously by Paul Newman in *The Life and Times of Judge Roy Bean*). You can visit the **Judge Roy Bean Visitor Center** (⊠ *526 State Loop 25* ☎ *432/291–3340* ⊕ *www.txdot.gov*), which contains some colorful exhibits and artifacts

Extend Your Trip

From New Orleans: Along the Mississippi *(Ch. 2)*; The Great American Music Road Trip *(Ch. 7)*

From San Antonio: The Best of Texas; Texas Hill Country *(Ch. 5)*

From Tucson: The Best of Arizona *(Ch. 5)*

From San Diego: Pacific Coast Highway; The Best of Southern California *(Ch. 3)*

related to this legendary figure. You can also follow Torres Avenue a short way to a bluff overlooking the Rio Grande and a remote patch of Mexico across it—a historical marker notes that this was once a popular border crossing that traces back centuries.

Roadside Attraction: About 18 miles west of Langtry, a short detour from U.S. 90 on Highway 1865 leads to the ghost town of Pumpville, whose only building still in use is a tiny, well-maintained stone Baptist church that bills itself the "gospel west of the Pecos" and still draws a handful of ranchers, from as far as 50 miles away, each Sunday.

MARATHON

Do: This tiny, historic railroad town is most famous for being one of the key bases for a foray into the breathtaking wilderness of **Big Bend National Park** (☎ *432/477–2251* ⊕ *www.nps.gov/bibe*), with the northern Persimmon Gap entrance just 40 miles south. Stop at the main Panther Junction Visitor Center, and then spend half of your day hiking any of the well-marked trails amid the spectacular mountain peaks of Chisos Basin. Then make your way to the park's southwestern corner, where you can explore (on a 1.6-mile round-trip trail) Santa Elena

Canyon, whose sheer 1,500-foot walls were carved by the Rio Grande. Get there via the stunning Ross Maxwell Scenic Drive, which curls for some 30 miles past silent deserted homesteads, grand overlooks, and the Castolon Historic District's ancient old adobe buildings.

Eat & Drink: When the sun sets, the intimate **12 Gage Restaurant** at the Gage Hotel (✉ 102 N.W. 1st St. ☎ 432/386–4205 ⊕ www.gagehotel.com) is Marathon's most memorable and romantic place for dinner (consider the hefty rib-eye steak with Hatch green chili cream corn). Also run by the Gage and set in an 1880s mercantile, the nearby **Brick Vault Brewery and Barbecue** (✉ 102 N.W. 1st St. ☎ 432/386–7538 ⊕ www.brickvaultbreweryandbbq.com) is a more casual microbrewery serving reliably good Texas-style barbecue.

Stay: Cowboy, Native American, and Hispanic cultures are reflected in the furnishings and artwork of the gorgeously restored and historic **Gage Hotel**, built in the 1920s by renowned architect Henry Trost.

Breakfast: Yet another excellent dining option adjacent to and run by the Gage Hotel, **V6 Coffee Bar** (✉ 109 N.E. 1st St. ☎ 432/308–6877 ⊕ www.gagehotel.com) is a good bet for hearty breakfast fare like biscuits with jalapeño gravy or avocado toast.

Day 9: Marathon, TX, to El Paso, TX

250 miles (4 hours without traffic and stops)

Follow U.S. 90 through the colorful towns of Alpine and Marfa, and then up to the tiny railroad town of Van Horn, where you'll pick up I–10 to El Paso.

ALONG THE WAY

Town: The cultural oasis of Marfa enjoys a devoted following among artists, hipsters, LGBTQIA+ folks, and free spirits, thanks to its clutch of avant-garde galleries, ranch-chic restaurants, indie hotels, and endless opportunities for people-watching—from poetry readings to gallery openings to bar-hopping. Its relative proximity to Big Bend as well as the Davis and Guadalupe mountain ranges has made this offbeat design mecca a favorite destination with hikers and other outdoors enthusiasts, too. You can tour one of the world's largest permanent installations of contemporary art at the **Chinati Foundation** (✉ 1 Cavalry Row ☎ 432/729–4362 ⊕ www.chinati.org), which displays works by American minimalist Donald Judd and others in buildings spread over 340 acres.

Eat & Drink: The hearty fare, potent coffee, and fresh-squeezed juices at Marfa's **Asters Cafe and Bakery** (✉ 215 Highland St. ☎ 432/295–0833 ⊕ www.asterscafeandbakery.com), a small patio café across from the Presidio County Courthouse, will help you fuel up for a day of hiking or art touring.

Shop: Marfa's arty vibe shines through in its clutch of distinctive shops. **Cobra Rock Boot Company** (✉ 211 S. Dean St. ⊕ www.cobrarock.com) is beloved for its bespoke leather boots while **Wrong Marfa** (✉ 110 Highland St. ☎ 432/729–1976 ⊕ www.wrongmarfa.com) carries distinctive pottery, drawings, and housewares. Check out the extensive selection of books, jewelry, and well-curated sundries at **Hey I Like It Here** (✉ 105 S. Highland Ave. ☎ 432/729–3700 ⊕ heyilikeithere.com) in the Hotel Saint George, and vintage wear, skin and body products, and whimsical cards at **Raba Marfa** (✉ 212 E. San Antonio St. ☎ 432/295–0064 ⊕ www.rabamarfa.com).

EL PASO

Do: With an attractive desert location fringed by mountains, this friendly city forms a culturally vibrant borderland region that encompasses neighboring Ciudad Juárez, Mexico, and Las Cruces, New Mexico. With distinctive hotels and restaurants (many of them set in artfully restored Victorian and early-20th-century buildings), and excellent museums, downtown El Paso is in the midst of an exciting revitalization. Make a point of visiting the superb (and free) **El Paso Museum of Art** (✉ *1 Arts Festival Plaza* ☎ *915/212–0300* ⊕ *www.epma.art*), which features a striking array of contemporary and historic Latin American, Spanish, and native artworks. Within Franklin Mountains State Park's 37 square miles of majestic scenery, you'll discover more than 100 miles of hiking trails—the southern section offers amazing views of the city below.

Eat & Drink: A culinary jewel of downtown's cultural district, **Anson 11** (✉ *303 N. Oregon St.* ☎ *915/504–6400* ⊕ *www.anson11.com*) offers both a refined dining room that turns out creatively prepared American dishes and a more casual bistro where you might tuck into a flatbread pizza or the kitchen's signature meat loaf with smoked-tomato gravy. Downtown has some cool spots for drinks, including **Craft and Social** (✉ *305 E. Franklin Ave.* ☎ *915/401–1909* ⊕ *www.craftandsocial.com*), a stylish but unpretentious lounge that stands out for its well-curated beer and wine list.

Stay: The city's 1912 grande dame, **Hotel Paso Del Norte** (✉ *10 Henry Trost Ct.* ☎ *915/534–3000* ⊕ *www.marriott.com*), offers a stunning historic design, superb restaurants, a hip bar, and a luxurious spa.

Breakfast: Bright and cheerful **Salt + Honey Bakery Café** (✉ *1125 Texas Ave.* ☎ *915/313–4907* ⊕ *www.saltandhoneyep.com*) is a great place to kick off your day with a well-crafted espresso drink and the Mediterranean-inspired all-day brunch and sandwich menu.

Day 10: El Paso, TX, to Silver City, NM

180 miles (3 hours, 30 minutes without traffic and stops)

Southern New Mexico is one section of this drive where there's a great payoff in venturing a little off the beaten path. Your day starts straightforwardly with a drive up I-10 to Las Cruces, then picks up I-25 north, passing through the self-proclaimed world capital of green chilis, Hatch, before turning onto Highway 152—the Geronimo Scenic Byway— through the tiny, picturesque mountain towns of Hillsboro and Kingston, before catching U.S. 180 the final stretch to Silver City.

ALONG THE WAY

Town: The largest city in the Mesilla Valley, fast-growing Las Cruces is home to New Mexico State University and adjacent to the historic village of Old Mesilla, which was established by a group of Mexican residents when the territory of New Mexico was acquired by the United States in 1848. The town's Old Mesilla Plaza and Historic District has seen celebrations, weddings, bloody political battles, and the milestone trial of Billy the Kid. Walk through to admire the many mid-19th-century adobe buildings, many of them now housing distinctive shops, restaurants, and bars.

Eat & Drink: Southern New Mexico has a surprisingly good winemaking scene, with Mesilla's **Luna Rossa Winery & Pizzeria** (✉ *1321 Avenida de Mesilla* ☎ *575/526–2484* ⊕ *www.lunarossawinery.com*) among the best. At the winery's casual restaurant, you can sample great vino alongside terrific pizzas, pastas, panini sandwiches, and homemade gelato.

Detour: Reached via U.S. 70 east, the northern section of **Organ Mountains–Desert Peak National Monument** (✉ *Aguirre Springs Rd.* ☎ *575/525–4300* ⊕ *www.blm.gov/visit/omdp*) is just 15 miles east of Las Cruces and offers dozens of great hikes through stunning, jagged mountains.

SILVER CITY

Do: This artsy little mountain town began as a mining hub, was the boyhood home of Billy the Kid, and today supports a sizable population of artists, academics, and free spirits. You can spend the afternoon walking around the community's historic downtown and dropping by the funky galleries of the Yankee–Texas Arts & Cultural District. Or get behind the wheel and take in the stunning alpine scenery of the surrounding Gila National Forest.

Eat & Drink: Little Toad Creek Brewery & Distillery (✉ *200 N. Bullard St.* ☎ *575/956–6144* ⊕ *www.littletoadcreek.com*) is in the center of downtown in a handsome historic building and serves tasty pub fare, like green-chili cheese fries and smoked pulled pork tacos, not to mention well-crafted drinks. The most historic and arguably the most colorful spot in the area, though, is the **Buckhorn Saloon & Opera House** (✉ *32 Main St.* ☎ *575/538–9911* ⊕ *www.facebook.com/buckhornsaloonandoperahouse*), which is 10 miles north of town in the pretty mountain hamlet of Pinos Altos. It offers live music and old-fashioned melodramas in an atmospheric 1860s building with pressed-tin ceilings and a fireplace.

Stay: Within walking distance of downtown galleries and restaurants, the **Murray Hotel** (✉ *200 W. Broadway St.* ☎ *575/956–9400* ⊕ *www.murray-hotel.com*) is a neatly restored 1930s art deco gem with compact, tastefully appointed rooms.

Breakfast: For first-rate espresso drinks on a relaxing patio in the colorful Yankee–Texas Arts & Cultural District, check

out **Tranquilbuzz Coffee House** (✉ *300 N. Arizona St.* ☎ *575/956–6476* ⊕ *www.tranquilbuzz.com*).

Day 11: Silver City, NM, to Bisbee, AZ

170 miles (3 hours without traffic and stops)

Drive southwest on Highway 90 through Lordsburg, then Highway 80 south and west through the very southeastern corner of Arizona to Bisbee.

ALONG THE WAY

Town: There aren't a whole lot of formal attractions on the drive from Silver City to Bisbee, and that's part of the charm—the great views of the Big Burro Mountains in New Mexico, the Chiricahua Mountains in Arizona, and miles of sweeping expanses of cactus-studded desert make for a lovely drive. But just outside the otherwise very sleepy town of Lordsburg, the once thriving mining town of **Shakespeare** (☎ *575/542–9034* ⊕ *www.shakespeareghosttown.com*) attracted some of the West's fiercest outlaws—Billy the Kid and Black Jack Ketchum among them. These days you can take a guided tour of this well-preserved ghost town said to have its share of haunted buildings.

Eat & Drink: By far the most intriguing spot for dinner and drinks along this route is **Saddle & Spur Tavern** (✉ *1046 G Ave.* ☎ *520/364–4481* ⊕ *www.thegadsdenhotel.com*), inside the gorgeous early 1900s Gadsden Hotel in the border town of Douglas, Arizona. The filling steak-centric southwestern fare is quite good, and the smartly decorated tavern is a stunner.

BISBEE

Do: Another quirky community that thrived during its copper-mining boom years in the early 20th century, Bisbee was for a time one of the biggest cities between the Mississippi River and the

Pacific. In the 1970s and 1980s, artists, hippies, and free spirits began settling here, buying and fixing up its colorful Victorian buildings and homes, which cling to the often steep hills that rise up around downtown. You can learn about the town's colorful history at the excellent **Bisbee Mining and Historical Museum** (✉ *5 Copper Queen Plaza* ☎ *520/432–7071* ⊕ *www.bisbeemuseum.org*) or on an underground tour of the Copper Queen Mine—these 75-minute excursions are led by knowledgeable and entertaining retired Phelps Dodge miners and go some 1,500 feet into the mine.

Eat & Drink: Informal burger joints, Mexican restaurants, and coffeehouses are the norm in Bisbee, but upscale **Cafe Roka** (✉ *35 Main St.* ☎ *520/432–5153* ⊕ *www.caferoka.com*) stands out from the pack for its creative, locally sourced contemporary Mediterranean—mostly Italian—fare. Among several colorful saloons, the subterranean **Bisbee Social Club** (✉ *67 Main St.* ☎ *520/366–3898* ⊕ *www.bisbeesocialclub.com*) impresses with its well-crafted cocktails.

Stay: A great option if you're seeking some extra space to kick around in and appreciate having a fully equipped kitchen, **Canyon Rose Suites** (✉ *11 Sowles Ave.* ☎ *520/432–5098* ⊕ *www.canyonrose.com*) is set inside a former boarding house in the stately Allen Block Building.

Breakfast: The considerable lore of the **Bisbee Breakfast Club** (✉ *75 Erie St.* ☎ *520/432–5885* ⊕ *www.bisbeebreakfastclub.com*), which you'll find set along a row of old buildings in the town's historic Lowell district, has spawned a small empire of restaurants around the state. But the original location has the most colorful personality, and the homestyle cooking—chicken-fried steak with eggs and spicy sausage gravy, cinnamon French toast, chorizo rancheros—will provide plenty of sustenance for the day ahead.

Day 12: Bisbee, AZ, to Tucson, AZ

110 miles (2 hours without traffic and stops)

Head northwest on Highway 80 to Tombstone, then cut across Highway 82 to Sonoita, a scenic drive through the Santa Rita Mountains and Coronado National Forest, and follow Highway 83 north to I-10, which leads west to Tucson.

ALONG THE WAY

Town: Immortalized in western lore and Hollywood movies (*Gunfight at the O.K. Corral*, *Tombstone*, *Wyatt Earp*), the bustling little hamlet of Tombstone prospered almost unimaginably in the 1880s thanks to a highly profitable silver mining boom and today makes for a fun, if slightly cheesy, stop to soak up the colorful history of the Earp brothers, Clanton gang, and Doc Holliday. Hop out for a stroll along historic Allen Street, where you can stop by the Gunfighter Hall of Fame and watch entertaining gunfight reenactments three times a day at the **O.K. Corral** (✉ *326 E. Allen St.* ☎ *520/457–3456* ⊕ *www.okcorral.com*).

Eat & Drink: As you continue west through the Santa Cruz Mountains, you'll enter one of the state's best-known (if underrated outside of Arizona) wine regions, Sonoita, which has about a dozen vintners. Some of these are outstanding and well worth a stop for a taste, including the self-described "off-grid" producer **Rune Wines** (✉ *3969 AZ-82* ☎ *520/338–8823* ⊕ *www.runewines.com*), where you can sip on a backyard terrace overlooking the mountains.

TUCSON

Do: Arizona's second-largest city offers immediate proximity to gorgeous natural scenery—it's a favorite destination of hikers, golfers, and spa goers. But it's also a youthful, laid-back college town (home to the University of Arizona) with plenty of cool cafés and bars, as well as myriad offbeat shops, especially along Historic Fourth Avenue. The must-see in this sunny city is **Saguaro National Park** (✉ 3693 S. Old Spanish Tr. ☎ 520/733–5153 ⊕ www. nps.gov/sagu), whose eastern and western units bracket Tucson. Arriving from the east, pick up a trail map at the Rincon Mountain Visitor Center. Drive south along the paved Cactus Forest Drive to the Javelina picnic area, where you'll see signs for the Freeman Homestead Trail, an easy 1-mile loop that winds through a stand of mesquite as interpretive signs describe early inhabitants in the Tucson basin.

Eat & Drink: Tucson offers one of the more diverse dining scenes along this itinerary, but don't overlook the city's stellar Mexican food, which South Tucson's **Mi Nidito** (✉ 1813 S. 4th Ave. ☎ 520/622–5081 ⊕ www.miniditorestaurant.com) has been serving since 1952. Cap off the evening with classic cocktails at the dark and alluring **Owls Club** (✉ 236 S. Scott Ave. ☎ 520/207–5678 ⊕ www.owlsclub-west.com).

Stay: Offering wallet-friendly rates and a handy location just off I–15, the vintage-cool **Hotel McCoy** (✉ 720 W. Silverlake Rd. ☎ 844/782–9622 ⊕ www. hotelmccoy.com) has its own modern art gallery, bookstore, and plenty of engaging common spaces.

Breakfast: Downtown's **5 Points Market & Restaurant** (✉ 756 S. Stone Ave. ☎ 520/623–3888 ⊕ www.5point-stucson.com) is an attractive spot (with a great patio) to fuel up on smoked-salmon Benedicts and chilled rice pudding with ponzu sauce, coconut, and cashews.

Day 13: Tucson, AZ, to Anza-Borrego Desert State Park, CA

365 miles (5 hours, 30 minutes without traffic and stops)

The best approach for this drive is mostly along I–10 and I–8, across southern Arizona via Yuma. Just before you reach the small city of El Centro, drive north on Highway 111, then turn west in Brawley on Highway 78 to **Anza-Borrego Desert State Park Visitor Center** (✉ 200 Palm Canyon Dr. ☎ 760/767–4205 ⊕ www. parks.ca.gov).

ALONG THE WAY

Town: Once a thriving port on the Colorado River back when it was navigable (before the advent of numerous dams), the town of Yuma borders California as well as the adjoining Mexican states of Baja California and Sonora. Give yourself about an hour to explore the **Yuma Territorial Prison State Historic Park** (✉ 220 Prison Hill Rd. ☎ 928/783–4771 ⊕ www. azstateparks.com), the hilltop site of the late-19th-century prison where as many as six inmates inhabited a tiny cell. Nearby, **Colorado River State Historic Park** (✉ 201 N. 4th Ave. ☎ 928/329–0471 ⊕ www.coloradoriverpark.com) preserves the grounds and some buildings from an 1860s U.S. Army depot and interprets the natural history of the 1,450-mile river.

Eat & Drink: Close to the Colorado River and Yuma's historic parks, **Prison Hill Brewing** (✉ 278 S. Main St. ☎ 928/276–4001 ⊕ www.prisonhillbrewing.com) occupies a handsome vintage downtown building with ample sidewalk seating and a large indoor dining room. Share an appetizer sampler of pretzels, sausage, fried chicken, and homemade beer cheese, and save room for the stout-chocolate brownies à la mode.

ANZA-BORREGO DESERT STATE PARK

Do: At about 586,000 acres, this stunning desert landscape, part of the UNESCO-designated Mojave and Colorado Deserts Biosphere Reserve, is larger than most of the country's national parks. Anza-Borrego itself has plenty to keep you busy, including some 500 miles of unpaved roads, some suitable for standard cars, others—including the famed road to Fonts Point—better suited to four-wheel drive. Start by picking up maps at the excellent park visitor center (be sure to check out its colorful desert garden), then drive a short way to Borrego Palm Canyon Campground, where you can embark on the Panoramic Overlook Trail, a short, moderately hilly 1.5-mile out-and-back trek with a payoff of spectacular 360-degree views. Another favorite scramble is the Slot, a steep but rewarding 0.8-mile hike through a narrow ravine of massive rock formations. As you explore the park, keep your eyes peeled for bighorn sheep, coyotes, and rattlesnakes. Later in the day, drive just north of the area's main town, Borrego Springs, to view the more than 130 massive bronze Sky Art sculptures—which include a sabertooth cat, a velociraptor, and a giant serpent—created by Mexican-American artist Ricardo Breceda that dot the sweeping 1,500-acre grounds of **Galleta Meadows** (⊠ 1700–1844 Borrego Springs Rd. ☎ 760/767–5555 ⊕ www.underthesunfoundation.org).

Eat & Drink: In tiny Borrego Springs, you'll find a few mostly simple options, including long-running **Carlee's Place** (⊠ 660 Palm Canyon Dr. ☎ 760/767–3262 ⊕ www.carleesplace.com), a lively roadhouse known for its massive menu of down-home American comfort fare, including hefty charbroiled steaks.

Stay: With a clothing-optional pool and close proximity to the park, adults-only **Borrego Valley Inn** (⊠ 405 Palm Canyon Dr. ☎ 760/767–0311 ⊕ www.borregovalleyinn.com) is an inviting place to unwind after a day of driving or hiking through the desert. Camping enthusiasts take note: you're welcome to pitch a tent anywhere in the state park, and with so little light pollution, the stargazing is pretty incredible.

Breakfast: Centrally located **Red Ocotillo** (⊠ 721 Avenida Sureste ☎ 760/767–7400 ⊕ www.redocotillo.com) is a good place in the morning for eggs Benedict or blueberry-buttermilk pancakes.

Day 14: Anza-Borrego Desert State Park, CA, to San Diego, CA

90 miles (2 hours without traffic and stops)

The last day of your adventure entails a relatively short drive through the desert mountains east of San Diego, but it's a memorable drive. Head south on Highway S3, then southwest on Highway 78 to Julian. From there, follow Highway 79 south as it cuts directly through the desert peaks, oak woodlands, and giant lake in the heart of Cuyamaca Rancho State Park. Then pick up I–8 east, for the final leg to San Diego.

ALONG THE WAY

Town: A quirky Victorian gold rush town, Julian lies just over the mountains from Anza-Borrego and bursts with antiques shops, galleries, old-timey stores, and cafés specializing in fruit—especially apple—pies.

Eat & Drink: By far the area's most acclaimed stop for lunch, **Jeremy's on the Hill** (⊠ 4354 CA-78 ☎ 760/765–1587 ⊕ www.jeremysonthehill.com) in quaint Wynola specializes in farm- and ranch-to-table burgers, meat loaf, and salads.

SAN DIEGO

Do: Congratulations! You've made it all the way from coast to coast, and what better way to celebrate the completion of this journey than by taking in a grand view of the Pacific Ocean. For a vista perched high on a sea cliff that also takes in Point Loma Peninsula, San Diego Bay, and the downtown skyline, head to **Cabrillo National Monument** (✉ 1800 Cabrillo Memorial Dr. ☎ 619/523–4285 ⊕ www.nps.gov/cabr). Or to see a gorgeous inlet with a white-sand beach, tidal pools, and often a view of barking sea lions lazing on the rocks, drive to La Jolla Cove, the centerpiece of the affluent seaside community of La Jolla.

Eat & Drink: Close to Cabrillo National Monument and anchoring a mixed-use development on the site of a former navy training campus on San Diego Bay, **Liberty Public Market** (✉ 2820 Historic Decatur Rd. ☎ 619/487–9346 ⊕ www.libertypublicmarketsd.com) is a fabulous food hall brimming with gourmet vendors and several hip sit-down bars and eateries. When in San Diego, do make a point of eating fish tacos, which you can grab on the go at inexpensive takeout places like the local chain **Oscars Mexican Seafood** (✉ 646 University Ave. ☎ 619/230–5560 ⊕ www.oscarsmexicanseafood.com).

Stay: To be close to the festive energy of downtown's historic Gaslamp Quarter and hip East Village districts, book a room at the swanky **Pendry San Diego** (✉ 550 J St. ☎ 619/738–7000 ⊕ www.pendry.com), with its rooftop pool, artfully decorated rooms, and outstanding on-site restaurants and bars. On the coast, the California craftsman–style **Lodge at Torrey Pines** (✉ 11480 N. Torrey Pines Rd. ☎ 858/453–4420 ⊕ www.lodgetorreypines.com) has an absolutely stunning cliff-top location with ocean views, a celebrated golf course, and access to the wonderful trails of Torrey Pines State Natural Reserve.

Breakfast: A beloved tradition for breakfast for several decades, **Big Kitchen Cafe** (✉ 3003 Grape St. ☎ 619/234–5789 ⊕ www.judysbigkitchen.com) in Golden Hill is a delight for its colorful art-filled dining room and hefty omelets (the one with avocado, cream cheese, and chives is a favorite).

Route 66

Written by Aimee Heckel

Historic Route 66 is the most famous highway in the United States, making it a must-drive for road-trippers and history buffs alike. The "Mother Road" dates back to 1926 and connects Chicago with Los Angeles (technically neighboring Santa Monica). The original road covered nearly 2,500 miles, winding through small towns in various states and quickly becoming synonymous with a particular vision of Americana. The road and the communities it crosses have changed a lot over the years, with improvements, new sections, and growth (much of the original route is now covered over with modern interstates), but you can still plan an adventurous trip from Illinois to California, hitting many of the historical highlights along the way.

At a Glance

Start: Chicago, IL

End: Santa Monica, CA

Miles Traveled: 2,300 miles

Suggested Duration: 9 days

States Visited: Arizona, California, Illinois, Missouri, New Mexico, Oklahoma, Texas

Key Sights: Cadillac Ranch; Gateway Arch National Park; Grand Canyon National Park; London Bridge; Petrified Forest National Park

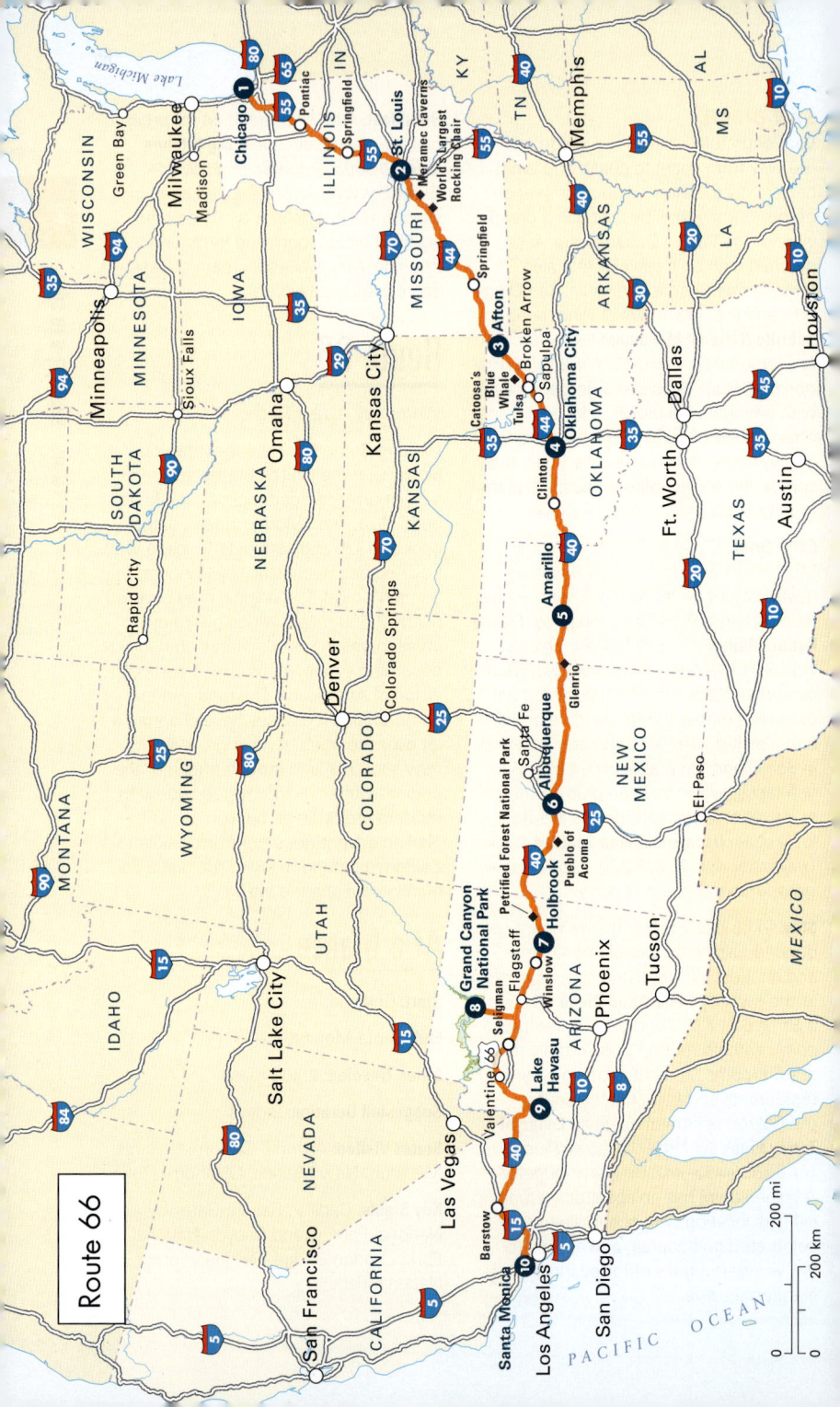

Route 66

Best Time to Go: Midwestern roads can be treacherous in the wintertime, so make this a warm-weather trip.

Day 1: Chicago, IL, to St. Louis, MO

300 miles (4 hours, 40 minutes without traffic and stops)

Start your trip in the Midwest's biggest city, Chicago, where major airports like O'Hare offer plenty of rental car options. As you leave the city, I–55 is dotted with Route 66 attractions, and you can follow them all the way into St. Louis. This is the official starting point of Route 66; while much of the country was still dirt roads, Illinois was the first to pave its part of the famous route.

ALONG THE WAY

Photo Op: Just over an hour and a half outside Chicago, the small town of Pontiac is home to the **Illinois Route 66 Hall of Fame and Museum** (✉ *110 W. Howard St.* ☎ *815/844–4566* ⊕ *www.il66assoc. org*), a fitting introduction to the adventure you've just embarked on. Even if you don't have time to explore the museum itself, be sure to stop for a photo of the world's largest Route 66 road sign outside the museum.

Town: Check out the self-guided **Living Legends Tour** in Springfield, Illinois (⊕ *visitspringfieldillinois.com*), where you can learn about Route 66 via Springfield's local entrepreneurs.

Eat & Drink: Have a hot dog on a stick for lunch at Springfield's **Cozy Dog Drive In** (✉ *2925 S. 6th St.* ☎ *217/525– 1992* ⊕ *www.cozydogdrivein.com*) opened in 1949 on Route 66. The casual eatery of today is located next door to the original site, now a historic landmark.

ST. LOUIS

Do: Route 66 runs right through St. Louis, Missouri, where you can visit the historic landmark the Chain of Rocks

Bridge. While in the area, see a true natural wonder, the **Meramec Caverns** (✉ *1135 MO-W* ☎ *573/468–2283* ⊕ *www. americascave.com*), "Missouri's buried treasure." And, of course, no visit to St. Louis is complete without a visit to **Gateway Arch National Park** (✉ *11 N. 4th St.* ☎ *314/655–1600* ⊕ *www.nps.gov/ jeff*), home to the city's famous arch.

Eat & Drink: While St. Louis has a vast dining scene, from elegant to budget-friendly, a one-of-a-kind, relaxed option is **Crown Candy Kitchen** (✉ *1401 St. Louis Ave.* ☎ *314/621–9650* ⊕ *crowncandykitchen.net*) located north of downtown. Decorated in 1930s style, the eatery makes its own (very delicious) candy.

Stay: Treat yourself to a memorable night at the elegant, art-filled **21c Museum Hotel St. Louis** (✉ *1528 Locust St.* ☎ *314/940– 2333* ⊕ *www.21cmuseumhotels.com/ stlouis*), which lies just north of verdant Gateway Mall.

Breakfast: Amid the handsome old buildings of the historic Central West End, close to Forest Park and the campus of Washington University, **Kingside Diner** (✉ *236 N. Euclid Ave.* ☎ *314/454– 3957* ⊕ *www.kingsidediner.com*) is a beloved old-school eatery known for buttermilk pancakes and cheddar drop biscuits smothered in sausage gravy.

Day 2: St. Louis, MO, to Afton, OK

325 miles (5 hours without traffic and stops)

I–44 follows the track of old Route 66 from Missouri to Oklahoma, through small towns and big cities, valleys and hills.

ALONG THE WAY

Roadside Attraction: As you approach Fanning, Missouri, be sure to check out the World's Largest Rocking Chair on Route 66. Yes, it's exactly what it sounds like.

Town: You've visited Springfield, Illinois, so why not Springfield, Missouri? This Springfield has the **Route 66 Springfield Visitor Center** (✉ 815 E. St. Louis St. ☎ 800/678–8767 ⊕ www.springfield-mo.org) and the well-preserved Rock Fountain Court Historic District, a group of stone cabins facing Route 66 that used to be public lodging.

Eat & Drink: In Springfield, stop by **Civil Kitchen** (✉ 107 Park Central Sq. ☎ 417/501–8456 ⊕ www.facebook.com/civilsgf), a hip but relaxed restaurant overlooking downtown's regal Park Central Square, for creative takes on traditional American dishes and craft beers.

Nature: The Springfield area has more than 100 parks and is known for its trails—a good excuse to get out and stretch your legs. A good intro trail to the area is **Wilson's Creek Greenway** (✉ 3825 W. Farm Rd. 146 ☎ 417/864–2015 ⊕ ozarkgreenways.org).

AFTON

Do: While it might be easy to drive right past this tiny town in Oklahoma, it's a Route 66 mecca, with classic Route 66 architecture and nostalgic attractions.

Eat & Drink: The best place to eat in Afton: **Nowhere** (✉ 300 S. 1st St. ☎ 918/919–4111 ⊕ www.facebook.com/nowhereonroute66). That's not cheekiness; it's the actual name of a tasty local barbecue joint. Nowhere on Route 66 (the full name, for its location right on the historical road) offers hand-rubbed, wood-smoked meats and an impressive collection of specialty sandwiches. Add some fried green beans and spicy pickles for a true American meal.

Shop: Shop a pecan grove at Afton's **Miller Pecan Company** (✉ 21853 U.S. 69 ☎ 918/257–6887 ⊕ www.millerpecancompany.com). Bet you've never had blackstrap molasses or scuppernong jelly before.

Stay: About 15 miles east of town in Wyandotte, the **River Bend Casino and Hotel** (✉ 100 Jackpot Pl. ☎ 918/678–4946 ⊕ www.riverbendcasino.com) offers attractively furnished rooms along with two restaurants. Even if you're not much on gaming, this is a comfortable choice.

Breakfast: Green Country Cafe (✉ 21601 U.S. 69 ☎ 918/257–5140) is a sweet, small-town restaurant with excellent pies, but the classic breakfast dishes won't disappoint either. If you're there too early for dessert, grab a slice of pie to go for a midday snack.

Day 3: Afton, OK, to Oklahoma City, OK

180 miles (2 hours, 45 minutes without traffic and stops)

Take I-44 down past Tulsa and Broken Arrow, Oklahoma, to Oklahoma City. The longest driveable length of Route 66 runs through Oklahoma. Keep your eyes open for landmarks, such as the Bridge No. 18 at Rock Creek, part of the Historic Route 66 in Sapulpa.

ALONG THE WAY

Roadside Attraction: Another Route 66 roadside attraction that can't be missed is Catoosa's Blue Whale, an 80-foot-long sperm whale made out of concrete and pipe.

Town: Tulsa, the second-largest city in Oklahoma, may be best known for its art deco architecture, but it's also home to several Route 66 markers, such as the 11th Street Arkansas River Bridge and the cottage-style Vickery Phillips 66 Station. If you have time, a visit to the city's **Greenwood Cultural Center** (✉ 322 N. Greenwood Ave. ☎ 918/596–1020 ⊕ www.greenwoodculturalcenter.org) is an essential stop to learn more about the 1921 Tulsa Massacre and the history of Greenwood, once America's Black Wall Street.

Eat & Drink: Get a tasty seafood lunch at Tulsa's **White River Fish Market and Restaurant** (✉ *1708 N. Sheridan Rd.* ☎ *918/835–1910* ⊕ *www.whiteriverfishmarket.com*). Yes, some of the best food in this landlocked state is surprisingly from the sea.

OKLAHOMA CITY

Do: Do your best cowboy impression at the **National Cowboy and Western Heritage Museum** (✉ *1700 N.E. 63rd St.* ☎ *405/478–2250* ⊕ *www.nationalcowboymusuem.org*), which boasts more than 28,000 western and Native American art and artifacts.

Eat & Drink: Pop's Soda Ranch (✉ *660 U.S. Rte. 66* ☎ *405/927–7677* ⊕ *www.pops66.com*) in nearby Arcadia is exactly the kind of mom-and-pop stop you want to eat at on a road trip like this. Just look for the massive, neon, glowing soda bottle as you cruise down 66.

Stay: The Route 66 road trip is all about time travel, and you can continue that at the **Colcord Hotel** (✉ *15 N. Robinson Ave.* ☎ *405/601–4300* ⊕ *www.colcordhotel.com*), built in 1909 originally as a skyscraper office tower. Today, it's a swanky luxury hotel.

Breakfast: The Colcord has several different restaurants on-site, including Flint, a terrific option for fluffy vanilla pancakes and breakfast tacos.

Day 4: Oklahoma City, OK, to Amarillo, TX

260 miles (4 hours without traffic and stops)

Continue along I–40 east. You'll find scattered small towns along the way with frequent Route 66 sites, such as old service stations, as you make your way into Texas.

Extend Your Trip

From St. Louis: Along the Mississippi *(Ch. 2)*; The Best of the Ozarks *(Ch. 6)*

From Albuquerque: The Best of New Mexico *(Ch. 5)*

From Grand Canyon: The Best of Arizona *(Ch. 5)*

From Los Angeles: The Pacific Coast Highway; The Best of Southern California *(Ch. 3)*

ALONG THE WAY

Town: Clinton, Oklahoma, is located on Route 66. Stop here to tour (and take some great selfies at) the **Oklahoma Route 66 Museum** (✉ *2229 W. Gary Blvd.* ☎ *580/323–7866* ⊕ *www.okhistory.org*) and to learn more about the state's part in the historic road.

Eat & Drink: The **Route 66 Cafe at the Market** (✉ *301 W. Gary Blvd.* ☎ *580/445–7008* ⊕ *www.rte66cafe.com*) in Clinton not only pays homage to the Mother Road, but it also has mouthwatering, old-fashioned comfort food. Take your pick from the meat loaf, catfish fry, chicken-fried steak, and homemade Frito pie, all just like Grandma used to make (okay, maybe not the Frito pie).

AMARILLO

Do: When in Amarillo, you have to take photos at one of the country's most famous roadside attraction, the **Cadillac Ranch** (✉ *13651 I–40 Frontage Rd.* ☎ *833/330–2650* ⊕ *www.facebook.com/1974cadillacranch*), where a row of Caddys curiously balance upright, noses down in the ground and tail fins up in the air.

Eat & Drink: Everything is bigger in Texas, right? Then order a 72-ounce steak at the **Big Texan Steak Ranch** (⊠ *7701 I–40 E* ☎ *806/372–6000* ⊕ *www.bigtexan.com*).

Stay: If you attempt the 72-ounce-steak challenge, you will be waddling back to your bed. Luckily, there's a motel and "horse motel" (yes, for your horses) on-site. The **Big Texan Motel** (⊠ *7701 I–40 Access Rd.* ☎ *806/372–6000* ⊕ *www.bigtexanmotel.com*) was built to look like an old Wild West town, complete with a Texas-shaped swimming pool.

Breakfast: Ye Olde Pancake Station (⊠ *2800 Virginia Circle* ☎ *806/355–0211* ⊕ *www.pancakestation.com*) is where the locals start their day. There's more than pancakes; you can actually order green eggs and ham (the green here is green chili).

Day 5: Amarillo, TX, to Albuquerque, NM

290 miles (4 hours without traffic and stops)

I–40 will shoot you straight west to New Mexico, passing a handful of Route 66 landmarks as you go.

ALONG THE WAY

Town: An unincorporated town that straddles the Texas-New Mexico border, Glenrio is where you can see the Historic Route 66 roadbed in a mid-century ghost town of the American West.

Eat & Drink: Russell's Truck and Travel Center (⊠ *11583 Frontage Rd. 4132* ☎ *575/576–8700*) in tiny Glenrio is a convenience store as well as an authentic Route 66 diner. It's not fancy, but it's the real deal.

ALBUQUERQUE

Do: There's so much to do in Albuquerque, but the **ABQ BioPark** (⊠ *903 10th St. SW* ☎ *505/768–2000* ⊕ *www.cabq.gov*) is a true wonderland for animal lovers. Round out the day with a sunset ride on

the **Sandia Peak Tramway** (⊠ *30 Tramway Rd. NE* ☎ *505/856–1532* ⊕ *www.sandiapeak.com*).

Eat & Drink: Campo at Los Poblanos (⊠ *4803 Rio Grande Blvd. NW, Los Ranchos de Albuquerque* ☎ *855/486–1380* ⊕ *www.lospoblanos.com*) is the definition of farm-to-table; it's located on an organic farm in the Rio Grande River valley.

Stay: Stay in the **Hyatt Regency Tamaya Resort and Spa** (⊠ *1300 Tuyuna Trail, Santa Ana Pueblo* ☎ *505/867–1234* ⊕ *www.hyatt.com*) for a luxurious experience with a focus on Native American culture (it's on the Santa Ana Pueblo), or at the **Hotel Parq Central** (⊠ *806 Central Ave. SE* ☎ *505/242–0040* ⊕ *www.hotelparqcentral.com*) for a unique and historical experience; the latter is a former infirmary transformed into an elegant hotel with a sultry rooftop bar.

Breakfast: Swing by the healthy and hip **Grove Cafe and Market** (⊠ *600 Central Ave. SE* ☎ *505/248–9800* ⊕ *www.thegrovecafemarket.com*) for a fresh breakfast in a bright, enclosed patio.

Day 6: Albuquerque, NM, to Holbrook, AZ

230 miles (30 hours, 30 minutes without traffic and stops)

I–40 West takes you to Arizona, past pink cliffs, wide-open spaces, tiny towns, and the Continental Divide, which is also the highest point on Route 66.

ALONG THE WAY

Detour: If you want to immerse yourself in Native American culture and the Pueblo of Acoma, take a small detour (about 20 minutes) to Sky City, New Mexico. Start at the **Sky City Cultural Center and Haak'u Museum** (⊠ *Haaku*

Rd. ☎ 505/552–7861 ⊕ www.acomasky-city.org) and learn about the oldest continuously inhabited settlement in North America.

Eat & Drink: Taste authentic Acoma food at the **Yaak'a Cafe** inside the Sky City cultural center. In addition to traditional fare, you can also find modern American food, all made by the tribe.

Photo Op: The **Rio Puerco Bridge** (✉ 14311 Central Ave NW ⊕ www.nps.gov) in Rio Puerco, New Mexico, is located west of Albuquerque on Route 66, after a scenic drive into the valley. You can walk across the bridge, which is on the National Register of Historic Places, and take photos of the old Highway 66 fading into the desert beyond.

HOLBROOK

Do: In the Holbrook area, take some time to enjoy the fairy tale–esque **Petrified Forest National Park** (☎ 928/524–6228 ⊕ www.nps.gov/pefo) and glimpse some fossils.

Eat & Drink: Locals love **Colonel Mustard Hot Dogs** (✉ 459 Navajo Blvd. ☎ 928/241–1034 ⊕ www.colonelmustardhotdogs.com) for its setting in a converted mid-century service station and its filling Chicago dogs and hot Italian beef sandwiches.

Stay: Spend the night in the **Wigwam Motel** (✉ 811 W. Hopi Dr. ☎ 928/524–3048 ⊕ www.sleepinawigwam.com), which doubles as a museum and has a parking lot filled with vintage automobiles. Accommodations are in a famously Instagrammable concrete teepee.

Breakfast: Mr. Maestas (✉ 502 Navajo Blvd. ☎ 928/524–6000) serves reliably good Mexican and American dishes in the morning inside a quirky dining room festooned with old photos and Route 66 memorabilia.

Day 7: Holbrook, AZ, to Grand Canyon National Park, AZ

175 miles (2 hours, 30 minutes without traffic and stops)

Follow I–40 to the Grand Canyon, past the city of Flagstaff, Arizona's famous red rocks, and the Coconino National Forest's thick pine trees. Although the route to the Grand Canyon veers away from the traditional Route 66, it's still a must-see for a true vision of America.

ALONG THE WAY

Town: Although this stretch of the drive is short and straightforward, a bonus site along the way is the 11-acre architectural treasure, the **La Posada Hotel** (✉ 303 E. 2nd St. ☎ 928/289–4366 ⊕ www.laposada.org) in Winslow, Arizona. Stroll through the grounds and pick up a souvenir.

Shop: La Posada's Trading Post and Book Store is a great place to find Mimbres design replica pottery, southwestern jewelry, and Native American crafts.

Eat & Drink: The La Posada Hotel houses **The Turquoise Room** (✉ 303 E. 2nd St. ☎ 928/289–2888 ⊕ www.theturquoiseroom.net), one of the finest restaurants in the region. It specializes in southwestern cuisine.

GRAND CANYON NATIONAL PARK

Do: Witnessing the 10-mile-wide **Grand Canyon** (✉ Grand Canyon National Park Visitor Center, South Entrance Rd. ☎ 928/638–7888 ⊕ www.nps.gov/grca) is awe-inspiring, even life-changing. Explore it via hiking, riding a mule, biking, or even rafting down the Colorado River.

Eat & Drink: The best restaurant by the Grand Canyon is hands down **El Tovar** on the South Rim (✉ 1 El Tovar Rd. ☎ 928/638–2631 ⊕ www.

2

Trips of a Lifetime **ROUTE 66**

Did You Know?

Sure-footed mules take riders along the rim for half-day trips and down into the Grand Canyon for longer excursions. Two-day trips include an overnight stay at Phantom Ranch on the canyon floor.

grandcanyonlodges.com), which serves both international and southwestern cuisine. It's also a bit expensive. If you're on a budget, you can also find food trucks on the South Rim.

Stay: Stay at the beautiful El Tovar Hotel on the South Rim. Let's be honest: you're going to want to stay here for a few days, thanks to the Euro-style hunting lodge feel and canyon-view rooms.

Breakfast: Grab a quick coffee and a light breakfast at the **Canyon Coffee House at The Fountain** (✉ *9 Village Loop Dr.* ☎ *928/638–2631* ⊕ *www.grandcanyonlodges.com*), inside the Bright Angel Lodge.

Day 8: Grand Canyon National Park, AZ, to Lake Havasu, AZ

240 miles (3 hours, 45 minutes without traffic and stops)

Head from one natural delight to another via the simple I–40 route, which takes you from the Grand Canyon to Lake Havasu City.

ALONG THE WAY

Town: The small town of Seligman, Arizona, calls itself a "birthplace" of Route 66. It feels like you've stepped back in time with the retro signs and classic cars.

Eat & Drink: When in Seligman, you must dine at **Delgadillo's Snow Cap** founded in the 1950s (✉ *301 AZ-66* ☎ *928/422–3291*), with quirky menu items like Oink Burgers, "male" or "female" sundaes, and a "cheeseburger with cheese."

LAKE HAVASU

Do: In Lake Havasu, visit the world-famous **London Bridge** (✉ *1340 McCulloch Blvd.* ⊕ *www.londonbridgetour.com*). It was built in the 1830s in London and moved to Arizona in the 1960s. This surprising beachfront resort in the middle

of the desert state boasts ample hiking, boating, biking, fishing, golfing, and special events—so much that you may want to extend your trip here for a few days.

Eat & Drink: Lake Havasu has a good selection of food, mostly casual. A brewery can provide a great glimpse into a community, so refuel at award-winning **Barley Brothers Restaurant and Brewery** (✉ *1425 McCulloch Blvd. N* ☎ *928/505–7837* ⊕ *www.barleybrothers.com*). With wood-fired-oven pizza, local brews, and a view of London Bridge, you can't go wrong.

Stay: It's an Arizona rite of passage to go camping on the lake, although there are other lodging options if you don't feel like roughing it, like the hip boutique **Heat Hotel** (✉ *1420 McCulloch Blvd. N* ☎ *928/854–2833* ⊕ *www.heathotel.com*) overlooking Bridgewater Channel.

Breakfast: Fill up on breakfast at the Lake Havasu City **Black Bear Diner** (✉ *1900 McCulloch Blvd. N* ☎ *928/855–2013* ⊕ *www.blackbeardiner.com*). This restaurant claims the "biggest portions for the hungriest bears," such as a 10-ounce "Bigfoot Chicken Fried Steak and Eggs" that's a whopping 2,580 calories.

Day 9: Lake Havasu, AZ, to Santa Monica, CA

300 miles (5 hours without traffic and stops)

There are two different routes from Havasu to Santa Monica, both similar in time and distance. Choose I–40 so you can make one final, historical stop in Barstow, California.

ALONG THE WAY

Town: Barstow, California, is home of the former Harvey House Railroad Depot, originally built in 1885. Today it's the **Route 66 Mother Road Museum** (✉ *681 N. 1st*

Ave. ☎ 760/255–1890 ⊕ www.route-66museum.org), featuring a spread of old photos and artifacts.

Eat & Drink: While in Barstow, you can snag some great Mexican food. **Lola's Kitchen** (✉ 1244 E. Main St. ☎ 760/255–1007), a hidden gem in a strip mall, has tasty green chilis that are worth the stop.

SANTA MONICA

Do: Wrap up your Route 66 road trip by spending a day exploring Los Angeles before ending your adventure with a photo op in the neighboring city of Santa Monica at **Santa Monica Pier,** where the famous "End of the Trail" sign marks the official end to your journey; you can even add your name to the list of fellow Route 66 travelers at the nearby information booth.

Eat & Drink: Finalize this history buff's journey where the French dip sandwich is said to have been invented, at L.A.'s **Philippe the Original** (✉ 1001 N. Alameda St. ☎ 213/628–3781 ⊕ www.philippes.com).

Stay: On Santa Monica's busy Main Street, the **Sea Shore Motel** (✉ 2637 Main St. ☎ 310/392–2787 ⊕ www.seashore-motel.com), family-owned since 1972, is a throwback to roadside motels in a trendy neighborhood.

Breakfast: Founded by Santa Monica natives, **Huckleberry Bakery and Café** (✉ 1014 Wilshire Blvd. ☎ 310/451–2311 ⊕ www.huckleberrycafe.com) brings together the best ingredients from local farmers and growers to craft diner-style comfort food with a chic twist. Everything is made on-site, even the hot sauce and almond milk.

The East Coast's Best Beaches

Written by Brandon Schultz

California may be known for its surfing and laid-back coastal attitude, but many of the country's best beaches are actually found on the East Coast, where more than 2,000 miles of coastline are dotted with scores of popular seaside destinations. For a highlights tour of the East Coast's best beaches south of New Jersey, follow this trail from Miami to Delaware, stopping in each state along the way at least once. It'll take at least eight days to hit them all, but don't be afraid to stay longer in any given spot or hit a few extra shores along the way. There's plenty to see in each town, and so many more gorgeous beaches along the route.

■ **TIP→** This route ends in Delaware so to truly experience the best of the East Coast, extend your trip even longer by linking it with two other road trips: The Best of Long Island and the Jersey Shore (*Ch. 8*) and Coastal New England (*Ch. 8*).

At a Glance

Start: Miami Beach, FL

End: Rehoboth Beach, DE

Miles Traveled: 1,450 miles

Suggested Duration: 8 days

States Visited: Delaware, Florida, Georgia, Maryland, North Carolina, South Carolina, Virginia

Key Sights: Myrtle Beach; the Outer Banks; Palm Beach; Tybee Island; Virginia Beach

Best Time to Go: If you want to hit all the beaches at the height of activity with all local businesses open, you'll need to visit in summer. The earlier you go, the less soaring and scorching the temperatures will be, and some crowds may be marginally smaller. Keep in mind that the summer will also mean accommodations book up quickly, so plan accordingly.

Day 1: Miami, FL, to Cocoa Beach, FL

210 miles (3 hours, 45 minutes without traffic and stops)

Miami International Airport (MIA), with more than a dozen car rental agencies, should be your point of entry for this adventure; Fort Lauderdale (FLL) may seem close, but traffic from here could easily add an additional hour to your day. When leaving Miami, it's a simple drive up I-95 N to Route 404, which will take you island-hopping through Thousand Islands to Cocoa Beach.

ALONG THE WAY

Town: About two hours from Miami, stop in West Palm Beach for a culture break. There's plenty of dining and shopping around the Palm Beaches, but the **Norton Museum of Art** (✉ 1450 S. Dixie Hwy. ☎ 561/832–5196 ⊕ www.norton. org) in West Palm is worth the stop alone. Here you'll find more than 8,000 pieces between the collection's five primary focuses: American, Chinese, European, contemporary, and photography.

Eat & Drink: While in West Palm Beach, grab a bite at **Batch New Southern Kitchen & Tap** (✉ 223 Clematis St. ☎ 561/708-0000 ⊕ www.batchsouthernkitchen. com), where local ingredients supply from-scratch recipes of modern southern dishes like shrimp and grits, chicken and waffles, and an entire mac and cheese menu. Garden-fresh cocktails mixed with craft American spirits are a hit here.

Shop: West Palm's Antique Row is brimming with hidden treasures, but the bargains are found at **Tanger Outlets Palm Beach** (✉ 1751 Palm Beach Lakes Blvd. ☎ 561/515–4400 ⊕ www.tanger. com/palmbeach), also in West Palm.

COCOA BEACH

Do: Cocoa Beach is best known for two things: surfing and space. The **Florida Surf Museum** (✉ 4275 N. Atlantic Ave. ☎ 321/446–1583 ⊕ www.floridasurf-museum.org) provides a good look into the state's surfing history for serious devotees, but the casually curious may have more fun simply watching the surfers at Westgate Cocoa Beach Pier. Transitioning from the sea to the sky, Cocoa Beach is equally famed as the gateway to the **Kennedy Space Center** (✉ Space Commerce Way, Merritt Island ☎ 855/433–4210 ⊕ www.kennedyspacecenter.com) at Cape Canaveral. There are plenty of tours and exhibits available year-round, but you'll create a lifelong memory if you time your visit to catch a rocket launch.

Eat & Drink: Drop by **Q's Crackin' Crab & Seafood Kitchen** (✉ 5240 N. Atlantic Ave. ☎ 321/613–4044 ⊕ www.qscrack-incrab.com) for a signature seafood boil drenched in garlic butter or one of a vast array of mixed seafood platters with lobster, crab, and shrimp dominating the menu. For the classic local cocktail experience, head back to Cocoa Beach Pier and visit the **Rikki Tiki Tavern** (✉ 401 Meade Ave. ☎ 321/783–7549 ⊕ www. resort.to) at the very tip, 800 feet from the shore, for cocktails over the ocean and under the thatched roof.

Stay: If a hotel can be both retro and contemporary, **Beachside Hotel & Suites** (✉ 3901 N. Atlantic Ave. ☎ 321/783–2221 ⊕ www. beachsidehotelcocoabeach.com) is it. Grab a complimentary surfboard and head to the beach 300 feet away or snag a cruiser for some more land-focused exercise. If exertion is out of the question, just float on the lazy-river-style pool.

The East Coast's Best Beaches

9 Rehoboth Beach
Bethany Beach
Indian River Bay
8 Fenwick Island
Ocean City

Chincoteague National
Wildlife Refuge

7 Virginia Beach

6 Kill Devil Hills
Roanoke Island

5 Myrtle Beach

4 Tybee Island

3 Jekyll Island

2 Cocoa Beach

1 Miami

Breakfast: Follow your nose to **Sunrise Bread Company** (✉ 315 S. Hopkins Ave., Titusville ☎ 321/268–1009 ⊕ www. sunrisebread.com) for baked goods and breakfast sandwiches on your way out of Cocoa Beach. You'll also find plenty of specialty coffees and smoothies to power you for your drive today.

Day 2: Cocoa Beach, FL, to Jekyll Island, GA

240 miles (3 hours, 30 minutes without traffic and stops)

Head back to I–95 north and continue up the coast until you reach Route 520 east. From here, it's a quick jaunt to the ocean to reach Jekyll Island across the East River. Don't forget that there's a small toll to access the island—you can pay with cash or a credit card.

ALONG THE WAY

Town: About an hour before Jekyll Island, make a stop in Jacksonville, Florida, the country's largest city by surface area. Jacksonville is home to a handful of notable art and history museums, a couple of historic forts, plenty of parks, and its top attraction, the **Jacksonville Zoo and Gardens** (✉ 370 Zoo Pkwy. ☎ 904/757–4463 ⊕ www.jacksonvillezoo.org).

Eat & Drink: Chow down on tacos and margaritas at **TacoLu** (✉ 1712 Beach Blvd. ☎ 904/249–8226 ⊕ www.tacolu. com) in Jacksonville Beach. This local favorite offers classics like Baja fish tacos and carnitas alongside a serious tequila list in a festive atmosphere of colorful art and murals.

JEKYLL ISLAND

Do: The former playground of America's wealthiest families, you'll still find plenty of lovely "cottages" (mansions, to any sane person) on Millionaire's Row, but the island today is better known for its impressive natural gifts. From the eerie beauty of epic **Driftwood Beach**

(☎ 800/933–2627 ⊕ www.goldenisles. com), where the still-standing remains of 200-year-old oaks and pines line the coast, to the **Georgia Sea Turtle Center** (✉ 214 Stable Rd. ☎ 912/635–4444 ⊕ www.gstc.jekyllisland.com), where you can get up close with the rehabbing patients, Jekyll Island is ideal for a quiet escape.

Eat & Drink: To enjoy live music at a waterfront location, have dinner at **The Wharf** (✉ 371 Riverview Dr. ☎ 912/635–3612 ⊕ www.jekyllwharf.com). Located on the Historic District pier, the view is idyllic any time of day, but can be particularly dramatic at sundown. Directly across the island (a whopping 4-minute drive or 20-minute walk), **Tortuga Jacks** (✉ 201 Beachview Dr. N ☎ 912/342–2600 ⊕ www. tortugajacks.com) also offers waterfront bites and sips and is a top choice if you're road-tripping with a pet.

Stay: Settle into the **Beachview Club Hotel** (✉ 721 Beachview Dr. N ☎ 912/635–2256 ⊕ www.beachviewclubjekyll.com) to experience quiet coastal living on Jekyll Island. The outdoor pool is shaded by live oaks and the shoreline is just steps beyond.

Breakfast: Snag coffee or an indulgent frappe to go from **The Pantry at Jekyll Island Club Resort** (✉ 371 Riverview Dr. ☎ 888/445–3179 ⊕ www.jekyllclub. com). It's a short drive for Day 3, so consider a simple breakfast order like the Jekyll cinnamon roll or a danish.

Day 3: Jekyll Island, GA, to Tybee Island, GA

110 miles (2 hours without traffic and stops)

Continue up I–95 north to I–16 east and cross the Wilmington River and Bull River on your way to Tybee Island.

Georgia's Jekyll Island is a peaceful place filled with nature excursions.

ALONG THE WAY

Photo Op: Just off I–95 in Townsend, the self-proclaimed "Smallest Church in America" offers a quaint photo op with its tiny chapel and miniature bell tower among the (much taller) trees.

Town: Savannah is one of the most alluring cities in the South and it's directly on your route to Tybee, so don't miss the chance to stop. Stroll River Street, gawk at the unnamed fountain in **Forsyth Park** (✉ 2 W. Gaston St. ☎ 912/351–3841 ⊕ www.savannahga.gov), and ogle the majestic mansions surrounding many of the 22 square parks found within a single square mile of downtown Savannah.

Eat & Drink: Mrs. Wilkes Dining Room

(✉ 107 W. Jones St. ⊕ www.mrswilkes.com) remains the top table in Savannah, but the no-reservations system makes it difficult for day-trippers to score a seat. Feel free to stop by and check—miracles can happen—but you're guaranteed a great meal at **Sisters of the New South** (✉ 2605 Skidaway Rd. ☎ 912/335–2761 ⊕ www.thesistersofthenewsouth.

com), a "meat and three" eatery with traditional sides like collard greens, red rice, and green beans. The peach cobbler is famous here, and sweet tea is a must.

Detour: Make a pit stop at **Bonaventure Cemetery** (✉ 330 Bonaventure Rd., Thunderbolt ☎ 912/651–6843 ⊕ www.savannahga.gov) on your way out of Savannah. This waterfront cemetery isn't just the titular "garden" of *Midnight in the Garden of Good and Evil* and the location of one of the book's most important scenes, it's also a gorgeous collection of stunning monuments and swaying Spanish moss hanging from towering oaks.

TYBEE ISLAND

Do: Just beyond Savannah, Tybee is a barrier island with both ocean and river beaches, the most popular of which is South Beach with its soft-sand shoreline. Beach bums will prefer the ocean beaches while fishing fans should head to the river beaches, and the historic 18th-century lighthouse and **Tybee Island Marine Science Center** (✉ 37 Meddin

Dr. ☎ 912/786–5917 ⊕ www.tybeema-rinescience.org) should appeal to all.

Eat & Drink: Embrace the island vibe with a meal at the **Crab Shack** (✉ 40 Estill Hammock Rd. ☎ 912/786–9857 ⊕ www.thecrabshack.com). What started as a charter boat company and marina slowly expanded as the owners began cooking up the day's catch; it's now a waterfront restaurant serving fresh seafood daily.

Stay: If you loved the Crab Shack, consider staying at the owners' Airbnb, Purple Haze, within walking distance of the restaurant and also overlooking the water (the restaurant's website has a direct link to the listing). If you prefer a more traditional stay, try the **Admiral's Inn** (✉ 1501 Butler Ave. ☎ 912/786–0700 ⊕ www.admiralsinntybee.com) for a three-star night with an outdoor pool.

Breakfast: There's a bit of a longer drive coming up, so treat yourself to a full meal at **Sunrise Breakfast** (✉ 1511 Butler Ave. ☎ 912/786–7473 ⊕ www.sunrisesavannah.com), where the Hash Brown Deluxe is the star of the signature menu. Potatoes are piled with broccoli, mushrooms, onions, and tomatoes, and you can add all manner of meats or eggs for protein.

Day 4: Tybee Island, GA, to Myrtle Beach, SC

220 miles (4 hours, 30 minutes without traffic and stops)

Instead of staying on I-95 north for most of the trip into South Carolina, stick to U.S. 17, which will take you through Charleston and its nearby collection of popular islands and beaches.

ALONG THE WAY

Town: Charleston itself would make an excellent stop, and if you're in a rush to make it to Myrtle Beach, by all means just take a half hour or so to wander

---

Extend Your Trip

From Miami: The Best of Southern Florida *(Ch. 7)*

From Cocoa Beach: The Best of Northern and Central Florida *(Ch. 7)*

From Myrtle Beach or the Outer Banks: The Best of the Carolinas *(Ch. 7)*

From Rehoboth Beach: The Best of Long Island and the Jersey Shore *(Ch. 8)*

---

around the city's cobblestone streets that ooze with southern charm. But if you have some time to spare, any of the city's outlying islands make a fine detour, from golf-famous Kiawah Island to historic Sullivan's Island. But don't miss rural Edisto Island, where you'll find magnificent stands of age-old oaks festooned with Spanish moss, and side roads that lead to Gullah hamlets and aging wooden churches. A driving tour around **Botany Bay Heritage Preserve** (✉ 1066 Botany Bay Rd. ⊕ www.dnr.sc.gov) passes through impoundments and maritime forest and past saltwater marsh, making it one of the most diverse and car-accessible coastal habitats in the Southeast.

Eat & Drink: Once a 1940s-era filling station (the pumps are still outside), **Whaley's** (✉ 2801 Myrtle St. ☎ 843/869–2161 ⊕ www.whaleyseb.com) on Edisto Island has been converted into a fun and eclectic bar and restaurant. The menu ranges from bar food like Buffalo wings and burgers to local shrimp, crab cakes, and pan-seared mahimahi.

MYRTLE BEACH

Do: Myrtle Beach is the crown jewel of the 60 miles of beach that make up South Carolina's Grand Strand. Light brown sands, gentle waves, and mild water temps make the beach itself enjoyable for all ages, but there's plenty of off-sand fun to be had, too. The main action is found at **Broadway at the Beach** (✉ *1325 Celebrity Circle* ☎ *843/444–3200* ⊕ *www.broadwayatthebeach.com*), which is actually on Lake Broadway, where you could spend anywhere from an hour to a day touring attractions, catching shows, and riding amusements like the SkyWheel, one of the tallest Ferris wheels in the nation.

Eat & Drink: If you packed a dressy outfit and are in the mood for steak and lobster, **The Library** (✉ *6613 N. Kings Hwy.* ☎ *843/448–4527* ⊕ *www.thelibraryrestaurantsc.com*) should be your dinner reservation of choice in Myrtle Beach. For a more casual place, choose **Hook & Barrel** (✉ *8014 N. Kings Hwy. B* ☎ *843/839–5888* ⊕ *www.hookandbarrelrestaurant.com*) for honey-glazed salmon, crab cakes, or filet mignon. Continue the tiki trend of this trip with after-dinner drinks at **8th Avenue Tiki Bar** (✉ *708 N. Ocean Blvd.* ☎ *843/712–2340* ⊕ *www.8thavetikibar.net*) on the boardwalk.

Stay: Aside from the view, there's a very practical reason to spring for a beachfront property in Myrtle Beach: there aren't a lot of public restrooms along the water, so you'll want easy access to your hotel if you'll be spending all day on the sand (especially if you're enjoying cocktails or beer). **Island Vista Resort** (✉ *6000 N. Ocean Blvd.* ☎ *843/449–6406* ⊕ *www.islandvista.com*) is an affordable option that also comes with its own indoor and outdoor pools and plenty of other creature comforts.

Breakfast: Start the day with a hearty breakfast at retro-cool **Lulu's Cafe** (✉ *1903 N. Ocean Blvd.* ☎ *843/712–1890* ⊕ *www.luluscafe.com*), a palm-flanked diner by the beach serving crab cake Benedicts, banana-pecan pancakes, and boozy brunch cocktails.

Day 5: Myrtle Beach, SC, to Kill Devil Hills, NC

310 miles (5 hours, 30 minutes without traffic and stops)

If you've fallen in love with I–95 north and want to continue on the same path, you could take this to U.S. 64 east, but there's a slightly shorter route today. You'll save about 15 minutes if you take Route 31 north instead, hugging the coast a bit tighter.

ALONG THE WAY

Roadside Attraction: Perhaps the weirdest and wildest pit stop on the East Coast, **South of the Border** (⊕ *www.sobpedro.com*) is a wonderland of towering, colorful figures (animal and human), neon lights, souvenir shopping, and roadside dining. You'll need to take the I–95 north route (or an alternative path up U.S. 501 north from Myrtle Beach) to hit this one, found immediately before the North Carolina border, but you won't regret it.

Town: Roughly 80 miles into your drive, take a break in Wilmington, North Carolina. The 230-block Historic District is packed with architecture that oozes southern grace as you say good-bye to the true South with today's drive. Don't miss the sprawling **Airlie Gardens** (✉ *300 Airlie Rd.* ☎ *910/798–7700* ⊕ *www.airliegardens.org*) for a romantic location that has attracted a slew of film and television crews.

Eat & Drink: Grab some pub fare at **Fork 'N' Cork** (✉ *122 Market St.* ☎ *910/228–5247* ⊕ *www.theforkncork.com*) in Wilmington. Start with fried pickles or crispy Brussels sprouts before choosing from a dozen burgers or sandwiches. If you're aiming to have seafood with every meal on this beach itinerary, give the Rattlesnake Bites a try; they're shrimp-and-corn-stuffed, deep-fried jalapeños served with habanero jelly.

Nature: Croatan National Forest

(☎ 252/638–5628 ⊕ www.fs.usda.gov) is the only coastal forest in the East, and you'll find it around the halfway point between Myrtle Beach and the Outer Banks, ideally situated for a brief stretch break.

KILL DEVIL HILLS

Do: The Outer Banks refers to 175 miles of barrier islands off the coast of North Carolina, and the numerous beaches have varying appeals. Kitty Hawk is one of the best for general interest, from surfing or lying on the beach to nature walks on nearby trails; there's something for everyone here. But Kill Devil Hills is a solid choice with great surfing, restaurants, and hotels. And don't miss nearby Roanoke Island, site of the first English settlement in 1585, all of whose inhabitants mysteriously vanished without a trace.

Eat & Drink: If you're ready for oysters, it's off to **Awful Arthur's** (☒ 2106 N. Virginia Dare Trail ☎ 252/441–5955 ⊕ www.awfularthursobx.com) you go. This Kill Devil Hills institution was the first oyster bar in the Outer Banks and is still riding high in popularity. The ocean-view lounge, a surprisingly rare occurrence in the Outer Banks, certainly adds to the appeal.

Stay: The **Sea Ranch Resort** (☒ 1731 N. Virginia Dare Trail ☎ 252/441–7126 ⊕ www.searanchresort.com) is a no-fuss stay in Kill Devil Hills with clean, spacious rooms, many of which include ocean views and private balconies. The Beachside Bistro with its oceanfront deck is great for evening drinks, too.

Breakfast: Miller's Seafood & Steakhouse (☒ 1520 S. Virginia Dare Trail ☎ 252/441–7674 ⊕ www.millersseafood.com) may not sound like a breakfast bonanza, but it's the top choice in Kill Devil Hills for a filling breakfast, with plenty of lighter options, too.

Day 6: Kill Devil Hills, NC, to Virginia Beach, VA

90 miles (1 hour, 40 minutes without traffic and stops)

Breaking from tradition, there's no I–95 north option today. Take Route 168 north to I–264 east, and stop when you reach the coast.

ALONG THE WAY

Town: Between canals, rivers, and lakes, Chesapeake, Virginia, has more waterways than you can see in a day, but that shouldn't stop you from dropping by to check a few out. You'll also find the lush **Chesapeake Arboretum** (☒ 624 Oak Grove Rd. ☎ 757/382–6411 ⊕ www.cityofchesapeake.net), a planetarium, a couple of farms, and the **Great Dismal Swamp** (☒ 3100 Desert Rd., Suffolk, VA ☎ 757/986–3705 ⊕ www.fws.gov).

Eat & Drink: Have lunch at **Baker's Crust Artisan Kitchen** (☒ 1244 Greenbrier Pkwy. ☎ 757/547–2787 ⊕ www.bakerscrust.com) in Chesapeake. Start with tuna and avocado *poke* or mozzarella *arancini* then dive into the sandwich menu, Neapolitan pizzas, farm-fresh salads, street tacos, or burgers. If that's not enough, there's a specialty entrée selection, too. More than a dozen signature drinks round out the craft cocktail menu (try the Bourbon Brûlée).

VIRGINIA BEACH

Do: Wide beaches along the boardwalk are the top feature of Virginia Beach, but there's a thriving locavore scene fed by numerous area farms, plenty of public art, an 18th-century lighthouse, and the fascinating Edgar Cayce's Association for Research and Enlightenment. **First Landing State Park** (☒ 2500 Shore Dr. ☎ 757/412–2300 ⊕ www.dcr.virginia.gov), Virginia's most visited, is the site of the first landing by English colonists in 1607, before they moved on to Jamestown.

Eat & Drink: Dine at **Heirloom** (✉ *2484 N. Landing Rd.* ☎ *757/689–3339* ⊕ *www.heirloomvb.com*) for an upscale taste of the city's fresh bounty. Start with a Virginia apple and baby kale salad with she-crab soup, then move on to the steamer pot of crab, shrimp, clams, and sausage or southern fried chicken with pimento mac and cheese and local collards.

Stay: For a special treat, check in to **The Historic Cavalier** (✉ *4200 Atlantic Ave.* ☎ *757/425–8555* ⊕ *www.marriott.com*) and surround yourself with artful luxury at this Autograph Collection property. If you'd rather save a bit, **The Founders Inn and Spa** (✉ *5641 Indian River Rd.* ☎ *757/424–5511* ⊕ *www.hilton.com*) offers fuss-free accommodations within a brick manor accented by formal English gardens.

Breakfast: Stop by **The Bee & the Biscuit** (✉ *1785 Princess Anne Rd.* ☎ *757/800–5959* ⊕ *www.beebiscuit.com*) for a memorable breakfast. Whether you opt for the breakfast tostada on a blue-corn tortilla, crumbled bacon pancakes, or bay crab Benedict, be sure to add an order of biscuits with honey butter and jam to your selection.

Day 7: Virginia Beach, VA, to Ocean City, MD

245 miles (1 hour, 40 minutes without traffic and stops)

Cross the Chesapeake Bay via U.S. 13 north to Old Ocean City Boulevard for a straightforward path directly into Ocean City, Maryland.

ALONG THE WAY

Town: Make a quick stop in Cape Charles, Virginia, just beyond the Chesapeake Bay Bridge-Tunnel. Cape Charles Beach offers the opportunity to satisfy yesteryear seaside nostalgia with ice cream on the boardwalk, a quiet pier, and spotting fish along the coast.

Eat & Drink: While in Cape Charles, peek into **Coastal Baking Co.** (✉ *555 Mason Ave.* ☎ *757/331–2482* ⊕ *www.coastalbaking-co.com*) for flaky turnovers, mini Bundt cakes, and seasonal cupcakes. If you're still hungry despite your big breakfast, there are more serious menu items here, but it's more fun to indulge in a few baked goods.

Nature: The **Chincoteague National Wildlife Refuge** (✉ *8231 Beach Rd.* ☎ *757/336–6122* ⊕ *www.fws.gov*), located on the Virginia part of Assateague Island, features more than 14,000 acres of beach, dunes, marsh, and maritime forest, all home to an incredible amount of wildlife. The refuge is most famous for its resident wild ponies, which have lived on the island for hundreds of years. You can see the ponies by hiking the 7½-mile Service Road or taking a tour bus or scenic boat tour.

OCEAN CITY

Do: Ocean City, Maryland, sits on a strip of land between the Atlantic Ocean and Isle of Wight Bay, offering tons of beach and water sport opportunities. Most visitors enjoy the lively boardwalk, and Trimper's Rides of Ocean City has been a rite of passage for area vacationers for decades. If you're an avid fisherperson, you might want to take the chance to land a white marlin while you're here.

Eat & Drink: Ocean City's atmosphere is on the casual/party side, so embrace the grab-and-go culture with dinner at **OC Street Food** (✉ *11505 Coastal Hwy.* ☎ *443/664–6322* ⊕ *www.ocstreet-foodmd.com*), offering an array of New York City street foods at the beach. Choose from kebabs, gyros, and pita platters, and don't forget the ice cream.

Stay: If you're looking for quieter nights, head toward Condo Row above 85th Street and rent a condo away from the hotels located in the much busier, party-forward southern end of Ocean City. If you do prefer a proper hotel,

Castle in the Sand Hotel (✉ 3701 Atlantic Ave. ☎ 410/289–6846 ⊕ www. castleinthesand.com) offers reasonable beachfront rooms with standard amenities.

Breakfast: Soriano's Coffee Shop (✉ 306 S. Baltimore Ave. ☎ 410/289–6656 ⊕ www. sorianoscoffeeshop.com) is your go-to morning stop before heading out of Ocean City. Cream chipped beef is the house specialty, but there are plenty of breakfast sandwiches and all the staples you'd expect from pancakes to omelets.

Day 8: Ocean City, MD, to Rehoboth Beach, DE

28 miles (50 minutes without traffic and stops)

Take Route 528 north, which becomes Route 1 north, as you travel up the scenic Delmarva Peninsula and through Delaware Seashore State Park. When you're ready to head home, the closest major airport is in Philadelphia, about two hours away.

ALONG THE WAY

Town: Make a stop in Fenwick Island, Delaware, to check out the **Discover-Sea Shipwreck Museum** (✉ 708 Coastal Hwy. ☎ 302/539–9366 ⊕ www.discoversea.com). There you'll be able to explore a collection of artifacts (such as coins, weapons, and a "mermaid") that were recovered from shipwrecks that occurred in the mid-Atlantic region and from around the world.

Eat & Drink: At **Bluecoast Seafood Grill** (✉ 30904 Coastal Hwy. ☎ 302/539–7111 ⊕ www.bluecoastseafoodgrill.com) in Bethany Beach, Delaware, the seafood is fresh, the dishes are beautifully yet simply prepared, and the wine list has been expertly curated.

Nature: This stretch of Delaware coast is also home to canals, ponds, and creeks,

as well as the Indian River Bay. Rent a kayak or a stand-up paddleboard and explore the bay on your own or with an outfitter like Ocean View's **EcoBay Kayak & SUP** (✉ 30048 Cedar Neck Rd. ☎ 302/841–2722 ⊕ www.ecobaykayak.com). You can also opt for a leisurely hike on the Prickly Pear Trail, an easy 3½-mile loop that offers views of pine trees, meadows, and the bay.

REHOBOTH BEACH

Do: Delaware's beach towns are perhaps some of the country's most underrated, offering no-frills and low-key fun among sparkling water, inviting beaches, and indisputably good vibes. Rehoboth Beach is one of the most popular, so be sure to spend some time on its relaxing sandy shores. Stroll the Rehoboth Beach Boardwalk, an old-fashioned boardwalk with shops, restaurants, and saltwater taffy shops. If you're lucky, you might be able to catch some live music at the **Rehoboth Beach Bandstand** (✉ Rehoboth Ave. ☎ 302/644–2288 ⊕ www.rehobothbandstand.com).

Eat & Drink: Check out **La Fable** (✉ 26 Baltimore Ave. ☎ 302/227–8510 ⊕ www. bonjourfable.com), a traditional French-style bistro in the heart of downtown Rehoboth. The menu features classic French dishes such as escargot, duck confit, and *boeuf bourguignon,* all served in an intimate, romantic environment. Afterward, shift back into beach-town mode with a couple of after-dinner drinks at **Rehoboth Ale House** (✉ 15 Wilmington Ave. ☎ 302/278–7433 ⊕ www.rehobothalehouse.com), where you'll find an impressive collection of rotating craft beers as well as a menu of delicious craft cocktails.

Stay: The **Bellmoor Inn and Spa** (✉ 6 Christian St. ☎ 302/227–5800 ⊕ www. thebellmoor.com) creates a luxurious experience for its guests. Amenities include a spa, a pool, a shuttle that takes guests directly to the beach, and beach chair and umbrella rentals. For classic beach-town charm outfitted with contemporary tastes in mind, try the **Ocean Glass Inn** (✉ 37299 Rehoboth Ave. ☎ 302/227–2844 ⊕ www.oceanglassinn.com).

Breakfast: Start your last morning on a healthy note with breakfast at **Greenman Juice Bar & Bistro** (✉ 12 Wilmington Ave. ☎ 302/227–4909 ⊕ www.greenmanjuicebar.com), where you can enjoy the homemade quiche or coconut rice porridge with a fresh juice or smoothie on the cozy patio.

The Appalachian Trail

Written by Andrew Collins

Short of becoming one of the approximately 800 thru-hikers who spend four to seven months walking the entire 2,193-mile Appalachian Trail every year, perhaps the best way to experience this fabled mountain route is by driving alongside it. To be clear, much of the trail climbs, plunges, twists, and turns through remote wilderness that has never been penetrated by roads, threading the often steep spine of the massive East Coast mountain range for which it's named. Even driving the "AT" takes some effort and often entails following narrow two-lane country roads through remote parts of the 14 states it passes through from northern Georgia to northern Maine.

With all that in mind, this itinerary gamely chases—rather than truly paralleling—the Appalachian Trail, crisscrossing it at dozens of access points where you can hop out, lace up your boots, and join the 3 million or so casual recreationists who hike at least a segment of the AT each year. The existence of the Appalachian Trail feels like a miracle today, given the rapid commercial development of the eastern United States since it was established in 1937. It passes within just 50 miles of Washington, D.C., and New York City, and it sometimes meanders within earshot of 18-wheelers grinding along interstate highways. But for most of the way, it provides a genuine detour from civilization—a rare opportunity to see America as it might have looked at the time of the nation's founding.

At a Glance

Start: Atlanta, GA

End: Millinocket, ME

Miles Traveled: 1,920 miles

Suggested Duration: 13 days

States Visited: Connecticut, Georgia, Maine, Maryland, Massachusetts, New Hampshire, New Jersey, New York, North Carolina, Pennsylvania, Tennessee, Vermont, Virginia, West Virginia

Key Sights: Great Smoky Mountains National Park; Shenandoah National Park; Harpers Ferry National Historical Park; Bear Mountain State Park; Mount Washington

Best Time to Go: This route climbs over some of the highest elevations in the eastern United States and ends in a part of Maine known for its frigid winters, so it's best to drive it during the warmer months, from around May through October.

Day 1: Atlanta, GA, to Helen, GA

90 miles (2 hours without traffic and stops)

Home to one of the country's busiest airports, Atlanta is the perfect gateway to the Appalachians. Once you get past city traffic, Route 400 and U.S. 19 provide a direct and easy path up into the region's foothills. At Dahlonega, turn east onto Route 115 and pass through Cleveland, picking up Route 75 to Helen.

The official southern start to the Appalachian Trail is Springer Mountain, but most hikers begin their adventure at the scenic Amicalola Falls State Park.

ALONG THE WAY

Town: Leafy and lively Dahlonega, home to the University of North Georgia and a burgeoning wine-making scene, was the site of a major gold rush boom in the late 1820s and 1830s, a legacy you can learn about at the **Dahlonega Gold Museum** (⊠ 1 Public Sq. N ☎ 706/864–2257 ⊕ www. gastateparks.org/dahlonegagoldmuseum). It's set inside a splendidly restored 1836 former courthouse that overlooks a town square fringed by colorful boutiques, winery tasting rooms, and cheerful cafés. At **Consolidated Mine** (⊠ 185 Consolidated Gold Mine Rd. ☎ 706/864–8473 ⊕ consolidatedgoldmine.com), the East Coast's largest gold mine during its 19th-century heyday, you can take a 40-minute tour through underground tunnels and past antique mining equipment.

Eat & Drink: With tall windows overlooking Dahlonega's town square, genial **Bourbon Street Grille** (⊠ 90 Public Sq. N ☎ 706/864–0086 ⊕ www.thebourbonstreetgrille.com) serves Creole and Cajun fare, including beignets and chicory-infused coffee. Around the corner, stop by lively **Spirits Tavern** (⊠ 19 E. Main St. ☎ 706/482–0580 ⊕ www. spirits-tavern.com) for Southern pub fare and well-poured cocktails.

Detour: It takes a little effort, but from Dahlonega you're only about 20 miles from the southern start of the Appalachian Trail. It's a picturesque half-hour drive west to get to where most hikers gear up, both mentally and physically, for their trek: **Amicalola Falls State Park** (⊠ 418 Amicalola Falls State Park Rd. ☎ 706/265–8888 ⊕ www.amicalolafallslodge.com). Here you can take a selfie beneath the stone arch where most hikers start their adventure, and then go hiking along the Appalachian Approach trail, which leads to the AT's official start at Springer Mountain. It's an arduous 15½-mile round-trip undertaking, so unless you're planning to camp overnight, it's best just to hike a couple of miles of it. There's also a lodge with comfy guest rooms back in the state park, which is also home to a stunning 729-foot-tall waterfall.

The Appalachian Trail

Roadside Attraction: Just off Route 75 near Cleveland, you'll pass a huge green revival building called **Babyland General Hospital** (✉ *300 NOK Dr.* ☎ *706/865–2171* ⊕ *www.cabbagepatchkids.com*). You won't find any real medical doctors or human patients inside this former health clinic. Instead, you'll encounter staff dressed in medical garb helping customers adopt Cabbage Patch Kids. Babyland is, in fact, the fictional birthplace of these distinctive (some might say creepy) dolls.

HELEN

Do: In an effort to boost tourism in the late 1960s, this folksy mountain town reimagined itself with an endearingly kitschy Bavarian theme. Most of Helen's buildings sport gingerbread trim and high, pitched roofs, and you'll find no shortage of souvenir shops stocked with German tchotchkes along with chalet-style beer gardens and sausage houses. The town also hosts a raucous Oktoberfest. To experience the region's considerable natural beauty, visit **Unicoi State Park** (✉ *Unicoi Bottoms Rd.* ☎ *706/878–2201* ⊕ *www.unicoilodge.com*), with its easy trail to oft-photographed Anna Ruby Falls; the park also offers ziplining and stand-up paddleboarding.

Eat & Drink: Overlooking the Chattahoochee River and set amid the cute shops of historic Nacoochee Village, **Habersham Winery** (✉ *7025 S. Main St.* ☎ *706/878–9463* ⊕ *www.habershamwinery.com*) is one of Georgia's oldest and most prolific vintners. Sample the excellent wines and order a meal from whichever food truck is on hand. Waitstaff clad in Bavarian costumes serve hearty German classics such as jaeger schnitzel and *schweinebraten* at **Hofbrauhaus Restaurant** (✉ *9001 N. Main St.* ☎ *706/878–2248* ⊕ *www.hofbrauhaushelenga.net*)—request a seat on the riverside patio. **Bigg Daddy's Restaurant & Tavern** (✉ *807 Edelweiss Strasse* ☎ *706/878–2739* ⊕ *www.biggdaddys.com*) is a convivial place to hoist beer steins.

Stay: The reasonably priced **Heidi Motel** (✉ *8820 N. Main St.* ☎ *706/878–2689* ⊕ *www.heidimotel.com*) has simple, spotless rooms set around an old-fashioned windmill. In the countryside north of town, **Valhalla Resort** (✉ *688 Bahn Innsbruck* ☎ *706/878–2200* ⊕ *www.valhallaresorthotel.com*) is one of the region's cushiest properties, with a full-service spa, a golf course, and a pool.

Breakfast: Start the day with a smoothie, chai tea, or salted-caramel apple pancakes at friendly **2 Wolves Tearoom** (✉ *8065 S. Main St.* ☎ *706/892–2958*).

Day 2: Helen, GA, to Bryson City, NC

93 miles (2 hours without traffic and stops)

Drive north up Route 75 and cross into North Carolina along the eastern shore of Lake Chatuge, then pick up U.S. 64 east, which climbs through Nantahala National Forest, crossing the Appalachian Trail at Winding Stair Gap. After visiting the town of Franklin, make the similarly hilly and scenic drive up U.S. 23 and U.S. 74 to Bryson City.

ALONG THE WAY

Nature: With a trailhead just off U.S. 64 about 18 miles east of Lake Chatuge, the vertiginous section of the Appalachian Trail from Winding Stair Gap to Siler Bald is a beauty. The full 9-mile out-and-back hike takes about five hours and has an elevation gain of nearly 2,000 feet, but the final stretch to Siler Bald offers eye-popping panoramic views.

Town: Inhabited for at least 1,000 years by the Cherokee until the U.S. government forced them to relocate to western North Carolina's Qualla territory in 1819, Franklin, North Carolina, is an attractive alpine community with a walkable downtown. You can learn about the region's numerous mines at the **Gem & Mineral Museum** (✉ 25 Phillips St. ☎ 828/369–7831 ⊕ www.fgmm. org), located in a converted jailhouse, and discover the story behind kilts and other Scottish textiles at the **Scottish Tartans Museum & Heritage Center** (☎ 86 E. Main St. ☎ 828/524–7472 ⊕ scottishtartansmuseum.org). On the east side of downtown, walk around **Nikwasi Mound** (✉ 524 E. Main St.), a grassy bluff that served as an important Cherokee cultural and spiritual center for centuries, and then stretch your legs along the serene **Little Tennessee River Greenway** (✉ 573 E. Main St. ☎ 828/369–8488 ⊕ www.littletennessee.org), a 5-mile multiuse path along the river.

Eat & Drink: Stop for lunch in Franklin at **Gracious Plates on Main** (✉ 46 E. Main St. ☎ 828/369–2690 ⊕ www.graciousplatesonmain.com), which serves lamb meatballs, tempura shrimp, and other eclectic small plates. Then treat yourself to a scoop of ice cream or a flavored latte at **Crabtree General Store & Coffee Vault** (✉ 41 Iotla St. ☎ 828/524–3660 ⊕ www.facebook.com/crabtreegeneralstore).

BRYSON CITY

Do: A popular gateway to Great Smoky Mountains National Park as well as a hub for white-water rafting, Bryson City is a tiny, amiable town that landed on the map when the Western North Carolina Railroad established a route through town in 1884. The trains ceased operations a century later, and thus was born the **Great Smoky Mountains Railroad** (✉ 45 Mitchell St. ☎ 800/872–4681 ⊕ www. gsmr.com), a scenic passenger line that now offers trips in historic trains from Bryson City's vintage depot along the Tuckasegee River to Dillsboro and through the dramatic Nantahala Gorge. To experience an adrenaline-fueled rush along the roiling Nantahala River, book a white-water rafting adventure with **Nantahala Outdoor Center** (✉ 13077 U.S. 19 ☎ 828/785–5082 ⊕ www.noc.com), which also offers tubing, kayaking, mountain biking, and ziplining.

Eat & Drink: Located at Nantahala Outdoor Center and with seating overlooking the river, laid-back Big Wesser serves up tasty barbecue, brisket chili, and Key lime pie, and River's End Restaurant doles out pizzas, burgers, and other pub grub. **Mountain Layers Brewing Company** (✉ 90 Everett St. ☎ 828/538–0115 ⊕ www. mountainlayersbrewingcompany.com) is arguably the best of the town's craft breweries; rotating food trucks provide sustenance.

Stay: Built in 1908 beside the gold-dome former courthouse (now a museum and visitor center), the redbrick **Everett Hotel** (✉ 16 Everett St. ☎ 828/488–1976 ⊕ www.theeveretthotel.com) has 10 elegantly appointed suites and a rooftop terrace with a fireplace. Plan a meal in the romantic restaurant specializing in seasonal modern southern fare.

Breakfast: The biscuits with sausage gravy are a favorite dish at cheerful **La Dolce Vita Bakery** (✉ 191 Everett St. ☎ 828/488–5888 ⊕ www.dolcebryson.com), which also serves espresso drinks and boozy brunch cocktails.

Day 3: Bryson City, NC, to Blowing Rock, NC

195 miles (5 hours without traffic and stops)

Today you'll visit one one of the highest-elevation stretches of the Appalachian Trail, in Great Smoky Mountains National Park, before crossing into Tennessee and driving through touristy but colorful Gatlinburg. Then you'll head east on U.S. 321 through Greeneville and Johnson City, traversing the border back into North Carolina and driving a short stretch of the famous Blue Ridge Parkway to the picture-perfect mountain town of Blowing Rock.

ALONG THE WAY

Nature: A visit to **Great Smoky Mountains National Park** (✉ *107 Park Headquarters Rd., Gatlinburg, TN* ☎ *865/436–1200* ⊕ *www.nps.gov/grsm*), which ranges across more than 520,000 acres of towering peaks and undeveloped deciduous and coniferous forests, is a must. Begin by checking out exhibits at the attractive **Oconaluftee Visitor Center** (✉ *1194 Newfound Gap Rd., Cherokee, NC* ☎ *828/497–1904* ⊕ *www.nps.gov/grsm*) and, behind it, the historic buildings that make up the Mountain Farm Museum. Continue north through the park on scenic Newfound Gap Road, taking the side route to the highest point on the Appalachian Trail, 6,643-foot-elevation Clingmans Dome, where an observation tower provides fantastic views. After crossing into the Tennessee side of the park, drive the serene 6-mile Roaring Fork Motor Nature Trail, stopping to make the quick hike to beguiling Grotto Falls.

Town: Gatlinburg, Tennessee, has plenty of attractions that some might consider a bit hokey—Ripley's Aquarium of the Smokies, the Hollywood Stars Museum, and Dollywood just up the road in Pigeon Forge—plus some popular distilleries. One of the most enjoyable ways to get your bearings in this hilly town is to drive up to Gatlinburg Scenic Overlook, located west of town on Gatlinburg Bypass. Another lofty draw is **Gatlinburg SkyPark** (✉ *765 Parkway* ☎ *865/436–4307* ⊕ *www.gatlinburgskypark.com*), where you can ride a chairlift 1,800 feet above sea level and saunter across the continent's longest pedestrian-only cable bridge. **Ober Gatlinburg Amusement Park & Ski Area** (✉ *1339 Ski Mountain Rd.* ☎ *865/436–5423* ⊕ *www.obermountain.com*) also offers lots of fun diversions for visitors of all ages.

Eat & Drink: Tennessee Jed's (✉ *631 Parkway* ☎ *865/412–1131* ⊕ *www.tennesseejeds.com*), in Gatlinburg, has built a devoted following for its ginormous sandwiches.

Essential Listening

The audiobook of Bill Bryson's 1998 memoir *A Walk in the Woods* provides an insightful and funny account of attempting to thru-hike the Appalachian Trail.

BLOWING ROCK

Do: The stretch of the Blue Ridge Parkway that leads to Blowing Rock contains several impressive sites, among them **Grandfather Mountain** (✉ *9872 Rte. 105 S, Banner Elk, NC* ☎ *828/963–9522* ⊕ *www.ncparks.gov*), with its mile-high swinging bridge, and **Linn Cove Viaduct** (✉ *3218 Blue Ridge Pkwy., Newland, NC* ☎ *828/348–3400* ⊕ *www.nps.gov/blri*), a winding 1,243-foot-long bridge that clings to Grandfather Mountain's face. At **Julian Price Memorial Park** (✉ *Milepost 297 Blue Ridge Pkwy.* ☎ *828/963–5911* ⊕ *www.blueridgeheritage.com*), you can rent a kayak or canoe to paddle around pretty Price Lake. Amid the fine galleries and cafés of downtown Blowing Rock, the **Blowing Rock Art and History Museum** (✉ *159 Ginny Stevens La.* ☎ *828/295–9099* ⊕ *www.blowingrockmuseum.org*) specializes in works that showcase the folkways and landscapes of Appalachia.

Eat & Drink: At friendly **Sunset & Vine** (✉ *150 Sunset Dr.* ☎ *828/414–9111* ⊕ *www.blowingrockwine.com*) wine shop, pick out a bottle along with some cheese and charcuterie—the knowledgeable staff will serve it to you at one of the café tables. Next door at **Blowing Rock Brewing Company** (✉ *152 Sunset Dr.* ☎ *828/414–9600* ⊕ *www.blowingrockbrewing.com*), try one of the old-world ales (*märzen, kölsch,* and others) paired with a baked soft pretzel or a bison burger.

Stay: Set on 87 wooded acres next to an alpine lake, posh **Chetola Resort** (✉ 185 Chetola Lake Dr. ☎ 828/295–5500⊕ www.chetola.com) is a perfect destination for a bit of pampering, with spa treatments and refined dining. With a rustic but stylish look, reasonably priced and family-friendly **Mountain Inn & Log Cabins** (✉ 827 Main St. ☎ 828/295–7991 ⊕ www.mountainaireinn.com) is steps from downtown retail and restaurants.

Breakfast: The expansive flagstone terrace of **Social on Main** (✉ 870 Main St. ☎ 828/414–9440 ⊕ www.socialonmainbr.com) is a pleasant place to savor chicken and waffles or biscuit breakfast sandwiches on a sunny morning.

Day 4: Blowing Rock, NC, to Roanoke, VA

240 miles (5 hours without traffic and stops)

Today's route ventures onto smaller roads to cross the AT in a couple of places. First, head north from Blowing Rock toward Marion, Virginia, via the intersection with the trail in Mount Rogers National Recreation Area. Then take I-81 east to Route 100 to the small town of Pearisburg, where you can once again access the trail. Continue east on U.S. 460 down through Blacksburg, returning to I-81 the rest of the way to Roanoke.

ALONG THE WAY

Eat & Drink: A great lunch stop midway through your drive, the **Wooden Pickle** (✉ 120 E. Main St. ☎ 276/783–2300 ⊕ www.woodenpicklefoodandspirits.com) in Marion, Virginia, turns out tasty salads, soups, and sandwiches.

Nature: Some of the most challenging but stimulating Appalachian Trail hikes in the Southeast can be found in southwestern Virginia, including the 4½-mile trek to the 5,729-foot summit of **Mount Rogers**

(✉ 3714 Rte. 16, Marion, VA ☎ 276/783–5196 ⊕ www.fs.usda.gov), and the 4-mile out-and-back scramble up to **Angel's Rest** (✉ 523 Rte. 793) in Pearisburg, which entails a climb of more than 1,600 feet but rewards hikers with fabulous vistas.

Town: Best known as the home of Virginia Tech university, the small but fast-growing city of Blacksburg is steeped in the agrarian heritage of southwestern Virginia. Adjacent to VT's rolling green campus, **Historic Smithfield** (✉ 1000 Merry Oak Way ☎ 540/231–3947 ⊕ www.historicsmithfield.org) contains a meticulously preserved 1700s farmhouse and its many outbuildings, fields, and gardens. Tours tell the story of both the owners and the enslaved Africans who were forced to toil here. At nearby **Hahn Horticulture Garden** (✉ 200 Garden La. ☎ 540/231–5970), explore 6 acres of beautifully laid out flower beds and plantings.

ROANOKE

Do: One of the cultural and economic hubs of the southern Appalachians, Roanoke enjoys a captivating setting on the Blue Ridge Parkway and the Roanoke River. Take in the view from beneath the 88½-foot-tall illuminated (at night) star in **Mill Mountain Park** (✉ 2198 Mill Mountain Spur ☎ 540/853–2236 ⊕ www.playroanoke.com), which offers several family-friendly attractions, including a great zoo. In Roanoke's historic city center, browse the acclaimed collections at the sleekly modern **Taubman Museum of Art** (✉ 110 Salem Ave. SE ☎ 540/342–5760 ⊕ www.taubmanmuseum.org) and the dazzling historic photos of vintage American railroad scenes at the **O. Winston Link Museum** (✉ 101 Shenandoah Ave. NE ☎ 540/982–5465 ⊕ www.roanokehistory.org), which occupies a former train station. Then check out the myriad vendors who proffer their goods daily at **Historic Roanoke City Market** (✉ Market Sq. SE ☎ 540/342–2028 ⊕ www.downtownroanoke.org).

Eat & Drink: Downtown's see-and-be-seen **Lucky Restaurant** (✉ *18 Kirk Ave. SW* ☎ *540/982–1249* ⊕ *www.eatatlucky. com*) serves globally inspired southern fare and boasts one of the best wine lists in the region. Afterward, wind down the evening at **Stellina** (✉ *104 Kirk Ave. SW* ☎ *540/400–7315* ⊕ *www.fortunatoroanoke.com*) with an inventive cocktail.

Stay: Treat yourself to a restful and romantic night in one of the three warmly appointed rooms at the **Black Lantern Inn** (✉ *1526 Franklin Rd. SW* ☎ *540/206–3441* ⊕ *www.blacklanterninn.com*); rates include a full organic breakfast. **The Liberty Trust** (✉ *101 S. Jefferson St.* ☎ *540/299–5100* ⊕ *www.libertytrusthotel.com*) has 54 fashionable rooms in a restored 1910 bank building, but drawbacks include noise from passing trains and a lack of on-site parking (though there's a garage nearby).

Breakfast: In a vintage storefront in hip Grandin Village, **Scratch Biscuit Company** (✉ *1820 Memorial Ave. SW* ☎ *540/855–0882* ⊕ *www.scratchbiscuit.com*) serves its fluffy namesake with a variety of fixings, from country ham and eggs to Cajun fried catfish.

Day 5: Roanoke, VA, to Luray, VA

200 miles (5 hours without traffic and stops)

Today's drive mostly along two of America's most scenic roads, the Blue Ridge Parkway and Shenandoah National Park's Skyline Drive, traces the twisting contours of the Appalachian Mountains. You can access the Appalachian Trail at a number of points on this route. Note that there's no fee for driving the Blue Ridge Parkway, but Shenandoah National Park charges a $30 entrance fee. To get to Luray, exit Skyline Drive at Thornton Gap and drive west 10 miles on U.S. 221.

ALONG THE WAY

Eat & Drink: Set inside a bucolic lodge with glorious views of azure Abbott Lake, **Peaks of the Otter Lake View Restaurant** (✉ *85554 Blue Ridge Pkwy., Bedford, VA* ☎ *540/586–1081* ⊕ *www.peaksofotter.com*) is a favorite stop for lunch along the Blue Ridge Parkway.

Town: Although there aren't any towns per se along the Blue Ridge Parkway, at mile 63.7—just north of the village of Big Island—you can stop at the **James River Visitor Center** (☎ *434/299–5496* ⊕ *www. nps.gov/blri*), which lies at the lowest point of the parkway. The grounds are lovely for a riverside picnic, and exhibits shed light on the canal system and locks that once made this waterway a critical transportation route. You can stroll along a pedestrian underpass that runs beneath the bridge that carries the parkway across the river.

LURAY

Do: A boutique-filled mountain town bisected by lazy Hawksbill Creek, Luray makes an excellent base for visiting magnificent **Shenandoah National Park** (✉ *540/999–3500* ⊕ *www.nps.gov/ shen*) and its alluring Skyline Drive, which spans 105 miles along a high ridge through the Appalachians, offering numerous spots for picnicking, viewing wildlife, and hiking. At many points you can hop onto a portion of the Appalachian Trail, a favorite being the 1-mile loop at Blackrock Summit. Other highlights along Skyline Drive include Little Devil Stairs and Signal Knob. On the edge of the town of Luray, set aside an hour or two to explore the most extensive cave system in the eastern United States at **Luray Caverns** (✉ *101 Cave Hill Rd.* ☎ *540/743–6551* ⊕ *www.luraycaverns.com*).

Eat & Drink: Inside the national park, **Pollack Dining Room at Skyland** (✉ *Mile 41, Skyline Dr.* ☎ *877/847–1919* ⊕ *www. goshenandoah.com*) serves up reliably good American fare (save room for the beloved blackberry ice cream pie) and fantastic views. In downtown Luray, count on the **Chop House Bistro** (✉ *132 E. Main St.* ☎ *540/860–5605* ⊕ *www.chop-bistro.com*)—which occupies a gorgeously renovated historic home—for rarefied contemporary American fare, including juicy steaks.

Stay: There are two rustic mid-century lodgings along Skyline Drive in Shenandoah National Park: **Big Meadows Lodge** (✉ *Mile 51, Skyline Dr.* ☎ *877/847–1919* ⊕ *www.goshenandoah.com*) and **Skyland** (✉ *Mile 41, Skyline Dr.* ☎ *877/847–1919* ⊕ *www.goshenandoah.com*). They both offer simple motel-style or cabin accommodations and epic mountain vistas. Just outside the park in Luray, **Brookside Cabins** (✉ *2978 U.S. 211 E* ☎ *540/743–5698* ⊕ *www.brooksidecabins.com*) is an endearing little compound of 1940s bungalows overlooking a babbling brook.

Breakfast: Gathering Grounds Patisserie (✉ *24 E. Main St.* ☎ *540/743–1121* ⊕ *www.ggrounds.com*) serves prodigious portions of pies, scones, and breakfast fare, along with smoothies and espresso drinks.

Day 6: Luray, VA, to Hagerstown, MD

124 miles (3 hours without traffic and stops)

Return from Luray to Shenandoah National Park and continue driving north along the final stretch of Skyline Drive to Front Royal, Virginia. Then take a series of local roads through the mountains in order to join up with the Appalachian Trail at Trumbo Hollow, Sky Meadows State Park, or Snicker Gap. At Berryville, pick up U.S. 340 northeast into West Virginia to visit Harpers Ferry National Historical Park, and then cross the Potomac River into Maryland and take Route 67, Route 66, and U.S. 40 to Hagerstown.

ALONG THE WAY

Nature: Driving from Front Royal north through Virginia on local roads, you can make relatively easy AT hikes at several points, including **Trumbo Hollow** (✉ *13167 John Marshall Hwy., Linden, VA*), **Sky Meadows State Park** (✉ *11012 Edmonds La., Delaplane, VA* ☎ *540/592–3556* ⊕ *www.dcr.virginia.gov*), and **Snickers Gap** (✉ *Blue Ridge Mountain Rd., Bluemont, VA*).

Town: With a strategic setting as the northernmost point of the Confederacy, the hilly river hamlet of Harpers Ferry, West Virginia, played a pivotal role in the Civil War. What brought the town the greatest infamy was a failed raid by abolitionist John Brown on the federal armory, an event highlighted at the compelling **Harpers Ferry National Historical Park** (✉ *171 Shoreline Dr.* ☎ *304/535–6029* ⊕ *www.nps.gov/hafe*).

Eat & Drink: Vintage signs and memorabilia hang from the timber rafters of **The Rabbit Hole** (✉ *186 High St.* ☎ *304/535–8818* ⊕ *www.rabbitholewv.com*), which serves finely crafted gastropub fare and has a breezy terrace overlooking the rivers and hills surrounding Harpers Ferry.

Photo Op: After passing directly through Harpers Ferry National Historical Park, the Appalachian Trail traverses the photogenic **1894 Winchester and Potomac Bridge** (✉ *Shenandoah and Potomac Sts.*) into Sandy Hook, Maryland.

HAGERSTOWN

Do: Situated amid the limestone ridges of the Appalachian Valley in western Maryland, this small city has long been a center of transportation, a history you can learn more about at the **Chesapeake & Ohio Canal National Historical Park** (✉ *142 W. Potomac St.* ☎ *301/739–4200* ⊕ *www.nps.gov/choh*) in nearby Williamsport. Other draws include the **Washington County Museum of Fine Arts** (✉ *401 Museum Dr.* ☎ *301/739–5727* ⊕ *www.wcmfa.org*), with its estimable collection of American landscape paintings, and the **Pennsylvania Dutch Market** (✉ 1583 Potomac Ave. ☎ 240/420–8555 ⊕ www.padutchmarket.com), which carries traditional Amish foods and crafts. It's just a 25-minute drive east to **Catoctin Mountain Park** (✉ 14707 Park Central Rd., Thurmont, MD ☎ 301/663–9388 ⊕ www.nps.gov/cato), a grand expanse of peaks and forest overseen by the National Park Service and bisected by the AT. The U.S. presidential retreat, Camp David, is also located inside the park.

Eat & Drink: Rik's Cafe (✉ 1065 Maryland Ave. ☎ 301/302–7541 ⊕ rikscafexperience.com) serves a wide-ranging menu, from seared ahi tacos with mango-avocado salsa to maple-glazed pork chops, in a casually elegant space, while **Broad Axe** (✉ 28 W. Franklin St. ☎ 301/733–8454 ⊕ www.facebook.com/broadaxelive) is a festive venue for gastropub fare, drinks, and music.

Stay: On the east side of town a short drive from the Appalachian Trail sections in South Mountain State Park, the gracious **Beaver Creek Inn & Spa** (✉ 20432 Beaver Creek Rd. ☎ 301/302–7777 ⊕ www.beavercreekinnandspa.com) offers plenty of perks, including a welcome bottle of wine, a gourmet breakfast, and an extensive menu of spa services.

Breakfast: A high-ceilinged, bi-level space with exposed brick walls and ample seating, **District Provision & Supply** (✉ 6 Rochester Pl. ☎ 301/791–1717 ⊕ www.eat-district.com) serves creative brunch fare from a weekly changing menu.

Day 7: Hagerstown, MD, to Stroudsburg, PA

205 miles (4 hours without traffic and stops)

After heading east on Route 77 from Hagerstown to Catoctin Mountain Park, take U.S. 15 north into Pennsylvania to Harrisburg. Here you'll hop onto I–81 and then I–78 to Bethlehem, before taking Route 33 to Stroudsburg.

ALONG THE WAY

Town: A vibrant city of around 75,000 in eastern Pennsylvania, Bethlehem has undergone a dramatic comeback in recent years. Its downtown contains the well-preserved colonial buildings of the Moravian community that settled here in the 1740s. You can learn about this rich heritage at the **Historic Bethlehem Museums & Sites**—stop at the visitor center inside **Schropp Dry Goods Shoppe** (✉ 505 Main St. ☎ 610/691–6055) to book a guided tour or pick up a map to explore on your own. Across the Lehigh River in the South Side district that was dominated by the 10-acre Bethlehem Steel factory from 1857 until it shuttered in 2003, you can learn about the region's—and the nation's—tumultuous manufacturing history at the superb **National Museum of Industrial History** (✉ 602 E. 2nd St. ☎ 610/694–6644 ⊕ www.nmih.org).

Eat & Drink: In Bethlehem's bustling Steel Stacks district, excellent eateries abound, including **Social Still Distillery** (✉ 530 E. 3rd St. ☎ 610/625–4585 ⊕ www.social-still.com), which is inside a century-old bank building and serves a diverse menu of international favorites, like pad Thai and shrimp and grits. Nearby **Bonn Place Brewing** (✉ 310-14 Taylor St. ☎ 610/419–6660 ⊕ www.bonnplace.com) is a cozy place to savor British-style lagers and ales.

STROUDSBURG

Do: This year-round base for recreation and family fun in the Poconos and the Delaware Water Gap National Recreation Area has an inviting small-town vibe. There's hiking, fall foliage viewing, and skiing close by at 1,306-acre **Big Pocono State Park** (✉ 980 Camelback Rd., Tannersville, PA ☎ 570/894–8336 ⊕ www.dcnr.pa.gov) and adorable animals to pet at **Quiet Valley Living Historical Farm** (✉ 347 Quiet Valley Rd. ☎ 570/992–6161 ⊕ www.quietvalley.org).

Eat & Drink: With a name like **Garlic** (✉ *907 Main St.* ☎ *570/350–6868* ⊕ *www.garli-crestaurantbar.com*), it's no surprise that this refined downtown restaurant turns out well-seasoned food—the Korean barbecue chicken and Cajun shrimp tortellini are standouts.

Stay: Offering 88 unfussy, well-priced rooms, **The Penn Stroud** (✉ *700 Main St.* ☎ *570/421–2200* ⊕ *www.thepenn-stroud.com*) dates to the 1830s and lies right in the center of this bustling town.

Breakfast: Drop by downtown's **Farmhouse Eatery** (✉ *728 Main St.* ☎ *570/534–0995* ⊕ *www.farmhousepoconos.com*) to dine on lobster Benedict or bourbon peach bacon waffles beneath a pressed-tin ceiling hung with crystal chandeliers.

Day 8: Stroudsburg, PA, to Pawling, NY

145 miles (3 hours, 30 minutes without traffic and stops)

After crossing the Delaware River from Stroudsburg, take I–80 into northwestern New Jersey and then stick mostly with smaller local roads to visit sections of the Appalachian Trail at Culvers Gap near Branchville and at Greenwood Lake, just over the border in New York. Continue east around the dense forests of Harriman State Park and up to Bear Mountain Park, before crossing the Hudson River and cutting north into the cute town of Cold Spring. From here, it's about a 45-minute drive east to Pawling.

ALONG THE WAY

Eat & Drink: An easy walk from the Appalachian Trail crossing at Culvers Gap in Branchville, New Jersey, the venerable **Mountain House Tavern** (✉ *19 U.S. 206* ✉ *973/250–3300* ⊕ *www.mountain-housenj.com*) serves made-from-scratch American dishes in a historic dining room overlooking Kittatinny Lake.

Nature: One of the most memorable and accessible places to hike the AT is New York's **Bear Mountain State Park** (✉ *3006 Seven Lakes Dr., Tomkins Cove, NY* ☎ *845/786-2701* ⊕ *www.parks.ny.gov*), where a 3.8-mile loop ascends a 1,300-foot summit affording panoramic views up and down the Hudson River. Just east of the park, the Appalachian Trail continues across the Instagram-worthy Bear Mountain Bridge, with its 360-foot-tall towers. When completed in 1924, it was the world's longest suspension bridge.

Town: Cold Spring is a graceful colonial village with impressive views across the Hudson River toward the imposing campus of the U.S. Military Academy at West Point. Go for a stroll amid the now-peaceful industrial ruins of **West Point Foundry Preserve** (✉ *80 Kemble Ave.* ⊕ *www.scenichudson.org*), and set aside time to explore the bountiful greenery and Georgian-style mansion of **Boscobel House and Gardens** (✉ *1601 Rte. 9D* ☎ *845/265-3638* ⊕ *www.boscobel.org*). Near here, the Appalachian Trail fringes the 75-acre grounds of the stunning mid-century modern estate **Manitoga** (✉ *584 Rte. 9D, Garrison, NY* ☎ *845/424–3812* ⊕ *www.visitmanitoga.org*), tours of which are available by advance reservation.

PAWLING

Do: The main drag of this diminutive hamlet has a handful of interesting indie retailers. Just outside town, the 4½-mile loop hike around tranquil Nuclear Lake, part of it along the Appalachian Trail, is a stunner with only a moderate elevation gain.

Eat & Drink: Set inside a courtly turn-of-the-century brick building, **McKinney and Doyle Fine Foods Cafe** (✉ *10 Charles Colman Blvd.* ☎ *845/855–3707* ⊕ *www.mckinneyanddoyle.com*) serves artfully plated salads, pastas, and small plates.

Stay: Minimalist decor and ultra-plush bedding are hallmarks of the

10-room **Station Inn** (✉ *7 Memorial Ave.* ☎ *845/266–6262* ⊕ *www.stationinnpawling.com*), which is in the heart of the village.

Breakfast: It's hard enough to resist the whimsical logo (a twinkle-toed grizzly) of the **Dancing Bear Cafe** (✉ *10 E. Main St.* ☎ *845/493–0931* ⊕ *www.dancingbearcafe.com*), but just wait until you lay eyes on the pastry case filled with heavenly delicacies, including apricot scones and chunky apple-cinnamon muffins. Among the more substantial offerings, try the stick-to-your-ribs steak and eggs.

Day 9: Pawling, NY, to Lenox, MA

72 miles (2 hours without traffic and stops)

Follow Route 22 northeast from Pawling toward Bulls Bridge, Connecticut, and then take U.S. 7 north through Kent and West Cornwall, before turning northwest at Route 112 to get to the Litchfield Hills village of Salisbury. Turn north onto Route 41 and cross into Massachusetts, returning to U.S. 7 at Sheffield and taking your time as you pass through the inviting Berkshires towns of Great Barrington and Stockbridge en route to Lenox.

ALONG THE WAY

Town: A quintessential Litchfield Hills country village, Kent lies just over the New York–Connecticut border and is flanked to the west by the Appalachian Trail. North of the neatly kept downtown, U.S. 7 passes by a few quirky attractions, including the **Connecticut Antique Machinery Museum** (✉ *31B Kent Cornwall Rd.* ☎ *860/927–0050* ⊕ *www.camamuseum.org*) and neighboring **Eric Sloane Museum** (✉ *31 Kent Cornwall Rd.* ☎ *860/927–2150* ⊕ *www.facebook.com/ericsloanemuseum*), which preserves the studio of its namesake artist as well as an 1820s iron furnace. Farther

north, **Kent Falls State Park** (✉ *462 Kent Cornwall Rd.* ☎ *860/927–3238* ⊕ *www.ctparks.com*) has a trail leading to a small cascade and is an idyllic spot for picnicking.

Photo Op: With its red wood-frame exterior, the circa-1860s **West Cornwall Covered Bridge** (✉ *Rte. 128 at U.S. 7*) is one of the prettiest bridges in New England.

Eat & Drink: Drop by **JP Gifford Market** (✉ *12 N. Main St.* ☎ *860/592–0200* ⊕ *www.jpgifford.com*) in Kent to pick up gourmet breakfast or lunch items to go and enjoy at Kent Falls State Park. Among the many trendy restaurants in Great Barrington, Massachusetts, the **Prairie Whale** (✉ *178 Main St.* ☎ *413/528–5050* ⊕ *www.prairiewhale.com*) is set inside a smartly restored house and serves sophisticated, locally sourced food and drink.

LENOX

Do: A summer and weekend vacation town that's drawn monied New Yorkers and Bostonians since the 19th century, this countrified bastion of Berkshires beauty is best known today for **Tanglewood** (✉ *297 West St.* ☎ *413/637–5180* ⊕ *www.bso.org/tanglewood*), the celebrated 200-acre concert venue that serves as the summer home of the Boston Symphony Orchestra. You can also get an up-close look at some of the area's palatial country estates that are now open for tours, including **The Mount** (✉ *2 Plunkett St.* ☎ *413/551–5111* ⊕ *www.edithwharton.org*)—the former residence of novelist Edith Wharton—and **Ventfort Hall Gilded Age Mansion & Museum** (✉ *104 Walker St.* ☎ *413/637–3206* ⊕ *gildedage.org*).

Eat & Drink: Lenox abounds with upmarket eateries, including **Bistro Zinc** (✉ *56 Church St.* ☎ *413/637–8800* ⊕ *www.bistrozinc.com*), which turns out classic French dishes like *moules frites* and duck confit, and the urbane wine bar **Brava** (✉ *65 Church St.* ☎ *413/637–9171* ⊕ *www.bravalenox.com*).

Stay: Made up of three colonial buildings, the **Cornell Inn** (✉ *203 Main St. ☎ 413/637–4800 ⊕ www.cornellbb. com*) strikes a pleasing balance between old-world and contemporary, its rooms decorated with bold colors and whimsical accents. Friendly owners, tasty food offerings, and moderate rates are among its attributes. **Life House Berkshires** (✉ *194 Pittsfield Rd. ☎ 855/967–5695 ⊕ www. lifehousehotels.com*), part of the hip boutique brand, has been fashioned out of a 1970s motor lodge. The posh rooms have Le Labo bath products and beautifully curated furnishings.

Breakfast: Cute, art-filled **Haven Bakery** (✉ *8 Franklin St. ☎ 413/637– 8948 ⊕ www.havencafebakery.com*) is a cheerful option to start your day. The salmon scramble and huevos rancheros both satisfy.

Day 10: Lenox, MA, to Woodstock, VT

135 miles (3 hours, 30 minutes without traffic and stops)

Continue your journey north through the Berkshires via U.S. 7 and Route 8 to Mount Greylock and North Adams, then head west on Route 2, picking up U.S. 7 again and following it north into Vermont. At the town of Manchester, turn northeast onto Route 30, crossing the Appalachian Trail at Bromley Mountain, and then follow Route 11, Route 100, Route 100A, and U.S. 4 to Woodstock for a curvy and gorgeous drive through Green Mountain National Forest.

ALONG THE WAY

Nature: Arguably the most stunning stretch of the Appalachian Trail in Massachusetts climbs over the 3,491-foot summit of **Mount Greylock** (✉ *Rockwell Rd. ☎ 413/499–4262 ⊕ www.mass. gov*), the state's highest point. You can hike to the Massachusetts Veterans

War Memorial Tower at the top, or make things easy and drive there.

Town: In 1999, the formerly downcast mill town of North Adams suddenly became a much-talked-about cultural destination when its massive shuttered electrical plant was masterfully reimagined as the **Massachusetts Museum of Contemporary Art** (✉ *1040 Mass MoCA Way ☎ 413/662– 2111 ⊕ www.massmoca.org*), an airy 280,000-square-foot space with riveting art exhibits. A few miles west, Williamstown is a college town with two more outstanding destinations for viewing art: the **Williams College Museum of Art** (✉ *15 Lawrence Hall Dr. ☎ 413/597–2429 ⊕ art-museum.williams.edu*) and **Clark Art Institute** (✉ *225 South St. ☎ 413/458– 2303 ⊕ www.clarkart.edu*), with a dramatic wing by the renowned architect Tadao Ando.

Eat & Drink: Right beside Mass MoCA, **Bright Ideas Brewing** (✉ *111 Mass MoCA Way ☎ 413/346–4460 ⊕ www.bright-ideasbrewing.com*) is set in a colorful, art-filled space with tasty beer—you're welcome to bring in food from nearby eateries. Williamstown's wildly popular **Mezze Bistro** (✉ *777 Cold Spring Rd. ☎ 413/458–0123 ⊕ www.mezzeres-taurant.com*) is a go-to for fresh and flavorful Mediterranean cuisine.

Roadside Attraction: One of the more unexpected sites you'll encounter as you drive through the pastoral countryside of southern Vermont is the **Bennington Battle Monument** (✉ *15 Monument Circle, Bennington, VT ☎ 802/447–0550 ⊕ www.benning-tonbattlemonument.com*), a 306-foot-tall obelisk erected in 1891. Take the elevator to the top for dazzling views of the mountains as well as Bennington College.

WOODSTOCK

Do: Woodstock possesses a small-town graciousness that's arguably unmatched even in a state that embodies quaintness. Saunter around the oblong village green, passing through the adorable

Middle Covered Bridge, which traverses the gurgling Ottauquechee River. The conservation-minded Rockefeller family spearheaded the town's ambitious preservation efforts. A direct result is **Marsh-Billings-Rockefeller National Historical Park** (✉ 69 Old River Rd. ☎ 802/457–3368 ⊕ www.nps.gov/mabi), a 555-acre estate laced with idyllic carriage roads. Venture across the street to explore **Billings Farm and Museum** (☎ 802/457–2355 ⊕ www.billingsfarm.org), one of New England's oldest operating farms.

Eat & Drink: The maker of mouthwatering, sustainably sourced burgers and other tempting fare, **Worthy Kitchen** (✉ 442 Woodstock Rd. ☎ 802/457–7281 ⊕ www.worthyvermont.com) also boasts one of the state's most impressive craft beer lists. For classic cocktails with a decidedly French bent, grab a seat at a marble café table inside **Au Comptoir** (✉ 4 Mechanic St. ☎ 802/299–5435 ⊕ www.aucomptoirvt.com).

Stay: The regal **Woodstock Inn & Resort** (✉ 14 The Green ☎ 800/448–7900 ⊕ www.woodstockinn.com) has been an exemplar of understated luxury since Laurance and Mary Rockefeller purchased and made over the property in the late 1960s. Features include a golf course, a spa, tennis courts, and upscale dining. The sweetly updated **Sleep Woodstock Motel** (✉ 4324 W. Woodstock Rd. ☎ 802/332–6336 ⊕ www.sleepwoodstock.com) lies just west of town, overlooking a scenic stretch of the Ottauquechee.

Breakfast: In a delightful Greek revival cottage in the center of town, **Mont Vert Cafe** (✉ 28 Central St. ☎ 802/457–7143 ⊕ www.monvertcafe.com) has earned a wildly enthusiastic following for its organic all-day breakfasts, including lox-and-schmear bagels and the decadent Monte Vert Cristo with local maple syrup.

Day 11: Woodstock, VT, to Gorham, NH

148 miles (3 hours, 30 minutes without traffic and stops)

On this serpentine drive across New Hampshire's White Mountain National Forest, prepare for plenty of twists and turns. After crossing the Vermont border into Hanover, New Hampshire, follow Route 10 north to Orford, and then meander east on Route 25A and Route 118 to I–93 and Franconia Notch State Park. Then follow U.S. 3 to U.S. 302 and drive south through Crawford Notch State Park. In Glen, turn north onto Route 16 and drive along the eastern flanks of Mount Washington and the Presidential Range to get to Gorham.

ALONG THE WAY

Town: After curving up around the north side of Woodstock, the Appalachian Trail passes by the superb, kid-approved **Montshire Museum of Science** (✉ 1 Montshire Rd., Norwich, VT ☎ 802/649–2200 ⊕ www.montshire.org) before crossing a short bridge over the Connecticut River into Hanover, home of the genteel campus of Dartmouth College. There, the well-curated **Hood Museum of Art** (✉ 6 E. Wheelock St. ☎ 603/646–2808 ⊕ hoodmuseum.dartmouth.edu) is worth a visit.

Eat & Drink: Many intrepid hikers are fans of **Base Camp Cafe** (✉ 3 Lebanon St. ☎ 603/643–2007 ⊕ www.basecampcafenewhampshire.com) in Hanover, which doles out big portions of boldly flavored Nepalese cooking.

Nature: Franconia Notch State Park (✉ Daniel Webster Hwy. ☎ 603/823–8800 ⊕ www.nhstateparks.org) abounds with recreational opportunities, including hiking along some particularly rugged stretches of the Appalachian Trail. For an easier jaunt, stroll through the park's Flume Gorge.

GORHAM

Do: Follow scenic U.S. 302 around the west side of hulking 6,288-foot Mount Washington into Bretton Woods, New Hampshire, where you can book a ride on the **1858 Cog Railway** (✉ *3168 Base Station Rd., Bretton Woods* ☎ *603/278–5404* ⊕ *www.thecog.com*) to the mountain's summit, which is also traversed via a challenging section of the Appalachian Trail. Or take Route 16 along the east side of the mountain, where you can drive the exhilarating **Mount Washington Auto Road** (✉ *1 Mt. Washington Auto Rd.* ☎ *603/466–3988* ⊕ *www.mt-washington.com*) to the top.

Eat & Drink: Nonna's Kitchen (✉ *19 Exchange St.* ☎ *603/915–9203* ⊕ *www.nonnasgorham.com*) is another of New Hampshire's popular dining choices for hungry hikers, who appreciate the homemade pastas as well as the filling veal piccata. **Big Day Brewing** (✉ *20 Glen Rd.* ☎ *603/915–9006* ⊕ *www.bigdaybrewing.com*) is a festive place to relax on the patio with a hoppy IPA; live bands often perform.

Stay: The upscale and contemporary **Glen House** (✉ *979 Rte. 16* ☎ *603/466–3420* ⊕ *www.theglenhouse.com*) lies at the foot of the Mount Washington Auto Road and across the street from Great Glen Trails Outdoor Center, where you can book a variety of outdoor activities, from kayaking to hiking. Dining on the terrace affords grand views of the White Mountains. One of the most popular and accessible of several northern New England lodgings operated by the Appalachian Mountain Club, the **AMC Joe Dodge Lodge at Pinkham Notch** (✉ *Rte. 16* ☎ *603/466–2721* ⊕ *www.outdoors.org*) offers no-frills rustic rooms (private and dorm-style) located steps from the AT.

Breakfast: The friendly **Bear Taphouse & Cafe** (✉ *115 Main St.* ☎ *603/301–5161* ⊕ *www.thebearingorham.com*) fits the bill for delicious, filling sustenance before a day of hiking through the rugged White Mountains.

Day 12: Gorham, NH, to Rangeley, ME

87 miles (1 hour, 45 minutes without traffic and stops)

Take U.S. 2 east from Gorham across the border to Bethel, Maine, and continue east. At Rumford, turn north onto Route 17 to get to the alpine lake town of Rangeley.

ALONG THE WAY

Town: An outdoor sports hub with a handsome village green and a good selection of places to eat and spend the night, Bethel, Maine, is home to popular Sunday River ski and snowboard resort. Be sure to check out the excellent interactive exhibits and geological displays, including a cool collection of meteorites, at the **Maine Mineral and Gem Museum** (✉ *99 Main St.* ☎ *207/824–3036* ⊕ *mainemineralmuseum.org*).

Eat & Drink: Bethel's **Le Mu Eats** (✉ *119 Main St.* ☎ *207/824–1155* ⊕ *www.facebook.com/lemueats*) stands out among the region's many pubs and taverns for its innovative cuisine, such as pho-style risotto with braised short rib and cornbread with smoked honey butter.

Photo Op: As you drive north on Route 17, aka Rangeley Lakes National Scenic Byway, pull off at the Height of Land scenic overlook to admire the dazzling scenery. This is a favorite spot for admiring the fall foliage, and you can even hike a bit of the Appalachian Trail, which crosses the road here.

RANGELEY

Do: The largest town amid a constellation of six giant lakes that have long drawn ardent enthusiasts of fishing, hiking, and cross-country skiing, Rangeley is a rugged, unpretentious community beloved for its natural beauty. The **Outdoor Heritage Museum** (✉ *8 Rumford Rd., Oquossoc, ME* ☎ *207/864–3091* ⊕ *www.*

historicrangeley.org) has illuminating exhibits on the region's human and natural history. For a great view of nearby Moose-lookmeguntic Lake, hike just over a mile to the fire tower that crowns Bald Mountain.

Eat & Drink: In addition to great beer, **Furbish Brew House** (✉ *2541 Main St.* ☎ *207/864–5847* ⊕ *www.instagram. com/furbishbrewhouse*) offers up creatively topped wood-fired pizzas and gastropub fare, and has outdoor seating with lovely lake views.

Stay: A classic 1907 hotel on the shore of tranquil Haley Pond, the sky-blue clapboard **Rangeley Inn** (✉ *2443 Main St.* ☎ *207/864–3341* ⊕ *www.therangeley-inn.com*) stands out for its broad veranda, period-furnished common rooms, and convivial restaurant and fireside tavern.

Breakfast: Start your morning off well with a Greek yogurt parfait drizzled with local honey or a slice of quiche at **Classic Provisions Rangeley** (✉ *2455 Main St.* ☎ *207/864-2717* ⊕ *www.classicprovisionsrangeley.com*), which has attractive seating on a landscaped patio.

Day 13: Rangeley, ME, to Millinocket, ME

188 miles (4 hours, 30 minutes without traffic and stops)

Take Route 16 northeast from Rangeley to Stratton, and then Route 27 southeast through the Carrabassett Valley to Kingfield. Then head east to Solon and weave through Maine's North Woods through Bingham, Mayfield Corner, Abbot, and Monson up to Greenville and the southern shore of Moosehead Lake. From here it's a somewhat rugged drive on unpaved but well-maintained Katahdin Iron Works Road through the Appalachian Mountain Club 100 Mile Wilderness to reach Route 11, just north of Brownville, which continues the final stretch to Millinocket, the gateway to Baxter State Park.

ALONG THE WAY

Town: On the main road to Greenville, the small former slate-quarrying town of Monson is traversed by the Appalachian Trail and hugs the shore of Lake Hebron. A significant investment in restoring the town's buildings has led to a renaissance that has added some buzzy galleries and eateries. Engaging stops include the **Monson General Store** (✉ *12 Greenville Rd.* ☎ *207/997–3800* ⊕ *www.facebook. com/monsongeneral*), which stocks handmade gifts and gourmet goods, and the informative museum at the **Monson Historical Society** (✉ *6 Tenney Hill Rd.* ☎ *207/876–3073* ⊕ *www.monsonmehistoricalsociety.com*).

Eat & Drink: Among Monson's widely acclaimed eateries, the high-end **Quarry** (✉ *15 Tenney Hill Rd.* ☎ *207/997–3486* ⊕ *www.facebook.com/thequarrymonson*) earns kudos for its beautifully presented farm-to-table cuisine. **Lakeshore House Lodge & Pub** (✉ *9 Tenney Hill Rd.* ☎ *207/997–7069* ⊕ *www.thelakeshorehouse.com*) is a more casual option, dispensing well-prepared comfort food and often featuring live music.

Detour: At 75,000 acres, Moosehead Lake is the largest body of water situated fully within New England. It's anchored on its south shore by the laid-back town of Greenville, where you can take a half-day cruise around the lake in a 1914 steamship from the wharf at the **Moosehead Marine Museum** (✉ *12 Lily Bay Rd.* ☎ *207/695–2716* ⊕ *www.katahdin-cruises.com*). Another fun activity is making the picturesque 20-mile drive up Route 6 to Rockwood, where you can catch a 15-minute ferry across Moosehead Lake to **Mount Kineo State Park** (✉ *Ferry from 62 Village Rd.* ☎ *207/941–4014* ⊕ *maine.gov*). It's famed for its soaring 700-foot-tall cliffs, which you can hike up to on a 3.4-mile loop trail. Lunch is served in the park's historic restaurant and bar, which overlooks the historic 9-hole golf course.

MILLINOCKET

Do: Throughout the hardscrabble mill town of Millinocket, you can almost always see Maine's highest summit, 5,267-foot Mount Katahdin, rising in the distance. The northern terminus of the Appalachian Trail, this dramatic peak anchors **Baxter State Park** (✉ *Baxter Park Rd.* ☎ *207/723–5140* ⊕ *www.baxterstatepark.org*), an immense wilderness that's more than five times larger than Acadia National Park. Actually hiking to the top is a serious undertaking, but there are several appealing and more manageable hikes in the park, including a relaxing ramble around Daicey Pond. Several reputable companies offer guided rafting and tubing trips on the Penobscot River including **Northern Outdoors** (☎ *207/663–4466* ⊕ *www.northernoutdoors.com*).

Eat & Drink: The laid-back **Sawmill Bar & Grill** (✉ *9 Millinocket Rd.* ☎ *207/447–6996* ⊕ *www.sawmillgrillme.com*) is a dependable choice for pizzas, pork ribs, and other traditional comfort fare.

Stay: A great choice if you're looking to play in the wilderness, **Twin Pines at NEOC** (✉ *30 Twin Pines Rd.* ☎ *207/723–5523* ⊕ *www.neoc.com*) is about 10 miles northwest of town on the shore of pristine Millinocket Lake and offers cabins and multi-bedroom vacation homes. The myriad guided activities include rafting, mountain-biking, and ascending to the summit of Mount Katahdin. The contemporary, light-filled **5 Lakes Lodge Bed & Breakfast** (✉ *46 Marina Dr.* ☎ *207/723–5045* ⊕ *www.5lakeslodge.com*) has six sumptuous rooms and enjoys a charmed lakefront setting.

Breakfast: Fuel up on flapjacks with maple syrup and breakfast burritos at the **Appalachian Trail Cafe** (✉ *210 Penobscot Ave.* ☎ *207/723–6720* ⊕ *www.facebook.com/appalachiantrailcafe*), a homey downtown storefront space considered by many to be the unofficial last stop of the Appalachian Trail.

Along the Mississippi River

Written by Stratton Lawrence

On the west side of Yellowstone National Park, a small spring emerges in Montana. Across the country, the Allegheny River descends from the Pennsylvania mountains. And in Minnesota, at Lake Itasca, a river forms and heads south. Fed by a watershed spanning 31 states, the Mississippi River is the circulatory system of our nation, and exploring its route reveals a clear view of America. It is 2,320 miles from the Gulf of Mexico to Lake Itasca, where the Upper Mississippi River forms, laying claim as the river's official headwaters. This artery helps to define the borders of 10 states, and even of our nation, through historic moments like the Louisiana Purchase.

Today's Mississippi River is not the one that pioneers encountered. Levees line the majority of its banks, preventing Big Muddy from overflowing into the floodplain that once formed wetlands along much of the route. The river's transformation into a controlled canal for barges has changed its character, but it still shows glimpses of its might when it overflows—and in the river's northern reaches where natural floodplain forests still exist.

What's most impressive about a drive up the Big River is the culture that emerged along its banks, from Cajun cuisine in Louisiana and soul music in Memphis to Mark Twain's literary portraits of Americana in Missouri. This road trip traces the mighty Mississippi from New Orleans (75 miles before the river spills into the Gulf of Mexico) to Minneapolis, where the river forms the heart of the city.

At a Glance

Start: New Orleans, LA

End: Minneapolis, MN

Miles Traveled: 1,400 miles

Suggested Duration: 7 days

States Visited: Illinois, Iowa, Louisiana, Minnesota, Mississippi, Missouri, Tennessee, Wisconsin

Key Sights: Delta Blues Museum; Gateway Arch; Graceland; Mark Twain's Boyhood Home; Mississippi National River and Recreation Area

Best Time to Go: In summer, you'll swelter through the early days of the trip, but a good sweat feels appropriate in the Mississippi Delta. As you head north, you'll reach weather divinity, and find that more restaurants and attractions are open and accessible than during the cold winter months.

Day 1: New Orleans, LA, to Natchez, MS

170 miles (3 hours without traffic and stops)

Take I–10 west to Baton Rouge, where you'll pick up U.S. 61 north to Natchez. U.S. 61 runs the length of the river and will be a constant companion on this trip.

ALONG THE WAY

Town: Before your trip starts, spend two or three days in the Big Easy. Eat Chicken Creole Captain at **Palm & Pine** (✉ *308 N. Rampart St.* ☎ *504/814–6200* ⊕ *www. palmandpinenola.com*). Discover the origins of the cocktail at **Sazerac House** (✉ *101 Magazine St.* ☎ *504/910– 0100* ⊕ *www.sazerachouse.com*), and prep yourself for the trip by getting rowdy at the **Rivershack Tavern** (✉ *3449 River Rd.* ☎ *504/834–4938* ⊕ *www.*

rivershacktavern.com). Then load up on coffee and beignets at **Café Du Monde** (✉ *800 Decatur St.* ☎ *504/525– 4544* ⊕ *www.cafedumonde.com*) and hit the road.

Eat & Drink: Halfway between Baton Rouge and the Mississippi state line, the **St. Francisville Inn** (✉ *5720 Commerce St.* ☎ *225/635–6502* ⊕ *www.stfrancisvilleinn.com*) in St. Francisville drapes the southern hospitality on as heavy as the Spanish moss on the trees outside. The French Creole cuisine here is a memorable treat.

NATCHEZ

Do: The **Natchez National Historical Park** (✉ *Melrose Montebello Pkwy.* ☎ *601/446–5790* ⊕ *www.nps.gov/ natc*) encompasses the city's waterfront district, including exhibits at Fort Rosalie, a strategic site for the French, British, and Spanish explorers who controlled the region through different eras. There are also well-maintained mansions and former plantations along the river, including the Melrose estate, a brick mansion whose surviving structures include a cabin where the plantation's enslaved people lived.

Eat & Drink: Watch boats ply the river while noshing on oysters Bienville at the **Magnolia Grill** (✉ *49 Silver St.* ☎ *601/446– 7670* ⊕ *www.magnoliagrill.com*), where the catfish is served chargrilled and spicy.

Stay: With views of the river from many of the rooms, **Hotel Vue** (✉ *130 John R. Junkin Dr.* ☎ *601/653–2521* ⊕ *www. choicehotels.com*) is a comfortable place to lay your head. Its star attraction is the top-floor restaurant and cocktail bar with a glass wall overlooking the Mississippi.

Breakfast: Get up early to hit the **Donut Shop** (✉ *501 John R. Junkin Dr.* ☎ *601/442–2317*) before they run out of the day's batch of hot glazed goodness, and grab a beef tamale to take with you on the road.

Along the Mississippi

Day 2: Natchez, MS, to Clarksdale, MS

220 miles (4 hours without traffic and stops)

Take U.S. 61/278 north all the way to Clarksdale, through the heart of the Mississippi Delta. In Rolling Fork, you have the option of shifting to Route 1 to more closely follow the river, visiting Greenville and Rosedale along the way.

ALONG THE WAY

Detour: Indianola, B. B. King's birthplace, is a 10-minute detour that's worth the stop to tour the **B. B. King Museum** (✉ *400 2nd St.* ☎ *662/887–9539* ⊕ *www.bbkingmuseum.org*) and pay homage at his grave. Across the street, you can load up on catfish, shrimp, and the Earlberta burger at **The Blue Biscuit** (✉ *501–503 2nd St.* ☎ *662/645–0258* ⊕ *www.thebluebiscuit.com*) if you're hungry.

Photo Op: Stop in Leland, Jim Henson's boyhood home, to tour the **Birthplace of Kermit the Frog Museum** (✉ *415 S. Deer Creek Dr. E* ☎ *662/686–7383* ⊕ *www.birthplaceofthefrog.com*) and pose with everyone's favorite friendly green amphibian.

Eat & Drink: Just north of Cleveland, **Airport Grocery** (✉ *3608 U.S. 61* ☎ *662/843–4817* ⊕ *www.airportgrocerycleveland.com*) is a laid-back blues joint known for pork barbecue, chili cheese tamales, and catfish hoagies. Or if you find yourself in Greenville after 5 pm, the original **Doe's Eat Place** (✉ *502 Nelson St.* ☎ *662/334–3315* ⊕ *www.doeseatplace.com*) is the finest place in the Delta for a hearty steak. Then stick around to catch a show at the **Walnut Street Blues Bar** (✉ *128 S. Walnut St.* ☎ *662/378–2254*), a staple along the Mississippi Blues Trail.

Essential Listening

Start your trip with Satchmo setting the mood. Let Louis Armstrong sing and play you to Baton Rouge, before pivoting to a modern-day horn man, Trombone Shorty. Once you head into the Mississippi Delta, aka blues country, add Robert Johnson's "Me and the Devil Blues" and B. B. King's "Everyday I Have the Blues" to the playlist. As you approach Memphis, put Elvis, Sam and Dave, Otis Redding, and Isaac Hayes in the rotation.

CLARKSDALE

Do: Start by taking the Clarksdale Walk of Fame self-guided tour, where the many stars that called this small town home are memorialized, including Sam Cooke, Son House, and Tennessee Williams. After immersing yourself in Robert Johnson and Muddy Waters at the **Delta Blues Museum** (✉ *1 Blues Alley* ☎ *662/627–6820* ⊕ *www.deltabluesmuseum.org*), head next door to the **Ground Zero Blues Club** (✉ *387 Delta Ave.* ☎ *662/621–9009* ⊕ *www.groundzerobluesclub.com*), a happening blues joint that's co-owned by Morgan Freeman.

Eat & Drink: The menu at **Hooker Grocer & Eatery** (✉ *316 John Lee Hooker La.* ☎ *662/624–7038* ⊕ *www.hookergrocer.com*) is sophisticated southern, with international flair (think gumbo meets chicken *karaage*), but the blues vibe is pure Delta, with live music on indoor and outdoor stages.

Stay: Travelers Hotel (✉ *212 3rd St.* ☎ *662/483–0693* ⊕ *www.stayattravelers.com*) has come a long way since it housed itinerant railroad workers a century ago—today, it's a boutique space with modern, Instagram-worthy furnishings and a lobby bar that serves as a community hub.

Breakfast: Meraki Roasting Company (✉ *282 Sunflower Ave.* ☎ *662/351–2233* ⊕ *www. merakiroasting.com*) is more than a coffee shop—it's an in-house mentorship program for young locals to build entrepreneurial experience through a 16-week employment program. It's also home to Big River Bagels (order a smear of the honey vanilla cream cheese).

Day 3: Clarksdale, MS, to Memphis, TN

75 miles (1 hour, 30 minutes without traffic and stops)

It's a short drive up U.S. 61 today, leaving plenty of time to explore Memphis.

ALONG THE WAY

Photo Op: Before leaving Clarksdale, stop by the old intersection of U.S. 61 and U.S. 49, where a three-guitar sculpture marks the place where blues legend Robert Johnson allegedly sold his soul to the devil to gain his guitar-playing abilities.

Detour: Before cruising into downtown Memphis, spend a few hours south of town at **Graceland** (✉ *Elvis Presley Blvd.* ☎ *901/332–3322* ⊕ *www.graceland. com*). If you're not an Elvis fan, you will be after touring the hip-shaking legend's mansion, airplane, and gardens while tracing his remarkable career.

Eat & Drink: After your quick drive, head straight for **Sunrise Memphis** (✉ *670 Jefferson Ave.* ☎ *901/552–3168* ⊕ *www. sunrise901.com*) for hearty sandwiches like the Hen House, or the Crunchy Tiger Hidden Salad.

MEMPHIS

Do: Tour the **Stax Museum of American Soul Music** (✉ *926 E. McLemore Ave.* ☎ *901/261–6338* ⊕ *www.staxmuseum.org*), where you'll be floored by

how many soul music hits emerged from the studio known as Stax Records, from Booker T. & the MGs to Otis Redding to the Staples Singers. The pièce de résistance is Isaac Hayes's Cadillac Eldorado with fur carpeting and 24-carat-gold trim. Leave time to tour **Mud Island River Park** (☎ *901/312–9190* ⊕ *www.memphisriverparks.org*), where a scale model of the lower Mississippi stretches over 2,000 feet.

Eat & Drink: The barbecue scene in Memphis is legendary, and **Charlie Vergos' Rendezvous** (✉ *52 S. 2nd St.* ☎ *901/523–2746* ⊕ *www.hogsfly.com*) is a multilevel temple to smoked pork. Order a rack of ribs and ask for a table in the subterranean basement for an experience that feels like slipping 70 years back in time. Or dine on modern southern fare with global influences at **The Beauty Shop** (✉ *966 Cooper St.* ☎ *901/272–7111* ⊕ *www. thebeautyshoprestaurant.com*), which occupies a storefront that once held a beauty salon where Priscilla Presley had her hair done.

Stay: Prepare for the most memorable hotel of your trip—**The Peabody Memphis** (✉ *149 Union Ave.* ☎ *901/529–4000* ⊕ *www.peabodymemphis.com*) sparkles from top (where the resident ducks live in their rooftop Royal Duck Palace) to the bottom (where the magnificent lobby features a fountain that said ducks swim in each day). Arrive in time to sip a cocktail as the ducks march to the elevator at 5 pm. Rooms are spacious, with stately furniture and details.

Breakfast: Inside the Peabody, the **Capriccio Grill's** (✉ *149 Union Ave.* ☎ *901/529–4199* ⊕ *www.peabodymemphis.com*) Italianate art and decor feel like stepping into Old Europe, and thoughtful breakfast entrées like almond toast and an Elvis Smoothie (peanut butter yogurt and bananas served with banana nut bread) will fuel the drive ahead.

Day 4: Memphis, TN, to St. Louis, MO

290 miles (4 hours, 30 minutes without traffic and stops)

Today's drive leaves the Delta behind as you head into the Mississippi River Valley. I-55 north runs directly to St. Louis, although you have plenty of options for detours and stops to experience the river along the way.

ALONG THE WAY

Town: Just minutes off I-55, New Madrid is a charming Missouri town situated along a horseshoe bend in the river. It's best known as the site of a major fault that led to massive earthquakes in 1811. Take the five-minute walk from Riverside Park to an observation deck with terrific views of the river. Check out the engaging exhibits on the town's Civil War history and its great earthquake at the **New Madrid Historical Museum** (✉ *1 S. Main St.* ☎ *573/748–5944* ⊕ *www.newmadridmuseum.com*), and tour the 19th-century mansion at the **Hunter-Dawson State Historic Site** (✉ *312 Dawson Rd.* ☎ *573/748–5340* ⊕ *www.mostateparks.com*).

Detour: The southernmost point in Illinois, Cairo is a town that's well past its prime, but it's a fascinating place to visit, both historically and geographically. The flood-prone city sits on a peninsula at the confluence of the Ohio and Mississippi Rivers. At **Fort Defiance Park** (✉ *Fort Defiance Rd.* ☎ *618/734–4127* ⊕ *www.stateparks.com*), you can see where the rivers and the state lines of Illinois, Missouri, and Kentucky all come together. If time allows, continue south to **Columbus Belmont State Park** (✉ *350 Park Rd., Columbus, KY* ☎ *270/677–2327* ⊕ *www.parks.ky.gov*), an important Civil War site along a tranquil stretch of the river.

Eat & Drink: The Kozy (✉ *710 U.S. 61* ☎ *573/483–2898* ⊕ *www.thekozymo.com*), in the little town of Bloomsdale,

Missouri, serves creative comfort fare—think burgers with wild mushrooms and goat cheese and pulled pork eggs Benedict—in an airy, family-friendly bungalow with a shaded front porch.

ST. LOUIS

Do: After taking in the view from 630 feet at **Gateway Arch National Park** (✉ *11 N. 4th St.* ☎ *314/655–1600* ⊕ *www.nps.gov/jeff*), spend the afternoon at **City Museum** (✉ *750 N. 16th St.* ☎ *314/231–2489* ⊕ *www.citymuseum.org*), an all-ages playground that includes an endless array of fun things to climb over and through, from a 10-story spiral staircase slide and a series of caves to the MonstroCity, an outdoor complex of cages and stairs that's capped by an airplane.

Eat & Drink: St. Louis has several foods unique to the city: slingers (eggs, a beef patty, and hash browns, covered with chili), toasted ravioli, and St. Louis–style pizza (thin crust with gooey cheese). Grab a classic pie from **Pizza-A-Go-Go** (✉ *6703 Scanlan Ave.* ☎ *314/781–1234* ⊕ *pizzaagogostl.wixsite.com/pizzaagogostl*), breaded and fried ravioli from **Anthonino's Taverna** (✉ *2225 Macklind Ave.* ☎ *314/773–4455* ⊕ *www.anthoninos.com*), and a breakfast slinger from **Gotham and Eggs** (✉ *3139 S. Grand Blvd.* ☎ *314/833–8355* ⊕ *www.gothamandeggs.com*).

Stay: Union Station is an architectural landmark that's now home to the St. Louis Aquarium, several restaurants, and the modern, well-appointed **Union Station Hotel** (✉ *1820 Market St.* ☎ *314/231–1234* ⊕ *www.hilton.com*). Check in by 5 pm to see the 3-D light show on the vaulted ceiling in the Grand Hall.

Breakfast: Egg (✉ *3100 Locust St.* ☎ *314/899–0036* ⊕ *www.eggstl.com*) has two locations where you can score their delicious hashes (meat, veggies, and eggs over potatoes), Tunisian-style *shakshuka*, and breakfast tacos. On weekends, be sure to make a reservation.

The Gateway Arch in St. Louis stands proud over the Mississippi River.

Day 5: St. Louis, MO, to Davenport, IA

280 miles (4 hours, 30 minutes without traffic and stops)

Leave St. Louis on I–64 west before taking U.S. 61 to Hannibal, Missouri. After taking some time to explore, cross the river to reach I–172, passing through Carthage, Missouri, and a brief stretch on U.S. 136 before taking U.S. 67 north to Davenport.

ALONG THE WAY

Eat & Drink: If you're up for the scenic route, take Route 100 from St. Louis along the east bank of the river, and stop for lunch at **Grafton Oyster Bar** (✉ *215 Water St.* ☎ *618/786–3000* ⊕ *www. graftonoysterbar.com*) in Grafton, Illinois, a floating restaurant that takes cues from New Orleans. The signature appetizer is a savory shrimp-and-alligator-sausage cheesecake.

Town: Hannibal is as quaint and purely American as one can imagine. Visit **Mark Twain's Boyhood Home Museum** (✉ *415 N. Main St.* ☎ *573/221–9010* ⊕ *www. marktwainmuseum.org*), cruise the river on a paddleboat, and see the statue of Huck Finn and Tom Sawyer. Finally, climb the **Mark Twain Memorial Lighthouse** (✉ *E. Rock St.* ☎ *573/221–0154* ⊕ *www.hannibalparks.org*) for a sweeping view of the river and town.

Roadside Attraction: Along the river in Quincy, Illinois, sits **Villa Kathrine** (✉ *532 Gardner Expy.* ☎ *217/224–3688* ⊕ *www. quincyparkdistrict.com*), an impressive but odd late-19th-century mansion built by an eccentric millionaire who drew inspiration from his travels to Morocco. The home now serves as the tourist information center for Quincy.

DAVENPORT

Do: Take a walk through the **Vander Veer Botanical Park** (✉ *215 W. Central Park Ave.* ☎ *563/326–7818* ⊕ *www.davenportiowa.com*), which includes a grand walkway lined with trees and a conservatory with seasonal blooms. In the evening, catch a concert or theatrical performance at the historic **Adler Theatre** (✉ 136 E. 3rd St. ☎ 563/326–8500 ⊕ www.adlerdavenport.com) before walking the Davenport Skybridge after dark, when it lights up with multicolored LEDs.

Eat & Drink: Front Street Brewery (✉ 421 W. River Dr. ☎ 563/324–4014 ⊕ www.frontstreetbrew.com) has midwestern craft beer clout, brewing an array of porters, pales, and light ales since opening in 1992. Their kitchen serves upscale pub grub, and the taproom lets you sip a pint in view of the river.

Stay: Hotel Blackhawk (✉ 200 E. 3rd St. ☎ 563/322–5000 ⊕ www.marriott.com) is a classy, modern hotel in a renovated historic building, with many rooms offering views of the river. There's an on-site old-timey barber shop, and a bowling alley on the bottom floor that's known for its martinis.

Breakfast: You can expect a little more creativity from the menu than its name might suggest at **The Diner** (✉ 421 W. River Dr. ☎ 563/323–0895 ⊕ www.thedinerqc.com), where extensive breakfast options include Bonnie's Huggabunch, a deconstructed bacon cheeseburger with eggs, sandwiched between pancakes.

Day 6: Davenport, IA, to La Crosse, WI

190 miles (3 hours, 30 minutes without traffic and stops)

Your route today is due north on U.S. 61 to Dubuque, Iowa, where you'll hop across the water to Route 35 to more closely follow the river. After passing Prairie du Chien, Wisconsin, you'll enjoy a largely undeveloped 50 miles with constant river views.

ALONG THE WAY

Roadside Attraction: Just west of Davenport is the world's largest truck stop, **Iowa 80 TA** (✉ 755 W. Iowa 80 Rd. ☎ 563/284–6961 ⊕ www.iowa-80truckstop.com), with room for 900 trucks to park. In addition to everything you could ever need for a truck, there are plenty of T-shirts and gimmicky souvenirs.

Roadside Attraction: In Port Byron, Illinois, a 30-foot-tall statue of a man riding a vintage penny-farthing bicycle (dubbed *Will B. Rolling*) highlights a stroll or ride along the Great River Bike Trail.

Town: Set along scenic hills and bluffs overlooking the river, Dubuque is an excellent way station. Tour the **National Mississippi River Museum & Aquarium** (✉ 350 E. 3rd St. ☎ 563/557–9545 ⊕ www.rivermuseum.org), where the exhibits include fish native to the river and the National Rivers Hall of Fame. Then take the short ride on the **Fenelon Place Elevator** (✉ 491 W. 4th St. ☎ 563/582–6496 ⊕ www.fenelonplaceelevator.com), which takes you up a steep hill to the former mansion of a businessman who built the small railway to avoid the walk up and down.

Eat & Drink: Valley Fish & Cheese (✉ 304 S. Prairie St. ☎ 608/326–4719 ⊕ www.facebook.com/valleyfishcheese) in Prairie du Chien prides itself on "good, quality oddball stuff." That might mean snapping turtle jerky or a delicious filet of hickory-smoked perch. Owner "Mississippi Mike" Valley fishes on the Mississippi to harvest the smoked fish for sale in the rustic building that's adorned floor to ceiling with river effects and memorabilia.

Nature: The Upper Mississippi River National Wildlife and Fish Refuge stretches for much of the river on today's drive, allowing you to see more of the Mississippi as it looked before levees. Near the end of the drive, walk or bike the Shady Maple Interpretive Trail in Goose Island County Park to explore a healthy floodplain forest.

LA CROSSE

Do: Get your bearings in La Crosse by heading to the top of Grandad Bluff, a cliff that overlooks the city and the Mississippi nearly 600 feet below. Then cruise by the 54-foot-tall **World's Largest Six Pack** (✉ *3rd St. S*), adorned with La Crosse Lager labels. Finally, head to **Riverside Park** (✉ *100 State St.* ☎ *608/789-7533* ⊕ *www.explorelacrosse.com*) and the adjacent **Riverside International Friendship Gardens** (✉ *405 E. Veterans Memorial Dr.* ☎ *608/789-7533* ⊕ *www.riverside-gardens.org*). Stroll through the gardens before a walk or jog along the river.

Eat & Drink: Treat yourself to fine dining with a view at **The Waterfront** (✉ *328 Front St. S* ☎ *608/782-5400* ⊕ *www.thewaterfrontlacrosse.com*), a seafood-oriented white-tablecloth spot known for steaks, impeccable service, and views of the Mississippi from the pleasant patio.

Stay: The most impressive residence in town—built for a lumber baron in the late-19th-century—is now the **Castle La Crosse Bed and Breakfast** (✉ *1419 Cass St.* ☎ *844/726-5808* ⊕ *www.castlecrossebnb.com*). This towering home with a stone facade feels legitimately regal, from the grand staircase to the spacious, luxuriously appointed rooms.

Breakfast: Grounded Patio Café (✉ *308 Main St.* ☎ *608/784-5282* ⊕ *www.groundedlax.com*) is a local favorite for coffee, smoothies, and egg sandwiches, including sandwich specialties like the Tuscan Sunrise with turkey, tomato, Swiss, and pesto on an English muffin.

Day 7: La Crosse, WI, to Minneapolis, MN

160 miles (3 hours without traffic and stops)

You've got options today, but skip the interstate on your last day of driving. Flank the river along U.S. 61 unless you're stopping for pizza at Suncrest Gardens. In Red Wing, Minnesota, cross the river to Hager City, before picking up U.S. 10 north of Hastings.

ALONG THE WAY

Town: Winona, Minnesota, is a pleasant riverfront college town where you can stretch your legs with a hike around the city's lake, go birding in the floodplain forest of Aghaming Park, or cool off with a swim in the river at Latsch Island Beach.

Eat & Drink: If you're traveling on a Friday or Saturday, plan on a late lunch at **Suncrest Gardens** (✉ *S2257 Yaeger Valley Rd.* ☎ *608/626-2122* ⊕ *www.suncrestgardensfarm.com*) in Cochrane, Wisconsin, where the "Pizza Farm" bakes pies in a wood-fired oven, made from ingredients grown right on the farm. Stick around for live music, or rent a room in the farmhouse on Airbnb and stay the night.

Nature: The National Park Service maintains and protects 72 miles of riverfront between Ramsey and Hastings, Minnesota. As you approach St. Paul, floodplain valleys curve into bluffs, offering one of the best opportunities for exploration via kayaking and canoeing on the river.

Roadside Attraction: If you head through Red Wing, the town's eponymous shoe company created the **World's Largest Boot** (✉ *315 Main St.*), a 20-foot-tall size 638½ that required 80 cowhides to source its leather.

MINNEAPOLIS

Do: Brace yourself for city life by escaping into the green heart of Minneapolis at the 200-acre **Minnehaha Regional Park** (✉ *4801 S. Minnehaha Dr.* ☎ *612/230-6400* ⊕ *www.minneapolisparks.org*), where a picture-perfect waterfall crashes 53 feet on its way downstream to the Mississippi. Then visit the **Minneapolis Sculpture Garden** (✉ *725 Vineland Pl.* ☎ *612/375-7600* ⊕ *www.walkerart.org*) to pose with the city's famous *Spoonbridge and Cherry* sculpture. See one more example of oversized art by driving into the heart of the city to see the **Bob Dylan mural** (✉ *1 S. 5th St.*), depicting the musician at three stages in his career.

Eat & Drink: The dining scene in Minneapolis could fill weeks of exploration, but experience a taste from one of its most inventive kitchens at **Spoon and Stable** (✉ *211 N. 1st St.* ☎ *612/224– 9850* ⊕ *www.spoonandstable.com*), where the gorgeous presentations of entrées like trout and dry-aged duck breast insist that you photograph your food. In St. Paul, **The Lexington** (✉ *1096 Grand Ave.* ☎ *651/289–4990* ⊕ *www.thel-exmn.com*) is an upscale dining stalwart that's reinvented itself to remain relevant with dishes like walleye cakes and hot Brussels sprouts (but they still serve their smoked chicken pot pie).

Stay: You don't have to stay at the Foshay Tower—home to the posh **W Minneapolis** (✉ *821 S. Marquette Ave.* ☎ *612/215– 3700* ⊕ *www.marriott.com*)—to take in the views of the city from the rooftop observation deck, but crash here and you may take frequent trips to the 30th floor. On weekends, the "living room" transforms into a hip club with live DJs.

Breakfast: Breakfast options in the Twin Cities are as wide and inviting as dinner, but **Nolo's** (✉ *515 N. Washington Ave.* ☎ *612/800–6033* ⊕ *www.noloskitchen.com*) stands out by offering a signature breakfast fried rice, doused in yum yum sauce, and breakfast tacos that opt for crunch over soft tortillas.

The Great American Baseball Road Trip

Written by Mark Sullivan

For hardcore baseball fans, nothing beats a trip to some of the country's best ballparks, right? We've upped the ante a bit with this tour, throwing in some cool side trips, a couple of must-see museums, and a few bits of history about the game that you should know. You'll check out restaurants and pubs where you can discuss the big game with other sports fans, and stay at hotels that are walking distance to the stadiums (and sometimes look down onto the fields).

Just keep in mind that this itinerary doesn't factor in extra time if you really want to get to know the big cities like Chicago, Pittsburgh, and Boston. So feel free to add days in any of the baseball-loving cities along the way.

At a Glance

Start: Kansas City, MO

End: Boston, MA

Miles Traveled: 1,776 miles

Suggested Duration: 8 days

States Visited: Illinois, Iowa, Massachusetts, Michigan, Missouri, New York, Pennsylvania

Key Sights: Fenway Park; National Baseball Hall of Fame; Negro Leagues Baseball Museum; PNC Park; Wrigley Field

Best Time to Go: If you're actually planning to see a baseball game while on this trip (and you should), you'll need to make the trek during baseball season, from April through September.

Day 1: Kansas City, MO

Fly into Kansas City and spend your first day of the trip exploring the city's unique, baseball-loving history. In the morning, pick up your rental car to hit the road.

KANSAS CITY

Do: In Kansas City's historic 18th and Vine District, once the heart of the city's African American community, you'll find the fantastic **Negro Leagues Baseball Museum** (✉ *1616 E. 18th*

The Great American
Baseball Road Trip

St. ☎ 816/221–1920 ⊕ www.nlbm.com).
The well-regarded museum chronicles
the 100-year history of the historic
league, formed in 1920 because players
were banned from all-white teams. It has
plenty about the hometown team, the
Kansas City Monarchs, as well as Negro
League greats like John Henry Lloyd,
Satchel Paige, and Jackie Robinson (who
played for the Monarchs).

In the same complex is the **American Jazz
Museum** (⊠ 1616 E. 18th St. ☎ 816/474–
8463 ⊕ www.americanjazzmuseum.org),
which has its own baseball connection;
18th and Vine was one of the only neighborhoods where Black players could find
lodging, and they frequented the jazz
clubs in the neighborhood. Of course,
you'll also want to head to **Kauffman
Stadium** (⊠ 1 Royal Way ☎ 816/921–
8000 ⊕ www.kansascity.royals.mlb.com)
to catch a game with the Kansas City
Royals. The crown-shaped scoreboard
and a gushing outfield fountain make this
park memorable. Don't miss the on-site
Hall of Fame Museum.

Eat & Drink: There's absolutely no doubt
about where you should eat here:
Arthur Bryant's BBQ (⊠ 1727 Brooklyn
Ave. ☎ 816/231–1123 ⊕ www.arthurbry-
antsbbq.com), the place that perfected
Kansas City–style barbecue. It's in the
18th and Vine District, so it's perfect
timing after a trip to the Negro Leagues
Baseball Museum. Just north of downtown, **Chappell's Restaurant and Sports
Museum** (⊠ 323 Armour Rd. ☎ 816/421–
0002 ⊕ www.chappellskc.com) is jam-
packed with baseball memorabilia.

Stay: Located with a handsome
downtown landmark, the grand **Hotel
Phillips** (⊠ 106 W. 12th St. ☎ 816/221–
7000 ⊕ www.hilton.com) is on the
National Register of Historic Places. The
art deco styling is impressive, especially
in the ornate lobby. There's a tucked-away
speakeasy for late-night imbibing.

Breakfast: Fortify yourself for the day's
long drive with a stop at the upscale
Blue Bird Bistro (⊠ 1700 Summit
St. ☎ 816/221–7559 ⊕ www.bluebirdbis-
tro.com), where everything is made with
locally grown and organic ingredients.

Day 2: Kansas City, MO, to Dyersville, IA

*367 miles (5 hours, 40 minutes without
stops or traffic)*

I–35 speeds you north from Kansas City
to Des Moines. From there, continue
north on I–35 or head diagonally through
the farm towns on U.S. 65. Either
way you'll connect to U.S. 20, which
takes you to Dyersville, Iowa, with its
small-town vibe and picturesque brick
buildings.

ALONG THE WAY

Town: Des Moines, Iowa, may not have
a major league team, but locals couldn't
care less. They cheer on the Iowa Cubs, a
minor league team affiliated with the Chicago Cubs, at downtown's **Principal Park**
(⊠ 1 Line Dr. ☎ 515/243–6111 ⊕ www.
iowacubs.com). It has a great riverfront location and it's a perfect place to
experience the local joy of a minor league
stadium.

Eat & Drink: Not far from Principal Park,
downtown's **Waterfront Seafood Market**
(⊠ ClockTower Sq., 2900 University
Ave. ☎ 515/233–5106 ⊕ www.waterfront-
seafoodmarket.com) expertly straddles
the line between classic and contemporary with fresh fish prepared in a variety
of ways.

DYERSVILLE

Do: The real reason the rural town of
Dyersville is on the map is the ***Field
of Dreams* Movie Site** (⊠ 28995 Lansing Rd. ☎ 563/875–8404 ⊕ www.
fieldofdreamsmoviesite.com), a baseball
diamond built for one of the most famous
baseball movies of all times, *Field of*

Dreams. In the Kevin Costner film, an Iowa farmer plows up a cornfield to make a baseball diamond because he hears a mysterious voice whispering, "If you build it, he will come," and indeed, long-dead baseball players appear to play a game in the movie. And in real life, the building of the field has also brought hordes of tourists: the site is now one of the most popular attractions in Iowa.

Eat & Drink: At **Textile Brewing Company** (✉ *146 2nd St. NE* ☎ *563/207–0357* ⊕ *www.textilebrews.com*), the name refers to the sewing factory that operated on the premises more than a century ago. Order a craft beer—the American-style lager named for the town is a favorite—and then pub grub like flatbreads topped with barbecued chicken or chorizo.

Stay: Baseball fans will want to book a night at the *Field of Dreams* **Farm House** (✉ *28995 Lansing Rd.* ☎ *563/875–8404* ⊕ *www.fieldofdreamsmoviesite.com/home-rental*), the three-bedroom home that had a starring role in *Field of Dreams*. It sits near the famous field, so you can stroll over after the crowds have left.

Breakfast: A plaque on the wall here reads "Welcome Friends and Family," and you'll certainly feel right at home when you settle in for breakfast at the **Dyersville Family Restaurant** (✉ *226 1st Ave. E* ☎ *563/875–0033* ⊕ *dyersvillefamilyrestaurant.com*). It sits in Dyersville's historic downtown.

Day 3: Dyersville, IA, to Chicago, IL

204 miles (3 hours, 30 minutes without traffic and stops)

Take U.S. 20 east past Dubuque, Iowa, eventually reaching Rockford, Illinois. From there, I–90 takes you directly to Chicago.

ALONG THE WAY

Town: Galena, Illinois, is one of the most charming small towns between Dyersville and Chicago. The well-preserved 19th-century buildings hold more than 100 boutiques where you can shop to your heart's content. Pick up some baseball memorabilia at **Country Crafts and Sports** (✉ *113 S. Main St.* ☎ *815/776–0067* ⊕ *www.countycraftandsports.com*).

Eat & Drink: On Main Street in Galena is the intriguingly named **Fritz and Frites** (✉ *317 N. Main St.* ☎ *815/777–2004* ⊕ *www.fritzandfrites.com*), a storefront bistro that's a little bit German and a little bit French. It's basically Alsatian food, and it's all delicious. Look for the black-and-white awning.

CHICAGO

Do: There's plenty to do in the Windy City, but for this trip, head straight to **Wrigley Field** (✉ *1060 W. Addison St.* ☎ *773/404–2827* ⊕ *www.mlb.com/cubs/ballpark*), one of baseball's best and most historic stadiums. It's easy to see why Chicago Cubs fans are so, well, fanatic about this beauty from 1914: the classic bright-red marquee over the entrance, the scoreboard that's still turned by hand, and the outfield wall covered with ivy. Tours of the park and dugouts are given from April to October.

And don't miss the **Chicago Sports Museum** (✉ *835 N. Michigan Ave.* ☎ *312/202–0500* ⊕ *www.chicagosportsmuseum.com*), where an interactive exhibit lets you learn to throw a curve ball with Cy Young Award winner Steve Stone. There's also a massive trove of memorabilia related to the Cubs' historic 2016 World Series win, including manager Joe Maddon's famous "We Did Not Suck" T-shirt (for non–baseball fans: they hadn't won the World Series in a record 108 years).

Eat & Drink: A surprisingly sophisticated sports bar, **Harry Caray's 7th Inning Stretch** (✉ *Water Tower Pl., 835 N. Michigan Ave.* ☎ *312/202–0500* ⊕ *www.*

harrycarays.com) is named for the beloved announcer for the Chicago Cubs. Yes, that's a photo of President Barack Obama on the wall; he was one of hundreds of celebrities who've come to pay tribute to Caray. For decades, the family-owned-and-operated **Slugger's World Class Sports Bar** (✉ *3540 N. Clark St.* ☎ *773/248–0055* ⊕ *www.sluggersbar.com*) has long been a favorite on game day. The location, around the corner from Wrigley Field, can't be beat.

Stay: Once a private men's club, the **Chicago Athletic Association** (✉ *12 S. Michigan Ave.* ☎ *312/940–3552* ⊕ *www.chicagoathletichotel.com*) has been transformed into one of the city's most opulent places to stay. It hasn't totally gotten rid of the masculine vibe—for example, the Game Room bar is filled with billiard tables, a shuffleboard court, and a bocce bay. If that's not your scene, head to the solidly soundproofed Cherry Circle Room.

Breakfast: Not far from Wrigley Field, the Lakeview location of the old-school Scandinavian-inspired diner **Ann Sather** (✉ *909 W. Belmont Ave.* ☎ *773/348–2378* ⊕ *www.annsather.com*) serves scrumptious salmon-dill omelets and Swedish pancakes with lingonberries.

Day 4: Chicago, IL, to Detroit, MI

283 miles (4 hours without traffic and stops)

Believe it or not, I–94 takes you almost the entire way to Detroit. Along the way, you can catch glimpses of Lake Michigan during the first half of the trip.

ALONG THE WAY

Town: Kalamazoo, Michigan, is within easy driving distance for both Cubs and Tigers fans, but locals prefer to cheer on the Kalamazoo Growlers, who play in a summer collegiate baseball league. Their

Extend Your Trip

From Chicago: All the Great Lakes *(Ch. 6)*

From Detroit: Underrated Cities of the Midwest *(Ch. 6)*

From Pittsburgh: A Frank Lloyd Wright Tour *(Ch. 6)*

From Boston: Retracing the American Revolution *(Ch. 2)*; The Best of New England *(Ch. 8)*

home is **Homer Stryker Field** (✉ *251 Mills St.* ☎ *269/337–8191* ⊕ *www.homer-stryker-field.lany.io*), where you'll be so close to the action, you can hear the chatter in the dugout.

Eat & Drink: The name might make you think they'd give baseball fans the cold shoulder, but Kalamazoo's **Niskers Char-Grill & Slap Shot Hockey Bar** (✉ *5051 W. Main St.* ☎ *269/903–2427* ⊕ *www.niskerschargrill.com*) is for sports lovers of all stripes. No matter what the big game is that day, it's on the big-screen TVs at this friendly pub.

DETROIT

Do: Detroit might just be the most sports-loving city in America. It's the only downtown that's home to teams from all four major sports: baseball (the Tigers), football (the Lions), basketball (the Pistons), and hockey (the Red Wings). But the Tigers—which formed in 1901 and were charter members of the American League—hold a special place in the hearts of Detroiters. With a Ferris wheel with cars shaped like baseballs and a carousel with 30 hand-painted tigers, **Comerica Park** (✉ *2100 Woodward Ave.* ☎ *313/962–4000* ⊕ *www.detroit.tigers.mlb.com*) has a personality few other fields can match. The left-field concourse is dominated by statues of many of the greats—Al Kaline, Ty Cobb, and Hank Greenberg—who led the Tigers to winning seasons. The Beer Hall, with a 70-foot-long bar serving many microbrews, is the place to celebrate a victory or commiserate about a defeat.

Eat & Drink: After a Tigers home game, a free shuttle bus transports fans to **Tommy's Detroit Bar & Grill** (✉ 624 3rd Ave. ☎ 313/965–2269 ⊕ www.tommysdetroit.com), where locals rave over the corned beef that's made right on the premises. Order it as a sandwich with Thousand Island dressing or as part of the belly-busting "Monstah" burger. In the evening, **Thomas Magee's Sporting House and Whiskey Bar** (✉ 1408 E. Fisher Service Dr. ☎ 313/263–4342 ⊕ www.thomasmagees.com) is a lively tavern serving a long list of beers and a whiskey of the month.

Stay: Within walking distance of Comerica Park is the sultry **Siren** (✉ 1509 Broadway St. ☎ 313/277–4736 ⊕ www.thesirenhotel.com), a boutique hotel located in the 1926 Wurlitzer Building. Splurge for the Penthouse, a lofty retreat with double-height windows looking out onto the ballpark.

Breakfast: Inside Downtown's Chrysler House, **Dime Store** (✉ 719 Griswold St. ☎ 313/962–9106 ⊕ www.eatdimestore.com) is reputed to have the city's best brunch. Don't worry if you're not there during a weekend—the peach cobbler French toast and all the other favorites are also on the regular breakfast menu.

Day 5: Detroit, MI, to Pittsburgh, PA

286 miles (4 hours, 15 minutes without traffic and stops)

I–75 and I–80 take you around the southern shores of Lake Erie and past Cleveland, Ohio. How can you be so close to a baseball-loving city like that and not stop by? It's just a quick detour on I–90. Then take I–77 south to return to I–80, which brings you to Pittsburgh.

ALONG THE WAY

Town: Cleveland's crowning glory is **Progressive Field** (✉ 2401 Ontario St. ☎ 216/420–4487 ⊕ www.mlb.com/guardians/ballpark), a neoclassical ballpark that is consistently ranked among the best in the country by baseball fans. The stadium has got its flaws, like way too many skyboxes, but the handsome facade and views of the skyline make it memorable.

Eat & Drink: One thing you should know about Cleveland is that there are two famous mustards in town: Authentic Stadium Mustard, favored at the NFL's Cleveland Browns Stadium, and Bertman Original Ballpark Mustard, the winner at Progressive Field. Since this is a baseball trip, head to **Mabel's BBQ** (✉ 2050 E. 4th St. ☎ 216/417–8823 ⊕ www.mabelsbbq.com), not far from Progressive Field, to sample Bertman mustard in any variety of burgers or sandwiches, either on its own or incorporated into a delectable barbecue sauce.

PITTSBURGH

Do: Known mostly for its Gilded Age history thanks to its role as an early-20th-century industrial city, Pittsburgh is also home to **PNC Park** (✉ 115 Federal St. ☎ 412/321–2827 ⊕ www.mlb.com/pirates/ballpark), one of MLB's most intimate ballparks, with only two decks so you're never too far from the action. Unlike the beer-soaked scene at some stadiums, the home field of the Pittsburgh Pirates is somewhere to bring the whole family. Kids are even encouraged to run the bases after Sunday games.

The Pirates used to play at Forbes Field, where second baseman Bill Mazeroski famously hit a home run over the left-center outfield wall in game seven of the 1960 World Series, defeating the

Wrigley Field has been home to the Chicago Cubs since 1916.

Yankees. The stadium is long gone, but the **Forbes Field Wall** (✉ *Roberto Clemente Dr.*) still stands on the campus of the University of Pittsburgh. Have your photo taken in front of the wall, still marked with the number 406 to show how far Mazeroski sent the ball.

The **Western Pennsylvania Sports Museum** (✉ *1212 Smallman St.* ☎ *412/454–6000* ⊕ *www.heinzhistorycenter.org*), part of the John Heinz History Center, has lots of interesting exhibits, but nothing tops the one focusing on the history of the Negro Leagues. Pittsburgh was once home to both the Homestead Grays and the Pittsburgh Crawfords, making it the center of the circuit. Check out a glove belonging to pitcher Satchel Paige, whose legendary career with the Cleveland Indians came after decades of playing in the Negro Leagues for teams like the Chattanooga Black Lookouts.

Eat & Drink: A stone's throw from PNC Park, **Proper** (✉ *139 7th St.* ☎ *412/281–5700* ⊕ *www.properpittsburgh.com*) is a brick-oven pizzeria with some creative combinations like the Black & Gold, topped with cracked black pepper and slices of Yukon Gold potatoes. Across the river, **Redbeard's on Sixth** (✉ *144 6th St.* ☎ *412/261–2324* ⊕ *www.redbeardspgh.com*) is known for its mural of legendary ballplayers. The names of the burgers are all clever baseball references, too.

Stay: Talk about a room with a view: the sumptuous **Renaissance Pittsburgh Hotel** (✉ *107 6th St.* ☎ *412/562–1200* ⊕ *www.marriott.com*) gazes down on the mighty Allegheny River and the infield at PNC Park. This place is packed when there's a home game, so book well ahead.

Breakfast: Pamela's Diner (✉ *60 21st St.* ☎ *412/281–6366* ⊕ *www.pamelasdiner.com*) brags about serving the "breakfast of champions." Try the hearty Pittsburgh Hash, fried with Lyonnaise potatoes, kielbasa, and sauerkraut and topped with Swiss cheese.

Day 6: Pittsburgh, PA, to Williamsport, PA

199 miles (3 hours, 15 minutes without traffic and stops)

Heading east from Pittsburgh, U.S. 22 takes you to I–99. Take this to State College, home of Penn State, then hop on I–80 for the rest of the trip to Williamsport.

ALONG THE WAY

Town: In the town of State College, a favorite activity every summer is catching a State College Spikes game, a collegiate summer baseball team that is part of the MLB Draft League. The team plays at **Medlar Field at Lubrano Park** (✉ *112 Medlar Field* ☎ *814/272–1711* ⊕ *www.mlbdraftleague.com/state-college*) on the campus of Pennsylvania State University.

Eat & Drink: Not far from Medlar Field is the **Sowers Harvest Café** (✉ *421 E. Beaver Ave.* ☎ *814/867–1007* ⊕ *www.sowersharvest.cafe*), a favorite with students. The emphasis at this bustling eatery is food that is good and good for you, so there are a lot of healthy sandwiches and salads.

WILLIAMSPORT

Do: If it's August, stop at **Howard J. Lamade Stadium** (✉ *100 Borderline Rd.* ☎ *570/326–1921* ⊕ *www.littleleague.org/world-series*) in Williamsport, home to the Little League World Series, where thousands of fresh-faced baseball players return year after year for their shot at the championship. The stadium, built in 1959, holds 40,000 fans, and even more stake out a spot on the hill rising up beyond the outfield. The rest of the year, check out the **World of Little League Museum** (✉ *525 U.S. 15, South Williamsport* ☎ *570/326–3607* ⊕ *www.littleleague.org/world-of-little-league*).

Eat & Drink: Grab a table on the umbrella-shaded patio beside **Barrel 135** (✉ *Residence Inn by Marriot Williamsport, 135 W. 3rd St.* ☎ *570/322–7131* ⊕ *www.barrel135.com*), a chic eatery with a globe-trotting menu (think Jamaican jerk chicken and Korean barbecue) and interesting beers on tap.

Stay: One of the region's most eye-catching lodgings is Williamsport's 19th-century **City Hall Grand** (✉ *454 Pine St.* ☎ *570/215–2810* ⊕ *www.cityhallgrandhotel.com*). Outside it's a little like a castle, but inside the loftlike spaces have a cool, contemporary vibe. The Little League Room, with some historic photos of the ballfield, is stunning.

Breakfast: On Southern Avenue, **The Buttery Biscuit** (✉ *715 W. Southern Ave.* ☎ *570/601–4558* ⊕ *www.facebook.com/thebutterybiscuit570*) is the kind of place that locals don't like to share with out-of-towners. This diner knows how to make a stick-to-your-ribs meal.

Day 7: Williamsport, PA, to Cooperstown, NY

199 miles (3 hours, 30 minutes without traffic and stops)

You're headed into the mountains today, so be prepared for lots of twists and turns on this route. Basically, you take U.S. 15 north of Williamsport, changing to Route 14 when you reach Trout Run, Pennsylvania. This road takes you through hamlets like Roaring Branch and Cedar Ledge on your way to Waverly, New York, where you change to Route 17 on your way to the college town of Binghamton, New York (on Route 17, be on the lookout for signs celebrating the local Maine-Endwell team for winning the Little League World Series in 2016). From here, it's I–88 and Route 28 to Cooperstown.

ALONG THE WAY

Eat & Drink: Facing the Susquehanna River, the waterfront community of Owego, New York, is a pleasant place to stop for lunch. Try the **Owego Kitchen** (✉ *13 Lake St.* ☏ *607/223–4209* ⊕ *www. theowegokitchen.com*), a funky little spot that attracts students from the local university. The "Not Your Mom's Tuna Salad Sandwich" spices things up with albacore tuna and Jamaican relish.

COOPERSTOWN

Do: A mecca for baseball lovers, Cooperstown is home to the **National Baseball Hall of Fame** (✉ *25 Main St.* ☏ *888/425–5633* ⊕ *www.baseballhall.org*). This don't-miss destination is jam-packed with memorabilia from the earliest days of baseball. One of the most interesting exhibits documents the challenges Black players faced before and after Jackie Robinson was recognized as the first Black player in the major leagues when he joined the Brooklyn Dodgers in 1947. (It also documents how a formerly enslaved man named Moses Fleetwood Walker actually broke the color line in 1884.) If you're in town in May, catch the annual Hall of Fame Classic at **Doubleday Field** (✉ *1 Doubleday Ct.* ☏ *607/547–2270* ⊕ *www.doubledayfield.com*), a handsome ballfield dating back to 1920.

Eat & Drink: Named for the man who supposedly invented baseball, **Doubleday Café** (✉ *93 Main St.* ☏ *607/547–5468* ⊕ *www. doubledaycafe.com*) occupies one of several beautiful brick buildings on Cooperstown's main street. If you're thinking it serves pub grub, you'd be right. But it also has seriously delicious dinner specials that make it seem like fine dining.

Stay: A seven-minute walk from Main Street, **The Otesaga Resort Hotel** (✉ *60 Lake St.* ☏ *607/547–9931* ⊕ *www.otesaga.com*) feels a world away. The back of this colonial-style showplace faces Blackbird Bay, which you'll enjoy from one of the rockers on the wraparound porch. Many of the traditionally decorated rooms and suites share the same stellar views.

Breakfast: With its own coffee bean roaster in the corner, **Stagecoach Coffee** (✉ *31 Pioneer St.* ☏ *607/547–6229* ⊕ *www. stagecoachcoffee.com*) is an eye-opening experience. Bagels range from the "Usual" (cream cheese and tomato slices) to the "Unusual" (add avocado) to the "Ultimate" (add bacon).

Day 8: Cooperstown, NY, to Boston, MA

238 miles (3 hours, 45 minutes without traffic and stops)

From Cooperstown, Route 166 takes you east to Warnerville, where you'll switch to I–88. Around the town of Rotterdam, you'll hop on I–90, detour onto I–87 to stick to the outskirts of New York's capital city of Albany, then return to I–90 for the entire way to Boston. It's a pretty drive, especially if you happen to be here in early October, the height of leaf-peeping season.

ALONG THE WAY

Detour: It doesn't seem right to have a baseball-focused trip and not mention the New York Yankees, one of the MLB's most historic teams that has seen some of the sport's most famous players as well as the team with the most World Series wins (27 since being established in 1901). The original House That Ruth Built was torn down and rebuilt in 2009, but the new **Yankee Stadium** (✉ *1 E. 161st St., The Bronx* ☏ *718/293–4300* ⊕ *www. mlb.com/yankees/ballpark*) incorporated some of the designs of its predecessor and offers plenty of insight into Yankee history. The Bronx stadium is a two-hour-plus, often traffic-filled drive south of Albany, so it's best added as a full extra-day side trip, but it's a can't-be-missed experience for any baseball fan.

Town: Several towns claim to be the inspiration for Ernest L. Thayer's 1888 ode to baseball, "Casey at the Bat," but Holliston, Massachusetts, has perhaps the most compelling case. Thayer grew up in nearby Worcester, and his family owned a wool mill less than a mile from the baseball diamond in the Holliston neighborhood called Mudville. Take a selfie with the statue of "Mighty Casey" while you're here.

Eat & Drink: On Railroad Street in Mudville, **Casey's Publichouse** (✉ *81 Railroad St., Holliston* ☎ *508/429–4888* ⊕ *www.caseyspublichouse.com*) memorializes the fictional ballplayer and his team, the Mudville Nine. The atmosphere is relaxed, and the menu is a step or two above your typical pub grub.

BOSTON

Do: Even if you're not a baseball fan, you haven't really visited Boston until you've visited **Fenway Park** (✉ *4 Jersey St.* ☎ *877/733–7699* ⊕ *www.mlb.com/redsox/ballpark*). The home of the Red Sox since 1912, baseball's best-loved ballpark has a stately entrance at street level that makes it feel like part of the neighborhood. Seats atop the "Green Monster," the 37-foot left field wall that's a goal for many batters, come at a premium, but it's hard to find a seat here that doesn't give you a great vantage point. Tours are a great way to get to know the place. They're usually given every hour on the hour, but they end four hours before the opening pitch on game day.

Eat & Drink: The founder of **Bennett's Sandwich Shop** (✉ *1348 Boylston St.* ☎ *857/239–9736* ⊕ *www.bennetssandwichshop.com*) had an unsuccessful tryout with the Red Sox when he was in high school, but that didn't stop him from offering the luscious lobster rolls to fans leaving Fenway Park. If you didn't score tickets to the game, head to **Bleacher Bar** (✉ *82A Landsdowne St.* ☎ *617/262–2424* ⊕ *www.bleacherbarboston.com*), with an unbeatable view of Fenway Park's third base. It's always packed, but that's part of the appeal.

Stay: A short stroll from Fenway Park, the upscale **Hotel Commonwealth** (✉ *500 Commonwealth Ave.* ☎ *617/933–5000* ⊕ *www.hotelcommonwealth.com*) has views of the scoreboard from some rooms. The accommodations are luxurious, and the service is top-notch. If you're looking for something a bit more reasonably priced, the rock-and-roll-theme **Verb Hotel** (✉ *1271 Boylston St.* ☎ *617/566–4500* ⊕ *www.theverbhotel.com*) is just as close to the ballpark. There's a pretty pool in the courtyard where a cool crowd gathers.

Breakfast: On fashion-forward Boylston Street, hip **Pavement Coffeehouse** (✉ *1334 Boylston St.* ☎ *857/263–7355* ⊕ *www.pavementcoffeehouse.com*) roasts its own beans, so you're guaranteed a primo cup of joe. The pastries are delectable, too.

Civil War Battlefields and History

Written by Barbara Noe Kennedy

As the bloodiest war in American history, the Civil War ravaged the United States from 1861 to 1865, pitting brother against brother, father against son, and neighbor against neighbor, all while fighting to end the chattel slavery that the country was built on from its inception. Today the bloody battlefields have been preserved in a mantle of peaceful escape, where one can—and must—learn from the past. From Gettysburg in the North all the way to Vicksburg in the South, and then across to Charleston, this epic drive explores the history and realities of the periods before, during, and after the Civil War. Along the way, an array of fascinating stops includes unsung towns, beloved dining establishments, and lesser-known sites that tell the fuller story of the war that will appeal to hardcore history buffs and high school students alike.

At a Glance

Start: Harrisburg, PA

End: Charleston, SC

Miles Traveled: 2,263 miles

Suggested Duration: 10 days

States Visited: Georgia, Maryland, Mississippi, North Carolina, Pennsylvania, South Carolina, Tennessee, Virginia, West Virginia

Key Sights: Appomattox Court House National Historical Park; Gettysburg National Battlefield; Harpers Ferry; McLeod Plantation Historic Site; Vicksburg National Battlefield

Best Time to Go: This trip is possible year-round, though spring is always lovely, with blossoms adding ephemeral color to the now-peaceful battlefields. Travel can be tough in the north during winter months.

Day 1: Harrisburg, PA, to Gettysburg, PA

38 miles (45 minutes without traffic and stops)

With the closest sizable airport to Gettysburg, the state capital Harrisburg is a good place to pick up a rental car and begin your journey. Be sure to start your Civil War adventure with a visit to the city's Smithsonian-affiliated **National Civil War Museum** (✉ *1 Lincoln Circle* ☎ *717/260–1861* ⊕ *www.nationalcivilwarmuseum.org*). Follow U.S. 15 southwest through green countryside and rolling hills as you make your way to one of America's most hallowed grounds.

ALONG THE WAY

Town: About 15 miles southwest of Harrisburg, U.S. 15 cuts through the historic agricultural town of Dillsburg, packed with old-time charm. Stroll the historic streets and pick up apples, berries, and nectarines at family-owned **Mount Airy Orchards** (✉ *522 E. Mt. Airy Rd.* ☎ *717/432–2544* ⊕ *www.mtairyorchards.com*).

Eat & Drink: In Dillsburg, grab a bite at the landmark **Baker's Diner** (✉ *515 N. U.S. 15* ☎ *717/432–8800* ⊕ *www.bakersdinerpa.com*), which has served homestyle meals in its cozy eatery since 1958.

Detour: Veer off at Straban Township for 12 miles on PA-394 to Cashtown, where Confederate officers used the **Cashtown Inn** (✉ *1325 Old Rte. 30* ☎ *717/334–9722* ⊕ *www.cashtowninn.com*) as their headquarters before Gettysburg broke out in July 1863; the basement served as a field hospital during the battle. The brick building has been preserved as a four-room inn and tavern serving refined American dishes.

GETTYSBURG

Do: Gettysburg is a picturesque town that's all about the famous battle that occurred here on July 1–3, 1863, turning the tide of the Civil War in favor of the Union. Get a solid introduction at the **Gettysburg National Military Park Museum and Visitor Center** (✉ *1195 Baltimore Pike* ☎ *717/334–1124* ⊕ *www.nps.gov/gett*); visit museums and historic houses in downtown Gettysburg (including the Jennie Wade House, which tells the story of the only civilian killed during the battle); tour the battlefield by bus, Segway, horseback, bike, or self-guided auto tour; and visit the cemetery where Lincoln gave his famous Gettysburg Address.

Eat & Drink: Built in 1776, the **Dobbin House Tavern** (✉ *89 Steinwehr Ave.* ☎ *717/334–2100* ⊕ *www.dobbinhouse.com*) served as a Confederate sniper roost due to its prime view over

Cemetery Hill. Today it's a popular tavern and restaurant featuring colonial-style cuisine in a historic location (try the baked king's onion soup or primal rib of beef).

Stay: The region has tons of adorable inns and B&Bs in historic buildings, including the peaceful **Baladerry Inn** (✉ 40 Hospital Rd. ☎ 717/337–1342 ⊕ www.baladerryinn.com) and the **Lightner Farmhouse** (✉ 2350 Baltimore Pike ☎ 717/321–3771 ⊕ www.lightnerfarmhouse.com); both served as field hospitals during the battle. The upscale, acclaimed **Hotel Gettysburg** (✉ 1 Lincoln Sq. ☎ 717/337–2000 ⊕ www.hotelgettysburg.com), established in 1797, has beautifully appointed historic rooms with modern trimmings.

Breakfast: The Lincoln Diner (✉ 32 Carlisle St. ☎ 717/334–3900 ⊕ www.thelincolndiner.com) is a popular spot among locals and visitors alike for its homestyle comfort food and desserts.

Day 2: Gettysburg, PA, to Harpers Ferry, WV

71 miles (1 hour, 30 minutes without traffic and stops)

Follow U.S. 15 and U.S. 340 south through hilly green countryside speckled with farms and small towns as you make your way to Harpers Ferry, known as the site of an 1859 raid by famed abolitionist John Brown.

ALONG THE WAY

Nature: Right off U.S. 15 near Thurmont, Maryland, leafy trails wind through **Catoctin Mountain Park** (✉ 14707 Park Central Rd. ☎ 301/663–9388 ⊕ www.nps.gov/cato), filled with waterfalls, thick woods, and scenic vistas. Camp David hides somewhere nearby (search the skies for tell-tale helicopters).

Town: The 18th-century historic district in Frederick, Maryland, is filled with

museums like the **National Museum of Civil War Medicine** (✉ 48 E. Patrick St. ☎ 301/695–1864 ⊕ www.civilwarmed.org), public artwork, galleries, innovative restaurants, and upscale boutiques.

Eat & Drink: In Frederick, **Showroom** (✉ 882 N. East St. ☎ 301/835–7628 ⊕ www.showroomfrederick.com) is a modern take on a classic diner, occupying an old car dealership.

Attraction: A relatively unknown but significant battle unfolded in July 1864 on the fields at **Monocacy National Battlefield** (✉ 5201 Urbana Pike ☎ 301/662–3515 ⊕ www.nps.gov/mono), south of Frederick. Though the Confederates won, the time they spent fighting delayed them from possibly capturing the nation's capital.

Detour: On September 17, 1862, the bloodiest single day of battle unfolded at Antietam, located southwest of Frederick via U.S. 40 and Route 34. Learn all about it at the **Antietam National Battlefield** (✉ 302 E. Main St., Sharpsburg, MD ☎ 301/432–5124 ⊕ www.nps.gov.anti), take a self-guided driving tour around the battlefield, and walk several bucolic trails (including Snavely's Ford Creek). You can also see the sites by kayaking Antietam Creek.

HARPERS FERRY

Do: Located at the confluence of the Shenandoah and Potomac Rivers, this mountain town was where John Brown attempted to initiate a revolt of enslaved people by taking over the town's federal arsenal in 1859; the mission failed and Brown was captured and eventually executed, but the event is considered an important precursor to the Civil War. His "fort" (the old firehouse), along with other related sites, have been preserved as part of **Harpers Ferry National Historical Park** (✉ 171 Shoreline Dr. ☎ 304/535–6029 ⊕ www.nps.gov/hafe). There's also great hiking (including the soaring Marye's Heights Trail, with a fabulous bird's-eye view over Harpers Ferry), the

Gettysburg was the site of the most famous battle of the Civil War as well as Lincoln's Gettysburg Address.

John Brown Museum, and Jefferson Rock, where the third president stated in 1785: "The scene is worth the voyage across the Atlantic."

Eat & Drink: Kelley Farm Kitchen (✉ *1112 Washington St., Bolivar, WV* ☎ *304/535–9976* ⊕ *www.kelleyfarmkitchen.com*) offers hearty vegan cuisine, including all-day breakfasts, amazing Impossible burgers, and addictive garlic knots.
Bolivar Bread Bakery (✉ *914 Washington St., Bolivar, WV* ☎ *304/535–8108* ⊕ *www.bolivarbread.com*) is popular for its small-batch artisan bread, biscuits, and pastries—it's a perfect place to stock up on snacks for the road.

Stay: The **Light Horse Inn** (✉ *1084 Washington St., Bolivar, WV* ☎ *877/468–4236* ⊕ *www.lighthorseinn.com*) provides a nature escape in the heart of town, occupying a historic house with early American flair.

Breakfast: Battle Grounds Bakery & Coffee (✉ *180 High St.* ☎ *304/535–8583* ⊕ *www.facebook.com/battlegroundsbakery*) has delicious breakfast sandwiches, fresh baked goods, and what many say is the best coffee around.

Day 3: Harpers Ferry, WV, to Alexandria, VA

250 miles (4 hours, 25 minutes without traffic and stops)

Drive through pastoral Loudoun County, Virginia, via several local routes as you head to Manassas, and then on to Alexandria.

ALONG THE WAY

Attraction: Washingtonians flocked to Manassas, Virginia, in 1861 with picnic baskets and wine to watch the first major Civil War battle in Virginia. As the battle became unruly they fled, with any thought of a quick war swiftly extinguished. The visitor center at **Manassas National Battlefield** (✉ *6511 Sudley*

Rd. ☎ 703/361–1339 ⊕ www.nps.gov/ mana) has a good overview of both Manassas I and II, which unfolded in 1862; there are also walking trails and a self-guided auto route.

Detour: After Robert E. Lee left his Virginia home and plantation, Arlington House, to command the Confederate army, the Union confiscated the property and converted it into a burial site. Today the renovated house stands in the center of **Arlington National Cemetery** (☎ 877/907–8585 ⊕ www.arlingtoncemetery.mil), where nearly 400,000 Americans who died during wartime, as well as many notable Americans (including William Howard Taft and John F. Kennedy), are interred in its 624 acres. It's about 20 minutes north of Alexandria via the George Washington Memorial Parkway.

ALEXANDRIA

Do: Alexandria was the first Southern city to be taken by the Union in May 1861, and there are plenty of historic sights to explore. The Carlyle House served as a field hospital (and the basis for the PBS series *Mercy Street*); the Stabler-Leadbeater apothecary shop sold residents everything from liquid opium to dental equipment and windowpanes; the site of Union Fort Ward harbors well-preserved earthen walls and a small museum; and over 1,800 African Americans who escaped from bondage during the Civil War are buried at the Contrabands and Freedmen Cemetery Memorial on Washington Street. Don't miss the **Freedom House Museum** (✉ 1315 Duke St. ☎ 703/746–4554 ⊕ www.alexandriava. gov), which was the headquarters of the nation's largest domestic slave-trading firm until Union forces took the city; today it gives an important look into the realities of chattel slavery before the Civil War.

If you have time, cross the river into Washington, D.C., where President Abraham Lincoln was assassinated on April

Extend Your Trip

From Richmond: The Blue Ridge Parkway (*Ch. 7*)

From Atlanta or Charleston: The Civil Rights Trail (*Ch. 7*)

From Charleston: The Best of the Carolinas (*Ch. 7*)

15, 1865, at Ford's Theatre. He died at Petersen House across the street, now part of a fascinating museum that examines the Civil War in light of his murder.

Eat & Drink: King Street has a plethora of acclaimed restaurants offering a range of prices and styles. The **Fish Market** (✉ 105 King St. ☎ 703/836–5676 ⊕ www. fishmarketva.com) is the place to go for Chesapeake crab cakes and Virginia oysters while the **Tasting Room** (✉ 1600 King St. ☎ 703/894–3434 ⊕ www.archerhotel. com) is a favorite inside the hip Archer Hotel that serves Penn Cove mussels and crisp-skinned snapper with rock shrimp and shellfish butter.

Stay: The first officer killed in the war, Elmer Ellsworth, died at the Marshall House on King Street, which today is boutique hotel the **Alexandrian** (✉ 480 King St. ☎ 703/549–6080 ⊕ www. marriott.com). The **Morrison House** (✉ 116 S. Alfred St. ☎ 703/838–8000 ⊕ www. marriott.com), in a Federalist building with a literary theme, is another cozy historic choice.

Breakfast: Royal Restaurant (✉ 730 N. St. Asaph St. ☎ 703/548–1616 ⊕ www. royalrestaurantva.com) has been serving hearty traditional breakfasts for more than 100 years.

Day 4: Alexandria, VA, to Richmond, VA

105 miles (1 hour, 50 minutes without traffic and stops)

Today's drive is a straight shot down truck-hoarding, traffic-filled I–95.

ALONG THE WAY

Nature: Miles of tranquil trails lace **Prince William Forest Park** (✉ *18170 Park Entrance Rd.* ☎ *703/221–7181* ⊕ *www. nps.gov/prwi*), a 15,000-acre oasis of oaks, maples, and poplars near Triangle, Virginia.

Attraction: The state-of-the-art **National Museum of the Marine Corps** (✉ *1775 Semper Fidelis Way* ☎ *703/432–1775* ⊕ *www. usmcmuseum.com*) relates American history through the eyes of the U.S. Marines. You'll know it by the dramatic, tilted, steel mass—inspired by the flag raisings at Iwo Jima—rising just off I–95 in Triangle.

Town: The historic town of Fredericksburg on the Rappahannock River has both Revolutionary and Civil War history (George Washington's mother lived here). Four major battles unfolded in the vicinity of Fredericksburg over the course of two years, providing an interesting look at changing war tactics. Highlights include the Sunken Wall in Fredericksburg, Spotsylvania's Bloody Angle, and the house where Stonewall Jackson died.

Eat & Drink: Mason Dixon Café (✉ *2100 Princess Anne St.* ☎ *540/371–1950* ⊕ *www.masondixoncafe.com*) in Fredericksburg is a favorite local spot, offering sandwiches, burgers, and full-fledged entrées.

RICHMOND

Do: The longtime capital of Virginia is experiencing a cultural revival in its architecturally rich streets. The city was also the capital of the Confederacy during the Civil War, a history it attempts to reckon with via several historic sites. The **Richmond National Battlefield Park** (✉ *470 Tredegar St.* ☎ *804/771–2145* ⊕ *www. nps.gov/rich*) comprises 13 Civil War sites, including battlefields and miles of defensive fortifications; its expansive visitor center is housed in an old wool mill overlooking the James River.

Eat & Drink: Try the seasonal, southern delights at **Shagbark** (✉ *4901 Libbie Mill E. Blvd.* ☎ *804/358–7424* ⊕ *www. shagbarkva.com*), or slurp down fresh Chesapeake bivalves at **Rappahannock Oyster Company** (✉ *320 E. Grace St.* ☎ *804/545–0565* ⊕ *www.rroysters. com*). If you have time, see what appeals in Carytown or Scott's Addition, just two of the city's many up-and-coming neighborhoods filled with restaurants, shops, and cafés.

Stay: The **Jefferson Hotel** (✉ *101 W. Franklin St.* ☎ *804/788–8000* ⊕ *www. jeffersonhotel.com*) exudes historic elegance with chandeliers, gilded trim, and Tiffany stained-glass windows. **Quirk Hotel** (✉ *201 W. Broad St.* ☎ *804/340–6040* ⊕ *www.destinationhotels.com*) has turned a 1916 luxury department store into a hip retreat.

Breakfast: Dot's Back Inn (✉ *4030 MacArthur Ave.* ☎ *804/266–3167* ⊕ *www. dotsbackrichmond.com*) is a retro diner with all the classics (and an amazing crab cake Benedict).

Day 5: Richmond, VA, to Appomattox, VA

92 miles (1 hour, 40 minutes without traffic and stops)

Today head west across central Virginia on U.S. 360, Route 307, and U.S. 460.

ALONG THE WAY

Detour: The 10-month siege at Petersburg, Virginia, from June 1864 to April 1865, resulted in Richmond's fall and set the path to surrender at Appomattox. Preserved as **Petersburg National Battlefield** (✉ 5001 Siege Rd. ☎ 804/732–3531 ⊕ www.nps.gov/pete), the site offers a visitor center discussing the siege (including the infamous Battle of the Crater), self-guided auto routes, and living history demonstrations.

APPOMATTOX

Do: General Robert E. Lee surrendered to General Ulysses S. Grant on April 9, 1865, at the McLean House in the village of Appomattox Court House, signaling the end of the Civil War. **Appomattox Court House National Historical Park** (✉ 111 National Park Dr. ☎ 434/352–8987 ⊕ www.nps.gov/apco) has 27 structures restored to their 1865 look, including the parlor where the war-ending documents were signed.

Eat & Drink: The **Babcock House** (✉ 250 Oakleigh Ave. ☎ 434/352–7532 ⊕ www.babcockhouse.com) is a popular stop for burgers, sandwiches, meat loaf, and other hearty entrées as well as Sunday brunch (it's also a B&B). **Carmine's Pizzeria** (✉ 1952 Church St. ☎ 434/352–4444 ⊕ www.facebook.com/carminesitalianpizzeria) serves New York–style pizza by the pie or by the slice.

Stay: The five-room **Longacre of Appomattox** (✉ 1670 Church St. ☎ 434/352–9251 ⊕ www.longacreofappomattox.com) offers English-style charm in the Virginia countryside.

Breakfast: Granny Bee's (✉ 179 Main St. ☎ 434/352–2259 ⊕ www.facebook.com/grannybeesrestaurant) serves good old-fashioned heartiness. For something lighter, check out **Baine's Books and Coffee** (✉ 205 Main St. ☎ 434/229–8157 ⊕ www.bainesbooks.com).

Day 6: Appomattox, VA, to Chattanooga, TN

440 miles (6 hours, 40 minutes without traffic and stops)

After enjoying Appalachian scenery on U.S. 460, bite the bullet today for the long-haul drive on interstate highways, via I–81, I–40, and I–75.

ALONG THE WAY

Nature: Stretch your legs on the peaceful trails along the New River in Virginia's **New River Trail State Park** (✉ 116 Orphanage Dr. ☎ 276/699–6778 ⊕ www.dcr.virginia.gov); it's about 10 miles south of I–81 at Max Meadows off I–77. The fishing there is superb, too.

Roadside Attraction: Although Dr. Charles T. Pepper didn't invent the spicy, cherry root beer–esque soda, he did give his name to it—he had offered the real inventor, Charles Alderton, his first job, who then named his liquid invention in his former boss's honor. You'll find his pilgrimage grave site at Mountain View Cemetery in Rural Retreat, Virginia, just west of the I–77 interchange.

Town: In the outdoorsy town of Abingdon, Virginia, jump on the 34.3-mile Virginia Creeper rail-to-recreation trail or attend a performance at the **Barter Theatre** (✉ 127 W. Main St. ☎ 276/628–3991 ⊕ www.bartertheatre.com), the nation's longest-running professional theater, performing since 1933.

Eat & Drink: Dead End BBQ (✉ 3621 Sutherland Ave. ☎ 865/212–5655 ⊕ www.deadendbbq.com) in Knoxville, Tennessee, stands out for its award-winning, nationally recognized fare that takes you back to the dead-end street where the owners originally served barbecue to neighbors.

Trips of a Lifetime CIVIL WAR BATTLEFIELDS AND HISTORY

CHATTANOOGA

Do: Some of the Civil War's hardest-fought battles unfolded in and around Chattanooga, with the Union repelling the Confederacy back to Georgia in 1863, in effect paving the way for Sherman's March to the Sea. Civil War veterans established the **Chickamauga and Chattanooga National Military Park** (✉ *3370 Lafayette Rd., Fort Oglethorpe, GA* ☎ *706/866–9241* ⊕ *www. nps.gov/chch*) in 1889, making it the nation's oldest (and at nearly 10,000 acres, the largest) military park. Tour the park on your own or with a park ranger, visit two different visitor centers, hike trails, and more.

Eat & Drink: The burgers at **Tremont Tavern** (✉ *1203 Hixson Pike* ☎ *423/266–1996* ⊕ *www.tremonttavern.com*) have a cult following, though if you're hungry for fried chicken, **Champy's World Famous Fried Chicken** (✉ *526 E. Martin Luther King Blvd.* ☎ *423/752–9198* ⊕ *www.champy-schicken.com*) is the place to go.

Stay: Sleep in a Victorian-era luxury sleeper car at the **Hotel Chalet** (✉ *92 Choo Choo Ave.* ☎ *423/266–5000* ⊕ *www. thehotelchalet.com*); standard suites are available as well. The hotel is a hub of activity, with several on-site restaurants and a distillery.

Breakfast: Family-owned **Bluegrass Grill** (✉ *55 E. Main St.* ☎ *423/752–4020* ⊕ *www.bluegrassgrillchattanooga. com*) on Main Street is beloved for its homemade diner favorites; try the alderwood-smoked salmon frittata or corned beef—or tofu—hash.

Day 7: Chattanooga, TN, to Shiloh, TN

220 miles (3 hours, 50 minutes without traffic and stops)

Follow I–24 north and U.S. 64 west on a rustic drive to Shiloh National Military Park.

ALONG THE WAY

Eat & Drink: You're in whiskey country, so, of course, you need to visit the **Jack Daniels Distillery** (✉ *280 Lynchburg Hwy.* ☎ *931/759–6357* ⊕ *www.jackdaniels.com*) in Lynchburg, Tennessee, 25 miles north of Winchester via Route 50. A variety of sampling tours are offered. Around the corner, the distillery's **Miss Mary Bobo's Restaurant** (✉ *295 Main St.* ☎ *931/759–7394* ⊕ *www.missmarybobos.com*) serves standard southern fare for lunch.

SHILOH

Do: Shiloh may mean "place of peace," but in 1862, these pristine lands saw a pivotal battle that resulted in a Union victory and killed more soldiers than in all previous Civil War battles combined (23,746 casualties over two days). Today the 5,000-acre **Shiloh National Military Park** (✉ *1055 Pittsburg Landing Rd.* ☎ *731/689–5696* ⊕ *www.nps. gov/shil*) offers interpretive centers, a self-guided auto tour, ranger programs, living history exhibits, and special events. Don't miss Fraley Field, where the battle began; the Hornet's Nest, where Union troops held back waves of Confederates; and Pittsburg Landing, where Grant received reinforcements that turned the tide for the North.

Eat & Drink: You won't find a more authentic place for fried catfish than **Hagy's Catfish Hotel** (✉ *1140 Hagy La.* ☎ *731/689–3327* ⊕ *www.catfishhotel. com*) in Savannah, Tennessee, where the southern delicacy is served on the banks of the Tennessee River alongside hush puppies, coleslaw, and fries. The original shack, built in 1825 by ancestor-settler Henry Hagy, was occupied by Union forces during the Battle of Shiloh before opening as a restaurant in 1938.

Stay: There aren't tons of choices in the area surrounding Shiloh, but the **Lodge at Pickwick Landing** (✉ *120 Playground Loop* ☎ *731/689–3135* ⊕ *www.*

tnstateparks.com) in Counce offers basic rooms with river views.

Breakfast: Dae Break (✉ *990 Pickwick Rd. S* ☎ *731/438–3461*) in Savannah has everything you want in a homestyle breakfast joint.

Day 8: Shiloh, TN, to Vicksburg, MS

300 miles (4 hours, 45 minutes without traffic and stops)

Hop onto U.S. 45 south to the fabled Natchez Trace Parkway, one of the nation's most scenic byways. You'll enjoy 60 miles of historic sites, hiking enclaves, and bountiful springtime azaleas before veering off at Mathiston, Mississippi, following U.S. 82 to I–55 to I–20 southwest, finally bringing you into Vicksburg.

ALONG THE WAY

Town: The **Civil War Interpretive Center** (✉ *501 W. Linden St.* ☎ *662/287–9273* ⊕ *www.nps.gov/shil*) in Corinth, Mississippi, about 23 miles southwest of Shiloh, stands on the site where the Battle of Corinth took place just a few months after Shiloh, offering videos, interactive exhibits, and multimedia presentations. In addition, the **Corinth Contraband Camp** (✉ *800 N. Parkway St.* ☎ *662/287–9273* ⊕ *www.nps.gov/shil*) commemorates the settlement where formerly enslaved African Americans fled to safety behind Union lines; a quarter-mile path leads past six life-size bronzes depicting denizens of the camp. Historic buildings filled with boutiques and art galleries line Fillmore Street.

Town: Honor the king of rock 'n' roll at the **Elvis Presley Birthplace** (✉ *306 Elvis Presley Dr.* ☎ *662/841–1456* ⊕ *www.elvispresley-birthplace.com*) in Tupelo, Mississippi, on the Natchez Trace Parkway, where he was born in 1935 and learned to play the guitar. **Tupelo National Battlefield** (✉ *2005 W. Main St.* ☎ *662/680–4025* ⊕ *www.nps.gov/tupe*)

recalls the Battle of Tupelo on July 13–15, 1864, in which the Union successfully kept the Confederates from interfering with Sherman's March to the Sea.

Eat & Drink: Hal and Mal's (✉ *200 Commerce St.* ☎ *601/948–0888* ⊕ *www.halandmals.com*) in Mississippi's capital city of Jackson is a honky-tonk serving music and drinks alongside soul food.

VICKSBURG

Do: In May 1863, Vicksburg was the last major Confederate stronghold on the Mississippi River, and the Union's decisive victory in the Siege of Vicksburg in July 1863 (along with the recent win at Gettysburg) is considered a turning point in the war. **Vicksburg National Military Park** (✉ *3201 Clay St.* ☎ *601/636–0583* ⊕ *www.nps.gov/vick*) has more than 1,400 monuments and markers, restored and original trenches, and a cemetery.

Eat & Drink: Authentic tastes of the South include **10 South Rooftop Bar & Grill** (✉ *1301 Washington St.* ☎ *601/501–4600* ⊕ *www.10southrooftop.com*), a casual rooftop bar with views over the Mississippi; **Beechwood Restaurant** (✉ *4451 Clay St.* ☎ *601/636–3761* ⊕ *www.beechwoodrestaurantandlounge.com*), an old-timey favorite serving steaks and seafood; and **Bovina Café** (✉ *191 Tiffentown Rd.* ☎ *601/636–6802*), beloved for its soul food.

Stay: Many of the town's historic abodes have been converted to inns and B&Bs, including **Anchuca** (✉ *1010 1st E. St.* ☎ *601/661–0111* ⊕ *www.anchuca.com*), a Greek revival mansion outfitted with period antiques, and **Cedar Grove Mansion Inn** (✉ *2200 Oak St.* ☎ *601/636–1000* ⊕ *www.cedargrovemansion.com*), overlooking the Mississippi River.

Breakfast: The Tomato Place (✉ *3229 U.S. 61* ☎ *601/661–0040* ⊕ *www.thetomatoplace.com*) is known for its fried green tomatoes, bread pudding, and welcoming atmosphere.

Day 9: Vicksburg, MS, to Atlanta, GA

420 miles (6 hours, 20 minutes without traffic and stops)

It's freeway-driving all the way today via I–20, with some serious mileage to get under your belt before reaching Atlanta.

ALONG THE WAY

Nature: Encircling Shadow Lake an hour east of Vicksburg, **Roosevelt State Park** (✉ *2149 Rte. 13, Morton, MS* ☎ *601/732–6316* ⊕ *www.mdwfp.com*) offers hiking, fishing, and camping in a peaceful forest that ignites with autumn foliage.

Town: Boutiques and restaurants in the artsy, 20-block Northport Historic District in Northport, Alabama, occupy 19th- and early-20th-century buildings; walking tours are offered.

Town: Though it's Alabama's largest city, Birmingham has a small-town feel. Stop here for the Birmingham Civil Rights District, where you can delve into African American history, and **Sloss Furnaces National Historic Landmark** (✉ *20 32nd St. N* ☎ *205/254–2025* ⊕ *www.slossfurnaces.org*), where two blast furnaces long fired the city's steel industry.

Eat & Drink: Some of the South's best fried chicken can be found at **Café Dupont** (✉ *113 20th St. N* ☎ *205/322–1282* ⊕ *www.cafedupont.net*) in Birmingham.

ATLANTA

Do: This humming metropolis has museums, luxury shopping, and great food and art scenes. As the site of the 1864 Battle of Atlanta and the starting point for Sherman's March to the Sea, it has plenty of Civil War sights, too, including the **Atlanta History Center's Cyclorama** (✉ *130 W. Paces Ferry Rd. NW* ☎ *404/814–4000* ⊕ *www. atlantahistorycenter.com*), which depicts the battle, and **Kennesaw Mountain National Battlefield Park** (✉ *900 Kennesaw*

Mountain Dr. ☎ *770/427–4686* ⊕ *www. nps.gov/kemo*), where Sherman's Atlanta campaign started.

Eat & Drink: If you're looking for something upscale in this culinary haven, **Miller Union** (✉ *999 Brady Ave. NW* ☎ *678/733–8550* ⊕ *www.millerunion.com*) is an ode to modern southern cuisine. Or go the picnic route and swing by **Ponce City Market** (✉ *675 Ponce De Leon Ave. NE* ☎ *404/900–7900* ⊕ *www. poncecitymarket.com*), a vibrant food hall. Dine-in restaurants include W. H. Stiles Fish Camp and H&F Burger.

Stay: The late neo-futuristic architect John Portman designed downtown's **Hyatt Regency** (✉ *265 Peachtree Rd. NE* ☎ *404/577–1234* ⊕ *www.hyatt.com*) in 1967 and updated it before his death in 2017 with personal touches including pieces from his own art collection. The **Hotel Clermont** (✉ *789 Ponce De Leon Ave. NE* ☎ *470/485–0485* ⊕ *www. hotelclermont.com*) is a funky stay in a century-old building near Ponce City Market.

Breakfast: R. Thomas' Deluxe Grill (✉ *1812 Peachtree St. NW* ☎ *404/881–0246* ⊕ *www.rthomasdeluxegrill.net*) on Peachtree Street has been serving healthy breakfasts for more than 30 years. The **Silver Skillet** (✉ *200 14th St. NW* ☎ *404/874–1388* ⊕ *www.silverskillet.com*) has been around even longer (since 1956), and is always packed with patrons enjoying skillet country ham, fried seasoned catfish strips, and other southern classics.

Day 10: Atlanta, GA, to Charleston, SC

300 miles (4 hours, 45 minutes without traffic and stops)

Today has more freeway driving in store, heading southeast on I–20 and I–26 as you end your trip where the Civil War first started.

ALONG THE WAY

Town: Augusta, Georgia, is known as the host of the Masters golf tournament, but it's also the birthplace of James Brown and offers a revitalized Broad Street and a bucolic Riverwalk to explore. You can also take a cruise on the Augusta Canal.

Eat & Drink: Just one of the many exciting food options in Columbia, South Carolina, the **Motor City Supply Company Bistro** (⊠ 920 Gervais St. ☎ 803/256–6687 ⊕ www.motorsupplycobistro.com) offers casually upscale meals like steamed mussels and Dijon-fried eggplant.

Attraction: Located just outside Charleston, **McLeod Plantation Historic Site** (⊠ 325 Country Club Dr. ☎ 843/762–9514 ⊕ www.ccprc.com) is the only former plantation in the area where the visitor experience is focused on the lives of the enslaved people who toiled here. Guided and self-led tours are organized around a "Transition to Freedom" program that imagines what life was like for the people working on the cotton plantation and the ramifications these injustices still have on society today. The site is an essential reminder of what the Civil War was really fought over: the desire of Southern plantation owners to keep enslaving people.

CHARLESTON

Do: Charleston is a bevy of historic houses, thriving restaurants, and booming art galleries all found along cobblestone streets. The Civil War officially kicked off at Fort Sumter, in Charleston Harbor, on April 12, 1861, when a shot fired from Fort Johnson across the way initiated a 34-hour battle. The fort has been preserved as the **Fort Sumter and Fort Moultrie National Historical Park** (☎ 843/883–3123 ⊕ www.nps.gov/fosu), accessible by ferry from downtown Charleston.

Eat & Drink: Charleston has a legendary food scene, and you'd have to actively try to have a bad meal while here. **Graze** (⊠ 863 Houston Northcutt Blvd., Mt. Pleasant, SC ☎ 843/606–2493 ⊕ www.grazecharleston.com), **Husk** (⊠ 76 Queen St. ☎ 843/577–2500 ⊕ www.huskrestaurant.com), and **Xiao Bao Biscuit** (⊠ 224 Rutledge Ave. ⊕ www.xiaobiscuit.com) are just a few of the city's best, while **Edmund's Oast** (⊠ 1081 Morrison Dr. ☎ 843/727–1145 ⊕ www.edmundsoast.com) is a cutting-edge brewery/dining dynamo.

Stay: Charleston reigns in the world of refined inns and B&Bs. **Charleston Place** (⊠ 205 Meeting St. ☎ 800/611–5545 ⊕ www.charlestonplace.com) is all marble, antiques, and chandeliers while the **French Quarter Inn** (⊠ 166 Church St. ☎ 866/812–1900 ⊕ www.fqicharleston.com) is a little more cozy but still luxurious.

Breakfast: Hannibal's Soul Kitchen (⊠ 16 Blake St. ☎ 843/722–2256 ⊕ www.hannibalkitchen.com) is the go-to for a seafood breakfast, while **Three Little Birds Café** (⊠ 65 Windermere Blvd. ☎ 843/225–3065 ⊕ www.threelittlebirdcafe.com) believes in "Peace, Love, and Pancakes"—and has a lovely porch to dine on during nice weather.

Retracing the American Revolution

Written by Brandon Schultz

At its most basic, the birth of the United States can be defined by the years of the American Revolutionary War, but it's important to understand the foundation built in the more than 150 years leading up to the rebellion and the country's rapid development in the years following. Whether you're a historian or a history newbie, this road trip will explore the origins of the United States, from its first British settlement to the first and last major engagements of the Revolution. You'll end among the awe-inspiring museums and monuments of Washington, D.C., where you'll uncover the modern evolution of the capital, originally ordered by Congress with the Residence Act in 1790.

At a Glance

Start: Boston, MA

End: Washington, D.C.

Miles Traveled: 906 miles

Suggested Duration: 8 days

States Visited: Maryland, Massachusetts, New Jersey, New York, Pennsylvania, Virginia, Washington, D.C.

Key Sights: Colonial Williamsburg; The Freedom Trail; Independence Hall; Jamestown; Washington Crossing Historic Park

Best Time to Go: Various stops along this route have stronger connections to different seasons (Washington's Crossing is best reimagined in snowy winter, while Philadelphia will be in its full Revolutionary glory in July), but autumn would be the most agreeable average for the destinations as a whole. The only month that you should completely avoid is December, as Colonial Williamsburg is typically closed for the whole month.

Day 1: Boston, MA

If you're flying to the trip's starting point, you'll arrive at Boston Logan International Airport. It's just a 10-minute drive from there to downtown Boston, and you should plan to spend a full day in the city before hitting the road.

Do: From the Boston Tea Party to the ride of Paul Revere (whose house still stands in the city's North End), Boston's connections to the American Revolutionary War are legendary. At the very least, you'll want to visit the **Bunker Hill Monument & Museum** (✉ 43 Monument Sq., Charlestown ☎ 617/242–7275 ⊕ www.nps.

gov/bost), the **Boston Tea Party Ships & Museum** (✉ 306 Congress St. ☎ 617/338–1773 ⊕ www.bostonteapartyship. com), **Granary Burial Ground** (✉ Tremont St. ⊕ www.boston.gov) where Sam Adams and Paul Revere are buried, **Old North Church** and the **Paul Revere House** (✉ 19 North Sq. ☎ 617/523–2338 ⊕ www. paulreverehouse.org), the **Boston Massacre site** (✉ Corner of State and Congress Sts. ☎ 617/357–8300 ⊕ www. bostonmassacre.net), and **USS Constitution** (✉ Bldg. 22, Charlestown Navy Yard ☎ 617/426–1812 ⊕ www.ussconstitutionmuseum.org), which is the world's oldest ship still afloat. If you're up for a 2½-mile walk, you could follow the **Freedom Trail** (⊕ www.thefreedomtrail.org) for 16 significant sites, including most of the ones mentioned above.

Eat & Drink: Abigail's Tea Room (✉ 306 Congress St. ☎ 866/955–0667 ⊕ www. bostonteapartyship.com) at the Boston Tea Party Ships & Museum offers a fun period experience for a cup of tea and a light lunch. For dinner with a historic twist, try the **Green Dragon Tavern** (✉ 11 Marshall St. ☎ 617/367–0055 ⊕ www.green-dragonboston.com). The original Union Street location, where Paul Revere, John Hancock, and other Sons of Liberty met, is gone, but the tradition lives on in the current location on Marshall Street.

Shop: Faneuil Hall (☎ 617/523–1300 ⊕ faneuilhallmarketplace.com) has been a beloved Boston marketplace since the 1740s, and certainly played its part in Revolutionary history with the likes of Samuel Adams and George Washington addressing crowds here. Today you'll find four large markets, including the foodie favorite known as Quincy Market.

Stay: Although Boston doesn't have any hotels that date back to the Revolution, there are quite a few elegant 19th-century properties, including **The Liberty** (✉ 215 Charles St. ☎ 617/224–4000 ⊕ www.marriott.com), a stunningly transformed former

Retracing the
American Revolution

jailhouse near the Charles River and just a short walk from the Boston Common.

Breakfast: Stop by **Render Coffee** (✉ *563 Columbus Ave.* ☎ *617/262–4142* ⊕ *www. rendercoffeebar.com*) in the South End before heading out of town. Build your own breakfast sandwich (try the rosemary, potato, and egg) and grab a cup of premium coffee.

Day 2: Boston, MA, to Saratoga, NY

200 miles (3 hours, 15 minutes without traffic and stops)

Take I–90 west across Massachusetts and into New York, turning onto I–87 north shortly before reaching Saratoga.

ALONG THE WAY

Town: You can't take a Revolutionary War road trip without stopping at the site of the war's first engagement in Lexington, just outside Boston. Explore **Minute Man National Historical Park** (✉ *174 Liberty St., Concord, MA* ☎ *978/369–6993* ⊕ *www. nps.gov/mima*) to uncover the momentous events of April 19, 1775. If you have spare time after the park, check out the 17th-century taverns in town.

Eat & Drink: If you're ready for a second cup of coffee and a quick lunch, stop at **Sturbridge Coffee House** (✉ *407 Main St., Sturbridge, MA* ☎ *508/347–2288* ⊕ *www. sturbridgecoffeehouse.com*) about an hour beyond Lexington. Largely considered the best local coffee in town, this amiable shop also happens to be two minutes from **Old Sturbridge Village** (✉ *1 Old Sturbridge Village*

Rd. ☎ 800/733–1830 ⊕ www.osv.org),
a living history museum recreating late
18th-century life (a great spot to stroll
with your brew and to-go sandwich).

Roadside Attraction: You'll find the
largest cuckoo clock in New England
in Sturbridge, just 5 miles off I–90. The
functional clock stands over 20 feet tall
and is "hidden" in the Secret Garden
of **The Bird Store and More** (✉ 4 Cedar
St. ☎ 508/347–2473 ⊕ www.thebird-
storeandmore.com). The quirky clock
itself is also a shop, and the cuckoo
appears hourly from 9 am to 6 pm.

SARATOGA

Do: Fast-forward from the beginning of the
war to its decisive turning point with the
Battles of Saratoga. At **Saratoga National
Historical Park** (✉ 648 Rte. 32, Stillwater,
NY ☎ 518/670–2985 ⊕ www.nps.gov/
sara), you'll find the site of the British
Army's first-ever surrender, which helped
the colonists secure the international aid
that would ultimately support victory.

Eat & Drink: Just a 10-minute drive from
the park, **Sweet Lou's Bistro** (✉ 161 Broad
St. ☎ 518/507–6013 ⊕ www.sweetlous-
deli23.com) is a Schuylerville favorite for
quality plates with no pretension. Choose
from the signature corned beef and pastrami menu, or try something a little less
classic, like a grilled macaroni-and-cheese
sandwich with bourbon bacon.

Stay: Reserve one of the lakeview rooms
at **The Nest on Saratoga Lake** (✉ 511 Rte.
9P ☎ 518/306–5531 ⊕ www.browns-
beachresort.com) for a special sunset
experience. This quaint inn is the coziest
stay you'll find within 10 minutes of Saratoga National Historical Park.

Breakfast: The Merc (✉ 430 Broadway ☎ 518/886–8479 ⊕ www.
themercsaratoga.com) occupies a
handsome downtown space with paneled
walls and pressed-tin ceilings. A favorite
late-morning destination, it's known for its
Saratoga Spritz brunch cocktail and buttermilk biscuits with sage-sausage gravy.

Essential Listening

Study up on all that's to come on
your trip by listening to Season 2 of
Mike Duncan's podcast, *Revolutions*.
This season covers the American
Revolution, so you'll gain increased
perspective throughout your
journey as you progress with both
the itinerary and the series.

Day 3: Saratoga, NY, to Morristown, NJ

*180 miles (3 hours without traffic and
stops)*

Head back down I–87 south into New
Jersey and follow I–287 most of the way
to your next destination.

ALONG THE WAY

Town: Make a stop in Albany, the capital
of New York. The oldest residence in the
city is the Quackenbush House, dating to
around 1730, but the most famous house
around is quickly becoming the **Schuyler
Mansion** (✉ 32 Catherine St. ☎ 518/434–
0834 ⊕ www.parks.ny.gov), a name
brought back to national fame with
Broadway's *Hamilton*. At **First Church**
(✉ 110 N. Pearl St. ☎ 518/463–4449),
you'll also be able to glimpse the oldest
pulpit in America, brought to the United
States in 1656.

Eat & Drink: The Hollow Bar + Kitchen (✉ 79
N. Pearl St. ☎ 518/426–8550 ⊕ www.
thehollowalbany.com) in downtown
Albany offers classic pub fare like chicken
tenders, chili, and nachos alongside fresh
takes like Buddha bowl salad, vegan
meat loaf, and a risotto of the day.

Detour: New Bridge Landing (✉ 1209
Main St., River Edge, NJ ☎ 201/343–
9492 ⊕ www.bergencountyhistory.org)

From Fanueil Hall to Bunker Hill, Boston is filled with Revolution-era sights.

is a little-known North Jersey spot about 15 minutes off today's route, but the tiny town had tremendous hypothetical impact on the Revolution and stands as a reminder of one of life's most important lessons. Here, a tactical retreat by Washington is widely believed to have saved the Continental Army from a rebellion-crushing defeat in 1776. The original bridge is gone, but the current edition (circa 1889) still has a spot on the National Register of Historic Places. Three colonial houses also remain nearby.

MORRISTOWN

Do: America's first national historical park (established in 1933), **Morristown National Historical Park** (✉ *30 Washington Pl.* ☎ *973/543–2016* ⊕ *www.nps.gov/morr*) is a bit unusual in that it's home to four separate sites, not all connected, which each played a part in the war. The most interestingly (and mysteriously) named is Fort Nonsense, but the most significant are the Ford Mansion and adjacent Washington's Headquarters Museum. The surviving mansion was home to Washington during the infamous "hard winter" and the museum tells the story of his remarkable leadership in keeping an army together and motivated through harsh conditions. Don't miss the replica soldier huts at Jockey Hollow.

Eat & Drink: Despite the name, **Jockey Hollow Bar & Kitchen** (✉ *110 South St.* ☎ *973/644–3180* ⊕ *www.jockeyhollowbarandkitchen.com*) has nothing to do with the historical park, but the four dining spaces inside the former Vail Mansion demand a visit for the seafood, famous house-made pastas, or both. The wine list is equally significant.

Stay: If you're feeling a bit presidential after today's itinerary, finish the day with a dignified stay at **The Madison Hotel** (✉ *1 Convent Rd.* ☎ *800/526–0729* ⊕ *www.themadisonhotel.com*). The reasonably priced four-star hotel is stately inside and out, and offers both an indoor pool and an elegant steak house worth peeking into even if you're not dining.

Breakfast: The breakfast menu at **The Artist Baker** (✉ *16 Cattano Ave.* ☎ *973/267–5540* ⊕ *www.theartistbaker.com*) changes daily, but you can always count on a hot cup of specialty coffee and irresistible pastries from this top local bakery.

Day 4: Morristown, NJ, to Philadelphia, PA

85 miles (1 hour, 30 minutes without traffic and stops)

It's a quick drive through the rest of New Jersey today, heading south toward I–95 south, taking you directly into Philadelphia.

ALONG THE WAY

Town: Just before crossing the Delaware River into Pennsylvania, stop at **Washington Crossing Historic Park** (✉ *355 Washington Crossing Pennington Rd., Titusville* ☎ *609/737–0623* ⊕ *www.state.nj.us*) in New Jersey. Then called Johnson's Ferry, this is the spot where Washington famously crossed the river on the icy Christmas night of 1776 in a surprise attack that tipped the scales back in the Continental Army's favor.

Eat & Drink: Cross the bridge for lunch at **Washington Crossing Inn** (✉ *1295 General Washington Memorial Blvd., Washington Crossing* ☎ *215/493–3634* ⊕ *www.washingtoncrossinginn.com*) in Pennsylvania. (Both states have a Washington Crossing on either side of the river.) Affordable meals are served inside the refined home preserved from the early 19th century; weekend brunch is especially adored here.

Detour: A half-hour detour on your way to Philly, **Valley Forge National Historical Park** (✉ *1400 N. Outer Line Dr., King of Prussia, PA* ☎ *610/783–1077* ⊕ *www.nps.gov/vafo*) was the site of the Continental Army's winter encampment after the British took Philadelphia. The site became the equivalent of America's fourth-largest city as 12,000 soldiers (and several hundred women and children) built 1,500 cabins. This is where Washington resupplied, retrained, and reinspired the entire army during a brutal winter that temporarily halted fighting.

PHILADELPHIA

Do: Tomorrow you'll catch the museums and historical sites that only offer daytime hours, but this evening you can stroll the historic streets of Old City, including the impossibly picturesque Elfreth's Alley, the oldest continuously inhabited residential street in the country. You can also stroll by Benjamin Franklin's grave at **Christ Church Burial Ground** (✉ *340 N. 5th St.* ☎ *215/922–1695* ⊕ *www.christchurchphila.org*) and toss a penny on it for luck (he's the one who coined the adage "A penny saved is a penny earned.").

Eat & Drink: While in Old City, dine at **The Olde Bar** (✉ *125 Walnut St.* ☎ *215/253–3777* ⊕ *www.theoldebar.com*) if you like seafood. This oyster bar and retro cocktail lounge is always a stylish choice. Otherwise, head to **Amada** (✉ *217–219 Chestnut St.* ☎ *215/625–2450* ⊕ *www.amadarestaurant.com*) for modern Spanish tapas from the same chef.

Stay: If you're looking for a period stay, book a room at **Morris House Hotel** (✉ *225 S. 8th St.* ☎ *215/922–2446* ⊕ *www.morrishousehotel.com*). This boutique hotel was originally built in 1787 and is a National Historic Landmark with easy access to many of the city's historic sites.

Breakfast: Pop over to the **Reading Terminal Market** (✉ *1136 Arch St.* ☎ *215/922–2317* ⊕ *www.readingterminalmarket.org*) for breakfast. This huge facility is one of the oldest public markets in the country and frequented by locals and tourists daily. At breakfast, the must-try bites are the homestyle cooking of several Pennsylvania Dutch vendors, including Dutch Eating Place.

Day 5: Philadelphia

Stay put today. You'll need to spend a full day in Philadelphia to catch even a sampling of its impact on early America.

Do: You won't find a city with deeper ties to the Revolution than Philadelphia, so even a full day here will still require a highlights tour. Don't miss: **Independence Hall** (✉ 520 Chestnut St. ☎ 215/965–2305 ⊕ www.nps.gov/inde); the **Liberty Bell** (✉ 526 Market St. ☎ 215/965–2305 ⊕ www.nps.gov/inde); the **National Constitution Center** (✉ 525 Arch St. ☎ 215/409–6600 ⊕ www.constitutioncenter.org); the **Museum of the American Revolution** (✉ 101 S. 3rd St. ☎ 215/253–6731 ⊕ www.amrevmuseum.org); **Carpenter's Hall** (✉ 320 Chestnut St. ☎ 215/925–0167 ⊕ www.carpentershall.org), site of the First Continental Congress; and **Declaration House** (✉ 700 Market St. ☎ 215/965–2305 ⊕ www.nps.gov/inde), where the Declaration of Independence was written. For a bit of fun that's more a space of legend than fact, you can also tour the **Betsy Ross House** (✉ 239 Arch St. ☎ 215/629–4026 ⊕ www.historicphiladelphia.org).

Eat & Drink: Have a sandwich at **High Street Restaurant** (✉ 101 S. 9th St. ☎ 215/625–0988 ⊕ www.highstreetphilly.com). The breads are baked in-house and the fillings range from roast pork with broccoli rabe (a Philly staple) to poached salmon with roasted red pepper and olive tapenade. Or you can take a detour to nab a classic Philly cheesesteak at **Jim's Steaks** (✉ 400 South St. ☎ 215/928–1911 ⊕ jimssouthstreet.com). You've probably heard that the real battle of the best Philly cheesesteak is between Geno's and Pat's, but Jim's is a sleeper favorite and is a bit closer to the city center.

Breakfast: 3J's Cafe (✉ 317 Market St. ☎ 215/309–3140 ⊕ www.3jscafephilly.com) has plenty of breakfast sandwiches, jazzed-up pancakes, and, of course, avocado toast, but the breakfast specialties may provide more of the sustenance you need for the long drive ahead. Consider the loaded breakfast bowl with tofu scramble or some biscuits and sausage gravy with eggs and fried chicken.

Day 6: Philadelphia, PA, to Williamsburg, VA

290 miles (4 hours, 45 minutes without traffic and stops)

Hop on I–95 south and settle in for the nearly five-hour drive down to Williamsburg. It's a long one, but you just had a day off from driving so you should be ready for it.

ALONG THE WAY

Town: The capital of the United States is simply the location of the U.S. Congress and, for a brief period of about two months ending in February 1777, that was Baltimore. There's plenty to see in this harbor city, but no actual battle action was seen here during the Revolution, despite the construction of **Fort McHenry National Monument** (✉ 2400 E. Fort Ave. ☎ 410/962–4290 ⊕ www.nps.gov/fomc) in anticipation of a British approach. The fort did see action during the War of 1812, though, and is where Francis Scott Key penned "The Star-Spangled Banner," which would become the young country's national anthem.

Eat & Drink: Five minutes from Fort McHenry, have lunch at **Hull Street Blues Café** (✉ 1222 Hull St. ☎ 410/727–7476 ⊕ www.hullstreetblues.com). This small, local favorite takes full advantage of its river/harbor location with a seafood focus, and any meal should begin with the cream of crab soup.

Attraction: Sprawling **Mount Vernon** (✉ 3200 Mount Vernon Memorial Hwy. ☎ 703/780–2000 ⊕ www.mountvernon.org), the plantation and home of George and Martha Washington, serves as a reminder of the complex legacy of our first president and many of the Founding Fathers: leaders in the American Revolution, and, simultaneously, enslavers of hundreds of people. Washington was a student of landscape design and agriculture who transformed his estate into gardens and fields for observation and production. Even if you don't go inside the revered house, exploring the waterfront grounds is a worthwhile peek into Washington's masterful manipulation of nature. You should also make time to explore the various outbuildings in which enslaved people ran Mount Vernon's many operations. You can learn more about these enslaved people—who represented 90% of Mount Vernon's residents at the time of Washington's death—by visiting one of their living quarters on the property, such as Pioneer Farm.

WILLIAMSBURG

Do: By the time you arrive, many of Williamsburg's Colonial attractions will be closed, but you'll spend a full day here tomorrow, so don't fret. In the meantime, enjoy a low-key evening and consider getting to know the area casually with something fun like a candlelight ghost tour.

Eat & Drink: Colonial Williamsburg is the place to embrace full immersion, so kick it off right with dinner at **Josiah Chowning's Tavern** (✉ 109 E. Duke of Gloucester St. ☎ 800/447–8679 ⊕ www.colonialwilliamsburghotels.com). The menu is inspired by colonial pub grub and the restaurant itself is designed as an authentic 18th-century alehouse, complete with period-appropriate entertainment like balladeers and old-timey games nightly.

Stay: Keep the theme going strong with a stay at **Colonial Houses Historic Lodging** (✉ 136 Francis St. E ☎ 844/280–4578 ⊕ www.colonialwilliamsburghotels.com). These colonial reproductions will blast you to the past with furniture and

decor, but you won't have to leave modern luxuries and conveniences behind. Best of all, guests receive discounts and special incentives for Colonial Williamsburg.

Breakfast: Williamsburg is also a college town, and that means there's a proper breakfast scene. Among the most popular is the no-fuss **Colonial Pancake House** (✉ 301 Page St. ☎ 757/253–5852 ⊕ www.colonialpancake.com), which specializes in piles of pancakes and waffles, with plenty of other traditional breakfast-nook fare available.

Day 7: Williamsburg, VA

Today's the day to catch all that Colonial Williamsburg has to offer while the sun's up, so skip the highway and traverse the cobblestone streets on foot. You'll continue onward tomorrow.

Do: Colonial Williamsburg is an enormous living history museum that represents the era when the town was the capital of the 18th-century Virginia colony. More than 300 acres are populated not just with architecture, but period actors strolling the streets and working in shops that were relevant to the once-thriving town. Strolling through town is free, but most historic houses, shops, and performances are ticketed. Start with a visit to the **Colonial Williamsburg Visitor Center** (✉ 101 Visitor Center Dr. ☎ 888/965–7254 ⊕ www.colonialwilliamsburg.org) to map your afternoon based on your personal interests, like blacksmithing, letterpress printing, or, if you're a Loyalist, ogling the personal effects of British nobility at Governor's Palace (Thomas Jefferson also lived here when he was governor after the war).

Eat & Drink: Have one last dose of Williamsburg-style immersion with a final dinner at **King's Arms Tavern** (✉ 416 E. Duke of Gloucester St. ☎ 855/240–3278 ⊕ www.colonialwilliamsburghotels.

com), where servers in period dress present updated plates inspired by 18th-century recipes that would have been served when the original tavern opened in 1772.

Breakfast: AromasWorld (✉ 431 Prince George St. ☎ 757/221–6676 ⊕ www. aromasworld.com) serves an extensive menu of house-roasted specialty coffees and teas with deliciously fresh baked bites. Breakfast is served until noon and, if you're making a later start today, you could also pick up some sandwiches for lunch.

Day 8: Williamsburg, VA, to Washington, DC

150 miles (2 hours, 30 minutes without traffic and stops)

Backtrack today by taking I–95 north up to the nation's capital, Washington, D.C., where you'll find flights to just about anywhere in the country from Ronald Reagan Washington National Airport, Dulles International Airport, or even Baltimore/Washington International Airport.

ALONG THE WAY

Town: There are two worthwhile spots to stop today and, if you still have the energy, it's recommended to hit both. Though they're in opposite directions from Williamsburg, they're only about 30 minutes apart from each other; it's certainly possible to see it all, but feel free to choose just one for a more relaxed day. To the west, your first option is **Jamestown** (✉ 1368 Colonial Pkwy. ☎ 757/856–1250 ⊕ www.historic-jamestowne.org), where you can explore the ruins of the first European settlement in the colonies (this area is called Historic Jamestowne) as well as re-creations of the fort with a Powhatan village at a living history museum (this area is called Jamestown Settlement). To the east, you'll find the site of the last major

battle of the Revolution, a fitting final day stop. The Siege of Yorktown resulted in a captured British Army and prompted negotiations to end the war. You can visit the battlefield at **Colonial National Historical Park** (☎ 757/898–2410 ⊕ www. nps.gov/colo).

Eat & Drink: Depending where you head today, you could grab a bite at **Dale House Café** (✉ 1367 Colonial National Historic Pkwy. ☎ 757/229–1170 ⊕ www. historicjamestowne.org) on the James River in Historic Jamestowne or at **Water Street Grille** (✉ 323 Water St. ☎ 757/369–5644 ⊕ www.waterstreetgrille.net) on Yorktown Beach. If you're starting early because you plan to hit both stops, visit Yorktown second and snag a snack and a craft beer with a view at Water Street Grille before journeying onward.

WASHINGTON, D.C.

Do: Since it didn't quite exist until after the Revolution, the U.S. capital has admittedly little to do with the early days of the nation, but it still provides a fascinating perspective on where these revolutionary efforts led. Consider **Daughters of the American Revolution Memorial Hall** (✉ 1776 D St. NW ☎ 202/628–1776 ⊕ www. dar.org); the **National Museum of American History** (✉ 1300 Constitution Ave. NW ☎ 202/633–1000 ⊕ www.american-history.si.edu), where you'll find Washington's uniform and Jefferson's desk; **Larz Anderson House** (✉ 2118 Massachusetts Ave. NW ☎ 202/785–2040 ⊕ www. societyofthecincinnati.org); and, of course, the Washington and Jefferson memorials. One essential stop is the phenomenal **National Museum of African American History and Culture** (✉ 1400 Constitution Ave. NW ☎ 844/750–3012 ⊕ www.nmaahc. si.edu), which seeks to view American history through the African American experience, giving insight into how chattel slavery was deeply entwined with our country's founding and the contributions African Americans made to the Revolutionary War.

Eat & Drink: Have an elegant final dinner at **The Bazaar** (✉ *1100 Pennsylvania Ave. NW* ☎ *202/868–5088* ⊕ *www.thebazaar. com*) in the Waldorf Astoria Washington DC. In the lavish 1899 building that originally served as D.C.'s General Post Office, you can feast on the eclectic, creative fare of celebrated chef José Andrés.

Stay: Rest up at the **Dupont Circle Hotel** (✉ *1500 New Hampshire Ave. NW* ☎ *202/483–6000* ⊕ *www.doylecollection.com*) for a chic reentry to the present day. In this neighborhood, you'll also find the gorgeous embassies of many U.S. allies—a testament to the international powerhouse that rose from the struggles and successes of the American Revolutionary War.

Breakfast: Depending on your departure time, you may be able to squeeze in an egg sandwich or *huevos revueltos* at **Emissary** (✉ *2032 P St. NW* ☎ *202/748–5655* ⊕ *www.emissarydc.com*), but if time is tight you can at least score your caffeine of choice from the neighborhood coffeehouse and wake up on the way to the airport.

Chapter 3

THE WEST COAST

3

Updated by
Margot Bigg

WELCOME TO THE WEST COAST

TOP REASONS TO GO

★ **Big Sur:** The Pacific Coast Highway is scenic the whole way through, but nothing matches the rugged beauty and winding coastal roads of Big Sur.

★ **Santa Monica Pier:** More than just an old-school amusement park, Santa Monica's famed pier along the Pacific Ocean offers family fun and gorgeous coastal views.

★ **Yosemite National Park:** By merely standing in Yosemite Valley and turning in a circle, you can see more natural wonders in a minute than you could in a full day pretty much anywhere else.

★ **Olympic National Park:** Edged on all sides by water, the forested landscape of Olympic National Park is remote and pristine, capturing the particular beauty of the Pacific Northwest.

★ **The Willamette Valley:** Oregon's famed wine country delivers some of the country's best wine alongside stunning scenery and charming small towns.

1 The Pacific Coast Highway and Highway 101. A drive up the entire West Coast of the United States is completely unforgettable.

2 The Best of Northern California. San Francisco, Lake Tahoe, Yosemite, and more.

3 The Best of Central and Southern California. Los Angeles, Joshua Tree, Orange County, and more.

4 California's National Parks. Hit up every single one of California's nine national parks in one epic trip.

5 The Best of the Pacific Northwest. See the hip cities and stunning landscapes of Washington and Oregon.

6 Wine Countries of the Pacific Northwest. Several of the country's best wine regions are found in its northwest corner.

Whether you're looking for curving coastlines overlooking an endless expanse of ocean, treks through misty forests where ancient trees stand guard, or desert landscapes containing rocky monoliths that seem to rise from the sand, the country's West Coast offers some of the most unforgettable road trip adventures in the whole world.

The Pacific Coast Highway and Highway 101

Written by Shoshi Parks

The drive along the famous Pacific Coast Highway, from San Diego to Seattle, will take you from the sunny beaches in Southern California through redwood trees and into Oregon, characterized by windswept vistas and forest-flanked beaches. Continue north and you'll soon find yourself in the rainforests of Olympic National Park before heading inland to Seattle. With epic views, diverse culinary offerings, majestic hiking trails, and thriving cities, this marvelous coastal stretch is one you won't forget.

At a Glance

Start: San Diego, CA

End: Seattle, WA

Miles Traveled: 1,622 miles

Suggested Duration: 12 days

States Visited: California, Oregon, Washington

Key Sights: Golden Gate Bridge; Hearst Castle; Lewis & Clark National Historic Park; Los Angeles County Museum of Art; Redwood National Park

Best Time to Go: This trip is gorgeous all year long (especially along the Pacific Coast Highway), but you'll get the best weather in the Pacific Northwest in summer and early fall.

Day 1: San Diego, CA, to Los Angeles, CA

125 miles (2 hours without traffic and stops)

California-dream your way out of San Diego and along the southernmost stretch of the Pacific Coast Highway. Pass through Orange County's classic beach communities before heading slightly inland to the heart of Los Angeles.

ALONG THE WAY

Town: Take a walk along the wooden Oceanside Pier, one of the state's longest, in Oceanside and catch a wave at South Carlsbad State Beach. Swing by the **California Surf Museum** (✉ *312 Pier View Way* ☎ *760/721–6876* ⊕ *www.surf-museum.org*) for a look at the popular Southern California sport and the legendary athletes who have made their mark.

Eat & Drink: A few blocks inland from Oceanside Pier, **The LAB Collaborative** (✉ *201 N Cleveland St. Suite 109* ☎ *442/266–2436* ⊕ *thelaboce-anside.com*) serves up massive portions of pub fare classics with a twist. The menu is loaded with seafood options, from chimichurri-marinated surf and turf to Thai baked salmon, along with steaks, salads, and vegan sloppy joes.

Nature: Get out on the water, post up at **Doheny State Beach** (✉ *25300 Dana Point Harbor Dr.* ☎ *949/496–6171* ⊕ *www.dohenystatebeach.org*), or walk the trails at **Dana Point Headlands Conservation Area** (✉ *34558 Scenic Dr.*) to get a glimpse of the majestic mammals that frequent these waters. Whale-watching tours depart from Dana Point Harbor.

LOS ANGELES

Do: The options for things to do in Los Angeles are virtually endless. Wander through massive **Griffith Park** (✉ *4730 Crystal Springs Dr.* ☎ *323/913–4688* ⊕ *www.laparks.org*) or stop by the **La Brea Tar Pits** (✉ *5801 Wilshire Blvd.* ☎ *213/763–3499* ⊕ *www.tarpits.org*) for a glimpse of prehistoric Los Angeles. Some of the country's best modern art is housed at the **Los Angeles County Museum of Art** (✉ *5905 Wilshire Blvd.* ☎ *323/857–6000* ⊕ *www.lacma.org*), and you can get a glimpse of Hollywood history and movie magic at the **Academy Museum of Motion Pictures** (✉ *6067 Wilshire Blvd.* ☎ *323/930–3000* ⊕ *www.academymuseum.org*).

Eat & Drink: Dig into Korean fried chicken and *banchan* at Grand Central Market hot spot **Shiku** (✉ *317 S. Broadway* ☎ *213/365–7211* ⊕ *www.shikulosangeles.com*) or Middle Eastern specialties from beloved chef Ori Menashe at **Bavel** (✉ *500 Mateo St.* ☎ *213/232–4966* ⊕ *www.baveldtla.com*). After dinner, **The Slipper Clutch** (✉ *351 S. Broadway* ☎ *213/201–3838* ⊕ *www.theslipperclutch.com*), a downtown Los Angeles bar inspired by New York punk rock, offers highballs and craft beer with a side of pinball.

Stay: Los Angeles is huge and getting from one neighborhood to another can be a major time-suck, so choose the location of your hotel carefully. In Koreatown, between Hollywood and Downtown, the boutique **LINE LA** (✉ *3515 Wilshire Blvd.* ☎ *213/381–7411* ⊕ *www.thelinehotel.com*) boasts local art and hosts regular events. Downtown's **Hotel Figueroa** (✉ *939 S. Figueroa St.* ☎ *213/627–8971* ⊕ *www.hotelfigueroa.com*) opened in 1926 as a place for professional women travelers to stay in an era where most hotels would turn unaccompanied women away; today, all are welcome in this lovely Spanish colonial spot.

Breakfast: Get a classic L.A. diner breakfast at the **House of Breakfast** (✉ *3728 W. Olympic Blvd.* ☎ *323/731–5405*).

Day 2: Los Angeles, CA, to San Luis Obispo, CA

189 miles (3 hours without traffic and stops)

Navigate north up the Pacific Coast Highway toward celebrity hangout Santa Barbara. Outside the city, you enter the state's lesser-known wine country and pass through Solvang, one of California's quirkiest towns, before returning to the coast and San Luis Obispo.

The Pacific Coast Highway and Highway 101

Victoria
Bellingham
North Cascades Nat'l Park
Olympic National Park
Everett
97
Olympic National Park
12
13 Seattle
WASHINGTON
Ocean Shores
Tacoma
Spokane
Aberdeen
12
Olympia
Ellensburg
90
Astoria
11
Mount Rainier Nat'l Park
Yakima
Lewiston
Cannon Beach
26
Vancouver
82
Tillamook
Portland
84
Pendleton
Lincoln City
Salem
Newport
10
20
OREGON
Cape Perpetua
Eugene
395
Bend
Coos Bay
Bandon
Crater Lake Nat'l Park
20
20
101
Medford
Brookings
9
199
Crescent City
Klamath Falls
Boise
84
Klamath
IDAHO
Redwood National and State Parks
5
Eureka
8
395
Ferndale
299
Lassen Volcanic Nat'l Park
Legend of Bigfoot Gift Shop
101
Redding
Elko
80
Leggett
Mendocino
7
Chico
Bowling Ball Beach
1
101
Reno
Jenner
80
Lake Tahoe
Carson City
50
Bodega Bay
Sacramento
Ely
Tomales Bay
6
Point Reyes Station
Point Reyes National Seashore
Bolinas
Golden Gate Bridge Vista Point
Oakland
NEVADA
San Francisco
5
Half Moon Bay
San Jose
Yosemite National Park
CALIFORNIA
1
Santa Cruz
Monterey
Salinas
Kings Canyon National Park
Death Valley Nat'l Park
Carmel
Bixby Creek Bridge
101
Fresno
395
Big Sur
4
Julia Pfeiffer Burns State Park
5
Hearst Castle
99
Las Vegas
Cambria
Sequoia National Park
Morro Bay
3
San Luis Obispo
Bakersfield
1
15
Solvang
Arroyo Burro County Beach Park
5
Lancaster
Santa Barbara
101
Joshua Tree Nat'l Park
40
Los Angeles
2
Palm Springs
Long Beach
Dana Point Headlands Conservation Area
Salton Sea
10
Doheny State Beach
Oceanside
Pacific Ocean
San Diego
1
8
Tijuana
Yuma

0   100 mi
0   100 km

ALONG THE WAY

Town: In Santa Barbara, see what's blooming at the **Santa Barbara Botanic Garden** (✉ *1212 Mission Canyon Rd.* ☎ *805/682–4726* ⊕ *www.sbbg.org*) or visit the Old Mission (✉ *2201 Laguna St.* ☎ *805/682–4713* ⊕ *www.santabaramission.org*), one of California's original 18th-century Spanish missions. There's plenty of shopping to be done downtown.

Eat & Drink: The longtime local favorite **La Super-Rica Taqueria** (✉ *622 N. Milpas St.* ☎ *805/963–4940* ⊕ *www.facebook. com/lasuperricataqueria*) in Santa Barbara packs authentic flavor and is the perfect introduction to Southern California tacos.

Nature: Sprawl out on the sand or take a swim at **Arroyo Burro County Beach Park** (✉ *2981 Cliff Dr.* ☎ *805/687– 3714* ⊕ *www.countyofsb.org*), called Hendry's Beach by locals.

Roadside Attraction: The bizarre wine country town of Solvang is equal parts Danish village and Disney movie.

SAN LUIS OBISPO

Do: There are vineyards galore just outside San Luis Obispo in the Edna Valley. Join an organized wine tour or plan your own with a wine-touring map available at the Old Edna Townsite. A historic Mission, the **Mission San Luis Obispo de Tolosa** (✉ *751 Palm St.* ☎ *805/781– 8220* ⊕ *www.missionsanluisobispo. org*) still stands in the Old Town Historic District.

Eat & Drink: The craft eatery **Taste!** (✉ *2900 Broad St.* ☎ *805/200– 2978* ⊕ *www.taste2900.com*), which serves everything from classic burgers to pork banh mi, has been winning awards in SLO since it opened in 2014. At the **Sidecar Cocktail Co.** (✉ *1040 Broad St.* ☎ *805/439–3563* ⊕ *www.sidecarcocktail.company*), sip on margaritas and tiki drinks or enjoy some of the best comfort food in town.

Essential Listening

Make your way through Southern California with the classic surf rock tunes of *The Beach Boys Greatest Hits.*

Stay: The popular themed rooms at the world-famous **Madonna Inn** (✉ *100 Madonna Rd.* ☎ *805/543–3000* ⊕ *www. madonnainn.com*) include everything from "Yosemite Rock" to "Love Nest." The kitschy on-site Silver Bar Cocktail Lounge is worth a visit whether you are staying here or not.

Breakfast: Over 100 different delectable doughnut flavors are available every day (including vegan and gluten-free options) at **SloDoCo Donuts** (✉ *793F Foothill Blvd.* ☎ *805/782–9766* ⊕ *www.slodoco. com*).

Day 3: San Luis Obispo, CA, to Big Sur, CA

107 miles (2 hours, 15 minutes without traffic and stops)

Head north past Cambria and toward the rocky bluffs, towering redwoods, and rushing waterfalls of Big Sur, where the California coast puts on one of its most spectacular shows.

ALONG THE WAY

Eat & Drink: Get fresh seafood plucked straight from Morro Bay at **The Galley Seafood Grill & Bar** (✉ *899 Embarcadero* ☎ *805/772–7777* ⊕ *www.galleymorrobay.com*), a waterfront restaurant on the Morro Bay Embarcadero.

Town: The laid-back beach town of Cambria extends from beautiful Moonstone Beach to a quaint downtown peppered with antiques shops and boutiques.

Roadside Attraction: On the top of a hill looking out over the Pacific, lavish **Hearst Castle** (✉ *750 Hearst Castle Rd., San Simeon* ☎ *800/444–4445* ⊕ *www.hearstcastle.org*), built for publishing magnate William Randolph Hearst by early 19th-century architect extraordinaire Julia Morgan, has more than 40 bedrooms, 61 bathrooms, indoor and outdoor swimming pools, and 127 acres of gardens. The only way to visit the castle and its gardens is by joining one of the many tours, which depart from the visitor center at the base of the hill (it's wise to book ahead). A full-sized movie theater at the center screens a film about the castle's backstory.

Photo Op: The descendants of the zebras (yes, zebras) once kept at Hearst Castle are often visible from the side of Highway 1 in San Simeon.

BIG SUR

Do: Get a look at Big Sur's McWay Falls from Highway 1, then hit the trail at **Julia Pfeiffer Burns State Park** (✉ *52801 Rte. 1* ☎ *831/667–1112* ⊕ *www.parks.ca.gov*) or the water at **Sand Dollar Beach** (✉ *Rte. 1* ☎ *805/434–1996* ⊕ *www.parks.ca.gov*) or **Andrew Molera State Park** (✉ *45500 Rte. 1* ☎ *831/667–2315* ⊕ *www.parks.ca.gov*).

Eat & Drink: Nepenthe (✉ *48510 Rte. 1* ☎ *831/667–2345* ⊕ *www.nepenthe.com*) isn't the cheapest spot in town, but its location alone, crowning the top of a ridge overlooking the Pacific, is worth the splurge. Get a cocktail or enjoy a full dinner of steak and seafood out on the patio.

Stay: If you have the gear for a night under the stars, snag a campsite at Julia Pfeiffer Burns State Park. To get a reservation, plan to book as far in advance as possible. Otherwise, the **Big Sur Lodge** (✉ *47225 Rte. 1* ☎ *831/667–3100* ⊕ *www.bigsurlodge.com*) is a clean, comfortable option. But if you've got cash to burn, you won't regret a night

at the epic **Post Ranch Inn** (✉ *47900 Rte. 1* ☎ *831/667–2200* ⊕ *www.postranchinn.com*).

Breakfast: Cozy **Deetjen's Restaurant** (✉ *48865 Rte. 1* ☎ *831/667–2378* ⊕ *www.deetjens.com*) serves up hearty breakfast burritos, airy buttermilk pancakes, and tasty eggs Benedict in a rustic lodge setting.

Day 4: Big Sur, CA, to San Francisco, CA

149 miles (3 hours without traffic and stops)

Travel on toward San Francisco. As you pass the artist colony of Carmel and the town of Monterey (the setting for John Steinbeck's 1945 novel *Cannery Row* and the more modern HBO series *Big Little Lies*), stick to Highway 1 and the beach towns that line the coast of the Bay Area. This route adds 30 minutes to the trip but is a much more interesting drive than going up Highway 101.

ALONG THE WAY

Photo Op: Cross the world-famous Bixby Creek Bridge on the northern end of Big Sur then pull over to get the perfect shot.

Town: Tiny Carmel has long drawn artists with its charm. Explore the town's galleries and boutiques and, if you have the time, take a quick detour down the aptly named 17-Mile Drive for lovely views and a look at how the other half lives.

Eat & Drink: Stop at the roadside favorite **Sam's Chowder House** (✉ *4210 Rte. 1* ☎ *650/712–0245* ⊕ *www.samschowderhouse.com*) in Half Moon Bay for a bowl of clam chowder on the patio.

SAN FRANCISCO

Do: From the "Painted Ladies" (Victorian homes) of the Haight to the back alleys of the largest Chinatown outside Asia, San Francisco is one of the country's most enchanting cities. The murals

One of the most photographed spots along the coast, Bixby Bridge has amazing views of Big Sur.

in the Mission neighborhood, North Beach's **Coit Tower** (✉ 1 Telegraph Hill Blvd. ☎ 415/249–0995 ⊕ www.sfrecpark. org), and downtown museums such as the **San Francisco Museum of Modern Art** (✉ 151 3rd St. ☎ 415/357–4000 ⊕ www. sfmoma.org) are among the many must-sees.

Eat & Drink: Get a modern take on Chinese food at **Mister Jiu's** (✉ 28 Waverly Pl. ☎ 415/857–9688 ⊕ www.misterjius. com) or a San Francisco–style burrito from a city favorite, **La Taqueria** (✉ 2889 Mission St. ☎ 415/285–7117 ⊕ www. lataqueriasf.com). After dinner, head to Haight Street for a drink at Persian institution **Zam Zam** (✉ 1633 Haight St. ☎ 415/861–2545) or craft-cocktail favorite **The Alembic** (✉ 1725 Haight St. ☎ 415/666–0822 ⊕ www.alembicsf. com).

Stay: The stylish **Proper Hotel** (✉ 45 McAllister St. ☎ 415/735–7777 ⊕ www. properhotel.com) near the Civic Center is a carefully orchestrated gallery of art and design with a popular rooftop bar, while

the boutique **Hotel Kabuki** (✉ 1625 Post St. ☎ 415/922–3200 ⊕ www.jdvhotels. com) in Japantown will swath you in its Zen aesthetic.

Breakfast: Before heading over the Golden Gate Bridge to Marin, grab a satisfying southern breakfast at **Brenda's French Soul Food** (✉ 652 Polk St. ☎ 415/345–8100 ⊕ www.frenchsoulfood.com) in the Tenderloin.

Day 5: San Francisco, CA, to Tomales Bay, CA

50 miles (1 hour, 40 minutes without traffic and stops)

It's a short drive today over the Golden Gate Bridge and up Highway 1 to the Point Reyes National Seashore and the oyster-rich waters of Tomales Bay.

ALONG THE WAY

Photo Op: Cross the Golden Gate then pull over at the **Golden Gate Bridge Vista Point** (⊕ www.goldengatebridge.org) for a view of the architectural marvel in all its glory.

Detour: The "hidden" town of **Bolinas,** a small surfing community in a cove of Bolinas Bay, is about a 10-minute drive from Highway 1. The community abuts Mount Tamalpais and you can hike straight from town into the redwoods that sprout from Marin's tallest mountain.

Town: The tiny, historic town of **Point Reyes Station** has a handful of pleasant shops and restaurants. It's a lovely stop before hitting the wild lands of the national seashore a few miles down the road.

Eat & Drink: One of Northern California's best cheese purveyors, **Cowgirl Creamery** (⊠ 80 4th St. ☎ 415/663–9335 ⊕ cowgirl-creamery.square.site) in Point Reyes Station is the perfect stop. Pick up a round of Mt. Tam, the creamery's flagship triple cream, along with bread, charcuterie, and wine for lunch alfresco.

TOMALES BAY

Do: Head to **Point Reyes National Seashore** (☎ 415/464–5137 ⊕ www.nps.gov/pore), an unusual mix of historical ranching and dairy lands and protected wilderness. See the wild Tule elk at Tomales Point, whale-watch from the 150-year-old Point Reyes Lighthouse, and get a look at the elephant seal colony at Chimney Rock.

Eat & Drink: When you've had your fill of Point Reyes, hit the road to drive up the inland side of Tomales Bay. **The Marshall Store** (⊠ 19225 Rte. 1 ☎ 415/663–1339 ⊕ www.themarshallstore.com), a roadside joint with barbecued oysters, Dungeness crab sandwiches, and other delights from the bay, is always worth a stop.

Stay: About four miles up the road from the Marshall Store, **Nick's Cove** (⊠ 23240 Rte. 1 ☎ 415/663–1033 ⊕ www.nickscove.com) has well-appointed cabins that hang out over the calm Tomales waters. Nick's also has a fantastic farm-to-table restaurant (and its own hillside farm, The Croft, a historic boathouse for sipping cocktails, and a small beach with a fire pit for roasting marshmallows after dark).

Breakfast: It's a 10-mile drive to Valley Ford and the **Estero Cafe** (⊠ 14450 Rte. 1 ☎ 707/876–3333 ⊕ www.estero.cafe), a local café with a knack for breakfast.

Day 6: Tomales Bay, CA, to Mendocino, CA

129 miles (3 hours without traffic or stops)

It's a day of spectacular views and quaint coastal towns as you continue up the Pacific Coast Highway toward Mendocino.

ALONG THE WAY

Town: In Bodega Bay, tool around town on a bike or rent a kayak for a few hours on the water. Four miles from the coast is the village of Bodega, the filming location for Alfred Hitchcock's 1963 film *The Birds.*

Eat & Drink: In Jenner, the Russian River meets the sea. Find stunning views of both at the intimate **River's End Restaurant** (⊠ 11048 Rte. 1 ☎ 707/865–2484 ⊕ www.ilovesunsets.com), which specializes in local seafood and seasonal produce.

Nature: In Point Arena, Bowling Ball Beach is littered with perfectly round boulders carefully carved by the waves.

MENDOCINO

Do: This laid-back town is a mecca for artists and gallery owners. Check out the **Mendocino Art Center** (⊠ 45200 Little Lake St. ☎ 707/937–5818 ⊕ www.mendocinoartcenter.org), then browse some of the many galleries in town. If you prefer your art in liquid form, there are a number of wineries in nearby Anderson Valley.

Eat & Drink: Farm-to-table California cuisine is on the menu at the cozy **Trillium Cafe** (✉ *10390 Kasten St.* ☎ *707/937–3200* ⊕ *www.trilliummendocino.com*). End the night with a shot and a beer at **Dick's Place** (✉ *45070 Main St.* ☎ *707/937–6010*), a dive over a century old.

Stay: The **Blue Door Inn** (✉ *10481 Howard St.* ☎ *707/937–4892* ⊕ *www.innsofmendocino.com*) is an elegant Victorian bed-and-breakfast with a modern aesthetic. Many of the rooms have fireplaces, soaking tubs, and views of the Pacific.

Breakfast: Grab a coffee and breakfast (or just a pastry for the road) at the **Goodlife Cafe & Bakery** (✉ *10483 Lansing St.* ☎ *707/937–0836* ⊕ *www.goodlifecafemendo.com*).

Day 7: Mendocino, CA, to Eureka, CA

143 miles (3 hours without traffic or stops)

Today's route takes you away from the coast and into the weird and wonderful world of rural Northern California on the Redwood Highway stretch of Highway 101. At the day's end, you're back at the coast in Eureka, a city that rose to prominence during the gold rush era.

ALONG THE WAY

Town: Leggett is crawling with unusual attractions just kitschy enough to be fun. Drive through a massive sequoia at the **Chandelier Drive-Through Tree** (✉ *67402 Drive Thru Tree Rd.* ☎ *707/925–6464* ⊕ *www.drivethrutree.com*) or take home a Sasquatch effigy from the **Legend of Bigfoot Gift Shop** (✉ *2500 U.S. 101, Garberville* ☎ *707/247–3332*).

Eat & Drink: The roadside café **The Peg House** (✉ *69501 U.S. 101* ☎ *707/925–6444* ⊕ *www.thepeghouse.com*) in Leggett has a large patio, live music, and burgers and oysters hot off the grill.

Roadside Attraction: All of Leggett's roadside attractions are amusing, but **Confusion Hill** (✉ *75001 U.S. 101* ☎ *707/925–6456* ⊕ *www.confusionhill.com*) takes the cake. Built for mid-century road-trippers, this mysterious spot is home to the "gravity house," the "chipalope," and the world's tallest freestanding redwood chainsaw carving.

Detour: The well-maintained Victorian town of Ferndale is so picturesque that it has shown up in a number of movies and TV shows, including 1995's *Outbreak* and 2001's *The Majestic*. It's also got a spectacular hillside cemetery as creepy as it is lovely. You'll find Ferndale a 10-mile drive toward the coast from Highway 101.

EUREKA

Do: The entire town of Eureka has been named a historic landmark, but the best-preserved blocks are located in Old Town. Explore the neighborhood on foot and don't forget to check out the **Carson Mansion** (✉ *143 M St.* ☎ *707/443–5665* ⊕ *www.ingomar.org*), considered one of the grandest Victorian homes in the United States.

Eat & Drink: The sophisticated yet unstuffy **Humboldt Bay Provisions** (✉ *205 G St.* ☎ *707/672–3850* ⊕ *www.humboldtbayprovisions.com*) deals in fresh local oysters and handcrafted cheeses, meats, breads, and desserts. For a more laid-back meal, hit the **Lost Coast Brewery Taproom** (✉ *1600 Sunset* ☎ *707/267–9651* ⊕ *www.lostcoast.com*), where they've got a menu full of sandwiches, salads, and appetizers along with some of the best beer in town.

Stay: Get your own slice of Victorian heaven with a night's stay at the historic **Carter House Inn** (✉ *301 L St.* ☎ *800/404–1390* ⊕ *www.carterhouse.com*).

Breakfast: Fill up on breakfast favorites like French toast, biscuits and gravy, and eggs Benedict at the **Greene Lily Cafe** (✉ *307 2nd St.* ☎ *707/798–6083* ⊕ *www.thegreenlilycafe.com*).

Day 8: Eureka, CA, to Brookings, OR

106 miles (2 hours, 10 minutes without traffic or stops)

Bouncing back and forth from coast to forest, today's drive takes you north through Redwood National and State Parks and over the Oregon state border.

ALONG THE WAY

Nature: Redwood National and State Parks (☎ 707/464–6101 ⊕ www.nps.gov/redw) are a collection of protected spaces stretching almost 50 miles from Crescent City to Orick, California. Walk among the giant redwood trees in Jedediah Smith Redwoods, visit lush Fern Canyon in Prairie Creek Redwoods, and watch the Roosevelt elk graze near Gold Bluffs Beach.

Eat & Drink: Fill up on sandwiches, soups, and salads at the **Log Cabin Diner** (✉ 301 Rte. 169 ☎ 707/482–0400) in Klamath, California. After lunch, say hello to the emus that live next door.

Town: Stop in at Crescent City, California, to check out the beautiful **Battery Point Lighthouse** (✉ 235 Lighthouse Way ☎ 707/464–3089 ⊕ www.delnortehistory.org), one of the oldest on the West Coast. In town, you'll find plenty of shops and galleries to peruse as well as cafés and restaurants.

BROOKINGS

Do: The redwoods and coastal views don't stop at the Oregon border. In Brookings, take a hike along the **Oregon Redwoods Trail** (☎ 541/247–3600 ⊕ www.fs.usda.gov) and admire the rock formations rising out of Lone Ranch Beach.

Eat & Drink: Indulge in seafood at local favorite, the **Pacific Sushi & Grill** (✉ 613 Chetco Ave. ☎ 541/251–7707 ⊕ www.pacifisushi.com). At the **Oxenfre Public House** (✉ 631 Chetco Ave. ☎ 541/813–1985 ⊕ www.oxenpub.com), a

gastropub serving local organic food late into the night.

Stay: Wake up with a view of the Pacific at the comfortable and modern **Beachfront Inn** (✉ 16008 Boat Basin Rd. ☎ 541/469–7779 ⊕ www.beachfrontinn.com).

Breakfast: Get pancakes and other classic breakfast dishes at the rustic diner **Mattie's Pancake House** (✉ 15975 U.S. 101 ☎ 541/469–7211).

Day 9: Brookings, OR, to Newport, OR

205 miles (4 hours, 15 minutes without traffic or stops)

The Oregon Coast pulls out all the stops today as you head north from Brookings, through the fishing town of Bandon, past the Oregon Dunes National Recreation Area, and on to Newport.

ALONG THE WAY

Town: Once a major fishing hub on the Oregon Coast, Bandon now caters more to tourists with fun shops, harborside eats, and a cheese-producing creamery, **Face Rock** (✉ 680 2nd St. SE ☎ 541/347–3223 ⊕ www.facerockcreamery.com).

Eat & Drink: Nosh on award-winning fish tacos, Dungeness crab rolls, and local oysters at the no-frills **Tony's Crab Shack** (✉ 155 1st St. SE ☎ 541/347–2875 ⊕ www.tonyscrabshack.com) by the water in Bandon.

Photo Op: The rocky coastline in Cape Perpetua forms delightful natural fountains and churns at the Spouting Horn and Thor's Well.

NEWPORT

Do: See otters and fish endemic to this region of the Pacific at the **Oregon Coast Aquarium** (✉ 2820 S.E. Ferry Slip Rd. ☎ 541/867–3474 ⊕ www.aquarium.org) or walk along the town's historic bayfront where seafood processing has been ongoing for over 100 years. At the northern end of town, the **Yaquina Head Lighthouse** (✉ *750 N.W. Lighthouse Dr.* ☎ *541/574–3100* ⊕ *www.blm.gov*) stands tall above Nye Beach's long stretch of sand.

Eat & Drink: Splurge on a dinner of seafood prepared with unique international flavors at **Local Ocean** (✉ *213 S.E. Bay Blvd.* ☎ *541/574–7959* ⊕ *www.local-ocean.net*), then head to the historic local dive, the **Bay Haven Inn** (✉ *608 S.W. Bay Blvd.* ☎ *541/265–7271*). Before going in, stop across the street to visit the colony of sea lions that post up at the harbor.

Stay: Let the sounds of the sea lull you to sleep at the **Ocean House Bed & Breakfast** (✉ *4920 N.W. Woody Way* ☎ *541/265–3888* ⊕ *www.oceanhouse.com*) at Nye Beach or enjoy a stay at the **Whaler** (✉ *155 S.W. Elizabeth St.* ☎ *541/272–3630* ⊕ *www.whalernewport.com*), a cozy motel with ocean views and a private balcony in every room.

Breakfast: The hole-in-the-wall **Cafe Stephanie** (✉ *411 N.W. Coast St.* ☎ *541/265–8082* ⊕ *www.facebook.com/nyebeach-cafestephanie*) serves an excellent daily breakfast menu with options like quiche, crepes, and breakfast burritos.

Day 10: Newport, OR, to Astoria, OR

133 miles (3 hours without traffic or stops)

Highway 101 sweeps inland today, passing through the outer edge of Tillamook State Forest before heading back to the coast and the site where Lewis and Clark first saw the Pacific. The day's drive ends in Astoria, a port town and one of the stars of 1985's *The Goonies*.

ALONG THE WAY

Eat & Drink: Brake for some cheese (and a tour) at the **Tillamook Creamery** (✉ *4165 N. Hwy. 101* ☎ *503/815–1300* ⊕ *www.tillamook.com*) in Tillamook. The on-site café sells multiple iterations of mac and cheese along with pizza, sandwiches, and ice cream.

Town: Go for a stroll along Cannon Beach, a wide swath of golden sand punctuated by massive monoliths, including the 235-foot-tall Haystack Rock.

ASTORIA

Do: Learn about Lewis and Clark's epic adventure to discover the West in the early 19th century and peek inside their winter shelter, Fort Clatsop, at the **Lewis & Clark National Historic Park** (✉ *92343 Fort Clatsop Rd.* ☎ *503/661–2471* ⊕ *www.nps.gov/lewi*). In town, Goonies fans will get a kick out of the **Oregon Film Museum** (✉ *732 Duane St.* ☎ *503/325–2203* ⊕ *www.oregon-filmmuseum.org*), while aficionados of architecture and design will enjoy the **Flavel House Museum** (✉ *714 Exchange St.* ☎ *503/325–2203* ⊕ *www.astoriamu-seums.org*).

Eat & Drink: Astoria's food-and-drink scene is best known for its seafood and beer, both of which you can find tasty versions of at the **Buoy Beer Company** (✉ *1 8th St.* ☎ *503/325–4540* ⊕ *www.buoybeer.com*). For a quick and hearty meal, head to takeaway-only **Bowpicker Fish & Chips**, housed in a converted boat (✉ *1634 Duane St.* ☎ *503/791–2942* ⊕ *www.bowpicker.com*).

Stay: Find modern elegance for a song at the boutique **Hotel Elliot** (✉ *357 12th St.* ☎ *503/325–2222* ⊕ *www.hotele-lliott.com*) or check in at the stylish **Selina Commodore Hotel** (✉ *258 14th St.* ☎ *786/485–0498* ⊕ *www.selina.com*), a historic property downtown.

Breakfast: Delicious breads and seasonal, organic breakfast dishes are made fresh daily at the worker's collective, the **Blue**

Scorcher Bakery & Cafe (✉ *1493 Duane St.* ☎ *503/338–7473* ⊕ *www.bluescorcher.coop*).

Day 11: Astoria, OR, to Olympic National Park, WA

132 miles (2 hours, 45 minutes without traffic or stops)

Take in the last of the ocean views on your last day driving the coast. Then cross over the Washington border and head north to Lake Quinault in Olympic National Park.

ALONG THE WAY

Town: In the industrial harbor town of Aberdeen, Washington, you'll find several homages to Kurt Cobain, who grew up here in the 1970s and 1980s. See memorials to the musician above and below the bridge in Kurt Cobain Memorial Park and get a look at his **childhood home** (✉ *1210 E. 1st St.*).

Eat & Drink: Have a pint alongside high-quality gastropub fare at the more-than-a-century-old **8th Street Ale House** (✉☎ *207 8th St.* ☎ *360/612–3455* ⊕ *www.8thstreetalehouse.com*) in Hoquiam.

Detour: It's about a 15-minute drive from the fork in the road north of Gray's Harbor City to Ocean Shores, a well-loved summer vacation spot with an endless beach.

OLYMPIC NATIONAL PARK

Do: Although you won't be able to see the entirety of **Olympic National Park** (☎ *360/565–3130* ⊕ *www.nps.gov/olym*), a place that covers more than a million acres of diverse landscape, you can explore its lower reaches. Head for Lake Quinault, where you can swim, fish, or boat in the lake or hike the Quinault Rain Forest Trail.

Eat & Drink: Dine on the delights of the Pacific Northwest at **The Salmon House Restaurant** (✉ *516 S. Shore Rd.* ☎ *360/288–2535* ⊕ *www.rainforestresort.com*) at the Rainforest Resort. Their menu includes house-smoked salmon, steak, pasta, and selections from their full bar.

Stay: A perfect remnant of mid-century Americana, the waterfront **Lake Quinault Lodge** (✉ *345 S. Shore Rd.* ☎ *888/896–3818* ⊕ *www.olympicnationalparks.com*) has a wide lawn set with Adirondack chairs, outdoor games, and a swimming dock. Or find camping nearby at the **Falls Creek Campground** (✉ *S. Shore Rd.* ☎ *360/288–0203* ⊕ *www.recreation.gov*).

Breakfast: Grab breakfast with a view of the lake in the Lake Quinault Lodge's Roosevelt Room.

Day 12: Olympic National Park, WA, to Seattle, WA

154 miles (2 hours, 45 minutes without traffic and stops)

On the last day of your road trip, backtrack to Aberdeen, then head east through the state capital of Olympia and then north on I–5 to the bustling city of Seattle.

ALONG THE WAY

Town: Make a stop in the Washington state capital, Olympia, for a tour of the legislature and supreme court or check out the **Monarch Sculpture Park** (✉ *8431 Waldrick Rd. SE* ☎ *360/264–2408* ⊕ *www.monarchsculpturepark.org*) and its many outdoor works of art. If you're traveling with kids, they'll get a kick out of the **Hands On Children's Museum** (✉ *414 Jefferson St. NE* ☎ *360/956–0818* ⊕ *www.hocm.org*).

Eat & Drink: Order an oh-so-satisfying sandwich or salad at the popular **Lucky Lunchbox** (✉ *2826 Capitol Blvd. SE* ☎ *360/259–8164* ⊕ *www.theluckylunchbox.com*) in Olympia.

SEATTLE

Do: Whether it's your first time in Seattle or your 100th, the city's greatest hits—including the delicate sculptures at the **Chihuly Garden & Glass Museum** (✉ 305 Harrison St. ☎ 206/753–4940 ⊕ www. chihulygardenandglass.com), the bustling seafood market **Pike Place** (✉ 85 Pike St. ☎ 206/682–7453 ⊕ www.pikeplace-market.org), and the famed **Space Needle** (✉ 400 Broad St. ☎ 206/905–2100 ⊕ www.spaceneedle.com)—never get old. Options a little farther off the beaten track include a visit to the Fremont Troll, the **Museum of Pop Culture** (✉ 325 5th Ave. N ☎ 206/770–2700 ⊕ www.mopop.org), and the interconnecting tunnels of the **Seattle Underground** (✉ 102 Cherry St. ⊕ www. undergroundtour.com).

Eat & Drink: Seattle's food scene is nothing short of fantastic. Find excellent Latin American and Cuban food at **Mojito** (✉ 7545 Lake City Way NE ☎ 206/525–3162 ⊕ www.mojitoseattle.com), masterful Indian at Pioneer Square's **Nirmal's** (✉ 106 Occidental Ave. S ☎ 206/683–9701 ⊕ www.nirmalseattle.com), and fresh seafood at **Matt's in the Market** (✉ 94 Pike St. ☎ 206/467–7909 ⊕ www. mattsinthemarket.com). Sip martinis and more at **Bathtub Gin & Co.** (✉ 2205 2nd Ave. ☎ 206/728–6069 ⊕ www. bathtubginseattle.com), an unpretentious basement speakeasy in Belltown.

Stay: Get an affordable night's stay at the colorful, art-accented **Maxwell Hotel** (✉ 300 Roy St. ☎ 206/286–0629 ⊕ www. staypineapple.com) at the base of Queen Anne Hill. The **Alexis Royal Sonesta Hotel** (✉ 1007 1st Ave. ☎ 206/624–4844 ⊕ www.sonesta.com) epitomizes the aesthetic of the Pacific Northwest, with contemporary style and a palette of marine blues and forest greens.

Breakfast: Start the day off with a comforting spread from **Fat's Fried Chicken and Waffles** (✉ 2726 E. Cherry St. ☎ 206/602–6863 ⊕ www.fatschickenandwaffles.com).

Essential Listening

Grunge may not be king in Seattle anymore, but Washington state still has a special place in its heart for Nirvana and the album that brought them into the mainstream, *Nevermind*.

The Best of Northern California

Written by Shoshi Parks

Northern California is among the country's most spectacular regions, as you'll surely see if you follow this drive. This itinerary takes you from San Francisco and the Napa Valley to Lake Tahoe and Yosemite National Park, and then on to Monterey Bay. In between the dramatic Pacific coastline to the west and the rugged Sierra Nevada to the east, you'll find three major cities, incredible ecological diversity, and some of the best wine regions in the world.

At a Glance

Start: San Francisco, CA

End: San Jose, CA

Miles Traveled: 880 miles

Suggested Duration: 9 days

States Visited: California

Key Sights: Golden Gate Bridge; Lake Tahoe; Napa Valley; Winchester Mystery House; Yosemite National Park

The Best of
Northern California

Best Time to Go: Thanks to Northern California's mild Mediterranean climate, this trip is just as enjoyable in the dead of winter as it is in the heat of summer.

Day 1: San Francisco, CA, to Bodega Bay, CA

53 miles (1 hour, 30 minutes without traffic and stops)

Your first day takes you from the San Francisco Airport north on Highway 101 and into the city of San Francisco. After seeing the sights, drive down Park Presidio and cross the majestic Golden Gate Bridge. Continue north through Marin, then head west to Tomales Bay and Bodega Bay just beyond.

ALONG THE WAY

Town: San Francisco is worth a full day of exploration (or more), but if you're just passing through on the way to Bodega Bay, you can still do a quick circuit of some of the city's greatest hits. Check out the old-school Italian neighborhood North Beach, Coit Tower, and the cable cars on Russian Hill, or visit Mission Dolores, the painted ladies of NoPa and Haight Street, and scenic **Golden Gate Park** (☎ 415/831–2700 ⊕ www.sfrecpark. org).

Eat & Drink: San Francisco is hands down one of the best food cities in the country. In the North Beach area, try pizza from a 13-time world champion at **Tony's Pizza Napoletana** (✉ 1570 Stockton St. ☎ 415/835–9888 ⊕ www.tonyspiz-zanapoletana.com). For hearty Mexican fare, head to **Taquería El Farolito** in the

Mission (✉ 2779 Mission St. ☎ 415/824–7877 ⊕ www.elfarolitosf.com). Over in NoPa, check out **Che Fico Alimentari** (✉ 834 Divisadero St. ☎ 415/416–6980 ⊕ www.cheficoalimentari.com), a nationally renowned Italian salumeria.

Photo Op: There's no better photo op than the Golden Gate Bridge, especially when the fog rolls through in the afternoon. Pull over at the **Golden Gate Bridge Vista Point** (⊕ www.goldengatebridge.org) on its northern side for the best view.

Detour: Cross to the western side of Tomales Bay near the adorable town of Point Reyes Station for a visit to **Point Reyes National Seashore** (☎ 415/464–5137 ⊕ www.nps.gov/pore), where there are miles of beach, hiking trails that weave among herds of endangered Tule elk, and a historic lighthouse.

BODEGA BAY

Do: Rent a kayak and hit the water or take a tour with **Blue Waters Kayaking** (✉ 11401 Rte. 1 ☎ 415/669–2600 ⊕ www.bluewaterskayaking.com) after dark for a chance at seeing glowing bioluminescence in Tomales Bay. If you prefer to stay on dry land, try your hand at shucking the area's famous oysters at the rustic-hip **Hog Island Oyster Farm** (✉ 20215 Shoreline Hwy. ☎ 415/663–9218 ⊕ www.hogislandoysters.com) in Marshall (reservations recommended).

Eat & Drink: The no-frills **Marshall Store** (✉ 19225 Rte. 1 ☎ 415/246–9306 ⊕ www.themarshallstore.com) has fantastic raw and barbecued oysters, not to mention rolls piled high with Dungeness crab. For a more extensive meal of fresh local seafood and farm-fresh produce, continue up the road to **Nick's Cove** (✉ 23240 Rte. 1 ☎ 415/663–1033 ⊕ www.nickscove.com), a historic roadhouse that's a destination in itself.

Stay: Spend the night in the beautifully renovated bayside cottages at Nick's Cove or head up the road to **The Lodge at Bodega Bay** (✉ 103 Rte.

1 ☎ 707/875–3525 ⊕ www.lodgeatbodegabay.com), a comfortable hotel with sweeping views of the shoreline.

Breakfast: Feast on crab cakes and a view at **Spud Point Crab Co.** (✉ 1910 Westshore Rd. ☎ 707/875–9472 ⊕ www.spudpointcrabco.com) or grab coffee and a bagel at **Roadhouse Coffee** (✉ 1580 Eastshore Rd.), both in Bodega Bay.

Day 2: Bodega Bay, CA, to Napa, CA

42 miles (1 hour without traffic and stops)

Drive east on Adobe Road over the hills and into Sonoma County. Spend some time in historic downtown Petaluma, then continue east through the famed vineyards of Napa Valley on Routes 116 and 121.

ALONG THE WAY

Town: In Petaluma, you'll find a fetching historic downtown rife with Victorian-era homes, boutiques, and antiques stores. For a self-guided walking tour, stop in at the **Petaluma Visitors Center** (✉ 210 Lakeville St. ☎ 707/769–0429 ⊕ www.visitpetaluma.com).

Eat & Drink: While in town, stop for lunch at Petaluma's cozy riverside **Wild Goat Bistro** (✉ 6 Petaluma Blvd. N ☎ 707/658–1156 ⊕ www.wildgoatbistro.com) or the **Tea Room Cafe** (✉ 316 Western Ave. ☎ 707/765–0199 ⊕ www.tearoomcafe.com), a sweet bakery where breakfast and sandwiches are served all day.

Roadside Attraction: Tour one of the best-preserved early-19th-century adobes left in California at the **Petaluma Adobe State Historic Park** (✉ 3325 Adobe Rd. ☎ 707/762–4871 ⊕ www.parks.ca.gov), which was once the seat of an agricultural empire owned by General Mariano Guadalupe Vallejo.

The Golden Gate Bridge is perhaps California's most recognizable landmark.

NAPA

Do: Wine taste the day away in the vineyards of Napa Valley. It would take you weeks to get through even just the best of the best, but you can't go wrong with the mid-century modern vibes of **Ashes & Diamonds** (⊠ *4130 Howard La.* ☎ *707/666–4777* ⊕ *www.ashesdiamonds.com*), the French château–inspired sparkling purveyor **Domaine Carneros** (⊠ *1240 Duhig Rd.* ☎ *707/257–0101* ⊕ *www.domainecarneros.com*), picturesque **Bouchaine Vineyards** (⊠ *1075 Buchli Station Rd.* ☎ *707/252–9065* ⊕ *www.bouchaine.com*), and style-drenched **Clos du Val** (⊠ *5330 Silverado Trail* ☎ *707/261–5212* ⊕ *www.closduval.com*).

Eat & Drink: Nibble on Spanish tortillas, smoky garlic shrimp, and paella at downtown Napa's tapas restaurant **Zuzu** (⊠ *829 Main St.* ☎ *707/224–8555* ⊕ *www.zuzunapa.com*), or head a few miles north to Santa Helena for pork chops, cioppino, and burrata at **Longmeadow Ranch's Farmstead Restaurant** (⊠ *738 Main St.* ☎ *707/963–4555* ⊕ *www.longmeadowranch.com*).

Stay: Stay the night in Napa's glamorous boutique **Archer Hotel** (⊠ *1230 1st St.* ☎ *707/690–9800* ⊕ *www.archerhotel.com*) or check in at the somewhat more affordable but equally lovely **Blackbird Inn** (⊠ *1755 1st St.* ☎ *707/226–2450* ⊕ *www.blackbirdinnnapa.com*) or **Cedar Gables Inn B&B** (⊠ *486 Coombs St.* ☎ *707/224–7969* ⊕ *www.cedargablesinn.com*).

Breakfast: Find a mouthwatering breakfast of Benedicts, griddle cakes, and flatbreads at the farm-style **Boon Fly Cafe** (⊠ *4048 Sonoma Hwy.* ☎ *707/299–4870* ⊕ *www.boonflycafe.com*).

Day 3: Napa, CA, to Sacramento, CA

113 miles (1 hour, 15 minutes without traffic and stops)

Today's drive heads east through the rich agricultural lands of the northern Central Valley and into the state capital, Sacramento.

ALONG THE WAY

Town: Davis, home to one of the University of California campuses, is a weird and wonderful haven rooted within the rural farmlands of the Central Valley. Perhaps not surprisingly, some of the best things to do here are plant-and-animal-based. Take a peaceful walk through the **UC Davis Arboretum and Public Garden** (✉ 448 La Rue Rd. ☎ 530/752–4880 ⊕ www.arboretum.ucdavis.edu), visit hawks and owls at the **California Raptor Center** (✉ 1340 Equine La. ☎ 530/752–6091 ⊕ www.crc.cetmed.ucdavis.edu), or learn about pollinators at the **UC Davis Honey Bee Haven** (✉ Bee Biology Rd. ☎ 530/867–9429 ⊕ www.beegarden.ucdavis.edu).

Eat & Drink: There are plenty of affordable eats in Davis, including *poke* and sushi burritos at **Good Friends Hawaiian Poke** (✉ 400 G St. ☎ 530/231–5537) and tacos at **Taqueria Davis** (✉ 505 L St. ☎ 530/758–8453 ⊕ www.taqueriadavis.com).

SACRAMENTO

Do: In recent years, California's state capital has finally come into its own as a city worth spending some time in. While here, get a look at the city's past at the **Old Sacramento State Historic Park** (✉ 111 I St. ☎ 916/445–7387 ⊕ www.parks.ca.gov) on the banks of the Sacramento River. The **Crocker Art Museum** (✉ 216 O St. ☎ 916/808–7000 ⊕ www.crockerart.org) near the waterfront has an impressive collection of work from artists throughout California and beyond.

Eat & Drink: Sacramento has some excellent Asian eateries, including the Vietnamese/Thai **Lemon Grass Restaurant** (✉ 601 Munroe St. ☎ 916/486–4891 ⊕ www.lemongrassrestaurant.com) and **Kru Contemporary Japanese Cuisine** (✉ 3135 Folsom Blvd. ☎ 916/551–1559 ⊕ www.krurestaurant.com). For authentic Mexican fare with a plant-based twist, head to **El Cantaro Vegan Taqueria** (✉ 9123 Kiefer Blvd. ☎ 916/898–2691). After dinner, you'll find creative cocktails at the mid-century-evoking **Ten Ten Room** (✉ 1010 10th St. ☎ 916/272–2888 ⊕ www.tentenroom.com) or the vintage dive **B-Side** (✉ 1430 S St. ☎ 916/706–1830 ⊕ www.b-sidesacramento.com).

Stay: The sophisticated **Kimpton Sawyer Hotel** (✉ 500 J St. ☎ 916/545–7100 ⊕ www.sawyerhotel.com) comes with a third-floor pool deck and cocktail lounge while the modern **The Exchange** (✉ 1006 4th St. ☎ 916/931–3300 ⊕ www.hilton.com) downtown has a rooftop restaurant-bar.

Breakfast: Breakfast with the locals at the bizarrely wonderful diner **Pancake Circus** (✉ 2101 Broadway ☎ 916/452–3322 ⊕ www.pancakecircus.net).

Essential Listening

Get the lowdown on wine culture with an audiobook of *Cork Dork: A Wine-Fueled Adventure Among the Obsessive Sommeliers, Big Bottle Hunters and Rogue Scientists Who Taught Me to Live for Taste* by Bianca Bosker.

Day 4: Sacramento, CA, to Tahoe City, CA

113 miles (2 hours without traffic and stops)

Head into the foothills of the Sierra Nevada Mountains and through some of the earliest gold-mining camps in the state. At Truckee, where the Donner Party infamously overwintered in 1846, turn south onto U.S. 89. It will take you all the way to the shores of Lake Tahoe.

ALONG THE WAY

Town: A mining camp during California's mid-19th-century gold rush, Auburn's carefully restored Old Town is a blast from the past outfitted with restaurants, boutiques, and a fantastic old firehouse. In the **Placer County Historical Museum** (✉ 101 Maple St. ☎ 530/889–6500 ⊕ www.placer.ca.gov) inside the monumental Placer County Courthouse, get a look at the raw gold that made Northern California known around the world.

Eat & Drink: In Auburn, fill up on grown-up pub fare and beer at the craft brewery **Auburn Alehouse** (✉ 289 Washington St. ☎ 530/885–2537 ⊕ www.auburnalehouse.com) or enjoy Texas-style barbecue at the **Smokey Pit** (✉ 160 Harrison Ave. ☎ 530/889–9080 ⊕ www.smokeypitbarbeque.com).

Nature: Stop for a hike at legendary Donner Lake in Truckee, where the Donner Party resorted to cannibalism to survive a brutal winter stuck in the Sierra Nevada Mountains. In **Donner Memorial State Park** (✉ 12593 Donner Pass Rd. ☎ 530/582–7892 ⊕ www.parks.ca.gov), you'll find a monument to those early settlers and the mellow 2½-mile round-trip Lakeshore Interpretive Trail.

TAHOE CITY

Do: For those who love the outdoors, Tahoe is a world-class playground in both summer and winter. In the winter months, rent yourself some skis or a snowboard and head to **Northstar** (✉ 5001 Northstar Dr. ☎ 530/562–2267 ⊕ www.northstarcalifornia.com) or **Palisades Tahoe** (✉ 2600 Alpine Meadows Rd. ☎ 800/403–0206 ⊕ www.palisadestahoe.com). In summer, hike, kayak, or get some sun at Kings Beach. Floating down the Truckee River in an inner tube is an unbeatable way to spend a hot afternoon.

Eat & Drink: Dig into pizzas and wings at **Front Street Station Pizza** (✉ 205 W. River Rd. ☎ 530/583–3770 ⊕ www.frontstreetpizzaca.com) or go highbrow at **Wolfdale's Cuisine Unique** (✉ 640 N. Lake Blvd. ☎ 530/583–5700 ⊕ www.wolfdales.com), a lake-view restaurant with surf-and-turf delights like seared bay scallops and lingcod.

Stay: Stay the night amid the modern mountain stylings of **Basecamp Tahoe City** (✉ 955 N. Lake Blvd. ☎ 530/580–8430 ⊕ www.basecamphotels.com), or find panoramic views of the lake at **Sunnyside Lodge** (✉ 1850 W. Lake Blvd. ☎ 530/583–7200 ⊕ www.sunnysidelodge.com).

Breakfast: Wake up to breakfast burritos and Benedicts at the adorable **Fire Sign Cafe** (✉ 1785 W. Lake Blvd. ☎ 530/583–0871 ⊕ www.firesigncafe.com).

Day 5: Tahoe City, CA, to Murphys, CA

148 miles (3 hours, 15 minutes without traffic and stops)

Skirt along the western side of Lake Tahoe on U.S. 89 then head west on Route 88 to Route 49, the scenic Golden Chain Highway. From there you'll head south through historic gold rush towns, stopping for the night in Murphys, a charismatic village populated with wineries, boutiques, and restaurants.

ALONG THE WAY

Nature: Before leaving Tahoe, stop at Emerald Bay, one of the most beautiful areas of the lake. Hike to the bottom of the hill to see **Vikingsholm** (☎ 530/525–9530 ⊕ www.vikingsholm.com), a castle built on the lake's shore in the 1920s. For a fun adventure, rent a kayak and paddle out to the lake's only island, Fanette, where the ruins of a teahouse used by the castle's mistress still remain.

Town: In Jackson, one of the deepest gold mines in the world is also one of the last where the original mill still remains. See the inner workings of the **Kennedy Gold Mine** (✉ *12594 Kennedy Mine Rd.* ☎ *209/223–9542* ⊕ *www.kennedygoldmine.com*) on a guided tour or walk the self-guided trail on your own.

Eat & Drink: Fill up on everything from prime rib to deep-fried pickles at **Brickhouse Brews** (✉ *140 Main St.* ☎ *209/223–3580* ⊕ *www.facebook.com/BrickhouseBrews*) in Jackson.

MURPHYS

Do: Many of the historic towns in Gold Country are cute, but Murphys takes the cake. Before strolling around town, hit one of the many local wineries, starting with **Ironstone Vineyards** (✉ *1894 6 Mile Rd.* ☎ *209/728–1251* ⊕ *www.ironstonevineyards.com*) just a few minutes down Route 4. On a tour through the nearby **Mercer Caverns** (✉ *1665 Sheep Ranch Rd.* ☎ *209/728–2101* ⊕ *www.mercercaverns.net*), you can get a glimpse of what Calaveras County looks like from under the earth.

Eat & Drink: For such a small town, Murphys has a surprising number of fantastic eateries. Find an unexpected pairing of authentic Mexican and classic Italian dishes at **Gabby's Cuisine** (✉ *260 Jones St.* ☎ *209/813–7043* ⊕ *www.gabbscuisinemurphys.com*), carefully crafted seared mahimahi and lamb shank at **Alchemy** (✉ *191 Main St.* ☎ *209/728–0700* ⊕ *www.alchemymurphys.com*), and Vietnamese favorites at the **Asian Cafe** (✉ *64 Mitchler St.* ☎ *209/728–8898*).

Stay: Spend the night at the romantic **Victoria Inn** (✉ *402 Main St.* ☎ *209/728–8933* ⊕ *www.victoriainn-murphys.com*) or at the clean and comfortable **Murphys Inn Motel** (✉ *76 Main St.* ☎ *209/728–1818* ⊕ *www.murphysinnmotel.com*).

Breakfast: Grab breakfast at **Grounds Restaurant** (✉ *402 Main St.* ☎ *209/728–8663* ⊕ *www.groundsrestaurant.com*), where the coffee is fresh and the waffles are fluffy.

Day 6: Murphys, CA, to Yosemite National Park, CA

67 miles (1 hour, 30 minutes without traffic and stops)

From Murphys continue down the Gold Chain Highway to its terminus at Yosemite Junction. From there, you'll travel east on Route 120 all the way to one of the country's most stunning national parks.

ALONG THE WAY

Town: Columbia State Historic Park (✉ *22708 Broadway St.* ☎ *209/588–9128* ⊕ *www.parks.ca.gov*), a re-created gold-mining village about 20 miles south of Murphys, is kitschy fun, and the old-timey candy shop is not to be missed.

Eat & Drink: Stop by Columbia's historic **St. Charles Saloon** (✉ *22801 Main St.* ☎ *209/288–2258* ⊕ *www.stcharlessaloon.com*) for a pint and the best pizza in town.

Photo Op: In Groveland, don't miss the oldest continuously operating saloon in the state, the **Iron Door** (✉ *18761 Main St.* ☎ *209/962–8904* ⊕ *www.irondoorsaloon.com*).

YOSEMITE NATIONAL PARK

Do: Take in the sights by car or lace up your boots and hit the trails and head to **Yosemite National Park** (☎ *209/372–0200* ⊕ *www.nps.gov.yose*). Yosemite Valley is where you'll find the park's most famous landmarks, including Bridalveil Fall, Half Dome, and El Capitan, but if you're traveling in the summer, the sights along Tioga Road are just as spectacular (and less crowded).

Eat & Drink: Casual eats can be found at several spots around Yosemite Valley, including the **Curry Village Pizza Deck** (✉ *9010 Curry Village Dr.* ⊕ *www.travelyosemite.com*) and the **Village Grill** (✉ *Yosemite National Park Rd.* ☎ *209/372–0200* ⊕ *www.travelyosemite.com*). For more upscale dining, check out **The Mountain Room** in the Yosemite Valley Lodge (✉ *9006 Yosemite Lodge Dr.* ☎ *888/413–8869* ⊕ *www.travelyosemite.com*) or **The Ahwahnee Dining Room** (✉ *1 Ahwahnee Dr.* ☎ *209/372–1489* ⊕ *www.travelyosemite.com*).

Stay: If you have the gear, car camping or even backpacking in Yosemite is well worth the effort. You'll have to make a reservation if you want to stay in a campground, but wilderness permits to camp in the backcountry are readily available. If you'd prefer a comfortable bed, try the elegant Ahwahnee or the more affordable **Yosemite Valley Lodge** (✉ *9006 Yosemite Lodge Dr.* ☎ *888/413–8869* ⊕ *www.travelyosemite.com*).

Breakfast: Coffee and light bites are available at **Degnan's Kitchen** (✉ *9015 Village Dr.* ☎ *888/413–8869* ⊕ *www.travelyosemite.com*) in Yosemite Village and **Base Camp Eatery** (✉ *9006 Yosemite Lodge Dr.* ☎ *888/413–8869* ⊕ *www.travelyosemite.com*) in the Yosemite Valley Lodge.

Day 7: Yosemite National Park, CA, to Half Moon Bay, CA

174 miles (3 hours, 15 minutes without traffic and stops)

On your longest drive of the road trip, today you'll shoot straight west out of the Sierras, through the Central Valley and back into the Bay Area. Cross the San Mateo–Hayward Bridge over the San Francisco Bay and continue to the Pacific coast and the town of Half Moon Bay.

ALONG THE WAY

Town: Around Livermore, you'll find an under-the-radar wine region known for its Chardonnay, Sauvignon Blanc, and Petite Sirah. Among the best local wineries are **Page Mill Winery** (✉ *1960 S. Livermore Ave.* ☎ *925/456–7676* ⊕ *www.*

pagemillwinery.com), **McGrail Vineyards and Winery** (✉ *5600 Greenville Rd.* ☎ *925/215–0717* ⊕ *www.mcgrailvineyards.com*), and **BoaVentura de Caires Winery** (✉ *9309 Tesla Rd.* ☎ *925/606–9672* ⊕ *www.boaventuravineyard.com*).

Eat & Drink: Soak up the wine with a big bowl of ramen or udon at **Kiseki** (✉ *1510 N. Vasco Rd.* ☎ *925/292–9664* ⊕ *www.eatkiseki.com*) in Livermore, or stop in San Mateo across the bay for Filipino pork knuckles and beef *salpicao* at **Avenida Restaurant** (✉ *201 E. 3rd Ave.* ☎ *650/781–3637* ⊕ *www.avenidarestaurant.net*).

Detour: Before crossing the bay, take a detour to the vibrant city of Oakland. Picnic at Lake Merritt, visit the shops along Temescal Alley or Piedmont Avenue, and visit the always innovative **Oakland Museum of California** (✉ *1000 Oak St.* ☎ *510/318–8400* ⊕ *www.museumca.org*).

HALF MOON BAY

Do: Separated from the core of Silicon Valley by rolling hills, the beach enclave of Half Moon Bay remains quiet and surprisingly idyllic. Here you can ride horses on the beach with **Sea Horse Ranch** (✉ *1828 Cabrillo Hwy. N* ☎ *650/726–9903* ⊕ *www.seahorseranch.org*), surf the waves at world-famous Mavericks, and relax on the sand at **Gray Whale Cove State Beach** (☎ *650/726–8819* ⊕ *www.parks.ca.gov*).

Eat & Drink: Almost anywhere you go in Half Moon Bay, seafood is on the menu. Try the famous chowder beachside at **Sam's Chowder House** (✉ *4210 Rte. 1* ☎ *650/712–0245* ⊕ *www.samschowderhouse.com*), or gorge on cioppino and fried scallops at the **Flying Fish Grill** (✉ *211 San Mateo Rd.* ☎ *650/712–1125* ⊕ *www.flyingfishgrill.net*).

Stay: Let the sound of the ocean lull you to sleep at the **Beach House** at Half Moon Bay (✉ *4100 Cabrillo Hwy. N* ☎ *650/712–0220* ⊕ *www.beach-house.com*) or the

Cypress Inn on Miramar Beach (✉ *407 Mirada Rd.* ☎ *650/726–6002* ⊕ *www. cypressinn.com*). Or if you don't mind a splurge, you can hobnob with celebrities at the glamorous **Ritz-Carlton Half Moon Bay** (✉ *1 Miramontes Point Rd.* ☎ *650/712–7000* ⊕ *www.ritzcarlton. com*).

Breakfast: Start your morning with crepes from **Mavericks Creperie** (✉ *146 San Mateo Rd.* ☎ *650/713–5298* ⊕ *www. maverickscreperie.com*).

Day 8: Half Moon Bay, CA, to Monterey, CA

90 miles (2 hours without traffic and stops)

Travel south along the Pacific Coast Highway. The ocean will be your quiet companion most of the way to Monterey.

ALONG THE WAY

Photo Op: The **Pigeon Point Light Station** (✉ *210 Pigeon Point Rd.* ☎ *650/879– 2120* ⊕ *www.parks.ca.gov*) in Pescadero has kept its lonely watch over this section of the Pacific coast since 1872.

Town: Ride one of the country's oldest wooden roller coasters, the Giant Dipper, at Northern California's last remaining beachside amusement park, the **Boardwalk** (✉ *400 Beach St.* ☎ *831/423– 5590* ⊕ *www.beachboardwalk.com*) in Santa Cruz.

Eat & Drink: While in Santa Cruz, fuel up on food-truck fare and beer from local favorite **Humble Sea Brewing Co.** (✉ *820 Swift St.* ☎ *831/621–2890* ⊕ *www.hum-blesea.com*); you can watch the surfers hang ten as you eat.

Nature: Hike to a magical sea cave on Fern Grotto Beach (or along any number of other trails) at **Wilder Ranch State Park** (✉ *1401 Coast Rd.* ☎ *831/423–9703* ⊕ *www.parks. ca.gov*) on Highway 1.

Essential Listening

Listen to *Cannery Row*, John Steinbeck's novel about workers in the sardine factories that once formed the economic backbone of Monterey. Or if you're a *Big Little Lies* fan, make sure you listen to the televison show's haunting theme song "Cold Little Heart" by Michael Kiwanuka as you approach the coastal town.

MONTEREY

Do: Rent a bike and ride the waterfront Monterey Bay Coastal Trail, hunt for starfish and sea urchin in the tide pools at **Asilomar State Beach** (✉ *Sunset Dr.* ☎ *831/646–6440* ⊕ *www.parks. ca.gov*), tour the boardwalk-like Cannery Row, or go whale-watching. Though the tickets are costly, the **Monterey Bay Aquarium** (✉ *886 Cannery Row* ☎ *831/648– 4800* ⊕ *www.montereybaysquarium.org*) is not to be missed.

Eat & Drink: Dig into a heaping plate of Italian-style seafood at **Monterey's Fish House** (✉ *2114 Del Monte Ave.* ☎ *831/373–4647* ⊕ *www.monterey-fishhouse.com*) or old-school surf and turf at the eccentric **Sardine Factory** (✉ *701 Wave St.* ☎ *831/373–3775* ⊕ *www. sardinefactory.com*) near Cannery Row. Late night, sip cocktails over the fire pit at the **Pearl Hour** (✉ *214 Lighthouse Ave.* ☎ *831/657–9447* ⊕ *www.pearl-hour.com*) or craft beer at downtown's **Alvarado Street Brewery** (✉ *426 Alvarado St.* ☎ *831/655–2337* ⊕ *www.asb.beer*).

Stay: Just a few steps from Cannery Row, the renovated **Wave Street Inn** (✉ *571 Wave St.* ☎ *831/375–2299* ⊕ *www. wavestreetinnmonterey.com*) has a comfortable coastal vibe. Down the bluff in Pacific Grove, you can spend the night overlooking the bay in the gorgeous Victorian **Seven Gables Inn** (✉ *555 Ocean View Blvd.* ☎ *831/372–4341* ⊕ *www. thesevengablesinn.com*).

Breakfast: Housed in a historic adobe downtown, the buzzy **Alta Bakery** (✉ *502 Munras Ave.* ☎ *831/920–1018* ⊕ *www. altamonterey.com*) makes incredible coffee, breakfast pastries, and breads.

Day 9: Monterey, CA, to San Jose, CA

72 miles (1 hour, 20 minutes without traffic and stops)

On the last day of your road trip, you'll retrace your steps up the coast to Santa Cruz then cut through redwoods that tower over the Santa Cruz Mountains on winding Route 17. Over the hill, stop in swanky Los Gatos before traveling on to San Jose. The airport and its rental car agencies are conveniently located near the city's central core.

ALONG THE WAY

Town: Located at the base of the Santa Cruz Mountains, Los Gatos is as cute as they come. Stroll past the shops and eateries of North Santa Cruz Avenue, stopping anywhere that catches your fancy.

Eat & Drink: While in Los Gatos, lunch on mango red curry and spicy eggplant basil at the Asian-fusion restaurant **Golden Triangle Cuisine** (✉ *217 N. Santa Cruz Ave.* ☎ *408/402–5092* ⊕ *goldentrianglecuisine.weebly.com*). If you need a caffeinated or sugary pick-me-up, stop by **Manresa Bread** (✉ *276 N. Santa Cruz Ave.* ☎ *408/402–5372* ⊕ *www.manresabread.com*), the accessible bakery offshoot of a Michelin-starred restaurant in town.

SAN JOSE

Do: In massive, sprawling San Jose, there are a wide variety of museums, parks, and oddities to keep you occupied. Take a tour of the bizarre **Winchester Mystery House** (✉ *525 S. Winchester Blvd.* ☎ *408/247–2000* ⊕ *www.winchestermysteryhouse.com*), explore modern art at the **San Jose Museum of Art** (✉ *110 S. Market St.* ☎ *408/271–6840* ⊕ *www.sjmusart.org*) or the smaller but more cutting-edge **Institute of Contemporary Art** (✉ *560 S. 1st St.* ☎ *408/283–8155* ⊕ *www.icasanjose. org*), or hike through the ghost town of a mercury-mining settlement at **Almaden Quicksilver County Park** (✉ *21785 Almaden Rd.* ☎ *408/268–3883* ⊕ *www.sccgov. org*).

Eat & Drink: Find a wide range of tasty, affordable eats at the downtown **San Pedro Square Market** (✉ *87 N. San Pedro St.* ⊕ *www.sanpedrosquaremarket. com*), gourmet Mexican fusion at Willow Glen's **Zona Rosa** (✉ *1411 The Alameda* ☎ *408/275–1411* ⊕ *www.zonarosadining.com*), or flavorful Ethiopian at **Walia Ethiopian Cuisine** (✉ *2208 Business Circle* ☎ *408/645–5001* ⊕ *www.waliaethiopian.com*). Celebrate your last night on the road with cocktails from the **Haberdasher** (✉ *43 W. San Salvador St.* ☎ *408/792–7356* ⊕ *www.haberdashertogo.com*).

Stay: Spend your final night at the storied **Hotel De Anza by Hyatt** (✉ *233 W. Santa Clara St.* ☎ *408/286–1000* ⊕ *www.hyatt. com*) downtown or the sophisticated hacienda-style **Hotel Valencia Santana Row** (✉ *355 Santana Row* ☎ *855/596–3396* ⊕ *www.hotelvalencia-santanarow. com*).

Breakfast: Have a farewell breakfast of tri-tip and hash or French toast at the **Park Station Hashery** (✉ *1701 Park Ave.* ☎ *408/320–1711* ⊕ *www.parkstationhashery.com*).

The Best of Central and Southern California

Written by Amber Gibson

This eight-day road trip from Big Sur to San Diego spans some of California's most breathtaking landscapes, navigating from forests to beaches and deserts, all while driving down the Pacific Coast Highway with unobstructed views of the dramatic coastline below. Along the way, taste luscious wines in Paso Robles and Santa Barbara and experience big-city living in Los Angeles and San Diego. This region of the country marks the ideal balance between urban and rural, adventure and relaxation, simplicity and luxury.

At a Glance

Start: Monterey, CA

End: San Diego, CA

Miles Traveled: 900 miles

Suggested Duration: 8 days

States Visited: California

Key Sights: Big Sur; Joshua Tree National Park; Pebble Beach; San Diego Zoo; Santa Monica Pier

Best Time to Go: The weather in Southern California is great year-round, but Joshua Tree and Palm Springs can get mighty hot in summer.

Day 1: Monterey, CA, to Big Sur, CA

40 miles (1 hour, 20 minutes without traffic and stops)

Rent a car from one of the half-dozen car-rental providers located at Monterey Regional Airport (if you'd rather fly direct, San Jose International Airport is about an hour and 20 minutes from Monterey).

Enjoy a leisurely hour-long drive along the coast through Andrew Molera State Park and Julia Pfeiffer Burns State Park.

ALONG THE WAY

Detour: Relish the scenic 17-mile drive through Pebble Beach, best known for its championship golf courses, raw white beaches, and rugged coastal cliffs. Admission is $10.50 per vehicle, but the fee is reimbursed with a $35 purchase at Pebble Beach Resorts restaurants. The gates are open to the public from sunrise to sunset.

Town: Clint Eastwood was once mayor of Carmel-by-the-Sea, where he legalized ice-cream cones, although high heels are still verboten without a permit from city hall. The quirky seaside town is home to art galleries aplenty and storybook cottages.

BIG SUR

Do: Between **Julia Pfeiffer Burns State Park** (✉ *52801 Rte. 1* ☎ *831/667–1112* ⊕ *www.parks.ca.gov*) and **Andrew Molera State Park** (✉ *45500 Rte. 1* ☎ *831/667–2315* ⊕ *www.parks.ca.gov*), there are dozens of hikes you can take to discover secluded coves, rushing waterfalls, and blossoming meadows. **Limekiln State Park** (✉ *63025 Rte. 1* ☎ *805/434–1996* ⊕ *www.parks.ca.gov*) is much smaller, but the abandoned limestone kilns and easy beach access make it worth a visit.

Eat & Drink: Big Sur Deli (✉ *47520 Rte. 1* ☎ *831/667–2225* ⊕ *www.bigsurdeli.com*) has been serving hearty sandwiches, salads, pastries, and deli staples for over three decades.

Stay: Deetjen's Big Sur Inn (✉ *48865 Rte. 1* ☎ *831/667–2377* ⊕ *www.deetjens.com*) was built in the 1930s and the cozy rooms and cabins are listed on the National Register of Historic Places. Guests are forced to unplug and focus on the surrounding nature—there are no TVs, Wi-Fi, or cell phone coverage on the property. If Internet and cell service are

The Best of Central and Southern California

a must, **Glen Oaks Big Sur** (✉ 47080 Rte. 1 ☎ 831/667–2105 ⊕ www.glenoaks-bigsur.com) has more modern amenities and an equally immersive atmosphere.

Breakfast: Enjoy a substantial meal of pancakes and huevos rancheros at the **Ripplewood Cafe** (✉ 47047 Rte. 1 ☎ 831/667–2242 ⊕ www.ripplewoodresort.com).

Day 2: Big Sur, CA, to Paso Robles, CA

140 miles (2 hours, 30 minutes without traffic and stops)

Cruise along the legendary Pacific Coast Highway in the lane closest to the ocean, passing through Cambria and Cayucos before cutting inland at Morro Bay to Paso Robles.

ALONG THE WAY

Photo Op: Snap a pic of the opulent hilltop **Hearst Castle** (✉ 750 Hearst Castle Rd., San Simeon ☎ 800/444–4445 ⊕ www.hearstcastle.org) built by media magnate William Randolph Hearst, which is now a National Historic Landmark.

Eat & Drink: Stop by **Cambria Coffee Roasting Company** (✉ 761 Main St. ☎ 805/927–0670 ⊕ www.cambriacoffeesales.com) in Cambria to try meticulously brewed single-origin coffee from Central America. Farther south, get lunch at **Ruddell's Smokehouse** (✉ 101 D St. ☎ 805/995–5028 ⊕ www.smokerjim.com) in Cayucos, where they smoke their own oysters, salmon, and albacore tuna for tasty tacos with a beach view.

Town: Morro Bay is a sleepy, foggy beach town located on a natural harbor. It's popular with fishermen and surfers, although you'll want to rent a wet suit to catch waves in these cold waters. Visit Morro Rock Beach to see the famous volcanic stone that helped early sailors navigate the coast. Peregrine falcons, harbor seals, sea otters, and sea lions can often be spotted at this nature reserve.

PASO ROBLES

Do: There are more than 200 wineries in Paso Robles, including **Opolo Vineyards** (✉ 7110 Vineyard Dr. ☎ 805/238–9593 ⊕ www.opolo.com), which also has an adjacent distillery, and **Booker Vineyard** (✉ 2644 Anderson Rd. ☎ 805/237–7367 ⊕ www.bookerwines.com), where you can play bocce ball and escape the heat in underground wine caves. As the sun begins to set, head to **Sensorio** (✉ 4380 Rte. 46 ☎ 805/226–2497 ⊕ www.sensoriopaso.com), a multi-acre immersive art experience filled with over 100,000 color-changing lights.

Eat & Drink: Niner Wine Estates (✉ 2400 Rte. 46 ☎ 805/239–2233 ⊕ www.ninerwine.com) offer a full-service restaurant overlooking their Malbec and Cabernet Sauvignon vineyards. They also make their olive oil, sourdough focaccia, farmer's cheese, and ice cream in-house. Or pick up a picnic of dairy-free cheese and crackers at **The Vreamery** (✉ 1835 Spring St. ☎ 805/975–0052 ⊕ www.thevreamery.com).

Stay: Allegretto Vineyard Resort (✉ 2700 Buena Vista Dr. ☎ 805/369–2500 ⊕ www.allegrettovineyardresort.com) resembles an opulent Tuscan villa decorated with an amalgamation of globally inspired art and sculptures. Across its 20 acres, manicured Mediterranean gardens, grapevines, lavender plants, and olive trees thrive.

Breakfast: Spearhead Coffee (✉ 619 12th St. ☎ 805/296–3328 ⊕ www.spearheadcoffee.com) roasts its own beans, including a local whiskey-infused variety, and uses homemade syrups in its inventive lattes, like the Cortijo, sweetened with condensed milk and clove.

Day 3: Paso Robles, CA, to Santa Barbara, CA

130 miles (2 hours, 30 minutes without traffic and stops)

After a brief glimpse of the Pacific at Pismo Beach, take the 101 and cut across inland before ending back with ocean views in Santa Barbara.

ALONG THE WAY

Town: San Luis Obispo is an energetic college town that's the cultural and commercial hub of the Central Coast. Its dynamic downtown is easily walkable, with numerous local boutiques and public art installations along Higuera Street. The city's ambitious climate action plan includes becoming carbon neutral by 2035 and it's protected a 54,000-acre greenbelt around the city from development.

Eat & Drink: Load up on carbs at **Bob's Well Bread Bakery** (✉ 550 Bell St. ☎ 805/344–3000 ⊕ www.bobswellbread.com) in Los Alamos. The breads here, including baguettes and *pain au levain* for sandwiches, are all made with natural starters in old-world European traditions resulting in a satisfying crust and springy crumb.

Photo Op: The small village of Solvang is famous for its Danish-style architecture, including thatched-roof cottages and four wooden windmills.

SANTA BARBARA

Do: Known as the American Riviera, Santa Barbara invented the concept of an urban wine trail, with nearly 30 tasting rooms to choose from, concentrated in the Presidio and eclectic Funk Zone neighborhoods. **Au Bon Climat** (✉ 813 Anacapa St. ☎ 805/963–7999 ⊕ www.

aubonclimat.com) makes world-class Pinot Noir and Chardonnay while **Margerum Santa Barbara Tasting Room** (✉ *19 E. Mason St.* ☎ *805/845–8435* ⊕ *www.margerumwines.com*) has elegant Rhône blends and a standout food menu, too. For nondrinkers, **Los Padres Outfitters** (✉ *Asegra and Greenwell Ave.* ☎ *805/755–8687* ⊕ *www.lospadresoutfitters.com*) offers private guided horseback rides on the beach for all experience levels, allowing you to splash into the ocean along the cragged bluffs.

Eat & Drink: Secret Bao (✉ *1201 Anacapa St.* ☎ *805/259–3226* ⊕ *www.secretbaosb.com*) is a fun stop for fast-casual contemporary Korean food while vegetarian restaurant **Satellite SB** (✉ *1117 State St.* ☎ *805/364–3043* ⊕ *www.satellitesb.com*) has bountiful salads and toasts topped with Balsamic-smoked shiitake mushrooms and accompanied by an intriguing selection of natural wines. For dinner, share authentic Spanish tapas and heaping bowls of paella among friends at **Loquita** (✉ *202 State St.* ☎ *805/880–3380* ⊕ *www.loquitasb.com*). Don't skip the Basque cheesecake for dessert.

Stay: El Encanto, A Belmond Hotel (✉ *800 Alvarado Pl.* ☎ *805/845–5800* ⊕ *www.belmond.com*) is the grand dame of Santa Barbara's luxury resorts, originally opened in 1918 and later restored to its Spanish colonial revival glory, with bungalows tucked away amid 7 acres of lush gardens and bougainvillea-draped walls. Centrally located **Palihouse** (✉ *915 Garden St.* ☎ *805/564–4700* ⊕ *www.palisociety.com*) has a preppy vintage vibe and quaint courtyard. All 24 rooms at this boutique property have gas fireplaces, balconies or terraces, and a minibar well-stocked with local snacks.

Breakfast: Cajé Coffee Roasters (✉ *1316 State St.* ⊕ *www.caje.coffee*) has the best blended coffee drinks, smoothies, and acai bowls in town. For a taste of Paris, visit **Bree'osh** (✉ *2700 De La Vina St.* ☎ *805/770–2238* ⊕ *www.breeosh.*

com) in Montecito, run by a soigné French couple and serving exquisitely laminated croissants and *kouign-amann* (a sweet Breton cake).

Day 4: Santa Barbara, CA, to Los Angeles, CA

100 miles (2 hours without traffic and stops)

Meander along the coastline for a leisurely drive before heading east on I–10 to downtown Los Angeles.

ALONG THE WAY

Eat & Drink: Little Dom's Seafood (✉ *686 Linden Ave.* ☎ *805/749–7400* ⊕ *www.ldseafood.com*) in Carpinteria is the premier place for local seafood fresh from the docks, including live Santa Barbara *uni*, local halibut, and yellowfin tuna, freshly prepared with Ojai olive oil and vibrant Calabrese pepper sauce. Plus, pastry chef Ann Kirk makes the best biscotti this side of the Atlantic and incredible small-batch gelato. If you're in a hurry, the market next door has sandwiches, prepared salads, and Italian cookies to take away.

Photo Op: El Matador's powerful rock formations are a popular spot for engagement photos and coastline drone shots.

Town: Scores of A-list celebrities, from Julia Roberts to Lady Gaga, call Malibu home. Stretch your legs at one of the famous beaches, like Zuma Beach, where the original *Baywatch* was filmed.

LOS ANGELES

Do: The Broad (✉ *221 S. Grand Ave.* ☎ *213/232–6250* ⊕ *www.thebroad.org*) is one of L.A.'s finest museums, offering free general admission and rotating exhibitions of contemporary art. Golden hour at **Griffith Observatory** (✉ *2800 E. Observatory Rd.* ☎ *213/473–0800* ⊕ *www.griffithobservatory.org*) is the best vantage point for 360-degree views of the city, including the Hollywood Sign.

Eat & Drink: The patio at **Piccalilli** (✉ *3850 Main St.* ☎ *424/298–8450* ⊕ *www.piccalillila.com*) is a pleasant place for people-watching in Culver City, where you can enjoy miso pork jowl, smashed Szechuan cucumbers, and tomato curry with garlic naan. Los Angeles also has the best vegan food scene in the country, and **Pura Vita** (✉ *8274 Santa Monica Blvd.* ☎ *323/688–2303* ⊕ *www.puravitalosangeles.com*) in West Hollywood serves vegan Italian food that even carnivores love. The pizza, lasagna, arancini, and eggplant parmigiana are undeniably good, and great for the planet.

Stay: Hotel Figueroa (✉ *939 S. Figueroa St.* ☎ *213/627–8971* ⊕ *www.hotelfigueroa.com*) first opened in 1926 as a safe haven for solo female travelers who couldn't check into most hotels without a male chaperone. Today the hotel continues to champion local women in the arts, and the notorious coffin-shaped pool is a cheeky nod to burying the patriarchy. **JW Marriott Los Angeles L.A. LIVE** (✉ *900 W. Olympic Blvd.* ☎ *213/765–8600* ⊕ *www.marriott.com*) is a great hotel for families, located next to the Staples Center, with spacious rooms and a lively rooftop pool. **Downtown L.A. Proper** (✉ *100 S. Broadway* ☎ *213/806–1010* ⊕ *www.properhotel.com*) is the coolest new property in downtown, with a Mexican modernism–inspired design by Kelly Wearstler and restaurants by L.A. dining doyennes Suzanne Goin and Caroline Styne.

Breakfast: Aussie all-day café **Strings of Life** (✉ *609 N.W. Knoll Dr.* ☎ *424/313–8136* ⊕ *www.sol-losangeles.com*) in West Hollywood combines the best of both worlds: specialty coffee and chef-driven food. Crispy potato cake with smoked salmon, mango coconut chia pudding, and fluffy omelets are a few breakfast favorites.

Day 5: Los Angeles, CA, to Palm Springs, CA

152 miles (2 hours, 30 minutes without traffic and stops)

Hit the road early to maximize your time in Joshua Tree National Park, then trace your route back to Palm Springs, where you'll spend the night.

ALONG THE WAY

Roadside Attraction: Life-size dinosaurs Dinny the Brontosaurus and Mr. Rex are visible from the freeway as you pass through **Cabazon** (✉ *50770 Seminole Dr.* ☎ *909/272–8164* ⊕ *www.cabazondinosaurs.com*). The surrounding open-air museum includes robotic dinosaurs, gemstone and fossil panning, and a gift shop inside Dinny's belly.

Eat & Drink: Coachella Valley produces more than 90% of the dates grown in the United States, and **Shields Date Garden** (✉ *80-225 Rte. 111* ☎ *760/347–0996* ⊕ *www.shieldsdategarden.com*) is a great place to sample them all: golden Zahidi dates, amber-color Halawi dates, firm Deglet Noor dates, and soft caramel-like Medjool dates. Try the supersweet date milkshake and pick up an assortment to go—they're the perfect road trip and hiking snack.

Nature: Enter **Joshua Tree National Park** (☎ *760/367–5500* ⊕ *www.nps.gov/jotr*) through the less crowded south entrance off I-10 east of Indio. You can see a lot just driving through, including Joshua trees galore, molten magma monoliths, and the cholla cactus garden. If you have the time and stamina, there are hundreds of granite rock formations for rock climbing and bouldering, too. Cell phone service is weak, so consider picking up a physical map at the Cottonwood Visitor Center before wandering off to explore the desert scenery.

Did You Know?

Found only in Arizona, California, Nevada, and Utah, the Joshua tree (*Yucca brevifolia*) is actually a member of the agave family. Native Americans used the Joshua tree's hearty foliage like leather, forming it into everyday items like baskets and shoes. Later, early settlers used its core and limbs for building fences to contain their livestock.

PALM SPRINGS

Do: The **Palm Springs Aerial Tramway** (✉ *1 Tram Way* ☎ *760/325–1391* ⊕ *www. pstramway.com*) offers spectacular views of the entire valley along Chino Canyon to Mt. San Jacinto State Park from the world's largest rotating tram car. The 10-minute ride brings you up to 8,516 feet with restaurants, a natural history museum, and more than 50 miles of hiking trails.

Eat & Drink: Visit **Copley's** on Palm Canyon (✉ *621 N. Palm Canyon Dr.* ☎ *760/327– 9555* ⊕ *www.copleypalmsprings.com*) for a romantic dinner alfresco on Cary Grant's former estate. **Wildest Restaurant & Bar** (✉ *72990 El Paseo* ☎ *760/636– 0441* ⊕ *www.wildestrestaurant.com*) has creative vegan options like sautéed king oyster mushroom "scallops" along with excellent seafood and grass-fed steaks.

Stay: The intimate bungalows at adults-only **L'Horizon Palm Springs** (✉ *1050 E. Palm Canyon Dr.* ☎ *760/323– 1858* ⊕ *www.lhorizonpalmsprings.com*) are a quintessential example of the mid-century modern architecture that Palm Springs is famous for. Geometric tiled courtyards at **Villa Royale** (✉ *1620 S. Indian Trail* ☎ *760/327–2314* ⊕ *www. villaroyale.com*), beloved by movie stars during Hollywood's golden age, burst with color and raw desert beauty. The **Ritz-Carlton Rancho Mirage** (✉ *68900 Frank Sinatra Dr.* ☎ *760/321–8282* ⊕ *www. ritzcarlton.com*) is a family-friendly option with the most luxurious spa in Palm Springs and fantastic hiking right on the property.

Breakfast: Breakfast at **Cheeky's** (✉ *622 N. Palm Canyon Dr.* ☎ *760/327– 7595* ⊕ *www.cheekysf10.com*) is practically a rite of passage in Palm Springs, thanks to its bacon bar and hangover-halting mimosas.

Day 6: Palm Springs, CA, to Santa Monica, CA

130 miles (2 hours, 30 minutes without traffic and stops)

The drive today isn't too long if you make sure to avoid peak traffic times. Just be sure to arrive in Santa Monica in time for sunset on the pier.

ALONG THE WAY

Town: Claremont is the most endearing small town between the desert and Los Angeles. You can play hundreds of unique instruments from around the globe at musician Ben Harper's **Folk Music Center** (✉ *220 Yale Ave.* ☎ *909/624– 2928* ⊕ *www.folkmusiccenter.com*) and wander across 86 acres of native California plants at the **California Botanic Garden** (✉ *1500 N. College Ave.* ☎ *909/625– 8767* ⊕ *www.calbg.org*).

Eat & Drink: Destroyer (✉ *3578 Hayden Ave.* ☎ *310/360–3860* ⊕ *www.destroyer. la*) in Culver City is the more casual sister restaurant to avant-garde fine-dining Vespertine, with elevated breakfast fare like buttery smoked cod on Icelandic seeded rye bread and sunchoke sourdough waffles with creamed kale and country ham. Sip a sweet-potato latte and grab a pastry from the case to go.

SANTA MONICA

Do: An afternoon at the **Santa Monica Pier** (✉ *200 Santa Monica Pier* ☎ *310/458– 8900* ⊕ *www.santamonicapier.org*) will bring you back to the 1920s, when the Pleasure Pier and its amusement park attractions thrived. Take a ride on the historic merry-go-round and the world's only solar-powered Ferris wheel, or sign up for trapeze school if you're feeling daring. Download the Secret Story Tour app and solve digital puzzles while unlocking secrets from the pier's past.

Eat & Drink: Pasjoli (✉ *2732 Main St.* ☎ *424/330–0020* ⊕ *www.pasjoli.com*) is a sophisticated bistro that transports you to Paris, imbuing the freshest local California produce with precise French technique. Dishes range from delicate blue crab and poached rhubarb to signature pressed duck straight from Escoffier's culinary bible, an indulgence for two that must be ordered in advance.

Stay: Many of the guest rooms at **Viceroy Santa Monica** (✉ *1819 Ocean Ave.* ☎ *310/260–7500* ⊕ *www.viceroy-hotelsandresorts.com*) offer panoramic Pacific Ocean views and marble bathrooms featuring luxury toiletries from ROIL and Natura Bissé. Reserve one of six open-air cabanas in advance for poolside rest and relaxation. Just down the road, reduce your energy consumption at eco-friendly **Shore Hotel** (✉ *1515 Ocean Ave.* ☎ *310/458–1515* ⊕ *www.shorehotel.com*), a LEED-Gold-certified hotel with a solar-reflecting roof and heated swimming pool powered by solar energy. Finally, the historic **Fairmont Miramar Hotel & Bungalows** (✉ *101 Wilshire Blvd.* ☎ *310/576–7777* ⊕ *www.fairmont.com*) has been a pied-à-terre for Hollywood royalty for a century—Greta Garbo even lived here for four years.

Breakfast: Urth Caffe Santa Monica (✉ *2327 Main St.* ☎ *310/314–7040* ⊕ *www.urthcaffe.com*) serves organic coffee, fresh pastries, and hearty breakfast staples, with plenty of clearly labeled plant-based and gluten-free options available.

Day 7: Santa Monica, CA, to Laguna Beach, CA

70 miles (2 hours without traffic and stops)

Be sure to check the traffic before departing today. Highway 1 is usually significantly slower, but with prettier ocean views than if you cut inland on I–405. Both routes are a straight shot to Laguna Beach.

ALONG THE WAY
Eat & Drink: Dog Haus Biergarten (✉ *7811 Edinger Ave., Huntington Beach* ☎ *714/894–4287* ⊕ *bellaterra.doghaus.com*) has a good selection of beer on draft and serves German-style sausages, burgers, hot dogs, and plant-based meats on slightly sweet King's Hawaiian rolls.

Town: Newport Beach has plenty to offer to nature lovers, shopaholics, and the young at heart. **Crystal Cove State Beach** (✉ *8471 N. Coast Hwy.* ☎ *949/494–3539* ⊕ *www.crystalcovestatepark.org*) is one of the more pristine and rustic beaches in Orange County, with an underwater park for scuba divers and snorkelers. **Fashion Island** (✉ *401 Newport Center Dr.* ☎ *949/721–2000* ⊕ *www.fashionisland.com*) is Orange County's premier luxury shopping center, and **Balboa Fun Zone** (✉ *600 E. Bay Ave.* ☎ *949/675–8915* ⊕ *www.ocfunzone.com*) has been a family favorite since the 1930s, with a nautical museum, arcade games, whale-watching, and chocolate-dipped ice-cream Balboa Bars.

LAGUNA BEACH
Do: Explore the tide pools at Crescent Bay Beach, Rockpile Beach, and Thousand Steps to discover colorful marine life including anemones, hermit crabs, and sea stars. Main Beach and Treasure Island are some of the most easily accessible tide pools in the area. You'll want to visit at low tide and keep an eye on the swell. Sea kayaking is another way to get up close with ocean critters in the protected Laguna Beach State Marine Preserve.

Eat & Drink: Choose from a huge range of ingredients, from shrimp tempura to bamboo shoots, to create your own ramen or udon bowl at **Gu Ramen Taps and Tapas** (✉ *907 S. Coast Hwy.* ☎ *949/715–0825* ⊕ *www.guramen.com*). The "tapas" options served here run the gamut, from cream cheese wontons to Japanese-style deviled eggs.

Stay: Nestled in the Aliso and Wood Canyons, **The Ranch at Laguna Beach** (✉ *31106 Coast Hwy.* ☎ *949/499–2271* ⊕ *www.theranchlb.com*) is all about laid-back luxury, with a 9-hole golf course and access to Aliso Beach via a pedestrian walkway, where you can relax under turquoise umbrellas and roast s'mores by beach bonfires at night. Sustainability is core to their mission; in order to lower their carbon footprint, they compost, crush glass bottles to fill bunkers, use reclaimed water for irrigation, and more.

Breakfast: Blk Dot Coffee (✉ *656 N. Coast Hwy.* ☎ *949/371–0288* ⊕ *www.blkdot-coffee.com*) is a fun stop for breakfast and Vietnamese coffee, including unique specialty drinks like iced sea salt foam–topped coffee and the Vietnamese Tiger, gussied up with brown sugar syrup and black jelly.

Day 8: Laguna Beach, CA, to San Diego, CA

70 miles (1 hour, 40 minutes without traffic and stops)

This gorgeous drive down the coastline on Historic Highway 101 is short and scenic, past Camp Pendleton and on to San Diego.

ALONG THE WAY

Town: Sea walls divide the series of small sandy beaches that line Carlsbad, a town with fun for the whole family, including prestigious golf courses, hidden lagoons, delicious eats at the **Windmill Food Hall** (✉ *890 Palomar Airport Rd.* ☎ *760/214–9127* ⊕ *www.windmillfoodhall.com*), and **LEGOLAND** (✉ *1 Legoland Dr.* ☎ *888/690–5346* ⊕ *www.legoland.com*) for the kids.

Shop: Enjoy health-conscious shopping at **One Paseo** (✉ *3725 Paseo Pl.* ☎ *858/523–2298* ⊕ *www.onepaseo.com*) in Del Mar, an outdoor development featuring chic homegrown brands like Shop Good for clean beauty, Roark for outdoorsy menswear, and Pigment for home decor and flora.

SAN DIEGO

Do: Torrey Pines Gliderport (✉ *2800 Torrey Pines Scenic Dr.* ☎ *858/452–9858* ⊕ *www.flytorrey.com*) is the largest tandem flight center in the country, and all ages and physical abilities can soar like a bird above the seaside cliffs in a peaceful tandem flight. If you prefer to see the mighty Pacific by sea, book a leisurely sunset cruise with **San Diego Sailing Tours** (✉ *1450 Harbor Island Dr.* ☎ *619/786–0173* ⊕ *www.sandiegosailingtours.com*) and see the historic vessels at the Maritime Museum up close. And, of course, be sure to pay a visit to Balboa Park and the famous **San Diego Zoo** (✉ *2920 Zoo Dr.* ☎ *619/231–1515* ⊕ *www.zoo.sandiegozoo.org*).

Eat & Drink: Addison (✉ *5200 Grand Del Mar Way* ☎ *858/314–1900* ⊕ *www.addisondelmar.com*) is the most glamorous fine-dining experience in town, and the tasting menu will surprise you with novel dishes like white asparagus ice cream drizzled with extra-virgin olive oil. **Ironside Fish & Oyster** (✉ *1654 India St.* ☎ *619/269–3033* ⊕ *www.ironsidefishandoyster.com*) is another delicious pick for fresh local seafood including peel 'n' eat Baja shrimp, rockfish ceviche, roasted yellowtail collar, and ruby-red bigeye tuna filets. Save room for dessert at **Stella Jean's Ice Cream** (✉ *4404 Park Blvd.* ☎ *619/501–8252* ⊕ *www.stella-jeans.com*), where scoops of colorful mango sticky rice, *ube pandesal* toffee, and matcha pistachio await.

Stay: Fairmont Grand Del Mar (✉ *5300 Grand Del Mar Ct.* ☎ *858/314–2000* ⊕ *www.fairmont.com*) is a sprawling Mediterranean estate with opulent Spanish, Venetian, and Moroccan architecture, a glamorous courtyard pool, golf, tennis, pickleball, and beds so comfortable you'll never want to get up. The gardens at hacienda-style **Estancia La Jolla** (✉ *9700 N. Torrey Pines Rd.* ☎ *855/430–7503* ⊕ *www.meritagecollection.com*) are filled with stylish succulents and host live musical performances.

Breakfast: The cacao waffle topped with coconut yogurt at **Parakeet Cafe** (✉ *1680 India St.* ☎ *619/255–1442* ⊕ *www.parakeetcafe.com*) is a decadently sweet way to start your day; there's also *shakshuka* with *labneh* or chilaquiles if you're looking for something savory.

California's National Parks

Written by Andrew Collins

From otherworldly desertscapes and soaring sequoias to eye-popping canyons and rocky islands, California contains some of the country's most celebrated national parks. You probably already know about the "bucket list" destinations like Yosemite and Death Valley, but on this journey north through inland California's Sierra Nevada mountain range and then back down along the state's breathtaking coastline, you'll also discover some of the park system's hidden treasures—underrated yet dazzling landscapes like Lassen Volcanic, Point Reyes, Pinnacles, and Channel Islands.

This itinerary covers a lot of ground, and you'll need at least 10 days to spend even a day at every park highlighted. If you're able to set aside two to three weeks, you'll be able to explore and appreciate the landscape more thoroughly.

At a Glance

Start: Los Angeles, CA

End: Los Angeles, CA

Miles Traveled: 2,300 miles

Suggested Duration: 10 days

States Visited: California

Key Sights: Bumpass Hell, Lassen Volcanic National Park; Generals Highway, Sequoia National Park; Keys View, Joshua Tree National Park; Newton B. Drury Scenic Highway, Redwood National and State Park; Yosemite Valley, Yosemite National Park

Best Time to Go: You can access parts of every California national park year-round, but the desert parks are better avoided during the sizzling hot June to August months, and access on some key park roads is limited in winter in Lassen Volcanic, Yosemite, and Sequoia and Kings Canyon.

Day 1: Los Angeles, CA, to Joshua Tree, CA

145 miles (3 hours without traffic and stops)

Grab your rental car at LAX, and then follow I–10 east to exit 117. Continue north on Route 62, which leads to the park's West Entrance, off Park Boulevard in the small town of Joshua Tree. This is a mostly prosaic freeway drive through suburbia, but Route 62 is a scenic and sometimes twisty route through Morongo Valley.

ALONG THE WAY

Town: The Coachella Valley's classic desert resort community—long famous with Hollywood folks and one of the country's top LGBTQIA+ destinations—Palm Springs is a popular gateway to Joshua Tree National Park, worth at least a short stop to stroll among its distinctive design shops, galleries, and eateries and maybe even to ride the thrilling **Palm Springs Aerial Tramway** (✉ *1 Tram Way* ☎ *760/325–1391* ⊕ *www.pstramway.com*), which carries passengers through Chino Canyon to an elevation of 8,516 feet, near the summit of Mt. San Jacinto.

Eat & Drink: Downtown Palm Springs pulses with inviting restaurants, many with sprawling patios cooled off on hot days by misting machines. One favorite is **Cheeky's** (⌧ *622 N. Palm Canyon Dr.* ☎ *760/327–7595* ⊕ *www.cheekysps.com*) for daily brunch and lunch, where you can order chilaquiles, buttermilk corn pancakes, and a "flight" of five types of bacon.

Shop: The Uptown Design District along North Palm Canyon Drive is a stretch of cool shops—including colorful **Trina Turk** (⌧ *891 N. Palm Canyon Dr.* ☎ *760/416–2856* ⊕ *www.trinaturk.com*) for swimwear and fashion, and 1950s-chic **The Shag Store** (⌧ *745 N. Palm Canyon Dr.* ☎ *760/322–3400* ⊕ *www.shagstore.com*) for art and housewares—specializing in the mid-century modern aesthetic for which Palm Springs is internationally famous.

JOSHUA TREE NATIONAL PARK

Do: An 800,000-acre expanse of the Mojave and Sonoran Deserts, **Joshua Tree National Park** (☎ *760/367–5500* ⊕ *www.nps.gov/jotr*) contains hundreds of the distinctive Joshua trees for which it is named. Joshua Tree's Park Boulevard extends for more than 50 miles through the park, and it's worth either starting or ending on this drive via the park's southeastern entrance off I-10. Must-sees that are easy to access from the main park road include the boulder-strewn paths around Skull Rock and the Jumbo Rocks Campground, and Hidden Valley and Cap Rock, which you can tour via easy loop trails dotted in places with Joshua trees. Be sure to make the 6-mile side drive to Keys View overlook, from which you can see the San Andreas Fault and the Salton Sea, and on clear days, the craggy mountain peaks of northern Mexico.

Eat & Drink: Near Yucca Valley, **Pappy & Harriet's Pioneertown Palace** (⌧ *53688 Pioneertown Rd., Pioneertown*

☎ *760/228–2222* ⊕ *www.pappyandharriets.com*) is located on an old Hollywood set that figured in dozens of movies in the 1940s and 1950s and is now an offbeat venue for watching live bands while eating stick-to-your-ribs burgers, steaks, and Tex-Mex fare. After dinner, stop to people-watch at retro-cool **The Virginian Cocktails** (⌧ *73643 Twentynine Palms Hwy.* ☎ *760/361–3050* ⊕ *www.facebook.com/virginiancocktails*).

Stay: If you stay in Palm Springs, consider one of the lodgings near the north end of town—which puts you a little closer to the park—such as stylish **Arrive Palm Springs** (⌧ *1551 N. Palm Canyon Dr.* ☎ *760/507–1650* ⊕ *www.arrivehotels.com*), with its chic vibe and an on-site ice-cream shop. Closer to the park, the funky, moderately priced **29 Palms Inn** (⌧ *73950 Inn Ave.* ☎ *760/367–3505* ⊕ *www.29palmsinn.com*) is set amid 70 acres of palm trees, with desert gardens, an art gallery, and a colorful restaurant.

Breakfast: Fuel your day at **JT Country Kitchen** (⌧ *61768 Twentynine Palms Hwy.* ☎ *760/366–8988* ⊕ *www.jtcountrykitchen.com*) in the town of Joshua Tree, a down-home diner where biscuits and gravy, breakfast burritos, French toast, and other breakfast treats are served all day.

Day 2: Joshua Tree, CA, to Death Valley, CA

240 miles (4 hours without traffic and stops)

The journey northward runs along both state highways and some unnumbered side roads, but all are paved and well-signed. Start in Twentynine Palms, turn north toward Baker via Amboy and Kelso, pick up Route 127 north to Death Valley Junction, and then take Route 190 west to the Furnace Creek area, in the heart of the park.

California's National Parks

ALONG THE WAY

Town: In tiny Shoshone, the **Crowbar Cafe & Saloon** (✉ *Old State Hwy. 127* ☎ *760/852–4123* ⊕ *www.shoshonevillage.com*) is filled with old mining paraphernalia and photos of the region, and is a colorful stop for enjoying flame-grilled rainbow trout, fish tacos, and other hearty western dishes.

Detour: There's not a lot to see or do—beyond soaking up the sweeping Mojave Desert vistas—along this remote route, but once you reach the town of Shoshone, about three hours into your drive, you have the option of accessing Death Valley via the southeastern route along Route 178 through stark yet desolately beautiful Badwater Basin. At 282 feet below sea level, this is the lowest point in the Western Hemisphere. As you continue north toward Furnace Creek, check out the dramatic rock formations at Natural Bridge and Devil's Golf Course. Traveling this route adds about an hour to the drive without stops.

DEATH VALLEY NATIONAL PARK

Do: At 5,270 square miles, **Death Valley** (☎ *760/786–3200* ⊕ *www.nps.gov.deva*) is the largest U.S. national park outside Alaska, and although its name hints at some of the hottest temperatures and most unforgiving terrain in the world, it's also a land of considerable diversity, with multicolored canyons, 11,000-foot peaks, undulating sand dunes, and fragrant wildflower meadows. Start with a drive along 9-mile Artist's Drive, admiring the brilliantly hued landscape, then continuing on to the rewarding 2-mile Golden Canyon Interpretive Trail. Next, check out Zabriskie Point, which takes in the park's dramatic, multihued hills, and Dante's View, a mile-high lookout in the Black Mountains from which you can see many of Death Valley's most remarkable features.

Eat & Drink: With its astounding valley views, the **Inn at Death Valley Dining Room** (✉ *Rte. 190* ☎ *760/786–2345* ⊕ *www. oasisatdeathvalley.com*) is the park's signature restaurant, serving innovatively prepared seasonal cuisine and refreshing prickly-pear margaritas.

Stay: Given how far Death Valley is from other cities, it's advisable to stay inside the park, which has a handful of options. It tends to book up early during busy periods, but the beautifully restored 1927 Inn at Death Valley is the most treasured of these. Offering simpler motel-style accommodations, **Stovepipe Wells Village Hotel** (✉ *51880 Rte. 190* ☎ *760/786–7090* ⊕ *www.stovepipedeathvalley. com*) is a more economical option with a peaceful location near striking Mesquite Flat Sand Dunes.

Breakfast: Located in Stovepipe Wells Village, **Panamint Springs Resort Restaurant** (✉ *40440 Rte. 190, Darwin* ☎ *775/482–7680* ⊕ *www.panamintsprings.com*) turns out a popular breakfast buffet and has an attractive patio with grand vistas of Panamint Valley.

Day 3: Death Valley, CA, to Sequoia and Kings Canyon, CA

325 miles (6 hours, 30 minutes without traffic and stops)

Because getting here entails a long drive, and Sequoia and Kings Canyon are actually two distinct but contiguous parks, it's worth developing a strategy before deciding on your exact route. Plan to spend one night in Kings Canyon's Grant Corner Village, arriving via Route 180 and limiting your time in Sequoia to the park's northern reaches.

ALONG THE WAY

Town: Bakersfield in California's Central Valley is a good place to break up today's journey. Highlights include an emerging Downtown Arts District and the **California Living Museum** (✉ *10500 Alfred Harrell*

Hwy. ☎ 661/872–2256 ⊕ www.calmzoo. org), which includes an exceptional zoo, botanical garden, and natural history museum.

Eat & Drink: An Italian grocery and restaurant that's been a fixture in Bakersfield since 1910, **Luigi's** *(⊠ 725 E. 19th St. ☎ 661/322–0926 ⊕ www.shopluigis. com)* remains a favorite place for big portions of hot-pastrami sandwiches, pasta Bolognese, and homemade cheesecake.

SEQUOIA AND KINGS CANYON NATIONAL PARKS

Do: These spectacular alpine parks each offer a different kind of landscape, with Sequoia all about the towering, ancient conifers—the world's largest trees—for which it's named, and Kings Canyon renowned for its sweeping alpine peaks and valleys. You can gain a real sense of Sequoia's awe-inspiring landscape by arriving on Route 198 through the Ash Mountain Entrance, and then climbing some 3,500 feet along Generals Highway where you can visit the engaging Giant Forest Museum, and stroll amid the sequoia trees in Round Meadow and along the Big Trees Trail. Other highlights include the famed 274.9-foot General Sherman Tree, which ranks among the world's oldest and highest trees, and climbing the stone steps to the scenic overlook from Moro Rock. To explore Kings Canyon, base yourself around Grant Grove Village with a short trek to Panoramic Point, a look at Grizzly Falls, and a stroll through magnificent Zumwalt Meadow, with its grand views of the Kings River and the Grand Sentinel and North Dome rock formations.

Eat & Drink: In Sequoia, **The Peaks Restaurant** inside Wuksachi Lodge *(⊠ 64740 Wuksachi Way ⊕ www.visitsequoia. com)* is famous for its giant fireplace and locavore-minded seasonal cuisine—reservations are essential. The top dining

Essential Listening

Driving through the sierras provides the perfect backdrop for listening to any of the several audiobooks by the preeminent 19th-century naturalist and oft-described "father of the national parks" system, John Muir, whose writings and conservation advocacy helped secure the designation of Sequoia and Yosemite National Parks. Great choices include *Our National Parks* and *Wilderness Essays.*

option in Kings Canyon, **Grant Grove Restaurant** *(⊠ 86728 Rte. 180 ☎ 866/807–3598 ⊕ www.visitsequoia.com)* has a large dining room overlooking expanses of sequoia trees; the kitchen turns out creative American cuisine with a focus on sustainable ingredients.

Stay: The lodging options in these parks are amazing thanks to their jaw-dropping designs, especially the grand, cedar-and-stone Wuksachi Lodge in Sequoia. The timber-frame **John Muir Lodge** *(⊠ 86728 Rte. 180 ☎ 866/807–3598 ⊕ www. visitsequoia.com)* in Kings Canyon has relatively simple rooms, but offers a bit of quiet away from the crowds of nearby Grant Grove Village.

Breakfast: Convenient options in the park include the aforementioned Grant Grove Restaurant in Kings Canyon, and the casual **Lodgepole Market, Deli, and Cafe** *(⊠ 63204 Lodgepole Rd. ☎ 559/565–3301 ⊕ www.visitsequoia.com)* in Sequoia.

Day 4: Sequoia and Kings Canyon, CA, to Yosemite, CA

150 miles (3 hours, 30 minutes without traffic and stops)

Take Route 180 west from Kings Canyon to Fresno, then follow Route 41 north, which leads directly to Yosemite's South Entrance and Wawona section.

ALONG THE WAY

Eat & Drink: The stylish **School House Restaurant & Tavern** (✉ *1018 S. Frankwood Ave.* ☎ *559/787–3271* ⊕ *www.schoolhousesanger.com*) in Sanger occupies a 1920s redbrick schoolhouse and turns out locally sourced fare, such as steak Cobb salads, spiced-lamb-and-beef burgers, and a house favorite: pear bread pudding with vanilla ice cream, candied walnuts, and fresh basil.

Town: In the heart of California's San Joaquin Valley, Fresno offers some standout attractions that make it worth a stop. Highlights include the fanciful grottoes and tunnels of **Forestiere Underground Gardens** (✉ *5021 W. Shaw Ave.* ☎ *559/271–0734* ⊕ *www.undergroundgardens.com*) and the considerable pre-Columbian Mesoamerican and Andean holdings of the **Fresno Art Museum** (✉ *2233 N. 1st St.* ☎ *559/441–4221* ⊕ *www.fresnoartmuseum.org*).

Photo Op: Inside the park, **Wawona Road** (✉ *Rte. 41*) continues north from the South Entrance up into Yosemite Valley. As you approach the valley, you'll pass through a tunnel, and the view as you emerge is mesmerizing.

YOSEMITE NATIONAL PARK

Do: One of the most celebrated landscapes in America, **Yosemite** (☎ *209/372–0200* ⊕ *www.nps.gov/yose*) ranges across nearly 1,200 square miles and could really be described as several parks in one. During a short stay, you can view the stands of imposing sequoia trees in Mariposa Grove in Wawona, which is the easiest area to access if coming from Fresno. And you can focus the rest of your time on the best-known sites of Yosemite Valley: admiring legendary El Capitan (the largest exposed-granite monolith on the planet), checking out the roaring triple cascades of 2,425-foot-tall Yosemite Falls, driving to the overlook atop Glacier Point for an astounding view of the valley, and embarking on one or two shorter hikes, such as the 3-mile Mist Trail to Vernal Fall or the 8.5-mile Panorama Trail from Glacier Point, which provides you terrific views of Half Dome. In summer, as you exit the park through the Eastern Entrance, you can drive the breathtaking 59-mile Tioga Road to Tuolumne Meadows and on to Lee Vining.

Eat & Drink: Dinner at the vaunted **Ahwahnee Dining Room** (✉ *1 Ahwahnee Dr.* ☎ *888/413–8869* ⊕ *www.travelyosemite.com*) is an unforgettable experience, where rarefied modern American cuisine is served beneath ornate chandeliers and a 34-foot ceiling.

Stay: Designed by Gilbert Stanley Underwood in the late 1920s, the grand stone-and-timber Ahwahnee is one of the country's singular national parks lodges. It's expensive and always booked well in advance, but it's absolutely worth the splurge. Outside the park, the town of Oakhurst has plenty of options, and you'll find some nifty lodgings in Groveland, Fish Camp, Mariposa, and other towns to the west as well.

Breakfast: Especially convenient if you're headed toward Tuolumne Meadows, the seasonal **White Wolf Lodge** (✉ *White Wolf Rd.* ☎ *888/413–8869* ⊕ *www.travelyosemite.com*) is a pleasingly rustic spot 30 miles northwest of Yosemite Valley, offering all-you-can-eat homestyle breakfasts.

Day 5: Yosemite, CA, to Lassen Volcanic, CA

281 miles (5 hours, 10 minutes without traffic and stops)

Although open only from around early June through late October, Yosemite's Eastern Entrance leads to the most scenic route to Lassen and allows you to explore Tuolumne Meadows. This route follows Route 120 east out of the park to the small town of Lee Vining, where you turn north on U.S. 395 and pass gorgeous Mono Lake, cutting up through Carson City and Reno, Nevada. U.S. 395 leads back into California, where you turn west in Susanville onto Route 36, which leads to Lassen's southern sections. The rest of the year, you'll have to leave Yosemite from the west, driving by way of Stockton via Routes 120 and 4. Then turn north on Route 99, continuing through Sacramento to Chico, and then following Route 32 to Route 36/89 west to the park's southerly Kohm Yah-mah-nee Visitor Center. These routes take roughly the same amount of time.

ALONG THE WAY

Nature: Not far from Yosemite's Eastern Entrance, Lee Vining is a cute, friendly village that's home to remote, enormous Mono Lake, with its eerie calcium-carbonate tufas (hoodoo-like rock formations), which you can get a better look at on free nature walks offered in summer through the **Mono Basin Scenic Area Visitor Center** (✉ *Lee Vining Creek Trail* ☎ *760/647–3044* ⊕ *www.fs.usda. gov*).

Eat & Drink: Many who pass through Reno give it no more than a quick look, perhaps taking in its glitzy skyline of neon-streaked casino towers, but "the biggest little city in the world" has a revitalized downtown with attractive promenades along the Truckee River and a number of excellent restaurants.

Old World Coffee Lab (✉ *104 California Ave.* ☎ *775/391–0189* ⊕ *www.oldworld-coffee.co*) is a hip stop for well-crafted espresso drinks and fresh bagels. Beside the river, **Sierra Street Kitchen and Cocktails** (✉ *50 N. Sierra St.* ☎ *775/686–6669* ⊕ *www.sierrastkitchen.com*) offers tasty internationally inspired tapas, creative sips, and live music some evenings.

LASSEN VOLCANIC NATIONAL PARK

Do: Although named for the now dormant plug volcano at its heart, which erupted dramatically in 1915, the 165-square-mile **Lassen Volcanic National Park** (☎ *530/595–4480* ⊕ *www.nps.gov/lavo*) is more diverse than its name suggests, offering miles of trails through dense alpine forests and wildflower meadows. The drive north along Lassen Park Highway is a gem, passing by the Devastated Area, which still shows evidence of the 1915 eruption, and leading to the gorgeous scenery around Manzanita Lake, where you can visit the excellent Loomis Museum and enjoy a stroll along the 1-mile Lily Pond Nature Trail. Other draws include the 3-mile round-trip Bumpass Hell Trail, which reveals some of the park's most exciting geothermal features, including steam vents, mud pots, and boiling lakes, and assuming you're fit for a 2,000-foot climb, undertaking the 2½-mile hike to the 10,457-foot summit of Lassen Peak.

Eat & Drink: Dining options in the park are limited, but the **Restaurant at Highlands Ranch Resort** (✉ *41515 Rte. 36 E, Mill Creek* ☎ *530/595–3388* ⊕ *www. highlandranchresort.com*), just outside the park's southern entrance, doles out sophisticated fare overlooking a pastoral meadow. You'll find a smattering of cafés and bars a bit east in the small town of Chester and larger community of Susanville, which is home to **Lassen Ale Works at the Boardroom** (✉ *702-000 Johnstonville Rd.* ☎ *530/257–4443* ⊕ *www.lassenaleworks.com*), a lively spot for gourmet pizza and distinctive craft beers.

Did You Know?

Found within Sequoia National Park, sequoias once grew throughout the northern hemisphere, until they were almost wiped out by glaciers. Some of the fossils in Arizona's Petrified Forest National Park are extinct sequoia species.

Stay: About 10 miles from the park's southern entrance, the upscale High-lands Ranch Resort is a standout for its plush bungalows, many with outdoor hot tubs. Inside the park, near the northern entrance, **Manzanita Lake Camping Cabins** (✉ *39489 Rte. 44, Shingletown* ☎ *530/779–0307* ⊕ *www.lassenlodging.com*) is a great, reasonably priced option comprising 20 rustic but handsome modern cabins.

Breakfast: In Chester, bright and cheerful **Cravings** (✉ *278 Main St.* ☎ *530/258–2229* ⊕ *www.facebook.com/chestercravings*) serves flavorful breakfast burritos and Belgian waffles.

Day 6: Lassen Volcanic, CA, to Redwood, CA

215 miles (4 hours without traffic and stops)

Redwood National Park comprises several different units spanning a 60-mile corridor from just above Trinidad north to Crescent City, almost to the Oregon border, with several key sites and visitor centers in between. From the Manzanita Lake section of Lassen, it's about 200 miles west via Routes 44 and 299. Then head north on U.S. 101 to reach the Thomas H. Kuchel Visitor Center, the southernmost in the park, before continuing north to explore the park.

ALONG THE WAY

Town: Redding is far Northern California's main hub, and it's worth a stop to visit its **Turtle Bay Exploration Park** (✉ *844 Sundial Bridge Dr.* ☎ *530/243–8850* ⊕ *www.turtlebay.org*), a highlight of which is the stunning Santiago Calatrava–designed Sundial Bridge, a metal-and-translucent-glass pedestrian walkway, suspended by cables from a single tower and spanning a broad bend in the Sacramento River.

Eat & Drink: The panorama from the patio and glass-walled dining room at **View 202** (✉ *202 Hemsted Dr.* ☎ *530/226–8439* ⊕ *www.view202redding.com*), which sits on a hilltop above the Sacramento River in Redding, takes in the snowcapped mountains in the distance. The modern American menu emphasizes grilled meats and fish from noted California purveyors but also includes bouillabaisse and homemade ravioli.

REDWOOD NATIONAL AND STATE PARKS

Do: Made up of both federal lands administered by the national park service and several state parks, the officially named **Redwood National Park and State Parks** (☎ *707/464–6101* ⊕ *www.nps.gov/redw*) is the definitive place to walk amid redwood trees, which can rise to more than 350 feet (they differ from sequoias in that they grow near the coast, and are taller but generally don't attain the same girth as their inland counterparts). The best place to spend the bulk of your time is the Prairie Creek Redwoods State Park section, which is just off U.S. 101. Here you can drive 10-mile Newton B. Drury Scenic Parkway, admiring trees along the way and stopping at several points—notably the Big Tree Wayside—for short hikes. Another highlight is driving to Gold Bluffs Beach and making the short ¼-mile hike into Fern Canyon, a magical 50-foot-canyon carpeted with deer, sword, and five-finger ferns—the dizzyingly lush landscape appeared famously in *Jurassic Park 2*. As you continue north, make the beautiful Coastal Drive Loop, a narrow and partially unpaved 9-mile journey through stands of redwoods with expansive vistas of the Pacific. Both a retro-kitschy must for photo ops and fun souvenirs, and an opportunity to explore the area's redwoods via a six-passenger gondola, Trees of Mystery sits right along U.S. 101. Upon pulling into this goofy place, you'll be greeted by a talking 49-foot-tall Paul Bunyan statue—and yes, Babe the Blue Ox stands dutifully beside him.

Eat & Drink: At the southern end of the park, the best dining is in the funky college town of Arcata and the North Coast's largest city, Eureka. **Cafe Brio** (✉ 791 G St. ☎ 707/822–5922 ⊕ www. cafebrioarcata.com) overlooks Arcata's town plaza, bakes its own breads, and serves superb focaccia sandwiches, leafy salads, and creative dinner fare. In Eureka's Old Town, **Cafe Waterfront** (✉ 102 F St. ☎ 707/443–9190 ⊕ www.cafewaterfronteureka.com) occupies an old former brothel and is well-regarded for its oyster burgers, chowders, steamed clams, and other locally caught seafood.

Stay: Eureka and Arcata have a wealth of accommodations, from chain properties to "Painted Ladies" Victorian B&Bs, including the **Carter House Inns** (✉ 301 L St. ☎ 707/444–8062 ⊕ www.carterhouse.com), which stands out for its central Old Town Eureka location. You'll also find some distinctive options near the park's core attractions, such as **Elk Meadow Cabins** (✉ 7 Valley Green Camp Rd. ☎ 707/302–8393 ⊕ www.elkmeadowcabins.com), a cluster of spacious, restored former millworkers' cabins with kitchens and a communal fire pit.

Breakfast: In Trinidad, **Beachcomber Cafe** (✉ 363 Trinity St. ☎ 707/677–0106 ⊕ www.beachcombertrinidad.com) is a great place to pick up bagels topped with chèvre, poached eggs, lox, and other delicious toppings, along with organic espresso drinks.

Day 7: Redwood National Park, CA, to Point Reyes National Seashore, CA

340 miles (6 hours without traffic and stops)

Today's drive is from coastal Humboldt County to coastal Marin County near San Francisco, most of it inland through magnificent old-growth forest on Highway 101. When you get to Petaluma, cut toward the coast via D Street and then Point Reyes–Petaluma Road, which takes you to Highway 1 and then the park's entrance.

ALONG THE WAY

Eat & Drink: You won't lack for notable dining options along this route, especially once you get to Sonoma County. **Catelli's** (✉ 21047 Geyserville Ave. ☎ 707/857–3471 ⊕ www.mycatellis.com) Italian restaurant in Geyserville beckons hungry diners with exceptional homemade pastas.

Town: One of several picturesque communities in the heart of Sonoma's Wine Country, Healdsburg has an attractive downtown anchored by a tree-shaded square. Here you'll find dozens of winery tasting rooms, fashionable boutiques, and fine restaurants. If you have a little extra time, venture west from town via Westside Road, where you can enjoy tastings at some of California's most esteemed wineries, such as **Gary Farrell** (✉ 10701 Westside Rd. ☎ 707/473–2909 ⊕ www.garyfarrellwinery.com).

POINT REYES NATIONAL SEASHORE

Do: The 71,000-acre **Point Reyes National Seashore** (✉ 415/464–5137 ⊕ www.nps.gov/pore), set on a lush, windswept peninsula in the Pacific, lies just 30 miles north of San Francisco but feels as though it could be galaxies away. It's a pristine patchwork of drives and hikes atop 100-foot sea cliffs, along pristine beaches, and past wildlife-rich estuaries. It's worth driving to the farthest point in the park, Lighthouse Visitor Center, for a trek over a dramatic headland where you can often spy gray whales just off the coast during the winter and spring migratory periods. Among the seashore's most scenic beaches, **Limantour Spit** is a gorgeous spot to watch the waves crash dramatically against the shore. Keep an eye out for harbor seals and all kinds of migratory birds, too.

Eat & Drink: Just north of the park with a magnificent location overlooking Tomales Bay, Hog Island Oyster Co.'s Marshall Oyster Farm and **The Boat Oyster Bar** (✉ *20215 Shoreline Hwy.* ☎ *415/663–9218* ⊕ *www.hogislandoysters.com*) is a delightful spot for locally harvested raw and barbecued oysters—you can even shuck and barbecue them yourself if you're feeling adventurous. Not far from the park entrance, the village of Point Reyes Station has several inviting restaurants, including **Side Street Kitchen** (✉ *60 4th St.* ☎ *415/663–0303* ⊕ *www.sidestreet-prs.com*) a casual indoor-outdoor spot serving huge hearty breakfasts (including tasty hot apple fritters) in the morning and rotisserie chicken, salads, and sandwiches at lunch and dinner.

Stay: Just south of Point Reyes Station, the **Olema House** (✉ *10021 Coastal Hwy. 1* ☎ *415/663–9000* ⊕ *www.olemahouse.com*) is a smartly restored 1860s stagecoach stopover that's close to the park. Another good option that's a little easier on the wallet, the **Cottages at Point Reyes Station** (✉ *13275 Sir Francis Drake Blvd., Inverness* ☎ *415/669–7250* ⊕ *www.cottagepointreyes.com*) offer cabins with fireplaces encompassing a gorgeous private 8-acre wildlife preserve.

Breakfast: In Point Reyes Station, don't miss the delectable blueberry-buttermilk scones, blackberry-lemon-pear muffins, and ham-and-cheese croissants at **Bovine Bakery** (✉ *11315 Rte. 1* ☎ *415/663–9420* ⊕ *www.bovinebakeryptreyes.com*), where you can also fuel up on espresso and chai lattes.

Day 8: Point Reyes National Seashore, CA, to Pinnacles, CA

170 miles (3 hours without traffic and stops)

Although it covers one relatively small (by national park standards) tract of about 26,600 acres, Pinnacles National Park feels like two separate places, as it's accessed from either the east or west, and there's no road connecting the two entrances. From Point Reyes National Seashore, take Highway 1 through the gorgeous Marin Headlands to U.S. 101, continue south over the Golden Gate Bridge through San Francisco, connect with I–280 south through Silicon Valley, pick up U.S. 101 southeast of San Jose, and then, if you're heading to the western side of the park, follow U.S. 101 to Soledad, and then turn east on Route 146. Or if you're entering the east side of the park, branch off the U.S. 101 south of Gilroy at exit 353 and take Route 25 south to Route 146. Note that the road to the western entrance is windy and meanders through some hilly terrain while the road to the eastern entrance is much more direct.

ALONG THE WAY

Town: One of the world's most beautiful cities needs no introduction, and sure enough, San Francisco is right on the way between these two parks. Once you cross the Golden Gate Bridge, hop onto Highway 1 and head south through the Richmond District. Pause for anywhere from an hour to a few hours in **Golden Gate Park** (☎ *415/831–2700* ⊕ *www.sfrecpark.org*), which is home to exceptional cultural treasures like the **de Young Museum** (✉ *50 Hagiwara Tea*

Garden Dr. ☎ 415/750–3600 ⊕ www.
deyoung.famsf.org) and **California Academy
of Sciences** (✉ 55 Music Concourse
Dr. ☎ 415/379–8000 ⊕ www.calacademy.
org).

Eat & Drink: Near San Francisco's Golden
Gate Park, you'll find a wealth of great
restaurants, especially in the Richmond
District (just north) and the Sunset
District (just south). Asian eateries are
particularly good in these parts, and a
couple of standouts are trendy **Burma
Superstar** (✉ 309 Clement St. ☎ 415/387–
2147 ⊕ www.burmasuperstar.com)
in the Richmond, and bare-bones **San
Tung** (✉ 1031 Irving St. ☎ 415/242–
0828 ⊕ www.santung.net) in the Sunset,
which is revered for its dry-fried chicken
wings and steamed dumplings.

PINNACLES NATIONAL PARK

Do: Upgraded in 2013 from a national
monument to a national park, **Pinnacles**
(☎ 831/389–4485 ⊕ www.nps.gov/pinn)
is nonetheless still somewhat underrated, despite being barely more than two
hours away from San Francisco. This
remarkable volcanic landscape is bisected by a ridge of jagged mountains. In
the eastern section of the park, you can
view the excellent exhibits at Bear Gulch
Nature Center, before embarking on the
Bear Gulch Trail to the famed Bear Gulch
Caves. On the western side, drive to the
Chaparral Trailhead area for a grand view
of the park's High Peak, and take the
2½-mile Balconies Cliffs-Cave Loop. For
any of these hikes to the park's caves,
make sure you pack a flashlight before
setting out.

Eat & Drink: Dining options are quite
limited near the park, but you'll find a
handful of inexpensive, informal options
in Soledad, including some excellent
Mexican restaurants, like **Taqueria Pache-
co** (✉ 325 Front St. ☎ 831/678–1808),
a no-frills spot with mouthwatering al
pastor, carne asada, and other tacos.
A little farther south in Kings City,
The Cork & Plough (✉ 200 Broadway

St. ☎ 831/386–9491 ⊕ www.facebook.
com/thecorkandplough) serves updated
comfort fare using locally sourced ingredients—from lamb burgers to braised-ox-
tail gnocchi—and features a great
selection of Monterey County wines.

Stay: The top lodging option near the
park, the **Inn at Pinnacles** (✉ 32025
Stonewall Canyon Rd. ☎ 831/678–
2400 ⊕ www.innatthepinnacles.com)
is just outside Soledad; it's a stunning
Mediterranean-inspired home set on 160
acres of vineyards.

Breakfast: There's not much near the
park, but up in Salinas, you can count
on the friendly folks at **First Awakenings**
(✉ 171 Main St. ☎ 831/784–1125 ⊕ www.
firstawakenings.net) to fill you up with
delicious ways to start the day, including
green chili and carnitas scrambles and
several varieties of eggs Benedict.

Day 9: Pinnacles, CA, to Channel Islands, CA

240 miles (4 hours without traffic and
stops)

It's a direct shot down the U.S. 101 to
reach the park's visitor center in the
small seaside city of Ventura.

ALONG THE WAY

Eat & Drink: Famous in the 19th century
for its hot springs resorts, Paso Robles is
today a font of superb wine country restaurants and tasting rooms. Among the
best eateries in town, upscale **Thomas
Hill Organics** (✉ 1313 Park St. ☎ 805/226–
5888 ⊕ www.thomashillorganics.com) is
one of the Central Coast's most vaunted
destinations for fine locavore-driven
cuisine. For a simpler and less expensive
meal, duck into the **Hatch Rotisserie & Bar**
(✉ 835 13th St. ☎ 805/221–5727 ⊕ www.
hatchpasorobles.com), a casual spot with
elevated comfort fare and a first-rate
drinks program.

Town: San Luis Obispo is home to prestigious California Polytechnic State University and has an attractive downtown anchored by the 18th-century **Mission San Luis Obispo de Tolosa** (✉ 751 Palm St. ☎ 805/781–8220 ⊕ www.missionsanluisobispo.org). It also anchors an ever-growing wine region, and you'll find numerous wineries and tasting rooms nearby.

CHANNEL ISLANDS NATIONAL PARK

Do: Visiting the **Channel Islands National Park,** a nautical park (☎ 805/658–5730 ⊕ www.nps.gov/chis) that comprises five islands off the coast of Santa Barbara, Ventura, and Oxnard, takes a little extra effort, as the only way to visit any of them is via a boat excursion (or your own private boat). A few different companies offer a variety of cruises to the archipelago, some specializing in scuba diving, kayaking, and other activities. If you have just a day, the best plan is to stop by the park **visitor center** (✉ 1901 Spinnaker Dr.) in Ventura, which features exhibits and shows a film about the islands, which range in size from 1-square-mile Santa Barbara to the quite extensive 96-square-mile Santa Cruz Island. You could then take an hour-long excursion on one of the **Island Packers** (✉ 1691 Spinnaker Dr. ☎ 805/642–1393 ⊕ www.islandpackers.com) high-speed catamarans to Santa Cruz Island. Once on the island, you can hike amid the unspoiled landscape of 2,500-foot mountains and dramatic canyons, viewing the many kinds of flora and fauna that thrive here and learning about the indigenous Chumash communities that once lived here.

Eat & Drink: There are no facilities on the islands, but **Andria's Seafood Restaurant & Market** (✉ 1449 Spinnaker Dr. ☎ 805/654–0546 ⊕ www.andriasseafood.com), in Ventura near the visitor center, overlooks the harbor and marina, and offers delicious clam chowder and fish-and-chips.

Stay: For convenience to the park visitor center and cruises to the islands, the **Ventura Beach Marriott** (✉ 2055 E. Harbor Blvd. ☎ 805/643–6000 ⊕ www.marriott.com) is an excellent choice.

Breakfast: Ventura's **Harbor Cove Cafe** (✉ 1867 Spinnaker Dr. ☎ 805/658–1639 ⊕ www.harborcovecafe.net) is next to the park visitor center and is a great option for picking up a breakfast burrito and coffee, as well as box lunches for the rest of your day, before setting sail for Santa Cruz Island.

Day 10: Channel Islands, CA, to Los Angeles, CA

70 miles (1 hour, 30 minutes without traffic and stops)

From Ventura, U.S. 101 is the fastest and most direct way into Los Angeles, but branching off onto coastal Highway 1 in Oxnard and continuing along it through Malibu and Santa Monica offers much prettier scenery, and depending on traffic, it doesn't necessarily take much longer.

ALONG THE WAY

Eat & Drink: A funky, old-school spot in Malibu that's perfect for a casual seafood feast, the **Reel Inn** (✉ 18661 Pacific Coast Hwy. ☎ 310/456–8221 ⊕ www.reelinnmalibu.com) is perhaps most famous for its mahimahi sandwiches and pepper-seared ahi salads.

Town: Santa Monica provides a scenic entry into metro L.A. and is notable for its pedestrian-friendly downtown (especially jacaranda-shaded Third Street Promenade and Santa Monica Place), old-school Santa Monica Pier, and gorgeous Santa Monica State Beach.

The Best of the Pacific Northwest

Written by Margot Bigg

With its gorgeous scenery, bohemian cities, celebrated regional fare, and world-famous beer and wine, the Pacific Northwest is like nowhere else in the country, or—frankly—on earth. This weeklong road trip will give you a solid sampling of what the region has to offer, taking you through temperate rain forests, along windswept beaches, up ancient mountains, and past crystalline lakes, hitting four national parks along the way. And while the great outdoors is what beckons many to this little corner of America, this itinerary will also give you plenty of time to hang out in cities such as Portland and Seattle, both of which have thriving culinary scenes and plenty of unique experiences.

At a Glance

Start: Seattle, WA

End: Seattle, WA

Miles Traveled: 1,850 miles

Suggested Duration: 8 days

States Visited: Oregon, Washington

Key Sights: Crater Lake National Park; Mount Rainier National Park; North Cascades National Park; Olympia National Park; the Space Needle

Best Time to Go: It's no secret that the Pacific Northwest gets a lot of rain, and it's a good idea to pack a waterproof jacket whatever time of year you visit. The driest weather tends to be in summer and early fall, and heavy winter snowfall in the mountainous parts of the region makes visiting national parks and other outdoor attractions challenging, even with four-wheel drive.

Day 1: Seattle, WA, to Port Angeles, WA

258 miles (6 hours without traffic and stops)

Pick up your rental car first thing in the morning and make your way to the Hoh River Rain Forest, one of the most photographed stretches of Olympic National Park. Then trace your route back part of the way to Port Angeles, where you'll spend your first night.

ALONG THE WAY

Town: At the base of the Olympic Mountains, Sequim is an old mill town overlooking the Strait of Juan de Fuca. Stop for a stroll or a bite to eat in the compact city center. If you come on a Saturday between May and October, don't miss the chance to browse for local produce and crafts at the **Sequim Farmers and Artisans Market** (✉ *152 W. Cedar St.* ⊕ *www.sequimmarket.com*).

Eat & Drink: Stick around Sequim for lunch at **Dockside Grill** (✉ *2577 W. Sequim Bay Rd.* ☎ *360/638–7510* ⊕ *www.docksidegrill-sequim.com*), which serves everything from fish-and-chips to oyster po' boys, all with fantastic views over the Sequim Bay.

Nature: Within the Hoh River Rain Forest, take in towering spruce and hemlock trees in this rainy stretch of **Olympic National Park** (☎ *360/565–3130* ⊕ *www.nps.gov/olym*). For the best views without much effort, consider a hike through the 0.8-mile-long Hall of Mosses loop trail.

PORT ANGELES

Do: Popular with weekending Seattleites, this cute coastal town offers lots of shops and dining, along with the **North Olympic History Center** (✉ *933 W. 9th St.* ☎ *360/452–2662* ⊕ *www.northolympichistory.org*) and the **Feiro Marine Life Center** (✉ *315 N. Lincoln*

The Best of the
Pacific Northwest

St. ☎ 360/417–6254 ⊕ www.feiromar-
inelifecenter.org).

Eat & Drink: It's always brunchtime at **New
Day Eatery** (✉ 102 W. Front St. ☎ 360/504–
2924 ⊕ www.newdayeatery.com), where
locals go to enjoy sandwiches, smoothies, and traditional breakfast treats.

Stay: Spread across two manicured
acres overlooking the sea, the Victorian
Sea Cliff Gardens Bed & Breakfast (✉ 397
Monterra Dr. ☎ 360/452–2322 ⊕ www.
seacliffgardens.com) features elegant,
antiques-filled rooms and suites, some
with whirlpool tubs. If you'd rather stay
inside Olympic National Park, the **Sol Duc
Hot Springs Resort** (✉ 12076 Sol Duc-Hot
Springs Rd. ☎ 888/896–3818 ⊕ www.
olympicnationalparks.com) offers cabins
and campsites plus a few sprawling hot
springs–fed pools.

Breakfast: At the **Oak Table Café** (✉ 292
W. Bell St. ☎ 360/683–2179 ⊕ www.
oaktablecafe.com) in nearby Sequim,
carefully crafted breakfasts and lunches
are the focus. Try the huge soufflé-style
apple-cinnamon pancakes.

Day 2: Port Angeles, WA, to Mount Rainier National Park, WA

*183 miles (4 hours without traffic and
stops)*

Head south along U.S. 101 to Olympia,
and then continue southeast all the way
to Mount Rainier National Park via the
town of Ashford.

ALONG THE WAY

Town: Although it's the capital of Washington State, Olympia is a little college city that's best known for its bohemian atmosphere and easy access to the great outdoors. Learn about wildlife at the **Wolf Haven International** (✉ *3111 Offut Lake Rd. SE, Tenino* ☎ *360/264–4695* ⊕ *www.wolfhaven.org*) wolf sanctuary or take a three-mile hike along the Ellis Cove Trail, which runs through the wetlands of **Priest Point Park** (✉ *2600 E. Bay Dr. NE* ☎ *360/753–8380* ⊕ *www.olympiawa.gov*).

Eat & Drink: Olympia is a great spot to stick around for lunch. For fresh, from-scratch Italian fare, consider **Mercato Ristorante** (✉ *111 Market St. NE* ☎ *360/528–3663* ⊕ *www.mercatoristorante.com*). This popular spot offers a solid menu of salads, antipasto, pasta, and pizza plus an always-solid wine list with plenty of regional and imported options.

MOUNT RAINIER NATIONAL PARK

Do: Mount Rainier National Park

(☎ *360/569–2211* ⊕ *www.nps.gov/mora*) is one of the most popular places for mountain climbing and backpacking in the Pacific Northwest, and for good reason. Its namesake perpetually snowcapped volcano is the fifth-highest mountain in the Lower 48 and has some 26 glaciers. It's divided into five sections, four with their own visitor centers. Most visitors stop at the main Henry M. Jackson Memorial Visitor Center, which offers educational exhibits, guided hikes, and a cafeteria. Also worth visiting is the Grove of the Patriarchs in the Ohanapecosh section of the park, with its old-growth trees believed to be over 1,000 years old.

Eat & Drink: At the top of Crystal Mountain, some 6,872 feet above sea level, **Crystal Mountain Resort's Summit House** (✉ *33914 Crystal Mountain Blvd.,*

Essential Listening

The Hoh Rainforest is the quietest place in the contiguous United States. Prepare yourself with *One Square Inch of Silence*, an audio preview of the pristine forest, courtesy of acoustic ecologist Gordon Hempton.

Enumclaw ☎ *360/663–3085* ⊕ *www.crystalmountainresort.com*) is worth visiting for the views alone. The menu here is simple but far from plain, with Wagyu beef burgers, wild game chili, and veggie curry wraps, plus chocolate mousse s'mores for dessert.

Stay: If you want to stay inside the park, the **National Park Inn** (✉ *47009 Paradise Rd. E* ☎ *360/569–2411* ⊕ *www.mtrainierguestservices.com*) is your best noncamping bet, with year-round accommodations and an inviting lobby with a big fireplace. For a romantic alternative, consider booking a cabin at nearby **Wellspring Spa** (✉ *54922 Kernahan Rd. E* ⊕ *www.wellspringspa.com*), which offers quiet cabins, spa services, cedar saunas, and two outdoor hot tubs.

Breakfast: Fuel up with a hearty breakfast at Ashford's **Copper Creek Restaurant** (✉ *35707 Rte. 706* ☎ *360/569–2799* ⊕ *www.coppercreekinn.com*), which dates to 1946, making it the oldest continuously operating restaurant in the state. The interiors are rustic and lodge-like down to the antler chandeliers and wood-paneled everything, and the food is hearty, with scrambles, French toast, pancakes, and biscuits and gravy on the menu.

Day 3 : Mount Rainier National Park, WA, to Portland, OR

222 miles (4 hours, 30 minutes without traffic and stops)

Head back to I–5 and drive south until you reach exit 22, for a detour to Mount St. Helens. After visiting the site, head back to I–5 and continue south until you reach Portland.

ALONG THE WAY

Town: If you need a place to stretch your legs, Longview is a great option. At the heart of the city, Lake Sacajawea is a sprawling man-made lake surrounded by parkland; there's even a small Japanese garden. The city is also home to a number of squirrel bridges, which allow squirrels to avoid traffic by crossing high above roads, from tree to tree—don't forget to look up!

Eat & Drink: Toeing the line between pub fare and gourmet cuisine, **The Office 842** (✉ 842 Washington Way ☎ 360/442–4647 ⊕ www.theoffice842.com) in Longview is a great place to break up your trip with some cheesy fondue or pizza-inspired naan flatbreads.

Detour: Famous for its 1980 eruption, Mount St. Helens is a must-see for anyone interested in national history. You can learn about the eruption at the **Johnston Ridge Observatory** (✉ 24000 Spirit Lake Hwy., Toutle, WA ☎ 360/274–2140 ⊕ www.fs.usda.gov), or explore the subterranean Ape Cave, the longest continuous lava tube in the continental United States.

PORTLAND

Do: Just south of the Oregon-Washington border, Portland is known for its free-spirited atmosphere, great dining, and ample opportunities to get out in nature. You don't even need to leave the city limits to experience the area's natural beauty, with highlights such as **Forest Park** (☎ 503/823–4492 ⊕ www.portlandoregon.gov), the **International Rose Test Garden** (☎ 503/238–7433 ⊕ www.trimet.org), and the **Lan Su Chinese Garden** (✉ 239 N.W. Everett St. ☎ 503/228–8131 ⊕ lansugarden.org) all within a few minutes' drive from downtown. Book lovers won't want to miss **Powell's City of Books** (✉ 1005 W. Burnside St. ☎ 800/878–7323 ⊕ www.powells.com), the world's largest new-and-used bookstore on the planet. If you'd rather spend more time in nature, make your way to the nearby Columbia River Gorge to check out **Multnomah Falls** (✉ 53000 E. Historic Columbia River Hwy.), the second-highest year-round waterfall in the United States.

Eat & Drink: For a gourmet evening, make a reservation at **ASTERA** (✉ 1407 SE Belmont St. ☎ 503/610–8076 ⊕ www.asterapdx.com), where a delightfully presented tasting menu showcasing the "horticultural cuisine of Cascadia" takes center stage.

Stay: Portland has tons of hotel options to choose from, ranging from the quirky to the swanky. If you're looking for an unusual stay, consider **McMenamins Kennedy School** (✉ 5736 N.E. 33rd Ave. ☎ 503/249–3983 ⊕ www.mcmenamins.com), an old schoolhouse turned hotel where you can sleep in refurbished classrooms. If you'd rather be downtown, the **Heathman Hotel** (✉ 1001 S.W. Broadway ☎ 503/241–4100 ⊕ www.heathmanhotel.com) is a Portland classic, with elegant rooms and a popular afternoon tea service. For a more contemporary vibe in the heart of the city, artsy **Woodlark** (✉ 813 S.W. Alder St. ☎ 877/239–0882 ⊕ www.provenancehotels.com/woodlark) features fresh rooms with sleek, modern decor spread across two historic buildings.

Even on the hottest days, Mount Rainier still glistens with snow.

Breakfast: Over the past couple of decades, Portland has gained a reputation for its doughnuts owing largely to the tourist-fave **Voodoo Doughnut** (✉ *22 S.W. 3rd Ave.* ☎ *503/241–4704* ⊕ *www. voodoodoughnut.com*) with its curiously shaped (and arguably gimmicky) pastries. But locals in the know are more likely to send you to **Blue Star Donuts** (✉ *672 S. Gaines St.* ☎ *503/954–3672* ⊕ *www.blue-stardonuts.com*), with its cakey, gourmet doughnuts, including some standout vegan options.

Day 4: Portland, OR, to Newport, OR

188 miles (4 hours without traffic and stops)

Head out to the Oregon coast via U.S. 26, which will take you through the forested Coastal Mountain Range before eventually joining up with U.S. 101. Stop in Cannon Beach before continuing south along the coast to Newport.

ALONG THE WAY

Town: One of the most popular and easily accessed towns on the Oregon coast, Cannon Beach is known for its art galleries, boutiques, and—unsurprisingly—seafood restaurants. It's also home to Haystack Rock, one of Oregon's oft-photographed natural features.

Eat & Drink: One of a handful of Pelican Brewing outlets along the coast, the **Pelican Brewing Company** (✉ *1371 S. Hemlock St., Cannon Beach* ☎ *503/908–3377* ⊕ *www.pelicanbrewing.com*) offers a wide variety of microbrews on tap and a menu of seafood-heavy pub fare, including a popular clam chowder.

Roadside Attraction: Oregon's cheesiest attraction, the **Tillamook Cheese Factory** (✉ *4165 N. U.S. 101, Tillamook* ☎ *503/815–1300* ⊕ *www.tillamook.com*) is open to visitors for free self-guided tours. After your tour, you'll get the chance to try all sorts of free cheese samples; just save room for ice cream, served at the Tillamook ice-cream parlor.

NEWPORT

Do: Famous for its Dungeness crab, Newport is one of the busier cities on the 101, with plenty more to do than just stroll the sand. Star attractions include the **Yaquina Head Lighthouse** (✉ *750 N.W. Lighthouse Dr.* ☎ *541/574–3100* ⊕ *www.blm.gov*) and the **Oregon Coast Aquarium** (✉ *2820 S.E. Ferry Slip Rd.* ☎ *541/867–3474* ⊕ *www. aquarium.org*), with its underwater tunnel and seabird aviary.

Eat & Drink: Offering some of the best views in Newport, the ocean-facing **Georgie's Beachside Grill** (✉ *744 S.W. Elizabeth St.* ☎ *541/265–9800* ⊕ *www.georgies-beachsidegrill.com*) serves a reasonably priced seafood-dominant menu in a casual setup.

Stay: One of the sleeker options on this stretch of the Oregon coast, the **Inn at Nye Beach** (✉ *729 N.W. Coast St.* ☎ *541/265–2477* ⊕ *www.innatenyebeach.com*) offers contemporary rooms, many with views out over the sea. For something a bit more secluded, the **Moolack Shores Inn** (✉ *8835 N. Coast Hwy.* ☎ *541/265–2326* ⊕ *www.moolackshores.com*) offers reasonably priced hotel rooms just north of town.

Breakfast: Start your day at the snug **Panini Bakery** (✉ *232 N.W. Coast St.* ☎ *541/272–5322*) for delicious espresso drinks, fresh-baked pastries, and freshly squeezed orange juice.

Day 5: Newport, OR, to Crater Lake National Park to Bend, OR

332 miles (6 hours, 30 minutes without traffic and stops)

Drive inland on U.S. 20 before continuing southeast to Crater Lake. From here, make your way north to Bend for the night.

ALONG THE WAY

Town: Home of the University of Oregon, Eugene is the state's second-largest city, and offers lots of great dining and green spaces without the crowds of Portland.

Eat & Drink: Eugene has had a strong hippie influence since the 1960s, and nowhere can this aesthetic be felt more than at the vegetarian **Morning Glory Café** (✉ *450 Willamette St.* ☎ *541/687–0709* ⊕ *www.morninggloryeugene. com*). The lunch menu focuses on soups, salads, and sandwiches while the café's sweet and savory breakfast offerings are served well into the afternoon.

Detour: Rather than heading straight for Bend, head south to the only national park in Oregon: **Crater Lake National Park** (☎ *541/594–3000* ⊕ *www.nps.gov/crla*). Spanning over 5 miles in length, and with a depth of 1,943 feet, this ancient caldera lake is the deepest in the country. To get the best views of the park, take time to drive the 33-mile-long Rim Drive, which loops along the lake, with plenty of spots to pull off for photos along the way. If you decide to linger for a day or two, you can take a boat out to Wizard Island, a cinder cone island that sits in the heart of the lake.

BEND

Do: Central Oregon's main economic hub, Bend is a small but quickly growing city celebrated for its sunny climate and easy access to year-round outdoor recreation. Along with a cute downtown area full of shops and restaurants, you'll find ample parks, hiking areas, and even a couple of museums—don't miss the **High Desert Museum** (✉ *59800 U.S. 97* ☎ *541/382–4754* ⊕ *www.highdesertmuseum.org*), a family-friendly cross between a living history museum and a zoo.

Eat & Drink: Housed in a Craftsman-style bungalow, **Ariana Restaurant** (✉ *1304 N.W. Galveston Ave.* ☎ *541/330–5539* ⊕ *www. arianarestaurantbend.com*) is a chef-owned fine-dining spot that offers European fare with a northwest twist, along with an extensive wine and cocktail menu.

Stay: Rather than stay right in downtown Bend, head a few miles out into the surrounding countryside for a night (or a few nights) at **Brasada Ranch** (✉ *16976 S.W. Brasada Ranch Rd., Powell Butte* ☎ *888/487–3563* ⊕ *www. brasada.com*), an 1,800-acre resort with spacious cabins and suites plus golf, horseback riding, multiple pools, a fantastic gourmet restaurant, and a luxury spa, all set against a backdrop of the snowcapped Cascade Range. If you're on a budget, the cozy **Pine Ridge Inn** (✉ *1200 S.W. Mount Bachelor Dr.* ☎ *800/600–4095* ⊕ *www.pineridgeinn.com*) features homey rooms with gas fireplaces, mini-refrigerators, and microwaves.

Breakfast: Before you hit the road, make a pit stop at **Lone Pine Coffee Roasters** (✉ *910 N.W. Harriman St.* ☎ *541/306–1010* ⊕ *www.lonepinecoffeeroasters. com*) for a fresh pastry and a cup of joe made from beans roasted on-site.

Day 6: Bend, OR, to Leavenworth, WA

311 miles (5 hours, 30 minutes without traffic and stops)

Head north back into Washington state on U.S. 97, and continue driving until you reach the Bavarian-inspired town of Leavenworth.

ALONG THE WAY

Photo Op: If you want an image that sums up the natural beauty of central Oregon, **Smith Rock State Park** (☎ *800/551–6949* ⊕ *www.oregonstateparks.org*) won't disappoint. This tuff and basalt monolith, located just off U.S. 97 is one of the most popular spots in the Pacific

Northwest for rock climbing. You can easily get a great shot of the rock from the parking area; keep your eyes peeled for bald eagles and raptors.

Town: Just north of the border with Washington, the little town of Goldendale serves local rural communities and travelers passing through on their way to or from local attractions such as the **Goldendale Observatory State Park** (✉ *1602 Observatory Dr.* ☎ *509/773–3141* ⊕ *www.goldendaleobservatory. com*) and the **Maryhill Winery** (✉ *9774 Rte. 14* ☎ *509/773–1976* ⊕ *www.maryhillwinery.com*).

Eat & Drink: Situated at the entrance of Goldendale's St. John the Forerunner Greek Orthodox Monastery, **St. John's Bakery** (✉ *2378 U.S. 97* ☎ *509/773–6650* ⊕ *www.stjohnmonastery.org*) provides an unusual alternative to the diner fare that dominates along U.S. 97, with everything from sweet baklava to savory lunch treats such as spanakopita and gyros. They also serve outstanding coffee.

Roadside Attraction: If you want to see England's most famous Neolithic site but don't want to fly across the Atlantic to do it, fear not: you can still get your Stonehenge fix in Goldendale at the **Stonehenge Memorial** (✉ *41-97 Stonehenge Dr.* ⊕ *www.maryhillmuseum.org*). This full-scale replica was built in 1918 as a World War I veterans memorial and offers views out over the Columbia River.

LEAVENWORTH

Do: Revamped in the 1960s to look like a Bavarian village (even the gas stations and chain restaurants use hand-painted signage), Leavenworth is most popular for its shopping, dining, and general atmosphere. It's especially popular around Christmastime, but the Kris Kringle vibes are year-round here, particularly at the **Nutcracker Museum** (✉ *735*

Front St. ☎ 509/548–4573 ⊕ www. nutcrackermuseum.com), which boasts around 3,000 nutcrackers, some dating back centuries. The town's location due east of Seattle also makes it a popular jumping-off point for regional outdoor activities, from winter snowshoeing to summer rock climbing.

Eat & Drink: It's always Oktoberfest at **München Haus Bavarian Grill and Beer Garden** (✉ 709 Front St. ☎ 509/548–1158 ⊕ www.munchenhaus.com), a popular sausage-and-beer joint on the northern end of town. The menu is dominated by sausages, including a few veggie options, all served with a huge range of mustards and other condiments, from apple cider vinegar sauerkraut to German curry ketchup.

Stay: A short drive from downtown Leavenworth, the lodge-style **Sleeping Lady Mountain Resort** (✉ 7375 Icicle Rd. ☎ 509/548–6344 ⊕ www.sleepingla-dy.com) offers rooms and cabins (some with bunk beds), plus an on-site spa with treatments and a dry sauna. If you're on a budget or visit during the holiday season, when accommodations can be hard to come by, there are also plenty of options in the nearby city of Wenatchee, about a 25-minute drive south of town.

Breakfast: In the heart of Leavenworth, the **Gingerbread Factory** (✉ 829 Front St. ☎ 509/548–6592 ⊕ www.ginger-breadfactory.com) serves espresso drinks and a variety of gingerbread cookies and houses as well as classic breakfast pastries such as marionberry scones and cinnamon rolls. There's also a small indoor seating area designed to resemble a forecourt (complete with an artificial tree adorned with heart-shaped cookie ornaments) for those who want to dine in.

Day 7: Leavenworth, WA, to North Cascades National Park, WA

249 miles (4 hours, 15 minutes without traffic and stops)

There are multiple ways to access North Cascades National Park. If you want to bring your car with you, take U.S. 2 to Everett and then take I–5 north to the North Cascades Highway. However, make sure to check road conditions ahead of time, as parts of both U.S. 2 and the North Cascades Highway frequently experience snow-related closures well into the spring months. You can also access the park by heading to Lake Chelan, about an hour's drive northeast of Leavenworth, and taking a passenger ferry four hours into the remote town of Stehekin, which is accessible only by boat, floatplane, or hiking 23 miles from the Cascade Pass Trailhead.

ALONG THE WAY

Town: Made famous by its appearance in the cult TV classic *Twin Peaks*, the town of Snoqualmie's biggest draw is 268-foot **Snoqualmie Falls,** which gushes dramat-ically into the Snoqualmie River below. There are a few observation decks at the top of the falls next to the parking lot, but many people like to hike down to the base for the full experience. Don't leave before checking out the displays and short film about the Snoqualmie Tribe at the visitor center.

Eat & Drink: Just above the falls, trib-ally owned **Salish Lodge & Spa** (✉ 6501 Railroad Ave. ☎ 425/888–2556 ⊕ www. salishlodge.com) is a great place to break up your journey, whether overnight or for a meal or even a spa service. The on-site restaurant serves up gourmet meals prepared from mostly local ingredients, including locally foraged fiddlehead ferns and honey produced on-site. Come for brunch to experience their extravagant "Honey from Heaven" service, in which servers drip honey onto your plate from many feet above.

NORTH CASCADES NATIONAL PARK

Do: Among the most remote natural areas in Washington state, the glacier-filled **North Cascades National Park** (📠 360/854–7200 ⊕ www.nps.gov/noca) features over half a million acres of alpine scenery and an extensive network of hiking trails. You can learn about the park and get hiking tips from Parks Service staff at the North Cascades Visitor Center, though it's only open in the summer. Another great place to get oriented is at the **North Cascades Environmental Learning Center** (✉ 1940 Diablo Dam Rd., Rockport 📠 360/854–2599 ⊕ www.ncascades.org) at Diablo Lake, where you can learn all about the local ecosystem or book a guided tour or canoe trip. If you end up visiting the Stehekin part of the park, you can get your bearings at the National Parks Service Golden West Visitor Center, a few minutes' walk from the passenger ferry port.

Eat & Drink: If you're staying in the Winthrop/Twisp area, **The Fainting Goat Restaurant** (✉ 207 White Ave., Winthrop 📠 509/996–3919) is a great place to grab dinner, with an affordable menu of pasta dishes and solid dessert offerings. The options in Stehekin are limited, and most visitors end up eating at either the Lodge at Stehekin's on-site restaurant or at the **Stehekin Valley Ranch** (📠 509/682–4677 ⊕ www.stehekinvalleyranch.com).

Stay: There aren't a ton of overnight options in and around the park, and many visitors end up renting independently owned cabins or camping in the Ross Lake area. A bit farther east, the towns of Winthrop and Twisp have a larger number of hotel options. Winthrop's **Sun Mountain Lodge** (✉ 604 Patterson Lake Rd. 📠 509/996–2211 ⊕ www.sunmountainlodge.com) is an excellent choice, and offers beautiful views and lots of outdoor activities. For something cheaper, **Idle-A-While Motel** (✉ 505 Methow Valley Hwy. 📠 509/997–3222 ⊕ www.idle-a-while-motel.com) in Twisp offers cabin-like rooms with mini-refrigerators and microwaves. If you're visiting the Stehekin portion of the park, the **North Cascades Lodge at Stehekin** (✉ 1 Stehekin Valley Rd. 📠 855/685–4167 ⊕ www.lodgeatstehekin.com) offers a wide range of accommodations ranging from hotel rooms to large cabins, and even a lake house.

Breakfast: If you're in Stehekin, the **Stehekin Pastry Company** (✉ Stehekin Valley Rd., 2 miles from Stehekin Ferry boat landing 📠 509/682–7742 ⊕ www.stehekinpastry.com) is one of the most popular spots in town, with a wide range of baked goods served fresh every morning. If you're staying in Twisp or Winthrop, head to the **Cinnamon Twisp Bakery** (✉ 116 Glover St. N, Twisp 📠 509/997–5030 ⊕ www.facebook.com/CinnamonTwispBakery) for a fresh bagel sandwich.

Day 8: North Cascades National Park, WA, to Seattle, WA

117 miles (2 hours, 15 minutes without traffic and stops)

If you're returning from the North Cascades Highway, head back the way you came until you reach I–5. Drive south to I–405 south, stopping in Woodinville before continuing south to the Evergreen Point Floating Bridge, from where you can cross Lake Washington into Seattle. If you've opted to visit Stehekin via Lake Chelan, you can take U.S. 2 east all the way to Woodinville and then continue on to Seattle.

ALONG THE WAY

Town: Home to more than 100 wineries, distilleries, and cideries, Woodinville is a must-visit for anyone itching to try some Pacific Northwest wine.

Eat & Drink: The Bistro at Hollywood Schoolhouse (✉ 14810 N.E. 145th St. ☎ 425/892–2575 ⊕ www.hollywoodschoolhousebistro.com) in Woodinville features a French-inspired menu created with local ingredients and, of course, a huge wine list. In the true Pacific Northwest style, there's even dog-friendly seating on the outdoor patio.

SEATTLE

Do: Seattle offers a ton to see and do, from visiting the first branch of Starbucks at **Pike Place Market** (✉ 85 Pike St. ☎ 206/682–7453 ⊕ www.pikeplacemarket.org) to strolling through some of its many area parks. And while Seattle is a relatively big city by Pacific Northwest standards, many of its star attractions are grouped together at the Seattle Center area, including the **Museum of Pop Culture** (✉ 325 5th Ave. N ☎ 206/770–2700 ⊕ www.mopop.org), **Chihuly Garden and Glass** (✉ 305 Harrison St. ☎ 206/753–4940 ⊕ www.chihulygardenandglass.com), and—of course—the **Space Needle** (✉ 400 Broad St. ☎ 206/905–2100 ⊕ www.spaceneedle.com).

Eat & Drink: Situated in the Queen Anne neighborhood, the romantic **Eden Hill Restaurant** (✉ 2209 Queen Anne Ave. N ☎ 206/708–6836 ⊕ www.edenhillrestaurant.com) offers whimsical tasting menus that change frequently, but always draw from the produce of the region.

Stay: In the heart of downtown Seattle, the elegant **Fairmont Olympic Hotel** (✉ 411 University St. ☎ 206/621–1700 ⊕ www.fairmont.com) offers some serious vintage charm, with gorgeous interior architecture that harkens back to when it opened in 1924. If you'd prefer something more intimate, the **Shafer Baillie Mansion Bed & Breakfast** (✉ 907 14th Ave. E ☎ 206/322–4654 ⊕ www.sbmansion.com) in the Capitol Hill area offers old-fashioned rooms done up with lavish antique furnishings, including four-poster beds.

Breakfast: In Seattle's Phinney Ridge area, north of downtown, **Coyle's Bakeshop** (✉ 8300 Greenwood Ave. N ☎ 206/257–4736 ⊕ www.coylesbakeshop.com) is the place to go if you've got a hankering for a croissant worthy of a French boulangerie or a big slice of cake. If you'd prefer a more savory start to the day, consider a rosemary cretzel, a hybrid between a croissant and a pretzel.

Wine Countries of the Pacific Northwest

Written by Margot Bigg

It should come as little surprise that some of the best wines in the country are produced in the Pacific Northwest; after all, much of this lush region is on the same latitude as France's most celebrated wine regions. Oregon and Washington, while notoriously rainy, are also blessed with the ideal balance of sunshine and rainfall to produce some fantastic varietals, particularly Pinot, Syrah, and Chardonnay.

This itinerary will introduce you to the Pacific Northwest's most important wine regions, while highlighting not-to-miss wineries, dining options, and attractions along the way. You'll start in southern Oregon before making your way north to the largest AVA (American Viticultural Area) in the state: the Willamette Valley, known for its relatively mild climate and world-famous Pinot Noirs. From there, you'll head north up to the Columbia Gorge AVA, which spans both Oregon and Washington on the north and south banks of the Columbia River, continuing

Wine Countries of the Pacific Northwest

on to Walla Walla and the Yakima Valley. Then it's on to Woodinville, a Seattle-area city that's centered on the wine industry, before wrapping your trip up with a visit to Seattle proper.

Finally, remember that the most important thing to keep in mind on this trip is to always drive responsibly. Alternate designated drivers each day, use car services to get to wineries from your hotels, or stick to the sip-and-spit method.

At a Glance

Start: Medford, OR

End: Seattle, WA

Miles Traveled: 859 miles

Suggested Duration: 6 days

States Visited: Oregon, Washington

Key Sights: Chateau Ste. Michelle; Hiyu Wine Farm; Maryhill Stonehenge; Prosser Vineyard & Winery; Seven Hills Winery

Best Time to Go: The best time to visit the Pacific Northwest is late spring through early autumn, when temperatures are pleasant and there's less chance of heavy rain. Late summer is particularly pretty for winery visits, when grapevines are at their most bountiful (though if you visit this time of year, you may find that the wine harvest has already begun). Note that while many wineries in the Pacific Northwest are open year-round, some do shutter for the winter holidays and a few even remain closed until early spring.

Day 1: Medford, OR, to Ashland, OR

51 miles (1 hour, 15 minutes without traffic and stops)

Start your trip in southern Oregon—the main airport for the region is in the city of Medford, but the pretty university town of Ashland makes for a better base. Although Ashland is only a 20-minute drive from Medford, a more scenic option is to take Route 238 down to the town of Jacksonville and the surrounding Applegate Valley before looping back up to Ashland for the evening.

ALONG THE WAY

Town: You can't take more than a few steps in the tiny town of Jacksonville without ending up in front of a winery. **Anchor Valley Wine Bar and Tasting Room** (✉ *150 S. Oregon St.* ☎ *541/702–2355* ⊕ *www.anchorvalleywine.com*) and **South Stage Cellars** (✉ *125 S. 3rd St.* ☎ *541/899–9120* ⊕ *www.southstagecellars.com*) are great options, while rosé lovers won't want to miss out on **Quady North** (✉ *255 E. California St.* ☎ *541/702–2123* ⊕ *www.quadynorth.com*). Not far from town in the surrounding Applegate Valley, **Cowhorn Vineyard** (✉ *1665 Eastside Rd.* ☎ *541/899–6876* ⊕ *www.cowhornwine.com*) is one of only a few certified biodynamic vineyards in the United States and offers beautiful Rhône-style wines served out on a patio or in their sustainably built tasting room.

Eat & Drink: Stick around Jacksonville for lunch at **C St. Bistro** (✉ *230 E. C St.* ☎ *541/261–7638* ⊕ *www.cstbistro.com*), which serves salads, soups, sandwiches, and pizzas made largely from locally sourced ingredients.

ASHLAND

Do: There's no shortage of wineries in and around Ashland, many clustered just to the east of town. Popular options include the expansive **Irvine & Roberts Vineyards** (✉ *1614 Emigrant Creek Rd.* ☎ *541/482–9383* ⊕ *www.irvinerobertsvineyards.com*), which specializes in wines normally associated with the Willamette Valley (think Pinots) and the long-established **Weisinger Family Winery** (✉ *3150 Siskiyou Blvd.* ☎ *541/488–5989* ⊕ *www.weisingers.com*), which has been producing wine in the region since 1988. If you're a performing arts fan, the **Oregon Shakespeare Festival** (✉ *15 S. Pioneer St.* ☎ *541/482–2111* ⊕ *www.osfashland.org*) is an Ashland must, showing multiple plays (not all Shakespeare) across three theaters from February through October of every year.

Eat & Drink: Sit down for a snazzy dinner at **Alchemy Restaurant and Bar** (✉ *35 S. 2nd St.* ☎ *541/488–1115* ⊕ *www.alchemyashland.com*), where you'll find everything from steak tartare to vegan burgers on the menu.

Stay: Ashland has its own thermal hot springs source and you can bathe in the waters from the comfort of your own hotel room's soaking tub at **Lithia Springs Resort** (✉ *2165 W. Jackson Rd.* ☎ *800/482–7128* ⊕ *www.lithiaspringsresort.com*) on the northern end of town. For something more traditionally elegant, the historic **Ashland Springs Hotel** (✉ *212 E. Main St.* ☎ *888/795–4545* ⊕ *www.ashlandspringshotel.com*) offers classically furnished rooms, a gorgeous lobby with stately chandeliers, and a fantastic on-site restaurant.

Breakfast: Start your day with a hearty breakfast at **Morning Glory** (✉ *1149 Siskiyou Blvd.* ☎ *541/482–2017* ⊕ *www.morninggloryashland.com*), where the options range from lemon ricotta stuffed French toast to Alaskan red crab omelets; they even do a breakfast risotto.

Day 2: Ashland, OR, to McMinnville, OR

267 miles (4 hours, 30 minutes without traffic and stops)

From Ashland, drive straight up I–5 until you reach the state capital, Salem. From here, head northwest to McMinnville, stopping at a few Willamette Valley wineries along the way.

ALONG THE WAY

Town: Oregon's second-largest city, Eugene, makes for a good midway stop, with good dining and shopping options and plenty of parks to stretch your legs. It's also home to a few excellent wineries, including **Sweet Cheeks Winery** (✉ *27007 Briggs Hill Rd.* ☎ *541/349–9463* ⊕ *www.sweetcheekswinery.com*) and the massive **King Estate Winery** (✉ *80854 Territorial Hwy.* ☎ *541/685–5189* ⊕ *www.kingestate.com*) just outside town.

Eat & Drink: Your best bet for lunch is at the **5th Street Public Market** (✉ *296 E. 5th Ave.* ☎ *541/484–0383* ⊕ *www.5stmarket.com*), a multilevel complex with a solid mix of shops and tasting rooms, plus restaurants offering everything from seafood to burritos. If it's a nice day, you may want to grab some cheese and charcuterie at the **Provisions Market Hall** (✉ *296 E. 5th Ave.* ☎ *541/606–4563* ⊕ *www.provisionsmarkethall.com*), a large specialty market with extensive deli offerings, a bakery, and a solid selection of wine from the Willamette Valley and beyond.

MCMINNVILLE

Do: There are countless possible ways to explore the Willamette Valley, with many of the wineries situated in and around the towns of Amity, Carlton, Dundee, Newberg, and McMinnville. One possible approach is to start at the Salem area's **Bryn Mawr Vineyards** (✉ *5935 Bethel Heights Rd. NW* ☎ *503/581–4286* ⊕ *www.brynmawrvineyards.com*),

notable for their hilltop views, continuing to **Maysara Winery** (✉ *15765 S.W. Muddy Valley Rd.* ☎ *503/843–1234* ⊕ *www.maysara.com*), a biodynamic winery with a strong focus on sustainability. From here, make your way northeast to Dundee's beloved **Argyle Winery** (✉ *691 Rte. 99 W* ☎ *503/538–8520* ⊕ *www.argylewinery.com*), known for its sparkling options, and then on to Utopia Vineyards (don't leave without grabbing a bottle of Estate Pinot). Continue to **The Carlton Winemakers Studio** (✉ *801 N. Scott St.* ☎ *503/852–6100* ⊕ *www.winemakersstudio.com*), a cooperative winery with 16 vintners, before dipping south to McMinnville for the evening.

Eat & Drink: The fanciest (and most expensive) restaurant in the Willamette Valley, **ōkta** (✉ *618 NE 3rd St.* ☎ *503/376–5353* ⊕ *www.oktaoregon.com*) offers 10-course dining experiences that evolve with the season. For a great overview of the best wines from the region and beyond, opt for the add-on pairing, meticulously developed by sommelier Ron Acierto.

Stay: There are plenty of excellent spots to stay throughout the Willamette Valley, from cozy winery B&Bs to reliable chain hotels. Downtown McMinnville options include sleek **Atticus Hotel** (✉ *375 N.E. Ford St.* ☎ *503/472–1975* ⊕ *www.atticushotel.com*) and quirky, budget-friendly **McMenamins Hotel Oregon** (✉ *310 N.E. Evans St.* ☎ *503/472–8427* ⊕ *www.mcmenamins.com*). Not far from the city, the **Vintages Trailer Resort** (✉ *16205 S.E. Kreder Rd., Dayton* ☎ *971/267–2130* ⊕ *www.the-vintages.com*) lets you spend the night in sleekly refurbished retro trailers from decades past. If you're more into pampering than glamping, splurge for a night or two at **The Allison Inn & Spa** (✉ *2525 Allison La.* ☎ *503/554–2525* ⊕ *www.theallison.com*) in nearby Newberg, which offers contemporary rooms with woodsy views, an award-winning spa, and fine dining at its much-lauded farm-to-fork restaurant, Jory.

Vineyards in Oregon's Willamette Valley are best known for producing Pinot Noirs.

Breakfast: Situated a short drive north of McMinnville in Dundee, **Red Hills Market** (✉ 155 S.W. 7th St. ☎ 971/832–8414 ⊕ www.redhillsmarket.com) offers everything from avocado toast dressed in locally produced olive oil to hearty plates of chilaquiles.

Day 3: McMinnville, OR, to Hood River, OR

100 miles (2 hours without traffic and stops)

Take Route 99 to I–5, stopping in Portland for lunch along the way. Then make your way out to Hood River via I–84, which runs parallel to the Columbia River in the Columbia Gorge.

ALONG THE WAY

Town: Oregon's biggest city of Portland definitely merits a stop along the way, even if just to pop into one of its best-known attractions, the gargantuan **Powell's City of Books** (✉ 1005 W. Burnside St. ☎ 800/878–7323 ⊕ www.powells.com). The so-called City of Roses is also home to one of the coolest wine shops out there, the quirky and unpretentious **Pairings Portland Wine Shop & Bar** (✉ 455 N.E. 24th Ave. ☎ 541/531–7653 ⊕ www.pairingsportland.com), which offers an ever-changing selection of wines from around the world, with heavy emphasis on organic and biodynamic options.

Eat & Drink: Portland offers an exceptionally large number of dining options for a city of its relatively modest size, but hitting up a food cart "pod" (a cluster of independent food carts, usually on a former parking lot) is arguably the most quintessential Portland dining experience. Among the more famous pods is **Cartopia** (✉ 1207 S.E. Hawthorne Blvd. ⊕ www.instagram.com/cartopiafoodcarts), in Southeast Portland, where you can get everything from Egyptian fare to meals based entirely on French fries, not to mention plenty of beer and wine. The heated, covered seating is a huge bonus on rainy Portland days.

Shop: Oregon doesn't have sales tax, which makes it a popular shopping stop for road-trippers from nearby states. For some of the best bargains, head to the **Columbia Gorge Outlets** (✉ *450 N.W. 257th Way, Troutdale* ☎ *503/669–8060* ⊕ *www. shopcolumbiagorgeoutlets.com*) on the edge of town, where you'll find tax-free factory outlets of brands such as Columbia Sportswear, Tommy Hilfiger, and even Coach.

Nature: The best-known attraction in the Columbia Gorge is also one of the most photogenic. At 620 feet tall, Multnomah Falls is the second-highest year-round waterfall in the United States, and while you can hike up to the top of the falls via a mile-long trail, the best photo ops are conveniently right by the parking lot.

HOOD RIVER

Do: Hood River's compact city center is a great place to start your visit, with plenty of tasting rooms within walking distance of one another; popular options include **Stoltz Winery** (✉ *514 State St.* ☎ *541/716–1330* ⊕ *www.stoltzwinery.com*) and **Evoke Winery Hood River Tasting Room** (✉ *708 Oak St.* ☎ *541/386–3700* ⊕ *www. evokewinery.com*). It's also worth dipping into the tasting room of **Hood River Distillers** (✉ *660 Riverside Dr.* ☎ *541/386–1588* ⊕ *www.hrdspirits.com*), the oldest distillery in the Northwest, to sample its range of whiskeys, gins, and vodkas. Then make your way down to **Marchesi Vineyards & Winery** (✉ *3955 Belmont Dr.* ☎ *541/386–1800* ⊕ *www. marchesivineyards.com*), known for its Italian-style options, and then on to **Hiyu Wine Farm** (✉ *3890 Acree Dr.* ☎ *541/436–4680* ⊕ *www.hiyuwinefarm.com*) to sample sustainably grown wines and ciders beautifully packaged in bottles with whimsical watercolor labels.

Detour: If you don't mind adding a little more driving to the beginning or end of your Hood River stay, it's worth taking a ride along the Hood River "Fruit Loop," a popular driving loop that takes you past a variety of produce stands and wineries, plus a bakery and a lavender farm. U-pick options are available throughout the warmer months; if you visit in the late summer or autumn, be sure to stock up on some of the region's famous pears and apples.

Eat & Drink: Smack in the heart of downtown Hood River, **Love & Hominy** (✉ *112 Oak St.* ☎ *541/716–1001* ⊕ *www.loveandhominy.com*) serves creative takes on tacos, with fusion offerings ranging from vaguely Thai-style options with peanut sauce and edamame to Mediterranean tacos that put the best of meze into a corn tortilla.

Stay: Hood River offers plenty of spots to stay across a range of price points. Solid options include the centrally located **Hood River Hotel** (✉ *102 Oak St.* ☎ *541/386–1900* ⊕ *www.hoodriverhotel.com*) and its hipster-chic rooms with local flair plus a 10-person bunkhouse for larger groups, and the budget-friendly **Adventure Lodge** (✉ *1306 Oak St.* ☎ *541/239–2391* ⊕ *www.adventurelodge.co*); it has motel-style digs updated with sleek decorative touches.

Breakfast: Start your day Scandinavian style at the Hood River branch of Portland's beloved **Broder Øst** (✉ *102 Oak St.* ☎ *541/436–3444* ⊕ *www.brodereast. com*). The huge breakfast menu features dishes such as chèvre-stuffed Norwegian lefse and *unnipurro*, a Finnish-style "oven porridge."

Day 4: Hood River, OR, to Walla Walla, WA

191 miles (3 hours, 15 minutes without traffic and stops)

Continue east along the Columbia River until you reach U.S. 12 in Wallula Junction, which will take you all the way to Walla Walla.

ALONG THE WAY

Photo Op: Situated at an elevation of around 700 feet and located between Hood River and The Dalles on the Historic Columbia River Highway, the **Rowena Crest Viewpoint** (✉ *6500 Historic Columbia River Hwy.* ☎ *800/551–6949* ⊕ *www. oregonstateparks.org*) is among the best places to snap an epic photo of the Columbia River Gorge. Better still, it's fully accessible by road, so while you could theoretically hike up to it, you certainly don't need to.

Town: Just east of Hood River, The Dalles is worth a stop for anyone interested in local history. Noteworthy attractions include the **Fort Dalles Museum and Anderson Homestead** (✉ *500 W. 15th St., at Garrison St.* ☎ *541/296–4547* ⊕ *www. fortdallesmuseum.org*), the **Columbia Gorge Discovery Center & Museum** (✉ *5000 Discovery Dr.* ☎ *541/296–8600* ⊕ *www. gorgediscovery.org*), and Sunshine Mill, a former wheat mill that now houses the Quenett and Copa Di Vino wineries.

Eat & Drink: Stop for lunch and a wine tasting at **Maryhill Winery's Bistro** (✉ *9774 Rte. 14* ☎ *509/773–1976* ⊕ *www. maryhillwinery.com*), which offers classic options such as charcuterie, cheese, and dips along with crab cakes, steamer oysters, and substantial sandwiches.

Roadside Attraction: On the Washington side of the Columbia River, flanked on the west by a large cow field, sits an exact replica of Stonehenge, known as the **Maryhill Stonehenge** (✉ *41-97 Stonehenge Dr.* ⊕ *www.maryhillmuseum.org*). It was built in the early 20th century as a World War I memorial. Like its namesake, the copy is oriented so that its altar stone matches up with the summer solstice sunrise.

WALLA WALLA

Do: Walla Walla has a huge number of wineries right within its city limits, and it's easy enough to go wine tasting without having to get behind the wheel, especially if you're staying downtown. Worthwhile choices include the **Echolands Winery Tasting Room** (✉ *7 W. Alder St.* ☎ *541/679–2109* ⊕ *www.echolandswinery.com*), **Kontos Cellars** (✉ *10 N. 2nd Ave.* ☎ *509/204–2141* ⊕ *www.kontoscellars.com*), and **Dama Wines** (✉ *123 E. Main St.* ☎ *509/525–2299* ⊕ *www. damawines.com*). If you do want to get out and explore the region, L'Ecole No. 41 Winery, Caprio Cellars, and Valdemar Estates Winery are all worth the short drives, as is the Port of Walla Walla Incubators, a collection of start-up wineries situated in a collection of old World War II buildings, located right next to the regional airport.

Eat & Drink: In the heart of the city center, **TMACs** (✉ *80 N. Colville St.* ☎ *509/522–4776* ⊕ *www.tmacsww.com*) serves Italian-inspired meals that rely heavily on locally sourced produce, plus a changing selection of rich desserts.

Stay: Among Walla Walla's most historic buildings, the **Marcus Whitman Hotel** (✉ *6 W. Rose St.* ☎ *509/525–2200* ⊕ *www. marcuswhitmanhotel.com*) has been hosting travelers since first opening back in 1928; today it features classic rooms plus an on-site restaurant and a wine lounge. For something more contemporary, the **Finch** (✉ *325 E. Main St.* ☎ *509/956–4994* ⊕ *www.finchwallawalla.com*) has bright, modern rooms in an unfussy, boutique environment. If you'd rather stay somewhere a bit more bucolic, **Eritage Resort** (✉ *1319 Bergevin Springs Rd.* ☎ *833/374–8243* ⊕ *www. eritageresort.com*) features beautiful, intimate suites with private patios and countryside views.

Breakfast: Grab a light breakfast at the **Colville Street Patisserie** (✉ *40 S. Colville St.* ☎ *509/301–7289* ⊕ *www. colvillestreetpatisserie.com*) before continuing your trip through wine country. Along with Danishes, cakes, and cookies, they offer unusual options such as goat cheese and herb croissants and kouign-amanns, butter pastries originating in the French region of Brittany.

Day 5: Walla Walla, WA, to Yakima, WA

83 miles (1 hour, 30 minutes without traffic and stops)

Backtrack west along U.S. 12 and continue until you reach the Tri-Cities of Kennewick, Pasco, and Richland. After stopping for a meal and maybe some wine, hop on I–82 and head northeast until you reach Yakima.

ALONG THE WAY

Town: Wine is a big deal in the Tri-Cities area; there are over 200 wineries in the region and it's home to Washington State University's **Ste. Michelle Wine Estates WSU Wine Science Center** (✉ *University Dr.* ☎ *509/372–7224* ⊕ *www.wine.wsu. edu*). If you have to choose just one winery, make it **Badger Mountain Vineyard** (✉ *1106 N. Jurupa St.* ☎ *509/627–4986* ⊕ *www.badgermtnvineyard.com*), Washington's first wine grape vineyard to earn USDA organic certification.

Eat & Drink: Stop for lunch at **Fiction Restaurant** (✉ *894 Tulip La.* ☎ *509/627–5000* ⊕ *www.bookwalterwines.com*), located at the J. Bookwalter Winery in Richland. The lunch menu here is dominated by salads, sandwiches, and pizzas, but there's also plenty of interesting appetizers for sharing, including panko-battered avocado fries.

YAKIMA

Do: After visiting the Tri-Cities, you'll head into the Yakima Valley, home to the oldest AVA in Washington. Start in the town of Prosser, dubbed the "birthplace of Washington wine," and home to 30-odd wineries; **14 Hands Winery** (✉ *660 Frontier Rd.* ☎ *509/786–5514* ⊕ *www.14hands.com*) and **Airfield Estates** (✉ *14450 Woodinville-Redmond Rd. NE* ☎ *425/877–1274* ⊕ *www.*

airfieldwines.com) both merit visits. Continue northeast to the town of Yakima, stopping at **Treveri Cellars** (✉ *71 Gangl Rd.* ☎ *509/877–0925* ⊕ *www.trevericellars.com*) in nearby Wapato before hitting Yakima's **Gilbert Cellars** (✉ *2620 Draper Rd.* ☎ *509/249–9049* ⊕ *www. gilbertcellars.com*) and **Tieton Cider Works** (✉ *619 W. J St.* ☎ *509/571–1430* ⊕ *www. tietonciderworks.com*). And if you need a break from wine tasting, drop into the **Yakima Valley Museum** (✉ *2105 Tieton Dr.* ☎ *509/248–0747* ⊕ *www.yvmuseum. org*), where you'll find a range of exhibits focused on local history, plus a few quirky highlights such as a collection of apple box labels and a "cabinet of curiosities" from around the world.

Eat & Drink: It's worth the 25-minute drive to nearby Tieton to visit **Nomad Kitchen & Mercantile** (✉ *700 Maple St.* ☎ *509/654–3345* ⊕ *www.nomad-mercantile.com*), where diners sit down at long communal tables (the servers do put some space between groups) to enjoy an ever-changing menu of seasonal dishes made from locally sourced ingredients.

Stay: Housed in an old Freemasons lodge dating to 1911, **The Hotel Maison** (✉ *321 E. Yakima Ave.* ☎ *509/571–1900* ⊕ *www. thehotelmaison.com*) is the swankiest option in town, with modernly furnished rooms and a well-equipped fitness center. For something more low-key (and pet friendly), **The Hotel Y** (✉ *1700 N. 1st St.* ☎ *509/248–5650* ⊕ *www.thehotely. com*) offers modern rooms with exterior entrances, some with wet bars and microwaves.

Breakfast: Essencia Artisan Bakery and Chocolaterie (✉ *4 N. 3rd St.* ☎ *509/575–5570* ⊕ *www.facebook.com/EssenciaArtisanBakery*) is a good spot for breakfast, with à la carte pastries and breakfast sandwiches as well as set breakfasts that come with fresh fruit and tea, coffee, or juice.

Day 6: Yakima, WA, to Seattle, WA

167 miles (2 hours, 45 minutes without traffic and stops)

Continue north along I–82, which merges with I–90 and will take you northwest, all the way to Bellevue. From here, head north to the city of Woodinville to visit some of its celebrated wineries before making your way south to Seattle.

ALONG THE WAY

Town: A major hub for Washington wine, Woodinville is home to many of the state's top tasting rooms, including the oldest of the lot: **Chateau Ste. Michelle** (✉ *14111 N.E. 145th St.* ☎ *425/488–1133* ⊕ *www.ste-michelle.com*). The city consists of four key districts, each with its own unique feel and plenty of wineries and bottle shops: the sleek Hollywood District, the more industrial Warehouse District, the sprawling West Valley, and the compact downtown.

Eat & Drink: Pair your lunch with some of Washington's finest wines at **Purple Café and Wine Bar** (✉ *14459 Woodinville-Redmond Rd. NE* ☎ *425/483–7129* ⊕ *www. purplecafe.com*). The menu includes sandwiches, pastas, fresh seafood, and a smattering of vegan dishes. While the wine list features bottles from around the world, the majority of offerings are local favorites.

SEATTLE

Do: Wine lovers won't want to miss **SODO Urbanworks** (✉ *3931 1st Ave. S* ☎ *206/973–1983* ⊕ *www.sodo-urbanworks.com*), an industrial complex that's been transformed into a one-stop shop for wine lovers, with many of the city's best tasting rooms under one roof. If you find yourself in the Capitol Hill area, be sure to drop in for a drink at the sleek **Aluel Cellars** (✉ *801A E. Thomas St.* ☎ *206/329–5994* ⊕ *www.aluelcellars.*

com) or pick up a few bottles at **European Vine Selections** (✉ *522 15th Ave. E* ☎ *206/323–3557* ⊕ *www.evswines. com*). If you want to get a feel for the city beyond its wine scene, head to the Seattle Center; there you'll find major attractions like the Space Needle, Chihuly Garden and Glass, and the Museum of Pop Culture.

Eat & Drink: Housed in the Melrose Market, a cluster of automotive buildings that have been revamped into a shopping and dining district, **Marseille** (✉ *1531 Melrose Ave.* ☎ *206/659–1845* ⊕ *www.marseille-foodandwine.com*) offers seasonal fine dining and an extensive wine list. There's even an on-site bottle shop in case you want to pick up a bottle or two before leaving.

Stay: For Lake Washington and Seattle skyline views, book an upper-floor room at the sleek **Hyatt Regency Bellevue on Seattle's Eastside** (✉ *900 Bellevue Way NE* ☎ *425/462–1234* ⊕ *www.hyatt. com*). It's located away from Seattle's congestion in the Bellevue Collection shopping and dining district, an ideal spot if you want easy access to dining and drinking options without having to drive home afterward. Another good choice is the **Ballard Inn** (✉ *5300 Ballard Ave. NW* ☎ *206/789–5011* ⊕ *www.ballardinn-seattle.com*) in the hip Ballard neighborhood, which offers beautifully furnished rooms that mix 1920s vintage vibes with modern fixtures.

Breakfast: Wrap your trip up with a hearty breakfast at **The Fat Hen** (✉ *1418 N.W. 70th St.* ☎ *206/782–5422* ⊕ *www.thefahenseattle.com*), which serves seasonal dishes such as homemade granola, salmon toast, and egg-based breakfast skillets.

THE WEST AND THE ROCKIES

Updated by
Aimee Heckel

WELCOME TO THE WEST AND THE ROCKIES

TOP REASONS TO GO

★ **Yellowstone National Park:** The nation's first national park is still one of its most popular. Wait for Old Faithful to erupt or glimpse the stupendous Grand Prismatic Spring, the largest hot spring in the United States.

★ **Great Basin National Park:** With one of the country's least-visited parks, pine trees make up Nevada's ancient forest. The bristlecone pine is one of the world's longest-living trees and likely its oldest living organism.

★ **Arches National Park:** The sandstone arches here, famous symbols of the American West, have been carved by thousands of years of wind, water, and ice.

★ **The Million Dollar Highway:** These 25 miles in western Colorado take you on a spectacular journey through the San Juan Mountains.

★ **Deadwood:** The quintessential Wild West town still attracts visitors hoping to relive its rowdy and lawless past.

1 Big Sky Country. The wide-open spaces of Montana, Idaho, and Wyoming are any road-tripper's dream.

2 The Loneliest Road in America: Nevada's Route 50. Route 50 spans the entire middle of the country from coast to coast, but its most desolate stretch in Nevada is a perfect way to explore the state.

3 Utah's National Parks. These five parks highlight some of America's most stunning landscapes.

4 The Best of Colorado. The Centennial State is filled with Rocky Mountain adventures, Wild West lore, and glamorous ski towns.

5 The Ultimate Wild West Road Trip. Relive the legends and outlaws of the Old West on this epic trip that takes you to key spots in Arizona, Colorado, Wyoming, and South Dakota.

Defined by the Rocky Mountains, stunning expanses of open blue skies and unbelievable mountain ranges dot the landscapes of the American West. You'll find a high concentration of notable national parks here, all offering unforgettable vistas that make for road trips nothing short of gorgeous.

Big Sky Country

Written by Shoshi Parks

Circling the northern reaches of the Rocky Mountains, this road trip through Montana, Idaho, and Wyoming is one of the most stunning exhibitions of nature to be found in this world. Out here, the landscape is dense with national forests and national monuments lauded for their stunning beauty and cultural histories, not to mention three separate national parks: Glacier, Yellowstone, and Grand Teton. Over 10 days, the itinerary careens over mountain passes, through emerald forests, and along the banks of sapphire lakes and rivers. Although this route will knock the socks off just about anyone, for those willing to get out in nature to hike, kayak, and horseback ride, the word *epic* doesn't even begin to describe it.

At a Glance

Start: Bozeman, MT

End: Bozeman, MT

Miles Traveled: 1,582 miles

Suggested Duration: 10 days

States Visited: Idaho, Montana, Wyoming

Key Sights: Craters of the Moon National Monument; Eatons' Ranch; Glacier National Park; Grand Teton National Park; Yellowstone National Park

Best Time to Go: The elevation and mountains make Big Sky Country cold and snowy more than six months out of the year. Although there is some great winter-weather adventuring along this route, you'll get the most out of the itinerary if you travel between May 1 and September 30.

Day 1: Bozeman, MT, to Glacier National Park, MT

298 miles (5 hours without traffic and stops)

On your first day, head northwest out of Bozeman toward the Montana state capital, Helena, then north via I–15. By the time you hit U.S. 89, the views of Flathead National Forest and the Rocky Mountains are in full bloom.

The Best of
Big Sky Country

ALONG THE WAY

Town: Helena's Historic District, Last Chance Gulch, has a fascinating history rooted in the city's early pioneer and mining days. Take a self-guided walking tour through the neighborhood's 19th-century dry goods stores, hotels, and churches to get the backstory of what was once a remote outpost of the Wild West.

Eat & Drink: Fill up with a ham gobbler sandwich, French dip, or chef salad from Choteau's roadside **Outpost Deli** (✉ 824 Main Ave. N ☎ 406/466–5330 ⊕ www. outpost-deli-edan.io).

GLACIER NATIONAL PARK

Do: The massive peaks of the Continental Divide in northwest Montana are the backbone of Glacier National Park and its sister park in Canada, Waterton Lakes, which together make up the International Peace Park. From their slopes, melting snow and alpine glaciers yield the headwaters of rivers that flow west to the Pacific Ocean, north to the Arctic Ocean, and southeast to the Atlantic Ocean via the Gulf of Mexico. Coniferous forests, thickly vegetated stream bottoms, and green-carpeted meadows provide homes and sustenance for all kinds of wildlife. **Glacier National Park** (☎ 406/888–7800 ⊕ www.nps.gov/glac) has more than 700 miles of hiking trails to do solo or with a guide. Fish at the park's many lakes and rivers (no permit required) and take a drive down the famed Going-to-the-Sun Road, one of the country's most spectacular National Historic Landmarks.

Eat & Drink: Enjoy hearty, casual American fare like prime rib and wings at **Packers Roost** (✉ 9640 U.S. 2 ☎ 406/387–9922) and the **Glacier Distilling Company** (✉ 10237 U.S.

One of the most spectacular drives in the country is the Going-to-the-Sun Road in Glacier National Park.

2 E ☎ 406/387–9887 ⊕ www.glacierdistill-ing.com) next door in Coram.

Stay: Book a night at the historic **Belton Chalet** (✉ 12575 U.S. 2 ☎ 406/888–5000 ⊕ www.glacierparkcollection.com), an early-20th-century lodge in West Glacier. Or there are 13 campgrounds within Glacier National Park; the one at Kintla Lake is a bastion of solitude and beauty.

Breakfast: Get your caffeine fix and a breakfast wrap at **Montana Coffee Traders** (✉ 30 9th St. W ☎ 406/892–7696 ⊕ www.coffeetraders.com) in Columbia Falls, a local northwestern Montana chain.

Day 2: Glacier National Park, MT, to Missoula, MT

160 miles (3 hours without traffic and stops)

Make a stop in beautiful Whitefish before heading south along the eastern shore of Flathead Lake (Route 35) and into the city of Missoula.

ALONG THE WAY

Town: Whitefish considers itself Montana's "outdoor recreation playground," and for good reason. In winter, skiers flock to **Whitefish Mountain Resort** (✉ 1015 Glades Dr. ☎ 877/754–3474 ⊕ www.ski-whitefish.com) while during the warmer seasons, locals and visitors alike hit the hiking trails in the **Flathead National Forest** (☎ 406/758–5208 ⊕ www.fs.usda.gov) or the beachfront at Flathead Lake.

Eat & Drink: The Raven (✉ 15321 Rte. 35 ☎ 406/837–2836 ⊕ www.ravenbigfork.com), a waterfront restaurant in Big Fork, has an eclectic menu, craft cocktails, live music, and unparalleled views.

Nature: Get out on the water at Flathead Lake, the biggest freshwater lake west of the Mississippi. Rent a kayak or stand-up paddleboard in Woods Bay, go for a swim, or fish for trout and perch from shore.

MISSOULA

Do: The cultural center of northwest Montana, Missoula is home to the University of Montana, the Clark Fork River, and lots of restaurants, shops, and bars along the aptly named Hip Strip. Explore the ghostly remains of **Garnet** (☎ 406/329–3914 ⊕ www.garnetghosttown.org), an early gold-mining town, or soak up some culture at the **Missoula Art Museum** (✉ 335 N. Pattee St. ☎ 406/728–0447 ⊕ www.missoulaartmuseum.org). If you're visiting in winter, hit the slopes at the **Montana Snowbowl** (✉ 1700 Snow Bowl Rd. ☎ 406/549–9777 ⊕ www.montanasnowbowl.com). During the summer, they run zipline tours over the chairlifts.

Eat & Drink: Dig into traditional Mexican eats at the stylish restaurant and agave bar **The Camino** (✉ 125 N. Pattee St. ☎ 406/317–1260 ⊕ www.thecaminomissoula.com). At **Gild** (✉ 515 S. Higgins Ave. ☎ 406/926–3258 ⊕ www.gildbrewing.com), a brewpub on the Hip Strip, you'll find three separate floors of fun, each with their own bar and atmosphere.

Stay: The Missoula lodging scene is a long list of chain hotels and motels. The regional outfit, the **C'mon Inn** (✉ 2775 Expo Pkwy. ☎ 406/543–4600 ⊕ www.cmoninn.com), a lodge with an indoor courtyard and waterfall, is one of the better options.

Breakfast: Have a seat or take your coffee and breakfast to go at **Market on Front** (✉ 201 E. Front St. ☎ 406/541–0246 ⊕ www.marketonfront.com), a bustling café and market downtown.

Day 3: Missoula, MT, to Stanley, ID

256 miles (5 hours without traffic and stops)

Today's route takes you through hundreds of miles of national forest and across the border into Idaho.

ALONG THE WAY

Town: In Salmon, Idaho, take a rigorous hike to the **Goldbug Hot Springs** (☎ 208/765–5100 ⊕ www.idahohotsprings.com) for a soak or stop in at the **Sacajawea Interpretive, Cultural, and Education Center** (✉ 2700 Main St. ☎ 208/756–1188 ⊕ www.sacajaweacenter.org), which delves into the history of the Lewis and Clark Expedition and the Agaidika Shoshone-Bannock Nation from which Sacajawea, their Indigenous guide, hailed.

Eat & Drink: Tuck into a massive burger with all the fixings at **The Savage Grill** (✉ 907 Mulkey St. ☎ 208/756–2062 ⊕ www.facebook.com/SavageGrill) in Salmon.

STANLEY

Do: With access to the Sawhill Mountains and the Salmon River, Stanley is a good base for outdoor adventures on the Idaho frontier. Take an epic adventure on the Salmon River with one of Stanley's many white-water-rafting outfitters or keep your feet planted firmly on the hiking trails around Redfish, Stanley, and Sawtooth lakes.

Eat & Drink: The log cabin **Sawtooth Luce's** (✉ 105 Niece Ave. ☎ 208/774–3361 ⊕ www.sawtoothluces.com) serves quality comfort food with solid vegetarian options and outdoor seating. At the over 90-year-old **Rod-N-Gun Saloon** (✉ 730 Ace of Diamonds St. ☎ 208/774–2922 ⊕ www.therodandgun.com), you can unwind with a fireside cocktail.

Stay: The suites and private cabins of **Stanley High Country Inn** (✉ 525 Ace of Diamonds St. ☎ 208/774–7000 ⊕ www.stanleyinn.com) have a rustic aesthetic adorned with modern touches.

Breakfast: Have a traditional breakfast straight from the griddle at **Limbert's** (✉ 401 Redfish Lodge Rd. ☎ 208/774–3536 ⊕ www.redfishlake.com) in the Redfish Lake Lodge.

Day 4: Stanley, ID, to Sun Valley, ID

62 miles (1 hour, 10 minutes without traffic and stops)

Take in the beauty of the Sawtooth National Forest on today's short drive from Stanley to Sun Valley and the neighboring town of Ketchum.

ALONG THE WAY

Eat & Drink: Stretch your legs and grab a cold drink or a bite at the **Galena Lodge** (✉ *15187 Rte. 75* ☎ *208/726–4010* ⊕ *www.galenalodge.com*), a community-owned home base for skiers and hikers in the town of Galena in the Boulder Mountains.

Nature: Hike one of the Sawtooth National Forest's two national recreation trails—the Fishhook Creek Boardwalk at Redfish Lake or the Wood River Nature Trail at Wood River Campground—or take a scenic drive along the Ponderosa Pine Scenic Byway (Route 21) or the City of Rocks Backcountry Byway.

SUN VALLEY

Do: Forget any assumption you might have about Idaho—Sun Valley is a posh, all-season outdoor getaway. At the **Sun Valley Resort** (✉ *1 Sun Valley Rd.* ☎ *800/786–8259* ⊕ *www.sunvalley.com*), you can ski or snowboard in winter, while in summer you can golf, go for a horseback ride, or hike the trails of Bald Mountain.

Eat & Drink: Have an elegant dinner at Sun Valley's original dining room, **The Ram** (✉ *1 Sun Valley Rd.* ☎ *208/622–2225* ⊕ *www.sunvalley.com*), or indulge in Italian favorites at nearby Ketchum's relaxed yet elegant restaurant **Enoteca** (✉ *300 N. Main St.* ☎ *208/928–6280* ⊕ *www.ketchum-enoteca.com*). At the historic **Pioneer Saloon** (✉ *320 N. Main St., Ketchum* ☎ *208/726–3139* ⊕ *www.pioneersaloon.com*), meat is on the menu, along with plenty of liquor to wet your whistle.

Stay: One of Ketchum's newer properties, the **Limelight Hotel** (✉ *151 Main St. S* ☎ *208/726–0888* ⊕ *www.limelighthotels.com*) downtown has spacious guest rooms and large indoor and outdoor lounges. Art and design are woven into the fabric of **Hotel Ketchum** (✉ *600 N. Main St.* ☎ *208/471–4716* ⊕ *www.hotelketchum.com*), an affordably priced stay on Main Street.

Breakfast: Have breakfast at **The Kneadery** (✉ *260 N. Leadville Ave.* ☎ *208/726–9462* ⊕ *www.kneadery.com*) in Ketchum, a rustic eatery with Rocky Mountain–inspired takes on traditional dishes like Benedicts and omelets.

Day 5: Sun Valley, ID, to Jackson, WY

241 miles (4 hours, 30 minutes without traffic and stops)

Drive along the volcanic moonscape of Craters of the Moon National Monument and westward through southern Idaho until you hit Jackson, the southern gateway to Grand Teton National Park.

ALONG THE WAY

Nature: Explore the cinder cones and underground lava tubes of the spectacular **Craters of the Moon National Monument** (☎ *208/527–1335* ⊕ *www.nps.gov/crmo*), an alien landscape formed by fire.

Detour: A disaster at a nuclear power plant in 1961 played a part in turning Atomic City into a near ghost town (its current population is less than fifty people). Take a look at what's left on this quick 6-mile detour (about 10 minutes each way) on U.S. 26. Luckily visitors today are unlikely to encounter serious radiation exposure.

Town: In Idaho Falls, stroll along the River Walk to see the town's eponymous waterfall. If you don't intend to stop at Craters of the Moon, see similar lava formations at the bite-sized Hell's Half Acre just south of town.

Eat & Drink: Fuel up with refined American food at **Copper Rill Restaurant** (✉ *415 River Pkwy.* ☎ *208/529–5800* ⊕ *www. copperrill.com*) in Idaho Falls where you can dine in style along the river.

JACKSON

Do: Located at the base of the Tetons, Jackson is dense with art galleries and boutiques. The **National Museum of Wildlife Art** (✉ *2820 Rungius Rd.* ☎ *307/733–5771* ⊕ *www.wildlifeart. org*) has an impressive collection of artistic renderings of animals from around the world. Get your own look at those that frequent this region of Wyoming at the **National Elk Refuge** (✉ *675 E. Broadway Ave.* ☎ *307/733–9212* ⊕ *www.fws.gov*) on the edge of town.

Eat & Drink: Dig into plates piled high with mushroom pappardelle and chicken Parmesan at **Orsetto Italian Bar and Eatery** (✉ *161 Center St.* ☎ *307/203–2664* ⊕ *www.orsettojh.com*) or order a wood-fired pizza from **Hand Fire Pizza** (✉ *120 N. Cache St.* ☎ *307/733–7199* ⊕ *www.handfirepizza.com*), located in a historic theater. After dinner, belly up to the bar at the **Million Dollar Cowboy** (✉ *25 N. Cache St.* ☎ *307/733–2207* ⊕ *www.milliondollarcowboybar. com*), a lively western bar.

Stay: Get a room in the western-styled **Hotel Jackson** (✉ *120 N. Glenwood St.* ☎ *307/733–2200* ⊕ *www.hoteljackson.com*), once named Wyoming's most beautiful hotel by *Architectural Digest*, or find a more affordable stay at the **Wyoming Inn of Jackson Hole** (✉ *930 W. Broadway* ☎ *307/734–0035* ⊕ *www. wyominginn.com*), a contemporary hotel styled in leather and wood.

Breakfast: Snag a table inside a historic log cabin at **Cafe Genevieve** (✉ *135 E. Broadway Ave.* ☎ *307/732–1910* ⊕ *www. genevievejh.com*) or on the outdoor patio

for a breakfast made with fresh, seasonal ingredients.

Day 6: Jackson, WY, to Yellowstone National Park, WY

57 miles (1 hour, 15 minutes without traffic and stops)

Today's drive is one of the most epic legs of all, cruising seamlessly through Grand Teton National Park into Yellowstone National Park.

ALONG THE WAY

Nature: Natural beauty surrounds you as you drive north through **Grand Teton National Park** (☎ *307/739–3300* ⊕ *www. nps.gov/grte*), which demands at least a few hours of exploration. Some of the most popular sites and trails in the park include Jenny Lake, the Taggart Lake Trail, the Mormon Row Historic District and, of course, Grand Teton itself.

Eat & Drink: There aren't a whole lot of options for lunch in Grand Teton National Park, but **Leek's Pizzeria** (✉ *Leeks Marina Rd.* ☎ *307/543–2494* ⊕ *www.signalmtnlodge.com*) in nearby Colter Bay Village is worth a stop for tasty pies and a table with a view of Jackson Lake.

Photo Op: Grand Teton and Yellowstone are both teeming with wildlife. Keep your eyes peeled for bison, elk, moose, bears, and other incredible animals. If you plan to pull over for a photo, be sure to keep your distance (at least 75 feet is recommended for most wildlife and at least 300 feet for bears and wolves).

YELLOWSTONE NATIONAL PARK

Do: Considered one of the most spectacular national parks in the United States, **Yellowstone** (☎ *307/344–7381* ⊕ *www. nps.gov/yell*) is festooned with hot springs and geysers, including the granddaddy of them all, Old Faithful. Whether

4

The West and the Rockies **BIG SKY COUNTRY**

you plan to explore the backcountry on foot or to stick to the roads, you'll spend your day immersed in an epic natural world. Allow at least two hours to explore Old Faithful and the surrounding village. Eruptions occur approximately 90 minutes apart but can vary, so check with the visitor center for predicted times. Be sure to explore the surrounding geyser basin, including the 1½-mile Geyser Hill Loop, and Old Faithful Inn, from which you can watch the geyser erupt from the hotel's rear deck. A short drive north, make Grand Prismatic Spring in Midway Geyser Basin your can't-miss geothermal stop; farther north, near Madison, detour to the west along short Firehole Canyon Drive to see the Firehole River cut a small canyon and waterfall (Firehole Falls).

Eat & Drink: Have an upscale dinner of sustainable fresh fish and wild game at the **Lake Yellowstone Hotel Dining Room** (✉ *236 Yellowstone Lake Rd.* ☎ *307/344–7311* ⊕ *www.yellowstonenationalparklodges.com*). In the **Bear Pit Lounge** at the Old Faithful Inn (✉ *3200 Old Faithful Inn Rd.* ☎ *307/344–7311* ⊕ *www.yellowstonenationalparklodges.com*), sit back and relax with a cocktail and apps.

Stay: For the most authentic Yellowstone experience, spend the night under the stars. The quiet **Slough Creek Campground** (✉ *Slough Creek Campground Rd.* ☎ *307/344–7381* ⊕ *www.nps.gov/yell*) in Lamar Valley is a stone's throw from some of the best wildlife-watching in the park. For more luxurious accommodations, try the historic **Lake Yellowstone Hotel** (✉ *235 Yellowstone Lake Rd.* ☎ *307/344–7311* ⊕ *www.yellowstonenationalparklodges.com*).

Breakfast: Get in on a breakfast buffet (individual specialties are also available) at the **Obsidian Room** in the Old Faithful Snow Lodge (✉ *2 Old Faithful Rd.* ☎ *307/344–7311* ⊕ *www.yellowstonenationalparklodges.com*).

Day 7: Yellowstone National Park, WY, to Cody, WY

52 miles (1 hour without traffic and stops)

Continue through Yellowstone and out its eastern entrance then on toward Cody, a historic town with a Wild West pedigree.

ALONG THE WAY

Nature: Start your adventure early today to explore even more of Yellowstone. You can make your way to the park's northern entrance to explore Mammoth Hot Springs, massive natural travertine terraces where mineral water flows continuously, building an ever-changing display. Or head to Lookout Point, which offers impressive views of the Grand Canyon of Yellowstone, through which the Yellowstone River has formed one of the most spectacular gorges in the world, with steep canyon walls and waterfalls.

Eat & Drink: Food options are limited and can be spread out within Yellowstone, especially in the off-season, so be sure to pack a picnic for your driving adventures today.

CODY

Do: Named for showman Buffalo Bill Cody, the town of Cody takes great pride in its Wild West history. Check out the authentic cabins and artifacts from Wyoming's pioneer days at **Old Trail Town** (✉ *1831 Demaris Dr.* ☎ *307/587–5302* ⊕ *www.oldtrailtown.org*) or stop in at the **Buffalo Bill Center of the West** (✉ *720 Sheridan Ave.* ☎ *307/587–4771* ⊕ *www.centerofthewest.org*), a complex of five museums that includes the Buffalo Bill Museum, the Plains Indians Museum, and the Cody Firearms Museum.

Eat & Drink: Get an unlimited chuckwagon dinner and a show at **The Cody Cattle Company** (✉ *1910 Demaris*

Dr. ☎ 307/272–5770 ⊕ www.thecody-cattlecompany.com). After dinner, grab a pint in nearby Powell at **WyOld West Brewing Company** (✉ 221 N. Bent St. ☎ 307/764–6200 ⊕ www.wyoldwest.com), which also has a wide-ranging menu of sandwiches, burgers, pasta, and more.

Stay: A former working cattle ranch, **K3 Guest Ranch Bed & Breakfast** (✉ 30 Nielsen Trail ☎ 307/587–2080 ⊕ www.k3gues-tranch.com) offers western-themed accommodations and an all-inclusive breakfast cooked over a campfire on the patio.

Breakfast: Get your morning coffee and a light breakfast at friendly local favorite, **Rawhide Coffee Co.** (✉ 1155 Sheridan Ave. ☎ 307/578–8344 ⊕ www.raw-hidecoffeeco.com).

Day 8: Cody, WY, to Eatons' Ranch, WY

132 miles (2 hours, 30 minutes without traffic and stops)

Drift across northern Wyoming and into the pines of Bighorn National Forest. Eatons' Ranch has been flanking its eastern edge for over 140 years.

ALONG THE WAY

Town: Stop in the town of Greybull for a look at ancient dinosaur tracks in the painted badlands of Red Gulch and the bizarre rocks that form the geological anomaly Devil's Kitchen.

Eat & Drink: Get quesadillas and burritos with a family touch at **Los Gabanes Mexican Restaurant** (✉ 546 Greybull Ave. ☎ 307/765–2120 ⊕ www.facebook.com/losgabanesmx) in Greybull.

EATONS' RANCH

Do: This dude ranch in northeastern Wyoming is one of America's first. Located on the slopes of the Bighorn Mountains, **Eatons'** (✉ 270 Eaton Ranch

Rd., Wolf ☎ 307/655–9285 ⊕ www.eatonsranch.com) is one of the few ranches where more experienced riders can still take horses out without a guide (guided trail rides also happen twice a day). They also do overnight pack trips in the neighboring national forest.

Eat & Drink: All meals and a cocktail hour are included at Eatons' Ranch and served in the large, cheery dining room (Saturday is outdoor barbecue night). If you're hankering for more adult beverages, stop in at The Apartment Bar or purchase wine or beer from the ranch store.

Stay: Almost all guests stay in individual cabins on the property, each rustic but comfortable with full bathrooms. Larger cabins have two to three bedrooms, fireplaces, and porches. There are also three suites in the Main Ranch House.

Breakfast: For breakfast, you're back at the communal dining room, but if you sleep in and miss the meal, stop by the on-site coffee shop.

Day 9: Eatons' Ranch, WY, to Red Lodge, MT

184 miles (3 hours without traffic and stops)

Today's drive takes you up through the Crow Nation, past the site of one of the most infamous battles of the 19th-century American Indian Wars, then west toward Billings, Montana. From there, travel southwest toward Red Lodge on the outskirts of the Custer Gallatin National Forest.

ALONG THE WAY

Attraction: Follow the **Battle of Little Bighorn** where Custer had his last stand on a self-guided driving tour of the battlefield (✉ I–90 Frontage Rd., Crow Agency ☎ 406/638–2621 ⊕ www.nps.gov/libi).

Town: In the city of Billings, see the carefully maintained treasures of **Moss**

Mansion (✉ *914 Division St.* ☎ *406/256–5100* ⊕ *www.mossmansion.com*) or the contemporary **Yellowstone Art Museum** (✉ *401 N. 27th St.* ☎ *406/256–6804* ⊕ *www.artmuseum.org*). Just outside town, step into the ancient past at **Pictograph Cave State Park** (✉ *3401 Coburn Rd.* ☎ *406/254–7342* ⊕ *www.stateparks.mt.gov*), which boasts more than 100 rock paintings in three easy-to-access caves.

Eat & Drink: At **Walkers Grill** (✉ *2700 1st Ave. N* ☎ *406/245–9291* ⊕ *www.walkersgrill.com*) in Billings, you'll find a variety of dishes made with local ingredients, including steaks and seafood along with an extensive wine list.

RED LODGE

Do: In winter, the town of Red Lodge draws thousands to its well-loved ski resort, **Red Lodge Mountain** (✉ *305 Ski Run Rd.* ☎ *406/446–2610* ⊕ *www.redlodgemountain.com*). In warmer months, there are plenty of outdoor activities to be had, including hiking along the Lake Fork Trail and visiting the rehabilitated and rescued animals at the **Yellowstone Wildlife Sanctuary** (✉ *615 2nd St. E* ☎ *406/446–1133* ⊕ *www.yellowstonewildlifesanctuary.org*).

Eat & Drink: Dig into the flavors and aromas of Sicilian cuisine at the upscale **Piccola Cucina** (✉ *7 Broadway Ave. N* ☎ *406/446–1212* ⊕ *www.piccolacucinagroup.com*) at Ox Pasture or find a more laid-back experience (with multiple James Beard Foundation nominations) on the wide-ranging menu at **Prerogative Kitchen** (✉ *104 Broadway Ave. S* ☎ *406/445–3232* ⊕ *www.prerogativekitchen.com*).

Stay: Take in the mountain views from the cozy **Inn on the Beartooth** (✉ *6648 U.S. 212* ☎ *406/446–1768* ⊕ *www.innonthebeartooth.net*). Or in town, you'll find a great night's sleep within the wood-paneled rooms at the **Alpine Lodge** (✉ *1105 Broadway Ave.*

N ☎ *406/446–2213* ⊕ *www.alpinelodge.com*).

Breakfast: Wake up with traditional and international breakfast favorites from **The Wild Table** (✉ *113 Broadway Ave. N* ☎ *406/446–0226* ⊕ *www.thewildtable.com*).

Day 10: Red Lodge, MT, to Bozeman, MT

149 miles (2 hours, 30 minutes without traffic and stops)

The last leg of your journey, Red Lodge to Bozeman, is also one of the least eventful. Follow U.S. 212 to Route 421 and onto I–90 west through Livingston and on to Bozeman.

ALONG THE WAY

Town: Take a break with a history lesson in Livingston's railroad museum, the **Depot Center** (✉ *200 W. Park St.* ☎ *406/222–2300* ⊕ *www.livingstondepot.org*), or the **Yellowstone Gateway Museum** (✉ *118 W. Chinook St.* ☎ *406/222–4184* ⊕ *www.yellowstonegatewaymuseum.org*), which has exhibitions on the region's natural and cultural past.

Eat & Drink: Stop for a meal and a brew at the colorful **Neptune's** in Livingston (✉ *232 S. Main St.* ☎ *406/333–2400* ⊕ *www.neptunestaphouse.com*), which specializes in coastal cuisine and sushi.

BOZEMAN

Do: There is much to do in the university town of Bozeman. See an impressive collection of dinosaur fossils at the **Museum of the Rockies** (✉ *600 W. Kagy Blvd.* ☎ *406/994–2251* ⊕ *www.museumoftherockies.org*) or browse the shops and galleries downtown. If you're traveling in winter, hit the slopes at **Bridger Bowl Ski Area** (✉ *15795 Bridger Canyon Rd.* ☎ *406/587–2111* ⊕ *www.bridgerbowl.com*).

Eat & Drink: Grab dinner at the **Blackbird Kitchen** (✉ *140 E. Main St.* ☎ *406/586–0010* ⊕ *www.blackbirdkitchen.com*), a cute Italian spot with a wood-fired oven, or splurge on the last dinner of your road trip at **Open Range** (✉ *241 E. Main St.* ☎ *406/404–1940* ⊕ *www.instagram.com/openrangemontana*), a classic Montana steak house. End your night on the town at the Bozeman institution, the **Haufbrau House** (✉ *22 S. 8th Ave.* ☎ *406/587–4931*).

Stay: Book a room at the stylish **RSVP Hotel** (✉ *510 N. 7th Ave.* ☎ *406/404–7999* ⊕ *www.rsvphotel.co*) or **The Lark** (✉ *122 W. Main St.* ☎ *866/464–1000* ⊕ *www.larkbozeman.com*), a sunny downtown hotel with an outdoor wood-burning fireplace and a patio overlooking Main Street.

Breakfast: The Nova Cafe (✉ *312 E. Main St.* ☎ *406/587–3973* ⊕ *www.thenova-cafe.com*) in downtown Bozeman has a menu packed with both savory and sweet morning treats.

The Loneliest Road in America: Nevada's Route 50

Written by Stefanie Waldek

If you're looking for the cross-country road less traveled, you won't do better than U.S. 50, also called Highway 50, which spans more than 3,000 miles between West Sacramento, California, and Ocean City, Maryland, cutting right through the center of the United States. Its moniker is the "Loneliest Road in America," bestowed upon it by *Life* magazine. The most desolate, yet perhaps most interesting, stretch of the highway is its 300-mile span in Nevada, where the road crosses the expansive Great Basin Desert and passes through several quirky small towns.

"We warn all motorists not to drive there unless they're confident of their survival skills," said an AAA representative in the *Life* story. But Nevada's tourism board took that warning in stride, offering an official survival guide for drivers, complete with a "passport" that you can stamp in the major towns along the highway. As it turns out, the drive is not at all dangerous—just make sure to top up your gas tank every chance you get—but it does offer beautiful mountain and desert views, a taste of the historic Wild West, and a chance to visit Nevada's only national park.

At a Glance

Start: Las Vegas, NV

End: Las Vegas, NV

Miles Traveled: 1,122 miles

Suggested Duration: 6 days

States Visited: Nevada

Key Sights: The Bellagio; Eureka Opera House; the Extraterrestrial Highway; Great Basin National Park; Pyramid Lake

Best Time to Go: Several stops on this route are open only from spring to fall—stick to May or September for milder weather.

Day 1: Las Vegas, NV, to Carson City, NV

433 miles (7 hours without traffic and stops)

While by no means close to Highway 50, Las Vegas is a good place to fly into and pick up a rental car. To start your road trip, take I-95 N all the way to Carson City, making a few fun pit stops throughout the drive.

The Loneliest Road in America: Nevada's Route 50

ALONG THE WAY

Town: While most visitors to Beatty use the town as a base camp for nearby Death Valley National Park, it's also a great place to stretch your legs. Visit the retro **Atomic Inn** (✉ *350 S. 1st St.* ☎ *775/553–2250* ⊕ *www.atomicinnbeatty.com*) for a photo op, marvel at the Tom Kelly Bottle House (a historic building made entirely from glass bottles), or explore the ghost town of Rhyolite, known for outdoor art installations.

Roadside Attraction: Located near the intersection of I–95 and Route 266 is the infamous **Cottontail Ranch,** a now-abandoned legal brothel reportedly frequented by Howard Hughes. It closed in 2004 and has since been boarded up, but you can still make a quick stop to snap a photo or two.

Eat & Drink: Just shy of the halfway point of your drive today is the **Tonopah Brewing Company** (✉ *315 S. Main St.* ☎ *775/482–2000* ⊕ *www.tonopahbrewing.com*), which has a tasting room that's perfect for lunch and a cold beer.

CARSON CITY

Do: Welcome to Nevada's state capital and the start (or end, depending on your direction) of Highway 50 in the state. Try to get to town before 5 pm so you can stop by the **Carson City Visitor Center** (✉ *1900 S. Carson St.* ☎ *800/638–2321* ⊕ *www. visitcarsoncity.com*) to grab *The Official Hwy 50 Survival Guide*. If you arrive even earlier, try to visit one of the city's museums, like the **Nevada State Railroad Museum** (✉ *2180 S. Carson St.* ☎ *775/687–6953* ⊕ *www.carsonrailroadmuseum.org*), or simply stroll the walkable downtown and shop the boutiques.

Eat & Drink: Carson City is the largest town on this itinerary, and there's a wide variety of restaurants and bars to fill your evening. Try spiced-to-order dinner at Thai restaurant **The Basil Thai Creative** (✉ *311 N. Carson St.* ☎ *775/841–6100* ⊕ *www.thebasilthaicuisine.com*), followed by a round of beers at **The Tap Shack** (✉ *211 Rice St.* ☎ *775/350–7001*), where locals hang out.

Stay: In all honesty, Carson City isn't known for its hotels, but there are plenty of national chains that are perfectly serviceable, like the **Hampton Inn & Suites Carson City** (✉ *10 Hospitality Way* ☎ *775/885–8800* ⊕ *www.hilton.com*). If you're looking for a more boutique stay, use Airbnb, where you can find rooms in the historic St. Charles Hotel.

Breakfast: Whether you've got time for a sit-down breakfast or you're itching to get out on the road, make your first stop of the day **L.A. Bakery Café and Eatery** (✉ *1280 N. Curry St.* ☎ *775/885–2253* ⊕ *www.labakerycafe.com*). There are café options for a leisurely meal or you can simply grab a coffee and pastry to go.

Day 2: Carson City, NV, to Fallon, NV

62 miles (1 hour, 10 minutes without traffic and stops)

Today's your first day on historic Highway 50—but you should also take a little off-route detour to Pyramid Lake, just northwest of the town of Fernley, which is actually on Alternate U.S. 50 (a breakoff that connects the main highway to the major cross-country I-80).

ALONG THE WAY

Town: You should stop in two towns along the route today: Dayton and Fernley, both of which are stamp stops in your survival guide (they're about 40 minutes apart). In the former, pop into the **Historical Society of Dayton Valley** (✉ *135 Shady*

As you officially start your Highway 50 journey, listen to the *Nevada Magazine Radio Show* hour-long podcast episode about the route to get jazzed for what's to come.

La. ☎ *775/246–6316* ⊕ *www.hsdv.org*) to learn about the town's gold rush days (in 1849, a prospector discovered gold here for the first time in what would eventually become the state of Nevada). In the latter, stock up on food, supplies, and gas—the towns only get smaller from here on out.

Eat & Drink: Pop into **Black Bear Diner** (✉ *1190 E. Main St.* ☎ *775/835–8512* ⊕ *www.blackbeardiner.com*) for an old-fashioned road-trip lunch, and follow up with dessert at **Steve's Homemade Ice Cream** (✉ *1360 U.S. 95 N* ☎ *775/575–0500*), both in Fernley.

Detour: Head 25 miles north of Fernley to Pyramid Lake, one of the largest natural lakes in Nevada and all that's left of the former inland sea Lake Lahontan. The surreal scenery, including the unusual tufa rock formations, makes for a great photo op, but be sure to respect the landscape during your visit: this is sacred land to the Paiute tribe. Visit the **Pyramid Lake Paiute Tribe Museum and Visitors Center** (✉ *709 State St., Nixon* ☎ *775/574–1088* ⊕ *www.pyramidlake.us*) to learn more about the history and significance of the lake.

FALLON

Do: There are two major reasons to come to Fallon, population roughly 9,000: to taste the region's famous Hearts of Gold cantaloupe and to drink at **Frey Ranch** (✉ *1045 Dodge La.* ☎ *775/423–4000* ⊕ *www.freyranch.com*), a distillery.

You can also visit the **Churchill County Museum** (✉ *1050 S. Maine St.* ☎ *775/423–3677* ⊕ *www.ccmuseum.org*) to learn about the region's history.

Eat & Drink: If you think this trip is going to be all diners and fast food, think again. For dinner tonight, try **Vn Pho** (✉ *2183 W. Williams Ave.* ☎ *775/428–5858* ⊕ *www.vnphofallon.com*).

Stay: You're pretty limited to chain hotels in Fallon, and of the handful in town, the **Best Western Fallon Inn & Suites** (✉ *1035 W. Williams Ave.* ☎ *775/423–6005* ⊕ *www.bestwestern.com*) is one of the best options.

Breakfast: You can't go wrong with pastries or hot dishes at the **Courtyard Café and Bakery** (✉ *55 E. Williams Ave.* ☎ *775/423–5505* ⊕ *www.facebook.com/CourtyardCafeFallon*)—they're all delicious.

Day 3: Fallon, NV, to Austin, NV

111 miles (1 hour, 40 minutes without traffic and stops)

It's another day of traveling along Highway 50.

ALONG THE WAY

Photo Op: No, that 600-foot sand dune rising up from the rocky desert isn't a mirage: it's Sand Mountain, part of Sand Mountain Recreation Area.

Detour: Though it's about 60 miles off Highway 50, **Berlin-Ichthyosaur State Park** (☎ *775/964–2440* ⊕ *www.parks.nv.gov*) is a worthy detour—it has a ghost town and 225-million-year-old fossils of extinct marine reptiles (ichthyosaurs). The former mining town of Berlin was abandoned in 1911, and today its remnants can be explored by visitors to the park. As for the dinosaur bones? Those weren't discovered until 1928, but they're now on display in the Fossil House.

Eat & Drink: When you get back to Highway 50, stop for lunch at **Middlegate Station** (✉ *42500 Austin Hwy.* ☎ *775/423–7134* ⊕ *www.middlegatestation.com*), known for its Monster Burger Challenge, in which competitors must consume four pounds of food.

AUSTIN

Do: The former silver-mining town of Austin only has a couple of hundred residents today, but it was once the second-largest city in Nevada, with a population of 5,000. Visit the town's three 150-year-old churches and the ruins of Stokes Castle, the summer home of 19th-century railroad magnate Anson Phelps Stokes.

Eat & Drink: The Austin area is home to the legendary **Lucky Spur Saloon** (✉ *306 Kingston Canyon Rd.* ☎ *775/964–2000* ⊕ *www.facebook.com/luckyspursaloon*), frequently called the best bar in the middle of nowhere. Take in the views of Kingston Canyon from the worn leather bar stools or play a game of pool as you sip a local brew.

Stay: In town, your best bet is the quaint (read: clean, comfortable, and surprisingly modern) **Cozy Mountain Motel** (✉ *40 Main St.* ☎ *775/346–1566* ⊕ *www.facebook.com/CozyMountainMotel*). If you don't mind driving a little outside town, try the quirky **Paradise Ranch Castle Bed & Breakfast** (☎ *440/781–8768* ⊕ *www.paradiseranchcastle.com*).

Breakfast: Options are limited in Austin, but the **International Café & Bar** (✉ *59 Main St.* ☎ *775/964–1225*) has outdoor seating and hearty portions.

Day 4: Austin, NV, to Baker, NV

210 miles (3 hours, 30 minutes without traffic and stops)

You're driving east along Highway 50 all day today, straight through to the state line.

ALONG THE WAY

Photo Op: Just east of Austin is the **Hickison Petroglyph Recreation Area** (☎ 775/635–4062 ⊕ www.blm.gov), where you can see ancient petroglyphs along a ½-mile walking trail.

Town: Prepare to spend a bit of time in Eureka, known as "the Friendliest Town on the Loneliest Road." The former mining town is incredibly well preserved so be sure to check out the restored historic sites like the **Eureka Opera House** (✉ 31 S. Main St. ☎ 775/237–6006 ⊕ www. eurekacountynv.gov), the **courthouse** (✉ 10 S. Main St. ☎ 775/237–5263), the **Eureka Sentinel Museum** (✉ 10 N. Monroe St. ☎ 775/237–5010) in the former *Eureka Sentinel* newspaper building, and the **Jackson House Hotel** (✉ 251 N. Main St. ☎ 775/237–5247 ⊕ www.eurekagcinnandjacksonhouse.com), all of which date back to the late 19th century.

Eat & Drink: Stop for lunch at the **Owl Club Bar & Steakhouse** (✉ 61 N. Main St. ☎ 775/237–5280 ⊕ www.facebook. com/eurekaowlclub) or the **Urban Cowboy Bar and Grill** (✉ 121 N. Main St. ☎ 775/237–5774 ⊕ www.eurekaurbancowboy.com), both in Eureka.

Detour: Get a taste of the region's mining history with a quick visit to **Ward Charcoal Ovens State Historic Park** (☎ 775/289–1693 ⊕ www.parks.nv.gov), located just 6 miles off Highway 50 at Nevada Historical Marker No. 54, which denotes the Ward Mining District. Six massive beehive charcoal kilns from the 19th century still stand here, and you can take a peek inside them (legend has it they were used for shelter by stagecoach bandits).

BAKER

Do: This teensy town of fewer than 100 people is mostly known as the gateway to Great Basin National Park, so there's not a ton to do here beyond eat, drink, and gamble at the slot machines at the **Border Inn** (☎ 775/234–7300 ⊕ www. borderinncasino.com). The inn is a quirky motel where the rooms are on the Utah side of the border, but the office, "casino," and restaurant are on the Nevada side. At night, remember to look up— Great Basin National Park is a designated International Dark Sky Park, meaning it's ideal for stargazing.

Eat & Drink: Sugar, Salt & Malt (✉ 70 S. Baker Ave. ☎ 775/237–5726 ⊕ www. saltandsucre.com) offers a variety of options, including breakfast burritos, pizzas, and house-made ice cream sandwiches.

Stay: The **Stargazer Inn** (✉ 115 S. Baker Ave. ☎ 775/234–7323 ⊕ www.stargazernevada.com) is the place to stay in Baker, or you could head to the 375-acre **Hidden Canyon Retreat** (✉ 500 Hidden Canyon Rd. ☎ 775/234–7172 ⊕ www. hiddencanyonretreat.com), a ranch just outside town. If you'd like to overnight in Great Basin National Park itself, there are campsites open year-round.

Breakfast: The **Great Basin Café** (☎ 775/234–7200 ⊕ www.greatbasincafe. com) serves breakfast sandwiches, omelets, pancakes, and more, conveniently located inside the national park's visitor center.

Great Basin National Park is Nevada's only national park.

Day 5: Baker, NV, to Ely, NV

62 miles (1 hour without traffic and stops)

The majority of your day should be spent at Great Basin National Park. Afterward, you can make the short journey back west on Highway 50 to Ely.

ALONG THE WAY

Roadside Attraction: On the road between Baker and Great Basin is the Permanent Wave Society, a collection of punny folk art installations. Although a number of the sculptures were removed by the Nevada Department of Transportation in 2016, some pieces remain and can still be seen along the roadside.

Nature: Great Basin National Park (☎ 775/234–7331 ⊕ *www.nps.gov/grba*) is one of the least visited national parks in the country, meaning you can enjoy the natural beauty without large crowds. Take a guided tour through the famous Lehman Caves, hike to the summit of Wheeler Peak during the summer, and go cross-country skiing or snowshoeing in the winter.

Eat & Drink: The only restaurant in Great Basin is the **Great Basin Café** (✉ *100 Rte. 448* ☎ *775/234–7200* ⊕ *www.greatbasin-cafe.com*) in the Lehman Caves Visitors Center, and it's only open seasonally. If you're visiting during the off-season, bring a to-go lunch from Baker.

Detour: Just 15 minutes north of Ely is the **McGill Drugstore Museum** (✉ *11 S. 4th St.* ☎ *775/235–7276*), a former pharmacy that's been preserved with vintage goods on its shelves, therefore serving as somewhat of a time capsule.

ELY

Do: With a population of some 4,000 people, Ely is the biggest town around this neck of the woods. Its biggest year-round attraction is the **Nevada Northern Railway Museum** (✉ *1100 Ave. A* ☎ *775/289–2085* ⊕ *www.nnry.com*), while seasonal events like the White Pine County Fair and Horse Races in August and Race the

Rails in September, in which cyclists race steam locomotives, are quite popular.

Eat & Drink: If you've had enough diner food on this trip, experience some fine dining with a side of gimmicks at **Jailhouse Cell Block Steak House** (✉ 211 5th St. ☎ 775/289–3033 ⊕ www.jailhousecasino.com), part of the Jailhouse Motel & Casino complex, where you can also grab after-dinner drinks at the lounge or the sports bar, as well as gamble.

Stay: Hotels range from classic chains like the **La Quinta Inn & Suites by Wyndham Ely** (✉ 1591 Great Basin Blvd. ☎ 775/289–8833 ⊕ www.wyndhamhotels.com) to locally owned independent accommodations like the **Bristlecone Motel** (✉ 700 Ave. I ☎ 775/289–8838 ⊕ www.bristleconemotelnv.com).

Breakfast: Grab a coffee or a smoothie at **Flower Basket & Espresso Depot** (✉ 445 E. 11th St. ☎ 775/289–2828 ⊕ www.facebook.com/ElyFlowerBasket), a flower shop and café.

Day 6: Ely, NV, to Las Vegas, NV

244 miles (3 hours, 50 minutes without traffic and stops)

It's time to make the long trek back to Vegas. Take Route 318 and U.S. 93 south through a stretch of Nevada almost as desolate as Highway 50; you might know it as Area 51. Gas stations are once again few and far between, so make sure you set out on a full tank of gas today.

ALONG THE WAY

Roadside Attraction: You can't actually visit the highly classified Area 51, of course (officially known as Homey Airport, the restricted Air Force installation was finally revealed to actually exist in 2013), but the areas surrounding it have embraced the extraterrestrial mythos. Nevada Route 375 is actually called the Extraterrestrial

Highway. At Crystal Springs, take a quick hop on it until you reach the hamlet of Rachel and its collection of UFO-themed businesses.

Eat & Drink: The area's alien theme is most apparent at Rachel's **Little A'Le'Inn** (✉ 9631 Old Mill Rd. ☎ 775/729–2515 ⊕ www.littlealeinn.com). Even if you aren't hungry for a tasty "alien burger," a pilgrimage to this restaurant/bar is practically a requirement to earn those Area 51 bragging rights. While the food is typical diner fare such as chili and sandwiches, it's very reasonably priced, and the owners put some tender loving care into keeping their landmark shipshape.

LAS VEGAS

Do: Live it up on your last night of your trip by living large in Vegas. Take the traditional route and spend some time gambling in one of the major casinos (if you only have time for one, make it the Bellagio) or seeing a performance, like the Cirque du Soleil or whichever legendary musical artist currently has a residency. If nightlife isn't really your style, enjoy the **Mob Museum** (✉ 300 Stewart Ave. ☎ 702/229–2734 ⊕ www.themobmusuem.org) or the quirky **Neon Museum** (✉ 770 Las Vegas Blvd. N ☎ 702/387–6366 ⊕ www.neonmuseum.org)—basically a graveyard of old neon signs.

Eat & Drink: A premier Hong Kong–style Chinese restaurant on the Las Vegas Strip is **Mott 32** (✉ The Venetian, 3325 S. Las Vegas Blvd. ☎ 702/607–3232 ⊕ www.venetian.com), which offers its impeccable signature dish Peking duck, in addition to myriad dumplings and street food. Afterward, get a cocktail at the **Chandelier Bar in the Cosmopolitan** (✉ 3708 Las Vegas Blvd. S ☎ 702/698–7000 ⊕ www.cosmopolitanlasvegas.com), which offers innovative spins on an ever-changing menu of reinvented classics.

Stay: You can't go wrong spending the night at the **Bellagio** (✉ 3600 S. Las Vegas

Blvd. ☎ 888/987–6667 ⊕ bellagio.mgm-resorts.com) or **Mandalay Bay** (✉ 3950 Las Vegas Blvd. ☎ 877/632–7700 ⊕ mandalaybay.mgmresorts.com) with its 11 acres of pools, but for something more affordable, **Harrah's** (✉ 3475 S. Las Vegas Blvd. ☎ 800/214–9110 ⊕ www.caesars.com) on the Center Strip is old-school Vegas all the way.

Breakfast: Don't miss an indulgent breakfast with incredible views of the Bellagio Conservatory and Botanical Gardens at **Sadelle's Cafe** (✉ 3600 S. Las Vegas Blvd. ☎ 702/693–7075 ⊕ www.sadelles.com).

Utah's National Parks

Written by Stefanie Waldek

Utah is an outdoor adventurer's dream, with spectacular landscapes comprising towering buttes, snowcapped mountains, winding slot canyons, lush forests, and mysterious hoodoos. The state is home to five national parks, not to mention a number of national forests and national monuments, each offering a range of experiences, from easily accessible scenic drives to multiday hikes through the backcountry. The best part is you can see them all in just over a week. This nine-day road trip itinerary covers the highlights of each national park—and much more—but if your schedule allows, it's highly recommended to spread your time out to add even more time in each park.

At a Glance

Start: Salt Lake City, UT

End: Salt Lake City, UT

Miles Traveled: 1,125 miles

Suggested Duration: 9 days

States Visited: Arizona, Utah

Key Sights: Arches National Park; Bryce Canyon National Park; Canyonlands National Park; Capitol Reef National Park; Zion National Park

Best Time to Go: Summer might be the most popular time to visit Utah's national parks, but visiting in the spring or in the fall is a great choice, as the weather is mild and the crowds are thinner. You'll see the fewest crowds in winter, but be mindful of road and trail closures due to snow.

Day 1: Salt Lake City, UT, to Arches National Park, UT

230 miles (3 hours, 45 minutes without traffic and stops)

When your flight lands in Salt Lake City, don't dally—you'll want to get to Arches ASAP to maximize your time there. Pick up your rental car, and take I–15 south through the suburbs of Salt Lake City and Provo, veer east on U.S. 6 and I–70, and finally continue on U.S. 191 south.

ALONG THE WAY

Town: The approximate halfway point of today's drive is the town of Price. If you need a break to stretch your legs, consider visiting the **Utah State University Eastern Prehistoric Museum** (✉ 155 E. Main St. ☎ 800/817–9949 ⊕ www.usueastern.edu) to see some dinosaur bones.

Eat & Drink: If you can hold out for lunch, drive another hour to historic **Ray's Tavern** (✉ 25 S. Broadway ☎ 435/564–3511 ⊕ www.facebook.com/RaysTavern) in Green River for burgers, beer, and homemade pie.

ARCHES NATIONAL PARK

Do: As one of Utah's most popular parks, **Arches** (☎ 435/719–2299 ⊕ www.nps.gov/arch) has hikes for all levels, but favorites include Delicate Arch (the park's most famous arch), Double Arch (featured in Indiana Jones and the Last

More than 1.5 million visitors come to Arches annually, drawn its wind- and water-carved rock formations.

Crusade), and Landscape Arch (one of the longest arches on the planet).

Eat & Drink: There's no food to be found in the park, so you'll have to carry in any snacks or meals. If you're looking for a sit-down dinner, try **Desert Bistro** (✉ *36 S. 100 W* ☎ *435/259–0756* ⊕ *www.desert-bistro.com*) in Moab, just 5 miles outside the park, for exquisite fine dining.

Stay: You can either camp in the park itself or you can stay in a hotel in Moab. If you go the latter route, consider the luxe resort **Sorrel River Ranch** (✉ *Mile 17, Rte. 128* ☎ *435/259–4642* ⊕ *www.sorrelriver.com*); the boutique **Hoodoo Moab, Curio Collection by Hilton** (✉ *111 N. 100 W* ☎ *435/355–0595* ⊕ *www.hilton.com*); or the bed-and-breakfast **Sunflower Hill Inn** (✉ *147 N. 300 E* ☎ *435/259–2974* ⊕ *www.sunflowerhill.com*).

Breakfast: Fuel up for your day with a quintessential diner breakfast at the old-school **Moab Diner** (✉ *189 S. Main St.* ☎ *435/259–4006* ⊕ *www.moabdiner.com*).

Day 2: Arches National Park, UT, to Canyonlands National Park (Islands in the Sky), UT

26 miles (30 minutes without traffic or stops)

If you want to stay in a hotel, you'll keep Moab as your base tonight, so your route will be round-trip. Campers, however, can just take the one-way journey to Canyonlands. To get to Canyonlands' **Islands in the Sky Visitors Center** (✉ *Grand View Point Rd.* ☎ *435/259–4712* ⊕ *www.nps.gov/cany*) from Moab, you can take Route 313 for a quick highway drive, or you can opt for the slower scenic route on Route 279, which takes two hours and offers great photo ops. Just be sure you have all-wheel drive and aren't afraid of a few narrow switchbacks.

Utah's National Parks

ALONG THE WAY

Eat & Drink: You won't pass any restaurants between Moab and Canyonlands, so pack your lunch today.

Photo Op: On your way back to Moab, drive past the Potash Evaporation Ponds. They might not sound too interesting, but they're an incredible photo op—their brilliant turquoise waters pop against the orange-red rocks of the landscape. You can also catch sight of them from **Dead Horse State Park** (☎ 435/259–2614 ⊕ www.stateparks.utah.gov), the filming location of the epic finale of *Thelma & Louise*.

Nature: Along the scenic route, you'll pass the Corona Arch Trail, a 3-mile out-and-back hike that passes Bowtie Arch and Corona Arch. You can also tack on a 1.9-mile out-and-back diversion to Pinto Arch if you're feeling ambitious.

CANYONLANDS NATIONAL PARK (ISLANDS IN THE SKY)

Do: Canyonlands National Park (☎ 435/719–2313 ⊕ www.nps.gov/cany) is split into four sections, and the area known as Islands in the Sky is the closest to Moab and the most popular overall. A few highlights include hiking Mesa Arch, hiking or simply taking in the vistas of Grand View Point, and the panoramic views from Buck Canyon Overlook.

Eat & Drink: There's no food in Canyonlands either, so bring some with you; otherwise you'll have to head back to Moab for a meal. For dinner, check out **Moab Brewery** (⊠ 686 S. Main St. ☎ 435/259–6333 ⊕ www.themoabbrewery.com), one of the most popular spots in town. If beer's not your thing, don't worry—they've also opened an adjacent distillery.

Stay: Again, if you're not camping within the national park, you'll be staying in Moab. Make it easy on yourself and stay put at last night's accommodation.

Breakfast: Don't miss the eggs Benedict at Moab's breakfast-only **Jailhouse Café** (⊠ 101 N. Main St. ☎ 435/259–3900 ⊕ www.jailhousecafemoab.com), set in a late-19th-century home that was at one time the county courthouse.

Day 3: Canyonlands National Park (Islands in the Sky), UT, to the Needles, UT

100 miles (2 hours without traffic and stops)

Today you're headed to the more off-the-beaten-path district of Canyonlands called the Needles. From the Islands in the Sky Visitor Center, head back toward Moab, south on U.S. 191, then west on UT-211 to get to the **Needles Visitor Center** (⊠ Rte. 211 ☎ 435/259–4711 ⊕ www.nps.gov/cany).

ALONG THE WAY

Eat & Drink: Once again, outside of Moab, there aren't any restaurants along the route. Eat a hearty breakfast and pack a to-go lunch.

Roadside Attraction: As its name implies, **Hole N' the Rock** (⊠ 11037 U.S. 191 ☎ 435/686–2250 ⊕ www.theholeintherock.com) is a home carved right into a rock. Former owners Albert and Gladys Christensen began construction around 1940 and finished in 1952, opening a café and gift shop on-site. Today visitors can pay for a tour, shop for trinkets at the trading post, pick up an ice cream at the general store, or even pet some animals at the petting zoo.

Nature: If you're stopping for a picnic lunch, do so at Wilson Arch, just a five-minute hike off the highway. You can also see it from the road if you'd rather not stop.

Roadside Attraction: If you're fascinated by apocalyptic cults, don't miss the Home of Truth, a ghost town that was once a religious colony founded by Marie Ogden in the 1930s. The ruins are on private property, but you can see them from the road.

Photo Op: See more than 600 petroglyphs at **Newspaper Rock State Historic Monument** (✉ *Rte. 211* ☎ *435/587–1500* ⊕ *www.utahscanyoncountry.com*), many of which are on a massive 200-foot rock face; yes, it's almost like it's a printed newspaper.

CANYONLANDS NATIONAL PARK (THE NEEDLES)

Do: The Needles region includes quite a bit of backcountry terrain, meaning you should be an experienced hiker and driver (with a 4x4 vehicle) if you decide to tackle some of the more advanced trails and drives. But there are plenty of options for beginner- and intermediate-level visitors, too. Options include the Roadside Ruin loop, which takes you past an 800-year-old structure; the half-mile Cave Spring loop, which includes a stop at a 19th-century cowboy camp; and the much more advanced Elephant Hill, which offers vistas of the park's famous sandstone needles.

Eat & Drink: As you might have guessed, there are no restaurants in the park, so carry your food in. The closest spot for a dine-in meal is the town of Monticello; go for Asian fusion at **Ja-Roen Thai Sushi** (✉ *380 S. Main St.* ☎ *435/587–4000* ⊕ *www.facebook.com/jaroenthairest*).

Stay: If you're not camping in Canyonlands, book a stay at the quaint **Grist Mill Inn** (✉ *64 S. 300 E* ☎ *435/587–2597* ⊕ *www.thegristmillinn.com*) in Monticello, a B&B housed in a former flour mill built in 1933.

Breakfast: The Grist Mill Inn also runs a restaurant, the **Granary Bar and Grill** (✉ *64 S. 300 E* ☎ *435/587–2597* ⊕ *www.granarybarandgrill.com*), where breakfast is served to both guests and the public. It's also the spot for drinks at night.

Day 4: Canyonlands National Park, UT, to Page, AZ

215 miles (3 hours, 30 minutes without traffic and stops)

It's a bit of a haul between Canyonlands and Zion, the next national park on the itinerary, so take some time to explore the terrain: drive south on U.S. 191 and U.S. 163 through majestic Monument Valley, then continue on Route 98 west to Page, Arizona, where you can spend the night.

ALONG THE WAY

Roadside Attraction: As you approach the village of Mexican Hat, you'll spot its namesake to the northeast: a sombrero-like rock that towers over the landscape.

Photo Op: You know the scene in Forrest Gump when Forrest stops running? Well, you'll drive right past it on U.S. 163. Stop at the sign for Forrest Gump Point around mile 13, and make sure there are no cars coming before you run out into the middle of the road to snap a photo or record a video.

Nature: The big showstopper today is **Monument Valley Navajo Tribal Park** (☎ *435/727–5870* ⊕ *www.navajonationparks.org*), famous for its mitten-shaped buttes. The park is on Navajo land, and if you want to explore beyond the 17-mile Tribal Park Loop, also known as the Valley Drive, you'll have to secure a permit, hire a guide, or join a tour. The one exception is the self-guided Wildcat Trail, a 4-mile loop around the Mitten Buttes and Merrick Butte.

Town: About 40 minutes past Monument Valley, across the Arizona border, is the town of Kayenta, where you should pause to learn about the area's Navajo history and culture at the **Navajo Cultural Center of Kayenta** (✉ U.S. 160 ☎ 928/697–3170). Then head to the local **Burger King** (yes, Burger King) to see an exhibit about the Navajo Code Talkers of World War II, organized by the fast-food joint's owner, the son of a Navajo Code Talker (⊕ www.facebook.com/BurgerKingHighway160).

Eat & Drink: If you're not up for dining at Burger King, **Kayenta's Amigo Cafe** (✉ U.S. 163 ☎ 928/697–8448 ⊕ www.amigocafe-kayenta.com) serves Mexican, Navajo, and American cuisine for breakfast, lunch, and dinner.

PAGE

Do: Page is a base camp for a number of nearby outdoor activities, the most popular of which is touring **Antelope Canyon** (⊕ www.antelopecanyon.com). You're required to have a guide, and tours book up months in advance—don't expect to have the famous slot canyon all to yourself when you visit. Other Page attractions include Horseshoe Bend, Glen Canyon Dam, and Lake Powell.

Eat & Drink: For dinner, chow down at **Big John's Texas BBQ** (✉ 153 S. Lake Powell Blvd. ☎ 928/645–3300 ⊕ www.bigjohn-stexasbbq.com), then head to **State 48 Tavern** (✉ 614 N. Navajo Dr. ☎ 928/645–1912 ⊕ www.facebook.com/state48tavern) for drinks.

Stay: Most hotels in Page are chains, but just outside town is the renowned luxury resort **Amangiri** (✉ 1 Kayenta Rd., Canyon Point, UT ☎ 435/675–3999 ⊕ www.aman.com). For something more wallet-friendly, book a stay at **Grandview Inn Bed and Breakfast** (✉ 1601 Grandview St. ☎ 928/660–2614 ⊕ www.grand-view-inn.com).

Essential Listening

As you're on the way to Zion National Park, tune in to the "The Sound of Geology" episode of America's National Parks Podcast, which discusses the geologic history of the country's parks.

Breakfast: If your accommodation doesn't serve breakfast in the morning, head to **Hot N Sweet Coffee and Donut Shop** (✉ 36 S. Lake Powell Blvd. ☎ 928/612–2112) for a grab-and-go option.

Day 5: Page, AZ, to Zion National Park, UT

115 miles (2 hours, 15 minutes without traffic and stops)

Today, simply take U.S. 89 to Route 9, and you'll be at the gates of Zion in no time.

ALONG THE WAY

Roadside Attraction: You'll want to hurry to Zion in order to maximize your time there, but take a brief stop at Pahreah and the Old Pariah Townsite. Pahreah is an old ghost town, though all that remains is a graveyard. The Old Pariah Townsite was a filming location for a number of Westerns, and while the set no longer exists, the striated landscape is a sight to behold.

Town: Kanab is just past today's halfway point, and while most people are here to get out into nature, there are some quirky stops in town that are worth a visit, namely the seasonal **Little Hollywood Museum** (✉ 297 W. Center

St. ☎ 435/644–5337 ⊕ www.littleholly-woodmuseum.org).

Eat & Drink: Pop by the **Rocking V Cafe** (✉ 97 W. Center St. ☎ 435/644–8001 ⊕ www.rockingvcafe.com) in Kanab for a mix of comfort food and fine dining (including vegan options) in an art-filled historic building.

ZION NATIONAL PARK

Do: There's no way you could fit in all the highlights of **Zion** (☎ 435/772–3256 ⊕ www.nps.gov/zion) in a single-day visit, but definitely don't miss the Narrows, the Emerald Pools, and the Canyon Overlook. Remember that the park is one of the most visited in the country, meaning it's got the crowds—and the lines—to match.

Eat & Drink: Unlike the two other parks you've visited on this trip, there actually are food options inside Zion itself. There's the more upscale **Red Rocks Grill Dining Room** and the casual (and seasonal) **Castle Dome Café,** both of which are located at **Zion Lodge** (✉ 1 Zion Lodge ☎ 435/772–7700 ⊕ www.zionlodge.com).

Stay: Stay inside the park if you can—the historic Zion Lodge is the only accommodation within the park itself other than campgrounds. But if you can't score a reservation, there are dozens of hotels in the region, everything from sprawling resorts like **Zion Mountain Ranch** (✉ 9065 W. Hwy. 9 ☎ 866/648–2555 ⊕ www.zmr.com) to cozy, romantic B&Bs like **Under the Eaves Inn** (✉ 980 Zion Park Blvd. ☎ 435/772–3457 ⊕ www.undertheeaves.com).

Breakfast: There's no shortage of breakfast cafés in Springdale, but for the best coffee, go to **Deep Creek Coffee Co.** (✉ 932 Zion Park Blvd. ☎ 435/669–8849 ⊕ www.deepcreekcoffee.com).

Day 6: Zion National Park, UT, to Bryce Canyon National Park, UT

85 miles (1 hour, 45 minutes without traffic and stops)

Bryce Canyon (☎ 435/834–5322 ⊕ www.nps.gov/brca) is less than two hours away from Zion via an extremely beautiful drive—just head east along Route 9, then north on U.S. 89, and finally east on Route 12, a scenic byway and All-American Road.

ALONG THE WAY

Eat & Drink: Grab a bite at **Thunderbird Restaurant** (✉ 4530 S. State St. ☎ 435/648–2262 ⊕ www.thunderbirdutah.com), a stalwart in Mount Carmel Junction, serving classic American dishes and homemade pie.

Shops: Take a quick stop in Orderville to visit one of the several rock shops in town: you can buy rocks, jewelry, and refreshments before you hit the road again.

Detour: It's an ever-so-slight detour from the main route, but the town of Panguitch is a time capsule with a quintessential American Main Street lined with old buildings and vintage signs.

Nature: Stop in Red Canyon to hike the Pink Ledges Trail—it's just 0.7 miles long but has plenty of captivating scenery.

BRYCE CANYON NATIONAL PARK

Do: The easiest way to see some of Bryce Canyon's highlights is to traverse its 38-mile scenic drive, which stops at 13 viewpoints, including the popular Sunrise, Sunset, Inspiration, and Bryce points. If you have time for a hike, try the Navajo Loop Trail, a 1.5-mile loop into a slot canyon called Wall Street. You can also tack on the Queen's Garden Trail, which is 1.8 miles out and back.

Eat & Drink: There are several in-park restaurants, including the dining room at the **Lodge at Bryce Canyon** (☎ 435/834–8700 ⊕ www.brycecanyonforever.com), though they're all seasonal. For year-round dining, head to **Idk BBQ** (✉ 161 N. Main St. ☎ 435/679–8353 ⊕ www.idkbarbecue.com) in Tropic, just outside the park.

Stay: Pitch a tent at one of the park's campsites or spend the night at the Lodge at Bryce Canyon. Otherwise, you can stay in one of the many hotels, B&Bs, or rentals in the villages of Bryce and Tropic; one of the best is **Stone Canyon Inn** (✉ 1380 W. Stone Canyon La., Tropic ☎ 866/489–4680 ⊕ www.stonecanyoninn.com), a collection of guesthouses and bungalows.

Breakfast: Pick up a coffee and a pastry at **Bryce Canyon Coffee Co.** (✉ 21 N. Main St., Tropic ⊕ www.brycecanyoncoffeeco.com) for a to-go breakfast.

Day 7: Bryce Canyon National Park, UT, to Grand Staircase–Escalante National Monument, UT

50 miles (1 hour without traffic and stops)

Continue along Scenic Byway 12 to Grand Staircase-Escalante National Monument.

ALONG THE WAY

Eat & Drink: There are no restaurants between Tropic and Escalante (the only major towns on today's route), so be sure to pack a lunch today.

Detour: If you have the time, drive south on Kodachrome Road at Cannonville to head to **Kodachrome Basin State Park** (☎ 435/679–8562 ⊕ www.stateparks.utah.gov), home to 67 monolithic spires.

The park was named after the popular color film by the National Geographic Society during a 1948 survey.

Nature: Just to the northwest of Escalante is **Escalante Petrified Forest State Park** (✉ 710 Reservoir Rd. ☎ 435/826–4466 ⊕ www.stateparks.utah.gov), where you can hike through the petrified forest and see dinosaur bones and marine fossils.

GRAND STAIRCASE ESCALANTE NATIONAL MONUMENT

Do: Grand Staircase-Escalante National Monument (✉ 745 U.S. 89 ☎ 435/644–1300 ⊕ www.blm.gov) covers more than 1,500 square miles—it's larger than the five Utah national parks combined—so there's no way you can see it all in one go. But in a short period of time, you can explore a number of slot canyons (Zebra Slot, Peek-a-Boo Slot, and Spooky Slot, to name three), plus hike a number of trails, like Devil's Garden and Lower Calf Creek Falls.

Eat & Drink: For dinner, visit the **Esca-Latte Internet Cafe & Pizza Parlor** inside Escalante Outfitters (✉ 310 W. Main St., Escalante ☎ 435/826–4266 ⊕ www.escalanteoutfitters.com) for pizza and local beer.

Stay: It's primarily independent hotels in Escalante, each with its own personality. For a more unique stay, try **Escalante Yurts** (✉ 1605 Pine Creek Rd. ☎ 844/200–9878 ⊕ www.escalanteyurts.com) or **Escalante Escapes** (✉ 500 W. 200 N ☎ 435/668–2108 ⊕ www.escalanteescapes.com), which has luxurious tiny homes.

Breakfast: Kiva Koffeehouse (✉ 7386 Hwy. 12, between mile marker 73 and 74 ☎ 435/826–4550 ⊕ www.kivakoffeehouse.com) is a must-do when in Escalante—it has the best coffee for miles.

Day 8: Grand Staircase-Escalante National Monument, UT, to Capitol Reef National Park, UT

70 miles (1 hour, 30 minutes without traffic and stops)

The last national park of your trip, **Capitol Reef** (☎ 435/425–3791 ⊕ www.nps.gov/care) is an easy drive straight up Scenic Byway 12.

ALONG THE WAY

Town: Along the way, you'll drive through the town of Boulder. Make a stop at the **Anasazi State Park Museum** (✉ 460 Rte. 12 ☎ 435/335–7308 ⊕ www.stateparks.utah.gov) to visit an Ancestral Puebloan site and learn about the historic regional culture.

Eat & Drink: The seasonal **Hell's Backbone Grill & Farm** (✉ 20 Rte. 12 ☎ 435/335–7464 ⊕ www.hellsbackbonegrill.com) in Boulder has earned a number of James Beard nominations for its farm-to-table cuisine—it's by far one of the most popular restaurants along Scenic Byway 12.

Detour: One of the most scenic drives off Scenic Byway 12 is Burr Trail Road, a backway that travels through the picturesque Long Canyon. Note that a portion of the road isn't paved, so you should only traverse it in dry conditions with a 4x4 vehicle.

CAPITOL REEF NATIONAL PARK

Do: Travel along the Capitol Reef Scenic Drive for incredible vistas in practically every direction, then stop in the town of Fruita to pick fruit from orchards planted by pioneers in the 1800s. Along the drive, you might also want to hike the Grand Wash Trail, a 4½-mile out-and-back journey that passes Cassidy Arch, named for Butch Cassidy, who likely spent time hiding in the area.

Eat & Drink: There's no food inside Capitol Reef, so bring your own lunch or head to the **Capitol Burger** (✉ 12 W. Main St. ☎ 435/491–0742 ⊕ www.facebook.com/capitolburgertruck) food truck in nearby Torrey for very filling fare.

Stay: As with the other parks, you can camp in Capitol Reef or you can stay in a hotel in Torrey. At **Capitol Reef Resort** (✉ 2600 Rte. 24 ☎ 435/425–3761 ⊕ www.capitolreefresort.com), accommodations range from standard guest rooms and private cabins to Conestoga wagons.

Breakfast: The family-run **Wild Rabbit Cafe** (✉ 135 E. Main St. ☎ 435/425–3074 ⊕ www.thewildrabbitcafe.com) is a Torrey staple. While it's a great spot for breakfast, it also makes packed lunches for you to take into the park.

Day 9: Capitol Reef National Park, UT, to Salt Lake City, UT

235 miles (4 hours, 45 minutes without traffic and stops)

It's a long journey back to Salt Lake City today. Drive west on Route 24, then north on I–15. Once you hit the town of Nephi, get off the interstate to take the Nebo Loop Scenic Byway through the Uinta National Forest in the Wasatch Mountains. You'll meet back up with I–15 in Payson, and you can take that the rest of the way to Salt Lake City.

ALONG THE WAY

Detour: If you're feeling particularly ambitious, take a detour to **Goblin Valley State Park** (✉ Goblin Valley Rd., Green River ☎ 435/275–4584 ⊕ www.stateparks.utah.gov), an hour in the opposite direction from Salt Lake City, to see a landscape full of hoodoos that looks like they're from another planet (which explains why the Mars Desert Research

Station is located nearby). The park is an hour's drive east from Capitol Reef.

Eat & Drink: After your detour, backtrack toward Capitol Reef, then stop at the **Sunglow Restaurant and Motel** (✉ 91 E. Main St. ☎ 435/425–3821 ⊕ www. thesunglow.com) in Bicknell, where you can get a slice of its legendary pickle pie, among other unusual flavors like oatmeal and pinto bean.

Town: Stop in the town of Salina for a little break. Grab a bite at the **Famous Mom's Café** (✉ 10 E. Main St. ☎ 435/529–3921 ⊕ www.facebook.com/momscafe-salina), then stroll through the displays at **Miss Mary's Historical Museum** (✉ 204 S. 100 E ☎ 435/529–4108 ⊕ www.facebook. com/missmarysmuseum) or the **Art Robinson Truck Museum** (✉ 875 W. Main St.). For a more sobering history lesson, you can visit the **CCC & POW Camp** (✉ 700 E. Main St. ☎ 435/633–5167 ⊕ www.facebook.com/cccpowcamput), where a U.S. soldier infamously massacred German prisoners of war—the site now houses a museum remembering the event.

Nature: As you make your way along the Nebo Loop Scenic Byway, stop at the Devil's Kitchen for a quick hike to a scenic overlook.

SALT LAKE CITY

Do: Venture into Salt Lake's vibrant downtown, with its respected theater scene, farm-to-table restaurants, craft breweries and coffeehouses, and the impressive **City Creek Center** (✉ 50 S. Main St. ☎ 801/521–2012 ⊕ www. shopcitycreekcenter.com) retail plaza. Explore the city's namesake, the Great Salt Lake by car, on foot, or by bicycle. If you're here in summer, try floating off the beaches at Antelope Island—the water is so salty it's impossible to sink.

Eat & Drink: For dinner, enjoy the locally sourced ingredients and bold flavors at **Oquirrh** (✉ 368 E. 100 S ☎ 801/359–0426 ⊕ www.oquirrhslc. com) or the authentic Mexican cuisine at **Red Iguana** (✉ 736 W. North Temple ☎ 801/322–1489 ⊕ www.rediguana. com). Afterward, learn how SLC is trying to shed its teetotaler reputation with a drink at **Fisher Brewing Company** (✉ 320 W. 800 S ☎ 801/487–2337 ⊕ www.fisherbeer.com).

Stay: Splurge at the opulent **Grand America Hotel** (✉ 555 S. Main St. ☎ 800/304–8696 ⊕ www.grandamerica.com) or enjoy a night at the hip **AC Hotel by Marriott Salt Lake City Downtown** (✉ 225 W. 200 S ☎ 385/722–9600 ⊕ www. marriott.com).

Breakfast: The breakfast menu will wow you at **Pig & a Jelly Jar** (✉ 401 E. 90 S ☎ 385/202–7366 ⊕ www.pigandajelly-jar.com).

The Best of Colorado

Written by Aimee Heckel

A playground for nature lovers and outdoor enthusiasts, Colorado has majestic landscapes, raging rivers, and winding trails, all of which can be explored via the many scenic drives that make up the state's road system. In this 10-day road trip, you can truly explore the best of what Colorado offers: all four of the state's national parks, three major ski towns, and several different hot springs. You will visit Colorado's wine country and go on two of the most popular hikes (or more, if you're up for it). You will be awed by some of Colorado's natural wonders, such as the Cave of the Winds, the country's tallest sand dune, and the Garden of the Gods. And you'll also stop by tourist favorites, like Estes Park, Trail Ridge Road, and Grand Lake, all while keeping the driving time to four hours or less per day, so there's plenty of time to explore and enjoy all that Colorado has to offer.

The Best of Colorado

At a Glance

Start: Denver, CO

End: Denver, CO

Miles Traveled: 1,100 miles

Suggested Duration: 10 days

States Visited: Colorado

Key Sights: Black Canyon of the Gunnison National Park; Garden of the Gods; Great Sand Dunes National Park; Mesa Verde National Park; Rocky Mountain National Park

Best Time to Go: This trip includes mountain driving, which can be challenging in winter even for the most seasoned mountain driver. And some of the roads may not even be open during winter, so this trip is best suited for warmer weather (or be prepared for potential closures and detours).

Day 1: Denver, CO, to Boulder, CO

35 miles (50 minutes without traffic and stops)

Start your Rocky Mountain road trip by heading west from Denver on U.S. 6 to the classic mountain town of Golden, then head north on Route 93 to the vibrant college town of Boulder.

ALONG THE WAY

Town: Once the territorial capital of Colorado, Golden's growth was boosted by the high-tech industry as well as the **Molson Coors Brewery** (⌧ *13th and Ford Sts.* ☎ *866/812–2337* ⊕ *www.*

coorsbrewerytour.com) and the Colorado School of Mines. Although that growth has slowed down in recent years, it remains a top draw for outdoors and history enthusiasts, not to mention beer enthusiasts. Beer snobs will probably send you to any of Colorado's hundreds of microbreweries, but it's hard for any beer lover to resist a pilgrimage to Coors Brewery; founded in 1873, today it's the largest single-site brewery in the world.

Eat & Drink: Woody's Wood Fired Pizza (✉ 1305 Washington Ave. ☎ 303/277–1443 ⊕ www.woodysgolden.com) in Golden has a full menu, with pastas, chicken, calzones, and burgers, but it's the pizza, with its smoky, wood-fire-charred crust, that's the big draw.

BOULDER

Do: No place in Colorado better epitomizes the state's outdoor mania than Boulder, where sunny weather keeps locals busy through all seasons. For some of Boulder's prettiest views, head to **Chautauqua Park** (✉ Baseline Rd. and 9th St. ☎ 303/442–3282 ⊕ www.bouldercolorado.gov); nestled at the base of the Flatirons, the park is a launching point for 40 miles of hiking trails. You should also make time to explore Pearl Street, the city's hub and an eclectic collection of boutiques, bookstores, art galleries, cafés, bars, and restaurants.

Eat & Drink: Feast your eyes on the intricately carved walls, pillars, and ceiling at the **Boulder Dushanbe Teahouse** (✉ 1770 13th St. ☎ 303/442–4993 ⊕ www.boulderteahouse.com), a gift from Boulder's sister city Dushanbe, Tajikistan. Tajik artisans decorated the building in a traditional style, with ceramic Islamic art and a riot of colorful wood. The menu presents a culinary cross section of the world, with dishes including North African harissa chicken, spicy Indonesian peanut noodles, and Tajik shish kebab. Afterwards, spend some time trying out Boulder's many microbreweries, like

Avery Brewing Company (✉ 4910 Nautilus Ct. N ☎ 303/440–4324 ⊕ www.averybrewing.com).

Stay: Located in what looks like a two-level motel, the **Basecamp Boulder Hotel** (✉ 2020 Arapahoe Ave. ☎ 303/449–7550 ⊕ www.basecampboulder.com) is designed to be the base camp for your adventures—and it's as unique as Boulder, with a bouldering wall in the lounge, kombucha and local beer on tap in the lobby bar, bicycles guests can borrow, a canvas map of Boulder on guest room walls, and a dry sauna.

Breakfast: The Laughing Goat Coffeehouse (✉ 1709 Pearl St. ⊕ www.thelaughinggoat.com) is bohemian-style café that serves bagels, muffins, pastries, and oatmeal for breakfast; try the locally roasted, organic espresso, too.

Day 2: Boulder, CO, to Grand Lake, CO

84 miles (2 hours, 30 minutes without traffic and stops)

Today's drive takes you up U.S. 36 west, past the mountain town of Lyons, and up the mountain to Estes Park, the gateway to Rocky Mountain National Park. After exploring one of the country's most popular (and beautiful) national parks, you'll end the day in Grand Lake, a mountain town that's usually less crowded than Estes Park.

ALONG THE WAY

Town: Estes Park boasts a postcard-worthy old town lined with charming shops and restaurants; wildlife, in particular elk, often wander the streets. Estes also has a solid craft beer and distillery scene and is home to the famous, dramatic **Stanley Hotel** (✉ 333 E. Wonderview Ave. ☎ 970/577–4000 ⊕ www.stanleyhotel.com), where it's said author Stephen King was inspired to write *The Shining*.

Eat & Drink: While Estes Park's old town area is fun for window-shopping, ice cream, and taffy, head to **The Post Chicken & Beer** (✉ *333 E. Wonderview Ave.* ☎ *970/287–5001* ⊕ *www.postchickenandbeer.com*), where you can find gluten-free fried chicken and award-winning beers.

Nature: Rocky Mountain National Park (☎ *970/586–1206* ⊕ *www.nps.gov/romo*) is one of Colorado's four national parks, with 415 square miles of incredible trails, mountains, and wildlife. Take a scenic drive up Trail Ridge Road, the highest paved road in any national park, as well as North America's highest paved through-road.

GRAND LAKE

Do: Whereas Estes Park is the gateway to the Rocky Mountain National Park in the east, Grand Lake is considered the park's western gateway and it's a less crowded, but no less gorgeous, place to stop for the night. Located in the heart of this small mountain town is Colorado's largest natural lake.

Eat & Drink: Sagebrush BBQ and Grill (✉ *1101 Grand Ave.* ☎ *970/627–1404* ⊕ *www.sagebrushbbq.com*) is where to go for tasty local barbecue, as well as a relaxed western atmosphere: peanut shells on the floor, games on the TVs, and cowboy decor on the walls. You can even dare to try "Rocky Mountain oysters" here, which aren't oysters at all, but fried bull testicles.

Stay: Grand Lake must be experienced in a cabin. **Grand Mountain Rentals** (✉ *1028 Grand Ave.* ☎ *970/627–1131* ⊕ *www.grandmountainrentals.com*) is a locally owned company that can connect travelers with luxury lakeside properties.

Breakfast: The **Blue Water Bakery Cafe** (✉ *928 Grand Ave.* ☎ *970/627–5416* ⊕ *www.bluewaterbakery.com*) is a relaxed bakery and café with scrambles, burritos, and more—not to mention beautiful lake views and excellent coffee.

Day 3: Grand Lake, CO, to Vail, CO

110 miles (2 hours without traffic and stops)

Mountain driving can be challenging if you're new to it, but the scenery is absolutely worth the effort. Today you're heading south toward Colorado's stretch of famous ski towns, but you can stop for a dip in the natural springs to ease your muscles along the way.

ALONG THE WAY

Town: Relax in the natural mineral water at the **Hot Sulphur Springs Resort and Spa** (✉ *5609 Spring Rd.* ☎ *970/725–3306* ⊕ *www.hotsulphursprings.com*) in Hot Sulphur Springs. Here, seven natural springs emerge from a large fissure, filling more than 20 pools and baths at various temperatures.

Eat & Drink: Stop for lunch in the town of Dillon, home to Lake Dillon, one of the state's largest man-made reservoirs. At popular **Dillon Dam Brewery** (✉ *100 Little Dam St.* ☎ *970/262–7777* ⊕ *www.dambrewery.com*), one of the largest brewpubs in the Rockies, you can belly up to the horseshoe-shaped bar and sample ales and lagers while you munch on burgers, sandwiches, or pub grub.

VAIL

Do: Vail is one of the nation's biggest and most popular ski destinations with more than 5,300 acres and over 200 trails, but it's a five-star outdoor adventure year-round. You'll also find fine dining, a Swiss-inspired downtown, the **Walking Mountains Science Center** (✉ *318 Walking Mountains La., Avon* ☎ *970/827–9725* ⊕ *www.walkingmountains.org*), and great hiking.

Eat & Drink: Vail has such a great food scene that it's tough to narrow it down, but **Mountain Standard** (✉ *193 Gore Creek Dr.* ☎ *970/476–0123* ⊕ *www.*

mtnstandard.com) is at the top. Enjoy well-prepared New American food and local beer in the cozy restaurant on the banks of the river, right in the heart of downtown.

Stay: Although Vail is known for its ample luxury lodging options, a favorite way to stay is just outside town in nearby Wolcott, in luxury "glamping" tents by **Collective Retreats** (✉ 4098 Rte. 131 ☎ 970/445–2033 ⊕ www.collective-treats.com). Relax away from the crowds under unobstructed stars before retreating to your comfortable bed underneath an antler chandelier; toilets and running water are included in this not-so-camping experience.

Breakfast: Made-to-order breakfast is part of your stay at Collective Retreats, or you can head back into Vail for champagne brunch at the French brasserie **Vintage** (✉ 12 Vail Rd. ☎ 970/479–0175 ⊕ www.vintage-vail.com). Bacon-wrapped figs, crab Benedicts, croque madames and monsieurs, and huckleberry bacon French toast are highlights, paired, of course, with breakfast cocktails.

Day 4: Vail, CO, to Aspen, CO

100 miles (2 hours without traffic and stops)

The mountainous drive from Vail to Aspen isn't far, but it passes right through Glenwood Springs. Take an extended break here for a relaxing soak in the hot springs, a hike, and a locally crafted cocktail.

ALONG THE WAY

Town: Glenwood Springs is home to the world's largest hot springs pool, as well as several other places to relax in the area's natural mineral water. **Iron Mountain Hot Springs** (✉ 281 Centennial St. ☎ 970/945–4766 ⊕ www.

ironmountainhotsprings.com) is on the banks of the Colorado River, and the **Yampah Vapor Caves** (✉ 709 E. 6th St. ☎ 970/945–0667 ⊕ www.yampahspa.com) will take you underground to a dark and steamy hideaway.

Nature: One of Colorado's most beloved hikes is Hanging Lake Trail in Glenwood Canyon. This National Natural Landmark consists of a series of blue waterfalls spilling into a crystal lake; the lake even appears to be magically suspended off the edge of a cliff. Just note that you need reservations and a permit to experience it.

Eat & Drink: The **Colorado Ranch House** (✉ 704 Grand Ave. ☎ 970/945–9059 ⊕ www.coranchhouse.com), a Western-inspired, modern-American restaurant, serves cocktails made with alcohol from the local Woody Creek Distillers, as well as unique spins on classic dishes with locally sourced protein (think duck wings and an elk quesadilla); the Rocky Mountain ruby red trout is always a winner.

ASPEN

Do: Aspen Snowmass is one of the world's most famous skiing destinations, but skiing is not all Aspen offers. Have a picnic in the scenic **John Denver Sanctuary** (✉ 470 Rio Grande Pl. ☎ 970/920–5120 ⊕ www.aspenrecreation.com), relax in a waterside garden on the Roaring Fork River, and stroll through Aspen's hoppin' downtown.

Eat & Drink: The Wild Fig (✉ 315 E. Hyman Ave. ☎ 970/925–5160 ⊕ www.thewildfig.com), right off the walking mall, feels like a European brasserie in Colorado. You can't leave Aspen without ordering the Fish in a Bag, the fish of the day expertly prepared and served in a brown paper bag.

Photo Op: One of the most photographed views in the nation is the famous **Maroon Bells** national landmark. Hike these

Don't leave Colorado without snapping a photo of the peaks of the famous Maroon Bells.

popular mountains (there are several different trails of varying difficulty levels) or simply snap a selfie with them in the background.

Stay: Aspen is for luxury, so do it right and book a stay in one of the **Cuvée Aspen** (⊕ *www.cuvee.com*) properties. These luxe estates come with personalized details, like dinner prepared by a private chef, an in-room massage, or a champagne bubble bath.

Breakfast: Grab breakfast or brunch at **Village Smithy** (⊠ *26 S. 3rd St.* ☎ *970/963–9990* ⊕ *www.villagesmithy.com*), a local favorite. In this historic building that used to be a blacksmith shop, you can enjoy deep-fried French toast made with a homemade baguette (or a tofu scramble if you're in the mood for something healthier).

Day 5: Aspen, CO, to Palisade, CO

115 miles (2 hours without traffic and stops)

Let the exploration of the mountains continue as you venture past more ski towns and into wine territory (yep, Colorado makes wine!). You'll be backtracking up Route 82 west for the first leg of the trip, but make a stop in quirky Carbondale for lunch to break it up.

ALONG THE WAY

Detour: If you don't mind adding another hour onto your drive, one of the most scenic drives in Colorado is on Independence Pass, on Colorado Route 82 up and over the Continental Divide. Leaving from Aspen, it's in the opposite direction from Palisade, but in the fall, the yellow aspen leaves seem to transform the entire mountain into glittering gold, making the detour completely worth it.

Town: The artsy, outdoorsy town of Carbondale sits beneath Mt. Sopris (12,965 feet), and its Main Street is lined with century-old brick buildings that house clothing boutiques, art galleries, and excellent restaurants.

Eat & Drink: Bonfire Coffee (✉ *433 Main St.* ☎ *970/510–5327* ⊕ *www.bonfirecoffee.com*) is a craft coffee roaster known for its ethically and sustainably sourced coffees, which are roasted to order. The coffeeshop is located in a cozy, century-old, Wild West–style space.

Shop: "Cocktails with a conscience" is the motto at **Carbondale's Marble Distilling Co.** (✉ *150 Main St.* ☎ *970/963–7008* ⊕ *www.marbledistilling.com*), a zero-waste craft distillery named for the famous pieces of marble, from the neighboring town of Marble, used in the filtering process. Creative cocktails featuring homemade vodka, rye, whiskey, and bourbon are served, but you can also purchase bottles to take home with you.

PALISADE

Do: Palisade is home to most of Colorado's vineyards and a quarter of the state's wineries. Do a winery tour, taste small-batch wine, and also pick up some fresh peaches, another one of Palisade's claims to fame. Just remember to drive responsibly.

Eat & Drink: Palisade might be famous for its wine, but it also has a local brewery, the **Palisade Brewing Company** (✉ *200 Peach Ave.* ☎ *970/464–1462* ⊕ *www.palisadebrewingcompany.com*), with a full menu. If you're into spice, ask about the El Diablo Savory Cheesecake for dessert, made with ghost peppers, habanero peppers, jalapeños, sriracha, and pepper jack cheese, topped with an ancho/chipotle pesto.

Shop: Pick up a pie at **Palisade Pies** (✉ *3415 C ½ Rd.* ☎ *970/549–0347* ⊕ *www.facebook.com/Palisade-PieShop*), a family-owned shop that bakes pies packed with fresh fruit from their own orchard. On Sunday in mid-June through late September, don't miss the local farmers' market, where you can peruse produce, wine, and other local goods all in one spot.

Stay: Immerse yourself in Palisade's wine scene at **Wine Country Inn** (✉ *777 Grande River Dr.* ☎ *970/464–5777* ⊕ *www.coloradowinecountryinn.com*), which features breakfast and afternoon wine receptions (with private label wines) and vineyard views.

Breakfast: Start the day with pastries (including sweet rolls and pie) made with local fruits at the **Slice O' Life Bakery** (✉ *105 W. 3rd St.* ☎ *970/464–0577* ⊕ *www.facebook.com/sliceolifebakery*).

Day 6: Palisade, CO, to Telluride, CO

120 miles (2 hours, 30 minutes without traffic and stops)

All mountain drives through Colorado are scenic, so keep your camera on hand. This particular route takes you on Route 62 west to Route 134 south, which is part of the San Juan Skyway, one of the country's most stupendous drives.

ALONG THE WAY

Detour: A quick half hour west of Palisade, traveling on I–70 west, takes you to **Colorado National Monument** (✉ *Rim Rock Dr., Fruita* ☎ *970/858–3617* ⊕ *www.nps.gov/colm*), where sheer red-rock cliffs open to 23 miles of steep canyons and thin monoliths that sprout as high as 450 feet from the floor. Created between 65 million and 225 million years ago, the monument was designated in 1911 and has been popular with photographers, hikers, and those eager to drive its paved road, Rim Rock Drive, ever since. The 23-mile drive on the famed road will take you about an hour.

Nature: Another one of Colorado's famous parks, the **Black Canyon of the Gunnison National Park** (☎ 970/641–2337 ⊕ www. nps.gov/blca) is named for the black rocks lining its steep gorge, creating some of the steepest cliffs in the country.

Eat & Drink: Toast the canyon with a drink (and pizza, sausage, salad, and more) at the **High Alpine Brewing Company** (✉ 111 N. Main St. ☎ 970/642–4500 ⊕ www. highalpinebrewing.com) in Gunnison, a brewery located 7,700 feet above sea level.

TELLURIDE

Do: This European-influenced, historic town is considered one of the best ski destinations in North America thanks to its 300 inches of snow in the winter, and just as many days of sunshine per year. It's also home to one of Colorado's biggest annual music events, the Telluride Bluegrass Festival. To learn more about the city's mining history, make a visit to the **Telluride Historical Museum** (✉ 201 W. Gregory Ave. ☎ 970/728–3344 ⊕ www. telluridemuseum.org).

Eat & Drink: At dinnertime, take the Gondola up the mountain to **Allred's** (✉ San Sophia Station ☎ 970/728–7474 ⊕ www. tellurideskiresort.com) for the town's best food and views. Locally inspired fare such as elk, bison, and lamb feature prominently on the menu.

Stay: A grand stone-and-wood structure, the luxury ski-in ski-out **Inn at Lost Creek** (✉ 119 Lost Creek La., Mountain Village ☎ 970/728–5678 ⊕ www.innat-lostcreek.com) in the Mountain Village resembles an alpine lodge with contemporary furnishings.

Breakfast: Local institution **Baked** (✉ 127 S. Fir St. ☎ 970/728–4775 ⊕ bakedintel. com) serves fresh-baked goodies like sandwiches, pizza, and doughnuts.

Day 7: Telluride, CO, to Pagosa Springs, CO

170 miles (3 hours, 15 minutes without traffic and stops)

Today you can head out on Route 145, driving past scenic small towns that give you a taste of the old Wild West, as you make your way to Mesa Verde National Park, and then follow U.S. 160 on to Pagosa Springs. But if you don't mind an extra hour or so of driving time, loop back around the way you came from Telluride to take the Million Dollar Highway (aka U.S. 550) south from Ouray down to Mesa Verde. This awesome stretch of road climbs over Red Mountain Pass (arguably the most spectacular part of the 236-mile San Juan Skyway). As it ascends steeply from Ouray, the road clings to the cliffs hanging over the Uncompahgre River. Guardrails are few, hairpin turns are many, and behemoth RVs seem to take more than their share of road.

ALONG THE WAY

Nature: Explore ancient history at **Mesa Verde National Park** (☎ 970/529–4465 ⊕ www.nps.gov/meve), home to about 5,000 archaeological sites. This national park has some of the best-preserved Ancestral Pueblo cliff dwellings in the country.

Eat & Drink: By far the best place to eat in the park is the **Metate Room** (✉ 34879 U.S. 160, Mancos ☎ 970/529–4422 ⊕ www.visitmesaverde.com), a southwestern upscale restaurant attached to the Far View Lodge. Order a glass of wine and request a table outside on the rooftop (if you're there late enough, it's an excellent spot to watch the sunset).

Nature: As you leave Mesa Verde and head to Pagosa Springs, you can see **Chimney Rock** (✉ 3179 Rte. 151 ☎ 970/883–5359 ⊕ www.

chimneyrockco.org) from the highway, a national monument and archaeological site that was considered sacred by the Ancestral Puebloans. Stop and hike to the top; a half mile will reward you with 360-degree panoramic views.

PAGOSA SPRINGS

Do: Pagosa Springs has the world's deepest geothermal hot spring, certified by the *Guinness World Records*. You can't swim here (it's more than 1,000 feet deep), but you can enjoy its waters in many pools nearby.

Eat & Drink: Riff Raff Brewing Company (✉ *274 Pagosa St.* ☎ *970/264–4677* ⊕ *www.riffraffbrewing.com*) is a local brewery powered by the geothermal heat from the springs. How often can you say you had a beer that Mother Nature helped brew?

Stay: If you stay at the **Springs Resort and Spa** (✉ *323 Hot Springs Blvd.* ☎ *800/225–0934* ⊕ *www.pagosahotsprings.com*), you can wrap yourself in a big white spa robe and head directly for the 24 soaking pools that are terraced on several levels overlooking the San Juan River. As a hotel guest, you'll have 24-hour access.

Breakfast: The **Pagosa Baking Company** (✉ *238 Pagosa St.* ☎ *970/264–9348* ⊕ *www.pagosabakingcompany.com*) sells homemade goods and fresh, healthy breakfast offerings, from breakfast burritos to quiche.

Day 8: Pagosa, CO, to Great Sand Dunes National Park, CO

110 miles (2 hours without traffic and stops)

It's time to hit up Colorado's fourth and final national park, in quirky San Luis Valley, a region full of roadside attractions.

ALONG THE WAY

Roadside Attraction: Not far from the sand dunes is a strange sight to behold: the **UFO Watchtower** (✉ *Rte. 17, Center* ☎ *719/378–2296* ⊕ *theoriginalufowatchtower.com*), a supposed point of two energetic vortexes said to attract aliens. Come see for yourself if any aliens come to say hi and if not, leave a tribute for extraterrestrial guests in the sprawling yard of trinkets out front.

Nature: Another must-visit attraction nearby is the **Colorado Gators Reptile Park** (✉ *9162 La. 9 N, Mosca* ☎ *719/378–2612* ⊕ *www.coloradogators.com*); yes, hundreds of alligators live in southern Colorado.

GREAT SAND DUNES NATIONAL PARK

Do: The otherworldly **Great Sand Dunes National Park** (✉ *11999 Rte. 150* ☎ *719/378–6395* ⊕ *www.nps.gov/grsa*) seems out of place with mountains in the background and a creek running through them. You can even sled down the tallest sand dune in North America on a "sand-board."

Eat & Drink: Many people pack a picnic to enjoy in the dunes (you can even camp here), but another good bet in the valley is the **T Road Brewing Company** (✉ *120 W. Silver Ave., Crestone* ☎ *719/256–0431* ⊕ *www.troadbrewing.com*). It's nothing fancy, but the burgers and pizza do the job.

Stay: You can spend the night at **Rustic Rook Resort** (✉ *13254 La. 5 N* ☎ *719/270–1356* ⊕ *rusticrookresort.com*), which offers a glamping experience with comfortable tents that include private showers and wood stoves.

Breakfast: Food and coffee is included in your stay at Rustic Rook. The food features local ingredients and livestock whenever possible.

Day 9: Great Sand Dunes National Park, CO, to Colorado Springs, CO

194 miles (3 hours, 30 minutes without traffic and stops)

There are two routes to Colorado Springs; the shorter one takes you on U.S. 160 and up I–25 through historical towns like Pueblo, but the slightly longer route via Route 17 north to U.S. 285 and then U.S. 50 is much more scenic, taking you past several major mountains.

ALONG THE WAY

Town: The highlight of a stop in Cañon City is the Royal Gorge and its accompanying bridge, the highest bridge in the country and once the world's highest suspension bridge. Carved by the Arkansas River more than 3 million years ago, the Royal Gorge canyon walls tower up to 1,200 feet high. The 956-foot-high **Royal Gorge Bridge** (⊠ *4218 County Rd. 3A* ☎ *719/275–7507* ⊕ *www. royalgorgebridge.com*) sways on gusty afternoons and the river can be seen clearly between gaps in the boards, adding to the thrill of a crossing. You can walk across the bridge nearly 1,000 feet above the river, and then book a wild white-water-rafting trip in the Arkansas River to experience the bridge from below if there's time.

Eat & Drink: The **Whitewater Bar and Grill** (⊠ *45045 W. U.S. 50* ☎ *719/269– 1009* ⊕ *www.whitewaterbar.com*) is the ideal casual restaurant to break during an adventure-packed day. The vast backyard features sand volleyball, a playground for kids, horseshoes, fire pits, hammocks, and tons of tables with umbrellas—plus local beer, margaritas, and a full food menu.

COLORADO SPRINGS

Do: The contented residents of the Colorado Springs area believe they live in an ideal location, and it's hard to argue with them. The state's second-largest city has no shortness of outdoor and cultural adventures to enjoy. Immerse yourself in natural wonders at the **Cave of the Winds** (⊠ *100 Cave of the Winds Rd.* ☎ *719/685–5444* ⊕ *www.caveofthewinds.com*), a 500-million-year-old underground cave system, and then see more mountain magic aboveground at the **Garden of the Gods** (⊠ *Garden of the Gods Rd.* ⊕ *www.gardenofgods.com*), bizarre red-rock formations that tilt and balance in seemingly impossible ways. While you're here, be sure to take a train to the top of **Pikes Peak** (☎ *800/525– 2250* ⊕ *www.pikes-peak.com*), the most visited mountain in North America.

Eat & Drink: While there are plenty of incredible restaurants in Colorado Springs, a fun road-trip experience is to dine at the **Airplane Restaurant** (⊠ *1665 Newport Rd.* ☎ *719/570–7656*). A 1953 Boeing KC-97 tanker was converted into this quirky, casual restaurant, and you can sit in the cockpit and dine in the cabin.

Stay: It's expensive, but with its old-world style that emits pure luxury—including the signature pink building with the Mediterranean-style towers—**The Broadmoor** (⊠ *1 Lake Ave.* ☎ *800/755-5011* ⊕ *www. broadmoor.com*) continues to redefine itself with settings where guests can unwind and be pampered.

Breakfast: At **Adam's Mountain Café** (⊠ *26 Manitou Ave.* ☎ *719/685–1430* ⊕ *www. adamsmountaincafe.com*), join the locals in a cozy atmosphere with an emphasis on slow food made from scratch. The chef focuses on locally sourced and organic ingredients.

Day 10: Colorado Springs, CO, to Denver, CO

70 miles (1 hour, 15 minutes without traffic and stops)

This relatively quick highway drive on I–25 will shoot you back to Denver in no time flat. There's a lot to do in Colorado Springs, so it might be best to use this time to see anything you couldn't the previous day.

ALONG THE WAY

Town: Artsy, and very sleepy, Palmer Lake is a magnet for hikers who set out for the evergreen-clad peaks at several in-town trailheads. There are more good restaurants and working artists than one would expect from a population of about 2,800. The town developed around the railroad tracks that were laid here in 1871—the lake itself was used as a refueling point for steam engines.

Eat & Drink: Bella Panini (✉ *4 Rte. 105* ☎ *719/481–3244* ⊕ *www.bellapanini. com*) in Palmer Lake has a heavy Italian focus, but the chefs here aren't afraid to mix things up, whipping up such creative concoctions as crawfish-and-jalapeño pizza.

DENVER

Do: Wrap up your road trip with an art-filled day in Denver, the capital of Colorado. Visit the Golden Triangle Creative District, where you can see more than 16 different galleries and museums, including the **Denver Art Museum** (✉ *100 W. 14th Ave. Pkwy.* ☎ *720/865–5000* ⊕ *www.denverartmuseum.org*) and the **Clyfford Still Museum** (✉ *1250 Bannock St.* ☎ *720/354–4880* ⊕ *www. clyffordstillmuseum.org*). Hip Larimer Square is filled with boutiques, bars, and restaurants while taking a hike (and seeing a show, if you have the chance) at the **Red Rocks Park and Amphitheater** (✉ *18300 W. Alameda Pkwy.,*

Morrison ☎ *720/865–2494* ⊕ *www. redrocksonline.com*) is another must.

Eat & Drink: The most Colorado way to dine in Denver is at **Elway's** (✉ *2500 E. 1st Ave.* ☎ *303/399–5353* ⊕ *www. elways.com*), a steak house named after former Denver Broncos quarterback John Elway. The wine list is solid, the food is filling and tasty, and, in true Colorado fashion, the atmosphere is sophisticated but far from stuffy.

Stay: Complete your artsy day by staying at the **Art Hotel** (✉ *1201 Broadway* ☎ *303/572–8000* ⊕ *www.hilton. com*), a modern hotel that also houses an impressive, curated art gallery. You may even find a famous piece of art in your room. You can also spend the night at the visually striking and environmentally sustainable **Populus Hotel** (✉ *240 14th St.* ☎ *303/800–4240* ⊕ *www.populusdenver.com*).

Breakfast: Locals line up for blocks to get a table at **Snooze** (✉ *1701 Wynkoop St.* ☎ *303/825–3536* ⊕ *www.snoozeeatery.com*), a breakfast eatery. The upbeat, retro vibe is only second to its popular pineapple upside-down pancakes.

The Ultimate Wild West Road Trip

Written by Aimee Heckel

If you've ever dreamed of being a cowgirl or cowboy, this trip back in time is for you. Luckily for history fans, the American Wild West is still alive in states like New Mexico, Colorado, Arizona, Wyoming, and South Dakota. While many things have changed since the 1800s, western hospitality remains, as do tons of historical sites, saloons, working ranches, and ghost towns that created the classic vision of the Wild West that so many people still have today (helped along with many a Hollywood Western and even more recent television shows like *Westworld*). Throughout this 10-day adventure, you'll explore ghost towns of former mining communities, watch reenactments of shoot-outs, tip your hat at the same bars that once welcomed rebels and outlaws, and learn about America's history in the late 1800s as you journey through the country's most famous frontier towns. Each day is pretty driving-heavy with an average of four hours of driving per day, but it's the only way you'll be able to experience the best of the Wild West in just one trip.

At a Glance

Start: Tucson, AZ

End: Rapid City, SD

Miles Traveled: 2,160 miles

Suggested Duration: 9 days

States Visited: Arizona, Colorado, New Mexico, South Dakota, Wyoming

Key Sights: Buffalo Bill Center of the West; Deadwood, South Dakota; Dearfield Ghost Town; Mount Rushmore; Tombstone, Arizona

Best Time to Go: This is best as a warm-weather trip, because you won't love Wyoming's roads in a blizzard.

Day 1: Tucson, AZ, to Las Cruces, NM

325 miles (5 hours without traffic and stops)

Start your Wild West trip in southern Arizona, where many Hollywood Westerns have been filmed. Before you depart the city of Tucson, stop by Old Tucson just west of town for one of Hollywood's most popular filming locations (including *Three Amigos* and *Tombstone*). Today's drive to Las Cruces, New Mexico, is a straight shot east on I–10, but any true Western fan needs to make the hourlong detour down to Tombstone before you leave Arizona.

ALONG THE WAY

Town: Tombstone, aka the Town Too Tough to Die, is one of the most popular Wild West attractions, thanks to famous past residents like Doc Holliday and Wyatt Earp. Historic Allen Street is the site of the real 1881 gunfight at O.K. Corral, one of the Wild West's most famous shoot-outs that became the stuff of legend; you might even be able to catch a reenactment. Afterward, you can check out the replica gallows and other exhibits at the **Tombstone Courthouse State Historic Park** (✉ 223 E. Toughnut St. ☎ 520/457–3311 ⊕ www.azstateparks.com), visit the graves of outlaws at the **Boothill Graveyard** (✉ 408 Rte. 80 ☎ 520/457–2540 ⊕ www.discoverboothill.com), and look for ghosts at the supposedly haunted **Bird Cage Theatre** (✉ 535 E. Allen St. ☎ 520/457–3421 ⊕ www.tombstonebirdcage.com). Tombstone is packed with tour options if you want to stay a while.

Eat & Drink: The first meal of your trip needs to be at a saloon. Tip a pint at **Doc Holliday's Saloon** (✉ 517 E. Allen St. ☎ 520/457–2247 ⊕ www.facebook.com/DocHollidaysSaloon) or step back in time with a drink and a show at **Wyatt Earp's Oriental Saloon & Theater** (✉ 500 E. Allen St. ☎ 520/457–2407 ⊕ www.orientalsaloon.com).

LAS CRUCES

Do: The former stomping grounds of Billy the Kid, Las Cruces is the perfect place to feel like a cowboy for a day, thanks to the **New Mexico Farm & Ranch Heritage Museum** (✉ 4100 Dripping Springs Rd. ☎ 575/522–4100 ⊕ www.nmfarmandranchmuseum.org), which offers demos of cow milking, blacksmithing, and other ranching skills. You'll also enjoy wandering through Old Mesilla, a colorful village of historic adobe buildings and the former home of Billy the Kid.

Eat & Drink: Enjoy authentic, homemade Mexican food at **La Nueva Casita Cafe** (✉ 195 N. Mesquite St. ☎ 575/523–5434 ⊕ www.lanuevacasitacafe.com), a local favorite that dates back to the 1950s. After dinner, cruise around Main Street and the historic Mesquite District.

Stay: Immerse yourself in Spanish colonial style at the posh **Hotel Encanto de Las Cruces** (✉ 705 S. Telshor Blvd. ☎ 575/522–4300 ⊕ www.hotelencanto.com). Relax by the outdoor pool as the sun goes down.

Breakfast: Breakfast is included in your stay at the Encanto, or pop over to the **Cafe de Mesilla** (✉ 2190 Avenida de Mesilla ☎ 575/524–0000 ⊕ www.cafedemesilla.com), an adobe restaurant with classic New Mexican breakfast dishes you can enjoy on the patio. Try the Mesilla Morning Sandwich with green chilis.

Day 2: Las Cruces, NM, to Santa Fe, NM

280 miles (4 hours without traffic and stops)

Get a driving tour of the middle of New Mexico as you head north up Interstate 25.

ALONG THE WAY

Town: You'll drive through the big city of Albuquerque, so you may as well stop by the historic **San Felipe de Neri Church** (✉ 2005 N. Plaza St. NW ☎ 505/243–4628 ⊕ www.sanfelipedeneri.org) in Old Town Plaza. The still-running adobe church was built in 1793, dating back to the Spanish colonial period, and is one of the oldest surviving buildings in the city. Albuquerque's early Wild West history was notorious for having minimal law enforcement—the wild Wild West.

Eat & Drink: Fill 'er up at the **High Noon Restaurant and Saloon** (✉ 425 San Felipe St. NW ☎ 505/765–1455 ⊕ www.highnoonrestaurant.com) in Albuquerque's Old Town, housed in a historic 1785 building. The long-standing local restaurant serves ABQ's best hand-cut steaks and margaritas.

SANTA FE

Do: Santa Fe is the oldest capital city in the United States, and its history spanning Pueblo cultures and Spanish and Mexican rule is evident in its architecture and culture. But thanks to its role as the endpoint of the Santa Fe Trail, it's also a big draw for Wild West fans. Book a guided Jeep, bike, or walking tour with **Santa Fe Mountain Adventures** (☎ 505/988–4000 ⊕ www.santafemountainadventures.com), which will take you to see petroglyphs, historic ruins, and Ancestral Pueblo dwellings. The area surrounding Santa Fe is a popular filming location for Westerns, including *Godless*, *A Million Ways to Die in the West*, *No Country for Old Men*, and the remakes of *3:10 to Yuma*, *The Magnificent Seven*, and *True Grit*. Alternatively, you can take a detour an hour east to visit Las Vegas, New Mexico, once considered the most violent town in the Wild West.

Shop: Today Santa Fe is well-known for its art, with many artists showcasing a distinctly western style; you'll find examples at galleries like the **Sorrel Sky Gallery** (✉ 125 W. Palace Ave. ☎ 505/501–6555 ⊕ www.sorrelsky.com).

Eat & Drink: The expert culinary team at the romantic **Anasazi Restaurant & Bar** (✉ 113 Washington Ave. ☎ 505/988–3236 ⊕ www.rosewoodhotels.com) balances old-world techniques with southwestern spice in its approach to the menu. If you want a less formal vibe, dine in the more spacious, convivial bar or on the lively street-side patio.

Stay: The luxurious **Inn & Spa at Loretto** (✉ 211 Old Santa Fe Trail ☎ 505/988–5531 ⊕ www.hotelloretto.com) features architecture inspired by Taos Pueblo. The southwestern, homey boutique

The Ultimate
Wild West
Road Trip

hotel is just a few blocks from historic Santa Fe Plaza.

Breakfast: Start the day with a breakfast burrito smothered in spicy red chili at the casual diner **Tia Sophia's** (✉ *210 W. San Francisco St.* ☎ *505/983–9880* ⊕ *www. facebook.com/tiasophias*).

Day 3: Santa Fe, NM, to Durango, CO

215 miles (4 hours without traffic and stops)

It's time to giddy-up to Colorado, where today's drive will take you over a jaw-dropping mountain pass and past some photo-worthy attractions.

ALONG THE WAY

Town: Stop in Chama, New Mexico, where you can see (or ride, if time allows) the historic **Cumbres & Toltec Scenic Railroad** (☎ *888/286–2737* ⊕ *www. cumbrestoltec.com*). This coal-fueled steam train, built in 1880 for mining, is the country's most complete narrow-gauge railroad from that time. It chugs between Chama and Antonito, Colorado.

Eat & Drink: Pause in the hot-springs town of Pagosa Springs at **Riff Raff Brewing Company** (✉ *274 Pagosa St.* ☎ *970/264–4677* ⊕ *www.riffraffbrewing.com*), where you can get "earth-powered beer" (beer made via geothermal heat) and a goat burger smothered in onions and green chilis.

Nature: On U.S. 160, you'll pass the **Chimney Rock National Monument** (✉ *3179 Rte. 151, Chimney Rock* ☎ *970/883–5359* ⊕ *www.chimneyrockco.org*), a sacred rock formation that sticks straight up. You can hike this Ancestral Puebloan site or simply appreciate it from the highway.

Extend Your Trip

From Santa Fe: The Best of New Mexico *(Ch. 5)*

From Cody: Big Sky Country *(Ch. 4)*

From Rapid City: The Best of the Dakotas *(Ch. 6)*

DURANGO

Do: The Wild West wouldn't have been the Wild West without the invention of the railroad, so dedicate this leg of the trip to trains and make a visit to Durango, the truest railroad town in the West. Visit the free **Durango and Silverton Narrow Gauge Railroad and Museum** (✉ *479 Main Ave.* ☎ *888/872–4607* ⊕ *www.durangotrain.com*), with its railway dating back to the 1880s. If you don't have time for a full train ride, check out the inexpensive hour-long tour through the train yard.

Eat & Drink: For a raucous night, drink and dine at the **Diamond Belle Saloon,** an authentic Old West saloon with live ragtime piano located in the Strater Hotel (✉ *699 Main Ave.* ☎ *970/247–4431* ⊕ *www.strater.com*).

Stay: The **Strater Hotel** (✉ *699 Main Ave.* ☎ *970/247–4431* ⊕ *www.strater. com*), built in 1887, is a living history museum filled with Victorian antiques and an authentic Old West atmosphere. Or if you're looking for an off-the-beaten-path Old West escape, venture past Durango to **Dunton Hot Springs** (✉ *52068 Rd. 38, Dolores* ☎ *877/288–9922* ⊕ *www.duntondestinations.com*), a former mining town (established in 1885) that's been renovated into luxurious cabins (yes, the whole town). Stay in a real miner's hand-hewn log cabin, dine in a 19th-century farmhouse, and relax in private hot springs.

Breakfast: El Moro Tavern (✉ 945 Main Ave. ☎ 970/259–5555 ⊕ www.elmorotavern.com), home of "Durango's strangest shoot-out" in 1906, serves weekend brunch. Otherwise, walk down to the 11th Street Station food truck court for various breakfast options.

Day 4: Durango, CO, to Leadville, CO

About 290 miles (6 hours without traffic and stops)

Prepare for the most beautiful part of your road trip, along Colorado's Million Dollar Highway with fittingly million-dollar mountain views.

ALONG THE WAY

Town: Stop in historic Silverton, an old mining community and National Historic Landmark perched at 9,318 feet above sea level. The town is heaven for history buffs and outdoor lovers alike.

Eat & Drink: Silverton's **Bent Elbow Restaurant** (✉ 1114 Blair St. ☎ 970/387–5775 ⊕ www.thebent.com) is set inside an original Old West dining room and saloon, complete with a honky-tonk piano.

Nature: Pause as you enter Ouray, a fantasy-like mountain town built in a box canyon. You're surrounded by mountains on all sides, so take the time to explore by taking a jaunt to Box Canon Falls, where the turbulent waters of Clear Creek thunder 285 feet down a narrow gorge.

Detour: If you love a good ghost town, take a 45-minute detour to visit one of Colorado's finest: St. Elmo. This is one of Colorado's best-preserved ghost towns, with a dusty Main Street and saloon that looks straight out of a Western.

LEADVILLE

Do: Walk through the Victorian neighborhoods of the highest incorporated city in North America and a onetime

silver-mining boomtown. Don't miss the **National Mining Hall of Fame and Museum** (✉ 120 W. 9th St. ☎ 719/486–1229 ⊕ www.mininghalloffame.org), with fascinating replicas of mines.

Eat & Drink: The **Legendary Silver Dollar Saloon** (✉ 315 Harrison Ave. ☎ 719/486–9914 ⊕ www.legendarysilverdollarsaloon.com), located in a historical building that feels plucked from the 1800s, used to be a favorite hangout of John Henry "Doc" Holliday. Many features at the saloon (and restaurant) are original.

Stay: The **Delaware Hotel** (✉ 700 Harrison Ave. ☎ 800/748–2004 ⊕ www.delaware-hotel.com), in a Victorian brick building right in downtown, dates back to 1886. It's the last remaining grand hotel in town, and it's equal parts history museum and the crown architectural jewel of Leadville.

Breakfast: City on a Hill Coffee (✉ 508 Harrison Ave. ☎ 719/486–0797 ⊕ www.cityonahillcoffee.com) claims to be North America's highest-elevation coffee business. So you can check that off your bucket list while you eat breakfast.

Day 5: Leadville, CO, to Fort Collins, CO

160 miles (2 hours, 30 minutes without traffic and stops)

Try to plan this drive outside of rush hour and weekends, so you can make it down busy I–70 with less traffic.

ALONG THE WAY

Roadside Attraction: Visit the grave of William F. Cody (aka "Buffalo Bill") in **Lookout Mountain Park** (✉ 987 Lookout Mountain Rd. ☎ 720/865–0900 ⊕ www.denvergov.org), on the way down I–70. The on-site **Buffalo Bill Museum** (✉ 987½ Lookout Mountain Rd. ☎ 303/526–0744 ⊕ www.buffalobill.org) tells all about the famous buffalo hunter's life and the Wild West history in the region.

Town: Golden is one of Colorado's oldest frontier towns. **Golden History Tours** (☎ 720/432–1162 ⊕ www.goldenhistorytours.com) offers guided tours through the streets and parks, relaying some pretty wild (and true) tales.

Eat & Drink: Located in the historic 1913 Armory building in Golden, **Café 13** (✉ 1301 Arapahoe St. ☎ 303/278–2225 ⊕ www.cafe13golden.com) claims to be housed in one of the largest cobblestone buildings in the country. The menu is perfect for a healthy lunch of street tacos and sandwiches.

Detour: Swing east to Dearfield, a ghost town that used to be a Black-majority settlement. It was formed in 1910 as a proposed colony for African Americans and ended up being one of Colorado's most successful African American communities until the population started dwindling in the 1920s. The spot is a fascinating look at the often-unexplored role of African Americans in the Wild West.

FORT COLLINS

Do: A relaxing way to spend the evening in Fort Collins is wandering through its historic Old Town, which was the real-life inspiration for Disneyland's Main Street USA. Look for live music, ample shopping, and quirky shops, like **Nuance Chocolate** (✉ 214 Pine St. ☎ 970/484–2330 ⊕ www.nuancechocolate.com), a chocolatier that roasts and grinds chocolate beans nearby. It also claims to have the largest selection of single-origin chocolate in the world.

Eat & Drink: The Farmhouse at Jessup Farm (✉ 1957 Jessup Dr. ☎ 970/631–8041 ⊕ www.farmhousefc.com) feels like home, if home were a 130-year-old farmhouse converted into a rustic restaurant. Although the stairs squeak with age and the brick is exposed, the food is modern, hip, and local.

Stay: In town, stay at the historic **Armstrong Hotel** (✉ 259 S. College Ave. ☎ 970/484–3883 ⊕ www.thearmstronghotel.com),

with a pressed-tin ceiling and guest rooms furnished with antiques.

Breakfast: The **Silver Grill** (✉ 218 Walnut St. ☎ 970/484–4656 ⊕ www.silvergrill.com) in downtown Fort Collins is the classic greasy spoon, in all the best ways.

Day 6: Fort Collins, CO, to Atlantic City, WY

300 miles (4 hours, 45 minutes without traffic and stops)

Say adios to Colorado; U.S. 287 will usher you into Wyoming for a quieter stretch of the drive. While Wyoming is packed with Wild West destinations, this route will take you into the realm of ghost towns.

ALONG THE WAY

Town: Laramie, Wyoming, has historic buildings dating back to the 1800s, including a prison built on the river in 1872 where Old West outlaw Butch Cassidy was put behind bars.

Eat & Drink: The **Altitude Chophouse and Brewery** (✉ 320 S. 2nd St. ☎ 307/721–4031 ⊕ www.altitudechophouse.com) is Laramie's finest restaurant, specializing in American favorites that highlight a true western heritage (think beef brisket and prime rib).

Detour: The ghost town of **South Pass City** (☎ 307/332–3684 ⊕ wyoparks.wyo.gov) used to be a stop near the Oregon Trail. More than 30 historic structures have since landed the community on the National Register of Historic Places. Be sure to tour the Carissa mine shaft.

ATLANTIC CITY

Do: No, not that Atlantic City. Wyoming's version has a population of only about 57, but this tiny former mining camp in Wind River Country is the real-deal West, with preserved buildings and an old-fashioned, small-town energy you won't find in busier tourist sites. This is the place to unplug and unwind.

Eat & Drink: If you want to experience the Wild West, follow the dirt roads to the **Miner's Grubstake** (✉ 25 N. Granier Ave. ☎ 307/332–0915 ⊕ minersgrub-stakedredge.com), which calls its menu "good ol' home cookin'."

Stay: There's actually nowhere to stay in Atlantic City, but a short drive to Lander will bring you to the **Rock Shop Inn** (✉ 4260 Rte. 28 ☎ 847/873–2437 ⊕ www.rockshopinn.com), a secluded getaway with unique luxury cabins.

Breakfast: This is a small town with limited options, so head back to the Miner's Grubstake for a hearty American breakfast with an ever-popular Bloody Mary.

Day 7: Atlantic City, WY, to Cody, WY

200 miles (3 hours, 15 minutes without traffic and stops)

Wyoming roads can feel like ghost towns in and of themselves, so make sure you fill up on gas whenever you see a station. This wide-open drive north gets you closer to Yellowstone National Park and just past the Shoshone National Forest.

ALONG THE WAY

Town: Stop at Thermopolis, with the world's largest mineral hot springs, to unwind in the 104-degree healing waters at the **Hot Springs State Park Bath House** (✉ 168 Tepee St. ☎ 307/864–3765 ⊕ www.wyoparks.state.wy.us).

Eat & Drink: The **One Eyed Buffalo Brewing Company** (✉ 528 Broadway St. ☎ 307/864–3555 ⊕ www.oneeyedbuf-falobrewingwyo.com) in Thermopolis is a local brewery with a delicious menu (try the western-style charbroiled prime rib if it's on the menu).

CODY

Do: There's so much to do in this classic western town named after "Buffalo Bill" Cody. Start with a **Cody Trolley Tour** (✉ 1192 Sheridan Ave. ☎ 307/527–7043 ⊕ www.codytrolleytours.com), an hour-long tour on a funky green trolley through Cody's historic Old West and "new West" attractions. This provides an overview for what you might want to focus on in your short time here. In addition, cowboy culture lives on at the **Buffalo Bill Center of the West** (✉ 720 Sheridan Ave. ☎ 307/587–4771 ⊕ www.centerofthewest.org); round out your day with a visit to the on-site Plains Indian Museum.

Eat & Drink: The Cody Cattle Company (✉ 1910 Demaris Dr. ☎ 307/272–5770 ⊕ www.thecodycattlecompany.com) presents a family-style (read: bottomless) chuckwagon dinner and nightly western entertainment.

Stay: A Cody landmark, **Buffalo Bill's Irma Hotel** (✉ 1192 Sheridan Ave. ☎ 307/587–4221 ⊕ www.irmahotel.com) was built by Buffalo Bill himself. In the summer, you can see shoot-out reenactments in front of the hotel. Grab a drink at the famous bar, a gift to Buffalo Bill from Queen Victoria.

Breakfast: Go to **Granny's Restaurant** (✉ 1550 Sheridan Ave. ☎ 307/587–4829 ⊕ www.grannysrestaurantwy.com) for a home-cooked, American breakfast.

Day 8: Cody, WY, to Buffalo, WY

170 miles (3 hours without stops and traffic)

This day has you crossing Wyoming east on the highway, through lush forests.

ALONG THE WAY

Town: Ten Sleep, Wyoming, is named for its Native American history (the "ten sleeps," or "ten nights," refers to the

While Mount Rushmore is impressive, so is the stunning landscape of the Black Hills that surround it.

distance between the Sioux camps on the Platte River in the south and a Sioux campsite in the north). Today the town is known for its outdoor activities, particularly in the Big Horn Mountains, making it a popular destination for hikers, bikers, and rock climbers.

Eat & Drink: The **Ten Sleep Saloon and Restaurant** (⊠ *211 2nd St.* ☎ *307/366–2237* ⊕ *www.facebook.com/TenSleepSaloon*) is a surprisingly delicious American restaurant in a tiny town with a population of about 200.

BUFFALO

Do: Buffalo is a trove of history and a hospitable little town in the foothills below Big Horn Pass. Here cattle barons who wanted free grazing and homesteaders who wanted to build fences fought it out in the Johnson County Cattle War of 1892. Visit the nearby **Fort Phil Kearny Historic Site** (⊠ *528 Wagon Box Rd., Banner* ☎ *307/684–7629* ⊕ *www.wyoparks.wyo.gov*), home to two other major western battles: the Fetterman Fight of 1866 and Wagon Box Fight of 1867.

You can also check out the famous **TA Ranch** (⊠ *28623 Old Hwy. 87* ☎ *307/684–5833* ⊕ *www.taranch.com*), where you can see bullet holes in the barns where the Johnson County Cattle War ended. Another popular attraction is the **Jim Gatchell Museum** (⊠ *100 Fort St.* ☎ *307/684–9331* ⊕ *www.jimgatchell.com*), which explores the frontier history of the region. And a detour an hour and a half south will bring you to the Outlaw Caves, where Butch Cassidy and the Sundance Kid used to hide out.

Eat & Drink: Enjoy western hospitality at the **Occidental Saloon** (⊠ *18 N. Main St.* ☎ *307/684–8989* ⊕ *www.occidental-wyoming.com*) and order from the same bar where cowboys, desperados, and western legends gathered, gambled, and drank. Look up for the original bullet holes in the ceiling.

Stay: The 140-year-old **Occidental Hotel** (⊠ *10 N. Main St.* ☎ *307/684–0451* ⊕ *www.occidentalwyoming.com*), the oldest operating hotel in the state, has put up many a western legend, including Butch Cassidy and the Sundance Kid, Buffalo Bill, and Calamity Jane. A lot of this hotel remains in its original form, from the embossed ceilings to the antique chairs.

Breakfast: In the Occidental Hotel, the **Busy Bee Cafe** is a real spot that was a regular scene in the fictional western book and TV series *Longmire*. Order author Craig Johnson's "the usual": eggs, hash browns, toast or biscuit, and a ham steak.

Day 9: Buffalo, WY, to Rapid City, SD

220 miles (3 hours, 20 minutes without traffic and stops)

Hop on I-90 for a simple drive east to South Dakota, where you'll stop by one of the Wild West's most legendary towns and then head to Rapid City, the closest city with a major airport to return your rental car and head home.

ALONG THE WAY

Photo Op: Stop in Sundance, Wyoming, to take a photo next to the *Sundance Kid* statue; the Sundance Kid earned his name after he spent time in jail here for stealing a horse. It's also nice to take a small detour into nature and get a 360-degree panorama view from the old fire tower at Cement Ridge Lookout.

Town: Wind down your trip on a high note in Deadwood, South Dakota, the ultimate Wild West destination made even more famous thanks to the HBO television series of the same name. Walk through the historic downtown, visit the **Mount Moriah Cemetery** (✉ *10 Mt. Moriah Dr.* ☎ *605/722–0837* ⊕ *www.cityofdeadwood.com*), see some of the area's greatest historical treasures in the **Adams Museum** (✉ *54 Sherman St.* ☎ *605/578–1714* ⊕ *www.deadwoodhistory.com*), and

take the trolley to the **Adams House** (✉ *22 Van Buren St.* ☎ *605/578–3724* ⊕ *www.deadwoodhistory.com*).

Eat & Drink: Deadwood's spirit lives on at the city's oldest bar, the **Buffalo Bodega Complex** (✉ *658 Main St.* ☎ *605/578–1162* ⊕ *www.buffalobodega.com*).

RAPID CITY

Do: Rapid City is most famous for its proximity to **Mount Rushmore** (✉ *13000 Rte. 244, Keystone, SD* ☎ *605/574–2523* ⊕ *www.nps.gov/moru*), the iconic mountain carving with four presidential faces. But that's not the only mountain with a face in this region. See the world's largest in-progress mountain carving of Crazy Horse (☎ *605/673–4681* ⊕ *www.crazyhorsememorial.org*), an Oglala Sioux Indian chief who died in 1877.

Eat & Drink: Grab a hearty dish and beer at the state's first brewpub, **Firehouse Brewing Company** (✉ *610 Main St.* ☎ *605/348–1915* ⊕ *www.firehousebrewing.com*), located in a 1915 firehouse.

Stay: Go glamping with **Under Canvas** (✉ *24342 Ranch Rd., Keystone* ☎ *888/496–1148* ⊕ *www.undercanvas.com*) and their collection of luxury tents near the Black Hills National Forest just outside Rapid City. Sleep under the stars in an original gold-mining settlement, with unbelievable views of Mount Rushmore.

Breakfast: Under Canvas hooks you up with a locally sourced breakfast, or wrap up your trip with a classic American breakfast at the long-running **Colonial House Restaurant and Bar** (✉ *2315 Mt. Rushmore Rd.* ☎ *605/342–4640* ⊕ *www.colonialhousernb.com*).

Chapter 5

THE SOUTHWEST AND TEXAS

Updated by
Shoshi Parks

WELCOME TO THE SOUTHWEST AND TEXAS

TOP REASONS TO GO

★ **Grand Canyon National Park:** Seeing the Grand Canyon for the first time is an astounding experience. Witness the sandstone canyon walls, pine and fir forests, mesas, plateaus, volcanic features, and the Colorado River far below.

★ **The High Road to Taos:** The scenic drive between Taos and Santa Fe is one of the country's most famous, and most beautiful, routes.

★ **Monument Valley:** This remote corner of Arizona and Utah features famous sandstone buttes that dot the stunning landscape.

★ **Houston:** The biggest city in Texas is home to an incredibly diverse food scene and a world-class art scene.

★ **Fredericksburg:** You'll find plenty of charming small towns in Texas Hill Country, but only one is the region's winemaking center.

1 The Best of Arizona. A true southwestern adventure includes visits to Phoenix, the Grand Canyon, Sedona, and more.

2 The Best of New Mexico. The Land of Enchantment will wow with its desert landscapes and hip cities.

3 Native American Homelands of the Southwest. Explore the parts of Arizona, New Mexico, Utah, and Colorado that were and continue to be most sacred to the Navajo, Paiute, Hope, Ancestral Puebloan, and Acoma Pueblo peoples.

4 Enlightenment and Wellness in the Southwest. A trip that takes you to some of the funkiest and most spiritual places in the United States.

5 Dark Skies of the Southwest. This stretch of the region contains some of the most stunning night skies in the entire country.

6 The Best of Texas. An epic trek that spans Austin, San Antonio, and Houston as well as the state's far-west corners.

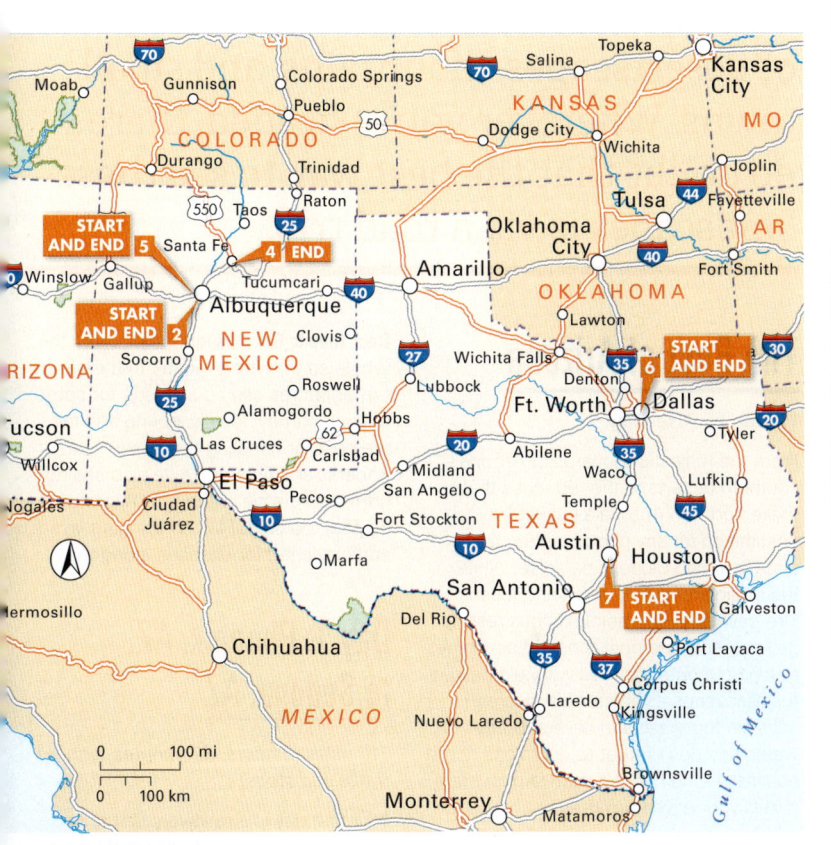

7 Texas Hill Country.
Between Austin and San
Antonio, explore the small
towns, wineries, and BBQ
joints that beckon
tourists.

From the red rocks of Arizona to the Gulf Coast of Texas, the southwestern United States is a stunning mash-up of desertscapes, mountains, and small towns. Wherever you're headed, there's no doubt that the best way to see these landscapes is via a road trip.

The Best of Arizona

Written by Elise Riley

From the majestic saguaros of Arizona's southern deserts to the red rocks that make northern Arizona a bucket-list destination for any photographer, this state is a road-tripper's paradise. While the urban areas of Phoenix and Tucson lure travelers with their luxurious resorts, golf courses, and near-constant sunshine, getting out onto the road will yield delightful discoveries. Grab some sunscreen, sensible footwear, and several bottles of water, and don't forget to download some podcasts—the nation's sixth-largest state awaits your adventurous eyes.

At a Glance

Start: Phoenix, AZ

End: Phoenix, AZ

Miles Traveled: 865 miles

Suggested Duration: 7 days

States Visited: Arizona

Key Sights: Heard Museum; Grand Canyon National Park; Kartchner Caverns State Park; Red Rock State Park; Saguaro National Park

Best Time to Go: This itinerary covers the whole state, which means that extreme temperatures can be an issue for some of your journey. Ideally, spring and fall are best for handling the desert heat of Phoenix and Tucson, while also seeing northern Arizona without temperatures dipping too cold. Plan on bringing layers and preparing for changes along the route.

Day 1: Phoenix, AZ, to Sedona, AZ

116 miles (2 hours, 30 minutes without traffic and stops)

Your first day is a relatively fast drive, but expect delays on Friday and Sunday, when desert dwellers leave the city en masse. I–17 is easy to access from Phoenix Sky Harbor International's rental car center, so hit the road and head north. You'll see a lot of cacti on your drive north and gradually—as the temperatures begin to drop—you'll also notice that they begin to disappear. The soil will also start getting redder as you make your way toward Sedona.

ALONG THE WAY

Eat & Drink: Pie is always a worthy diversion, right? The **Rock Springs Café** (✉ 35900 Old Black Canyon Hwy. ☎ 623/374–5794 ⊕ www.rock-springs.cafe) in Black Canyon City is a must-stop for bikers and road-trippers alike.

Roadside Attraction: An experimental community of artists, **Arcosanti** (✉ 13555 S. Cross L Rd., Mayer ☎ 928/632–7135 ⊕ www.arcosanti.org) remains a bit of a curiosity to visitors, and hasn't changed much in the 50 years since its founding. But this community of artisans crafts some of the most beautiful chimes and bells in the Southwest, which make for wonderful souvenirs.

Attraction: With such stiff competition from the Grand Canyon and Sedona, it's no surprise that **Montezuma Castle National Monument** (✉ Montezuma Castle Rd., Camp Verde ☎ 928/567–3322 ⊕ www.nps.gov/moca) rarely makes the must-do lists of Arizona attractions, but it's absolutely worth a visit. This 600-year-old structure was named by explorers who thought it had been erected by the Aztecs. Sinagua Native Americans actually built the five-story, 20-room cliff dwelling. Although you can't visit the cliff dwelling directly (the trail lets you view it from afar), you can still appreciate how impressive it is.

SEDONA

Do: Some people say Sedona simply needs to be breathed in for its mystical energy vortices. Others visit it to hike its trails and red-rock formations at the spectacular **Red Rock State Park** (✉ 4050 Red Rock Loop Rd. ☎ 928/282–6907 ⊕ www.azstateparks.com), while still more see it as a marketplace for arts and crafts. No matter your choice, simply open your eyes and take in the town, whether it's from your vehicle, by foot, or in the back of a Jeep on a guided tour. Must-visit spots include Bell Rock, Cathedral Rock, and the Chapel of the Holy Cross.

Eat & Drink: Its artistic vibe allows Sedona to naturally blend with the culinary community. Bars and coffee shops are aplenty, although you'll quickly discover that this town is small. One not-to-be-missed dinner destination is **Elote** (✉ 350 Jordan Rd. ☎ 928/203–0105 ⊕ www.elotecafe.com), which offers a modern twist on Mexican cuisine.

Stay: Sedona might be a tiny town, but the accommodations here run the gamut. Some of the finest resorts in the Southwest are here, like the superb **L'Auberge de Sedona** (✉ 301 L'Auberge La. ☎ 855/905–5745 ⊕ www.lauberge.com), but a hotel like **El Portal** (✉ 95 Portal La. ☎ 800/313–0017 ⊕ www.elportalsedona.com) checks just about every wish list. It's within walking distance of much of the area's shopping and nightlife, the staff is incredibly helpful, and the beautiful design includes authentic Tiffany and Roycroft pieces, French doors leading to balconies or a grassy central courtyard, stained-glass windows and ceiling panels, river-rock or tile fireplaces, and huge custom-designed beds.

Breakfast: Head to the **Coffee Pot** (✉ 2050 W. Rte. 89A ☎ 928/282–6626 ⊕ www.coffeepotsedona.com) to get your fuel for your journey north to the Grand Canyon.

Day 2: Sedona, AZ, to the Grand Canyon, AZ

109 miles (2 hours, 15 minutes without traffic and stops)

The best way to reach the Grand Canyon from Sedona is via Flagstaff, which is a relatively short morning drive. While the canyon's North Rim tends to be less crowded and has some underrated gems, the more popular South Rim of the Grand Canyon is the most accessible coming from Sedona.

ALONG THE WAY

Town: College-town enthusiasm and high-country charm make Flagstaff one of Arizona's most outdoors-friendly towns. Hiking, skiing, and climbing are local passions, and there are state and national parks to explore.

Eat & Drink: At **Tourist Home All Day Café** (✉ *52 S. San Francisco St.* ☎ *928/779–2811* ⊕ *www.touristhomecafe.com*) in Flagstaff, breakfast burritos, eggs Benedict, salads, and sandwiches all get a modern spin, and the quinoa falafel makes a great burger or vegan "hash-bowl." There's also an alluring selection of daytime cocktails.

Nature: A cinder cone that rises 1,000 feet, **Sunset Crater Volcanic National Monument** (✉ *6082 Sunset Crater Rd.* ☎ *928/526–0502* ⊕ *www.nps.gov/sucr*) was an active volcano 900 years ago. Its final eruption contained iron and sulfur, which give the rim of the crater its glow and thus its name. You can walk around the base, but you can't descend into the huge, fragile cone. The Lava Flow Trail, a half-hour, mile-long, self-guided walk, provides a good view of the evidence of the volcano's fiery power: lava formations and holes in the rock where volcanic gases vented to the surface.

GRAND CANYON NATIONAL PARK

Do: The **Grand Canyon** (☎ *928/638–7888* ⊕ *www.nps.gov/grca*) is easily the most visited site in Arizona and one of the most popular vacation destinations in the whole country. It's estimated that nearly 6 million people a year make the trek, so anticipate crowds. If possible, that's the best advice about any Grand Canyon–centered vacation: anticipate. Reservations open a year ahead of time for guided hikes, rafting trips, stays at historic hotels, you name it. If an immersive experience is what you desire, plan on preparing at least a year in advance to secure your spot. Luckily, it's certainly possible to visit the park and enjoy it within a single day. While the canyon can be enjoyed via several hikes and bike rides around the rim, the best experience is actually getting into the canyon itself. Your comfort and mobility levels will determine how far you travel into it, but there are several trails to choose from of varying difficulty levels—among the most popular are the Bright Angel Trail (moderate) and the Rim Trail (easy). Most are wide enough to walk comfortably in well-soled shoes. Just remember that the journey back up takes significantly longer and is significantly more difficult.

Eat & Drink: The Grand Canyon isn't exactly a destination for fine dining. But securing a sought-after reservation for a meal at one of the park's historic hotels could make for some beautiful memories. The historic **El Tovar** (✉ *1 El Tovar Rd.* ☎ *928/638–2631* ⊕ *www.grandcanyonlodges.com*) has a dining room that takes reservations 30 days in advance. It's the closest thing to a fine-dining experience you'll find for more than an hour's drive in any direction.

Stay: Historic South Rim hotels such as **Bright Angel Lodge** (✉ *9 Village Loop Dr.* ☎ *928/638–2631* ⊕ *www.grandcanyonlodges.com*) and El Tovar are the most sought after, and with good reason. If rooms are unavailable, accommodations in nearby Tusayan will be spartan, but sufficient. Remember, this leg of the journey is about viewing nature's majesty. Creature comforts take a break for this part.

Breakfast: Since cafés and brunch spots are limited here, it's best to enjoy breakfast at your hotel.

Day 3: The Grand Canyon, AZ, to Jerome, AZ

150 miles (3 hours without traffic and stops)

Head back south to the Verde Valley and its cluster of small towns via Route 64 and Route 89. This area of the state is certainly sleepy—it might make Sedona feel like a bustling metropolis—but the slowness of the Verde Valley is the point. Once a bustling area for copper mining, the valley is now known more for wine production, so plan on visiting some local wineries while you're here.

ALONG THE WAY

Town: The mountain town of Williams encompasses a nicely preserved half mile of historic Route 66. Sure, there are kitschy 1950s diners and souvenir shops, along with cowboys who enact staged gunfights on the streets, but you'll also find good restaurants, a few microbreweries, and outdoor activities like hiking, biking, and fishing.

Eat & Drink: For a nice taste of Route 66, enjoy a classic diner meal at **Cruisers Café 66** (✉ *233 W. Rte. 66* ☎ *928/635–2445* ⊕ *www.cruisers66.com*) in Williams.

JEROME

Do: A good place to base yourself in the Verde Valley, Jerome was once known as the Billion Dollar Copper Camp, but after the last mines closed in 1953, the booming population of 15,000 dwindled to 50 determined souls. Although its population has risen back to almost 500, Jerome still holds on to its "ghost town" designation, and several bed-and-breakfasts and eateries regularly report spirit sightings. It's also home to a bourgeoning art community. Learn about its history at **Jerome State Historic Park** (✉ *100*

Extend Your Trip

From Sedona: Enlightenment and Wellness in the Southwest *(Ch. 5)*

From the Grand Canyon: Route 66 *(Ch. 2)*

From Tucson: The Ultimate Wild West Road Trip *(Ch. 4)*

Douglas Rd. ☎ *928/634–5381* ⊕ *www.azstateparks.com*), visit its quirky galleries, and enjoy a visit to winery or two in nearby Cottonwood and Cornville, like **Page Springs Cellars** (✉ *1500 N. Page Springs Rd., Cornville* ☎ *928/639–3004* ⊕ *www.pagespringscellars.com*).

Eat & Drink: Thankfully, the Verde Valley's emergence as a wine producer also has blossomed a newfound reputation for culinary excellence. You'll be charmed by a meal at **Asylum Restaurant** in Jerome (✉ *200 Hill St.* ☎ *928/639–3197* ⊕ *www.asylumrestaurant.com*). Or for something a little more casual (and spooky), visit the **Haunted Hamburger** (✉ *410 Clark St.* ☎ *928/634–0554* ⊕ *www.thehauntedhamburger.com*).

Stay: Jerome's hotels most certainly lean into the town's paranormal reputation. The **Ghost City Inn** (✉ *541 Main St.* ☎ *928/634–4678* ⊕ *www.ghostcityinn.com*) and **Jerome Grand Hotel** (✉ *200 Hill St.* ☎ *888/817–6788* ⊕ *www.jeromegrandhotel.net*) both offer comfortable accommodations.

Breakfast: Everyone heads to the **Flatiron** (✉ *416 Main St.* ☎ *928/634–2733* ⊕ *www.theflatironjerome.com*) for coffee and breakfast in Jerome, and you should, too.

Day 4: Jerome, AZ, to Scottsdale, AZ

120 miles (2 hours without traffic and stops)

To reach southern Arizona, it's best to head back through Phoenix. But luckily, the Phoenix metro area also encompasses the whole of the East Valley, including upscale Scottsdale, which warrants a stop in its own right.

ALONG THE WAY

Eat & Drink: A classic Wild West town, Whiskey Row in Prescott still exudes turn-of-the-20th-century charm. For a lively frontier-style lunch, check out its historic **Palace Restaurant and Saloon** (☒ *120 S. Montezuma St.* ☎ *928/541–1996* ⊕ *www. facebook.com/WhiskeyRowPalace*). Legend has it that the patrons who saved the Palace's ornately carved 1880s Brunswick bar from a Whiskey Row fire in 1900 continued drinking at it while the row burned across the street. Whatever the case, the bar remains the centerpiece of the beautifully restored turn-of-the-20th-century structure, with a high, pressed-tin ceiling.

SCOTTSDALE

Do: Once an upscale Phoenix sibling, Scottsdale now flies solo as a top American destination. It's a bastion of high-end and specialty shopping, historic sites, elite resorts, restaurants, spas, and golf greens next to desert views. Don't miss the **Scottsdale Museum of Contemporary Art** (☒ *7374 E. 2nd St.* ☎ *480/874–4666* ⊕ *www.smoca.org*) as well as Frank Lloyd Wright's masterpiece **Taliesin West** (☒ *12621 N. Frank Lloyd Wright Blvd.* ☎ *480/860–2700* ⊕ *www.franklloydwright.org*), open for guided tours year-round. If you only have time to golf at one place, make it **Troon North** (☒ *10320 E. Dynamite Blvd.* ☎ *480/585–7700* ⊕ *www. troonnorthgolf.com*) while your top spa destination should be the Wells & Being

Spa at the **Fairmont Scottsdale Princess** (☒ *7575 E. Princess Dr.* ☎ *480/585–4848* ⊕ *www.fairmont.com*).

Eat & Drink: Dine at upscale steak house **Bourbon Steak** (☒ *7575 E. Princess Dr.* ☎ *480/585–2694* ⊕ *www.scottsdaleprincess.com*), the hip **Citizen Public House** (☒ *7111 E. 5th Ave.* ☎ *480/398–4208* ⊕ *www.citizenpublichouse. com*), or **The Mission** (☒ *3815 N. Brown Ave.* ☎ *480/636–5005* ⊕ *www.themissionaz.com*) for modern Latin cuisine. Afterwards, head to Old Town Scottsdale, a walkable area filled with bars and restaurants that encourages revelry year-round.

Stay: For a true Scottsdale resort experience, splurge for a night at the **Four Seasons Resort Scottsdale** at Troon North (☒ *10600 E. Crescent Moon Dr.* ☎ *480/515–5700* ⊕ *www.fourseasons.com*). For a slightly more affordable stay, check out the historic **Hotel Valley Ho** in Old Scottsdale (☒ *6850 E. Main St.* ☎ *480/376–2600* ⊕ *www.hotelvalleyho.com*).

Breakfast: Enjoy authentic French crepes, quiches, and tartes at **Chez Vous** (☒ *8787 N. Scottsdale Rd.* ☎ *480/443–2575*), tucked into a Scottsdale shopping center.

Day 5: Scottsdale, AZ, to Tucson, AZ

113 miles (2 hours without traffic and stops)

The most direct route you'll have in your entire journey, the drive from Scottsdale to Tucson is an easy two-hour trip south.

ALONG THE WAY

Town: The midway point of your drive today is Casa Grande, which gets its name from the **Casa Grande Ruins National Monument** (☒ *1100 W. Ruins Dr.* ☎ *520/723–3172* ⊕ *www.nps.gov/ cagr*). The lone place to sight-see on the

The Saguaro cacti that grow in Saguaro National Park are found only in the Sonoran Desert.

interstate, this national monument lets you see the ruins of a community dating back to 1450. Although you can't tour the Great House up close, rangers are available to answer questions and help explain how ancient communities thrived in the desert.

Nature: Before you reach Tucson, be sure to make time to spend a few hours in **Saguaro National Park** (☎ 520/733–5153 ⊕ www.nps.gov/sagu). The park's two distinct sections flank the city of Tucson. Perhaps the most familiar emblem of the Southwest, the towering saguaros are found only in the Sonoran Desert. Saguaro National Park preserves some of the densest stands of these massive cacti. Known for their height (often 50 feet) and arms reaching out in weird configurations, these slow-growing giants can take 15 years to grow a foot high and up to 75 years to grow their first arm. Take a drive on either the Bajana Loop Drive or the Cactus Forest Drive.

TUCSON

Do: Don't think of Tucson as Phoenix's younger sibling. Several degrees cooler than the scorching heat of Phoenix, Tucson also enjoys a slower pace and quite a different atmosphere. Thanks to its Western roots, university town vibe, and pop-culture connection to film, Tucson is an artist's haven. Don't miss the **Tucson Museum of Art and MOCA** (⊠ 265 S. Church Ave. ☎ 520/624–5019 ⊕ www.moca-tucson.org). An hour southwest of the city, it's worth it to make the trek to **Kitt Peak National Observatory** (⊠ Rte. 386, Sierra Vista ☎ 520/318–8726 ⊕ kpno.noirlab. edu), famous for its ideal conditions for stargazing.

Eat & Drink: Thanks to its proximity to Mexico, Tucson is a town where Mexican food should be enjoyed and savored repeatedly. The oldest restaurant in town is **El Charro Café** (⊠ 311 N. Court Ave. ☎ 520/622–1922 ⊕ www.elcharrocafe.com)—legend has it, the cheese crisp and chimichanga originated here. **Rollies Mexican Patio** (⊠ 4573 S. 12th

Ave. ☎ 520/300–6289 ⊕ www.rolliestuc-son.com) offers a much newer and more modern take on Mexican cuisine. And finally, at some point while in Tuscon, you must visit **Eegee's** (✉ 502 W. Ajo Way ☎ 520/792–1828 ⊕ www.eegees. com). Some might argue this is just a sandwich shop, but the real draw is the frozen-fruit drinks that have stained the lips of every Tucson child for generations.

Stay: While golf resorts are plentiful in Tucson, this part of Arizona edges out its competition in two very distinct ways: ranching and spas. Visit **Tanque Verde Ranch** (✉ 14301 E. Speedway Blvd. ☎ 520/296–6275 ⊕ www.tan-queverderanch.com) to stay on a work-ing, 640-acre guest ranch. For something a little more mind-body-spirit-oriented, **Canyon Ranch** (✉ 8600 E. Rockcliff Rd. ☎ 520/749–9655 ⊕ www.canyon-ranch.com) is regarded as one of the premier destination spas in the world. And if you're searching for something a little more middle-of-the-road, the **Ari-zona Inn** (✉ 2200 E. Elm St. ☎ 520/325–1541 ⊕ www.arizonainn.com) offers something a little more traditional.

Breakfast: Tucked inside the Stevens Home, part of the Tucson Museum of Art and Historic Block, **Café a la C'Art** (✉ 150 N. Main Ave. ☎ 520/628–8533 ⊕ www. cafealacarttucson.com) serves excel-lent breakfast frittatas, burritos, and pancakes.

Day 6: Tucson, AZ, to Tombstone, AZ

72 miles (1 hour, 15 minutes without traffic and stops)

It's a relatively quick drive out east to Arizona's ultimate Wild West town.

ALONG THE WAY

Nature: Get a workout and explore more than 2 miles of underground caves at **Kartchner Caverns State Park** (✉ 2980 S. Rte. 90, Benson ☎ 520/586–4100 ⊕ www.azstateparks.com), one of the only living cave systems in the world. Reservations are essential.

TOMBSTONE

Do: Channel your inner cowboy in this well-preserved western town with saloons, stagecoach rides, and a court-house. Visit the actual **O.K. Corral** (✉ 326 E. Allen St. ☎ 520/457–3456 ⊕ www. okcorral.com), learn about Wyatt Earp and the town's history at **Tombstone Courthouse State Historic Park** (✉ 223 E. Toughnut St. ☎ 520/457–3311 ⊕ www. azstateparks.com), and go on a ghost tour of the **Bird Cage Theatre** (✉ 535 E. Allen St. ☎ 520/457–3421 ⊕ www.tomb-stonebirdcage.com).

Eat & Drink: A meal at the historic **Crystal Palace Saloon** (✉ 436 E. Allen St. ☎ 520/457–3611 ⊕ www.crystalpal-acesaloon.com) is a must, as is enjoying a drink at **Big Nose Kate's Saloon** (✉ 417 E. Allen St. ☎ 520/457–3107 ⊕ bignoseka-testombstone.com).

Stay: Despite the town's touristy reputation, there aren't too many hotels in Tombstone. Your best bet is the **Tombstone Grand Hotel** (✉ 580 W. Randolph Way ☎ 520/457–9507 ⊕ tomb-stonegrand.com), nestled into a hill just outside town.

Breakfast: Get ready for hearty, gener-ous helpings of classic breakfast dishes at **Longhorn Restaurant** (✉ 501 E. Allen St. ☎ 520/457–3405 ⊕ www.thelong-hornrestaurant.com).

Day 7: Tombstone, AZ, to Phoenix, AZ

184 miles (2 hours, 55 minutes without traffic and stops)

You'll have to backtrack a bit on your last day of driving as you head back north to finally spend some time in Arizona's bustling capital city.

ALONG THE WAY

Town: Vineyards, tasting rooms, and horse ranches dot the gently rolling hills and grasslands of Sonoita. Key wineries to visit if you have the time include **AZ Hops & Vines** (✉ *3450 Rte. 82* ☎ *301/237–6556* ⊕ *www.azhopsandvines.com*) and **Callaghan Vineyards** (✉ *336 Elgin Rd., Elgin* ☎ *520/455–5322* ⊕ *www.callaghan-vineyards.com*).

Eat & Drink: While in Sonoita, take a lunch break from the wineries with a visit to **Copper Brothel Brewery** (✉ *3112 Rte. 83* ☎ *520/405–6721* ⊕ *www.copper-brothelbrewery.com*); it serves bar fare and craft beer.

PHOENIX

Do: The ultimate playground for adults, Phoenix encourages yearlong activity (yes, even in summer). Golfers flock here and compete for tee times as early as sunrise. If you're anticipating something a little slower, some of the finest spas in the nation call the "Valley of the Sun" home and have menus full of treatments for body and soul. And of course, nothing beats an afternoon poolside under some shade. For a little more culture in your stay in the Valley, consider some of the area's museums. **The Heard** (✉ *2301 N. Central Ave.* ☎ *602/252–8840* ⊕ *www. heard.org*) in downtown Phoenix offers the finest collection of Native American art in the world.

Eat & Drink: Much more than a town for chips and salsa, Phoenix is earning a reputation as a culinary destination.

Consider dining at **Richardson's** (✉ *6335 N. 16th St.* ☎ *602/265–5886* ⊕ *www. richardsonsnm.com*) for New Mexican fare in Central Phoenix or **Kai** (✉ *5594 W. Wild Horse Pass Blvd.* ☎ *602/225–0100* ⊕ *www.wildhorsepassresort.com*) for Native American–inspired fine dining.

Stay: Choose from hip and unabashedly quirky **Kimpton Hotel Palomar** (✉ *2 E. Jefferson St.* ☎ *602/253–6633* ⊕ *www. hotelpalomar-phoenix.com*) in downtown Phoenix or the luxurious **Sanctuary on Camelback Mountain Resort & Spa** (✉ *5700 E. McDonald Dr., Paradise Valley* ☎ *855/421–3522* ⊕ *www.gurneysresorts.com*).

Breakfast: Fresh, filling, and simply fantastic, the food at **Matt's Big Breakfast** (✉ *825 N. 1st St.* ☎ *602/254–1074*), an itty-bitty, retro-cool diner, is a great way to start any day.

The Best of New Mexico

Written by Aimee Heckel

A road trip through New Mexico is a journey through one of the most fascinating regions of the country; this nine-day loop starting and ending in Albuquerque hits many of the state's top attractions. You'll be amazed by the diverse natural wonders here, from underground caves and mineral-rich, natural hot springs to glistening white sand dunes you can "surf" on.

History and culture are also rich here, which you can see as you visit important sites like the Gila Cliff Dwellings and Bandelier National Monument. This trip offers a variety of experiences, from fine dining to hidden gems, and it pays special attention to New Mexico's art offerings. Immerse yourself in Georgia O'Keeffe's artwork, gallery hop in Santa Fe, and find inspiration around every corner.

At a Glance

Start: Albuquerque, NM

End: Albuquerque, NM

Miles Traveled: 1,540 miles

Suggested Duration: 9 days

States Visited: New Mexico, Texas

Key Sights: Bandelier National Monument; Carlsbad Caverns National Park; Gila Cliff Dwellings National Monument; High Road to Taos Scenic Byway; White Sands National Park

Best Time to Go: The weather in New Mexico is great in late spring, early summer, or fall, when temps are in the 70s and 80s. It can get pretty toasty during peak summertime, and it can snow in some regions in the wintertime, although any accumulation tends to melt pretty quickly.

Day 1: Albuquerque, NM, to Roswell, NM

252 miles (4 hours without traffic and stops)

This isn't the quickest route from Albuquerque to Roswell, but it permits a stop in Blue Hole, which is well worth the diversion. You'll take I-40 east to Santa Rosa, then work your way to U.S. 285, which will shoot you to Roswell.

ALONG THE WAY

Town: The Blue Hole of Santa Rosa is a natural wonder that seems to appear like a mirage in the New Mexico desert. This crystal-clear blue natural swimming pool is shockingly deep, boasting mysterious underground caves.

Eat & Drink: Get a taste of the historic Route 66 at the **Silver Moon Café** (✉ *2545 Rte. 66* ☎ *575/472–3162* ⊕ *www.facebook.com/silvermoonsantarosa*) in Santa Rosa, an old-school joint founded in the 1950s that feels like a step back in time.

Nature: If New Mexico's dry conditions have you craving more water, head to the **Santa Rosa Lake State Park** (✉ *Rte. 91* ☎ *575/472–3110* ⊕ *www.emnrd.state. nm.us*). Here you can go swimming, water skiing, and boating; you can even camp overnight if you want to extend your trip.

ROSWELL

Do: A truly underrated city, Roswell boasts its own zoo, a contemporary art museum, and another art museum that centers on southwestern work, but we all know what the city is really famous for: a supposed UFO crash in the 1940s. Learn more about it and tickle your supernatural curiosity at the **International UFO Museum and Research Center** (✉ *114 N. Main St.* ☎ *575/625–9495* ⊕ *www.roswellufomuseum.com*) and the **UFO Spacewalk** (✉ *116 E. 2nd St.* ☎ *575/910–2113* ⊕ *www.facebook. com/roswellufospacewalk*).

Eat & Drink: Part of the charm of Roswell is how hard it's leaned into the UFO kitsch. **Farley's Pub** (✉ *1315 N. Main St.* ☎ *575/627–1100* ⊕ *www.farleyspub. com*), a local chain, is adorned with sci-fi decor (such as posters and a wall of supernatural "heads") and serves casual wood-fired pizza, burgers, and ribs. The real draw here is the novelty decor more than the culinary expertise.

Stay: If you don't mind staying in a chain hotel, the **Holiday Inn Express & Suites Roswell** (✉ *3 Military Heights Dr.* ☎ *575/208–0736* ⊕ *www.ihg.com*) is your best bet for quality, but the inexpensive **Roswell Inn** (✉ *2101 N. Main St.* ☎ *575/623–6050* ⊕ *www.roswellinn. us*) is decorated with alien paraphernalia (it's about a mile from the UFO museum). Or for something even more memorable, look for a quirky vacation rental. Only in Roswell can you book an Airbnb that's actually a private 186-foot-deep, underground missile silo and a real-life Cold War relic.

Breakfast: The **Cowboy Cafe** (✉ *1120 E. 2nd St.* ☎ *575/622–6363* ⊕ *www.thecowboy. cafe*) plays into the town's extraterrestrial reputation with the Alien Omelet: ham, cheese, and green chili, smothered in "Roswell Sauce" and topped with a sunny-side-up egg.

Day 2: Roswell, NM, to Ruidoso, NM

200 miles (3 hours, 45 minutes without traffic and stops)

Although you can get from Roswell to Ruidoso (a straight shot west) in just over an hour, add to your journey with a side trip to the White Sands National Park (a little farther west than Ruidoso).

ALONG THE WAY
Attraction: White Sands National Park (✉ *19955 U.S. 70 W* ☎ *575/479–6124* ⊕ *www.nps.gov/whs*a) is named for its jaw-dropping (you guessed it) white sand dunes, comprised of shimmering, rare white gypsum—it's actually the world's biggest gypsum dune field. Hike through the dunes, go sand sledding on special saucers, or simply take photos of this majestic site in an 8-mile scenic drive.

Eat & Drink: There are no restaurants in the national park, but nearby Alamogordo

Extend Your Trip

From Las Cruces or Santa Fe: The Ultimate Wild West Road Trip *(Ch. 4)*

From Santa Fe or Taos: Enlightenment and Wellness in the Southwest *(Ch. 5)*

From Albuquerque: Route 66 *(Ch. 2)*; Native American Homelands of the Southwest *(Ch. 5)*

is home to authentic and filling Mexican food at **CJ's Si Senor Restaurant** (✉ *2300 N. White Sands Blvd.* ☎ *575/437–7879* ⊕ *www.facebook.com/AlamoSiSenor*). It doesn't get much better than a midday margarita after surfing the sand dunes.

RUIDOSO
Do: Ruidoso is an outdoor lover's paradise, with the nearby **Ski Apache!** resort (✉ *1286 Ski Run Rd., Alto* ☎ *575/464–3600* ⊕ *www.skiapache.com*) and **Lincoln National Forest** (✉ *3463 Las Palomas Rd.* ☎ *575/434-7200* ⊕ *www.fs.usda. gov*), packed with trails and waterfalls. History comes to life here, too, with 19th-century buildings and an old church.

Eat & Drink: Casa Blanca Restaurant and Bar (✉ *501 Mechem Dr.* ☎ *575/257–2495* ⊕ *www.casablancaruidoso.com*) is known for its mouthwatering fried green chili strips and green chili chicken enchiladas. This local gem has roots in the 1950s, when it started out of a private residence.

Stay: Immerse yourself in mountain life by staying in a cabin; the area has many to choose from. The luxurious **Ruidoso Mountain View Cabins** (✉ *Kirkman Circle* ☎ *575/222–2170* ⊕ *www.rentruidosocabins.com*) stand out for their views and location in the heart of the city, while still maintaining peace and privacy.

Breakfast: For giant portions in an intimate spot with a patio overlooking the river, locals love **Tina's Cafe** (✉ 2825 Sudderth Dr. ☎ 575/257–8930 ⊕ www.facebook.com/tinascaferuidoso). Don't miss the cinnamon rolls with bacon crumbles and maple icing ("pig candy style") or breakfast tacos stuffed with eggs.

Day 3: Ruidoso, NM, to Carlsbad Caverns, NM

170 miles (3 hours without traffic and stops)

The quickest route to Carlsbad Caverns will actually bring you back through Roswell, rather than winding through the Lincoln National Forest. But if you crave different scenery and have the time, head south and take U.S. 82 through the forest and connect back onto U.S. 285 for a slightly longer but scenic detour.

ALONG THE WAY

Town: Located within Lincoln National Forest, the town of Cloudcroft was established in 1898 when the El Paso–Northeastern Railroad crew laid out the route for the Cloud Climbing Railroad. Today, the mountain town has a kitschy, Old West atmosphere that's full of charm, along with countless trails and canyons on its outskirts; the Bridal View Falls and Grand View Trail are popular.

Eat & Drink: Superb wood-fired pizzas and craft beer are the draw at friendly, rustic **Cloudcroft Brewing Company** (✉ 1301 Burro Ave. ☎ 575/682–2337 ⊕ www.cloudcroft-brewing.com).

CARLSBAD CAVERNS NATIONAL PARK

Do: Carlsbad Caverns National Park (✉ 727 Carlsbad Caverns Hwy. ☎ 575/785–2232 ⊕ www.nps.gov/cave) will awe you with its more than 119 caves lined with

stalactites; when the sun goes down, you can see thousands of bats fly out of the caves. This is part of one of the best-preserved, exposed fossil reefs in the world, dating back to the Permian Period.

Eat & Drink: The **Yellow Brix Restaurant** (✉ 201 N. Canal St. ☎ 575/941–2749 ⊕ www.yellowbrixrestaurant.com) in Carlsbad serves fresh food all day (from sandwiches and salmon to prime rib and margarita chicken as well as brunch on the weekends) in a historic yellow-brick house built in the 1920s.

Stay: You can't stay in the park, so most visitors make the town of Carlsbad (20 miles away) their home base. Stay in **Fiddler's Inn** (✉ 705 N. Canyon St. ☎ 575/725–8665 ⊕ www.fiddlersinnbb.com), a country-style, family-run guesthouse in a century-old home, complete with a lovely garden and hot tub.

Breakfast: Breakfast is included in your stay at the Fiddler's Inn.

Day 4: Carlsbad Caverns, NM, to Las Cruces, NM

200 miles (3 hours without traffic and stops)

Get up early and take the straightforward route to Las Cruces on U.S. 62 toward El Paso, close to the Mexican border.

ALONG THE WAY

Detour: El Paso, Texas, is a quick, 10-minute detour; this unique city is the intersection of two different countries (the United States and Mexico) and three states (Texas, New Mexico, and the Mexican state of Chihuahua). Visit the **Ysleta Mission church** (✉ 131 S. Zaragoza Rd. ☎ 915/859–9848 ⊕ www.ysletadelsurpueblo.org), established in 1681 by Spanish refugees.

Within Carlsbad Caverns National Park, you'll find over 119 caves lined with stalactites.

Eat & Drink: Just southwest of Las Cruces, stop by **Luna Rossa Winery & Pizzeria** (✉ 1321 Ave. de Mesilla ☎ 575/526–2484 ⊕ www.lunarossawinery.com) in Old Mesilla to check out New Mexico's wine scene. Skeptics are sometimes surprised by the high quality of southern New Mexico wines, with Mimbres Valley's Luna Rossa among the region's most impressive vintners, specializing in estate-grown, mostly Italian and Spanish varietals like Dolcetto and Tempranillo.

LAS CRUCES

Do: Las Cruces has jaw-dropping scenery, a rich culture, fascinating history, and outdoor adventures galore. Don't miss the **Branigan Cultural Center** (✉ 501 N. Main St. ☎ 575/541–2154 ⊕ www.lascruces. gov) with its interesting history display and rotating exhibits housed in a 1935 Pueblo revival building.

Eat & Drink: Enjoy craft beer with a view over the Mesilla Valley at the **Pecan Grill and Brewery** (✉ 500 S. Telshor Blvd. ☎ 575/521–1099 ⊕ www.pecangrill. com). For dinner, try steak, chicken, or a burger grilled over pecan wood; in New Mexico style, always get your meats smothered in green chili.

Stay: The **Aguirre Spring Campground** (☎ 575/525–4300 ⊕ www.blm.gov/visit/ aguirre-spring-campground), perched high in the Organ Mountains, is the place to crash in Las Cruces. Campers get views of the Tularosa Basin and White Sands National Park.

Breakfast: Start the day with coconut French toast, green eggs and ham (that's eggs with basil-pesto sauce), or another unique dish on the patio at **The Shed** (✉ 810 S. Valley Dr. ☎ 575/525–2636 ⊕ www. ompctheshed.com) in Las Cruces. This from-scratch menu always surprises.

Day 5: Las Cruces, NM, to Silver City, NM

155 miles (3 hours without traffic and stops)

This leg is mostly highway and takes you past several small towns as you head into the national forest that contains the famous Gila Cliff Dwellings, where you can explore before settling for the night in Silver City. There are several routes to Gila, but the quickest starts with I–10.

ALONG THE WAY

Nature: The **Gila Cliff Dwellings National Monument** (✉ *26 Jim Bradford Trail* ☎ *575/536–9461* ⊕ *www.nps.gov/gicl*), located in the Gila National Forest, are mysterious, ancient Mogollon caves high above the canyon floor dating back to the late 1200s and early 1300s. See other artifacts, hike around the monument, and learn about the Mogollon, the wilderness, and the surrounding region in the museum.

Eat & Drink: Fuel up with tacos *al pastor* and carnitas burritos from **Sounds Good Cafe** (✉ *118 S. Gold Ave.* ☎ *575/652–0487*) in the town of Deming before heading north to the Gila National Forest.

SILVER CITY

Do: Silver City began as a tough and lawless mining camp in 1870, and struggled for a long time to become a more respectable— and permanent— settlement. Henry McCarty spent part of his boyhood here, perhaps learning some of the ruthlessness that led to his later infamy under his nickname Billy the Kid. Other mining towns in the area sparked briefly and then died, but Silver City eventually flourished and became the area's most populated. Learn more about its history at the **Silver City Museum** (✉ *312 W. Broadway St.* ☎ *575/538–5921* ⊕ *www.silvercitymuseum.org*).

Eat & Drink: Enjoy the best Texas-style barbecue in town at **Iron Door BBQ and Grill** (✉ *1123 N. Pope St.* ☎ *575/590–1495* ⊕ *www.facebook.com/irondoorbbq*). Served out of a little red trailer, just try to stop your mouth from watering as you wait for a taste of their smoky brisket, pork ribs, and jalapeño-apple sausage.

Stay: You can find a handful of lodging options near the national forest, but a fun choice is the rustic **Gila Hot Springs and Campground** (☎ *575/536–9944* ⊕ *www.gilahotspringscampground.com*) in Silver City. Relax in the natural hot springs, surrounded by the Gila Wilderness, just 4 miles from the national monument.

Breakfast: Diane's Restaurant and Parlor (✉ *510 N. Bullard St.* ☎ *575/538–8722* ⊕ *www.dianesrestaurant.com*) is run by an award-winning chef. The bakery side features more than 20 different types of bread, European pastries, and more. Get upscale food in the restaurant and casual, lighter fare and drinks at the parlor.

Day 6: Silver City, NM, to Truth or Consequences, NM

88 miles (2 hours without traffic and stops)

It's just over a two-hour drive from Silver City to Truth or Consequences on Route 152.

ALONG THE WAY

Photo Op: Stop in Mimbres, near mile marker 4 on Route 35 north, to visit a world-famous archaeological site. Explore 1,000-year-old ruins of the Mimbres people at the **Mimbres Culture Heritage Site** (✉ *12 Sage Dr.* ☎ *575/536–3333* ⊕ *www.mimbrescultureheritagesite.org*) and several 19th-century buildings.

TRUTH OR CONSEQUENCES

Do: Truth or Consequences is home to several naturally occurring hot spring pools, filled from an ancient rift in the Rio Grande. These thermal springs are some of the most mineral-rich in the country and are touted for their health benefits (not to mention a soothing break on a long road trip).

Eat & Drink: A long-standing local staple is **Los Arcos Steak and Lobster** (✉ *1400 N. Date St.* ☎ *575/894–6200* ⊕ *www. losarcossteakhouse.com*), which has been serving hand-cut steaks, seafood, and more since 1970. Enjoy dinner and a glass of wine on the patio, all while supporting a business run by a Truth or Consequences native.

Stay: The **Sierra Grande Lodge and Spa** (✉ *501 McAdoo St.* ☎ *877/288–7637* ⊕ *www.tedturner.com/sierra-grande-lodge-and-spa*) stands out for offering a full-service spa built above geothermal springs; private indoor and outdoor hot springs; locally crafted, organic skin care products in each room; and optional adventures like hot-air balloon rides.

Breakfast: The lodge's hot breakfast is included in your stay.

Day 7: Truth or Consequences, NM, to Santa Fe, NM

210 miles (3 hours without traffic and stops)

The route from Truth or Consequences to Santa Fe couldn't be simpler: just cruise up I–25. It's also worth it to make a stop at the Bosque Del Apache National Wildlife Refuge. The refuge is about 45 minutes north of Truth or Consequences, and the bird-watching you'll find there is unmatched.

ALONG THE WAY

Attraction: Bosque Del Apache National Wildlife Refuge (✉ *1001 Rte. 1, San Antonio* ☎ *575/835–1828* ⊕ *www.fws. gov*) is famous for the dramatic descent of migrating sandhill cranes in the fall. These 30,000 acres between the Chupadera and San Pascual mountains are an important stop year-round for all kinds of other birds, too.

SANTA FE

Do: Santa Fe is an art and culture paradise. Stroll through the downtown and its historic plaza, where restaurants, creative shops, and famous markets line the crooked streets. Canyon Road has lots of art galleries and there are several can't-miss museums like the **Georgia O'Keeffe Museum** (✉ *217 Johnson St.* ☎ *505/946–1000* ⊕ *www.okeeffemuseum.org*) and the **Museum of Indian Arts and Culture** (✉ *710 Camino Lejo* ☎ *505/476–1269* ⊕ *www.indianartsandculture.org*) located throughout the city. If you have time, don't miss **Meow Wolf** (✉ *1352 Rufina Circle* ☎ *866/636–9969* ⊕ *www. meowwolf.com*), a madly imaginative and completely immersive 22,000-square-foot collaborative art installation.

Eat & Drink: Santa Fe's foodie scene is as great as its art offerings, but a classic is **The Shed** (✉ *113½ E. Palace Ave.* ☎ *505/982–9030* ⊕ *www.sfshed. com*), located in an ancient adobe building downtown; it's been a local favorite since the 1950s. You must try the locally grown red chili enchiladas with a (strong) margarita.

Stay: The **Rosewood Inn of the Anasazi** (✉ *113 Washington Ave.* ☎ *505/988–3030* ⊕ *www.rosewoodhotels.com*) is ideally located right on the plaza (assuming you want to be in the heart of the action). This high-end, boutique hotel features incredible artwork throughout and top-notch service.

Breakfast: Start the day with breakfast *rellenos* on the patio at the **Tune-Up**

Café (✉ 1115 Hickox St. ☎ 505/983–7060 ⊕ www.tuneupsantafe.com); they also serve a mean brunch on the weekends.

Day 8: Santa Fe, NM, to Taos, NM

125 miles (2 hours, 45 minutes without traffic and stops)

After a stop at Bandelier National Monument, prepare for one of the most beautiful drives in the country. The 56-mile High Road to Taos Scenic Byway cuts through the Sangre de Cristo Mountains all the way to Taos. While the drive is just over 2½ hours, take your time to stop and explore the villages and farms along the way.

ALONG THE WAY

Detour: It takes less than an hour to drive the 40 or so miles from Santa Fe to **Bandelier National Monument** (✉ 15 Entrance Rd., Los Alamos ☎ 505/672–3861 ⊕ www.nps.gov/band). Here you can see the preserved homes of Ancestral Puebloans. A hike along the main loop should take about 90 minutes, and you can tackle additional trails for deeper immersion in the history and scenery.

Eat & Drink: Fill up with a farm-to-table dish like a bacon-wrapped filet or creative salad at local favorite, the **Blue Window Bistro** (✉ 1789 Central Ave. ☎ 505/662–6305 ⊕ www.labluewindowbistro.com) in nearby Los Alamos. Don't let its unpretentious location in a shopping center fool you; Blue Window has been popular for more than 40 years for a reason. Los Alamos is also an interesting place that deserves further exploration; it was the headquarters for the scientists in charge of the Manhattan Project, which led to the development of the atomic bomb (as seen in the 2023 film *Oppenheimer*).

Photo Op: Don't miss the most photographed church in New Mexico, the **San Francisco de Asis Church** (✉ 60 St. Francis Plaza ☎ 575/758–2754 ⊕ www.sfranchos.org), located in Rancho de Taos just outside Taos itself.

TAOS

Do: Taos provides a slow and scenic escape bursting with art, outdoor activities, and nature galore (including skiing in the winter). While here, pay a visit to the **Taos Pueblo** (✉ 120 Veterans Hwy. ☎ 575/758–1028 ⊕ www.taospueblo.com), the biggest group of multistory Pueblo dwellings in the country, and take a walk on the Rio Grande Gorge Bridge, where you can see the mighty river flow 650 feet underfoot.

Eat & Drink: Enjoy a meal at the **Love Apple** (✉ 803 Paseo Del Pueblo Norte ☎ 575/751–0050 ⊕ www.theloveapple.net), a farm-to-table restaurant housed in a former chapel. Tables are limited, but if you can land one, ask about the sweet-corn tamales with red-chili mole.

Stay: This B&B is a bit away from the action, but you'll appreciate the peaceful atmosphere at the **Adobe and Pines Inn** (✉ 4107 Rte. 68 ☎ 575/751–0947 ⊕ www.adobepines.com). The details here add up: Native American artifacts, mountain views, a historic adobe building, kiva fireplaces, and stunning gardens.

Breakfast: The **Farmhouse Cafe and Bakery** (✉ 1405 Paseo Del Pueblo Norte, El Prado ☎ 575/758–5683 ⊕ www.farmhouse-taos.com) serves tasty huevos rancheros and freshly baked cinnamon rolls with spectacular views.

The Taos Pueblo is the largest group of multistory Pueblo dwellings in the country.

Day 9: Taos, NM, to Albuquerque, NM

130 miles (2 hours, 30 minutes without traffic and stops)

This fast highway drive will bring you back onto busy I–25, past Santa Fe, and back to Albuquerque, but not before passing a few more key sights in the Santa Fe/Taos area.

ALONG THE WAY

Town: The tiny, very traditional village of Abiquiu was originally home to freed *genízaros*, Indigenous and mixed-race enslaved people who were forced to work in Spanish, Mexican, and American households well into the 1880s. Today it's best known as the location of the **Georgia O'Keeffe Home and Studio** (✉ *21120 U.S. 84* ☎ *575/467–2000* ⊕ *www.okeeffemuseum.org*), where the famed artist spent the last 50 years of her life, inspired by the region's stunning vistas and landscapes. You can also visit nearby

Ghost Ranch (✉ *280 Private Dr. 1708, U.S. 84* ☎ *505/685–1000* ⊕ *www.ghostranch.org*); O'Keeffe once lived on a small parcel of the 22,000-acre dude and cattle ranch that today serves as a retreat center offering O'Keeffe-focused tours to the public.

Eat & Drink: The inviting, art-filled restaurant at the **Abiquiú Inn** (✉ *21120 U.S. 84* ☎ *505/685–4378* ⊕ *www.abiquiuinn.com*) serves tasty New Mexican and American fare. Be sure to peek inside the adjoining art gallery featuring local work, and take a stroll through the graceful gardens.

Nature: Try to also pay a visit to **Kasha-Katuwe Tent Rocks National Monument** (✉ *Rte. 22, off I–25, Cochiti Pueblo* ☎ *505/331–6259* ⊕ *www.blm.gov/visit/kktr*), located just southwest of Santa Fe. The sandstone rock formations are a visual marvel, resembling stacked tents in a stark, water- and wind-eroded box canyon. The monument is managed in cooperation with Cochiti Pueblo, whose people call the area Kasha-Katuwe. It's an excellent choice for a day hike.

ALBUQUERQUE

Do: Albuquerque is adventure-packed, from water activities on the Rio Grande to vibrant art galleries. One surprise is the **Turquoise Museum** (✉ *400 2nd St. SW* ☎ *505/433–3684* ⊕ *www.turquoisemuseum.com*), where you can see some of the world's rarest pieces of turquoise and learn all about the stone; it's located in a mysterious Gothic castle that seems so out of place in this southwestern city. Another highlight is a visit to the **Petroglyph National Monument** (✉ *Western Trail NW* ☎ *505/899–0205* ⊕ *www.nps.gov/petr*). Beneath the stumps of five extinct volcanoes, this park encompasses more than 25,000 ancient Native American rock drawings inscribed on the 17-mile-long West Mesa escarpment overlooking the Rio Grande Valley.

Eat & Drink: Campo at Los Poblanos (✉ *4803 Rio Grande Blvd. NW* ☎ *855/486–1380* ⊕ *www.lospoblanos.com*) is an ultralocal, field-to-fork restaurant located on an organic farm in the Rio Grande Valley. The incredible menu is built around its own farm harvest as well as produce from other local purveyors. Say hello to the friendly barn cat who likes to walk guests to their car.

Stay: A newer gem in Albuquerque is the chic and luxurious **Hotel Chaco** (✉ *2000 Bellamah Ave. NW* ☎ *505/246–9989* ⊕ *www.hotelchaco.com*) right in Old Town, with a rooftop restaurant and bar, outdoor pool, and spacious rooms. It's located across from the hip Sawmill District, New Mexico's first food hall.

Breakfast: The **Grove Cafe and Market** (✉ *600 Central Ave. SE* ☎ *505/248–9800* ⊕ *www.thegrovecafemarket.com*) is all about supporting local farmers and products. Try sweet-potato hash outside on the enclosed patio in this colorful, popular restaurant.

Native American Homelands of the Southwest

Written by Shoshi Parks

From New Mexico's 19 Pueblos to the land of Navajo, the American Southwest is a patchwork of Native Nations. For thousands of years, these Indigenous communities have called the high desert home, and remnants of early cities and ceremonial centers still exist at sites like New Mexico's Chaco Culture National Historical Park and Colorado's Mesa Verde National Park. Despite the hardships of desert life and the aftermath of conquest and colonization, the Native American people of the Southwest haven't disappeared—far from it. From Albuquerque to Tuba City, Native people continue to carry on the traditions of their ancestors and forge new paths of self-expression and self-determination. Winding through five states, this epic itinerary is a breathtaking trip through the natural splendor of the American Southwest and the cultural heritage of its resilient Native American communities.

At a Glance

Start: Las Vegas, NV

End: Las Vegas, NV

Miles Traveled: 1,643 miles

Suggested Duration: 9 days

States Visited: Arizona, Colorado, Nevada, New Mexico, Utah

Key Sights: Acoma Pueblo; Grand Canyon-Parashant National Monument; Mesa Verde National Park; Monument Valley; Navajo Nation

Native American Homelands of the Southwest

Best Time to Go: This trip can be done any time of year, but for the best weather for camping and hiking, visit in spring or fall.

Day 1: Las Vegas, NV, to Page, AZ

280 miles (4 hours, 40 minutes without traffic and stops)

The Las Vegas sprawl melts into an endless painted desert of towering cliffs and terraces on the first day's drive toward Lake Powell and Page, Arizona.

ALONG THE WAY

Town: The quirky town of Kanab, Utah, on the outskirts of Grand Staircase-Escalante National Monument was once a popular filming location for Westerns and television series featuring celebrities from Clint Eastwood to the Rat Pack. See leftover sets from Kanab's Hollywood heyday at the **Little Hollywood Movie Museum** (✉ *297 W. Center St.* ☎ *435/644–5337* ⊕ *www.littlehollywoodmuseum. org*).

Eat & Drink: While in Kanab, grab a bite at the eclectic restaurant and art gallery, the **Rocking V Cafe** (✉ *97 W. Center St.* ☎ *435/644–8001* ⊕ *www.rocking-vcafe.com*). They've got a huge menu of sandwiches, salads, steaks, and more, all made with organic and natural ingredients.

Nature: At **Grand Staircase-Escalante National Monument** (✉ *745 U.S. 89* ☎ *435/644–1300* ⊕ *www.blm.gov*), a million acres of colorful cliffs and paper-thin slot canyons are waiting to be explored.

Detour: About an hour-and-a-half north of Kanab, the hoodoos grow in dense stands that fill the natural amphitheater at **Bryce Canyon National Park** (✉ *Rte. 63* ☎ *435/834–5322* ⊕ *www.nps.gov/brca*), part of the traditional tribal territory of the Paiute. The effect is otherworldly,

a landscape not found anywhere else on the planet. During long winters, Bryce Canyon's views are at their most spectacular and some of its snow-covered trails can be traversed via snowshoe. Summertime hikes will get you up close to the massive stone formations.

PAGE

Do: Possibly the world's most spectacular geological slots, **Antelope Canyon** (✉ *22 S. Lake Powell Blvd.* ☎ *855/574–9102* ⊕ *www.antelopecanyon.com*) has long been cherished by the Navajo. The tribe runs popular 90-minute tours through its rocky twists and turns several times a day. Advance reservations are recommended. Low-key Page makes a good base for exploring the canyon.

Eat & Drink: Dig into brisket, ribs, and pulled pork at **Big John's Texas Barbeque** (✉ *153 S. Lake Powell Blvd.* ☎ *928/645–3300* ⊕ *www.bigjohnstexasbbq.com*). Page isn't exactly known for its nightlife, but you'll find a good selection of beers on tap at the **State 48 Tavern** (✉ *614 N. Navajo Dr.* ☎ *928/645–1912* ⊕ *state48tavernpageaz.com*).

Stay: The **Lake Powell Motel** (✉ *750 S. Navajo Dr.* ☎ *928/645–9362* ⊕ *www.lake-powellmotel.net*) has both budget rooms and fully equipped apartments for a quiet night of rest. Get a few more amenities, including a pool, hotel bar, and views of beautiful Lake Powell at the **Lake Powell**

Resort (✉ *100 Lakeshore Dr.* ☎ *888/896–3829* ⊕ *www.lakepowell.com*).

Breakfast: Order a hearty home-style breakfast at local favorite, the **Ranch House Grille** (✉ *819 N. Navajo Dr.* ☎ *928/645–1420* ⊕ *www.ranch-housegrille.com*).

Day 2: Page, AZ, to Hovenweep National Monument, UT

204 miles (3 hours, 15 minutes without stops)

Green returns to the landscape as you travel over a rocky desert plateau and into the outskirts of southwestern Colorado's piñon forests where the skies are some of the darkest in the world. A detour will take you on one of the most incredible drives in the United States through Monument Valley.

ALONG THE WAY

Eat & Drink: A hip little adobe eatery, the **Amigo Cafe** (✉ *U.S. 163* ☎ *928/697–8448* ⊕ *www.amigocafekayenta. com*) in Kayenta, Arizona, specializes in Native American and southwestern favorites like Navajo tacos and green chili cheeseburgers.

Detour: Just 20 minutes north of Kayenta, Monument Valley's towering rock formations at **Monument Valley Tribal Park** (☎ *435/727–5870* ⊕ *www.navajona-tionparks.org*) rise like spires from the hallowed ground on the Navajo Nation.

Photo Op: The only place in the United States where you can stand in four states at the same time, **Four Corners Monument** (✉ *597 Rte. 597, Teec Nos Pos, AZ* ☎ *928/206–2540* ⊕ *www.navajona-tionparks.org*) isn't thrilling, but you can't beat the photo op.

HOVENWEEP NATIONAL MONUMENT

Do: Archaeologists are still working to explain the exact use of the unusual 800-year-old stone towers and "castles" at **Hovenweep National Monument** (☎ *970/562–4282* ⊕ *www.nps.gov/hove*). Walk among them, then settle in for an evening of stargazing at this certified International Dark Sky Park.

Eat & Drink: There are no stores or restaurants for miles. Come prepared with your own food and drinks.

Stay: Hovenweep's 31-site year-round campground is first-come, first-served.

Breakfast: Break your fast at the campsite or make a beeline for **Silver Bean** (✉ *410 W. Main St.* ☎ *970/529–3761* ⊕ *www. facebook.com/thesilverbean*), an hour's drive toward your next destination in Cortez, Colorado. This adorable coffee shop in a retro Airstream has hot and cold drinks, pastries, and breakfast burritos to eat on the artificial "lawn" or take away.

Day 3: Hovenweep National Monument, UT, to Mesa Verde, CO

76 miles (1 hour, 45 minutes without traffic and stops)

It's about an hour through bucolic ranch-lands and vineyards to Cortez, Colorado, before the climb to Mesa Verde begins. Even though the park's entrance is just ten miles from town, the drive up to the cliff dwellings is long, isolated, and quite beautiful.

ALONG THE WAY

Town: Colorado's gateway to the Southwest, the small town of Cortez has wineries, breweries, and the fascinating **Cortez Cultural Center** (✉ *25 N. Market St.* ☎ *970/565–1151* ⊕ *www.*

cortezculturalcenter.org), with exhibits on Ancestral Puebloan history and art by local and Native artisans. In summer, Native American dance performances take place regularly.

Eat & Drink: Relax with apps and a pint of pale ale from local brewery collective **WildEdge** (✉ *111 N. Market St.* ☎ *970/565–9445* ⊕ *www.wildedge-brewing.com*), in Cortez.

MESA VERDE NATIONAL PARK

Do: Take a self-guided tour of **Mesa Verde National Park** (✉ *34840 U.S. 160, Mancos* ☎ *970/529–4465* ⊕ *www.nps. gov/meve*) along the 6-mile Mesa Top Loop Road which offers views of 12 of Mesa Verde's most famous cliff dwellings, including the Spruce Tree House. These cliff dwellings were once home to the Ancestral Puebloan people, who left behind over 4,000 archaeological sites. Go inside the precarious Balcony House, Cliff Palace, or Long House on regular guided tours. Advance recommendations are highly recommended.

Eat & Drink: Wild game, fresh fish, and organic produce are on the menu at the nationally recognized **Metate Room** (✉ *34879 U.S. 160* ☎ *970/529–4422* ⊕ *www.visitmesaverde.com*) within the park, open April through October.

Stay: Perched on a shoulder of the Mesa Verde, the **Far View Lodge** (✉ *Mile Marker 15, Mesa Verde National Park* ☎ *970/529–4465* ⊕ *www.visitmesaverde.com*) gives guests a magnificent panorama view of the Four Corners that stretches as far as the eye can see. There are no TVs in the rooms, just private balconies and unbeatable views; it's open April through October.

Breakfast: Take coffee to go or sit down for a full breakfast at the Far View Terrace Café on the lodge's first floor.

Extend Your Trip

From Mesa Verde: The Best of Colorado *(Ch. 4)*

From Albuquerque: Route 66 *(Ch. 2)*; The Best of New Mexico *(Ch. 5)*

From Las Vegas: The Loneliest Road in Nevada: Route 50 *(Ch. 4)*

Day 4: Mesa Verde, CO, to Albuquerque, NM

266 miles (4 hours, 45 minutes without traffic and stops)

A southerly drive through the Pueblo lands of New Mexico takes you to Albuquerque.

ALONG THE WAY

Town: The small town of Aztec is home to **Aztec Ruins National Monument** (✉ *725 Ruins Rd.* ☎ *505/334–6174* ⊕ *www.nps. gov/azru*), a massive Puebloan great house and UNESCO World Heritage site that's over 900 years old. Explore the three-story structure built by the ancestors of New Mexico's 19 living Pueblo communities then walk the Old Spanish Trail into town.

Eat & Drink: For lunch in Aztec, pair a wood-fired pie or calzone with a frosty pint at **550 Brewing & Pizza Parlor** (✉ *119 N. Main Ave.* ☎ *505/636–2261* ⊕ *www. fivefiftypizzeria.com*).

Detour: For more of the Southwest's ancient splendor, take a 30-minute detour (25 miles each way) to **Bandelier National Monument** (✉ *15 Entrance Rd., Los Alamos* ☎ *505/672–3861* ⊕ *www.nps.gov/ band*) where an Ancestral Puebloan community lived, worked, and worshipped for around 350 years. Their descendants still remain, but were relocated to the banks of the Rio Grande in the 16th century following a long period of intense drought and social unrest.

ALBUQUERQUE

Do: Stroll through the streets of Albuquerque's Old Town or get a bird's-eye view of the city on the **Sandia Peak Tramway** (✉ 30 Tramway Rd. ☎ 505/856–1532 ⊕ www. sandiapeak.com). In October, keep your eyes trained on the skies above, when more than 500 colorful hot-air balloons take flight during the city's week-long **International Balloon Fiesta** (✉ 5000 Balloon Fiesta Pkwy. ☎ 855/725–1824 ⊕ www.balloonfiesta.com). In Isleta Pueblo on the northern edge of town, you can see one of the country's oldest churches, a gorgeous adobe mission parish established in 1622.

Eat & Drink: Tucked inside the **Indian Pueblo Cultural Center** (✉ 2401 12th St. NW ☎ 505/843–7270 ⊕ www.indian-pueblo.org), **Indian Pueblo Kitchen** serves Native-inspired dishes. Afterward, grab a southwestern-inspired pint at the rustic-modern **Bow & Arrow Brewing Company** (✉ 608 McKnight Ave. NW ☎ 505/247–9800 ⊕ www.bowandarrowbrewing. com).

Stay: One of Route 66's first motels, the restored **El Vado Motel** (✉ 2500 Central Ave. SW ☎ 505/361–1667 ⊕ www. elvadoabq.com) has a unique take on classic American road-trip culture complete with mid-century furnishings, local artwork, and a pool. On the northern edge of Albuquerque, the Sandia Pueblo operates the slick **Sandia Resort and Casino** (✉ 30 Rainbow Rd. NE ☎ 505/796–7500 ⊕ www.sandiacasino.com) with a golf course, spa, and a gorgeous view of the mountains.

Breakfast: Pull up a chair at **The Farmacy** (✉ 3718 Central Ave. SE ☎ 505/227–0330 ⊕ www.facebook.com/farmacyabq), a chic modern café with high-octane coffee and breakfast favorites like waffles and biscuits and gravy.

Day 5: Albuquerque, NM, to Chaco Canyon National Historic Park, NM

161 miles (3 hours without traffic and stops)

Head out of the city to Acoma, the oldest continuously occupied community in the United States, then back into the high desert for a visit to 1,000-year-old Chaco, once the Southwest's largest city.

ALONG THE WAY

Town: The stunning mesa-top village of Acoma, New Mexico, has survived drought, conquest, and colonization to earn the title of the oldest community in the United States. Members of the Acoma Pueblo still live here, thousands of feet in the sky, with no running water. The community's church and cemetery are its crown jewels, especially at Christmas when the paths are lit with candles for a midnight ceremony. The village can only be entered on guided tours, which leave from the **Sky City Cultural Center** (✉ Haaku Rd., Acoma Pueblo ☎ 800/747–0181 ⊕ www.acomaskycity.org) multiple times daily.

Eat & Drink: Don't be fooled by its location across from a truck stop. The no-frills **Spicy Bite** (✉ 1203-1299 Motel Dr. ☎ 505/356–0044 ⊕ www.facebook. com/5spicybite) in Milan, New Mexico, serves fresh and authentic Indian food.

CHACO CANYON NATIONAL HISTORIC PARK

Do: Explore the ruins of the once-great city of **Chaco Canyon** (✉ 1808 Rte. 7950 ☎ 505/786–7014 ⊕ www.nps.gov/chcu), which dominated the Southwest between AD 850 and 1250. Walk or drive the canyon loop, take a guided tour of Pueblo Bonito, or lace up your boots for a backcountry hike to some of Chaco's more remote sites.

Eat & Drink: There is no food in the park, but you can snag a cold drink and firewood in the visitor's center.

Stay: The **Gallo Campground** (⊕ *www. recreation.gov*, reservations necessary) is open year-round, and after dark, the night skies put on a spectacular display in this International Dark Sky Park.

Breakfast: This one's on you. Be sure to bring enough food and water for morning breakfast and coffee.

Day 6: Chaco Canyon National Historic Park, NM, to Chinle, AZ

170 miles (3 hours, 15 minutes without traffic and stops)

Travel through the Navajo Nation, stopping at the government seat at Window Rock, then on to the small town of Chinle, Arizona, which abuts the rugged, rocky Canyon de Chelly.

ALONG THE WAY

Detour: The bizarre rock formations of the Bisti Badlands form a landscape of desolation and solitude. Find them northwest of Chaco Canyon, a 40-mile drive into the desert (about 1 hour and 12 minutes each way).

Eat & Drink: At the down-home roadside diner **Jerry's Cafe** (⊠ *406 W. Coal Ave.* ☎ *505/722–6775*) in Gallup, New Mexico, dive into steaming plates of stuffed sopaipillas and chiles rellenos.

Town: Named for the near-perfect circle shaped by snow and rain in the red cliff behind the Navajo Nation's tribal headquarters, Window Rock has both an interesting museum and a moving memorial to World War II's Navajo Code Talkers. At

the **Ch'ihootso Indian Market Place** (⊠ *167A Rte. 264* ☎ *928/871–4698*) vendors sell everything from utilitarian goods to rugs and jewelry.

Shop: In operation for over 140 years, the **Hubbell Trading Post National Historic Site** (⊠ *1/2 Rte. 264, Ganado, AZ* ☎ *928/755–3475* ⊕ *www.nps.gov/hutr*) is a working trading post with exquisite handcrafted goods from local Navajo, Hopi, and Pueblo artisans. Stop by the visitor center to learn more about Hubbell's history, and take a walk around the grounds to visit its heritage Ganado sheep and Navajo hogans.

CHINLE

Do: With its painted rock formations and endless views, the **Canyon de Chelly National Monument** (☎ *928/674–5500* ⊕ *www.nps.gov/cach*) next door to Chinle is a geological wonder punctuated with ancient ruins. Take a self-guided or ranger-led hike or a scenic drive to the canyon's 10 overlooks.

Eat & Drink: The **Junction Restaurant** (⊠ *100 E. Main St.* ☎ *928/674–8443* ⊕ *www. junctionrestaurantaz.com*), adjacent to Chinle's Best Western, serves some of this small town's best food with a menu that includes Navajo tacos and posole. Keep in mind that by Navajo law, alcohol cannot be bought, sold, or transported on tribal lands.

Stay: The **Thunderbird Lodge** (⊠ *Rte. 7, Chinle* ☎ *928/674–5842* ⊕ *www.thunderbirdlodge.com*), owned and operated by the Navajo Nation, is a historic hotel with dependably clean and comfortable accommodations.

Breakfast: The Thunderbird Lodge Cafeteria next door to the lodge is inside a trading post more than a century old and has a wide selection of breakfast dishes, including tasty blue-corn pancakes.

Day 7: Chinle, AZ, to Tuba City, AZ

132 miles (2 hours, 30 minutes without traffic and stops)

Cross the Navajo border and enter the heart of the Hopi Nation, where a drive along the Hopi Arts Trail offers a glimpse of the artistic heritage and craftsmanship of a legendary Native community.

ALONG THE WAY

Eat & Drink: Get a taste of tribal specialties like Hopi hot beef and lamb stew at the **Hopi Cultural Center Restaurant** (✉ *Rte. 264* ☎ *928/734–2402* ⊕ *www. hopiculturalcenter.com*), located in the Hopi Cultural Center in Second Mesa.

Shop: Hopi artists are famed for their elaborately woven baskets, pottery, and silverwork. These are just some of the gorgeous pieces you'll find for sale along the **Hopi Arts Trail** (⊕ *www.hopiartstrail. com*) stretching between First Mesa and Tuba City.

TUBA CITY

Do: Several museums in Tuba City illuminate the Navajo experience, from stories of creation at the **Navajo Interactive Museum** (✉ *10 Main St.* ☎ *928/640-0684* ⊕ *www.discovernavajo.com*) to the role of the Navajo language in the Allied victory in World War II at the **Navajo Code Talkers Exhibit** (✉ *10 Main St.* ☎ *928/283–5441* ⊕ *www.discovernavajo.com*). Take home a piece of Native artistry from the **Tuba City Trading Post** (✉ *10 N. Main St.* ☎ *928/283–5441* ⊕ *www.discovernavajo.com*), which has been a working hub of commerce since 1870.

Eat & Drink: Tuba City doesn't have much in the way of food outside of fast-food restaurants. **Pizza Edge** (✉ *U.S. 160 and U.S. 264* ☎ *928/283–5938* ⊕ *www. pizzaedge.com*), a regional pizza chain with pizza, calzones, wings, and subs, is arguably the best of the bunch.

Stay: The **Moenkopi Legacy Inn & Suites** (✉ *U.S. 160 and U.S. 264* ☎ *928/283–4500* ⊕ *www.experiencehopi.com*), operated by the Hopi Nation, is a pleasant lodge accented with Native artwork and craftsmanship on the western edge of Hopi land. Amenities include a fitness center, pool, and kiva garden.

Breakfast: At **Hogan Espresso** (✉ *10 N. Main St.* ☎ *928/283–4545* ⊕ *www. facebook.com/hoganespressoandmore*), a cute little coffee shop with both indoor and outdoor seating, the coffee, pastries, and other fare are well worth a morning stop.

Day 8: Tuba City, AZ, to Grand Canyon-Parashant, AZ

233 miles (4 hours without traffic and stops)

Today you'll take a northern route through the painted cliffs and high elevation deserts of northern Arizona to reach Grand Canyon-Parashant National Monument.

ALONG THE WAY

Nature: The route to Grand Canyon-Parashant passes right through **Vermilion Cliffs National Monument** (⊕ *www.blm. gov*), home of The Wave, a stunning geological formation of crimson and gold that ripples across the Arizona desert. Enter the park's lottery online to score a permit to the site.

Town: The tiny town of Fredonia is worth a quick stop before heading into the rugged wilderness of Grand Canyon-Parashant. On North Main Street, check out the small but well curated **Red Pueblo**

Museum (✉ *900 U.S. 89A* ☎ *928/643–7777* ⊕ *www.facebook.com/redpueblomuseum*), which features everything from ancient Pueblo artifacts to an authentic pioneer-era log cabin.

GRAND CANYON-PARASHANT NATIONAL MONUMENT

Do: Less crowded than its national park counterpart, the views, hiking trails, and scenic drives at **Grand Canyon-Parashant National Monument** (☎ *435/688–3200* ⊕ *www.nps.gov/para*) in the traditional tribal lands of the Hualapai are no less spectacular.

Eat & Drink: Stock up on food and water in advance. There are no stores or potable water available within the monument.

Stay: Grand Canyon-Parashant has no developed campsites, but free backcountry camping is allowed throughout the park, including on the rim of the Grand Canyon. If you want to camp below the rim, you'll need a permit in advance.

Breakfast: At Grand Canyon-Parashant, the only breakfast for miles is the one you cook yourself.

Day 9: Grand Canyon-Parashant, AZ, to Las Vegas, NV

131 miles (2 hours, 15 minutes without traffic and stops)

Get your last look at the desert as you roll into the mighty city of Las Vegas and the end of the road.

ALONG THE WAY

Town: Quaint Boulder City, Nevada, is dotted with a small downtown historic district, small businesses, and parks (and no casinos—this is the only town in Nevada where gambling is illegal). Over the

hill from town, enormous Hoover Dam blocks the Colorado River as it enters Black Canyon. Backed up behind the dam is incongruous, deep-blue Lake Mead, the focal point of water-based recreation for southern Nevada and northwestern Arizona, and the major water supplier to seven southwestern states. The lake is ringed by miles of rugged desert country.

Nature: The breathtaking wonderland known as **Valley of Fire** (✉ *29450 Valley of Fire Rd., Overton, NV* ☎ *702/397–2088* ⊕ *www.parks.nv.gov*), with its red sandstone outcroppings, petrified logs, petroglyphs, and hiking trails, is along the northern reaches of Lake Mead.

Eat & Drink: The **Coffee Cup** (✉ *512 Nevada Hwy., Boulder City* ☎ *702/294–0517* ⊕ *www.worldfamouscoffeecup.com*) is a bustling breakfast-and-lunch diner that's been featured on Food Network's *Diners, Drive-Ins, and Dives*. Tourists line up on weekends for the quintessential small-town diner experience, complete with newspaper-strewn counter seating and the owners' family photos and water-sports memorabilia on the walls. It delivers on the food front too, with giant portions of favorites such as huevos rancheros, biscuits and gravy, and barbecue sandwiches.

LAS VEGAS

Do: You won't find much in the way of Indigenous culture in the City of Sin, but you will find a whole lot of debauchery. Head to big-name casinos on the strip like the **Bellagio** (✉ *3600 S. Las Vegas Blvd.* ☎ *888/987–6667* ⊕ *bellagio.mgmresorts.com*), the **Venetian** (✉ *3355 S. Las Vegas Blvd.* ☎ *866/659–9643* ⊕ *www.venetian.com*), and **Mandalay Bay** (✉ *3950 S. Las Vegas Blvd.* ☎ *702/632–7000* ⊕ *mandalaybay.mgmresorts.com*) or make your way downtown for a more vintage experience at **The Neon Museum** (✉ *770 Las Vegas Blvd.*

N ☎ 702/387–6366 ⊕ www.neonmuse-um.org), a graveyard for the city's retired neon signs.

Eat & Drink: Splurge on Cantonese delicacies at **Mott 32** (✉ 3325 S. Las Vegas Blvd. ☎ 702/607–3232 ⊕ www.mott32.com) in the Venetian, or keep things casual at the **Park MGM's Crack Shack** (✉ 3770 S. Las Vegas Blvd. ☎ 702/820–5991 ⊕ www.crackshack.com), a fried-chicken and sandwich joint with a fine-dining pedigree. The truly hungry will find what they're looking for at the **Wynn Las Vegas** (✉ 3131 S. Las Vegas Blvd. ☎ 702/770–7000 ⊕ www.wynn-lasvegas.com) and the **Rampart Casino** (✉ 221 N. Rampart Blvd. ☎ 702/507–5900 ⊕ theresortatsummerlin.com), which have some of the best buffets in town. Off the strip, get a swanky drink at the **Downtown Cocktail Room** (✉ 111 S. Las Vegas Blvd. ☎ 702/880–3696 ⊕ www.downtowncocktailroom.com) or a cold one at famed Rat Pack hangout **Atomic Liquors** (✉ 917 E. Fremont St. ☎ 702/982–3000 ⊕ www.atomic.vegas).

Stay: Get the resort experience at the **ARIA** (✉ 3730 S. Las Vegas Blvd. ☎ 866/359–7757 ⊕ aria.mgmresorts.com), which has a soaring modernist aesthetic, three outdoor pools, a spa, and the Jewel nightclub. Downtown, the classic **Golden Nugget Hotel & Casino** (✉ 129 Fremont St. ☎ 702/385–7111 ⊕ www.goldennugget.com) has 2,400 well-appointed guest rooms and a three-story waterslide that twists and turns through a 200,000-gallon shark tank.

Breakfast: Recharge with one of the breakfast sandwiches at **Eggslut** (✉ Boulevard Tower, 3708 S. Las Vegas Blvd. ☎ 702/698–2344 ⊕ www.cos-mopolitanlasvegas.com) or indulge in a French-inspired bistro-style brunch at **Bouchon** (✉ 3355 S. Las Vegas Blvd. ☎ 702/414–6200 ⊕ www.thom-askeller.com).

Enlightenment and Wellness in the Southwest

Written by Margot Bigg

The American Southwest has long been popular with spiritual seekers and those looking for healing and relaxation, and this itinerary will give you a whirlwind look at some of the best spiritual spots and wellness retreats the region has to offer. From New Agey towns like Ojai and Sedona to mystical national parks that exude otherworldly vibes, you'll experience hot springs, energy vortices, and famous ashrams, all guaranteeing you'll find at least some relaxation if not true spiritual transcendence.

At a Glance

Start: Los Angeles, CA

End: Santa Fe, NM

Miles Traveled: 1,340 miles

Suggested Duration: 8 days

States Visited: Arizona, California, New Mexico

Key Sights: Arcosanti; Cathedral Rock; El Santuario de Chimayó; Joshua Tree National Park; Petrified Forest National Park

Best Time to Go: This trip is doable year-round, but the weather in the region is at its most pleasant in the springtime and autumn. Summers can get very hot.

Day 1: Los Angeles, CA, to Ojai, CA

83 miles (1 hour, 30 minutes without traffic and stops)

From Los Angeles, take Highway 101 north to exit 70B. From here, it's about nine miles up Route 33 to the bohemian town of Ojai, known for its hot springs and spiritual centers.

ALONG THE WAY

Town: Just north of Santa Monica, the beach town of Malibu boasts 21 miles of sandy ocean beach plus plenty of cute boutiques, cafés, and restaurants. Popular attractions include the sea caves at **El Matador State Beach** (✉ *32220 E. Pacific Coast Hwy.* ☎ *310/457–8144* ⊕ *www. californiabeaches.com*) and the surfer-favorite Zuma Beach.

Eat & Drink: Overlooking the Pacific Ocean, **Malibu Farm** (✉ *23000 Pacific Coast Hwy.* ☎ *310/456–2852* ⊕ *www. malibu-farm.com*) offers a huge, eclectic menu with a solid selection of light seafood dishes alongside tacos, salads, and pizzas. Many of the items here are vegan and/or gluten-free, including some of the desserts.

OJAI

Do: Ojai's biggest draw is perhaps its easy access to natural hot springs. The best known is **Ecotopia** (✉ *2566 Matilija Canyon Rd.* ☎ *805/272–0011* ⊕ *www. ojaiecotopia.com*), a series of five pools located on the banks of the Matilija River. Art lovers will appreciate the **Beatrice Wood Center for the Arts** (✉ *8585 Ojai-Santa Paula Rd.* ☎ *805/646–3381* ⊕ *www. beatricewood.com*), while those with an interest in spirituality or eastern philosophy may want to stop by the **Krishnamurti Educational Center** (✉ *1098 McAndrew Rd.* ☎ *805/646–2726* ⊕ *www.kfa.org*), which frequently holds classes based on the teachings of Indian philosopher Jiddu Krishnamurti.

Eat & Drink: One of the most romantic options in town, the **Ranch House** (✉ *102 Besant Rd.* ☎ *805/646–2360* ⊕ *www. theranchhouse.com*) features New American fine dining and a solid wine menu, served in an enchanting tucked-away garden.

Stay: The twin properties collectively known as the **Iguana Inns of Ojai** (✉ *11794 N. Ventura Ave.* ☎ *805/646–5277* ⊕ *www. blueiguanainn.com*) do a great job of encapsulating the town's whimsical vibes, with art-filled rooms and beautiful gardens. Another quiet option, the **Ojai Retreat and Inn** (✉ *160 Besant Rd.* ☎ *805/646–2536* ⊕ *www.ojairetreat. com*) offers B&B-style rooms and cottages on a peaceful hilltop overlooking the Ojai Valley.

Breakfast: Start your day off at **Cafe Boku** (✉ *987 W. Ojai Ave.* ☎ *805/798–5822* ⊕ *www.bokusuperfood.com*), a health-conscious spot with a large open-air patio and a plant-forward breakfast menu offering burritos, avocado toasts, smoothies, and all sorts of fancy coffee drinks.

Day 2: Ojai, CA, to Joshua Tree, CA

212 miles (3 hours, 30 minutes without traffic and stops)

Head back toward Ventura, and then east toward Pasadena and on to funky Joshua Tree National Park, checking out some unusual local attractions along the way.

ALONG THE WAY

Town: Pasadena is a good spot to take a break, with its historic, walkable downtown area full of shops and restaurants, many housed in historic buildings. If you have a couple of hours to spare, you may want to check out the **Huntington Library, Art Collections, and Botanical Gardens** (✉ *1151 Oxford Rd., San Marino* ☎ *626/405–2100* ⊕ *www.huntington.*

org), with its extensive collection of European art and reference materials, plus its 16 sprawling themed gardens full of plant life from around the world.

Eat & Drink: Right in Old Town Pasadena, the local branch of L.A.'s beloved **Sage Vegan Bistro** (⊠ *41 Hugus Alley* ☎ *626/564–8111* ⊕ *www.sagevganbistro.com*) offers meat-free takes on popular dishes from around the world, plus sandwiches, salads, tacos, and pizzas. Around 90% of the produce here comes from local organic farmers and many of the items are gluten- and nut-free.

Roadside Attraction: Built in the late 1950s by UFOlogist George Van Tassel based on a blueprint he claimed came from extraterrestrial sources, the **Integratron** (⊠ *2477 Belfield Blvd., Landers* ☎ *760/364–3126* ⊕ *www.integratron.com*) is a 38-foot high white dome that resembles an observatory, albeit one constructed entirely of wood and fiberglass. Today the structure is used primarily for sound bath healings and other special events.

JOSHUA TREE NATIONAL PARK

Do: This area's main draw is **Joshua Tree National Park** (⊠ *74485 National Park Dr., Twentynine Palms* ☎ *760/367–5500* ⊕ *www.nps.gov/jotr*), located at the convergence of the Mojave and Colorado Deserts. The 1,235-mile expanse of wilderness is characterized by its otherworldly rock formations popular with rock climbers and its abundance of *Yucca brevifolia* plants, commonly referred to as Joshua trees. The area around the park has drawn free thinkers for decades, as evidenced by some of the more unusual area attractions. The Frank Lloyd Wright–designed **Joshua Tree Retreat Center** (⊠ *59700 Twentynine Palms Hwy.* ☎ *760/469–9764* ⊕ *www.jtrcc.org*) is one such spot, and offers spiritual teachings and retreats. Also worth checking out is the **Sky Village Swap Meet** (⊠ *7028 Theater

Extend Your Trip

From Joshua Tree: The Best of Southern California; California's National Parks *(Ch. 3)*

From Sedona: The Best of Arizona *(Ch. 5)*

From Taos or Santa Fe: The Best of New Mexico *(Ch. 5)*

Rd. ☎ *760/365–2104* ⊕ *www.skyvillageswapmeet.com*) in Yucca Valley, which offers a café and a weekend market, and is home to the Crystal Cave, a whimsical construction built with structural foam and filled with multihue crystals.

Eat & Drink: Housed in an old diner in Yucca Valley, north of Joshua Tree, **La Copine** (⊠ *848 Old Woman Springs Rd.* ☎ *760/289–8537* ⊕ *www.lacopinekitchen.com*) offers eclectic fine dining with a menu that changes by the season.

Stay: While you may just want to camp right in the national park, you certainly don't have to—there are plenty of lovely places to stay not far from the park entrance. For a rustic experience with a few more creature comforts, the **Castle House Estate** (⊠ *64278 E. Broadway, Joshua Tree* ☎ *760/853–1636* ⊕ *www.thecastlehouseestate.com*) offers a few shaded campsites as well as fully furnished yurts, a container home, a vintage RV, and a couple of "guard towers," two-story rooms designed to look like castle turrets. If you're a fan of design, consider booking a night at the **Lautner Compound** (⊠ *67710 San Antonio St., Desert Hot Springs* ☎ *760/832–5288* ⊕ *www.thelautner.com*), a collection of four vacation rentals designed back in 1947 by famed American architect John Lautner.

Breakfast: Get a hearty first meal of the day at **JT Country Kitchen** (✉ *61768 Twentynine Palms Hwy., Joshua Tree* ☎ *760/366–8988* ⊕ *www.jtcountrykitchen.com*), which offers down-home cooking like biscuits and gravy, omelets, and "world famous" buttermilk pancakes.

Day 3: Joshua Tree, CA, to Arcosanti, AZ

356 miles (5 hours, 30 minutes without traffic and stops)

Head south to Palm Springs and hop on I–10 until you reach the outskirts of Phoenix before heading north to the township of Arcosanti, which was started in the 1970s as an architectural experiment designed to address urban sprawl.

ALONG THE WAY

Town: Although it's best known for its annual gem-and-mineral show, the largest such conference on earth, Quartzite is a fun stopover year-round, thanks to a few quirky shops and plenty of hiking opportunities. For an unusual bit of history, stop by the **Hi Jolly Monument** (✉ *W. Elsie La. and Hi Jolly La.*). This pyramidal gravestone with a camel silhouette on top is the final resting place of Hadji Ali (nicknamed "Hi Jolly"), a camel driver who came to the United States in the mid-19th century as part of the U.S. Army's Camel Corps.

Eat & Drink: Dating back to 1918, **Rock Springs Café** (✉ *35900 Old Black Canyon Hwy.* ☎ *623/374–5794* ⊕ *www.rockspringscafe.com*) in Black Canyon City is the oldest independent restaurant in Arizona. Here you can chow down on all sorts of comfort food, from burgers to barbecued chicken, but the real draw is the wide variety of pies, from all-American apple pie to chocolate cherry cream.

Photo Op: Just north of Black Canyon City, the Sunset Point rest area offers well-maintained bathrooms and drinking fountains along with a gigantic sundial and great western views out over the desert.

ARCOSANTI

Do: Along with a gift shop full of their signature bells and an outdoor swimming pool, the experimental township **Arcosanti** (✉ *13555 S. Cross L Rd., Mayer* ☎ *928/632–7135* ⊕ *www.arcosanti.org*) offers one-hour guided tours of the site. They start with a short video in the gift shop/reception center and continue through the grounds; some add an extra hour to focus on architecture.

Eat & Drink: There's a simple café just downstairs from the visitor center, which offers buffet-style meals most days of the week; there are plenty of options for special diets available.

Stay: Arcosanti offers a range of on-site lodging, including simple guest rooms with private or shared bathrooms and a couple of suites that can be reserved via Airbnb. There's also a campsite, and dorm space is available for groups.

Breakfast: A buffet breakfast with toast, tea, coffee, cereal, and usually a hot dish is included with your stay at Arcosanti.

Day 4: Arcosanti, AZ, to Sedona, AZ

53 miles (1 hour without traffic and stops)

Continue north up I-17 until you reach Route 179, which will take you right to Sedona, known in New Age communities for its energy vortices.

ALONG THE WAY

Nature: One of the most recognizable geological formations in the Sedona area is the 12,000-foot-high Cathedral Rock, which is also a great place to take a hike; just wear solid shoes, as the trail can be slippery.

Sedona's Cathedral Rock is one of the most recognizable geological formations in the area.

Eat & Drink: Chow down on Mexican fare at Sedona's colorful **Elote Café** (✉ *350 Jordan Rd.* ☎ *928/203–0105* ⊕ *www.elotecafe.com*), named for Mexico's celebrated street corn.

SEDONA

Do: Sedona offers tons to do, from relaxing in one of the local spas and browsing crystal shops to taking a guided tour of the area's alleged vortexes. The cliffside Chapel of the Holy Cross is also a must-visit, both for its serene atmosphere and its unusual architecture.

Eat & Drink: At **Mariposa** (✉ *700 Rte. 89A* ☎ *928/862–4444* ⊕ *www.mariposasedona.com*), a Latin-inspired restaurant in one of Sedona's most picturesque locations, you can enjoy tapas, empanadas, and grilled selections with your Red Rocks view.

Stay: For a romantic splurge, it doesn't get more Sedona-chic than **L'Auberge de Sedona** (✉ *301 Little La.* ☎ *800/905–5745* ⊕ *www.lauberge.com*). If your budget is more modest, **Desert Quail**

Inn (✉ *6626 Rte. 179* ☎ *928/284–1433* ⊕ *www.desertquailinn.com*) is bare-bones but well-maintained.

Breakfast: Its whimsical garden seating is enough to make **Chocolatree** (✉ *1595 Rte. 89A* ☎ *928/282–2997* ⊕ *www.chocolatree.com*) a perfect way to start your day, but luckily they also have an extensive menu of gourmet health food, smoothies, espresso drinks, and, if you're in a brunchier mood, cocktails.

Day 5: Sedona, AZ, to Petrified Forest, AZ

137 miles (2 hours, 30 minutes without traffic and stops)

Head north along Route 89A to Flagstaff before joining I–40, which will take you to the ancient Petrified National Forest.

ALONG THE WAY

Town: Just a short drive from Sedona, Flagstaff is a good place to grab food or supplies. Take a little extra time to wander the Historic Downtown District right on Route 66 or head up to the **Lowell Observatory** (✉ *1400 W. Mars Hill Rd.* ☎ *928/774–3358* ⊕ *www.lowell.edu*) on the western side of town.

Eat & Drink: Sit down for some hearty English fare at Flagstaff's **Cornish Pasty Co.** (✉ *26 S. San Francisco St.* ☎ *928/440– 5196* ⊕ *www.cornishpastyco.com*), a pub restaurant featuring church pew bench–style seating and extensive draft beer options.

PETRIFIED FOREST NATIONAL PARK

Do: Within **Petrified Forest National Park** (☎ *928/524–6228* ⊕ *www.nps.gov/pefo*), petrified logs scattered about a vast pink-hued lunar-like landscape resemble a fairy-tale forest turned to stone. You can easily spend days exploring the park but if you're short on time, make sure to at least spend some time at the **Canyon de Chelly** (☎ *928/674–5500* ⊕ *www.nps. gov/cach*), home to more than 7,000 archaeological sites. You may even spot an ancient petroglyph.

Eat & Drink: If you don't want to eat at your hotel, you can save time and money by grabbing a meal at the **Painted Desert Diner** (✉ *1 Park Rd.* ☎ *928/524– 6228* ⊕ *www.nps.gov/pefo*).

Stay: Historic **La Posada Hotel** (✉ *303 E. 2nd St., Winslow* ☎ *928/289– 4366* ⊕ *www.laposada.org*) features old-fashioned rooms that exude a 1930s vibe. There's also an excellent on-site restaurant.

Breakfast: Stick around La Posada's **Turquoise Room** (✉ *303 E. 2nd St., Win- slow* ☎ *928/289–2888* ⊕ *www.thetur- quoiseroom.net*) for breakfast; you can grab your morning meal here.

Day 6: Petrified Forest, AZ, to Jemez Springs, NM

308 miles (4 hour, 45 minutes without traffic and stops)

Continue along I–40 until Albuquerque, then make your way north to Jemez Springs, known for its mineral-rich ther- mal waters.

ALONG THE WAY

Town: New Mexico's biggest city is a great spot to stop and stretch your legs or spend an afternoon. Attractions worth stopping for in Albuquerque include the **Petroglyph National Monument** (✉ *Western Trail NW* ☎ *505/899–0205* ⊕ *www.nps. gov/petr*), which is among the largest petroglyph sites on the continent, as well as the **Indian Pueblo Cultural Center** (✉ *2401 12th St. NW* ☎ *505/843– 7270* ⊕ *www.indianpueblo.org*), an expansive museum committed to pre- serving Pueblo culture and history.

Eat & Drink: Set in Albuquerque's Edo neighborhood, the **Grove Cafe & Market** (✉ *600 Central Ave. SE* ☎ *505/248– 9800* ⊕ *www.thegrovecafemarket.com*) offers a large all-day breakfast menu plus bistro-style salads and sandwiches at lunchtime. Many of the ingredients are sourced from local organic farmers. They also offer French macarons every Friday through Sunday.

JEMEZ SPRINGS

Do: This tiny settlement is a great place to break up your journey for the night. It offers easy access to a mix of devel- oped and wild hot springs. The village's **Bodhi Manda Zen Center** (✉ *1 Bodhi Dr.* ☎ *575/829–3854* ⊕ *www.bmzc.org*) attracts spiritual seekers and offers daily meditations for Zen practitioners as well as occasional retreats. Jemez Springs is also home to the historic **Jemez Historic Site** (✉ *18160 Rte. 4* ☎ *575/829– 3530* ⊕ *www.nmhistoricsites.org*), which features the remains of a 15th-century pueblo and a 17th-century Franciscan mission.

Eat & Drink: Although **Jemez Mountain Brewhouse** (✉ *17691 Rte. 126* ☎ *575/829–4222* ⊕ *www.jemezmountainbrewhouse.com*) is best known for its artisan pizza, they also have tasty apps like hot wings and roasted Brussels sprouts.

Stay: If you'd like to devote some time to soaking, **Jemez Hot Springs** (✉ *40 Abousleman Loop* ☎ *575/829–9175* ⊕ *www.jemezhotsprings.com*) is a good option. While you can come here as a day visitor, booking a stay at one of the on-site cottages is also an option.

Breakfast: Grab a cup of joe and a pastry at **Highway 4 Cafe & Bakery** (✉ *17502 Rte. 4* ☎ *575/829–4655* ⊕ *www.facebook.com/Hwy4cafe*) before you continue on toward Taos.

Day 7: Jemez Springs, NM, to Taos, NM

121 miles (2 hours, 45 minutes without traffic and stops)

Travel via state highways northeast toward Taos, taking a detour to explore Bandelier National Monument along the way.

ALONG THE WAY

Town: The atomic bomb was originally developed in little Los Alamos. Learn more about it (and about the region overall) at the **Los Alamos History Museum** (✉ *1050 Bathtub Row* ☎ *505/709–7794* ⊕ *www.losalamoshistory.org*).

Eat & Drink: One of the oldest spots in Los Alamos, **Blue Window Bistro** (✉ *1789 Central Ave.* ☎ *505/662–6305* ⊕ *www.labluewindowbistro.com*) boasts an extensive lunch menu with everything from tacos to calamari.

Detour: A short drive from Los Alamos, **Bandelier National Monument** (✉ *15*

Entrance Rd. ☎ *505/672–3861* ⊕ *www.nps.gov/band*) is worth visiting for its ancient Pueblo dwellings, some dating back almost 1,000 years. Highlights include a visitor center with displays of ancient artifacts as well as a network of well-maintained trails; the 1.2-mile-long Main Loop Trail will give you access to many of the monument's most important archaeological sites. Ladders are provided for those who want to climb up into a few of the ancient dwellings.

TAOS

Do: The most important site in Taos is **Taos Pueblo** (✉ *120 Veterans Hwy.* ☎ *575/758–1028* ⊕ *www.taospueblo.com*), a UNESCO World Heritage site and one of the oldest continuously inhabited spots in North America, with a history spanning over a millennium. Other not-to-miss spots include the Rio Grande Gorge Bridge, which offers fantastic views of the basalt canyon below, and the **San Francisco de Asís Mission Church** (✉ *60 St. Francis Plaza* ☎ *575/758–2754* ⊕ *www.sfranchos.org*), an 1816 adobe church that has provided inspiration for the likes of Ansel Adams and Georgia O'Keeffe. If you'd like to unwind at the end of your day, consider attending a meditation session with **Mindful Frontiers** (☎ *575/770–3683* ⊕ *mindfulfrontiers.net/community*) or booking an Ayurvedic treatment at **Auromesa** (✉ *101 Coyote Loop* ☎ *575/776–2212*), both in the Taos suburb of Arroyo Hondo.

Eat & Drink: Housed in a renovated 19th-century chapel, **The Love Apple** (✉ *803 Paseo Del Pueblo Norte* ☎ *575/751–0050* ⊕ *www.theloveapple.net*) offers a seasonal menu with ingredients sourced primarily from local farms. All the meals here are made from scratch, and there are plenty of options for people with dietary restrictions.

Stay: Right in the heart of Taos, overlooking its historic plaza, the luxurious **La Fonda on the Plaza** (✉ *108 S. Plaza* ☎ *575/758–2211* ⊕ *www.lafondataos.com*) features elegant rooms full of local touches and great views from its rooftop terrace restaurant. For an off-the-grid (and offbeat) alternative to staying in town, head a few miles north to the **Earthship Global Visitor Center** (✉ 2 Earthship Way, Tres Piedras ☎ 575/613–4409 ⊕ www.earthship. com), where you can spend the night in a cottage built primarily from upcycled tires and rammed earth, designed to have minimal impact on its natural surroundings. Self-guided tours are also available for day visitors.

Breakfast: Begin your day at **Bent Street Grille** (✉ 120 Bent St. ☎ 575/758–5787 ⊕ www.bentstreetgrille.com), which serves a southwestern-inspired breakfast menu all day, plus a smattering of freshly baked pastries.

Day 8: Taos, NM, to Santa Fe, NM

70 miles (1 hour, 30 minutes without traffic and stops)

Make your way south to Santa Fe, stopping at the Hacienda de Guru Ram Das along the way.

ALONG THE WAY

Town: Stop in Española to visit the **Hacienda de Guru Ram Das** (✉ 1A Ram Das Guru Pl. ☎ 505/753–6341 ⊕ www. espanolaashram.com), run by followers of Sikh Yogi Bhajan (of Yogi Tea fame). A variety of spiritual programs and educational activities are available.

Eat & Drink: Sit down for New Mexico-style tacos, fajitas, and—of course—sopaipillas at the **Sopaipilla Factory** (✉ 7 W. Gutierrez ☎ 505/455–2855 ⊕ www. sopaipillafactoryrestaurant.com) in northern Santa Fe. This local favorite in the town of Pojoaque offers abundant outdoor seating and a large vegetarian menu. All dishes are served with a free sopaipilla and a side of honey or honey butter.

Detour: El Santuario de Chimayó (✉ 15 Santuario Dr., Chimayo ☎ 505/351–4360 ⊕ www.holychimayo.us) is an adobe church that's often touted as the Lourdes of the Southwest. According to legend, a light appeared here on Good Friday in 1810—a hole was subsequently dug and a crucifix was unearthed. The dirt from the hole is believed to have healing properties to this day.

SANTA FE

Do: Santa Fe has a ton of things to see and do, from marveling at the ancient sacred artifacts at the **Museum of International Folk Art** (✉ 706 Camino Lejo, on Museum Hill ☎ 505/476–1204 ⊕ www. moifa.org) to wandering through the historic downtown, filled with whimsical shops and independent art galleries. Make sure to leave yourself plenty of time to immerse yourself in the fantastical at **Meow Wolf** (✉ 1352 Rufina Circle ☎ 866/636–9969 ⊕ www.meowwolf. com), a multimedia art attraction full of kaleidoscopic interactive exhibits.

Eat & Drink: If you're in the mood for a healthy yet tasty meal, make a beeline to **Ras Rody's Jamaican Vegan** (✉ 1320 Agua Fria St. ☎ 505/385–3011 ⊕ www.rasrody. com) food truck, just a few minutes' drive from downtown. Here you'll find an ever-changing menu of richly spiced Jamaican cuisine, fresh fruit juices, and delicious desserts.

Stay: Few properties compare to the **Inn of the Five Graces** (✉ 150 E. DeVargas St. ☎ 505/992–0957 ⊕ www.fivegraces. com), an elegant adobe-style luxury hotel with warm, sumptuous rooms and a mosaic-filled spa offering a range of Ayurveda-inspired massages and treatments. If your budget is a bit more modest, consider retiring to the relaxing **Ojo Santa Fe** (✉ 242 Los Pinos Rd. ☎ 877/977–8212 ⊕ ojosparesorts.com) on the south side of town, with its contemporary rooms and extensive spa. Don't miss the chance to soak in one of the private mineral-rich "ojito" soaking tubs.

Breakfast: Open for all three meals, **Cafe Pasqual** (✉ *121 Don Gaspar Ave.* ☎ *505/983–9340* ⊕ *pasquals.com*) serves fresh, Latin-inspired fare in a colorful space decorated with Mexican folk art and murals.

Dark Skies of the Southwest

Written by Andrew Collins

If you look at a light pollution map in the United States, you'll see that the Southwest is one of the few regions still largely dark at night. For both casual stargazers and ardent astronomy buffs, this swatch of high-desert plains and even loftier mountain ranges—particularly the states of New Mexico and Arizona—offer exceptional conditions for staring up at the galaxy. Founded in 1988 in Tucson, the nonprofit DarkSky International (formerly the International Dark-Sky Association) promotes the preservation of our dark skies through education and advocacy, and by designating International Dark Sky Places (IDSPs).

On this meandering loop through some of the most pristine landscapes of Arizona and New Mexico, you'll visit more than 20 IDSPs, including parks and communities. The route climbs over rugged 8,000-foot alpine passes, beside centuries-old Puebloan ruins, and through stunning national parks and secluded towns that offer evening astronomy and stargazing programs. This itinerary also visits a number of places that aren't yet officially designated by DarkSky International but nevertheless offer ideal conditions for falling asleep beneath the Milky Way, free from the glow of urban lights.

At a Glance

Start: Albuquerque, NM

End: Albuquerque, NM

Miles Traveled: 2,000 miles

Suggested Duration: 10 days

States Visited: Arizona, New Mexico

Key Sights: Chiricahua National Monument; Saguaro National Park; Grand Canyon National Park; Lowell Observatory; Valle del Oro National Wildlife Refuge; Valles Caldera National Preserve

Best Time to Go: Due to the significant elevation differences along this route, temperatures can swing more than 40 degrees on any given day, no matter the time of year. Each season has its pros and cons. Occasional snowstorms can render some areas temporarily inaccessible between November and April while late afternoon thunderstorms can cause flooding during the otherwise beautiful and lush (by desert standards) summer monsoon season. Spring and fall tend to have the most moderate temperatures, but the former can be windy and the latter is increasingly prone to wildfires.

Day 1: Albuquerque, NM, to Cloudcroft, NM

260 miles (5 hours without traffic and stops)

With a well-designed, mid-size airport offering flights from most major hubs in the western United States, Albuquerque makes an excellent start and endpoint for this adventure. The journey south mostly straddles the desert mountains that form an intermittent spine down the center of New Mexico. Just east of Albuquerque, take Route 337 and Route 542 south to visit Salinas Pueblo Missions National Monument in Mountainair. Then continue south on Route 55 and U.S. 54 to Carrizozo, east on U.S. 380 to Capitan, and south on local roads through Ruidoso to the high-mountain town of Cloudcroft.

Dark Skies
of the Southwest

ALONG THE WAY

Town: Made up of three units outside the arty high-desert village of Mountainair, **Salinas Pueblo Missions National Monument** (⊕ www.nps.gov/sapu) is the first DarkSky International–accredited stop on this itinerary. First explore the park's **Quarai Unit** (✉ 122 Manzano Quarai Rd. ☎ 505/847–2290), then learn more about these archaeological sites made up of extensively restored Ancestral Puebloan, and later Spanish colonial, ruins at the park's main **Visitor Center** (✉ 105 S. Ripley Ave. ☎ 505/847–2585). **Mountainair** has a few noteworthy arts spaces, including **La Galería @ the Shaffer** (✉ 103 W. Main St. ☎ 505/847–2888 ⊕ la-galeria-theshaffer.com). It's a 15-minute drive west on U.S. 60 to visit the national monument's smallest ruin, the **Abó Unit** (✉ 69 Ruins Rd. ☎ 505/847–2400). The largest and most impressive section, **Gran Quivira** (✉ 4030 Quivira Flats Rd. ☎ 505/847–2770) is a half-hour drive southeast of Mountainair, conveniently en route south toward Cloudcroft.

Eat & Drink: In downtown Mountainair, **B Street Market** (✉ 204 W. Broadway ☎ 505/847–2223 ⊕ www.bstreet-marketdeli.com) is a historic grocery dating back to 1903, stocked with gourmet snacks and a café-deli serving quesadillas and sandwiches.

Detour: From Capitan, it's a pretty 12-mile side track east to the verdant village where in 1878, the fabled outlaw Billy the Kid escaped from jail, killing a pair of deputies in the process. The **Lincoln Historic Site** (✉ Mile Marker 97, U.S. 380 ☎ 575/653–4025 ⊕ www.nmhistoricsites.org/lincoln)—comprising the original courthouse and jail, a museum, and a few other outbuildings—recounts the colorful, though violent, tale of the Lincoln County Wars.

CLOUDCROFT

Do: Sitting in the Sacramento Mountains at an elevation of 8,676 feet, the festive western village of Cloudcroft is one of the highest towns in the state. From the short and easy trails at the **Trestle Depot Recreation Area** (✉ E. Little Mexican Rd. ☎ 575/682–2551 ⊕ www.fs.usda.gov), you can see for miles down into the Tularosa Basin toward White Sands National Park. In town, the handful of streets are lined with cute souvenir shops, western-wear boutiques, galleries, and cafés. **Sacramento Mountains Museum** (✉ 1000 U.S. 82 ☎ 575/682–2932 ⊕ www.cloudcroftmuseum.com) contains a re-created Pioneer Village that depicts life here in the late 19th century.

Eat & Drink: Mad Jack's Mountain-top Barbecue (✉ 105 James Canyon Hwy. ☎ 575/682–7577 ⊕ www.madjacksbbq.com) has a devout following—and often long lines—for the tender slow-smoked brisket and prodigious beef ribs, while **Cloudcroft Brewing Company** (✉ 1301 Burro Ave. ☎ 575/682–2337 ⊕ www.cloudcroftbrewing.com) turns out filling pizzas and heady imperial red ales.

Stay: Built in 1899 by the Alamogordo and Sacramento Mountain Railway on a pine-shaded bluff, the colorfully painted and possibly haunted **Lodge at Cloudcroft** (✉ 601 Corona Pl. ☎ 575/682–2566 ⊕ www.thelodgeresort.com) enjoys a magical alpine setting. Rooms come in a variety of configurations, and there's a popular restaurant, a pool and hot tub, and one of the country's oldest golf courses.

Breakfast: Pop into airy and contemporary **High Rollin' Coffee** (✉ 109 James Canyon Hwy. ⊕ www.instagram.com/highrollincoffee) for a chocolate-lavender latte and an acai bowl or strawberry-chèvre toast.

Day 2: Cloudcroft, NM, to Willcox, AZ

290 miles (5 hours without traffic and stops)

After descending from Cloudcroft some 4,300 feet in less than 20 miles via U.S. 82, take U.S. 70 west—stopping to explore White Sands National Park and Organ Mountains–Desert Peaks National Monument—to Las Cruces. From here it's a straight shot west on I–10 to Willcox.

ALONG THE WAY

Nature: Between Alamogordo and Las Cruces, you'll pass by two wilderness areas of remarkable beauty, and although neither is a designated IDSP, both offer night-sky programs. **White Sands National Park** (✉ *19955 U.S. 70, Alamogordo* ☎ *575/479–6124* ⊕ *www.nps.gov/whsa*) contains just 40% of a massive 275-square-mile basin of rolling, snow-white dunes of gypsum. Explore the park on scenic Dunes Drive, with its myriad pullouts for short hikes, picnics, and opportunities for dune sledding. At **Organ Mountains–Desert Peaks National Monument** (✉ *Dripping Springs Rd.* ☎ *575/525–4300* ⊕ *www.blm.gov*), which consists of nearly a half-million acres of sheer, jagged peaks, you'll find myriad hiking trails, including the 4-mile round-trip Baylor Canyon Pass trek that takes you to a breathtaking overlook.

Town: New Mexico's second-largest city, Las Cruces (population 116,000) is a friendly interstate crossroads, a lively university town, and a hub of outdoor recreation. Walk around Old Mesilla, a neighborhood of chunky-walled adobe buildings that dates to before the United States acquired this former part of Mexico in 1848. You'll find indie shops and eateries here as well as a few miles north in the bustling downtown of Las Cruces proper. Just outside town, the impressive 47-acre **New Mexico Farm & Ranch Heritage Museum** (✉ *4100 Dripping Springs Rd.* ☎ *575/522–4100* ⊕ *www.nmfarmandranchmuseum.org*) traces the region's agriculture heritage back more than 4,000 years and features outstanding exhibits, a sheep and goat barn, a saddle-making studio, and much more.

Eat & Drink: With a covered patio and an art-filled dining room, **Salud! de Mesilla** (✉ *1800 Avenida de Mesilla* ☎ *575/323–3548* ⊕ *www.saludmesilla.com*) in Las Cruces serves big portions of inventively tweaked comfort food, from red chili poutine to fish-and-chips.

WILLCOX

Do: This small town in southeastern Arizona is home to an increasingly acclaimed winemaking scene but is most famous as the gateway to **Chiricahua National Monument** (✉ *12856 E. Rhyolite Creek Rd.* ☎ *520/824–3560* ⊕ *www.nps.gov/chir*), an underrated alpine jewel that contains the most dramatic portion of the mountain range for which this IDSP site is named. Drive the 8-mile park road—past hoodoos, spires, and other marvelously strange geological wonders—keeping an eye out for desert wildlife, including adorable raccoon-like coatis. A moderately challenging 1.8-mile round-trip hike leads to the 7,310-foot summit of Sugarloaf Mountain, where you can see for miles in every direction.

Eat & Drink: Tirrito Farm (✉ *6150 S. Kansas Settlement Rd.* ☎ *520/200–7270* ⊕ *www.tirritofarm.com*) is just a 30-mile drive from Chiricahua National Monument and features its own winery, brewery, and restaurant serving up tasty farm-to-table pizzas, burgers, and salads.

Stay: There are six luxury glamping domes, all with full bathrooms and climate control, at Tirrito Farm, as well as three luxurious casitas. In downtown Willcox, the **Arizona Sunset Inn & Suites** (✉ *340 S. Haskell Ave.* ☎ *520/766–3400* ⊕ *www.*

Mount Lemmon SkyCenter Observatory, just north of Tucson, features some of the biggest public telescopes in the country for stargazers.

arizonasunsetinn.com) has comfy and clean motel-style rooms.

Breakfast: Specialties at the down-home **Roadrunner Kafe** (✉ *700 Virginia Ave.* ☎ *520/253–6997* ⊕ *www.koa.com/ campgrounds/willcox*), which is attached to a popular KOA campground, include prickly pear–stuffed French toast and chicken-fried steak.

Day 3: Willcox, AZ, to Tucson, AZ

185 miles (3 hours, 30 minutes without traffic and stops)

After following Route 186 southeast into Chiricahua National Monument, head southwest, picking up U.S. 191 to the West Gleeson Road, a beautiful route through southern Arizona's mountainous landscape to Tombstone, where you'll pick up Route 82 west and Route 90 north to Kartchner Caverns State Park.

Continuing north, pick up I–10 for the last 45 minutes to Tucson.

ALONG THE WAY

Town: Although it's a bit touristy, there's no denying the fun of strutting through Wild West history on the gravel main drag of Tombstone, the high-desert town that will forever be famous as the site of the Gunfight at the O.K. Corral.

Eat & Drink: Among the several high-spirited Old West saloons in Tombstone, **Crystal Palace** (✉ *436 E. Allen St.* ☎ *520/457–3611* ⊕ *www.crystalpalacesaloon.com*) stands out for its tasty pub bites and its very impressive collection of Wild West photos and memorabilia.

Nature: Best known for its limestone caves filled with wonderfully strange-looking stalactites and stalagmites, **Kartchner Caverns State Park** (✉ *2980 Rte. 90, Benson* ☎ *520/586–4100* ⊕ *www. azstateparks.com/kartchner*) is an IDSP site that also has a few relatively easy above-ground trails and a hummingbird garden as well as monthly star parties.

Detour: Located a 45-minute drive down I–19 from Tucson, the DarkSky International–designated **Tumacácori National Historical Park** (✉ 1891 I–19 Frontage Rd., Tumacacori ☎ 520/377–5060 ⊕ www.nps.gov/tuma) contains three units, each with the protected ruins of a 17th-century Spanish colonial mission settlement. Rangers conduct evening programs aimed at giving visitors an idea of how the night sky would have appeared three centuries ago.

TUCSON

Do: Although it's a rather sprawling desert city, Tucson is the headquarters of DarkSky International and home to one of the most prominent IDSPs, **Saguaro National Park** (✉ 520/733–5153 ⊕ www.nps.gov/sagu), which comprises two units, East and West, both of which are quite far from urban lights. Protecting more than 2 million saguaro cacti, which dot the undulating Sonoran Desert landscape, the park can best be experienced on two scenic drives. In Saguaro East, start at the **Rincon Mountain Visitor Center** (✉ 3693 S. Old Spanish Trail) and follow the 8-mile Cactus Loop Drive. Then head to Saguaro West's **Red Hills Visitor Center** (✉ 2700 N. Kinney Rd.), making your way around the 5-mile Bajada Loop Drive, and then checking out the park's neighbor, the outstanding **Arizona-Sonora Desert Museum** (✉ 2021 N. Kinney Rd. ☎ 520/883–2702 ⊕ www.desertmuseum.org). Other astrotourism-related sights of interest include the fascinating **Pima Air & Space Museum** (✉ 6000 E. Valencia Rd. ☎ 520/574–0462 ⊕ www.pimaair.org) and, located high in the Santa Catalina Mountains north of the city, the **Mount Lemmon SkyCenter Observatory** (✉ 9800 E. Ski Run Rd. ☎ 520/626–8122 ⊕ www.skycenter.arizona.edu), which features the nation's largest dedicated public telescopes.

Eat & Drink: In the trendy Historic Fourth Avenue district, **Anello** (✉ 222 E. 6th St. ⊕ www.anello.space) serves up creatively topped wood-fired pizzas and seasonal vegetables in an urbane, intimate space. One of a few bars and eateries inside the beloved and historic Hotel Congress, **Tiger's Tap Room** (✉ 311 E. Congress St. ☎ 520/622–8848 ⊕ www.hotelcongress.com) is a great spot for cocktails and conversation.

Stay: In a quiet neighborhood relatively away from city lights, 69-room **Tanque Verde Ranch** (✉ 14301 E. Speedway Blvd. ☎ 520/296–6275 ⊕ www.tanqueverderanch.com) is a short drive from the East unit of Saguaro National Park. Amenities at this upscale dude ranch include cowboy cookouts, horseback rides, and yoga classes. Downtown's **Hotel Congress** (✉ 311 E. Congress St. ☎ 520/622–8848 ⊕ www.hotelcongress.com), a quirky property that dates to 1919, has reasonably priced rooms—a few of them allegedly haunted—and lots of fun common spaces.

Breakfast: Conveniently on the way from downtown to the West section of Saguaro National Park, **Barista del Barrio** (✉ 1002 N. Grande Ave. ☎ 520/244–5285 ⊕ www.baristadelbarrio.com) specializes in Mexican-influenced coffees (try the dulce de leche latte) and also serves delicious build-your-own breakfast burritos.

Day 4: Tucson, AZ, to Sedona, AZ

280 miles (5 hours, 45 minutes without traffic and stops)

Although it's possible to get from Tucson to Sedona in just three and a half hours via the interstate, this far more scenic route bypasses the urban sprawl of Phoenix and cuts through a pair of IDSPs—Oracle State Park and Tonto National Monument—via Route 77 through Globe and then Route 188 and Route 87 up over the dramatic Mogollon

Rim to Payson. Here a left turn onto Route 260 leads to Cottonwood, and Route 89A gets you the final stretch to Sedona.

ALONG THE WAY

Nature: As you drive through the mountains north of Tucson, stop by **Oracle State Park** (✉ *3820 E. Wildlife Dr., Oracle* ☎ *520/896–2425* ⊕ *www.azstateparks.com/oracle*) to explore its nature trails and the historic ranch house that now houses a visitor center and museum; if you're here at night, attend one of the telescope parties that helped Oracle become the first park in the state to earn DarkSky International status. Farther north outside the small town of Roosevelt, **Tonto National Monument** (✉ *26260 Rte. 188* ☎ *928/467–2241* ⊕ *www.nps.gov/tont*) contains cliff dwellings that date back more than 700 years and offers fascinating astronomy programs from its park amphitheater.

Detour: High above Verde Valley and offering panoramic views toward the red rocks of Sedona, endearing offbeat Jerome clings improbably to steep rocky slopes and is filled with colorfully restored late 19th-century buildings that date to its heyday as a center of copper mining. After dropping in population from 10,000 to fewer than 100, Jerome became a haunt for artists and hippies in the 1960s. Though still quite tiny, the town now has several unpretentious bars, cafés, shops, and galleries. Be sure to stop by **Jerome State Historic Park** (✉ *100 Douglas Rd.* ☎ *928/634–5381* ⊕ *www.azstateparks.com/jerome*), where engaging exhibits tell the story of this captivating community.

Town: An easygoing town in the Verde Valley, midway between funky Jerome and upscale Sedona, up-and-coming Cottonwood is a DarkSky International Community that's very much worth a visit in its own right. At the center of the increasingly respected **Verde Valley Wine Trail** (⊕ *www.vvwinetrail.com*), the town has several excellent tasting rooms. Just north, you can explore Ancestral Puebloan ruins at **Tuzigoot National Monument** (✉ *25 Tuzigoot Rd., Clarkdale* ☎ *928/634–5564* ⊕ *www.nps.gov/tuzi*) while nearby **Montezuma Castle National Monument** (✉ *Montezuma Castle Rd., Camp Verde* ☎ *928/567–3322* ⊕ *www.nps.gov/moca*) preserves an impressive five-story cliff dwelling built by the Indigenous Sinagua tribe in the 12th century.

Eat & Drink: Among the many wineries in Cottonwood, **Merkin Vineyards Tasting Room** (✉ *770 N. Verde Heights Dr.* ☎ *928/639–1001* ⊕ *www.merkintrattoria.com*) earns kudos for its romantic trattoria serving pasta and wood-fired pizzas.

SEDONA

Do: Although fast-growing, Sedona has worked hard to preserve its spectacular natural setting amid towering red rock buttes, spires, and other imposing geological formations. In 2014, the town became a DarkSky International Community. For a great view of the surrounding natural scenery, drive up to the overlook atop **Airport Mesa** (✉ *483 Airport Rd.*), where you can also hike a short trail for an even better perspective. But the best way to appreciate this amazing setting is to get up close to the local rock formations, either down in the valley at **Red Rock State Park** (✉ *4050 Red Rock Loop Rd.* ☎ *928/282–6907* ⊕ *www.azstateparks.com/red-rock*) or up in the narrow gorge—through which Route 89A climbs up toward Flagstaff—at **Slide Rock State Park** (✉ *6871 Rte. 89A* ☎ *928/282–3034* ⊕ *www.azstateparks.com/slide-rock*).

Eat & Drink: With a sprawling terrace overlooking cottonwood trees and the red rock scenery beyond, **Creekside American Bistro** (✉ *251 Rte. 179* ☎ *928/282–1705* ⊕ *www.creeksidesedona.com*) serves sophisticated contemporary American fare, such as braised short ribs with green chili grits.

Stay: **Amara Resort & Spa** (✉ *100 Amara La.* ☎ *928/282–4828* ⊕ *www.amararesort.com*) is set in a valley beside Oak Creek and surrounded by red rock cliffs, just steps from Sedona's tony downtown. It's a cushy place to relax, with a sublime full-service spa and trendy SaltRock Kitchen restaurant. About 8 miles up Route 89A near Slide Rock State Park, **Orchard Canyon on Oak Creek** (✉ *8067 N. Rte. 89A* ☎ *928/282–3343* ⊕ *www.enjoyorchardcanyon.com*) has 17 historic cabins and one of the best settings in the area for gazing up at the dark night sky.

Breakfast: Located beside gurgling Oak Creek, the **Pump House Station Urban Eatery** (✉ *313 Rte. 179* ☎ *928/862–4141* ⊕ *www.pumphousestation.com*) will help you to get your day off to a great start with its extensive menu of eggs Benedicts, omelets, and quiches.

Day 5: Sedona, AZ, to Grand Canyon Village, AZ

115 miles (2 hours, 30 minutes without traffic and stops)

Continue up picturesque Route 89A and then head west on I-40 to Williams, where Route 64 leads north to Grand Canyon Village.

ALONG THE WAY

Town: A popular gateway to the Grand Canyon, the unpretentious western town of Williams has a neat little downtown of preserved 19th- and early-20th-century buildings, including the **Grand Canyon Railway Depot** (✉ *280 N. Grand Canyon Blvd.* ☎ *800/843–8724* ⊕ *www.thetrain.com*), from which you can take two-and-a-half-hour rides on sleek mid-century trains to the Grand Canyon's South Rim.

Eat & Drink: Decked out with vintage Route 66 memorabilia and filled with cozy booths, **Anna's Canyon Cafe** (✉ *137 W. Railroad Ave.* ☎ *928/635–4907* ⊕ *www.grandcanyoncoffeeandcafe.*

Essential Listening

The audiobook of Paul Bogard's *The End of Night* is an eye-opening account of how most residents of the United States no longer see a truly dark night sky, and what steps we can take to restore the magic and importance of darkness.

com) in Williams makes an enjoyable midday stop for breakfast or lunch, or even just a cup of well-brewed coffee.

GRAND CANYON VILLAGE

Do: Although the view across the 6,000-foot-deep Grand Canyon is best appreciated during the day, this national park is also a brilliant setting for stargazing. An IDSP since 2019, **Grand Canyon National Park** (✉ *S. Entrance Rd.* ☎ *928/638–7888* ⊕ *www.nps.gov/grca*) offers myriad nighttime programs, including star parties at Mather Amphitheater and ranger-led constellation talks. During the day, be sure to check out the fascinating exhibits in the **Yavapai Geology Museum** (☎ *800/858–2808* ⊕ *www.grandcanyon.org*).

Eat & Drink: Set directly along the South Rim, the historic **El Tovar Dining Room** (✉ *1 El Tovar Rd.* ☎ *928/638–2631* ⊕ *www.grandcanyonlodges.com*) and the **Arizona Steakhouse** (✉ *10 Albright Ave.* ☎ *928/638–2631* ⊕ *www.grandcanyonlodges.com*) within Bright Angel Lodge are favorites for dining in the park.

Stay: El Tovar and Bright Angel Lodge are acclaimed because of their rim-side locations, but a somewhat underrated option that also enjoys a quiet, light-free setting is **Maswik Lodge** (✉ *202 Village Loop Dr.* ☎ *928/638–2631* ⊕ *www.grandcanyonlodges.com*), which is just a 10-minute walk from the canyon rim.

A visit to Lowell Observatory (even during the day) provides fascinating insights into our night sky.

Breakfast: Pick up a bagel breakfast sandwich or a breakfast burrito, along with espresso drinks and other picnic supplies, at **Grand Canyon Village Market & Deli** (✉ *1 Market Plaza Rd.* ☎ *928/638–2262* ⊕ *www.visitgrandcanyon.com*) to enjoy your first meal of the day at one of the South Rim's picnic areas.

Day 6: Grand Canyon Village, AZ, to Flagstaff, AZ

130 miles (3 hours without traffic and stops)

Take Route 64 east out of the Grand Canyon into the Navajo Nation to the small village of Cameron. Then head south on U.S. 89, detouring southeast along local roads to visit Wupatki and Sunset Crater national monuments, before picking up U.S. 89 for the final leg into Flagstaff.

ALONG THE WAY

Eat & Drink: Just north of the junction of Route 64 and U.S. 89, the **Cameron Trading Post** (✉ *466 U.S. 89, Cameron* ☎ *800/338–7385* ⊕ *www.camerontradingpost.com*) has been popular for buying Navajo- and Hopi-made textiles, dolls, and other artwork for more than a century. This rambling complex next to the dramatic Little Colorado River gorge also contains a welcoming restaurant decorated with Navajo rugs.

Nature: Wupatki National Monument (✉ *25137 Loop Rd.* ☎ *928/679–2365* ⊕ *www.nps.gov/wupa*) and **Sunset Crater Volcanic National Monument** (✉ *6082 Sunset Crater Rd.* ☎ *928/526–0502* ⊕ *www.nps.gov/sucr*) are a pair of IDSPs located along a picturesque high-desert road in the Navajo Nation. At Wupatki, you can walk amid four different sets of Ancestral Pueblo ruins that date as far back as AD 1100, the most extensive of which is behind the informative visitor center. About 20 miles south, Sunset Crater is an imposing volcano that last erupted nearly 1,000 years ago. Although you can't ascend up to the crater's edge, you can stroll along the easy 1-mile Lava Flow Trail, with its dramatic lava formations.

FLAGSTAFF

Do: Named the first DarkSky International Community in 2001, this lively college town set along a colorful stretch of historic Route 66 has taken a number of steps to reduce light pollution, including the establishment of a comprehensive city code on outdoor lighting standards. Just up the hill from downtown at **Lowell Observatory** (✉ 1400 W. Mars Hill Rd. ☎ 928/774–3358 ⊕ www.lowell.edu), you can gaze up at the solar system in the Giovale Open Deck Observatory and explore a number of historic buildings, including the one in which Clyde Tombaugh discovered Pluto in 1930. There's also the 40,000-square-foot Astronomy Discovery Center on Lowell's campus, showcasing state-of-the-art exhibits and an open-sky planetarium. An off-the-beaten-path attraction (free tours are by appointment) that fans of space exploration should check out is the **USGS Astrogeology Science Center** (✉ 2255 N. Gemini Dr. ☎ 928/556–7000 ⊕ www.usgs.gov/centers/astrogeology-science-center), which was created in 1963 to help train astronauts headed to the moon. Here you can view a moon rover that served as a training prototype and see exhibits about space exploration. Southeast of town, **Walnut Canyon National Monument** (✉ Walnut Canyon Rd. ☎ 928/526–3367 ⊕ www.nps.gov/waca) is an IDSP that preserves cliff dwellings that date back 900 years in a remote canyon.

Eat & Drink: Flagstaff has an impressive dining scene for a small city, and intimate **Tinderbox Kitchen** (✉ 34 S. San Francisco St. ☎ 928/226–8400 ⊕ www.tinderboxkitchen.com) is one of the finest options, known for its sublime seasonally sourced contemporary American cuisine and a well-curated wine list. After dinner, stroll over to the historic Monte Vista Hotel for a nightcap at **Rendezvous** (✉ 100 N. San Francisco St. ☎ 928/779–6971 ⊕ www.rendezvousflagstaff.com), one of a few social spaces in this rambling 1927 building with a photogenic neon sign.

Stay: Like the Monte Vista, the idiosyncratic **Weatherford Hotel** (✉ 23 N. Leroux St. ☎ 928/779–1919 ⊕ www.weatherfordhotel.com) has a colorful history and quirky, old-fashioned rooms that come in a range of configurations, often with claw-foot tubs and period antiques. There are three very popular bars on-site, some of them featuring live music. If you prefer quieter or more modern digs, book a room at the **Little America Hotel** (✉ 2515 E. Butler Ave. ☎ 928/779–7900 ⊕ flagstaff.littleamerica.com), a modern property with spacious rooms, a pool, and a fitness center.

Breakfast: Hip and stylish **Forêt Flg** (✉ 2 S. Beaver St. ☎ 928/214–7280 ⊕ www.foretflagstaff.com) serves inventive espresso drinks and elevated café fare, including pork porchetta sandwiches. The beloved **Toasted Owl Cafe** (✉ 12 S. Mikes Pike St. ☎ 928/774–5326 ⊕ www.thetoastedowl.com) is a popular go-to for its absolutely enormous breakfast and lunch portions, including hulking breakfast burritos smothered in cheese and green chili sauce. All of the wacky owl-themed tchotchkes inside are for sale.

Day 7: Flagstaff, AZ, to Gallup, NM

220 miles (3 hours, 30 minutes without traffic and stops)

Take I-40 east—making some side tracks south to Walnut Canyon National Monument, Meteor Crater National Landmark, and downtown Winslow—to Holbrook, and then follow U.S. 180 southeast to the south entrance of Petrified Forest National Park. Drive north on the park road and exit the park's north entrance back onto I–40, and continue an hour east to Gallup.

ALONG THE WAY

Roadside Attraction: Located on private land, **Meteor Crater Natural Landmark** (✉ *Meteor Crater Rd., Winslow, AZ* ☎ *800/289–5898* ⊕ *www.meteorcrater.com*) is one of the more curious sights of the Southwest. Although the $29 admission fee is rather steep, inside you'll find an engaging interactive space museum, and you can walk around a portion of this 3,900-foot-diameter crater that looks deceptively small but is actually as deep as a 60-story building.

Eat & Drink: Stop by the venerable, stunningly restored La Posada Hotel in Winslow to walk through the gardens, shop for southwestern art in the excellent gift shop, and have lunch in the elegant **Turquoise Room** (✉ *303 E. 2nd St.* ☎ *928/289–2888* ⊕ *www.theturquoiseroom.net*), with its stained-glass windows and colorful chandeliers.

Photo Op: Fans of classic rock, and the Eagles song "Take It Easy" in particular, will enjoy snapping selfies at the **Standing on a Corner Winslow Park** (✉ *Kinsley and E. 2nd Sts.* ☎ *480/326–3486* ⊕ *www.standinonthecorner.org*) in downtown Winslow.

Town: The nearest town to Petrified Forest National Park, Holbrook, Arizona, is an unassuming wayside with some wonderfully nostalgic Route 66 elements, including the famous **Wigwam Motel** (✉ *811 W. Hopi Dr.* ☎ *928/524–3048* ⊕ *www.sleepinawigwam.com*), with its 15 concrete teepees and parking lots filled with vintage 1940s and 1950s automobiles. **The Navajo County Historical Society Museum** (✉ *100 E. Arizona St.* ☎ *928/524–6558* ⊕ *www.holbrookazmuseum.org*) has interesting exhibits on Indigenous culture, ranching, and Route 66.

Nature: Although **Petrified Forest National Park** (✉ *1 Park Rd.* ☎ *928/524–6228* ⊕ *www.nps.gov/pefo*), including its scenic park road, is generally closed to the public at night, this IDSP does allow visitors to set out on backcountry nighttime hikes (you just have to obtain a free Dark Sky Overnight Permit).

GALLUP

Do: A center of commerce and trade for the surrounding Navajo Nation and other Indigenous tribes, Gallup is noted for its galleries and shops stocked with authentic Native-made crafts and gifts. One of the most famous, **Richardson's Trading Company** (✉ *223 W. Historic Rte. 66* ☎ *505/722–4762* ⊕ *www.richardsontrading.com*) has been going strong since 1913. Take a little time to walk around the nearby streets, admiring the murals and public art displays throughout this friendly town along Historic Route 66.

Eat & Drink: A simple and homey diner-style restaurant in downtown Gallup, **Jerry's Cafe** (✉ *406 W. Coal Ave.* ☎ *505/722–6775*) is a favorite for authentic chiles rellenos, beef enchiladas, and huevos rancheros.

Stay: Whether or not you spend the night at the legendary **Historic El Rancho Hotel** (✉ *1000 E. Rte. 66* ☎ *505/863–9311* ⊕ *www.elranchohotelgallup.com*), at least visit the two-story lobby whose walls are festooned with signed photos of the many Hollywood stars of yesteryear who stayed here while filming Westerns, including the likes of William Holden, Katharine Hepburn, and Gregory Peck. Be sure to also check out the large gift shop, and have dinner in either of the two on-site restaurants, both serving New Mexican classics. Rooms are simple but contain eye-catching western decor.

Breakfast: Stop inside the **Gallup Coffee Company** (✉ *201 W. Coal Ave.* ☎ *505/410–2505* ⊕ *www.gallupcoffeecompany. com*) for a breakfast sandwich or a bagel slathered in green chili cream cheese. This native-owned café serves excellent espresso drinks, too, and is set inside a restored 1920s Spanish colonial revival bank building.

Day 8: Gallup, NM, to Jemez Springs, NM

230 miles (4 hours, 15 minutes without traffic and stops)

Head southeast from Gallup on Route 602 and Route 53 to El Morro National Monument, and then continue east through the eerie lava beds of El Malpais National Monument to Grants, where you'll pick up I-40 east. Skirt the west side of Albuquerque by heading north on Route 45 and Route 528, and then take U.S. 550 northwest to San Ysidro, and finally Route 4 northeast through a red rock canyon to Jemez Springs.

ALONG THE WAY

Nature: Established in 1906 in part to preserve the meticulously carved signatures and notes left by Spanish colonial explorers as far back as 1605, **El Morro National Monument** (✉ *Rte. 53, Ramah* ☎ *505/783-4226* ⊕ *www. nps.gov/elmo*) contains a 200-foot-tall monolith called Inscription Rock—Ancestral Puebloans lived atop this and its neighboring cliffs in the 13th century. Set aside a couple hours to hike around the base of the rock, where you can view the inscriptions, and to climb the steps that have been chiseled into this dramatic formation. To enjoy this remote IDSP space after dark, you can overnight in the nine-site campground or attend one of the many night-sky events.

Detour: One of the most impressive archaeological sites in the Southwest, the extremely secluded **Chaco Canyon National Historical Park** (✉ *1808 Rte. 7950, Nageezi* ☎ *505/786-7014* ⊕ *www. nps.gov/chcu*) is 13 miles from the

nearest paved roads. It's worth trying to get here to view the vast Puebloan ruins, dating back to the mid-800s. The two unpaved roads into the park, especially the south approach that's most direct if coming from Gallup, often become impassable during the summer monsoon season due to heavy rains; always call the park to confirm road conditions before attempting to make the drive, which takes two hours from Gallup or two and a half hours from Jemez Springs by way of the better-maintained road off of U.S. 550 north of Cuba.

Town: A former mining town set along Old Route 66 that offers views of dramatic Mt. Taylor, Grants is a popular place to fill up on gas and grab a bite to eat, but its greatest draw are the otherworldly volcanic badlands of nearby **El Malpaís National Monument** (⊕ *www.nps.gov/elma*). The park's modern **visitor center** (✉ *1900 E. Santa Fe Ave.* ☎ *505/876-2783*) is a great place to learn about this 114,000-acre expanse of lava fields created when McCartys Crater erupted nearly 4,000 years ago. Along Route 53, coming from El Morro National Monument, you can stop and make an easy hike into Junction Cave, a 60,000-year-old lava tube. Another attraction just outside the park is **Ice Cave and Bandera Volcano** (✉ *12000 Ice Caves Rd.* ☎ *505/783-4303* ⊕ *www.icecaves. com*), which straddles the Continental Divide and features a historic trading post and perpetually icy underground cavern.

Eat & Drink: A retro-cool joint located inside a convenience store on the Laguna Pueblo, **Laguna Burger** (✉ *Rte. 66, New Laguna* ☎ *505/552-7762* ⊕ *www. thelagunaburger.com*) has gained an almost fanatical following for its green chili cheeseburgers. Other treats include barbecue pulled pork sandwiches and Frito pie dogs.

JEMEZ SPRINGS

Do: Popular with creative spirits and New Age enthusiasts, tiny Jemez Springs lies in a deep red-rock-walled canyon that's just an hour's drive north of Albuquerque but feels utterly remote. You can soak in the mineral-rich waters at **Jemez Hot Springs** (✉ *040 Abousleman Loop* ☎ *575/829–9175* ⊕ *www.jemezhotsprings.com*), which offers one- and two-hour soaking sessions. A bit farther up Route 4 you can visit the mammoth **Valles Caldera National Preserve** (✉ *39201 Rte. 4* ☎ *505/670–1612* ⊕ *www.nps.gov/vall*), an 89,000-acre IDSP that offers an extensive variety of recreational activities as well as nighttime programs. The park borders the western edge of **Bandelier National Monument** (✉ *15 Entrance Rd., Los Alamos* ☎ *505/672–3861* ⊕ *www.nps.gov/band*), with its well-preserved and easily accessible ancient cliff dwellings.

Eat & Drink: There are few dining options in town, but **Jemez Mountain Brewhouse** (✉ *17691 Rte. 4* ☎ *575/829–4222* ⊕ *www.jemezmountainbrewhouse.com*) turns out delicious artisan pizzas and local ales.

Stay: A peaceful eight-room inn set on the banks of the Jemez River, **Cañon del Rio** (✉ *16445 Rte. 4* ☎ *575/829–4377* ⊕ *www.canondelrio.com*) is a wonderful place to stare up at the dark night sky in the evening, either from your room's courtyard, the pool area, or the pathway alongside the river.

Breakfast: Highway 4 Coffee (✉ *17502 Rte. 4* ☎ *575/829–4655* ⊕ *www.facebook.com/hwy4cafe*) is a cute and reliable option for a caffeine pick-me-up and a light bite to eat in the morning.

Day 9: Jemez Springs, NM, to Las Vegas, NM

160 miles (3 hours, 30 minutes without traffic and stops)

Continue on Route 4 through Valles Caldera National Preserve and Bandelier National Monument to Pojoaque, and then take a portion of the famously photogenic "High Road to Taos" through Chimayó, Truchas, and Peñasco, and then drive southeast on Route 518 over the breathtaking Sangre de Cristo down to Las Vegas.

ALONG THE WAY

Detour: Under the dark skies of the Jemez Mountains, a team of scientists led by J. Robert Oppenheimer toiled in secrecy in the early 1940s to develop the world's first atomic bomb. You can learn about this complicated legacy in Los Alamos at **Manhattan Project National Historical Park** (✉ *475 20th St.* ☎ *505/661–6277* ⊕ *www.nps.gov/mapr*), where guided tours of some of the sites tell the story of this pivotal point in history. Learn more at the engaging **Los Alamos History Museum** (✉ *1050 Bathtub Row* ☎ *505/709–7794* ⊕ *www.losalamoshistory.org*) and **Bradbury Science Museum** (✉ *1450 Central Ave.* ☎ *505/667–4444* ⊕ *www.lanl.gov/museum*).

Town: A favorite community on the breathtaking High Road to Taos, Chimayó enjoys a celebrated tradition of Spanish colonial crafts, including rugs, woodcarvings, metalwork, and pottery. Great places to admire and buy these goods include **Ortega's Weaving** (✉ *53 Plaza Del Cerro* ☎ *505/351–4215* ⊕ *www.ortegasweaving.com*) and **Centinela Traditional Arts** (✉ *946 Rte. 76* ☎ *505/351–2180* ⊕ *www.chimayoweavers.com*). Built in 1816, the twin-belfried **El Santuario de Chimayó** (✉ *15 Santuario Dr.* ☎ *505/351–4360* ⊕ *www.holychimayo.us*) is a beautiful little church that's believed to have miraculous healing properties.

Eat & Drink: Set in a rambling late 1800s hacienda with tree-shaded patios and sky-lighted dining rooms, **Rancho de Chimayó** (✉ *300 Juan Medina Rd.* ☎ *505/351–4444* ⊕ *www.ranchodechimayo.com*) makes an enchanting stop for lunch or weekend brunch. The kitchen serves traditional New Mexico dishes, such as shredded-beef-stuffed sopaipillas.

LAS VEGAS

Do: Developed as a trade and transportation hub in the 1830s on the Old Santa Fe Trail and then further expanded in the late 19th century when the Atchison, Topeka and Santa Fe Railroad came through town, Las Vegas contains an impressive collection of well-preserved buildings that reflect that predominant architectural styles of early New Mexico, from Spanish colonial adobe to Italianate Victorian. Many of these stately old buildings now contain galleries, boutiques, and restaurants. The town is also a gateway to **Fort Union National Monument** (✉ *3115 Rte. 161, Watrous* ☎ *505/425–8025* ⊕ *www.nps.gov/foun*), an IDSP about 30 miles north. Here you can explore the remnants of an important 1850s fortification. Nighttime campfire talks, tours, and Night Wonders programs are offered.

Eat & Drink: The Skillet (✉ *623 12th St.* ☎ *505/563–0477* ⊕ *www.giant-skillet. com*) serves big portions of delicious comfort food—think brisket*barbacoa* bowls and churro sundaes—in a bustling dining room and on a shaded patio near Gallinas Creek. In the oldest neighborhood in Las Vegas, **El Rialto** (✉ *141 Bridge St.* ☎ *505/454–0037* ⊕ *www.facebook. com/elrialtolvnm*) is an inviting spot for well-prepared New Mexico classics, from chargrilled steaks to chicken flautas.

Stay: Las Vegas has a pair of stunning 19th-century hotels. The **Historic Plaza Hotel** (✉ *230 Plaza St.* ☎ *505/425–3591* ⊕ *www.plazahotellvnm.com*) overlooks the tree-shaded oval for which it's named, contains one of the best restaurants in town, and has appeared in a number of movies. Adjacent to the town's handsome vintage rail depot, the **Castaneda Hotel** (✉ *541 Railroad Ave.* ☎ *505/425–3591* ⊕ *www. castanedahotel.org*) sat dormant for decades before owners restored and reopened it as a 22-room lodging. The sweeping veranda is a lovely spot for evening cocktails.

Breakfast: In Las Vegas's newer late Victorian downtown, **Charlie's Spic & Span Bakery** (✉ *715 Douglas Ave.* ☎ *505/426–1921*) has been a favorite destination for filling breakfasts and people-watching since 1950.

Day 10: Las Vegas, NM, to Albuquerque, NM

135 miles (2 hours, 30 minutes without traffic and stops)

Take I–25 south and west from Las Vegas around breathtaking Glorieta Pass, skirting the south side of Santa Fe, and then follow enchanting Route 14—aka the Turquoise Trail—down along the eastern flanks of the Sandia Mountains to Albuquerque.

ALONG THE WAY

Detour: If you can extend your road trip by a day, consider making a side excursion into the sparsely settled high grasslands of northeastern New Mexico, where you'll find a pair of IDSPs. **Capulin Volcano National Monument** (✉ *46 Volcano Hwy., Capulin* ☎ *575/278–2201* ⊕ *www. nps.gov/cavo*) is centered around a pine-dotted cinder cone that last erupted around 60,000 years ago; you can hike a 1-mile paved loop around the crater's rim. And **Clayton Lake State Park** (✉ *141 Clayton Lake Rd., Clayton* ☎ *575/374–8808* ⊕ *www.emnrd.state.nm.us*) is popular for picnicking, viewing dinosaur footprints, and attending astronomy programs in its observatory. Clayton Lake has a campground, and you'll find a few lodging options relatively nearby in the town of Raton. From Las Vegas, it's a roughly six-hour round trip to visit both parks.

Town: A highlight of the beautiful drive along the Turquoise Trail, funky Madrid made its fortune during the late 19th century as a rather raucous coal-mining town. Like so many southwestern mining centers, it fell into a state of neglect after the mines closed and was then brought back to life toward the latter half of the 20th century by free spirits and creatives. Along the main drag, colorfully painted wood-frame houses now mostly contain art galleries and offbeat boutiques.

Eat & Drink: Attached to a mining museum and theater in Madrid, **The Mine Shaft Tavern** (✉ 2846 Rte. 14 ☎ 505/473–0743 ⊕ www.themineshafttavern.com) frequently comes up on lists of where to find the state's best green chili cheeseburger. There's often live music, too.

Roadside Attraction: High in the Sandia Mountains just northeast of Albuquerque, late artist Ross Ward established the endearingly odd **Tinkertown Museum** (✉ 121 Sandia Crest Rd., Sandia Park ☎ 505/281–5233 ⊕ www.tinkertown.com), a repository of carved miniatures, found objects, and western memorabilia.

ALBUQUERQUE

Do: Although located on the edge of New Mexico's largest metropolis, **Valle de Oro National Wildlife Refuge** (✉ 7851 2nd St. SW ☎ 505/248–6667 ⊕ www.fws.gov/refuge/valle_de_oro) became the first ever DarkSky International Urban Place in 2019. At night, this 570-acre green space that backs up to the Rio Grande is a fantastic place to observe the stars and planets during one of the well-attended astronomy programs. From the stunning

contemporary visitor center, trails lead through wetlands that attract a great variety of birdlife. In addition, Albuquerque has a number of outstanding attractions that appeal to curious minds, including the **New Mexico Museum of Natural History & Science** (✉ 1801 Mountain Rd. NW ☎ 505/841–2800 ⊕ www.nmnaturalhistory.org), which has exhibits on everything from dinosaurs to the exploration of Mars. You can also attend public stargazing programs at the **University of New Mexico Campus Observatory** (✉ 800 Yale Blvd. NE ☎ 505/277–1446 ⊕ observatory.unm.edu) and the **Rainbow Park Observatory** (✉ 301 Southern Blvd. SE ☎ 505/430–9604 ⊕ www.rrastro.org/Observatory/Observatory.html) in the suburb of Rio Rancho.

Eat & Drink: In downtown's hip Edo district, **Farina Pizzeria** (✉ 510 Central Ave. SE ☎ 505/243–0130 ⊕ www.farinapizzeria.com) is set inside a vintage storefront and serves exceptional blistered-crust pizzas with interesting toppings—there's a great wine list, too. Close to the city's colorful Old Town, the beautifully designed **Sawmill Market** (✉ 1909 Bellamah Ave. NW ☎ 505/563–4473 ⊕ www.sawmillmarket.com) is an expansive food hall set in a former lumber warehouse that offers a wide range of cuisines, from Spanish paellas to Japanese soft-serve ice cream.

Stay: In an imaginatively transformed 1920s hospital, the stylish **Hotel Parq Central** (✉ 806 Central Ave. SE ☎ 505/242–0040 ⊕ www.hotelparqcentral.com) has large, gorgeously appointed rooms and a rooftop bar with amazing views of downtown and the Sandia Mountains. In a quiet and historic neighborhood on the city's north side, the upscale **Los Poblanos Historic Inn** (✉ 4803 Rio Grande Blvd. NW ☎ 505/985–5000 ⊕ www.lospoblanos.com) has posh rooms, a terrific farm-to-table restaurant, and a relatively light-free setting.

Breakfast: Known for hearty breakfast dishes like chilaquiles and carne asada grits, the **Range Cafe Downtown** (✉ *320 Central Ave. SE* ☎ *505/243–1440* ⊕ *www.rangecafe.com*) is a colorful place to start the last morning of your adventure.

The Best of Texas

Written by Kristy Alpert

A road trip through the entire state of Texas may seem like an epic undertaking, and that's because it is. No other state in the United States has as many roadways, ranging from rural ranch-to-market roads lined with wildflowers to high-speed highways—including the fastest road in the nation, Route 130, where the speed limit is 85 mph. A direct line through the state would stretch a whopping 801 miles between its northern tip in the Panhandle to the southern banks of the Rio Grande, but the ultimate road trip through Texas isn't quite as linear. This journey through the Lone Star State is a winding route that highlights the state's best sights, cities, and natural scenery. Traverse the terraces of its award-winning wine country, cruise the coastal corridors along the Gulf of Mexico, bathe in the starry night sky above Big Bend National Park, and enjoy the wide-open plains as you discover the warmth and wonder of the "Great State of Texas."

At a Glance

Start: Dallas, TX

End: Dallas, TX

Miles Traveled: 2,587 miles

Suggested Duration: 10 days

States Visited: Texas, New Mexico

Key Sights: The Alamo; Big Bend National Park; Houston's Museum District; Marfa Lights Viewing Center

Best Time to Go: Either spring or falls works for optimal weather, but spring is bluebonnet season in Texas and truly a special time to visit the state.

Day 1: Dallas, TX, to Waco, TX

97 miles (1 hour, 30 minutes without traffic and stops)

The most direct route on I-35 east not only saves time but also passes through some of the most beloved roadside stops along the way. If coming from DFW International Airport, start on John W Carpenter Freeway (Route 114) before merging onto I–35 east near downtown Dallas. Don't forget to stock up on some of the city's famous gas station tacos from **Fuel City** (✉ *801 S. Riverfront Blvd.* ☎ *214/426–0011* ⊕ *www.fuelcity.com*) near the Convention Center District before leaving town.

ALONG THE WAY

Photo Op: The historic **Ellis County Courthouse** (✉ *100 S. Jackson St.*) in Waxahachie makes an impressive backdrop for a photo, which is why it has been featured in many films throughout the years, including *Tender Mercies* and *Bonnie and Clyde*. The gingerbread-house-like structure is listed on the National Register of Historic Places and dates back to 1897.

Detour: Between the months of March and April, the wildflowers on the sides of the road bloom in a glorious display of blue. During this "bluebonnet season" in Texas, bypass Waxahachie and head for Ennis instead to drive along the official **Texas Bluebonnet Trail** (⊕ *www.bluebonnettrail.org*).

Eat & Drink: No true Texan would make the trip between Dallas and Waco without stopping in at the **Czech Stop** (✉ *I–35, exit 353* ☎ *254/826–4161* ⊕ *www.czechstop.net*) in West for one of their delicious pastries. The small town of

The Best of Texas

West has been home to a thriving Czech community for over a century, and its downtown is filled with Czech bakeries and antiques stores. But it's hard to beat the convenience of a gas station–and–Czech bakery combination, especially since they make some of the best kolaches in Texas.

WACO

Do: Once simply known as the halfway marker between Dallas and Austin, Waco has seen a resurgence in recent years thanks to its role on the hit HGTV home makeover show *Fixer Upper*. The city is now a mecca for fans of Chip and Joanna Gaines, where stops include **Magnolia Market at the Silos** (✉ *601 Webster Ave.* ☎ *254/235–0603* ⊕ *magnolia.com*), **Black Oak Art Studio** (✉ *1619 Franklin Ave.* ☎ *254/732–1533* ⊕ *www.blackoakart.com*), and **Cottonland Castle** (✉ *3300 Austin Ave.*).

Eat & Drink: The cupcakes at **Silos Baking Co.** (✉ *601 Webster Ave.* ☎ *254/235–0603* ⊕ *magnolia.com/silos-baking-co*) are best eaten alfresco on the grounds of the expansive Magnolia complex, but for an old-school taste of Waco, pull in to dine on your dashboard at **Cupp's Drive Inn** (✉ *1424 Speight Ave.* ☎ *254/753–9364* ⊕ *www.cuppsdriveinn.com*).

Stay: HGTV fans can live their *Fixer Upper* dreams at the **Magnolia House** (✉ *323 S. Madison Ave., McGregor* ☎ *254/235–6111* ⊕ *www.magnolia.com/visit/stay*) vacation rental 20 minutes outside Waco. In town, the **Bed & Breakfast on White Rock Creek** (✉ *267 Ruby Dell La.* ☎ *254/799–9783* ⊕ *www.whiterockcreek.com*) is a great example of Waco's warm hospitality.

Breakfast: Everything served at **World Cup Cafe** (✉ *321 N. 15th St.* ☎ *254/757–1748* ⊕ *www.worldcupfairtrade.org*) is guaranteed Fair Trade, from the specialty coffee and the pecan praline pancakes to the chicken and biscuits.

Day 2: Waco, TX, to Austin, TX

102 miles (1 hour, 35 minutes without traffic and stops)

This all-interstate route along I–35 south is the quickest way into Texas's capital city.

ALONG THE WAY

Eat & Drink: Central Texas is often referred to as the Barbecue Belt, where famous barbecue joints like **The Salt Lick** (✉ *3550 E. Palm Valley Blvd., Round Rock* ⊕ *www.saltlickbbq.com*), **Kruez Market** (✉ *619 N. Colorado St., Lockhart* ☎ *512/398–2361* ⊕ *www.kreuzmarket.com*), and **Franklin Barbeque** (✉ *900 E. 11th St., Austin* ☎ *512/653–1187* ⊕ *www.franklinbbq.com*) often have lines that last for hours.

Town: A large, round rock in the low-water crossing section of Bushy Creek gave the town Round Rock its name in the mid-1800s, and the rock is still a reminder of the town's cattle-driving past. Today the town is home to a historic downtown shopping area and one of the best parks in the nation, the **Play for All Park** (✉ *151 N. A. W. Grimes Blvd.* ☎ *512/218–5540* ⊕ *www.roundrocktexas.gov*), where children of all abilities can play side by side without limitations.

Shop: Spend the afternoon scouring for deals on designer fashions and goods at the 125 stores of the **Round Rock Premium Outlets** (✉ *4401 I–35 N Frontage Rd.* ☎ *512/863–6688* ⊕ *www.premiumoutlets.com*).

AUSTIN

Do: Austin's reputation as the "Live Music Capital of the World" rings true with live performances from big-name artists popping up everywhere from **Waterloo Records** (✉ *600 N. Lamar Blvd.* ☎ *512/475–2500* ⊕ *www.waterloorecords.com*) to the **Cactus Café**

(✉ *2247 Guadalupe St.* ☎ *512/475–6515* ⊕ *www.cactuscafe.org*). Head to the South Congress (SoCo) District to see firsthand how local businesses strive to "Keep Austin Weird" through its quirky vintage stores, independent bookshops, and funky eateries.

Eat & Drink: Austin takes Tex-Mex to the next level with its own ATX-Mex staples like the Don Juan El Taco Grande breakfast taco at **Juan in a Million** (✉ *2300 E. Cesar Chavez St.* ☎ *512/472–3872* ⊕ *www.juaninamillion.com*) or the pecan-smoked brisket flautas at **Matt's El Rancho** (✉ *2613 S. Lamar Blvd.* ☎ *512/462–9333* ⊕ *www.mattselrancho.com*).

Stay: Snap a picture of the **Austin Motel's** (✉ *1220 S. Congress Ave.* ☎ *512/441–1157* ⊕ *www.austinmotel.com*) red-neon marquee before checking in to see why this quintessential Austin motel was once dubbed the "Phallus Palace." The former roadside motel has since become a playground for Austin's stylish set, where rooms feature retro-chic decor that vibes with the motel's mid-century modern look.

Breakfast: Breakfast is the most important meal of the day anywhere, but in Austin, it's sacred. **Joe's Bakery & Coffee Shop** (✉ *2305 E. 7th St.* ☎ *512/472–0017* ⊕ *www.joesbakery.com*) has been a favorite for huevos rancheros and breakfast tacos since it opened in 1935, while the more recent **Paperboy** (✉ *1203 E. 11th St.* ☎ *512/270–9980* ⊕ *www.paperboyaustin.com*) earned its reputation selling decadent breakfast sandwiches and creative pastries (like strawberry pink-peppercorn pop tarts) from a food truck before opening up a brick-and-mortar restaurant in East Austin.

Extend Your Trip

From Austin or San Antonio: Texas Hill Country *(Ch. 5)*

From San Antonio: Ultimate Cross Country Road Trip South *(Ch. 2)*

Day 3: Austin, TX, to Houston, TX

162 miles (2 hours, 35 minutes without traffic and stops)

U.S. 290 is a straight shot between Austin and Houston, with a short stretch of pay-by-mail tolls. Take exits as wanted, since this flyby road soars past some scenic backroads (like Old Potato Road near Paige) that meander through pastures of rusting oil drilling machinery and pick-your-own blackberry farms.

ALONG THE WAY

Eat & Drink: The 12-inch-platter-sized griddle cakes are legendary at **Maxine's Café and Bakery** (✉ *905 Main St.* ☎ *512/303–0919* ⊕ *www.maxinescafe.com*) in Bastrop, where you can order them stacked 12 high, but it's the homemade chicken-fried steak and freshly baked pies that keep locals coming back.

Nature: The pine trees at **Lost Pines of Bastrop State Park** (✉ *100 Park Rd. 1A* ☎ *512/321–2101* ⊕ *www.tpwd.texas.gov*) are unlike any others in the state. These Central Texas loblolly pines were separated by a prehistoric glacier and have adapted to thrive in their unique ecosystem of sandy and gravely soil alongside white-tailed deer, armadillos, and the endangered Houston toad.

Detour: Round Top is home to one of the best and oldest antiques fairs in the nation, the **Round Top Antiques Fair** (✉ 475 Rte. 237 S, Carmine ☎ 512/237–4747 ⊕ www.roundtoptexasantiques.com). The 30,000-square-foot Big Red Barn is just the start of this 100% antiques-and-vintage-only triannual fair, where professional porters and shippers help transport large items for shoppers.

Town: Although you don't have to stop in Brenham to sample homemade Blue Bell Ice Cream (it's available in most grocery stores throughout the state) from **The Little Creamery** (✉ 1101 S. Blue Bell Rd. ☎ 800/327–8135 ⊕ www.bluebell.com) in town, it's best if you do. Every Texan has a favorite Blue Bell flavor, so discover yours at the on-site ice-cream parlor before heading out for an artsy scavenger hunt to find the elaborate murals hiding just off the town's Main Street.

HOUSTON

Do: Houston's world-class arts scene extends from the extensive collection at the **Museum of Fine Arts** (✉ 1001 Bissonnet St. ☎ 713/639–7300 ⊕ www.mfah.org) to the exclusive and highly curated private works on display at the **Menil Collection** (✉ 1533 Sul Ross St. ☎ 713/525–9400 ⊕ www.menil.org). Explore the delicious side of Houston with a stroll through the city's Asiatown or space out on a visit to the **NASA Johnson Space Center** (✉ 2101 E. NASA Pkwy. ☎ 281/483–0123 ⊕ www.nasa.gov/johnson) visitor center.

Eat & Drink: Everything James Beard Award–nominee and native Houstonian Bobby Heugel touches is gold, and his dining credits in Houston include **Anvil Bar & Refuge** (✉ 1424 Westheimer Rd. ⊕ www.anvilhouston.com). **Ninfa's** (✉ 2704 Navigation Blvd. ☎ 713/228–1175 ⊕ www.ninfas.com) serves the city's top fajitas, and the dim sum menu at **Fung's Kitchen** (✉ 7320 Southwest Freeway ☎ 713/779–2288 ⊕ www.fungskitchen.com) is extensive and the service is fast.

Stay: Guests can enjoy sweeping views of the entire city from the **Post Oak Hotel's** (✉ 1600 W. Loop S ☎ 844/386–1600 ⊕ www.thepostoakhotel.com) elegant perch above Uptown Houston.

Breakfast: The servers at **Empire Café** (✉ 1732 Westheimer Rd. ☎ 713/528–5282 ⊕ www.empirecafe.com) can be found doling out hearty breakfast plates with French toast made from rustic Italian bread, crispy roasted potatoes smothered with mozzarella, and handcrafted cappuccinos all from inside these former gas station digs.

Day 4: Houston, TX, to South Padre Island, TX

377 miles (5 hours, 45 minutes without traffic and stops)

Make it to the shoreline in less than six hours by taking the U.S. 59 south and U.S. 77 route between these two cities.

ALONG THE WAY

Town: Victoria is the only county in Texas where all six flags have flown, and the town of Victoria has them all on display at **De Leon Plaza** (✉ 101 N. Main St.).

Eat & Drink: Victoria is also home to more than five of the barbecue restaurants along the highly underrated **Coastal Texas BBQ Trail** (⊕ www.discovervictoriatexas.com).

Nature: King Ranch (✉ 2205 Rte. 141 ☎ 361/592–8055 ⊕ www.king-ranch.com) in Kingsville is one of the biggest ranches in the world, where its 825,000 acres make it larger than the entire state of Rhode Island. Book a nature tour to explore the wildlife and rare birds that flock to what is often called "The Last Great Habitat."

SOUTH PADRE ISLAND

Do: This barrier island resort town is a birder's paradise, where a five-story watchtower offers views

The Alamo is still a symbol of Texan state pride.

of migrating birds at the **South Padre Island Birding Nature Center** (✉ *6801 Padre Blvd.* ☏ *956/761–6801* ⊕ *www. spibirding.com*). Assist in a sea turtle release at **Sea Turtle Inc.** (✉ *6617 Padre Blvd.* ☏ *956/761–4511* ⊕ *www. seaturtleinc.org*), charter a boat to look for dolphins, or paddleboard near the stunning *Cristo de los Pescadores* statue at **Isla Blanca Park** (✉ *33174 State Park Rd. 100* ☏ *956/761–5494* ⊕ *www.cameroncountytx.gov*).

Eat & Drink: Seafood is served on menus throughout the Gulf Coast, but in South Padre Island, it's "fresh catches only" at grab-and-go **Ceviche Ceviche** (✉ *1004 Padre Blvd.* ☏ *956/772–1555* ⊕ *www. facebook.com/cevichecevichesouthpadreisland*) and the marina-side **Sea Ranch Restaurant and Bar** (✉ *33330 State Park Rd. 100* ☏ *956/761–1314* ⊕ *www.searanchrestaurant.com*).

Stay: Waterfalls and palm trees dot the landscape throughout **Isla Grand Beach Resort's** (✉ *500 Padre Blvd.* ☏ *800/7292–7704* ⊕ *www.islagrand.com*) sprawling 10-acre property, located beachside in the southern portion of the island.

Breakfast: Specialty coffees and freshly baked pastries are available at **Yummies Bistro** (✉ *700 Padre Blvd.* ☏ *956/761–2526* ⊕ *www.facebook.com/yummies. bistro*) for dining in or they can be wrapped or poured in custom tumblers for easy snacking and sipping on the road.

Day 5: South Padre Island, TX, to San Antonio, TX

297 miles (4 hours, 30 minutes without traffic and stops)

I–37 is the fastest way out of town, which is why it's one of the few freeway hurricane evacuation routes for the Texas coast. Start on I–69 east and then follow I–37 north all the way to San Antonio.

ALONG THE WAY

Town: Robstown is the official birth-place of the popular poker game Texas Hold'em, although nowadays you're more likely to see locals holding a create-your-own fruit cup from the retro **Rod 'n' Roll's Treats and Eats** (✉ *324 W. Ave. J* ☎ *361/767–1323* ⊕ *www.rodnrolls.com*) than a deck of cards.

Detour: In April, the petite town of Poteet holds its annual Strawberry Festival and has been doing so since April 1948, where carnival rides, live concerts, and strawberry tastings fill the weekend schedule.

SAN ANTONIO

Do: Relive history with a visit to the **Alamo** (✉ *300 Alamo Plaza* ☎ *210/225–1391* ⊕ *www.thealamo.org*)—a pivotal battleground during the Texas Revolu-tion—and the four historic missions at the **San Antonio Missions National Historic Park** (✉ *6701 San Jose Dr.* ☎ *210/932–1001* ⊕ *www.nps.gov/saan*). The San Antonio River cuts through the bustling **River Walk promenade** (✉ *849 E. Com-merce St.* ☎ *210/227–4262* ⊕ *www. thesanantonioriverwalk.com*), where shoppers stroll alongside landscaped pathways to boutiques and brand-name stores, and restaurant goers dine river-side as boats of live music float by.

Eat & Drink: San Antonio is the birthplace of the puffy taco, a messy and crunchy deep-fried taco with all the fixin's. The taco was invented by brothers Henry and Ray Lopez, who each now own their own puffy taquerias, **Ray's Drive Inn** (✉ *822 S.W. 19th St.* ☎ *210/432–7171* ⊕ *www. raysdriveinn.net*) and **Henry's Puffy Tacos** (✉ *6030 Bandera Rd.* ☎ *210/432–7341* ⊕ *www.henryspuffytacos.com*).

Stay: The **Hotel Havana** (✉ *1015 Navarro St.* ☎ *210/222–2008* ⊕ *www.bunkhouse-hotels.com/hotel-havana*) is listed on the National Register of Historic Places, but this Cuban-chic boutique hotel has been restored to its grand dame glory with an eclectically modern spin.

Breakfast: Breakfast is served all day at the **Guenther House** (✉ *205 E. Guenther St.* ☎ *210/227–1061* ⊕ *www.guen-therhouse.com*), where their exclusive Founders Choice Coffee is brewed fresh and pastries are made from the restau-rant's own milled flour.

Day 6: San Antonio, TX, to Marfa, TX

405 miles (5 hours, 45 minutes without traffic and stops)

Drive through beautiful Texas Hill Country along I–10 west before entering the West Texas desert, where peace and quiet stretch on for miles.

ALONG THE WAY

Shop: The "Hill Country Mile" in Boerne follows the River Road Park and historic Main Street and offers a taste of Hill Country's best in one short, paved stretch of land. Make a quick stop to browse through stores of handcrafted jewelry, shop for homemade jams at the **Boerne Epicure Gourmet Market** (✉ *210 S. Main St.* ☎ *830/331–9355* ⊕ *www.facebook. com/boerneepicuregourmetmarket*), and pick through authentic antiques (and delicious homemade pickles) at **Fickle Pickles** (✉ *118 S. Main St.* ☎ *830/249–9306* ⊕ *www.ficklepickles.com*).

Town: Kerrville is one of Texas Hill Coun-try's best-kept secrets, where spring-fed creeks trickle through city parks and German heritage lives on through restau-rants, food trucks, and annual festivals. Walk along the mighty Guadalupe River in Louise Hays Park before grabbing a sandwich from **Greengrocers Deli** (✉ *225 W. Water St.* ☎ *830/257–3354* ⊕ *www. greengrocerdeli.com*) or a Bavarian pret-zel and craft beer at **Pint and Plow Brewing Company** (✉ *332 Clay St.* ☎ *830/315–7468* ⊕ *www.pintandplow.com*).

Roadside Attraction: The stones of **Stonehenge II** (✉ *120 Point Theatre Rd. S* ☎ *830/367–5121* ⊕ *www.hcaf.com/ stonehenge-ii*)—an exact replica of the British structure—were relocated stone by stone to their home along the Guadalupe River in Ingram. This unusual art piece shares space with replicas of Easter Island statues, also created by artist Al Shepperd.

Detour: Visit **Lost Maples Winery** (✉ *34986 Rte. 187* ☎ *830/966–5131* ⊕ *www. facebook.com/LMWinery*) and **Lost Maples State Natural Area** (✉ *37221 Rte. 187* ☎ *830/966–3413* ⊕ *www.tpwd.texas. gov*) in Vanderpool during the fall to catch glimpses of some of the best fall foliage in the state.

MARFA

Do: The entire town of Marfa is a social media post waiting to happen. This unlikely arts destination made headlines when acclaimed minimalist artist Donald Judd left New York City for the high desert of West Texas, where he transformed a former army base into a vibrant art museum now known as the **Chinati Foundation** (✉ *1 Cavalry Row* ☎ *432/729–4362* ⊕ *www.chinati.org*). Today the town is as stylish as it is quirky, where visitors can peruse the galleries at Ballroom Marfa, shop for designer shoes at Cobra Rock Boot Company, and then head out after the sun sets to watch for potential extraterrestrial activity at the **Marfa Lights Viewing Center** (✉ *U.S. 90* ☎ *432/729–4772* ⊕ *www.visitmarfa.com*).

Eat & Drink: Cochineal (✉ *107 W. San Antonio St.* ☎ *432/729–3300* ⊕ *www.cochinealmarfa.com*) puts a casual spin on fine dining while the wine garden at **Al Campo** (✉ *200 S. Russell St.* ☎ *432/729–2068* ⊕ *www.alcampomarfa.com*) plays with pairing wines with their award-winning queso and tacos.

Stay: Splurge on a stay at the **Saint George Hotel** (✉ *105 S. Highland Ave.* ☎ *432/729–3700* ⊕ *www.marfasaintgeorge.com*)

or give glamping a shot in the bohemian-chic tents, teepees, yurts, trailers, and casitas at **El Cosmico** (✉ *802 S. Highland Ave.* ☎ *432/729–1950* ⊕ *www.elcosmico. com*).

Breakfast: Ramona Tejada has welcomed celebrities (Matthew McConaughey is a fan) and cash-only customers in her home since she converted her kitchen into a breakfast joint off Route 67. She makes everything from scratch at **Marfa Burrito** (✉ *515 S. Highland Ave.*), including her salsas and hand-rolled tortillas.

Day 7: Marfa, TX, to Big Bend National Park, TX

129 miles (2 hours, 45 minutes without traffic and stops)

Head south on U.S. 67 until you reach the border town of Presidio, and then continue along Route 170 (aka River Road) to cruise beside the Rio Grande along the U.S. and Mexico border through Big Bend Ranch State Park.

ALONG THE WAY

Eat & Drink: Mexican food is a must on this stretch of the drive, and **El Changarrito** (✉ *79845 Rte. 170* ☎ *432/229–2274* ⊕ *www.facebook.com/ElChangarrito79845*) in Presidio offers some of the best tacos and *tortas* this side of the border. Try their tacos *de camaron* (shrimp) with a homemade *limonada con frutas* (fruit lemonade).

Town: The colorful characters that reside in Terlingua have breathed new life into this bona fide ghost town, where the quicksilver mines—and the community surrounding them—were abandoned just before World War II. Today the town is home to shipping container markets, quirky desert art installations, and one of the state's most eccentric chili cook-offs (held the first Saturday in November). But the most popular attraction is the front porch of the **Terlingua Trading Company**

(✉ *100 Ivey St.* ☎ *432/371–2234* ⊕ *www.facebook.com/TerlinguaTradingCompany*) for a sunset serenade and some good ol' fashioned talkin' as the sun drips below the desert skyline.

BIG BEND NATIONAL PARK

Do: Big Bend National Park (✉ *1 Panther Junction* ☎ *432/477–2251* ⊕ *www.nps.gov/bibe*) is jokingly referred to as "Texas's Gift to the Nation," but a visit to the 801,163 acres of native grasses, natural hot springs, and wild stargazing is no joke. Hike Santa Elena Canyon, canoe the Rio Grande, cruise along the Ross Maxwell Scenic Drive, and take in a sunset from "The Window" before settling in for some celestial entertainment at this International Dark Sky Park–certified gem.

Eat & Drink: The dining room at the **Chisos Mountains Lodge** (✉ *1 Basin Rural Station* ☎ *432/477–2291* ⊕ *www.chisosmountainslodge.com*) is the only full-service dining option in the park, where nightly specials are served alongside stunning views of the Chisos Basin.

Stay: The curated art and exquisite design of the **Willow House** (✉ *23112 Rte. 170, Terlingua* ☎ *432/213–2270* ⊕ *www.willowhouse.co*) make this design hotel an oasis in the desert, just 6 miles outside Big Bend National Park. Each of the hotel's 12 casitas have an unobstructed view of the Chisos Mountain Range, while the Main House is a meeting point for guests to come together for cocktails around a roaring fire.

Breakfast: At **La Posada Milagro Guesthouse's** (✉ *100 Milagro Way, Terlingua* ☎ *424/645–8017* ⊕ *www.laposadamilagro.com*) on-site coffee shop, the name Espresso y Poco Mas translates to "espresso and a little bit more," and the espresso speaks for itself while the "poco mas" ranges from French toast to fresh-squeezed orange juice.

Day 8: Big Bend National Park, TX, to El Paso, TX

330 miles (5 hours, 15 minutes without traffic and stops)

Although taking Route 118 north to I–10 west isn't the quickest route to El Paso, it's one of the more scenic drives through West Texas, as it passes by the craggy peaks of Mt. Livermore.

ALONG THE WAY

Town: Fort Davis is home to the **McDonald Observatory** (✉ *3640 Dark Sky Dr.* ☎ *432/426–3640* ⊕ *www.mcdonaldobservatory.org*), a research unit of the University of Texas at Austin. Tours begin with participants driving to the summit of Mt. Locke and Mt. Fowlkes, where the 10-meter mirror on the Hobby Eberly Telescope makes the neighboring 1-meter telescopes seem modest.

Eat & Drink: Broadway Cafe (✉ *404 Broadway St., Van Horn* ☎ *432/283–5090*) is the last stop in the Central time zone, but it should be your first choice for authentic homemade Mexican food.

Detour: Follow U.S. 90 west to catch a glimpse of the famous **Prada Marfa** (✉ *14880 U.S. 90* ☎ *432/729–3600* ⊕ *www.ballroommarfa.org*) in Valentine. Despite its retail facade, this Elmgreen & Dragset installation is a permanent land art project, where the door is always locked and the interior is forever featuring Prada's fall 2005 collection of bags and shoes.

EL PASO

Do: Discover the many sides of this border town by hiking through the rugged terrain of **Franklin Mountains State Park** and **Hueco Tanks State Park** (⊕ *www.tpwd.texas.gov*), uncovering new artists at the art school gallery within the **El Paso Museum of Art** (✉ *1 Arts Festival Plaza* ☎ *915/212–0300* ⊕ *www.elpasoartmuseum.org*), strolling through the bustling downtown markets, or getting lost in the colorful murals of historic El Segundo Barrio Street.

Eat & Drink: L&J Café (✉ *3622 E. Missouri Ave.* ☎ *915/566–8418* ⊕ *www.ljcafe.com*) has been family owned since 1927 and loved by many just as long for their homemade Mexican food and fresh chile de arbol salsa (be sure to buy some in the gift shop). Afterwards, head to **Elemi** (✉ *13500 Eastlake Blvd.* ☎ *915/532–2090* ⊕ *www.elemirestaurant.com*) for cocktails.

Stay: The **Plaza Hotel Pioneer Park** (✉ *106 W. Mills Ave.* ☎ *915/440–7666* ⊕ *www.plazahotelelpaso.com*) is one of the town's most impressive landmarks, where its "Pueblo Deco" architectural facade sets the stage for the 130 guest rooms within. Just a block over, the modern **Stanton House** (✉ *209 N. Stanton St.* ☎ *915/271–3600* ⊕ *www.stanton-house.com*) remains effortlessly cool throughout its chic open-concept common areas and tastefully curated guest rooms.

Breakfast: The perfect temperature for brewing coffee (210 degrees) inspired the name behind **2Ten Coffee Roasters** (✉ *3007 Montana Ave.* ☎ *915/745–8010* ⊕ *www.2tencoffeeroasters.com*). Their single-origin and blended beans are roasted in El Paso, where craft coffees are served alongside creative items like breakfast nachos and green chili and bacon sandwiches at their multiple cafés across town.

Day 9: El Paso, TX, to Lubbock, TX

342 miles (5 hours, 20 minutes without traffic and stops)

Take a shortcut through New Mexico along U.S. 62 east to avoid spending more than six hours on the road. Make sure to keep an eye out for the Salt Flats of Texas and Guadalupe Peak—the highest point in Texas—in Guadalupe Mountains National Park before crossing the state line into New Mexico.

ALONG THE WAY

Eat & Drink: The quirky decor and sassy signs in front of the **Cornudas Café** (✉ *180 U.S. 62* ☎ *915/964–2508*) in Salt Flat are a fitting welcome to this roadside restaurant, where menus are handwritten on brown paper sacks. You'd be hard-pressed to find a better burger west of the Pecos.

Town: The speed limit doesn't give Salt Flat its due justice (it remains 75 mph throughout the town's limits), but this curious little town is worthy of a slower look. Its ancient dry salt pan once spurred a war (El Paso Salt War), but today is part of the peaceful landscapes of **Guadalupe Mountains National Park** (✉ *400 Pine Canyon* ☎ *915/828–3251* ⊕ *www.nps.gov/gumo*).

Photo Op: Stop for a picture in front of the Texas State Line Monument in Carlsbad right before U.S. 62 east continues into New Mexico.

LUBBOCK

Do: This vibrant college town truly shines on game days, when the Goin' Band from Raiderland can be heard miles from the stadium and the tortilla shelves are empty throughout the town (throwing tortillas at Texas Tech football games has been a tradition since 1989). Explore Lubbock's musical past at the **Buddy Holly Center** (✉ *1801 Crickets Ave.* ☎ *806/775–3560* ⊕ *www.buddyhollycenter.org*), dedicated to the Lubbock-born musician, or learn about the town's World War II glider pilot training program at the **Silent Wings Museum** (✉ *6202 I–27* ☎ *806/775–3049* ⊕ *www.silentwingsmuseum.com*).

Eat & Drink: Lubbock is part of the Texas High Plains wine region—the second-largest American Viticultural Area in the state—and offers some great chances to taste some of the its finest vintages. Enjoy a glass or two at the **Funky Door**

Bistro & Wine Room (✉ *6801 Milwaukee Ave.* ☎ *806/687–0505* ⊕ *www.the-funkydoor.com*) and **McPherson Cellars Winery** (✉ *1615 Texas Ave.* ☎ *806/687–9463* ⊕ *www.mcphersoncellars.com*).

Stay: The **Cotton Court Hotel** (✉ *1610 Broadway St.* ☎ *806/758–5800* ⊕ *www.cottoncourthotel.com*) offers the quintessential Lubbock experience, where upscale accommodations and modern motel vibes are matched with curated antiques and industrial farmhouse decor.

Breakfast: The **Cast Iron Grill** (✉ *620 19th St.* ☎ *806/771–7690* ⊕ *www.castirongrill-lubbock.com*) is best known for its sweet southern pies, but between 7 and 10:30 am, it's all about their hash browns. Omelets at the grill are made with three eggs, but no one's going to judge you for ordering a slice of strawberry banana-split pie with your coffee instead.

Day 10: Lubbock, TX, to Dallas, TX

346 miles (5 hours without traffic and stops)

Notice the subtle changes along I–20 east as the landscape transitions from the high plains of the Panhandle to the prairies and lakes of North Texas along I–30 east.

ALONG THE WAY

Detour: The 10 Cadillacs submerged nose-down at **Cadillac Ranch** (✉ *13651 I-40 Frontage Rd.* ☎ *833/330–2650*) in Amarillo haven't moved since they were buried as an art installation in 1974 along historic Route 66. They have, however, changed in color, as visitors come armed with spray paint and accessories to leave their mark on this roadside attraction.

Eat & Drink: Owner Jay Stearns not only came up with the amazing recipes at **Jay's BBQ Shack** (✉ *602 S. 11th St., Abilene* ☎ *325/310–5511* ⊕ *www.jaysbbqshack.com*), he designed and made the pit he smokes them in, too. His two-handed tacos are Texas barbecue at its finest, but don't leave without trying his jalapeño hush puppies.

Town: Fort Worth is often associated with Dallas (i.e., Dallas/Fort Worth or DFW), but the city stands on its own with a scene that's a little bit western (the daily cattle drives at the **Stockyards National Historic District** [✉ *131 E. Exchange Ave.* ☎ *817/626–7921* ⊕ *www.fortworthstockyards.org*]) and a little bit urban (the vibrant shopping and entertainment throughout Sundance Square). See the only Michelangelo in the Americas at the **Kimbell Art Museum** (✉ *3333 Camp Bowie Blvd.* ☎ *817/332–8451* ⊕ *www.kimbellart.org*), marvel at the largest high-definition screen in the world at the **Texas Motor Speedway** (✉ *3545 Lone Star Circle* ☎ *817/215–8500* ⊕ *www.texasmotorspeedway.com*), or catch a film at the modern **Coyote Drive-In** (✉ *223 N.E. 4th St.* ☎ *817/717–7767* ⊕ *www.coyotedrive-in.com*) on Panther Island.

DALLAS

Do: Dallas plays host to the State Fair of Texas—the longest-running state fair in the United States—each September and October in Fair Park but welcomes visitors year-round with its urban parks, unrivaled shopping, and an arts district that's been rated the largest in the nation. Unearth the stories surrounding the JFK assassination at the **Sixth Floor Museum** (✉ *411 Elm St.* ☎ *214/747–6660* ⊕ *www.jfk.org*), view the outdoor murals in Deep Ellum, stroll the manicured grounds at the **Dallas Arboretum and Botanical Garden** (✉ *8525 Garland Rd.* ☎ *214/515–6615* ⊕ *www.dallasarboretum.org*), and take in a view of the entire city from the observation deck at **Reunion Tower** (✉ *300 Reunion Blvd. E.* ☎ *214/296–9950* ⊕ *www.reuniontower.com*).

Eat & Drink: Get your barbecue fix at **Pecan Lodge** (✉ *2702 Main St.* ☎ *214/748–8900* ⊕ *www.pecanlodge.com*) in

Texas Hill Country

Deep Ellum or enjoy the farm-fresh menu at **Petra and the Beast** (✉ *1901 Abrams Rd.* ☎ *214/484–2326* ⊕ *www. petraandthebeast.com*). For fine dining, head to **Fearing's Restaurant** (✉ *2121 McKinney Ave.* ☎ *214/922–4848* ⊕ *www. fearingsrestaurant.com*) to sample bold flavors from local celebrity and author of *The Texas Food Bible*, chef Dean Fearing.

Stay: Step inside Dallas's most beloved mansion turned luxury hotel at the **Rosewood Mansion on Turtle Creek** (✉ *2821 Turtle Creek Blvd.* ☎ *214/559–2100* ⊕ *www. rosewoodhotels.com*), where sumptuous guest rooms pay an upscale homage to the 1920s former residence. The rooftop pool above the Joule extends past the building's exterior, where swimmers can look out over the downtown streets below from a thick pane of glass.

Breakfast: The homestyle breakfast menu is extensive and served all day at **Original Market Diner** (✉ *4434 Harry Hines Blvd.* ☎ *214/521–0992* ⊕ *www.original-marketdiner.com*). Try their banana bread French toast or opt for a hearty helping of pork chops and eggs.

Texas Hill Country

Written by Kristy Alpert

The Texas Hill Country begins just north of San Antonio and stretches wide across the Edwards Plateau in Central Texas, where granite domes rise above grassy prairies of wildflowers as sparkling rivers ebb and flow along with the natural sway of the land. The pace of life is sweet and slow throughout this region, despite the vibrant energy and creativity from the eclectic mix of Anglo, German, and Spanish cultural influences.

Only in Hill Country are roadside stands just as likely to sell homemade kolaches and sizzling salsas as they are to sell fresh local produce, like the famous Hill Country peaches (in season May through August) and ripe red fruit from the native prickly pear cactus. Soak in the warmth along the windswept limestone hills of the region's three award-winning American Viticultural Areas (Texas Hill Country is also known as "Texas Wine Country") or cool down with a cold drink and an inflated tube while floating down the slow-flowing Guadalupe River.

At a Glance

Start: Austin, TX

End: Austin, TX

Miles Traveled: 297 miles

Suggested Duration: 6 days

States Visited: Texas

Key Sights: The Alamo; Barton Springs Pool; Cave Without a Name; Guadalupe River State Park; wineries of Fredericksburg

Best Time to Go: The colorful blooms of spring (specifically March to May) turn the hillsides into spectacular photo ops, but this route is captivating all year long.

Day 1: Austin, TX, to New Braunfels, TX

63 miles (1 hour, 25 minutes without traffic and stops)

Swap the traffic of I-35 south for the scenic backgrounds of the "Devil's Backbone" (a limestone ridge that runs through parts of Hill Country) by taking Route 1 Loop south to Ranch to Market Road 1826 toward Driftwood and then Ranch Road 12 to Wimberley. Then follow Purgatory Road (Route 306) as it winds through Gruene and crosses the Guadalupe River into New Braunfels.

ALONG THE WAY

Eat & Drink: The family recipes at **Salt Lick BBQ** (✉ *18300 Ranch to Market Rd. 1826* ☎ *512/858–4959* ⊕ *www.saltlickbq.com*) were first tested over hot coals on a pit made with rocks during the wagon trains of the mid-1800s and have been perfected over a similar, impressively constructed permanent pit in Driftwood. The barbecue here is famous throughout Texas, and the outdoor picnic seating beneath the shade of live oak trees fills up quickly on sunny afternoons.

Nature: The spring-fed swimming hole at **Jacob's Well Natural Area** (✉ *1699 Mt. Sharp Rd., Wimberley* ☎ *512/214–4593* ⊕ *www.hayscountytx.com*) allows swimmers—by reservation only between May 1 and September 30—into its crystal-clear waters and mystic underwater caves. Hiking around the area is free year-round and offers some challenging trails.

Detour: Devil's Backbone is regarded as the most haunted stretch of Texas highway, and the **Devil's Backbone Tavern** (✉ *4041 Farm to Market Rd. 32, Fischer* ☎ *830/964–2544* ⊕ *devilsbackbonetavern.com*), an authentic honky-tonk near Canyon Lake, is where ghostly tales and local legends are discussed below the sounds of the jukebox.

Town: The historic town of Gruene (pronounced "green") looks much like it did when German cotton farmers settled in during the late 1870s. Visit the oldest dance hall in Texas (Gruene Hall), shop for souvenirs and candy at the **General Store** (✉ *1610 Hunter Rd.* ☎ *830/629–6021*), or enjoy a meal on a patio overlooking the Guadalupe River at the **Gristmill River Restaurant** (✉ *1287 Gruene Rd.* ☎ *830/625–0684* ⊕ *www.gristmillrestaurant.com*).

NEW BRAUNFELS

Do: Taking its name from its German founder, Prince Carl of Solms-Braunfels, New Braunfels sits at the confluence of the Comal and Guadalupe Rivers, where visitors can float lazily down either river with rentals from countless local outfitters during warmer months or *pröst* with the town at the annual Wurstfest in November. Cool down at **Schlitterbahn Waterpark** (⊠ *400 N. Liberty Ave.* ☎ *830/625–2351* ⊕ *www.schlitterbahn.com*) or stay dry with a retro night out at **Stars & Stripes Drive-In Movie Theater** (⊠ *1178 Kroesche La.* ☎ *830/620–7469* ⊕ *www.driveinusa.com*) after strolling the shops, museums, and restaurants of downtown New Braunfels.

Eat & Drink: The atmosphere is lively and the schnitzel is crispy at **Krause's Café and Biergarten** (⊠ *148 S. Castell Ave.* ☎ *830/625–2807* ⊕ *www.krausescafe.com*), where the beer menu features local craft brews and imported German beers. Afterward, grab a seat in the outdoor living room at **Huisache Grill and Wine Bar** (⊠ *303 W. San Antonio St.* ☎ *830/620–9001* ⊕ *www.huisachegrill.com*) or sample your way through a tasting flight at **New Braunfels Brewing Company** (⊠ *180 W. Mill St.* ☎ *830/261–3463* ⊕ *www.nbbrewtx.com*).

Stay: Sleep inside a National Historic Landmark at the **Faust Hotel and Brewing Co.** (⊠ *240 S. Seguin Ave.* ☎ *830/625–7791* ⊕ *www.thefausthotel.com*) in downtown New Braunfels or sneak just outside of town to the opulent accommodations at **Gruene Mansion Inn** (⊠ *1275 Gruene Rd.* ☎ *830/629–2641* ⊕ *www.gruenemansioninn.com*).

Breakfast: Edouard Naegelin Sr. arrived in New Braunfels from Alsace-Lorraine in 1868 with a sack of flour and loads of ambition. His namesake bakery, **Naegelin's Bakery** (⊠ *129 S. Seguin Ave.* ☎ *830/625–5722* ⊕ *www.naegelins.com*), is the oldest bakery in Texas and

Extend Your Trip

From Austin or San Antonio: The Best of Texas *(Ch. 5)*

From San Antonio: The Ultimate Cross Country Road Trip South *(Ch. 2)*

the best place in town to grab a hot cup of coffee and a handcrafted pastry.

Day 2: New Braunfels, TX, to San Antonio, TX

34 miles (40 minutes without traffic and stops)

Today's quick ride breezes by on this interstate stretch along I–35 south.

ALONG THE WAY

Roadside Attraction: The **Animal World & Snake Farm Zoo** (⊠ *5640 S. I–35, New Braunfels* ☎ *830/402–4603* ⊕ *www.awsfzoo.com*) boasts one of the most diverse collections of snakes in the country, including a green anaconda and a black mamba.

Town: The town of Schertz winds its way from Randolph Air Force Base to the edge of the highway, where one of the largest flea markets in the United States is held on weekends at **Bussey's Flea Market** (⊠ *18738 N. I–35* ☎ *210/651–6830* ⊕ *www.busseysfm.com*). Picnic on the banks of Cibolo Creek or spend the afternoon walking the trails at **Crescent Bend Nature Park** (⊠ *12780 W. Schaefer Rd., Cibolo* ☎ *210/619–1850*).

Eat & Drink: Military members know how to pick a sandwich joint, and you'll notice the armed forces support by the patches that line the walls at **Youz Guyz** (⊠ *316 Pat Booker Rd.* ☎ *210/659–8930* ⊕ *www.*

facebook.com/YouzGuyzUC) in Universal City. The cheesesteaks at this unsuspecting location are on par with the best in Philly, and that's likely due to the fact that Joey Vento, of world-famous Geno's Steaks, is Youz Guyz's godfather.

SAN ANTONIO

Do: The San Antonio River breathes life into this vibrant city, flowing through the quaint pedestrian shops and restaurants of the **River Walk** (✉ 849 E. Commerce St. ⊕ www.thesanantonioriverwalk. com) and continuing on to the five UNESCO missions in the city (including Mission San Antonio de Valero, better known as **The Alamo** (✉ 300 Alamo Plaza ☎ 210/225–1391 ⊕ www.theala-mo.org). Walk the Skywalk on the Land Bridge at **Phil Hardberger Park Conservancy** (✉ 1021 Voelcker La. ☎ 210/492–7472 ⊕ www.philhardbergerpark.org) or discover why the city was designated a UNESCO Creative City of Gastronomy with **SA Food Tours** (✉ 711 Navarro St. ☎ 210/764–9467 ⊕ www.safoodtours. com).

Eat & Drink: The **Bottling Dept. Food Hall** (✉ 312 Pearl Pkwy., Bldg. 6 ☎ 210/564–9140 ⊕ www.atpearl.com) in the historic Pearl neighborhood puts a spotlight on local chefs serving international flavors at restaurants like Mi Roti and Brasserie Mon Chou Chou.

Stay: Hotel Emma's (✉ 136 E. Grayson St. ☎ 844/845–7384 ⊕ www.thehote-lemma.com) chic quarters once housed a brewery, but now this riverfront hotel is home to 145 guest rooms and suites, as well as some of the top dining options in town. This boutique hotel's location in the Pearl area gives guests easy access to the city's best restaurants, bars, cafés, and shops, not to mention the Pearl's twice-weekly farmers' market.

Breakfast: Brothers José and David Caceres have come a long way from selling their mother's prized pastries on the streets of Mexico City. Their restaurant,

Essential Listening

Waylon Jennings put this town on the map with his song "Luckenbach, Texas," and his longtime friend Willie Nelson has played the song for fans onstage at the Luckenbach Dance Hall.

La Panaderia Bakery Café (✉ 301 E. Houston St. ☎ 210/592–6264 ⊕ www. lapanaderia.com), has multiple locations throughout the city, all selling their exquisite pan dulces (sweet breads) and other handmade breads, like their tequila almond croissants and breakfast tortas (cakes) made with freshly baked birote bread.

Day 3: San Antonio, TX, to Boerne, TX

32 miles (40 minutes without traffic and stops)

The quickest route between San Antonio and Boerne on I-10 west takes you past the massive Six Flags Fiesta Texas theme park.

ALONG THE WAY

Town: The small town of Leon Springs takes travelers back in time with three historic buildings along its Historic District. The town was the site of the first officer training camp (established May 8, 1917) and the birthplace of the first ever Macaroni Grill Restaurant franchise.

Eat & Drink: Stop in for a bite at **The Original Rudy's** (✉ 24152 I-10, Leon Springs ☎ 210/653–7839 ⊕ www. leonspringsbbq.com) just outside San Antonio; as its name suggests, it's the original location of the beloved regional barbecue brisket and ribs chain.

BOERNE

Do: Explore Boerne's historical side at the **Kuhlmann-King Historical House**—an impressive 1880s home built by a German settler (✉ *402 E. Blanco Rd.* ☎ *210/275–8301* ⊕ *www.ci.boerne.tx.us*)—or at the **Dienger Trading Co.** (✉ *210 N. Main St.* ☎ *830/331–2225* ⊕ *www.thediengertradingco.com*), which now operates a boutique, bakery, and bistro from its carefully restored 1884 building. Soak in the sunshine at the **Cibolo Nature Center** (✉ *140 City Park Rd.* ☎ *830/249–4616* ⊕ *www.cibolo.org*) and create an urban scavenger hunt out of the town's **Art al Fresco trails** (⊕ *www.artalfresco.com*) before heading underground at the **Cave Without a Name** (✉ *325 Kreutzberg Rd.* ☎ *830/537–4212* ⊕ *www.cavewithoutaname.com*).

Eat & Drink: Peggy's on the Green (✉ *128 W. Blanco Rd.* ☎ *830/572–5000* ⊕ *www.peggysonthegreen.com*) serves southern food with an upscale twist inside a historic 19th-century stagecoach stop, while **Compadres Hill Country Cocina** (✉ *209 Lohmann St.* ☎ *830/331–2198* ⊕ *www.facebook.com/compadreshillcountrycocina*) specializes in smoked meats and Tex-Mex eats. Monday nights are for fish-and-chips at **Cibolo Creek Brewing** (✉ *448 S. Main St.* ☎ *830/816–5275* ⊕ *www.cibolocreekbrewing.com*), where plates are paired with pitchers of Boerne's finest craft brews.

Stay: The rooms at **The William** (✉ *170 S. Main St.* ☎ *361/420–1270* ⊕ *www.thewilliamboerne.com*) all feature New Orleans–style balconies that look out over Boerne's Main Street, while each of the rooms at **The Kendall** (✉ *128 W. Blanco Rd.* ☎ *830/249–2138* ⊕ *www.thekendalltx.com*) tells a unique story from the town's past, like the St. John's Suite inside a former chapel.

Breakfast: Set inside a historic building on Main Street, **The Boerne Grill** (✉ *143 S. Main St.* ☎ *830/249–4677* ⊕ *www.facebook.com/theboernegrill*) serves Hill Country coffee with local breakfast staples like smothered biscuits, *migas* (corn chips and eggs), and breakfast tacos.

Day 4: Boerne, TX, to Fredericksburg, TX

39 miles (40 minutes without traffic and stops)

Follow I–10 west through Comfort before turning onto U.S. 87 and traveling almost due north to Fredericksburg.

ALONG THE WAY

Town: Antiques shopping is almost a sport between Comfort's Front Street and High Street. At **The 8th Street Market** (✉ *523 8th St.* ☎ *830/431–5880* ⊕ *www.the8thstreetmarket.com*) inside the old 1940s-era Ford dealership, old and unexpected treasures line the interior as the smell of roasted coffee from the Comfort Coffee Co. wafts through the air. For an actual sporting experience, head to **Flat Rock Ranch** (✉ *Flat Rock Creek Rd.* ☎ *210/213–3006* ⊕ *www.flatrockranchtx.com*) for an afternoon of mountain biking.

Eat & Drink: Grab a glass of local Hill Country wine at **Bending Branch Winery** (✉ *142 Lindner Branch Trail* ☎ *830/995–2948* ⊕ *www.bendingbranchwinery.com*) in Comfort to sample some of Texas's award-winning vintages.

Detour: Venture out around sundown to Rocksprings to explore the **Devil's Sinkhole** (✉ *U.S. 377* ☎ *830/683–2287* ⊕ *www.tpwd.texas.gov*), the largest single-chamber cavern in the state, and watch in awe as more than 3 million Mexican free-tailed bats pour out from the eerie cavern (May through October).

FREDERICKSBURG

Do: Famous for its wine, wildflowers, shopping, and German heritage, Fredericksburg offers the chance to unwind or venture out into the heart

Visit Texas Hill Country in springtime so you can see the gorgeous Texas bluebonnets in bloom.

of Hill Country with its easy access to Enchanted Rock, the **Lyndon B. Johnson National Historical Park** (⌧ *100 Ladybird La., Johnson City* ☎ *830/868–7128* ⊕ *www.nps.gov/lyjo*), and the trails at **Wildseed Farms** (⌧ *100 Legacy Dr.* ☎ *830/990–8080* ⊕ *www.wildseedfarms.com*), the nation's largest working wildflower farm. Brush up on your World War II history at the **National Museum of the Pacific War** (⌧ *311 E. Austin St.* ☎ *830/997–8600* ⊕ *www.pacificwarmuseum.org*), shop around the boutiques of Main Street, pick your own peaches at **Jenschke Orchards** (⌧ *8301 U.S. 290* ☎ *830/997–8422* ⊕ *www.bestfredericksburgpeaches.com*), and taste your way through Hill Country at **Becker Vineyards** (⌧ *464 Becker Farms Rd.* ☎ *830/644–2681* ⊕ *www.beckervineyards.com*) and **Narrow Path Winery & Vineyards** (⌧ *6331 Ranch Rd. 1623, Stonewall* ☎ *830/998–1916* ⊕ *www.narrowpathwinery.com*).

Eat & Drink: The winemakers at **William Chris Vineyards** (⌧ *10352 U.S. 290, Hye* ☎ *830/998–7654* ⊕ *www.williamchriswines.com*) remain committed to pre-industrial methods of winemaking (i.e. open-air fermentation) from Texas-grown grapes. Feast on German fare made with local ingredients at **Otto's German Bistro** (⌧ *316 E. Austin St.* ☎ *830/368–0416* ⊕ *www.ottosfbg.com*) and stop in for samples at **Das Peach Haus** (⌧ *1406 S. U.S. 87* ☎ *830/997–8969* ⊕ *www.jelly.com*), home to Fischer & Wieser products like the locally beloved Original Roasted Raspberry Chipotle Sauce.

Stay: Named after a Texas legend (who is also the great-great-great-grandfather of current owner Alice Adair) James L. Trueheart, **The Trueheart Hotel**'s (⌧ *201 Llano St.* ☎ *830/992–3489* ⊕ *www.thetruehearthotel.com*) rooms are outfitted in a style that blends retro pop with western chic. Just down the road, the luxury B&B **Hoffman Haus** (⌧ *608 E.*

Barton Springs is one of the most popular outdoor experiences in Austin.

Creek St. ☎ 830/997–6739 ⊕ www.hoff-manhaus.com) boasts 23 rooms, each with the distinctly Hill Country aesthetic of crisp white linens and lavender bath products.

Breakfast: Breakfasts at **Nury's Restaurant** (✉ 714 S. Washington St. ☎ 830/992–3217 ⊕ www.nuryscuisine.com) range from classic pancakes and eggs to *huevos divorciados*, where two eggs are separated in neighboring sauces of homemade ranchero (red) and home-made tomatillo (green). Don't be shy about ordering pie for breakfast at the **Fredericksburg Pie Company** (✉ 108 E. Austin St. ☎ 830/990–6992 ⊕ www.fbgpie.com), where they serve locally roasted coffees like Texas Hill Country Pecan and the Fredericksburg Pie Company House Blend.

Day 5: Fredericksburg, TX, to Canyon Lake, TX

65 miles (1 hour, 20 minutes without traffic and stops)

Drive past the historic dance halls and hilly vineyards along U.S. 290 and Route 1888 before crossing the Blanco River and continuing along U.S. 281 south toward Canyon Lake.

ALONG THE WAY

Town: The slogan "Everybody's Somebody in Luckenbach" can be found on bumper stickers and T-shirts throughout this quirky town. Best known for the 1887 **Dancehall** (⊕ www.luckenbachtexas.com)—which still hosts regular dances and concerts and has become a rite of passage for many Texas musicians—the original general store and "feed lot" food stand are both worthy of a visit before continuing on.

Eat & Drink: The **Chess Club Café** (✉ *1020 U.S. 281 S* ☎ *830/833–4930* ⊕ *www. chessclubcafe.com*) in Blanco is only open 8 am to 2 pm Wednesday through Sunday, so come early and come hungry for specials like chicken-fried steak and scratch-made biscuits.

Roadside Attraction: The **Buggy Barn Museum** (✉ *1915 Main St.* ☎ *830/833–5708* ⊕ *www.buggybarnmuseum.com*) in Blanco is as niche as they come. More than 200 restored buggies, carriages, and wagons are on display, many of which have appeared in films like *True Grit, Abraham Lincoln: Vampire Hunter,* and *There Will Be Blood.*

Nature: There are 13 miles of hiking and biking trails throughout **Guadalupe River State Park** (✉ *3350 Park Rd. 31, Spring Branch* ☎ *830/438–2656* ⊕ *www.tpwd. texas.gov*), although most visitors are more focused on the 4 miles of river frontage. Toss a tube in the river for a peaceful float or hop in for a refreshing dip on a hot day.

CANYON LAKE

Do: Often referred to as the "Jewel of Texas Hill Country," Canyon Lake is a nature lover's playground, with hiking trails, boat docks, and campsites. Kayak on the lake, take a tour through the Canyon Lake Gorge, or explore the region's prehistoric past at **The Heritage Museum of the Texas Hill Country** (✉ *4831 Rte. 2673* ☎ *830/899–4542* ⊕ *www.theheritagemuseum.com*).

Eat & Drink: The tasting room at **La Cruz de Comal Wines** (✉ *7405 Rte. 2722* ☎ *830/899–2723* ⊕ *www.lacruzdecomalwines.com*) at the vineyards of Canyon Lake has a "Provence meets Texas Hill Country" feel, but the wines are purely Texan, with 100% of the grapes grown on the estate. Grab one of the healthy meal replacement shakes at the **Nutrition Shack** (✉ *14120 Rte. 306* ☎ *830/357–9155* ⊕ *www.facebook.com/NutritionShackCanyonLake*)

with delicious twists like the Fruity Pebble Protein Oats or the Sopaipilla Cheesecake Shake, or head to **Canyon City Grill** (✉ *14601 Rte. 306* ☎ *830/964–3640* ⊕ *www.canyoncitygrilltx.com*) for burgers and their famous "Texas Tots" beneath the oak trees.

Stay: The views from the lodge suites and the cathedral cabins at **Canyon Lakeview Resort** (✉ *872 Ledgerock Dr.* ☎ *210/787–1770* ⊕ *www.canyonlakeviewresort.com*) offer panoramic views of the resort's 80 miles of Canyon Lake shoreline. Days at this lakefront property are spent on the water, while evenings are spent around the boulder-lined fire pits soaking in the warmth of the area long after the sun goes down.

Breakfast: Inspired by the wild game and fresh-baked goods that mark the menu, **Wildflour Artisan Bakery & Grill** (✉ *2000 Rte. 2673* ☎ *830/964–2159* ⊕ *www. wildflourbakeryandgrill.com*) offers an authentic taste of Hill Country. Popular breakfast items include their whole-hog sausages and homemade biscuits with Paw Paw Bill's sausage gravy.

Day 6: Canyon Lake, TX, to Austin, TX

65 miles (1 hour, 15 minutes without traffic and stops)

Cross the Guadalupe River one final time before turning onto I–35 north for a quick drive back into Austin.

ALONG THE WAY

Town: Named for the nearby watering hole Manchaca Springs (referred to as "Manshack Springs"), where Tejano army officer turned Texas legend José Antonio Manchaca once camped, the town of Manchaca is very much still a watering hole along the route to Austin. Grab a drink at the **Manchaca Springs Saloon** (✉ *737 Rte. 1626* ☎ *512/845–9765* ⊕ *www.facebook.*

com/ManchacaSpringsSaloon) or taste some craft brews at **Texas Keeper Cider** (✉ *12521 Twin Creeks Rd.* ☎ *512/910–3409* ⊕ *www.texaskeeper.com*).

Eat & Drink: Celebrated barbecue-and-taco truck **Valentina's Tex-Mex BBQ** (✉ *308 S. Main St., Buda* ☎ *512/221–4248* ⊕ *www.valentinastexmexbbq.com*), located just north of Manchaca, slow-smokes their meats and hand-rolls their tortillas to create a delicious base for homemade salsas and sauces.

Detour: For a long time, **Dreamland** (✉ *2770 U.S. 290* ☎ *512/827–1279* ⊕ *www.dreamlanddstx.com*) in Dripping Springs was just that: a dream. The outdoor entertainment, recreation, and arts venue now puts sustainability first (rainwater collection tanks, Tesla charging stations, etc.), followed closely by their immense array of fun activities like lawn games, eccentric art installations, and a family-friendly beer garden.

AUSTIN

Do: With an average of more than 300 sunny days each year and live music venues that range from parks to patios, getting outside in Austin is the best way to soak in this capital city's vibe. Walk the 10-mile urban trail around Lady Bird Lake, swim in the spring-fed waters of **Barton Springs** (✉ *Barton Springs Rd.* ☎ *512/974–6300* ⊕ *www.austintexas.gov*), peruse the galleries at **Blanton Museum of Art** at the University of Texas at Austin (✉ *200 E. Martin Luther King Jr. Blvd.* ☎ *512/471–5482* ⊕ *www.blantonmuseum.org*), and get entertained at the many bars, restaurants, and venues along Austin's famous Sixth Street.

Eat & Drink: Asking an Austinite where to get the best tacos in town will lead to a lengthy debate, which you'll likely be discussing while in line—which can last up to four hours—for the award-winning brisket at **Franklin Barbecue** (✉ *900 E. 11th St.* ☎ *512/653–1187* ⊕ *www.franklinbarbecue.com*). But save yourself the debate (still get the brisket though—it's worth the wait) and head to **Veracruz All Natural** (✉ *111 E. Cesar Chavez St.* ☎ *512/665–2713* ⊕ *www.veracruzallnatural.com*), because their handmade tacos have a spot on everyone's "taco top 10."

Stay: Austin's **Proper Hotel** (✉ *600 W. 2nd St.* ☎ *512/628–1500* ⊕ *www.properhotel.com/austin*), a member of Design Hotels, is quintessential Austin at its finest, with local textiles and textures layered smartly inside its 244 modern rooms. For a fresh look into Austin's past, book a room inside the luxuriously restored 1928 mansion at the **Commodore Perry Estate** (✉ *4100 Red River St.* ☎ *512/817–5200* ⊕ *www.aubergeresorts.com*), an Auberge Resort.

Breakfast: Paperboy (✉ *1203 E. 11th St.* ☎ *512/910–3010* ⊕ *www.paperboyaustin.com*) takes breakfast seriously with its menu full of toasts, quiches, and migas to eat in-house or order to go from the restaurant's walk-up window.

Chapter 6

THE MIDWEST AND THE PLAINS

6

Updated by
Kristine Hansen

WELCOME TO THE MIDWEST AND THE PLAINS

TOP REASONS TO GO

★ **Badlands National Park:** This dramatic South Dakota landscape is home to steep canyons, bison, bighorn sheep, and stunning scenic viewpoints.

★ **Wisconsin's Door County:** Located on a scenic peninsula between Green Bay and Lake Michigan, Door County is one of the Midwest's most unforgettable regions, with outdoor adventures, antiques shops, and boutique wineries galore.

★ **Detroit:** Michigan's biggest city comes with fascinating museums, rich history, and lively food and art scenes.

★ **Mackinac Island:** For the ultimate Great Lakes experience, visit this island in the middle of Lake Huron, with nature trails, historic forts, and the often filmed Grand Hotel.

1 The Best of the Dakotas. Two of the country's least-visited states have an unexpected amount to offer.

2 Native American Homelands of the Great Plains. Explore Kansas, Oklahoma, and Nebraska through the tribes that live there today.

3 The Best of the Ozarks. The Ozark Mountains offer beautiful vistas and plenty of outdoor adventures in Arkansas, Missouri, Kansas, and Oklahoma.

4 The Best of the Heartland. Experience the ultimate Midwestern charm as you travel through the farmlands, lakes, and cities that make up Minnesota, Wisconsin, and Iowa.

5 Underrated Cities of the Midwest. See for yourself all the culture the Midwest has to offer, including incredible museums, delicious food scenes, and hip art communities.

6 All the Great Lakes. Hit up all five of the Great Lakes in one unforgettable trip.

7 A Frank Lloyd Wright Tour. From Chicago to Philadelphia, visit some of the famous architect's best works.

NUNAVUT

QUÉBEC   Québec City

MINNESOTA

Thunder Bay

Isle Royale National Park

Lake Superior

ONTARIO

Pictured Rocks Nat'l Lakeshore

Sault Ste. Marie

Ottawa

Montréal

35

inneapolis   WISCONSIN

St. Paul

39

Sleeping Bear Dunes Nat'l Lakeshore

MICHIGAN

75

Lake Huron

Toronto

L. Ontario

NY   VT

90

START AND END   4

Milwaukee

START AND END   6

Chicago

7   START

Detroit

Cleveland

Buffalo

Lake Erie

PENNSYLVANIA

New York

END   7

Philadelphia

Baltimore

IOWA

80

Des Moines

START AND END   5

OHIO

Columbus

70

Pittsburgh

NJ

DE

ILLINOIS

IN

Indianapolis

Cincinnati

Washington, D.C.

MD

Kansas City

70

55

St. Louis

Louisville

Lexington

WV

VA

Richmond

Norfolk

MISSOURI

65

75

KENTUCKY

Raleigh

ARKANSAS

40

Nashville

TENNESSEE

Charlotte

NC

Memphis

SC

Little Rock

3   START AND END

30

Atlanta

Charleston

Sheveport

55   MS

AL

GA

LA

20

Jackson

Montgomery

An expansive region covering the entire middle of the country, the Midwest and the Great Plains are lands of rolling farms, sweeping landscapes, rich Indigenous history, amazing architecture, and friendly residents. From the Great Lakes to the Ozarks, these lands were made to be explored via the wide-open road.

The Best of the Dakotas

Written by Cassandra Brooklyn

Collectively known as "The Dakotas," the supremely underrated states of North and South Dakota truly have something for everyone: rolling hills, underground cave systems, Wild West history, rich Native American culture, and national and state parks brimming with hiking, biking, kayaking, and wildlife-viewing. From rustic cabins and campgrounds to chic glamping sites and upscale hotels, the Dakotas have accommodations for every budget and every type of traveler, too.

Though this road trip itinerary visits seven cities in seven days, know that both North and South Dakota are overflowing with parks, museums, public art instillations, historic sites, and incredible eateries, so it's not a bad idea to consider extending your trip if possible.

At a Glance

Start: Sioux Falls, SD

End: Sioux Falls, SD

Miles Traveled: 1,240 miles

Suggested Duration: 7 days

States Visited: North Dakota, South Dakota

Key Sights: Badlands National Park; Crazy Horse National Memorial; Mount Rushmore; Theodore Roosevelt National Park; Wind Cave National Park

Best Time to Go: If you're hoping to do a lot of outdoor activities, spring and summer are the best times to take advantage of the stunning weather, as many destinations close for the winter. That being said, if you're a leaf-peeping connoisseur or winter sports buff, fall and early winter provide their own unique offerings in the Dakotas.

Day 1: Sioux Falls, SD, to Badlands National Park, SD

275 miles (4 hours without traffic and stops)

Today's drive is a straight shot across I–90, including several optional stops at quirky roadside attractions.

The Best of the Dakotas

ALONG THE WAY

Roadside Attraction: Stop at the **World's Only Corn Palace** (✉ 604 N. Main St. ☎ 605/995–8430 ⊕ www.cornpalace. com) in Mitchell at the beginning of your route (70 miles from Sioux Falls) and at the six-ton Giant Prairie Dog at the end (20 miles before Wall).

Photo Op: The town of Chamberlain is the home of the impressive **Dignity of Earth & Sky** Sculpture (☎ 605/347–5776 ⊕ www. lampherestudio.com/dignity), a statue dedicated to the Lakota and Dakota people of South Dakota. The sculpture depicts a 50-foot Lakota woman with a traditional star quilt.

Detour: Twenty minutes south of the town of Wall (the gateway town to Badlands National Park) lies **Minuteman Missile National Historic Site** (☎ 05/433–5552 ⊕ www.nps.gov/mimi), home to

a visitor center and two former Launch Control facilities, a reminder that nuclear missiles were in the Great Plains during the Cold War.

BADLANDS NATIONAL PARK

Do: You can drive the 39-mile Scenic Byway within **Badlands National Park** (☎ 605/433–5361 ⊕ www.nps.gov/badl) in about an hour, but you'll want to spend the most time along Sage Creek Rim Road (on the western edge of the loop), as it's one of the best places to see bison, bighorn sheep, pronghorns, and prairie dogs. The remoteness of the park makes it perfect for backcountry hikers and campers who want to escape the crowds and explore the wilderness far from trails and roads. Badlands bike tours can also be arranged. There's also almost no light pollution here, so the astronomy and night sky viewing is also incredible. If you're a fan of astronomy, plan your visit for July, when the area hosts the annual Badlands Astronomy Festival.

Eat & Drink: Fewer than 800 people live in the town of Wall, but 2 million people stop at its famous **Wall Drug** (✉ *510 Main St.* ☎ *605/279–2175* ⊕ *www.walldrug.com*) each year for food, photos, and shopping. It's about 10 minutes from the Badlands, so the town is a popular place for affordable food and accommodations. Don't miss the doughnuts.

Stay: Cedar Pass Lodge (✉ *20681 Rte. 240* ☎ *855/765–0737* ⊕ *www.cedar-passlodge.com*) is located within Badlands National Park, but it books up fast, so plan ahead. Staying within the park may be a bit more expensive, but it's worth the splurge, as it allows you to enjoy sunrises and sunsets right from your window. If you prefer to stay outside the park, check out **Badlands Frontier Cabins** (✉ *1101 Glenn St.* ☎ *605/279–2619* ⊕ *www.frontiercabins.com*) in Wall.

Breakfast: Head to Cedar Pass Lodge Restaurant (part of the Cedar Pass Lodge) and try the fry bread topped with *wojapi*, a Native American berry sauce.

Day 2: Badlands National Park, SD, to Mount Rushmore, SD

75 miles (1 hour, 30 minutes without traffic and stops)

Today is a relatively quick drive, but if you're a photographer and want to get the best light, be sure to get to Mount Rushmore before 11 am. Another good option is to drive 50 miles south of Mount Rushmore to explore Wind Cave National Park for the first half of the day, before heading north to check out Mount Rushmore for the last half.

Extend Your Trip

From the Badlands: Ultimate Cross Country Trip North *(Ch. 2)*

From Mount Rushmore or Sioux Falls: The Ultimate Wild West Road Trip *(Ch. 4)*

ALONG THE WAY

Shop: Native West Trading Co., near Interior, South Dakota, is a great place to purchase authentic, handcrafted items made by local Native artists.

Detour: Wind Cave National Park (☎ *605/745–4600* ⊕ *www.nps.gov/wica*) is home to one of the longest and most complex cave systems in the world. Aboveground there are hiking trails and an abundance of wildlife; while belowground, explore the cave, its maze of passages, and its unique honeycomb-like boxwork formations via candlelit tours. You could spend a couple of hours here before, or pay it a visit after, exploring Mount Rushmore (it's about an hour drive each way).

Eat & Drink: If you want to enjoy lunch in Wind Cave National Park, be sure to pack your own meal, because other than vending machines, the only dining venues inside park boundaries are the two picnic areas, one near the visitor center and the other at Elk Mountain Campground.

MOUNT RUSHMORE

Do: Hike the half-mile Presidential Trail to take in views of the **Mount Rushmore National Memorial** (✉ *13000 Rte. 244, Keystone* ☎ *605/574–2523* ⊕ *www.nps.gov/moru*). The Nature Trail also connects to the Presidential Trail and takes you to the Carver's Studio, where you can find the tools and models used in the construction of Mount Rushmore. From May through September, Mount

One of South Dakota's most stunning drives takes you through Badlands National Park.

Rushmore puts on evening light and music ceremonies that go through the history of the site.

Eat & Drink: While at Mount Rushmore, swing by the **Memorial Team Ice Cream** (⊠ 13000 Rte. 244 ☎ 605/574–2515 ⊕ www.mtrushmorenationalmemorial.com) and treat yourself to Thomas Jefferson's ice cream, made with the original recipe used in 1780 by America's third president. Jefferson is credited with bringing the first recipe for ice cream to what would become the United States. For a more substantial meal, **Skogen Kitchen** (⊠ 29 N 5th St. ☎ 605/673–2241 ⊕ www.skogenkitchen.com) in nearby Custer, is a Nordic-theme restaurant offering gourmet food that's typically hard to find in this area. Despite the high-end fare, the food is affordable and the restaurant has a casual outdoor patio that is pet friendly.

Stay: Under Canvas Glamping (⊠ 24342 Presidio Ranch Rd. ☎ 888/496–1148 ⊕ www.undercanvas.com) is just a few miles from Mount Rushmore and has on-site programming like yoga, nature walks, and bike tours.

Breakfast: Grapes & Grinds (⊠ 609 U.S. 16A ☎ 605/666–5142 ⊕ www.grapesgrinds.com) in Keystone offers the best of both worlds: coffee and wine. Start your day with a bagel and brew, and grab a bottle of wine for later.

Day 3: Mount Rushmore, SD, to Deadwood, SD

50 miles (1 hour, 10 minutes without traffic and stops)

You can spend the first half of the day exploring Custer State Park and/or the Crazy Horse Memorial, which are both not too far from Mount Rushmore. Then you'll head north to Deadwood, and no matter which route you take, the drive is beautiful, but the most spectacular route would be to take a detour along the Spearfish Canyon byway. That will add about an hour to the drive, but you'll pass beautiful waterfalls and gorgeous land-scapes. This route is particularly stunning when the leaves are changing in autumn.

ALONG THE WAY

Detour: Visit the rolling hills of **Custer State Park** (⊠ 13438 U.S. 16A ☎ 605/394–2693 ⊕ www.gfp.sd.gov), where roaming bison and towering granite spires line the route. The park is famous for its herd of 1,300 bison, which you can spot along the Wildlife Loop Road. It's the largest publicly owned bison herd in the country and the experience is similar to what you'd encounter in Yellowstone National Park. Each September, the park hosts its annual Buffalo Roundup, where wranglers on horseback round up the park's herd to be sorted and vaccinated. The park also offers mountain biking, fishing, paddle boating, mountain climbing, and some of the best hiking in the Black Hills. You could spend anywhere from a few hours to a few days hiking in the park.

Eat & Drink: For lunch, head to **Black Hills Burger and Bun Co.** (⊠ 441 Mt. Rushmore Rd. ☎ 605/673–3411 ⊕ www.blackhills-burgerandbun.com) in Custer, which serves homemade burgers, salads, and fun sides (think cheese curds and fried green tomatoes) using minimally pro-cessed ingredients.

Detour: Explore the living history and culture of South Dakota's Native Amer-ican tribes at the **Crazy Horse Memorial** (⊠ 12151 Ave. of the Chiefs, Crazy Horse ☎ 605/673–4681 ⊕ www.crazy-horsememorial.org). Designed to be the world's largest work of art (the face alone is 87 feet tall), this tribute depicts Crazy Horse, the legendary Lakota leader who helped defeat General Custer at Little Bighorn. A work in progress, thus far the warrior's head has been carved from the mountain, and the colossal head of his horse is beginning to emerge. It's worth spending a few bucks to take the bus to the base of the memorial. Also, don't miss the Indian Museum of North

Essential Listening

Listen to the audiobook *Bury My Heart at Wounded Knee* for an account of the "settling" of the American West from the perspec-tive of members of the Dakota, Ute, Sioux, Cheyenne, and other tribes.

America on-site, which is included with the admission to Crazy Horse.

DEADWOOD

Do: Explore the ultimate Wild West town of Deadwood, which real-life (and HBO) legends Wild Bill Hickcock and Calamity Jane called home. Wander the old streets where actors perform shoot-outs, tour the town in an old stagecoach, and try your hand at gold panning at the old **Broken Boot Gold Mine** (⊠ 1200 Pioneer Way ☎ 605/717–6848 ⊕ www.broken-bootgoldmine.com). The town is also known for rodeos, music jams, and all sorts of festivals, so check out special programming at **Outlaw Square** (⊠ 703 Main St. ☎ 605/578–1876 ⊕ www.outlawsquare.com) to find out what's going on.

Eat & Drink: For dinner, order a local craft beer and burger at **Deadwood's Saloon #10** (⊠ 657 Main St. ☎ 800/952–9398 ⊕ www.saloon10.com), where Wild Bill was famously shot during a poker game. You can even pay your respects at his grave, found in the town's Mount Moriah Cemetery. Upstairs at the saloon, you'll find the Deadwood Social Club, offering a finer dining experience.

Stay: Deadwood has loads of accom-modations at different price points and offering different amenities. If you want to stay in town, **SpringHill Suites by Marriott Deadwood** (⊠ 322 Main St. ☎ 605/559–1600 ⊕ www.marriott.com) is a good bet (it's connected to the

Cadillac Jack casino and within walking distance to museums), but if you want to stay in nature, book a lodge (two to seven bedrooms) at the **Executive Lodging of the Black Hills** (✉ *11842 U.S. 14A, Sturgis* ☎ *605/578–3555* ⊕ *www.vacasa.com/usa/Black-Hills-SD*).

Breakfast: While you're picking up coffee, pastries, and sandwiches at the **Pump House** (✉ *73 Sherman St.* ☎ *605/571–1071* ⊕ *www.pumphousecoffeecrew.com*), check out the blown-glass art being made next door at **Mind Blown Studio** (✉ *78 Sherman St.* ☎ *605/571–1071* ⊕ *www.mindblownstudio.com*).

Day 4: Deadwood, SD, to Medora, ND

220 miles (3 hours, 45 minutes without traffic and stops)

Enjoy beautiful rolling hills and wide-open prairie landscapes as you drive into North Dakota. About 30 minutes outside Deadwood, you will pass through the community of Belle Fourche, pronounced as "Bell Foosh." This town is considered to be along the geographic center of the United States.

ALONG THE WAY

Town: Stop by Sturgis, a sleepy town that livens up for three weeks of rallies during the annual **Sturgis Motorcycle Rallies** (⊕ *www.sturgismotorcyclerally.com*) each August. If you're not there for the rally, pop into the **Sturgis Motorcycle Museum & Hall of Fame** (✉ *999 Main St.* ☎ *605/347–2001* ⊕ *www.sturgismuseum.com*) to learn a bit about the town's motorcycle culture.

Eat & Drink: Much of the Belle Fourche area's economy is built on cattle, and when local ranchers and other residents want a good steak, they go to the **Branding Iron** (✉ *19079 U.S. 85* ☎ *605/892–2503*). This is a no-nonsense, saloon-style

facility with wood paneling on the walls, a bar, pool tables, lots of seating, and big food portions.

Detour: The 150-mile **Maah Daah Hey Trail** (☎ *701/225–5796* ⊕ *www.mdhta.com*) is an epic single-track trail carved through the North Dakota Badlands, showcasing some of the country's most unique and breathtaking terrain. Majestic plateaus, large expanses of rolling prairie, and rivers intertwine to offer any outdoors lover a taste of pure, unadulterated badlands.

MEDORA

Do: Medora is an outdoor enthusiast's dream, offering road biking, hiking, and camping, along with a downtown area full of shops and restaurants. Be sure to get to town by 7 pm so you can attend the live **Medora Musical** at 7:30 pm (✉ *3422 Chateau Rd.* ☎ *800/633–6721* ⊕ *www.medora.com*).

Eat & Drink: Dinner at the **Pitchfork Steak Fondue** (✉ *3422 Chateau Rd.* ☎ *800/633–6721* ⊕ *www.medora.com*) is a must. Here chefs load steaks onto a pitchfork and "fondue" them western style—basically, they're deep-fried in a vat of hot oil. Steaks are served with various sides, desserts, and drinks, and vegetarians can order a "Just the Fixin's" plate.

Stay: Luxury meets western charm at the **Historic Rough Riders Hotel** (✉ *301 3rd Ave.* ☎ *701/623–4444* ⊕ *www.medora.com*) in downtown Medora, but if you're looking for something more economical or pet friendly, check out the "tiny-house style" lodges at **Elkhorn Quarters** (✉ *400 E. River Rd. S* ☎ *800/633–6721* ⊕ *www.medora.com*).

Breakfast: Start your day with a cup of joe and fresh baked goods at the **Hidden Springs Java** (✉ *350 4th St.* ☎ *701/623–4700* ⊕ *www.facebook.com/HiddenSpringsJava*) or grab a proper breakfast at the **Cowboy Café** (✉ *215 4th St.* ☎ *701/623–4343*).

Day 5: Medora, ND, to Bismarck, ND

130 miles (2 hours without traffic and stops)

Today's route is an easy drive on I-94, with several potential detours and photo ops.

ALONG THE WAY

Nature: Bison, deer, prairie dogs, wild horses, and eagles are plentiful in **Theodore Roosevelt National Park** (☎ 701/623–4466 ⊕ www.nps.gov/thro), and a loop ride in the South Unit gets you up close with the wildlife. The park's 70,400 acres of breathtaking badlands are full of hiking trails, scenic overlooks, picnic spots, and campsites.

Photo Op: The best places for photo ops in Theodore Roosevelt National Park are Buck Hill and Wind Canyon. Also stop at the Painted Canyon for one last look (and a quick pic) of the park as you exit and head to Bismarck.

Eat & Drink: Pop into **Fluffy Fields Vineyard & Winery** (✉ 2708 21st St. E ☎ 701/483–2242 ⊕ www.fluffyfields.com) in Dickinson, North Dakota's first year-round winery, for a glass of wine on the patio to pair with the daily lunch and dessert specials (just keep in mind that the winery is closed Monday and Tuesday).

Detour: Beginning at exit 72 on I-94 near Gladstone is the Enchanted Highway, a 32-mile stretch that ends in the small town of Regent. Beginning with the *Geese in Flight* sculpture at exit 72, large metal sculptures are placed along the county highway, each with a parking area and kiosk. Some of the sculptures include *World's Largest Tin Family*, *Teddy Rides Again*, *Pheasants on the Prairie*, and *Grasshoppers in the Field*.

Roadside Attraction: About 30 miles before Bismarck, you'll pass *Salem Sue*, the "World's Largest Holstein Cow."

Detour: About 40 minutes north of Bismarck is **Fort Mandan** (✉ 838 28th Ave. SW, Washburn ☎ 701/462–8535 ⊕ www.parkrec.nd.gov), where Lewis and Clark met up with Sacagawea on their famous expedition. You can tour the historic site and walk in the footsteps of these legendary explorers.

BISMARCK

Do: Explore the art scene in downtown Bismarck, North Dakota's capital, by visiting several art galleries and colorful alley art in between Broadway and Main Avenue. Next, check out some of the outdoor attractions along the Missouri River walking path, which include the eagle sculptures, Steamboat Park, and **Chief Looking's Village Historic Site** (✉ 2023 Burnt Boat Rd. ☎ 701/222–6455). The grounds at the state capitol building have an arboretum trail with 75 species of trees, shrubs, and flowers. To learn about the state's geological, agricultural, industrial, and Native American history, visit the **North Dakota Heritage Center and State Museum** (✉ 612 E. Boulevard Ave. ☎ 701/328–2666 ⊕ www.statemuseum.nd.gov).

Eat & Drink: Bismarck is packed with great food and drink options. Grab a burger and brew at **Peacock Alley** (✉ 422 E. Main Ave. ☎ 701/221–2333 ⊕ www.peacock–alley.com) or sample the bison medallions at the **Pirogue Grille** (✉ 121 N. 4th St. ☎ 701/223–3770 ⊕ www.pirogue-grille.com). The brewery scene is also hoppin' and **Laughing Sun Brewing** (✉ 1023 E. Front Ave. ☎ 701/751–3881 ⊕ www.laughingsunbrewing.com) has plenty of options to tempt your palate and can also provide a tour.

Stay: Many standard and upscale hotels exist in the city, but for a unique lodging experience, head to **Fort Abraham Lincoln State Park** (✉ 4480 Fort Lincoln Rd. ☎ 701/667–6340 ⊕ www.parkrec.nd.gov), where you can overnight in a cabin or a teepee and wake up next to hiking trails.

Breakfast: Stop in at the **Terra Nomad** (✉ *514 E. Main Ave.* ☎ *701/751–2070* ⊕ *www.terranomadcompany.com*), a unique café in downtown Bismarck offering a holistic experience (and Instagram-worthy meals) to guests.

Day 6: Bismarck, ND, to Fargo, ND

245 miles (3 hours, 40 minutes without traffic and stops)

You may notice the flattened topography and fields that abound as you enter North Dakota's Red River valley.

ALONG THE WAY

Town: Visit **Frontier Village** (✉ *404 17th St. NE* ☎ *800/222–4766* ⊕ *www.discoverjamestownnd.com*) in the town of Jamestown to take a picture with the "World's Largest Buffalo" and to visit the **North American Bison Discovery Center** (✉ *500 17th St. SE* ☎ *800/807–1511* ⊕ *www.buffalomuseum.com*), where you can learn about the history and preservation of buffalo and even see an albino bison.

Eat & Drink: If you're ever going to try a bison burger, Jamestown is the perfect place to do it. Try one at the **Frontier Fort Bar & Grill** (✉ *1838 3rd Ave. SE* ☎ *701/252–7492*).

Photo Op: Stop by the **Fargo-Moorhead Convention and Visitors Bureau** (✉ *2001 44th St. S* ☎ *701/282–3653* ⊕ *www.fargomoorhead.org*) to take a picture with the original woodchipper from the movie *Fargo*. Also, if North Dakota is your last state to check off your bucket list (it seems like this happens a lot), you can join the "Saved the Best for Last" club at the visitor center; you get a commemorative T-shirt, an official certificate, and sometimes a round of applause from the staff.

Essential Listening

KILI Radio (90.1 FM) broadcasts from a local Lakota reservation, so you can hear old tribal music from powwows, modern tribal music, community affairs broadcasting, and commentary and conversations from elders and members of the Lakota Nation.

FARGO

Do: While it might have gotten the most hype from the Coen brothers' movie and television series of the same name, Fargo is North Dakota's largest city and visitors will find a lively cultural scene here. Art lovers will enjoy the unconventional **Plains Art Museum** (✉ *704 1st Ave. N* ☎ *701/551–6100* ⊕ *www.plainsart.org*) and the interactive and mural art spread across the city. Catch a live show at the **Fargo Theatre** (✉ *314 Broadway N* ☎ *701/239–8385* ⊕ *www.fargotheatre.org*), then head over to **Unglued** (✉ *1702 1st Ave.* ☎ *701/205–1597* ⊕ *www.ungluedmarket.com*), a craft market with 300 local artists.

Eat & Drink: Start with fried pickles at **Toasted Frog** (✉ *305 Broadway N* ☎ *701/478–7888* ⊕ *www.toastedfrog.com*), then enjoy bacon-wrapped bison meat loaf at **Mezzaluna** (✉ *309 Roberts St. N* ☎ *701/364–9479* ⊕ *www.dinemezzaluna.com*) in downtown Fargo.

Stay: The **Hotel Donaldson** (✉ *101 Broadway N* ☎ *701/478–1000* ⊕ *www.hoteldonaldson.com*) is definitely the most unique place to stay, as the rooms are designed around the work of regional artists and the hotel includes art galleries and hosts literary, artistic, and musical performances.

Breakfast: Jump-start your day at the **Twenty Below Coffee Co.** (✉ *14 Roberts St. N* ☎ *701/566–0977* ⊕ *www.20below.coffee*) in downtown Fargo, where you can get poached eggs, homemade bread, and killer coffee.

Day 7: Fargo, ND, to Sioux Falls, SD

245 miles (3 hours, 40 minutes without traffic and stops)

Today is an easy drive along I–29 so you'll have plenty of time to explore Sioux Falls when you arrive.

ALONG THE WAY

Detour: Explore **Fort Abercrombie** (✉ *935 Broadway N* ☎ *701/553–8513* ⊕ *www.history.nd.gov*), the first permanent U.S. military fort that was once known as "the Gateway to the Dakotas."

SIOUX FALLS

Do: Summer is the best time to catch free concerts and festivals in South Dakota's largest city, but public art installations, including the Sculpture Walk and Arc of Dreams, can be enjoyed year-round. On the first Friday of each month in summer (known as First Fridays), downtown streets come alive with music, discounts, and drink specials at restaurants, bars, and shops. You can also explore **Falls Park** (✉ *131 E. Falls Park Dr.* ☎ *605/367–7430* ⊕ *www.siouxfalls.gov*), where the Big Sioux River runs through a series of rock faces; don't miss the observation tower and the ruins of an old mill.

Eat & Drink: Named after the shish kebab–like grilled meat that is popular across southeastern South Dakota, **Urban Chislic** (✉ *431 W. 85th St.* ☎ *605/275–6328* ⊕ *www.urbanchislic.com*) is a fun, casual restaurant and bar. They specialize in chislic, but also have a full menu of burgers, sandwiches, and fun appetizers. For a sweet treat, head to **CH Patisserie**

(✉ *309 S. Phillips Ave.* ☎ *605/275–0090* ⊕ *www.chpastries.com*), owned by world-champion pastry chef Chris Hanmer.

Stay: Housed within a restored bank from 1918, **Hotel on Phillips** (✉ *100 N. Phillips Ave.* ☎ *605/274–7445* ⊕ *www.hotelonphillips.com*) is Sioux Falls' first boutique hotel; it combines classic charm with modern and elegant guest rooms.

Breakfast: At the **Phillips Avenue Diner** (✉ *121 S. Phillips Ave.* ☎ *605/335–4977* ⊕ *www.phillipsavenuediner.com*), you can enjoy classic breakfast dishes in a retro diner.

Native American Homelands of the Great Plains

Written by Shoshi Parks

Crisscrossed by rivers and rich with bison and waterfowl, the American prairie was once, and still remains, a place of essential Indigenous heritage and culture. Even before the Native nations of the Southeast were removed from their homelands en masse to Oklahoma along the Trail of Tears, the Pawnee, Osage, Comanche, Omaha, Ponca, Sac, Fox, and more called this land home. Although the people of the Plains fought hard against the westward expansion of the United States, one by one they succumbed to the brutal, genocidal tactics brandished by the U.S. Army and land-seeking settlers. But while the region's Indigenous people have been forced into reservations and faced the attempted destruction of their language, culture, and heritage, dozens of tribes remain, from Oklahoma and Kansas to Missouri and Nebraska. This road trip is a look at the heart of Indian Country: what was, what is, and what could have been.

At a Glance

Start: Oklahoma City, OK

End: Omaha, NE

Miles Traveled: 1,374 miles

Suggested Duration: 9 days

States Visited: Kansas, Missouri, Nebraska, Oklahoma

Key Sights: First Americans Museum; The Five Civilized Tribes Museum; Genoa Indian Industrial School Museum; Osage Nation Museum

Best Time to Go: This trip can be taken at any time of the year, but to get the most out of the region's wild, open spaces, travel between April and November.

Day 1: Oklahoma City, OK, to Sallisaw, OK

160 miles (2 hours, 30 minutes without traffic and stops)

After landing at Will Rogers Airport, you'll drive east today through the heart of Indian Country via I-40. Set the tone for your trip with a stop at the **First Americans Museum** (✉ *659 American Indian Blvd.* ☎ *405/ 594–2100* ⊕ *www.famok. org*) before leaving town. The architecturally stunning gallery shares the heritage, culture, and artwork of the 39 Native American nations in modern-day Oklahoma.

ALONG THE WAY

Town: Just outside OKC, stop by the **Citizen Potawatomi Nation Cultural Heritage Center** (✉ *1899 S. Gordon Cooper Dr.* ☎ *405/878–5830* ⊕ *www.potawatomi-heritage.com*) in Shawnee, which tells the story of the Potawatomi. The tribe was forced out of the Great Lakes region by the Indian Removal Act, first to Kansas and then on to Oklahoma, where they established their new nation in the 1870s.

Eat & Drink: Fill up on Nishnawbe fry bread tacos stuffed with meat, beans, and plenty of spice at **Firelake Frybread Taco** in Shawnee (✉ *1568 S. Gordon Cooper Dr.* ☎ *405/273–0108* ⊕ *www. facebook.com/frybreadtaco*).

Roadside Attraction: In Okemah, the birthplace of legendary folk musician Woody Guthrie, you'll find what's left of his boyhood home, the London House, and a mural to his legacy. His anthem "This Land Is Your Land" is just one example of how Indigenous people have been erased from the narrative of who belongs in America.

Nature: Six miles south of Vian, alligator snapping turtles, bald eagles, and waterfowl gather at the convergence of the Arkansas and Canadian Rivers in the **Sequoyah National Wildlife Refuge** (✉ *107993 S. 4520 Rd.* ☎ *918/773–5251* ⊕ *www.fws.gov*). Ancient Native American campsites found within the sanctuary date back almost 1,000 years.

SALLISAW

Do: Once part of the Cherokee Nation, Sallisaw today maintains a monument to the creator of the tribe's written language, Sequoyah. Visit his one-room cabin, a National Literary Landmark, built in 1829 and now called **Sequoyah's Cabin Museum** (✉ *470288 Rte. 101* ☎ *918/775–2413* ⊕ *www.visitcherokeenation.com*). Southeast of town on the Arkansas River, you'll find **Spiro Mounds** (✉ *18154 N. 1st St.* ☎ *918/962–2062* ⊕ *www.okhistory. org*), the remains of an ancient settlement that dates back to AD 800.

Eat & Drink: Head just south of town for some serious barbecue with an over 55-year pedigree at **Wildhorse Mountain BBQ** (✉ *110895 S. 4612 Loop* ☎ *918/775–9960* ⊕ *www.facebook. com/wildhorsemountainbbq*).

Stay: Sallisaw is light on lodging and what's there isn't great. Either get a cheap room at the **Quality Inn** (✉ *710 S. Kerr Blvd.* ☎ *918/774–0400* ⊕ *www.*

Native American Homelands of the Great Plains

choicehotels.com) or try the even more affordable, slightly nicer **Walnut Inn** (✉ *824 S. Paw Paw Rd.* ☎ *918/427–6600*), 15 miles away in Roland.

Breakfast: Stop by **Ruger's Grill** (✉ *118 E. Cherokee Ave.* ☎ *918/571–0391*) where classic breakfast favorites are served hot and fast every morning starting at 7 am.

Day 2: Sallisaw, OK, to Tahlequah, OK

76 miles (1 hour, 30 minutes without traffic and stops)

Head back west on I–40, then north on Route 351, to pass through the Muscogee (Creek) Nation before continuing on to the capital of the Cherokee Nation, Tahlequah.

ALONG THE WAY

Town: When the Five Civilized Tribes (the Cherokee, Chickasaw, Choctaw, Muscogee [Creek], and Seminole) were forced from their eastern homeland in the 1830s, the Muscogee (Creek) Nation settled here around modern-day Muskogee. The **Five Civilized Tribes Museum** (✉ *1101 Honor Heights Dr.* ☎ *918/683–1701* ⊕ *www.fivetribes.org*), in the original Indian Agency building from that era, tells the story of their history and displays the work of modern Native artists.

Eat & Drink: Nibble on sandwiches, salads, and cinnamon rolls inside the 100-year-old downtown Muskogee home that now holds the **Harmony House Lunch & Bakery** (✉ *208 S. 7th St.* ☎ *918/687–8653* ⊕ *www.harmonyhouse4lunch. com*).

Detour: Just 10 miles northeast of Muskogee, the Cherokee Nation operates the **Fort Gibson Historic Site** (✉ *907 N. Garrison Ave.* ☎ *918/478–4088* ⊕ *www.okhistory. org*). In the mid-19th century, the log fort served a prominent role in the forced

Essential Listening

Empire of the Summer Moon by S. C. Gwynne is a sweeping historical account of the 40-year struggle of the Comanche Nation to maintain control of their Oklahoma territory in the 19th century.

relocation of Native tribes and the battle for the West.

TAHLEQUAH

Do: Here in the capital of the Cherokee Nation, there are several museums dedicated to the heritage and practices of the tribe, including the **Cherokee National Prison Museum** (✉ *124 E. Choctaw St.* ☎ *918/207–3640* ⊕ *www.visitcherokeenation.com*), and the **Cherokee National Supreme Court Museum** (✉ *122 E. Keetoowah St.* ☎ *918/207–3508* ⊕ *www. visitcherokeenation.com*).

Eat & Drink: Indulge in catfish étouffée, sausage gumbo, and po' boys at **Linney Breaux's Cajun Eatery** (✉ *1095 E. 4th St.* ☎ *918/708–9461* ⊕ *www. linneybreauxs.com*). After dinner stop by **Dewain's Place** (✉ *303 S. Water Ave.* ☎ *918/931–1577* ⊕ *www.facebook. com/DewainsofTahlequah*), where the cocktails are strong and there's karaoke, live music, and plenty of games to keep you entertained.

Stay: In Tahlequah, chain hotels are the only option. Try the **Best Western NSU Inn** (✉ *101 Reasor St.* ☎ *918/431–0600* ⊕ *www.bestwestern.com*) or splurge on one of the priciest joints in town, the **Holiday Inn Express and Suites** (✉ *2142 Mahaney Ave.* ☎ *918/506–4545* ⊕ *www.ihg.com*).

Breakfast: Wake up with coffee and waffles at **Lift Coffee Bar** (✉ *309 N.*

In Oklahoma City, the First Americans Museum is a great place to start your trip and learn about the region's Native American nations.

Muskogee Ave. ☎ *918/316–7961* ⊕ *www.liftcoffeebar.net*).

Day 3: Tahlequah, OK, to Tulsa, OK

66 miles (1 hour, 15 minutes without traffic and stops)

Today's drive takes you through Sequoyah State Park, over the waters of Fort Gibson Lake, and on to Tulsa. Once known as the "oil capital of the world," Tulsa has more art deco architecture than almost anywhere else in the country. In the mid-19th century, it was at the crossroads of territory granted to three tribes removed from their eastern lands: the Muscogee (Creek), Cherokee, and Osage.

ALONG THE WAY

Nature: At **Sequoyah State Park** (✉ *17131 Park 10, Hulbert* ☎ *918/772–2545* ⊕ *www.travelok.com*), named for the great Cherokee chief, you can cruise Fort Gibson Lake in a paddle boat, play a round of golf, or book a trail ride at the Sequoyah Riding Stables.

TULSA

Do: In Tulsa, stop by **Greenwood Rising** (✉⊕ *23 N. Greenwood Ave.* ☎ *539/867–3173* ⊕ *www.greenwoodrising.org*), a state-of-the-art history center that memorializes the victims of the 1921 Tulsa Race Massacre and educates on the history of Tulsa's Black Wall Street. At **Gathering Place** (✉ *2650 S. John Williams Way E* ☎ *918/779–1000* ⊕ *www.gatheringplace.org*), arguably one of the best city parks in the United States, you can enjoy a variety of delightful trails, art installations, and playgrounds for visitors of all ages. As you travel through the city, keep an eye out for remnants of the golden age of Route 66 (like the 21-foot-tall space cowboy Buck Atom), especially along 11th Street.

Eat & Drink: Design your own buffet (perhaps with Nashville hot chicken, Jewish babka, pastrami reuben, and other superb options from pop-up chefs) at **Mother Road Market** (✉ *1124 S. Lewis*

Ave. ☎ *918/984–9009* ⊕ *www.mother-roadmarket.com*) or try the best Vietnamese in town at the beloved **Lone Wolf Banh Mi** (✉ *203 E. Archer St.* ☎ *918/728–7778* ⊕ *www.lonewolftulsa.com*). Afterward, sip tiki cocktails in a cushy booth at the classy-cool **Saturn Room** (✉ *209 N. Boulder Ave.* ☎ *918/794–9422* ⊕ *www.saturnroom.com*) or, for a more laid-back vibe, head to **Fassler Hall's** (✉ *304 S. Elgin Ave.* ☎ *918/576–7898* ⊕ *www.fasslerhall.com*) biergarten for a pint and a plate of mind-blowing duck-fat fries with gouda.

Stay: Spend the night in the chic hotel **The Mayo** (✉ *115 W. 5th St.* ☎ *918/582–6296* ⊕ *www.themayohotel.com*), which also has a popular roof-deck bar. On old Route 66, try **The Campbell Hotel** (✉ *2636 E. 11th St.* ☎ *855/744–5500* ⊕ *www.thecampbellhotel.com*).

Breakfast: Grab breakfast in the modern brick-walled diner **Chimera** (✉ *212 N. Main St.* ☎ *918/779–4303* ⊕ *www.chimeratulsa.com*), where the breakfast tacos are served all day long, or check out **Cirque Coffee** (✉ *1317 E. 6th St.* ☎ *918/933–4489* ⊕ *www.cirquecoffee.com*), a roaster with some of the best lattes and cold brews in town.

Day 4: Tulsa, OK, to Kansas City, KS

275 miles (4 hours, 40 minutes without traffic and stops)

Today's drive is the longest of your trip. Follow U.S. 75 north out of Tulsa, skirting the eastern edge of the Osage Nation. Break for bison at the Woolaroc Museum and Wildlife Preserve then continue north on Route 123 across the Kansas border and through the prairies to Kansas City.

ALONG THE WAY
Nature: At the **Woolaroc Museum and Wildlife Preserve** (✉ *1925 Woolaroc Ranch Rd.* ☎ *918/336–0307* ⊕ *www.woolaroc.org*) in Bartlesville, buffalo roam a

Essential Listening

Mary Glickman's *An Undisturbed Peace* is an unflinching novel about the devastation wrought by the Indian Removal Act and the journey along the Trail of Tears.

3,700-acre wildlife preserve just as they did before their near-eradication thanks to the westward expansion of America. A museum on the property houses Native American art and artifacts, along with other collections that pay tribute to the West.

Detour: About 20 miles northwest of Barnsdall, veer off course for a visit to the **Osage Nation Museum** (✉ *819 Grandview Ave.* ☎ *918/287–5441* ⊕ *www.osageculture.com*) in Pawhuska. In addition to featuring beautiful and fascinating art and artifacts, the museum is an active cultural and educational center for the tribe.

Town: See Laura Ingalls Wilder's famous books brought to life at the **Little House on the Prairie Museum** (✉ *2507 County Rd. 3000* ☎ *620/289–4238* ⊕ *www.lhopmuseum.com*) on the southern edge of Independence, Kansas.

Eat & Drink: Feast on fajita nachos and enchiladas rancheras at **El Pueblitos Mexican Restaurant** (✉ *1721 N. Penn Ave.* ☎ *620/331–5860*) in Independence.

KANSAS CITY
Do: In one of the largest cities in the Midwest, you'll find only a few remnants of Native people here. South of the city's center is the **Shawnee Indian Mission State Historic Park** (✉ *3403 W. 53rd St.* ☎ *913/262–0867* ⊕ *www.kshs.org*), what remains of a short-lived Native American residential school that forcibly re-educated children of the Shawnee, Delaware, and other Native nations in the

mid-1800s. In Riverview near downtown, visit the Huron Indian Cemetery, all that remains of the territory granted to the Wyandotte Nation in the 1840s.

Eat & Drink: Kansas City loves its barbecue. Do like the locals do and head to one of the city's best. Try **Joe's Kansas City Barbeque** (✉ *3002 W. 47th Ave.* ☎ *913/722–3366* ⊕ *www.joeskc. com*) or the classic **Gates BBQ** (✉ *1325 Emanuel Cleaver II Blvd.* ☎ *816/531– 7522* ⊕ *www.gatesbbq.com*). Wash down dinner with live music and a drink at **Red Eye** (✉ *6102 State Ave.* ☎ *913/334– 6700* ⊕ *www.red-eye-page.io*) or funeral home turned dive bar **Fat Matt's Vortex** (✉ *411 N. 6th St.* ☎ *913/296–7142*).

Stay: After a long day of driving, get a good night's rest at the boutique **Crossroads Hotel** (✉ *2101 Central St.* ☎ *816/897–8100* ⊕ *www.cross- roadshotelkc.com*) or the Gothic revival **Hotel Kansas City** (✉ *1228 Baltimore Ave.* ☎ *816/685–1228* ⊕ *www.hotelkc. com*), a former private social club for hobnobbing with presidents.

Breakfast: Wake up to salmon toast and Spanish tortillas at the **Happy Gillis Cafe & Hangout** (✉ *549 Gillis St.* ☎ *816/471– 3663* ⊕ *www.happygillis.com*).

Day 5: Kansas City, KS, to Nebraska City, NE

160 miles (2 hours, 45 minutes without traffic and stops)

Take I–29 out of Kansas City to U.S. 273, then head north on Highway 59 through St. Joseph, before getting back on I–29 to Nebraska City. Most of the drive travels the eastern bank of the Missouri River through the eponymous state. Before hitting Nebraska City, you'll briefly dip in and out of Iowa's southwest corner.

ALONG THE WAY

Photo Op: Make a pit stop at **O'Malley's Pub** (✉ *540 Welt St.* ☎ *816/640–5235* ⊕ *www. westonirish.com*) in Weston, Missouri's oldest bar, which is hidden underground within a moodily lit limestone brewery.

Nature: Walk the 1-mile Gosling Lake Trail loop in **Lewis and Clark State Park** (✉ *801 Lakecrest Blvd.* ☎ *816/579–5564* ⊕ *www. mostateparks.com*) on the Missouri River. The famed explorers passed through in 1804, some of the first white Americans to travel through the Native nations of the West.

Detour: It's less than a 10-minute detour from I–29 north of Weston to Atchison, home of the **Amelia Earhart Birthplace Museum** (✉ *223 N. Terrace St.* ☎ *913/367– 4217* ⊕ *www.ameliaearhartmuseum. org*) and the Amelia Earhart Earthworks, where the aviator's face is etched into a hillside overlooking Warnick Lake.

Town: In St. Joseph, Missouri, you'll find two memorials to things long gone: the **Jesse James Home Museum** (✉ *1201 S. 12th St.* ⊕ *www.ponyexpressjessejames. com*), where the outlaw was famously gunned down by Robert Ford in 1882, and the **Pony Express National Historic Trail and Museum** (✉ *914 Penn St.* ☎ *816/279– 5059* ⊕ *www.ponyexpress.org*), which is dedicated to the short-lived mail route that once connected the East to the West in the late 1850s and early 1860s.

Eat & Drink: In St. Joseph, dine at **Belle Epoque** (✉ *1141 Frederick Ave.* ☎ *816/301– 1418* ⊕ *www.facebook.com/thecafe- belleepoque*), a sweet little café with European vibes.

Roadside Attraction: The Presbyterian **Iowa and Sac & Fox Mission** (✉ *1737 Elgin Rd.* ☎ *785/442–3251* ⊕ *www.kshs.org*) in Highland served as a school for the tribe's children until they were moved off the land in the 1860s.

NEBRASKA CITY

Do: The **Arbor Day Farm** (✉ 2611 Arbor Ave. ☎ 402/873–8717 ⊕ www.arborday-farm.org) combines a state historical park, amusement park, and plenty of opportunities to commune with nature in the birthplace of America's tree-planting holiday. At the **Kregel Windmill Factory Museum** (✉ 1416 Central Ave. ☎ 402/873–1078 ⊕ www.kregelwindmillfactorymuse-um.org), learn about the forgotten minuti-ae of early-20th-century technology.

Eat & Drink: Enjoy barbecue (made right on the 260-acre farm) and apple-ci-der slushies at **Porter's at Arbor Day Farm** (✉ 2611 Arbor Ave. ☎ 402/873–8777 ⊕ www.arbordayfarm.org).

Stay: Spend the night in a Victorian home surrounded by more than 6 acres of pine trees at the **Whispering Pines Bed and Breakfast** (✉ 2018 6th Ave. ☎ 402/205–7003 ⊕ www.bbwhisperingpines.com) or in the attractive **Lied Lodge** (✉ 2700 Sylvan Rd. ☎ 402/873–8733 ⊕ www.arbordayfarm.org), a relaxing hotel evoca-tive of its natural surroundings.

Breakfast: Omelets, skillets, and biscuits and gravy await at the **Down-towner Casual Cafe** (✉ 715 1st Cor-so ☎ 402/713–5424 ⊕ www.facebook.com/TheDowntownerCasualCafe).

Day 6: Nebraska City, NE, to Kearney, NE

180 miles (2 hours, 45 minutes without traffic and stops)

Today's drive is a mostly straight shot west across the plains on I–80 with a stop in the hometown of the University of Nebraska–Lincoln.

ALONG THE WAY

Town: In Lincoln, visit the **Pioneers Park Nature Center** (✉ 3201 S. Codding-ton ☎ 402/441–7895 ⊕ www.lincoln.ne.gov) where the native beasts of the prairie, buffalo and elk, roam on more than 600 acres. The **International Quilt Museum** (✉ 1523 N. 33rd St. ☎ 402/472–6549 ⊕ www.internationalquiltmuseum.org) on the university campus has the world's largest collection of quilts, includ-ing those created by Indigenous quilters from around the United States.

Eat & Drink: In Lincoln, enjoy a burger at **Honest Abe's Burgers and Freedom** (✉ 126 N. 14th St. ☎ 402/261–4904 ⊕ www.grounduprestaurants.com) or grab a slice and a pint at **Yia Yia's Pizza and Beer** (✉ 1423 O St. ☎ 402/477–9166 ⊕ www.yiayiapizzandbeer.com).

KEARNEY

Do: The multimedia exhibit at the imposing **Great Platte River Road Arch-way** (✉ 3060 E. 1st St. ☎ 308/237–1000 ⊕ www.archway.org) tracks how white Americans expanded westward across the plains. At the **Fort Kearny State Historical Park** (✉ 1020 V Rd. ☎ 308/865–5305 ⊕ www.nps.gov), one of the stops on the Oregon Trail, you can learn more about the pioneers, Pony Express riders, gold prospectors, and Pawnee scouts who spent time at the site.

Eat & Drink: Find tasty bar-and-grill fare at **Cunningham's Journal** (✉ 610 Talmadge St. ☎ 308/237–5122 ⊕ www.cunning-hams–journal.com) or steak and seafood at upscale **Coppermill Steakhouse** (✉ 421 Talmadge St. ☎ 308/455–4580 ⊕ www.coppermillsteakhouse-kearney.com). After dinner pop into **Gillies** (✉ 1822 Central Ave. ☎ 308/236–9393 ⊕ www.facebook.com/gillieslive), a dive with cheap drinks and an outdoor patio.

Stay: The regional chain **New Vic-torian Inn & Suites** (✉ 903 2nd Ave. South ☎ 308/237–5858 ⊕ www.newvic-torianinn.com) offers cleanliness and comfort for a great value.

Breakfast: Start the day with a hearty homestyle breakfast at the **Breakfast Cart** (✉ 2524 1st Ave. ☎ 308/238–4210 ⊕ www.thebreakfastcart.com).

Day 7: Kearney, NE, to Niobrara, NE

209 miles (3 hours, 45 minutes without traffic and stops)

Head east along the Platte River, the banks of which attract hundreds of thousands of sandhill cranes each year. Past Grand Island, you'll travel north on U.S. 281 then stagger-step your way east and north to Royal then on to Niobrara and the beautiful Niobrara River.

ALONG THE WAY

Town: Wood River's **Crane Trust** (✉ *9325 S. Alda Rd.* ☎ *308/382–1820* ⊕ *www.cranetrust.org*) is dedicated to the conservation of the majestic sandhill crane, which migrates through the region every spring. Even if you're visiting in a different season, the Crane Trust's nature center is worth a visit.

Eat & Drink: In Grand Island, stop in at the cozy **Farmer's Daughters Cafe** (✉ *105 N. Walnut St.* ☎ *308/382–9794*) for coffee and a "brownbox" lunch.

Roadside Attraction: Encounter 12-million-year-old wildlife at the **Ashfall Fossil Beds State Historic Park** (✉ *86930 517th Ave.* ☎ *402/893–2000* ⊕ *www.ashfall.unl. edu*) in Royal where paleontologists are still at work uncovering the fossils left by a deadly volcanic ash fall.

NIOBRARA

Do: Native to the Niobrara River Valley region, the **Ponca Tribe** (✉ *2548 Park Ave.* ☎ *402/857–3519* ⊕ *www.poncatribe-ne.org*) operates a museum and educational trail in Niobrara. If you're traveling in August, don't miss their annual powwow, an extravaganza of dance and Native American heritage. While in Niobrara, have an adventure on its namesake river, where you can rent a canoe, tube, or kayak on your own or with a paddle guide.

Eat & Drink: Get a burger, cheese curds, and a stiff drink at the **Sportsmen's Bar** (✉ *25411 Park Ave.* ☎ *402/857–3340*) or a patty melt and chicken-fried steak at the sweetly cozy **Country Cafe** (✉ *89141 Rte. 14* ☎ *402/857–3544* ⊕ *www.eatcountrycafe.com*).

Stay: Stay the night at the **Whitetail River Lodge** (✉ *89140 Rte. 14* ☎ *402/857–3564* ⊕ *www.whitetailriverlodge.com*), an Amish-built log cabin bed-and-breakfast. If you're visiting between May and October, snagging a campsite or cabin at Niobrara State Park is well worth the effort.

Breakfast: Just south of Niobrara in Verdigre, dig into apricot "snails" and Czech pastries like cherry kolaches at **Verdigre Bakery** (✉ *405 S. Main St.* ☎ *402/668–2233* ⊕ *www.facebook.com/verdigrebakery*), family-run for over 15 years.

Day 8: Niobrara, NE, to Seward, NE

170 miles (3 hours without traffic and stops)

Travel south to Norfolk, the hometown of legendary comedian and *Tonight Show* host Johnny Carson, then on to Genoa, where a former residential school for re-educating Native American children has been preserved as a museum. Continue on to Seward via U.S. 81 or U.S. 34.

ALONG THE WAY

Town: In Norfolk, there's the **Norfolk Arts Center** (✉ *305 N. 5th St.* ☎ *402/371–7199* ⊕ *www.norfolkartscenter.org*) with an outdoor sculpture garden. While in Johnny Carson's childhood hometown, get a look at **where he grew up** (✉ *306 South 13th Street*).

Eat & Drink: While in Norfolk, get a sandwich, salad, or flatbread pizza at local favorite **Black Cow Fat Pig** (✉ *702 W.*

Norfolk Ave. ☎ 402/370–2172 ⊕ www. blackcowfatpigpubandsteak.com).

Roadside Attraction: In the 19th and early 20th centuries, the U.S. government worked to eradicate Native people by forcing their children to attend brutal boarding schools. Opened in 1884, the **Genoa Indian Industrial School** (✉ 209 E. Webster Ave. ⊕ www.genoaindianschool-museum.org) now operates as a museum dedicated to shedding light on this shameful chapter of American history.

Photo Op: At the end of today's road waits the largest time capsule in the world, a 45-ton vault buried in Seward in 1975.

SEWARD

Do: Seward has a historic downtown core lined with boutiques, galleries, and antiques shops. If you're visiting between May and September, stop in the **Inner Maker Art Village** (✉ 1693 224th Rd. ☎ 402/540–6929 ⊕ www.innermaker. com), which features jewelry and art crafted by members of local tribes and an assortment of books on Native American history.

Eat & Drink: Get dinner at **Rue 6** (✉ 123 S. 6th St. ☎ 402/646–9150), a gastropub with craft cocktails, flatbread pizzas, and skillet mac and cheese, or find corned beef and burgers at the bowling alley/karaoke bar **Sparetime Lounge & Grill** (✉ 123 S. 4th St. ☎ 402/643–3898). Thursday through Saturday, the **Bottle Rocket Brewery** (✉ 230 S. 5th St. ☎ 402/646–5847 ⊕ www.bottlerocketbrewing.com) pulls draughts until well after dark.

Stay: Spend the night in **Liberty House** (✉ 441 N. 5th St. ☎ 402/643–2555 ⊕ www.libertybbantiques.com), a quaint B&B, or get a room at the convenient **Cobblestone Hotel & Suites** (✉ 2575 Progressive Rd. ☎ 402/646–1004 ⊕ www.staycobblestone.com).

Breakfast: Fill up on breakfast bagel sandwiches and coffee at **Bagels & Joe** (✉ 522

Seward St. ☎ 531/727–2532 ⊕ www. bagelsandjoe.com).

Day 9: Seward, NE, to Omaha, NE

78 miles (1 hour, 15 minutes without traffic and stops)

Pass once more through Lincoln, then hop on I–80 headed for your final destination, Omaha (with a worthwhile last stop at the Wildlife Safari Park just off the interstate on Route 66). When it's time to catch your flight, you'll find the airport, OMA, on the city's northeast edge, along with major rental car companies.

ALONG THE WAY

Nature: Drive a 4-mile track through **Ashland's Wildlife Safari Park** (✉ 16406 292nd St. ☎ 402/944–9453 ⊕ www.wildlifesa-faripark.com), where North American bison, wolves, pelicans, and more roam freely.

Eat & Drink: Stop for breakfast or lunch (mostly sandwiches and waffles)—or splurge on an ice-cream sundae or cappuccino—at **Cheri O's** in Ashland (✉ 1404 Silver St. ☎ 402/944–4499 ⊕ www. cherioscoffee.com).

Photo Op: The beautifully designed **Holy Family Shrine** (✉ 23132 Pflug Rd. ☎ 402/332–4565 ⊕ www.holyfami-lyshrine.com) in Gretna is an Instagram-worthy stop.

OMAHA

Do: In this city of almost half a million, there's plenty to do, including visits to the **Durham** (✉ *801 S. 10th St.* ☎ *402/444–5071* ⊕ *www.durhammuseum.org*), a history museum in a repurposed art deco train station, and the **Joslyn Art Museum** (✉ *2200 Dodge St.* ☎ *402/342–3300* ⊕ *www.joslyn.org*). At the headquarters of the **Lewis and Clark Trail** (✉ *601 Riverfront Dr.* ☎ *402/661–1804* ⊕ *www.nps.gov/lecl*), learn more about the Native people with whom the Corps of Discovery communed, including the Omaha on whose homeland the city now sits.

Eat & Drink: Dine on comfort food made from local, seasonal ingredients at **Kitchen Table** (✉ *1415 Farnam St.* ☎ *402/933–2810* ⊕ *www.kitchentableomaha.com*), then toast to your last night at **Kaitei** (✉ *6109 1/3 Maple St.*), a speakeasy downstairs from a ramen shop in Benson, or the tiki bar **Laka Lono Rum Club** (✉ *1204 Howard St.* ☎ *402/786–8640*) in the Old Market District.

Stay: Rest up at one of Omaha's stylish downtown hotels, like the **Magnolia** (✉ *1615 Howard St.* ☎ *402/341–2500* ⊕ *www.magnoliahotels.com*).

Breakfast: Soak up your last night's celebration with banana bread French toast and a kimchi omelet at the hip **Saddle Creek Breakfast Club** (✉ *8734 Pacific St.* ☎ *402/932–5970* ⊕ *www.facebook.com/SCBCOmaha*).

The Best of the Ozarks

Written by Kristy Alpert

Often shadowed by the midwestern metropolises that surround it, the Ozark Mountains were once defined by their isolation; today that's one of the region's greatest assets. The hills of the Ozarks roll up from the beds of sparkling rivers and peak as the grand oak and hickory trees seem to sway on the ledge of limestone bluffs. The region winds its way through the southern portions of Missouri and into northern Arkansas and eastern Oklahoma, just barely touching the edge of southeastern Kansas. The air is as pure as the hearts of the people in the region, where mom-and-pop shops thrive alongside boutique hotels, chef-driven restaurants, and world-renowned art museums. A road trip through the region offers the chance to uncover the unique folklore, natural beauty, and undiscovered gems of the Ozarks.

At a Glance

Start: Little Rock, AR

End: Little Rock, AR

Miles Traveled: 1,388 miles

Suggested Duration: 9 days

States Visited: Arkansas, Kansas, Missouri, Oklahoma

Key Sights: Crystal Bridges Museum of National Art; Elephant Rocks State Park; Hot Springs National Park; the Lake of the Ozarks; Thorncrown Chapel

Best Time to Go: Travel in spring or autumn to see the Ozark foliage in all its true glory.

Day 1: Little Rock, AR, to Bentonville, AR

215 miles (3 hours, 10 minutes without traffic and stops)

The Clinton National Airport in Little Rock is the area's biggest airport, and where you'll be able to pick up a rental car to start your trip. Although the backroads between Little Rock and Bentonville pass through the heart of the Ozark National Forest, the highway route on I–40 and I–49 gets you there in less time and

The Best of
the Ozarks

takes you through Arkansas's little-known wine country.

ALONG THE WAY

Town: Take the exit on Route 64 to venture deep into the Arkansas Wine Trail in Altus, Arkansas. The region reminded immigrants Jacob Post and Johann Wiederkehr so much of their home German and Swiss wine regions that they settled in and began growing grapes in the late 1880s. Their wineries are still there today, along with about a dozen other wineries. A drive through the region is stunning, but a short lunch break or tasting makes this stop truly memorable.

Eat & Drink: Just 4 miles off the road in the heart of the Arkansas Wine Trail in Altus, you'll find winemaker and master sommelier Audrey House's award-winning **Chateau Aux Arc Vineyards and Winery** (⊠ 8045 Rte. 186 ☎ 479/468–4400 ⊕ www.chateau-auxarc.com). In the tasting room, visitors can sample complex blends, dry reds, and House's signature Cynthiana wines (which she pioneered to become the state grape of Arkansas).

BENTONVILLE

Do: Sam Walton put Bentonville on the map when he opened **Walton's 5&10** (⊠ 105 N. Main St. ☎ 479/277–8493 ⊕ www.walmartmuseum.com) in 1951, which would later inspire the world's first Walmart. The five-and-dime store is still there, attached to an authentic soda fountain that serves arguably the best butter pecan ice cream around. More recently, another member of the Walton family, Alice Walton, helped to open the architecturally stunning **Crystal Bridges Museum of American Art** (⊠ 600 Museum Way ☎ 479/418–5700 ⊕ www.

crystalbridges.org) and the family-friendly **Scott Family Amazeum** (✉ *1009 Museum Way* ☎ *479/696–9280* ⊕ *www.amazeum. org*).

Eat & Drink: Inside the **Hive at the 21c Museum Hotel** (✉ *200 N.E. A St.* ☎ *479/286–6575* ⊕ *www.thehivebentonville.com*) is a culinary journey through farm-fresh regional cuisine with many rotating dishes that give a nod to the Indian and Hmong families that have settled in Bentonville. For an ethereal eating experience, book a table at **The Preacher's Son** (✉ *201 N.W. A St.* ☎ *479/445–6065* ⊕ *www.thepreachersson.com*) for a gluten-free meal inside a renovated church that includes a speakeasy downstairs for after-dinner drinks.

Stay: The **21c Museum Hotel Bentonville** (✉ *200 N.E. A St.* ☎ *479/286–6500* ⊕ *www.21cmuseumhotels.com*) sits just off the main town square of downtown Bentonville and would be on the list of must–see places within the city even if you're not spending the night, thanks to its rotating gallery of art.

Breakfast: The biscuits are huge and the coffee is strong at the **Buttered Biscuit** (✉ *1403 S.E. Moberly La.* ☎ *479/319–4822* ⊕ *www.thebutteredbiscuit.co*); the strawberry cheesecake pancakes are a true indulgence.

Day 2: Bentonville, AR, to Eureka Springs, AR

44 miles (1 hour, 10 minutes without traffic and stops)

Arkansas's scenic Route 12 is without a doubt one of the most stunning drives in the state. The road doesn't stop winding once you pass Rogers, but you'll pass beneath canopied trees and over sparkling rivers.

ALONG THE WAY

Town: The boutiques and antiques stores of historic downtown Rogers alone are worth a stop, but now the town's brick-lined streets lead to an award-winning craft brewery, the **Ozark Beer Co.** (✉ *109 N. Arkansas St.* ☎ *479/636–2337* ⊕ *www. ozarkbeercompany.com*), and the headquarters for locally beloved **Onyx Coffee Lab** (✉ *101 E. Walnut St.* ☎ *479/899–6750* ⊕ *www.onyxcoffeelab.com*).

Eat & Drink: A short drive from downtown Rogers will put you face-to-face with Arkansas's only working watermill. The **War Eagle Mill** (✉ *11045 War Eagle Rd.* ☎ *866/492–7324* ⊕ *www.wareaglemill.com*) is a working gristmill (buy organic grain, cereal, and flour on-site), and its restaurant serves one of the best brunches in the state (breakfast and lunch are also available). Visit the third weekend in October for the mill's celebrated arts-and-crafts fair.

Nature: War Eagle Cavern (✉ *21494 Cavern Dr.* ☎ *479/789–2909* ⊕ *www.wareaglecavern.com*) is just a 2-mile drive off the main road, where you'll find the only lakeside cavern entrance in the state. Cave tours are available and take you deep within the caverns of this historic spot.

EUREKA SPRINGS

Do: More than 60 natural springs bubble and spring from this quirky Victorian town, where a series of winding staircases guide visitors up and down the steep terrain to boutique shops, family-owned restaurants (chain stores and restaurants are frowned upon), and miles of hiking trails. An active artist enclave colors the town with an artsy vibe, but it's the underground catacombs and sinister story behind the town's largest hotel that keep intrigue alive.

Eat & Drink: A bicycle sits on top of the marquee at **Sparky's Roadhouse Café** (✉ *147 E. Van Buren* ☎ *479/253–6001* ⊕ *www.sparkysroadhouse.com*), which is the first sign of this 1950s-style diner's funky decor. Come prepared to sign a waiver if you plan to sample their Stupid Hott Burger with homemade ghost chili salsa, or simply lounge with a cold beer on the open-air patio.

Stay: Known as "The Grand Ol' Lady of the Ozarks," the 1886 **Crescent Hotel and Spa** (✉ *75 Prospect Ave.* ☎ *855/725–5720* ⊕ *www.crescent–hotel.com*) features 72 guest rooms and four luxury lodges on its stunningly landscaped perch overlooking Eureka Springs. It's also known as the most haunted hotel in America, where nightly ghost tours uncover its haunting past.

Breakfast: The **Eureka Springs Coffee House** (✉ *11 N. Main St.* ☎ *479/239–2010* ⊕ *www.eurekaspringcoffee.com*) serves freshly baked cinnamon rolls and muffins alongside a variety of specialty coffee drinks made from Onyx Coffee Lab's signature roasts.

Day 3: Eureka Springs, AR, to Branson, MO

53 miles (1 hour, 10 minutes without traffic and stops)

The top end of what Arkansans call "the Pig Trail," Route 23 is one of the state's most scenic drives, with wildflowers in the spring and autumn colors shimmering in the fall. The road connects with the fastest way to get to Branson via Route 86 east and U.S. 65 north.

ALONG THE WAY

Detour: Before leaving Eureka Springs, take a detour to the **Thorncrown Chapel** (✉ *12968 U.S. 62* ☎ *479/346–0245* ⊕ *www.thorncrown.com*). The chapel is in the opposite direction from Branson, but the short detour to see this hidden glass chapel in the woods is worth it. The 48–foot chapel is one of three glass chapels in Arkansas, all designed by E. Fay Jones. The walk is short from the parking lot at the base of

Extend Your Trip

From St. Louis: Route 66 *(Ch. 2)*; Along the Mississippi *(Ch. 2)*; Underrated Cities of the Midwest *(Ch. 6)*

the hill, but the views are spectacular inside and outside of this absolutely inspiring structure.

Town: Ridgedale, Missouri, is home to the Top of the Rock, a scenic overlook at **Big Cedar Lodge** (✉ *190 Top of the Rock Rd.* ☎ *417/335–2777* ⊕ *www.bigcedar.com*) that offers four levels of viewing balconies to gaze out upon the Ozark Mountains and Table Rock Lake. Spend an hour or two soaking in the views before continuing on toward Branson.

Eat & Drink: The Buffalo Bar at Big Cedar Lodge offers the best views from its outdoor patio, where classic pub fare, as well as wood-fired lobsters and rib-eye steaks, fill the lunch menu.

BRANSON

Do: Branson offers authentic American small-town charm like few other towns can even imagine. Pies are sweeter in Branson, shopping is friendlier, and the entertainment is as clean as the streets of its historic downtown.

Eat & Drink: Branson Landing (✉ *100 Branson Landing Blvd.* ☎ *417/239–3002* ⊕ *www.bransonlanding.com*) is where the nightlife action happens in town, but for an authentic Branson meal, head to the **Farmhouse Restaurant** (✉ *119 W. Main St.* ☎ *417/334–9701* ⊕ *www.farmhouserestaurantbranson.com*) to fill up on chicken-fried steak, fried okra, and their famous blackberry cobbler.

Stay: The Branson Hotel (✉ *214 W. Main St.* ☎ *417/544–9814* ⊕ *www.thebransonhotel.com*) features nine rooms inside a renovated 1903 historic buildings and is reserved only for adults. For a more family-friendly option, check out the lakefront condos at **Still Waters Resort** (⊠ *21 Stillwater Trail* ☎ *800/777–2320* ⊕ *www.stillwatersresort.com*), overlooking Branson's Table Rock Lake.

Breakfast: Breakfast is served all day at **Billy Gail's Café** (⊠ *5291 Rte. 265* ☎ *417/338–8883* ⊕ *www.billygailsrestaurant.com*), where their Billion Dollar Bacon is hearty enough to be an entrée itself.

Day 4: Branson, MO, to St. Louis, MO

345 miles (6 hours, 15 minutes without traffic and stops)

Stick close to the border of Missouri and Arkansas along U.S. 160 east to Route 19 north before heading up U.S. 67 north for the chance to stop and explore Grand Gulf State Park and Elephant Rocks State Park.

ALONG THE WAY

Town: Thayer, Missouri, is just 10 miles from **Grand Gulf State Park** (☎ *417/264–7600* ⊕ *www.mostateparks.com*), which is more commonly known as the "Little Grand Canyon." The gulf itself stretches for a mile between canyon walls reaching 130 feet tall, where natural bridges and collapsed caves leave much to be explored.

Eat & Drink: Cross back over the border to Mammoth Springs, Arkansas, to dine alfresco by the mighty Spring River at **Wood's Riverbend Restaurant** (⊠ *80 Main St.* ☎ *870/625–9357* ⊕ *www.facebook.com/woodsriverbendrestaurant*). Breakfast is served all day long, but their barbecued ribs will keep you satisfied all the way to St. Louis.

Roadside Attraction: Elephant Rocks State Park (⊠ *7390 and 7406 Rte. 21* ☎ *573/546–3454* ⊕ *www.mostateparks.com*) is home to giant red granite boulders that have taken the shape of elephants. Use your imagination to make out the elephant shapes or simply climb to the top of the 27-foot-tall Dumbo rock for the ultimate bragging rights.

ST. LOUIS

Do: Set along the west bank of the Mississippi River, St. Louis is home to the only **National Blues Museum** (⊠ *615 Washington Ave.* ☎ *314/925–0016* ⊕ *www.nationalbluesmuseum.org*) in the country and offers amazing photo ops from either the bottom or top of the city's famous **Gateway Arch** (⊠ *11 N. 4th St.* ☎ *314/655–1600* ⊕ *www.nps.gov/jeff*). St. Louis is naturally suited for adventures, with its **Citygarden** (⊠ *801 Market St.* ☎ *314/241–3337*), **Meramec Caverns** (⊠ *1135 Hwy. W, Sullivan* ☎ *573/468–2283* ⊕ *www.americascave.com*), and nature reserves.

Eat & Drink: It's the local wild cherry wood used to smoke the meat at **The Shaved Duck** (⊠ *2900 Virginia Ave.* ☎ *314/776–1407* ⊕ *www.theshavedduck.com*) that makes all the difference at this award-winning St. Louis barbecue joint. You won't go wrong with anything from the smoker, but make sure to leave room for their decadent sides.

Stay: Pretend you're in England for a night with a stay at **The Cheshire** (⊠ *6300 Clayton Rd.* ☎ *314/647–7300* ⊕ *www.cheshirestl.com*); this historic boutique hotel features stained-glass windows, a Brit-style pub, an outdoor pool, and rooms named after British writers.

Breakfast: Breakfast is included with your stay at The Cheshire, and typically consists of scrambled eggs, hard-boiled eggs, fresh fruit, pastries, and coffee.

Day 5: St. Louis, MO, to Osage Beach, MO

166 miles (2 hours, 50 minutes without traffic and stops)

Not only does this route along I–44 put you on Historic Route 66 for part of the trip, but you'll also pass right by Onondaga Cave State Park, a National Natural Landmark.

ALONG THE WAY

Town: Check Cuba off your list … well, at least Cuba, Missouri; this small town is loaded with charisma. Drive along Cuba's Historic Route 66 for an outdoor art gallery of sorts as you pass by the town's 14 outdoor murals depicting famous moments in history.

Eat & Drink: Shelly's Route 66 Café (✉ 402 E. Washington St. ☎ 573/885–6000) in Cuba hasn't changed much since it first opened during the historic route's heyday. This classic diner serves hearty breakfasts and daily specials for lunch.

Photo Op: The dramatic stalagmites and impressive underground ponds within **Onondaga Cave State Park** (✉ 7556 Hwy. H ☎ 573/245–6576 ⊕ www. mostateparks.com) are just as photogenic as the Vilander Bluff natural area that sits above them; although you don't need to wait for a guide to access the panoramic views of the Meramec River at the top of Vilander Bluff.

OSAGE BEACH

Do: Osage Beach is just one of the quaint towns surrounding Lake of the Ozarks, where everything revolves around the water. Speedboats, pontoons, fishing boats, and Jet Skis can all be rented at an hourly rate, and even the local spas offer floating therapies.

Eat & Drink: Enjoy excellent views and casual bites at the **Redhead Lakeside Grill and Yacht Club** (✉ 1700 Yacht Club Dr. ☎ 573/693–1525 ⊕ www.

redheadlakesidegrill.com); you can even spend the day in the lakeside pool. Or enjoy drinks and bar food at **Shorty Pants Lounge and Marina** (✉ 1680 Autumn La. ☎ 573/302–1745 ⊕ www.shortypantslounge.com).

Shop: There are more than 35 stores mapped out along the **Osage Beach Outlet Marketplace** (✉ 4540 Osage Beach Pkwy. ☎ 573/348–2065 ⊕ www. premiumoutlets.com), where shoppers can score deals on designer handbags or grab a stylish swimsuit for the lake.

Stay: Margaritaville Lake Resort Lake of the Ozarks (✉ 494 Tan Tar A Dr. ☎ 573/348–3131 ⊕ www.margaritavilleresortlakeoftheozarks.com) may be owned by the estate of Floridian Jimmy Buffett but it successfully channels its lakeside setting with a tiki hut and boathouse grill.

Breakfast: The breakfast buffet at Margaritaville Lake Resort Lake of the Ozarks features options like a tropical fruit parfait or French toast stuffed with cannoli cream, providing more than enough fuel for your day of driving.

Day 6: Osage Beach, MO, to Baxter Springs, KS

170 miles (2 hours, 45 minutes without traffic and stops)

This long stretch of highway on I–44 goes by fast and ends with a stop along Historic Route 66.

ALONG THE WAY

Eat & Drink: Set along Route 66, 1950s-style **Iggy's Diner** (✉ 2400 Grand Ave. ☎ 417/237–0212 ⊕ www.iggysdiner. com) in Carthage, Missouri, serves breakfast, lunch, and dinner, and hand-dips the ice cream for their famous floats, malts, and shakes.

Roadside Attraction: Designed by Precious Moments creator Samuel J. Butcher, the **Precious Moments Chapel** (✉ 4321 S.

Chapel Rd. ☎ 800/543–7975 ⊕ www.
preciousmomentschapel.org) in Carthage
is a stand-alone chapel devoted entirely
to the Precious Moments characters
the artist created decades ago. Sistine
Chapel–style murals line the inside
of the building, while a gift shop sells
everything from exclusive figurines to
wedding accessories.

Nature: A long viewing platform at the
Schermerhorn Park and Cave (✉ 3501 S.
Main St. ☎ 620/783–2373) lets visitors
peek inside this half-mile-long cave,
where rare species of salamander are
protected by the EPA. The park is part
of the 55 square miles that comprise
the Ozarks of Kansas, and this little slice
of the state is ripe with caves, sinking
streams, and sinkholes.

BAXTER SPRINGS

Do: The historic town of Baxter Springs
is just a few miles from the OK-KS-MO
Tri-State Marker (you can stand in three
states at one time!), where it sits along
Route 66 with preserved gas stations
and vintage service buildings. The town's
Native American and Route 66 history
are explored within the **Baxter Springs
Heritage Center & Museum** (✉ 740 East
Ave. ☎ 620/856–2385 ⊕ www.baxter-
springsmuseum.org), where visitors
can begin a self-guided drive to 12
different sites along the town's Civil War
trail, including **Fort Blair** (✉ 198 E. 6th
St. ☎ 620/856–2385 ⊕ www.baxter-
springsmuseum.org).

Eat & Drink: Weston's **Route 66 Café**
(✉ 1737 Military Ave. ☎ 620/856–4414)
offers comfort diner food with friendly
service.

Stay: Little Brick Inn (✉ 1105 Military
Ave. ☎ 417/438–1234 ⊕ www.littlebrick-
inn.com) offers suite-sized accommodations, with plenty of antiques shops and
cafés right out the front door.

Breakfast: Breakfast is where **Weston's
Café** (✉ 1737 Military Ave. ☎ 620/856–
4414) really shines: the coffee is hot, the

biscuits are drenched in gravy, and pies
are made fresh daily.

Day 7: Baxter Springs, KS, to Tenkiller State Park, OK

*58 miles (2 hours, 35 minutes without
traffic and stops)*

Continue along Route 66 as you pass
over the Kansas border into Oklahoma
toward the Blue Whale of Catoosa (one
of the kitschier roadside attractions
along the route). From there you'll begin
to weave your way back and forth over
the Arkansas River before arriving in the
state park.

ALONG THE WAY

Eat & Drink: In Claremore, **Nut House
Deli** (✉ 26677 S. Rte. 66 ☎ 918/266–
1604 ⊕ www.nuthousedeli.com) offers
made-to-order sandwiches with quirky
names (like Cave Man, stuffed with roast
beef, ham, and bacon) perfect for a quick
lunch stop.

Town: The **Blue Whale of Catoosa** (✉ 2600
Rte. 66 ☎ 918/266–2505) may sound like
a mythical creature, but in the town of
Catoosa, it's a local legend. Made from
metal and cement, the whale was built
in a pond as a surprise anniversary gift in
the 1970s but became a secret swimming hole along Route 66. Swimming
is no longer allowed, but the spot is a
popular picnic area.

TENKILLER STATE PARK

Do: There are more than 130 miles of
shoreline surrounding Lake Tenkiller at
Tenkiller State Park (✉ 448159 E. 979 Dr.,
Vian ☎ 918/489–5641 ⊕ www.travelok.
com). Along with watersports and fishing, the clear waters of the lake provide
ideal conditions for scuba diving to the
lake's sunken treasures, including an
airplane fuselage, a school bus, a helicop-
ter, and two boats.

Hot Springs National Park is home to the most celebrated thermal waters in the country.

Eat & Drink: Boats and Jet Skis can pull right up to the floating deck at **Clearwater Café** (✉ *Lake Tenkiller State Park, Vian* ☎ *918/489–5655* ⊕ *www.facebook. com/clearwater.tenkiller*) at Pine Cove Marina on Tenkiller Lake, where steaks are cooked to order and onion rings come stacked a foot high.

Stay: RV and tent campgrounds line the park grounds, but it's the state park's 38 cabins that offer the best views along the lake.

Breakfast: There are few things sweeter than **Sweet Nana's Donuts** (✉ *207 E. Schley* ☎ *918/773–5003* ⊕ *www. facebook.com/sweetnanasdonuts*), other than maybe Nana herself. This mom–and–pop bakery serves full breakfasts (bacon, eggs, breakfast burritos, hot coffee, etc.), but the specialty doughnuts, maple bacon bars, and sausage rolls are among their best sellers.

Day 8: Tenkiller State Park, OK, to Hot Springs, AR

175 miles (3 hours, 30 minutes without traffic and stops)

Follow I–40 through Oklahoma and, just before crossing the Arkansas River, veer onto U.S. 71 south into Fort Smith, Arkansas, where you'll soon be driving out of the Ozarks and into Ouachita National Forest.

ALONG THE WAY

Town: Fort Smith is the third-most-populated city in Arkansas, and this quirky town offers everything from an amusement park ride in the middle of its downtown to a museum dedicated entirely to the spot where Elvis Presley got his first buzz cut when joining the army on March 25, 1958.

Eat & Drink: Whether you're craving a grilled cheese sandwich or the steak-and-egg special, **Benson's Grill** (✉ *2515 Rogers Ave.* ☎ *479/782–8181* ⊕ *www.bensons-grill.org*) in Fort Smith is a 24-hour diner serving breakfast, lunch, and dinner. Don't leave without ordering a slice of pie or cheesecake for dessert.

HOT SPRINGS

Do: In Central Arkansas's Ouachita Mountains, Hot Springs is home to some of the most prized thermal waters in the country (143 degrees and packed full of minerals). Run the bases around one of the first MLB Spring Training fields in the United States or soak in the gangster history inside **Hot Springs National Park** (✉ *369 Central Ave.* ☎ *501/620–6715* ⊕ *www.nps.gov/hosp*) at Bathhouse Row, where many of these historic hot spring bathhouses are still operational (they were once a favorite vacation spot for legendary criminals Al Capone, Lucky Luciano, and Bugsy Siegel).

Eat & Drink: Inside a renovated bathhouse, **Superior Bathhouse Brewery** (✉ *329 Central Ave.* ☎ *501/624–2337* ⊕ *www.superiorbathhouse.com*) serves upscale pub food and craft beers brewed from the thermal waters of the national park. Former speakeasy and mobster hangout **The Ohio Club** (✉ *336 Central Ave.* ☎ *501/627–0702* ⊕ *www.theohio-club.com*) is still a hot spot for nightlife in Hot Springs.

Stay: The chic **Hotel Hale** (✉ *341 Central Ave.* ☎ *501/760–9010* ⊕ *www.hotel-hale.com*) operates inside a renovated bathhouse along Bathhouse Row, where the boutique property features nine modern guest rooms with thermal water bathtubs.

Breakfast: Kollective Coffee and Tea (✉ *110 Central Ave.* ☎ *501/701–4000* ⊕ *www.facebook.com/kollectivecoffeetea*) is one of the top third-wave coffee shops in Arkansas, serving organic and local specialties (vegan options available) alongside locally roasted coffee.

Day 9: Hot Springs, AR, to Little Rock, AR

62 miles (1 hour, 25 minutes without traffic and stops)

Keep an eye out for roadside stands selling quartz crystals as you drive along Arkansas's scenic Route 7 toward Owensville, then cross through the last stretches of the Ouachita National Forest on Route 9 toward Paron before taking the scenic route into Little Rock on Kanis Road.

ALONG THE WAY

Nature: During a fall road trip, stop in at the **Roseberry Farms Pumpkin Patch** (✉ *12223 Rte. 9* ☎ *501/722–8545* ⊕ *www.roseberry–farms.com*) for an authentic Arkansas hayride and s'mores around the fire.

LITTLE ROCK

Do: Arkansas's capital is a city of tales and trails. The tales begin with **Little Rock Central High School,** a National Historic Site (✉ *2120 W. Daisy L. Gatson Bates Dr.* ☎ *501/374–1957* ⊕ *www.nps.gov/chsc*) on the U.S. Civil Rights Trail, and the trails begin with the **Big Dam Bridge** (✉ *4000 Cook's Landing Rd.*) that connects to 14 miles of winding trails along the city's River Trail system. The trail connects Little Rock's bustling River Market District to countless breweries and restaurants, and even provides pedestrian/cyclist access to the **Clinton Presidential Center** (✉ *1200 President Clinton Ave.* ☎ *501/374–4242* ⊕ *www.clintonlibrary.gov*).

Eat & Drink: Set inside a repurposed gas station, **The Fold: Botanas & Bar** (✉ *3501 Old Cantrell Rd.* ☎ *501/916–9706* ⊕ *www.thefoldlr.com*) serves modern Ark-Mex at its finest. The decor is retro chic and the tacos are served on handmade tortillas and filled with locally sourced ingredients. Order a ground-bison burrito and a homemade lemonade for the full experience.

Stay: The Empress of Little Rock (✉ *2120 S. Louisiana St.* ☎ *501/374–7966* ⊕ *www. theempress.com*) is listed on the National Register of Historic Places for its pure representation of Victorian architecture.

Breakfast: Out in the Argenta Arts District, Saturdays are for pancakes over at **Mugs Café** (✉ *515 Main St.* ☎ *501/379–9101* ⊕ *www.mugscoffeelr.com*). During the week, the hipster coffeehouse serves breakfast starting at 7 am and locally roasted coffee all day long.

The Best of the Heartland

Written by Kristine Hansen

America's heartland—a more appropriate nickname for the oft-labeled "flyover country" since midwesterners really are the nicest people you'll ever meet—may be flush with farmland, but it's also a supremely underrated destination for the arts, dining, and nature. On this nine-day trip, you'll explore a mix of college towns and metropolises that provide the perfect balance of nightlife and small-town charm. Get ready to paddle, bike, and stroll across the great states of Wisconsin, Iowa, and Minnesota, all while finding out what makes this region so unique.

At a Glance

Start: Milwaukee, WI

End: Milwaukee, WI

Miles Traveled: 1,655 miles

Suggested Duration: 9 days

States Visited: Iowa, Minnesota, Wisconsin

Key Sights: Apostle Islands National Lakeshore; Grant Wood's American Gothic House & Center; Milwaukee Art Museum; Rock Island State Park; Voyageurs National Park

Best Time to Go: Unless you want to snowmobile or cross-country ski, it's best to stick to a season free of snow and hazardous driving conditions. Spring and fall mean fewer crowds, but even then, you may need to pack a winter jacket, so summer is your best bet.

Day 1: Milwaukee, WI, to Madison, WI

80 miles (1 hour, 20 minutes without traffic and stops)

You literally cannot get lost driving between Wisconsin's two largest cities: the only way to travel on I–94 is west (Lake Michigan is a dead end to the east). Pick up your rental car at General Mitchell International Airport, a quick 15-minute drive south of downtown Milwaukee.

ALONG THE WAY

Detour: Built by Chicagoans during the turn of the last century, Lake Geneva (population 8,000) is Wisconsin's Lake Como (there's even a nearby lake called Lake Como) with the type of grand historic estates you'd find in Newport, Rhode Island. The 26-mile path around the namesake lake might seem daunting, but you'll get a good view from The Riviera, with its red-tile roof.

Eat & Drink: Don't knock the truck stop at the **Pine Cone Travel Plaza** (✉ *685 Linmar La.* ☎ *920/699–2766* ⊕ *www.pineconetravelplazamenu.com*) in Johnson Creek. The cream puffs are nearly the size of your head and there's an actual cheese department.

Nature: Even today, Wisconsin is home to a significant portion of the country's Native American population. At

The Best of the Heartland

Aztalan State Park (✉ N6200 County Rd. Q ☎ 608/873–9695 ⊕ www.dnr.wisconsin.gov), a National Historic Landmark in Jefferson, you can view remnants and a reconstruction of a Middle Mississippian village (from between AD 1000 and 1300) on a short walk.

MADISON

Do: Wander into the century-old **state capitol building** (✉ 2 E. Main St. ☎ 608/266–0382 ⊕ www.wisconsin.gov) for a free, self-guided tour (it actually has one of the largest domes in the world). Then ogle a genuine Thai pavilion (a gift from the Thai government to the University of Wisconsin, and the only such example in the continental United States) at the 16-acre **Olbrich Botanical Gardens** (✉ 3330 Atwood Ave. ☎ 608/246–4550 ⊕ www.olbrich.org).

Eat & Drink: You're in the Dairy State for a reason, right? At Memorial Union on the University of Wisconsin campus, enjoy a scoop of ice cream at **Daily Scoop** (✉ 800 Langdon St. ☎ 608/262–5959 ⊕ www.union.wisc.edu). It's crafted on campus and paired with a view of Lake Mendota from the sprawling terrace. For dinner, **The Old Fashioned** (✉ 23 N. Pinckney St. ☎ 608/310–4545 ⊕ www.theoldfashioned.com) is a tourist hot spot, but its cheese curds and beer cheese soup don't miss; it's the perfect place to try a Wisconsin old-fashioned, too (which replaces whiskey with brandy).

Stay: Because you're only here for one night, the view is a nonnegotiable amenity. Check into **The Edgewater** (✉ 1001 Wisconsin Pl. ☎ 608/535–8200 ⊕ www.theedgewater.com), a full-service resort towering above Lake Mendota.

Deep-fried cheese curds at Statehouse are a must, as is a walk on the hotel's pier.

Breakfast: As with every college town, Madison is loaded with coffee shops. On State Street (which connects the University of Wisconsin campus with Capitol Square), you'll find **Michelangelo's Coffee House** (✉ *114 State St.* ☎ *608/251–5299* ⊕ *www.michelangeloscoffeehouse. com*), a café-style concept with a black-and-white domed awning out front.

Day 2: Madison, WI, to Iowa City, IA

175 miles (3 hours without traffic and stops)

Leaving Wisconsin and taking U.S. 151 south all the way, you'll cut through the country's highest concentration of organic farms (in Vernon County, including the town of Viroqua) and cross the glorious Mississippi River in Dubuque, Iowa.

ALONG THE WAY

Eat & Drink: Wollersheim Winery, Distillery, and Bistro (✉ *7876 Rte. 188* ☎ *608/643–6515* ⊕ *www.wollersheim.com*) in Prairie du Sac, Wisconsin, is where Hungarian Agoston Haraszthy planted grapevines in the 1840s before founding California's oldest commercial winery, Buena Vista Winery in Sonoma.

Detour: Baraboo is home to Wisconsin's most popular state park, **Devil's Lake State Park** (✉ *S5975 Park Rd.* ⊕ *dnr.wisconsin. gov*). Rock climbers love it and so do swimmers. Even with just an hour to spare you can still fit in a hefty hike.

Roadside Attraction: Trust us, you have not seen anything like the quirky, weird, and wonderful **House on the Rock** (✉ *5754 Rte. 23* ☎ *608/935–3639* ⊕ *www. thehouseontherock.com*) in the town of Spring Green, Wisconsin. Alex Jordan—an admirer of then local architect Frank

Lloyd Wright, whose homestead (Taliesin) is just up the road—built this in 1960; it's cantilevered atop a rock and contains the world's largest indoor carousel.

IOWA CITY

Do: Ninety minutes southwest of Iowa City, you'll find the **American Gothic House & Center** (✉ *300 American Gothic St.* ☎ *641/652–3352* ⊕ *www.american-gothichouse.org*), the house in one of America's most famous paintings (*American Gothic* by Grant Wood, an Iowan painter). There's even a costume closet of denim and pitchforks so you can emulate the farming couple. Back in Iowa City, find out why UNESCO named it a City of Literature, in part due to the University of Iowa's Writers' Workshop (the nation's best creative writing program). Take a stroll on the "ped mall" (car-free street) or take a tour of the two university museums, the **Stanley Museum of Art** (✉ *160 W. Burlington St.* ☎ *319/335–1727* ⊕ *stanleymuseum.uiowa.edu*) and the **Museum of Natural History** (✉ *17 N. Clinton St.* ☎ *319/335–0480* ⊕ *mnh.uiowa.edu*).

Eat & Drink: You can count on a college town to go beyond burgers, and that's exactly what draws locals to **Thai Spice** (✉ *1210 S. Gilbert St.* ☎ *319/351–2581* ⊕ *www.facebook.com/thaispiceiowacity*) for comfort food or **Szechuan House** for spicy Chinese dishes (✉ *320 E. Burlington St.* ☎ *319/338–6788* ⊕ *www. szechuanhouseia.com*).

Stay: Despite Iowa's appreciation for the arts, funky and artsy hotels haven't quite arrived here yet. Dovetailing the tiny-house trend, bunk at the 700-square-foot Milk House at **Lucky Star Farm** (✉ *2625 Rte. 1 SW* ☎ *319/683–4042* ⊕ *www. theluckystarfarm.com*), an Airbnb located between Iowa City and Kalona in Johnson County. On the 20-acre working farm, you'll find llamas, goats, a chicken coop, a pond (borrow a stand-up paddleboard), and a fire pit.

Breakfast: In downtown Iowa City, the "Macpullman" at the **Pullman Bar & Diner** (✉ 17 S. Dubuque St. ☎ 319/338–1808 ⊕ www.pullmandiner.com) is a delicious riff on a fast-food favorite: sausage, egg, and cheese on an English muffin, topped with chipotle aioli.

Day 3: Iowa City, IA, to Eau Claire, WI

282 miles (5 hours without traffic and stops)

You have two options to head north out of Iowa City: I–380 north (the freeway) or the more scenic Route 1. Taking the latter option drops you along the Mississippi River on U.S. 151 north.

ALONG THE WAY

Attraction: Learn more about Grant Wood at the **Grant Wood Studio and Museum** (✉ 810 2nd Ave. SE ☎ 319/366–7503 ⊕ www.crma.org/grant–wood/grant–wood–studio) in Cedar Rapids, Iowa.

Eat & Drink: If you're lucky, you might get to enjoy a farm dinner at **A to Z Produce and Bakery** (✉ N2956 Anker La. ☎ 715/448–4802 ⊕ www.atozproduceandbakery.com) in Stockholm, Wisconsin. But if not, **Stockholm Pie & General Store** (✉ N2030 Spring St. ☎ 715/442–5505 ⊕ www.stockholmpieandgeneralstore.com) will satisfy.

EAU CLAIRE

Do: Rent a bicycle to further explore one of the Midwest's best examples of a renaissance. Check out **Tangled Up in Hue** (✉ 505 S. Barstow St. ☎ 715/855–0090 ⊕ www.tangledupinhue.com), with works by 100 artists, and the vibrant taproom at the **Brewing Projekt** (✉ 1807 N. Oxford Ave. ☎ 715/598–1836 ⊕ www.thebrewingprojekt.com). Don't miss the **Pablo Center at the Confluence** (✉ 128 Graham Ave. ☎ 715/832–2787 ⊕ www.pablocenter.org), an arts center along the

Extend Your Trip

From Madison, Milwaukee, or Iowa City: Underrated Cities of the Midwest *(Ch. 6)*

From Door County: All the Great Lakes *(Ch. 6)*

Chippewa River with live performances and rotating art exhibits.

Eat & Drink: Since its 1994 debut, **Mona Lisa's** (✉ 428 Water St. ☎ 715/839–8969 ⊕ www.monalisas.biz) in downtown Eau Claire has ranked high with locals for its artistically plated Italian dinners that are a mix of surf and turf.

Stay: Owned and operated by Justin Vernon (the Grammy Award–winning artist also known as Bon Iver), **The Oxbow Hotel** (✉ 516 Galloway St. ☎ 715/839–0601 ⊕ www.theoxbowhotel.com) lets you borrow records to play in your room and also hosts a farm-to-fork restaurant with outdoor seating and live music.

Breakfast: Whether you want to grab one of six signature croissants to go or dine in over egg entrées with a twist (like the Green Goddess or smoked salmon scramble), **The French Press** (✉ 2823 London Rd. ☎ 715/598–7017 ⊕ www.thefrenchpresseauclaire.com) is a little taste of Europe.

Day 4: Eau Claire, WI, to St. Cloud, MN

156 miles (2 hours, 30 minutes without traffic and stops)

Follow I–94 west to the Twin Cities (Minneapolis and St. Paul), then on to St. Cloud, named after Saint-Cloud, a city near Paris, France.

ALONG THE WAY

Photo Op: The **Minneapolis Sculpture Garden** (✉ *725 Vineland Pl.* ☎ *612/375–7600* ⊕ *www.walkerart.org*), part of the **Walker Art Center in Minneapolis,** is a great spot to stretch your legs and take in some art, including its most famous piece: a spoon cradling a cherry.

Eat & Drink: You can have a decent lunch, with a malt, at the three locations of **Snuffy's Malt Shop** (⊕ *www.snuffysmalt-shops.com*)—in Minnetonka, Edina, or Bloomington—for a fun dip back into the 1950s.

Town: A perennial pick for one of the most beautiful small towns in America, Stillwater, Minnesota, sits on the west bank of the St. Paul River. Check out the river and the town via the River City Sculpture Tour or pop in and out of antiques shops on Main Street.

ST. CLOUD

Do: If you like to kayak or canoe, the Beaver Islands (30 very small islands in the Mississippi River) are a fun outing. Prefer to keep dry and on land? The **Munsinger Clemens Gardens** (✉ *1515 Riverside Dr. SE* ☎ *320/257–5959* ⊕ *www.ci.stcloud. mn.us*) have been blooming and thriving since the 1930s on the banks of the Mississippi River. The White Garden is inspired by the famous Sissinghurst Castle Garden in Kent, England.

Eat & Drink: You'll find a range of options in St. Cloud, from Indian at **Star of India** (✉ *2812 W. Division St.* ☎ *320/281–3388* ⊕ *www.starofindiamn.com*) to Mongolian at **Mongo's Grill** (✉ *3701 W. Division St.* ☎ *320/253–2695* ⊕ *www. mongosgrill.com*). **Jules' Bistro** (✉ *921 W. St. Germain St.* ☎ *320/252–7125* ⊕ *www. julesbistrostcloud.com*), serving contemporary American cuisine, is a fine option, too.

Stay: Although St. Cloud's hotel cluster is dominated by chains, a suitable alternative is **Pillar Inn** (✉ *419 Main St.* ☎ *320/685–3828* ⊕ *www.thepillarinn.*

com) in nearby Cold Spring. Just three rooms are tucked into the Queen Anne beauty.

Breakfast: Skip Starbucks and go to **Rock Creek Coffeehouse** (✉ *214 2nd Ave. N* ☎ *320/281–5713* ⊕ *www.rockcreekcof-feehouse.com*) in nearby Sauk Rapids. It opens at 6 am, which is useful to know, as Voyageurs National Park is your next stop and you'll want lots of time to explore.

Day 5: St. Cloud, MN, to Voyageurs National Park, MN

247 miles (4 hours, 20 minutes without traffic and stops)

You're going to need nearly the full day at **Voyageurs National Park** (☎ *218/283–6600* ⊕ *www.nps.gov/voya*) as this natural paradise spanning 220,000 acres is not a drive-in type of park like Yellowstone or Yosemite. Fill up your coffee mug and get going early.

ALONG THE WAY

Eat & Drink: Hibbing is one of the few towns you'll pass through on Route 65 north and U.S. 53 north. Skip the breweries and pizza joints for more appropriate morning food: pastries at the fourth-generation-owned **Sunrise Bakery** (✉ *2601 1st Ave.* ☎ *218/263–4985* ⊕ *www.sunrise-bakery.com*).

VOYAGEURS NATIONAL PARK

Do: This isn't a park where you can pull up to the visitor center, grab a map, and head off on a quick hike. Guided boat tours (which take about two hours) are the recommended way to experience the vast park. Tours depart daily in the high season from Rainy Lake and Kabetogama visitor centers. For a deeper immersion, hire a local guide who can show you the park through overnight camping.

Eat & Drink: As remote as this park is, you can actually have lunch without leaving it, at the **Kettle Falls Hotel** (✉ 12977 Chippewa Trail ☎ 218/240–1724 ⊕ www.kettlefallshotel.com), accessible only by water. Otherwise, it's recommended you pack your own food in.

Stay: If your time is limited but you still want to see as much of the park as possible, then **Ebel's Voyageur Houseboats** (✉ 10326 Ash River Trail, Orr ☎ 218/374–3571 ⊕ www.ebels.com) allows you to squeeze in more time along—and above—the water. Or stay at **The Nomad Motel** (✉ 10 Riverview Blvd, International Falls ☎ 218/302–1096 ⊕ www.thenomadmotel.com), a 1950s-era motel with design details in the guest rooms like cane-back bed frames and sunburst mirrors.

Breakfast: Regardless of where you end up staying, packing your own breakfast or stopping at a fast-food stop once you hit the road is your best bet.

Day 6: Voyageurs National Park, MN, to Bayfield, WI

227 miles (4 hours without traffic and stops)

Once you hit Duluth, you'll drive around the rim of Lake Superior for the rest of the trip on U.S. 53 south and then again on Route 13 south.

ALONG THE WAY

Detour: To properly experience Boundary Waters Canoe Area Wilderness (just over 1 million acres in size) would take several days, but you can still get a sneak peek, particularly of the surrounding towns like Grand Marais, by traveling north on Route 61 north. Just be sure to allow enough time to get back on the route to Bayfield. From Duluth to Grand Marais is about four hours round–trip.

Essential Listening

Listen to the audiobook of Wisconsin memoirist Michael Perry's *Population 485*, a raw portrait of a small town (New Auburn, Wisconsin) told through the lens of his experiences as a volunteer firefighter.

Eat & Drink: Gronk's Grill & Bar (✉ 4909 E. 2nd St. ☎ 715/398–0333 ⊕ www.gronksgrill.com) in Superior, Wisconsin, hits you with humor before you've even taken your first bite. First, there's the faux sign for a "fish camp" on the log cabin exterior. Then, you'll see the His and Hers burgers (Gronk Burger is a breaded burger stacked with bacon and barbecue sauce while Ms. Gronk Burger is topped with deep-fried pickles).

BAYFIELD

Do: Thankfully it's possible to experience the **Apostle Islands National Lakeshore** (✉ 415 Washington Ave. ☎ 715/779–3397 ⊕ www.nps.gov/apis) on a day trip, even if you don't sail or have a kayak (although those can be rented in town if you wish to explore the caves). The Madeline Island Ferry Line takes you from Bayfield to Madeline in 25 minutes while the 2½-hour Grand Tour from **Apostle Islands Cruises** (✉ 2 Front St. ☎ 715/779–3925 ⊕ www.apostleisland.com) coasts by nearly all of the islands on a 55-mile sail.

Eat & Drink: For a progressive, orchard-driven feast, Bayfield is loaded with options, including **Blue Vista Farm** (✉ 34045 S. Hwy. J ☎ 715/779–5400 ⊕ www.bluevistafarm.com), **North Wind Organic Farm** (✉ 86760 Valley Rd. ☎ 715/779–3254 ⊕ www.northwindorganicfarm.org), and **Ericksen Orchard** (✉ 86600 Betzold

Rd. ☎ 715/913–0717 ⊕ www.ericksonorchard.com). The farm stands sell baked goods and cider, along with produce and fruit. For something more substantial, try a Lake Superior–caught whitefish sandwich at **Morty's Pub** (✉ 108 Rittenhouse Ave. ☎ 715/779–3996 ⊕ www.mortyspub.com), a block from the lake.

Stay: Wild Rice Retreat (✉ 84860 Old San Rd. ☎ 715/779–0178 ⊕ www.wildriceretreat.com) is the kind of wellness stay you might find in Sedona, Arizona, but with that Great Lakes friendliness. You can sign up for a guided retreat or create your own Zen with yoga classes. Accommodations are in the Treehaus, the Ricepod, or the Nest, all examples of modern architecture carved into a woodsy backdrop. With an expansive porch overlooking Lake Superior, **Old Rittenhouse Inn** (✉ 301 Rittenhouse Ave. ☎ 715/779–5111 ⊕ www.rittenhouseinn.com) is a historic B&B in downtown Bayfield that has won over many travelers.

Breakfast: Wonderstate Coffee (✉ 117 Rittenhouse Ave. ☎ 715/913–0330 ⊕ www.wonderstate.com) is the Bayfield outpost for the Viroqua-based coffee roaster. Along with coffee, they sell a variety of locally baked pastries.

Day 7: Bayfield, WI, to Green Bay, WI

279 miles (4 hours, 45 minutes without traffic and stops)

It's exciting to think you're in one of the northernmost areas of the United States, isn't it? Canada is, well, just to the north, separated from the continental United States by Lake Superior. Today you'll drive U.S. 51 south for the majority of the route, cutting through what Wisconsinites call "the North Woods" or simply "Up North."

ALONG THE WAY

Roadside Attraction: Wisconsin Concrete Park (✉ 8236 Rte. 13 ☎ 715/339–7282 ⊕ www.wisconsinconcretepark.org) in Phillips may be a bit of a detour, but if you like the slightly weird, and wish to understand one of Wisconsin's most overlooked art traditions (outsider art), it's worth the journey. On its 18 acres, you'll find 237 embellished mixed-media and concrete statues by the late Fred Smith.

Eat & Drink: Just outside the Menomonie Indian Reservation, **Jake's Supper Club** (✉ E5690 County Rd. ☎ 715/235–2465 ⊕ www.jakessupperclub.com) on Tainter Lake is an introduction to another Wisconsin tradition: the supper club. Portions are huge and the service is leisurely, so keep in mind that this is not an option if you're short on time. And despite the name, they open at 3:30 pm on weekdays and serve brunch on weekends.

GREEN BAY

Do: With only about 100,000 residents, Green Bay is a real anomaly for its size: it hosts an NFL team—the Green Bay Packers, who have earned 13 National Champion titles)—along with the **Green Bay Botanical Garden** (✉ 2600 Larsen Rd. ☎ 920/490–9457 ⊕ www.gbbg.org), the **NEW Zoo & Adventure Park** (✉ 4378 Reforestation Rd. ☎ 920/434–7841 ⊕ www.newzoo.org), the old-fashioned **Bay Beach Amusement Park** (✉ 1313 Bay Beach Rd. ☎ 920/448–3365 ⊕ greenbay.com), and the 700-acre **Bay Beach Wildlife Sanctuary** (✉ 1660 E. Shore Dr. ☎ 920/391–3671 ⊕ www.baybeachwildlife.com).

Eat & Drink: Even if you're not a Green Bay Packers fan, grab lunch or dinner at Lambeau Field's **1919 Kitchen & Tap** (✉ 1265 Lombardi Ave. ☎ 920/965–6970 ⊕ www.1919kitchenandtap.com). You can also sign up for a guided tour to learn more about the NFL's only community-owned team, tour the Packers Hall of Fame, and shop in the pro shop, with its staggering amount of NFL-inspired items.

Wisconsin's Door County is especially scenic during the fall.

Stay: Downtown Green Bay's gem is **Hotel Northland** (✉ 304 N. Adams St. ☎ 920/393–7499 ⊕ www.marriott.com), a restored historic property originally opened in the 1920s. Dinner is served in the Walnut Room with a bar that looks right out of *The Great Gatsby*.

Breakfast: The Creamery Downtown (✉ 114 Pine St. ☎ 920/489–8437 ⊕ www.thecreamerycafe.com) serves everything from homemade chai tea to Bloody Marys to get your day started, along with menu items such as a Benedict flight or a mushroom truffle omelet.

Day 8: Green Bay, WI, to Door County, WI

44 miles (45 minutes without traffic and stops)

This is your easiest and shortest driving day, but that's only because once you arrive in Sturgeon Bay, you'll be driving along the peninsula to experience the glory of Door County, an area similar in beauty and stature to New England's Nantucket. From Sturgeon Bay (the county seat to Northpoint (the northernmost tip), it's about a one hour drive covering 45 miles.

ALONG THE WAY

Eat & Drink: In Ephraim since 1906, **Wilson's Restaurant & Ice Cream** (✉ 9990 Water St. S ☎ 920/854–2041 ⊕ www.wilsonsicecream.com) is across the street from Green Bay (the body of water, not the city). It's where you can score an ice-cream cone or basket of greasy fare like burgers and fries.

Shop: People come to Door County to shop their hearts out, thanks to the region's many antique stores. **Summer Camp Antiques** (✉ 11996 Rte. 42 ☎ 920/854–8081 ⊕ www.summercampantiques.com) in Ellison Bay is highly curated and worth a stop if you don't like to dig too much.

Nature: Washington Island is home to a lavender field, **Fragrant Isle** (✉ 1350

Airport Rd. ☎ 920/847–2950 ⊕ www.
fragrantisle.com), where you can pick up
some dried lavender for the rest of your
journey. There are also lavender-laden
gardens you can stroll.

DOOR COUNTY

Do: Bypass the throngs of tourists in
Door County for a two-ferry trip to
Rock Island State Park (✉ 1924 Indian
Point Rd. ☎ 920/847–2235 ⊕ www.dnr.
wisconsin.gov). First, you need to get to
Washington Island: hop the Washington
Island Car Ferry from the northern tip of
Door County's peninsula, then the pas-
senger ferry from there. On Rock Island
is Pottawatomie Lighthouse, dating back
to 1836 and open for tours daily between
Memorial Day and Columbus Day. Just
note that cars and bicycles are not
allowed on Rock Island.

Eat & Drink: On Washington Island, **Red
Cup Coffee House** (✉ 1885 Detroit Harbor
Rd. ☎ 920/847–3304 ⊕ www.redcupkill-
ercoffee.com) is a nice stop to fuel up.
Fair Isle Books & Gifts, selling books and
fair-trade trinkets, is adjacent.

Stay: Outside of Sturgeon Bay, the
county's largest town, you won't find a
single chain hotel. Through Airbnb, you'll
find gems like a modernized log cabin
or contemporary farmhouse. **Roots Inn &
Kitchen** (✉ 2378 Maple Dr. ☎ 920/854–
5107 ⊕ www.rootsinnandkitchen.com) in
Sister Bay is an eclectic inn with just six
rooms and farm-to-table dining.

Breakfast: Is that a goat on the roof? Yep,
it is. **Al Johnson's** (✉ 10698 N. Bay Shore
Dr. ☎ 920/854–2626 ⊕ www.aljohnsons.
com) is a nod to Door County's Swedish
heritage, serving thin pancakes topped
with lingonberries. If there's a wait for
a table, shop in the attached boutique;
you might find a sweater or pair of socks
imported from Sweden or Norway.

Day 9: Door County, WI, to Milwaukee, WI

*165 miles (2 hours, 30 minutes without
traffic and stops)*

The fastest way back to Milwaukee is
to take I–43 south, but then you'd miss
another glimpse of Lake Michigan. Leaving Sturgeon Bay, instead take Route 42
south through towns like Kewaunee and
Algoma until you hit Manitowoc.

ALONG THE WAY

Town: An hour north of Milwaukee, Sheboygan is in the middle of a renaissance
thanks to its fabulous art museums like
the Art Preserve of the **John Michael
Kohler Arts Center** (✉ 3636 Lower Falls
Rd. ☎ 920/453–0346 ⊕ www.jmkac.org),
which celebrates the state's outsider
artists. A Sheboygan-style brat (this city
is the brat capital of the world) can be
sampled at **Al & Al's Steinhaus** (✉ 1502 S.
12th St. ☎ 920/452–5530 ⊕ www.alnals.
com) or you can pick some up for later
at **Johnsonville Marketplace** (✉ N6877 Rio
Rd. ☎ 920/453–5678 ⊕ www.johnsonvil-
lemarketplace.com).

Eat & Drink: This part of Wisconsin is
famous for smoked fish—try the smoked
chunk whitefish at **Schwarz Fish Company** (✉ 828 Riverfront Dr. ☎ 920/452–
0576 ⊕ www.schwarzfish.com) in
Sheboygan.

MILWAUKEE

Do: Take some time to explore the
Milwaukee Art Museum (✉ 700 N. Art
Museum Dr. ☎ 414/224–3200 ⊕ www.
mam.org), the **Harley Davidson Museum** (✉ 400 W. Canal St. ☎ 414/287–
2789 ⊕ www.harley-davidson.com), and
the **Pabst Mansion** (✉ 2000 W. Wisconsin
Ave. ☎ 414/931–0808 ⊕ www.pabst-
mansion.com), former home of Frederick Pabst, founder of Pabst Brewing.
Milwaukee is a big beer town after all,
so be sure to spend some time checking out its many breweries, including

Lakefront Brewery (✉ *1872 N. Commerce St.* ☎ *414/372–8800* ⊕ *www.lakefront-brewery.com*) and **Miller Brewery** (✉ *4251 W. State St.* ☎ *414/931–2337* ⊕ *www.millerbrewerytour.com*).

Eat & Drink: At the **Milwaukee Public Market** (✉ *400 N. Water St.* ☎ *414/336–1111* ⊕ *www.milwaukeepublicmarket.org*), vendors sell a wide variety of food, from plant-based meals served out of a converted VW bus to Middle Eastern cuisine. West Allis Cheese & Sausage Shoppe sells "orphans" (mini-wedges of Wisconsin cheese).

Stay: The sophisticated **Kimpton Journeyman Hotel** (✉ *310 E. Chicago St.* ☎ *888/536–9008* ⊕ *www.journeymanhotel.com*) has a hip rooftop bar with views of the city.

Breakfast: A rare daytime-only bar, **Uncle Wolfie's Breakfast Tavern** (✉ *234 E. Vine St.* ☎ *414/763–3021* ⊕ *www.unclewolfies.com*) serves a hip brunch menu, with options like bananas Foster oatmeal and biscuits and gravy.

Underrated Cities of the Midwest

Written by Kristine Hansen

Sure, everyone knows Chicago, but what about those "second cities" of the Midwest—places like Milwaukee, Indianapolis, St. Louis, and Louisville? This trip will take you to some of the most underrated spots in the region, including smaller towns like Madison, Iowa City, Grand Rapids, and Fort Wayne that deliver on college-town chill and big-city fun on a smaller scale. From regional foods, craft beer, and lesser-known art museums and cultural institutions to natural spaces like parks, lakes, and rivers and quaint Main Streets for eclectic shopping, it's time to experience what many dub "flyover country" with new eyes and a fresh perspective to stop those naysayers in their haughty tracks.

At a Glance

Start: Indianapolis, IN

End: Indianapolis, IN

Miles Traveled: 1,462 miles

Suggested Duration: 9 days

States Visited: Indiana, Iowa, Kentucky, Michigan, Missouri, Ohio, Wisconsin

Key Sights: Arab American National Museum; the Gateway Arch; Indianapolis Motor Speedway; Motown Museum; Muhammad Ali Center

Best Time to Go: Because this is the Upper Midwest, weather needs to be on your side, and if you opt for spring or fall, expect an even more vibrant aesthetic (fields of flowers or fall foliage) for your drive through the landscape.

Day 1: Indianapolis, IN, to Louisville, KY

115 miles (1 hour, 45 minutes without traffic and stops)

Fly into the Indianapolis International Airport and pick up a rental car before starting your road trip. On your first day, it's a straight shot down I–65 south. Between the two cities are rural areas and small towns for a nice easy day of driving.

ALONG THE WAY

Town: Love architecture? Columbus, Indiana, is home to a surprising number of modernist works, including three by Eero Saarinen: Miller House and Garden, North Christian Church, and the Irwin Bank Building.

Eat & Drink: Zaharakos (✉ *329 Washington St.* ☎ *812/378–1900* ⊕ *www.zaharakos.com*), in Columbus, has been in business since around 1900 and continues to

Underrated Cities of the Midwest

be a popular ice-cream shop for locals today. Before or after ordering, check out the second-floor museum's antique soda-fountain finds, dating back to the 1800s.

LOUISVILLE

Do: At night, walk over the **Big Four Bridge** (✉ 1101 River Rd. ☎ 502/574–3768 ⊕ www.ourwaterfront.org) above the Ohio River, connecting Kentucky with Indiana; this converted railroad bridge is pedestrian-only and lit up at night. Even if you're not a sports fan, diving into the history of baseball-bat manufacturing at **Louisville Slugger Museum & Factory** (✉ 800 W. Main St. ☎ 877/775–8443 ⊕ www.sluggermuseum.com) or learning about the late boxer Muhammad Ali at the **Muhammad Ali Center** (✉ 144 N. 6th St. ☎ 502/584–9254 ⊕ www.alicenter.org) is captivating.

Eat & Drink: Local chef (and former Top Chef contestant) Edward Lee has morphed into a celebrity in recent years, but you may be lucky and snag a reservation at **610 Magnolia** (✉ 610 W. Magnolia Ave. ☎ 502/636–0783 ⊕ www.610magnolia.com) or **Nami Modern Korean Steakhouse** (✉ 835 E. Main St. ☎ 502/690–2067 ⊕ www.nami-restaurant.com).

Stay: Tucked into 19th-century warehouses, the 91-room **21c Museum Hotel** (✉ 700 W. Main St. ☎ 502/217–6300 ⊕ www.21cmuseumhotels.com) is part art museum, part sweet stay, with sculptures and installations everywhere you look. Keep an eye out for a golden replica of Michelangelo's *David*.

Breakfast: Tres leches pancakes and dulce de leche French toast. Need we say more? **Con Huevos** (✉ 2339 Frankfort

Ave. ☎ 502/384–3027 ⊕ www.con-huevos.com) is a Louisville favorite.

Day 2: Louisville, KY, to St. Louis, MO

260 miles (3 hours, 50 minutes without traffic and stops)

I–64 takes you directly west to St. Louis. You'll pass through Evansville, Indiana, a college town (home to the University of Southern Indiana and the University of Evansville). Look for the Gateway Arch as you're cruising into and around St. Louis.

ALONG THE WAY

Nature: The southern section of the **Hoosier National Forest** (⊠ *811 Constitution Ave. Bedford, IN* ☎ *812/275–5987* ⊕ *www. fs.usda.gov*) overlaps with I–64 west. To reach it, exit in Saint Croix, Indiana, and take Route 37 south to Route 62 east for an easy 1-mile hike on the Celina Interpretive Trail, departing from the Celina boat ramp.

Eat & Drink: You'll find the most variety of nonchain restaurants in Evansville, Indiana. Craving a sweet snack? **Be Happy Pie Company** (⊠ *2818-B Mt. Vernon Ave.* ☎ *812/449–7718* ⊕ *www.behappypiecompany.com*) is one option, with five-inch pies and "pie bites" more suitable for one or two people.

ST. LOUIS

Do: St. Louis's 1,300-acre Forest Park (that's bigger than New York City's Central Park!) is home to the totally free-to-enter **St. Louis Art Museum** (⊠ *1 Fine Arts Dr.* ☎ *314/721–0072* ⊕ *www. slam.org*). Two other sculpture parks link nature with art (and, again, are free): **Laumeier Sculpture Park** (⊠ *12580 Rott Rd., Sappington* ☎ *314/615–5278* ⊕ *www.laumeiersculpturepark. org*) and **Citygarden Sculpture Park** (⊠ *801 Market St.* ☎ *314/241–3337* ⊕ *www.*

Essential Listening

The audiobook of Louisville chef Edward Lee's *Buttermilk Graffiti: A Chef's Journey to Discover America's New Melting-Pot Cuisine* will whet your palate for dinner in Derby City.

citygardensstl.org). To feel like a kid again, check out **City Museum** (⊠ *750 N. 16th St.* ☎ *314/231–2489* ⊕ *www. citymuseum.org*), an artful indoor reuse project that involves slides, climbing, and other interactive fun for all ages in a century-old warehouse.

Eat & Drink: If you're craving Italian, find toasted ravioli (breaded and deep-fried), a signature St. Louis dish, in The Hill neighborhood's restaurants, such as **Mama's on the Hill** (⊠ *2132 Edwards St.* ☎ *314/776–3100* ⊕ *www.mamasonthehill.com*). For a latte break, drop into **Winslow's Table** in University City (⊠ *7213 Delmar Blvd.* ☎ *314/725–7559* ⊕ *www.winslowstable.com*); don't skip the house-made pop tarts.

Stay: Angad Arts Hotel (⊠ *3550 Samuel Shepard Dr.* ☎ *314/561–0033* ⊕ *www. angadartshotel.com*) is the only hotel out there that will ask you what your mood is upon check-in … and then send you to a room awash in a color that matches.

Breakfast: Don't even think about leaving without sampling gooey butter cake. **The Mud House** (⊠ *2101 Cherokee St.* ☎ *314/776–6599* ⊕ *www.themudhousestl.com*)—a café in the cute and historic Cherokee District—features it on their menu, along with the signature "Mud Slinger" (vegetarian black bean chili, roasted potatoes, red onion, and cheddar) and a spicy tofu scramble.

Day 3: St. Louis, MO, to Iowa City, IA

260 miles (4 hours without traffic and stops)

U.S. 61 takes you directly north to Iowa. You may even find the temperature drops.

ALONG THE WAY

Town: Near Hannibal, Missouri, you'll find quite a few breweries and wineries with tasting rooms. **Cave Hollow West Winery** (✉ *217 Cave Hollow Rd.* ☎ *573/231–1000* ⊕ *www.cavehollow.westwinery. com*) makes wine inspired by Mark Twain's books while **Friendship Brewing Company** (✉ *422 N. Main St.* ☎ *573/600–9091* ⊕ *www.friendshipbrewco.com*) is located across the street from Twain's boyhood home.

Eat & Drink: Mount Pleasant, Iowa, is a nice place to stop for lunch, perhaps at **Sanity Coffee House** (✉ *104 S. Iris St.* ☎ *319/931–9594* ⊕ *www.mysanitycoffeehouse.com*), which serves espresso drinks, panini, milkshakes, and whoopie pies.

IOWA CITY

Do: Not every city has a pedestrian mall as pleasant as Iowa City: check out **Prairie Lights Books & Cafe** (✉ *15 S. Dubuque St.* ☎ *319/337–2681* ⊕ *www. prairielights.com*) for reading material and **Artifacts** (✉ *331 E. Market St.* ☎ *319/358–9617* ⊕ *www.artifacts-iowacity.com*) for unique vintage finds, from clothes to furnishings. About 15 minutes west of Iowa City is the **Herbert Hoover Presidential Library and Museum** (✉ *210 Parkside Dr.* ☎ *319/643–5301* ⊕ *www.hoover. archives.gov*). On the University of Iowa campus is the **Stanley Museum of Art** (✉ *160 W. Burlington St.* ☎ *319/335–1727* ⊕ *stanleymuseum.uiowa.edu*) and the **Museum of Natural History** (✉ *17 N. Clinton St.* ☎ *319/335–0480* ⊕ *mnh. uiowa.edu*).

Eat & Drink: College towns are full of casual, global-eating opportunities, such as **Oasis Falafel** (✉ *206 N. Linn St.* ☎ *319/358–7342* ⊕ *www.oasisfalafel. com*) or **Szechuan House** (✉ *320 E. Burlington St.* ☎ *319/338–6788* ⊕ *www.szechuanhouseia.com*). Close out the night with a drink at the **Vue Rooftop** (✉ *328 S. Clinton St.* ☎ *319/519–4650* ⊕ *www. vuerooftop-ic.com*), on the 12th floor of the Hilton Garden Inn Iowa City, with amazing views and a big-city vibe.

Stay: The modern suites at **Hotel Vetro** (✉ *201 S. Linn St.* ☎ *319/259–7111*) are the perfect, pampering spot to crash after a day on the go.

Breakfast: Stick a fork into soul food infused with midwestern ingredients at **Bluebird Diner** (✉ *330 E. Market St.* ☎ *319/351–1470* ⊕ *www.bluebird. cafe*), where the breakfast menu includes the Rajun Cajun omelet and Oeufs Louis XIV (eggs scrambled with black truffles).

Day 4: Iowa City, IA, to Madison, WI

175 miles (3 hours without traffic and stops)

Today you'll travel along the Great River Road, a 250-mile chunk of gorgeous scenery that includes Dickeyville, Wisconsin. Be sure to also take photos of the Mississippi River when you pass over it in Dubuque, Iowa.

ALONG THE WAY

Shop: The German-founded **Amana Colonies** (✉ *622 46th Ave., Amana* ☎ *319/622–7622* ⊕ *amanacolonies. com*) are a local's favorite day-trip destination for its gift shops, bakery, and café. Pick up a loaf of German dill or German black bread.

Detour: Mount Vernon, Iowa, is a small town and home to Cornell College.

Roadside Attraction: Dickeyville Grotto
(✉ 255–377 Great River Rd. ☎ 608/568–3119 ⊕ www.dickeyvillegrotto.com) in Dickeyville, Wisconsin, lies along U.S. 61 and is like nothing you've ever seen. Established by a priest between 1925 and 1930, it's a great example of the state's outsider art, where untrained artists used found objects (wood, rocks, and shells in this case) to create beautiful spaces.

Eat & Drink: In Mount Horeb, Wisconsin's Norwegian influence pops up in a few restaurants, including **Sjolind's Chocolate House** (✉ 219 E. Main St. ☎ 608/437–0233 ⊕ www.sjolinds.com), which also serves pastries and sipping chocolate.

MADISON

Do: You didn't come all this way to not try cheese. **Fromagination** (✉ 12 S. Carroll St. ☎ 608/255–2430 ⊕ www.fromagination.com) is a Parisian-inspired cheese shop on Capitol Square. Stroll State Street (its small collection of independent shops sell fair-trade goods and unique finds) to the University of Wisconsin–Madison and enjoy ice cream at **Memorial Union's Daily Scoop** (✉ 800 Langdon St. ☎ 608/262–5959 ⊕ www.union.wisc.edu) from its outdoor terrace hugging Lake Mendota. Then check out the continental United States's only Thai pavilion at **Olbrich Botanical Gardens** (✉ 3330 Atwood Ave. ☎ 608/246–4550 ⊕ www.olbrich.org).

Eat & Drink: L'Etoile (✉ 1 S. Pinckney St. ☎ 608/251–0500 ⊕ www.letoile–restaurant.com) is a farm-to-fork, finer-dining institution (founder Odessa Piper shopped the Dane County Farmers' Market across the street back in the 1970s), while its more casual sibling, **Graze** (✉ 1 S. Pinckney St. ☎ 608/251–2700 ⊕ www.grazemadison.com), is a block away.

Stay: Located a block off State Street and a few blocks from UW–Madison's Memorial Union, **Graduate Madison** (✉ 601 Langdon St. ☎ 608/257–4391 ⊕ www.

Extend Your Trip

From Louisville: The Great American Whiskey Road Trip *(Ch. 7)*

From St. Louis: Route 66 *(Ch. 2)*; Along the Mississippi *(Ch. 2)*; The Best of the Ozarks *(Ch. 6)*

From Iowa City, Madison, or Milwaukee: The Best of the Heartland *(Ch. 6)*

From Grand Rapids: A Frank Lloyd Wright Tour *(Ch. 6)*

graduatehotels.com) merges preppy-chic with laid-back fun. Enjoy drinks with cheese curds on the rooftop lounge.

Breakfast: Mickie's Dairy Bar (✉ 1511 Monroe St. ☎ 608/256–9476 ⊕ www.mickiesdairybar.com) on Monroe Street is a classic, no-frills breakfast institution, with omelets, shakes, and root-beer floats.

Day 5: Madison, WI, to Milwaukee, WI

79 miles (1 hour, 15 minutes without traffic and stops)

Once you're on I-94 east, just enjoy the drive and notice the quaint red barns and rolling green hills. Rarely is there traffic between Madison and Milwaukee, except for the towns bordering each.

ALONG THE WAY

Photo Op: No, that's not a space ship: the saucer-shaped building at the Johnson Creek exit (exit 267) off I-94 is the former Gobbler supper-club restaurant.

Eat & Drink: It may not be state fair season, but you can still snag the biggest cream puffs you've ever seen at the

Pine Cone Travel Plaza (✉ *685 Linmar La., Suite C, Johnson Creek* ☎ *920/699–2766* ⊕ *www.pineconetravelplazamenu. com*), also at exit 267.

MILWAUKEE

Do: With its soaring white wings over Lake Michigan, the Santiago Calatrava–designed Quadracci Pavilion of the **Milwaukee Art Museum** (✉ *700 N. Art Museum Dr.* ☎ *414/224–3200* ⊕ *www. mam.org*) is a stunner. Rent a shared bike from **Bublr** (✉ *161 W. Wisconsin Ave.* ☎ *414/931–1121* ⊕ *www.bublrbikes. org*) and cruise up Lincoln Memorial Drive along the lake. **Milwaukee Kayak Company** (✉ *318 S. Water St.* ☎ *414/301–2240* ⊕ *www.milwaukeekayak.com*) rents out kayaks and canoes at its Harbor District locale, providing a great way to experience the skyline from the Milwaukee River.

Eat & Drink: Food halls are where it's at here, either the mostly Black-owned eateries at **Sherman Phoenix** (✉ *3536 W. Fond Du Lac Ave.* ☎ *262/228–6021* ⊕ *www.shermanphoenix.com*) or the **Milwaukee Public Market** (✉ *400 N. Water St.* ☎ *414/336–1111* ⊕ *www. milwaukeepublicmarket.org*). Close down the night with a Pink Squirrel at a classic Milwaukee cocktail lounge like **At Random** (✉ *2501 S. Delaware Ave.* ☎ *414/481–8030* ⊕ *www.atrandommke.com*). Frozen custard is also a must here, either at **Leon's Frozen Custard** (✉ *3131 S. 27th St.* ☎ *414/383–1784* ⊕ *www.leonsfrozencustardmke.com*) or one of three locations of **Kopp's** (⊕ *www.kopps.com*).

Stay: Milwaukee is called Brew City for a reason: beer barons emigrated from Germany to here. Bunk at the 90-room **Brewhouse Inn & Suites** (✉ *1215 N. 10th St.* ☎ *414/810–3350* ⊕ *www. brewhousesuites.com*), within the former Pabst Brewery complex and home to antique copper kettles once used to make beer.

Breakfast: Since the 1970s, **Beans & Barley** (✉ *1901 E. North Ave.* ☎ *414/278–7878* ⊕ *www.beansandbarley.com*) on the East Side has managed to fuse Mexican with vegan and organic for all-day dining, along with old-fashioned pie slices and killer coffee in a sunny, high-ceilinged diner. Pick up snacks and a magazine for the ferry in the attached market.

Day 6: Milwaukee, WI, to Grand Rapids, MI

128 miles, including Lake Express Ferry across Lake Michigan (3 hours, 45 minutes without traffic and stops)

Today you're leaving part of the drive to the Lake Express ferry captain. The high-speed car ferry departs from the Port of Milwaukee (just south of the Hoan Bridge in Bay View) and drops you off in Muskegon, Michigan. From there, it's an easy 45-minute trip along I–96 east.

ALONG THE WAY

Photo Op: Be sure to scale a flight of stairs to the ferry's roof, but bring a jacket: it's cold and windy up there.

Eat & Drink: Dockers Fish House (✉ *3505 Marina View Point* ☎ *231/755–0400* ⊕ *www.dockersmuskegon.com*) in Muskegon serves lobster rolls, lobster fondue, smoked whitefish dip, and even milkshakes with a cool waterfront setting on Muskegon Lake.

Detour: Grand Haven, Michigan (22 miles from the ferry terminal), along the Lake Michigan shoreline, is that quintessential summer beach town with a boardwalk.

GRAND RAPIDS

Do: Called the GRAM by locals, the superb **Grand Rapids Art Museum** (✉ *101 Monroe Center St. NW* ☎ *616/831–1000* ⊕ *www.artmuseumgr.org*) has rotating exhibitions and a collection spanning eras. Stretch your legs at **Frederik Meijer Botanical Gardens & Sculpture Park**

(✉ *1000 E. Beltline Ave. NE* ☎ *616/957–1580* ⊕ *www.meijergardens.org*) or learn about a past president at **Gerald R. Ford Presidential Museum** (✉ *303 Pearl St. NW* ☎ *616/254–0400* ⊕ *www.fordlibrary-museum.gov*).

Eat & Drink: Opt for a local craft beer (Grand Rapids is nicknamed "Beer City USA") with dinner at **Stella's Lounge** (✉ *53 Commerce Ave. SW* ☎ *616/742–4444* ⊕ *www.stellaslounge.com*), known for its stuffed burgers, beer-battered avocados, and vintage arcade games. Afterwards, grab a drink at **Brewery Vivant** (✉ *925 Cherry St. SE* ☎ *616/719–1604* ⊕ *www.breweryvivant.com*), located within a former funeral chapel.

Stay: The **CityFlats Hotel** (✉ *83 Monroe Center St. NW* ☎ *616/608–1720* ⊕ *www.cityflatshotel.com*) has an eco-friendly mantra and a downtown location near shops, restaurants, and the GRAM.

Breakfast: That Early Bird (✉ *1445 Lake Dr. SE* ☎ *616/258–8350* ⊕ *www.thatearlybird.com*) serves breakfast nachos, curry hash, and horchata lattes—a fun switch on American-style breakfasts.

Day 7: Grand Rapids, MI, to Detroit, MI

157 miles (2 hours, 15 minutes without traffic and stops)

I–96 east takes you from Grand Rapids to Detroit, curling around the state capitol in Lansing.

ALONG THE WAY

Eat & Drink: A tad southwest of Grand Rapids lies **Farmhaus Farms** (✉ *9265 Kenowa Ave. SW* ☎ *616/320–2269* ⊕ *www.farmhausfarms.com*), where a family has been growing apples, peaches, and cherries since 1907. The market sells farm-fresh produce and sweet treats, including pies and apple dumplings.

Town: Jump off I–96 east to spot the Michigan Capitol Building in Lansing and perhaps snap a photo from the car. Guided hour-long tours are offered on weekdays and Saturday.

DETROIT

Do: Once famous for its car manufacturing, now it's the art scene here that attracts new residents and visitors alike. Spend some time gallery-hopping or visiting the **Detroit Institute of Arts** (✉ *5200 Woodward Ave.* ☎ *313/833–7900* ⊕ *www.dia.org*). The **Motown Museum** (✉ *2648 W. Grand Blvd.* ☎ *313/875–2264* ⊕ *www.motownmuseum.org*) and the **Arab American National Museum** (✉ *13624 Michigan Ave.* ☎ *313/429–2535* ⊕ *www.arabamericanmuseum.org*) in nearby Dearborn are two completely unique experiences you won't find elsewhere that help tell the region's full story.

Eat & Drink: You've heard of Detroit-style pizza (rectangular with a thick, chewy crust), so now's the time to try it; any **Jet's** (⊕ *www.jetspizza.com*) location will do. For a more upscale yet eclectic experience, book a table at **Grey Ghost Detroit** (✉ *47 Watson St.* ☎ *313/262–6534* ⊕ *www.greyghostdetroit.com*). And don't go to bed without slipping into a booth at the vintagey Candy Bar, inside **The Siren Hotel** (✉ *1509 Broadway St.* ☎ *313/277–4736* ⊕ *ash.world/hotels/the-siren*).

Stay: The Siren Hotel is a delightful throwback experience with its mid-century, golden-age-of-Hollywood decor while the **Detroit Foundation Hotel** (✉ *250 W Larned St.* ☎ *313/ 800–5500* ⊕ *www.detroitfoundationhotel.com*) offers hip industrial style in a former firehouse.

Breakfast: Detroit's West Village is home to Lisa Ludwinski's wildly popular **Sister Pie** (✉ *8066 Kercheval Ave.* ☎ *313/447–5550* ⊕ *www.sisterpie.com*) where breakfast as well as bakery items are available each morning.

The Detroit Institute of Arts features stunning murals from Diego Rivera.

Day 8: Detroit, MI, to Fort Wayne, IN

162 miles (2 hours, 35 minutes without traffic and stops)

From Detroit, I–75 south cuts through Toledo, Ohio, and weaves down to Fort Wayne.

ALONG THE WAY

Eat & Drink: It's rare to find a Hungarian restaurant in these parts, which is why you should pull over for lunch at **Tony Packo's Café** (✉ *1902 Front St.* ☎ *419/691–6054* ⊕ *www.tonypacko.com*) in Toledo, Ohio, since 1932. Enjoy the signature Hungarian hot dogs, pierogi, chicken paprikash, or an apple or cherry strudel.

Roadside Attraction: In Defiance, Ohio, you'll find a stack of five 1960s-era VW Bugs at **Pack Rat's Pawn Shop** (✉ *1938 E. 2nd St.* ☎ *419/782–7287* ⊕ *www.pack-ratpawnshop.com*), each decorated with further pizazz.

FORT WAYNE

Do: An outdoor sculpture park called **Promenade Park** (✉ *202 W. Superior St.* ☎ *260/427–6000* ⊕ *www.fort-wayneparks.org*) is a great place to chill and people-watch, with kayak rentals, canal boats, and swings. Love street art? Check out the Fort Wayne tourism website (⊕ *www.visitfortwayne.com*) for a handy interactive map that points you to the city's best.

Eat & Drink: For a town of only 267,000 residents, Fort Wayne is packed with such quality dining you may want to create a progressive meal during your short stay, ending with an Extreme Shake at **Just Cream** (✉ *338 E. Dupont Rd.* ☎ *260/449–1424* ⊕ *icecreamboutiquefw.square.site*).

Stay: The Bradley (✉ *204 W. Main St.* ☎ *260/428–4018* ⊕ *www.bradley-hotel.com*) is a Vera Bradley–themed hotel (a well-loved design shop in these parts). As you might expect, the brand's signature fabrics are on nearly every soft surface.

Breakfast: Duck into the tiny, 1950s-style **Cindy's Diner** (✉ 230 W. Berry St. ☎ 260/422–1957) for all-day breakfast and what's called "garbage" (hash browns, eggs, onions, cheese, and ham, all grilled together).

Day 9: Fort Wayne, IN, to Indianapolis, IN

126 miles (2 hours without traffic and stops)

For the final leg of the trip, it's an easy two-hour cruise south along I–69 south, an artery that connects the state's two largest (by population) cities.

ALONG THE WAY
Eat & Drink: Why wait until you reach Indianapolis to start the Indy Ice-Cream Trail? In business since 1870, **Graeter's** (✉ 864 S. Rangeline Rd. ⊕ www.graeters.com) is the only commercial ice-cream manufacturer to use French Pot freezers. Taste the frozen goodness for yourself at its location just north of Indy in Carmel.

INDIANAPOLIS
Do: Either stroll or rent a bike to experience a portion of the 8-mile-long **Indianapolis Cultural Trail** (⊕ www.indyculturaltrail.org), rimmed with art sculptures. Learn more about the Indy 500 at the **Indianapolis Motor Speedway Museum** (✉ 4750 W. 16th St. ☎ 317/492–6784 ⊕ www.imsmuseum.org), located at the famed track itself, or browse the collection (with works by Rembrandt, Hopper, Matisse, Picasso, and O'Keeffe) at the **Indianapolis Museum of Art** (✉ 4000 N. Michigan Rd. ☎ 317/923–1331 ⊕ www.discovernewfields.org), on the 152-acre Newfields campus.

Eat & Drink: At the state's oldest bar, the **Slippery Noodle Inn** (✉ 372 S. Meridian St. ☎ 317/631–6974 ⊕ www.slipperynoodle.com), you'll be able to tick off live blues music and dinner (from wings to pasta, plus burgers, subs, and salads) in one swoop.

Stay: Explore the nightlife in Indiana's largest city by booking a room downtown. **The Alexander** (✉ 333 S. Delaware St. ☎ 317/624–8200 ⊕ www.thealexander.com) has a great location and Instagram-worthy, mouth-blown glass pendant lighting at its on-site lounge, Plat 99.

Breakfast: The omelets at **Café Patachou** (✉ 225 W. Washington St. ⊕ www.cafepatachou.com) carry sassy names like "The Hippie with a Benz" while "broken yolks" are over-easy eggs on toast with a side of arugula salad. For a to-go treat for your plane ride, order a "Compost Cookie," inspired by Milk Bar owner Christina Tosi.

All the Great Lakes

Written by Kristine Hansen

If you grew up near a Great Lake, you were likely drilled with the HOMES acronym in grade school to keep them straight: Huron, Ontario, Michigan, Erie, and Superior. Filled with folklore (hello, shipwrecks!) and rimmed with lighthouses, cultural landmarks, and resort towns (not to mention a thriving surfing culture and wine regions), these five freshwater lakes easily marvel first-time visitors. No, you cannot see across the lakes and, yes, these waters are deep. Ticking off five lakes in 10 days might seem ambitious, but it's not impossible. Using this carefully crafted route, all the Great Lakes are seamlessly woven into an easy-to-follow itinerary packed with signature regional eats, blissful hikes, and natural wonders (like Niagara Falls and Indiana Dunes National Park).

At a Glance

Start: Chicago, IL

End: Chicago, IL

All the Great Lakes

Miles Traveled: 1,734 miles

Suggested Duration: 10 days

States Visited: Illinois, Indiana, Michigan, New York, Ohio, Ontario (Canada), Wisconsin

Key Sights: The Chicago Art Institute; Indiana Dunes National Park; Lake Erie Islands; Mackinac Island; Niagara Falls

Best Time to Go: Since this is the northernmost side of the country, avoid winter unless you get a kick out of frozen lakeshores. Summer is, of course, when the weather is best, but late spring or early fall only mean layers of clothing and thinner crowds.

Day 1: Chicago, IL, to Indiana Dunes National Park, IN

45 miles (1 hour without traffic and stops)

Your first day is also your easiest driving day, a quick one-hour trip traveling I–90 east toward Indiana. Flights into Chicago's O'Hare International Airport, one of the world's largest, are easy to come by and cars can be rented at the airport.

ALONG THE WAY

Eat & Drink: It's pretty much a sea of truck stops and fast-food drive-thrus along this route, but at the Calumet Avenue exit you will find a refreshing treat at **Jodi's Italian Ice Factory** (✉ *7322*

Calumet Ave. ☎ 219/803–2240 ⊕ www.
jodisice.com) in Hammond, Indiana, as
well as at **Dairy Belle** (✉ 7102 Calumet
Ave. ☎ 219/931–4550), a vintage ice-
cream stand.

INDIANA DUNES NATIONAL PARK

Do: Whether you're a trailblazer or stroller,
Indiana Dunes National Park (✉ 1050
N. Mineral Springs Rd. ☎ 219/395–
1882 ⊕ www.nps.gov/indu) offers hikes
for both. Hugging 15 miles of Lake Michigan shoreline, its 15,000 acres include 50
miles of trails. If you're into biking, pack
the bikes to explore the Calumet and Porter Brickyard Bike Trails. On the northern
tip of the park, **Old Lighthouse Museum**
(✉ 100 Heisman Harbor Rd. ☎ 219/872–
6133 ⊕ www.oldlighthousemuseum.
org) in Michigan City is the state's oldest
remaining lighthouse.

Eat & Drink: Don't be fooled: although
not as slick and spacious as, say, Goose
Island's Chicago taproom, **Burn'Em
Brewing** (✉ 1215 E. 2nd St. ☎ 219/217–
2337 ⊕ www.burnembrewing.com)
in Michigan City is a nice surprise for
sipping its craft beer in a down-home
environment, with a small outdoor patio.

Stay: With a restaurant and wine/martini
bar, and a five-minute walk to a private
beach, the 1924 **Duneland Beach Inn**
(✉ 3311 Pottawattomie Trail ☎ 219/874–
7729 ⊕ www.farinasupperclub.com) in
Michigan City is a posh place to spend
the night.

Breakfast: Inspired by regions around the
world, **Third Coast Spice Café** (✉ 761 Indian
Boundary Rd. ☎ 219/926–5858 ⊕ www.
thirdcoastspice.com) in Chesterton
serves breakfast dishes like Buffalo hot
hash and fun drinks like a cinnamon toast
latte.

Day 2: Indiana Dunes National Park, IN, to Cleveland, OH

*293 miles (4 hours, 40 minutes without
traffic and stops)*

Buckle up for your nearly five-hour ride to
what many call the North Coast, following I–90 east all the way.

ALONG THE WAY

Eat & Drink: Most people know South
Bend, Indiana, for the University of
Notre Dame (and presidential candidate,
former mayor, and Secretary of Transportation Pete Buttigieg) but the city
also has delicious restaurants, making
it the perfect spot to stop for lunch with
options like **Fiddler's Hearth** (✉ 127 N.
Main St. ☎ 574/232–2853 ⊕ www.fiddler-
shearth.com) and **West End Bakery** (✉ 414
W. 7th St. ☎ 574/225–1267 ⊕ www.face-
book.com/WestEndBakeryMishawaka) in
nearby Mishawaka, open since 1928.

Shop: Shipshewana, Indiana, off I–90
east and south of exit 101, is America's
largest Amish community. Pull over
to browse not only baked goods but
also handcrafted furniture at **Branden-
berry Amish Furniture** (✉ 1045 Rte.
5 ☎ 260/768–3270 ⊕ www.brandenber-
ryamishfurniture.com) and **Dutchman Log
Furniture** (✉ 7275 W. 200 N ☎ 260/366–
0702 ⊕ www.dutchmanlogfurniture.
com). If shabby-chic is more your
style, check out **Cherry Pickers** (✉ 160
Morton St. ☎ 574/612–4569 ⊕ www.
cherrypickersinc.com) and **2 Chicks and
a Chair** (✉ 155 Harrison St. ☎ 574/536–
6575 ⊕ www.facebook.com/2Chicksan-
daChair) for reclaimed finds.

CLEVELAND

Do: Few people know that Cleveland
has beaches and—gasp!—islands (hop
a ferry from Sandusky, an hour west of
Cleveland, to Lake Erie Islands, the chain
of 19 islands within Ohio; others in the

archipelago are in Canada, Michigan, New York, and Pennsylvania). Stroll Lake Erie's shoreline or just chill on the sand at **Edgewater Park** (☎ 216/635–3200 ⊕ www. clevelandmetroparks.com). If you're a music fan, don't miss the **Rock & Roll Hall of Fame** (✉ 1100 E. 9th St. ☎ 216/781–7625 ⊕ www.rockhall.com).

Eat & Drink: Michael Symon (of ABC's The Chew and five Food Network shows, including Iron Chef America) is Cleveland's most famous chef. Check out his food at **Mabel's BBQ** (✉ 2050 E. 4th St. ☎ 216/417–8823 ⊕ www.mabelsbbq. com) in downtown Cleveland—don't miss the banana cream pie.

Stay: Since the goal of this road trip is to see the Great Lakes, book a room with a Lake Erie view at **The Schofield Hotel** (✉ 2000 E. 9th St. ☎ 216/357–3250 ⊕ www.theschofieldhotel.com), a boutique hotel in a 1902 building that's a short walk to the lakefront.

Breakfast: Stray from the downtown area to the super cute **Luna Bakery & Cafe** (✉ 2482 Fairmount Blvd. ☎ 216/231–8585 ⊕ www.lunabakerycafe.com) in Cleveland Heights, for everything from a flaky, buttery croissant to a breakfast burrito or smoked salmon toast.

Day 3: Cleveland, OH, to Buffalo, NY

189 miles (3 hours without traffic and stops)

I-90 east takes you the entire way there, with a few tolls en route. You also pass through Pennsylvania.

ALONG THE WAY
Nature: Angola on the Lake, New York, is a popular vacation hamlet and second-home community, adjacent to **Lake Erie Beach Park** (✉ 9568 Lake Shore Rd., Angola ☎ 716/549–0970 ⊕ www. townofevans.org). It's the perfect spot

Essential Listening

Milwaukee writer Dan Egan's The Death and Life of the Great Lakes reads like a novel, pulling you into environmental problems like zebra-mussel invasions, but also the history of port traffic.

to stretch your legs and sink your toes in the sand.

Eat & Drink: Just before you hit Buffalo are several lakefront options, including an extensive lunch menu (including Maryland crab cakes, signature burgers, and Alaskan snow-crab legs) at **Rodney's** (✉ 4179 Lake Shore Rd. ☎ 716/627–5166 ⊕ www.rodneysonthelake.com) in Hamburg, right on the shoreline with outdoor seating.

BUFFALO
Do: The Frank Lloyd Wright–designed **Graycliff** (✉ 6472 Old Lake Shore Rd. ☎ 716/947–9217 ⊕ www.experiencegraycliff.org) hugs Lake Erie's bluffs in nearby Derby, 30 minutes south of downtown Buffalo. It offers four different tours, with the hour-long standard tour best for those pressed for time.

Eat & Drink: It's a fact: Buffalo's chicken wings are famous and delicious. There's even a Buffalo Wing Trail. Looking for something else that's tasty and quick? **West Side Bazaar** (✉ 1432 Niagara St. ☎ 716/464–6389 ⊕ www.westsidebazaar.com) is a project providing recent immigrants a boost for their food stands or artisans' booths.

Stay: One of the most intriguing hotels in Buffalo is also among its finest. **The Richardson Hotel** (✉ 444 Forest Ave. ☎ 716/493–2610 ⊕ www.therichardsonhotelbuffalo.com) is set on 42 sprawling acres in a Romanesque-style building that was once an asylum.

Breakfast: Flapjacks drizzled with New York maple syrup or mini-doughnuts and omelets at the vintage-y **Swan Street Diner** (⊠ *700 Swan St.* ☎ *716/768–1823* ⊕ *www.swanstreetdiner.com*)—tucked into a 1937 former diner car—will get you fueled for another day of driving.

Day 4: Buffalo, NY, to Niagara Falls, NY

20 miles (25 minutes without traffic and stops)

Don't be fooled by the short drive along I–190 north; you'll need all that extra time to explore Niagara Falls, which straddles the United States and Canada, and where Lake Erie drains into Lake Ontario. ⚠ **Don't forget to pack your passport if you plan to cross the border so you can return to New York with ease.** If you'd rather leave the car behind, book a one-day tour with **Gray Line** (☎ *877/285–2113* ⊕ *www.graylineniagarafalls.com*), which offers three different tours.

ALONG THE WAY

Eat & Drink: Tiny Lewiston, New York, is along the drive and boasts **Orange Cat Coffee Co.** (⊠ *703 Center St.* ☎ *716/754–2888*), perfect if you plan to depart Buffalo early in the day. Just look for the white house with the black shutters.

NIAGARA FALLS

Do: Two of the three famous falls are in the United States: Bridal Veil Falls and American Falls. The other (Horseshoe Falls, also called Canadian Falls and the largest) lies in Ontario, Canada. **Niagara Falls State Park** (⊠ *332 Prospect St.* ☎ *716/278–1794* ⊕ *www.niagarafallsstatepark.com*)—the country's oldest state park and championed into preservation by Frederick Law Olmsted—offers a mix of overlooks as well as trails to hike. Drop by the visitor center to get

Extend Your Trip

From Buffalo or Niagara Falls: The Best of New York State *(Ch. 8)*

From Sturgeon Bay: The Best of the Heartland *(Ch. 6)*

From Chicago: The Great American Baseball Road Trip *(Ch. 2)*; A Frank Lloyd Wright Tour *(Ch. 6)*

your bearings. Old Falls Street, USA, is a three-block shopping and entertainment district lined with Adirondack chairs and food vendors. Every Friday night during summer is a live music concert.

Eat & Drink: The Kasbah (⊠ *6130 Dunn St.* ☎ *905/357–1000* ⊕ *www.thekasbah.ca*) is a farm-to-table Greek, Italian, and Armenian restaurant owned by an Armenian émigré and boasting a patio. Leave decisions to the chef with the Kasbah Combo dinner menu. In a sea of chains, **Milestones on the Falls** (⊠ *6755 Fallsview Blvd., Niagara Falls, ON, Canada* ☎ *905/358–4720* ⊕ *www.milestonesonthefalls.com*) is refreshing, with views of the falls, bistro-type fare for lunch and dinner, and a nice wine list featuring Niagara selections.

Stay: Given that Niagara Falls is a popular group-tour spot and also attracts honeymooners, the lodging stock is a mix of quaint inns and chains. **Old Stone Inn Boutique Hotel** (⊠ *6080 Fallsview Blvd., Niagara Falls, ON, Canada* ☎ *905/357–1234* ⊕ *www.oldstoneinnhotel.com*), a former flour mill dating back to 1904, lies somewhere between, with a chic restaurant and bar flaunting steampunk decor.

Breakfast: Linger over three-egg omelets and Belgian waffles at the **Flying Saucer** (⊠ *6768 Lundy's La., Niagara Falls, ON, Canada* ☎ *905/356–4553* ⊕ *www.flyingsaucerrestaurant.com*), a quirky alternative to IHOP and Denny's with the same diner-like location.

Day 5: Niagara Falls, NY, to Bay City, MI

300 miles (4 hours, 50 minutes without traffic and stops)

Bypassing Detroit—via I-69 west in Michigan—to pass through Canada and reach this cozy town along Lake Huron's Saginawa Bay is a decision you won't regret. You'll pass through many cute towns, like Frankenmuth with its Bavarian-style architecture, on this easy-to-drive route relatively free of traffic congestion.

ALONG THE WAY

Eat & Drink: You can't leave Canada without sampling poutine. **Smoke's Poutinerie London** (✉ *551 Richmond St.* ☎ *519/810–5353* ⊕ *smokespoutinerie.com/store/smokes-poutinerie-london*) in London, Ontario, is a quick in-and-out option.

Town: The **Flint Institute of Arts** (✉ *1120 E. Kearsley St.* ☎ *810/234–1695* ⊕ *www.flintarts.org*) in Flint, Michigan, is the state's second-largest art museum with paintings by Mary Cassatt and John Singer Sargent, as well as ancient Asian objects dating as far back as the 11th century.

BAY CITY

Do: With just 33,000 residents, Bay City has a small-town vibe and access to beaches like **Bay City State Park** (✉ *3582 State Park Dr.* ☎ *989/684–3020*), home to Tobico Marsh, the largest remaining freshwater coastal wetlands along the Great Lakes. Craving some culture? **Saginaw Art Museum** (✉ *1126 N. Michigan Ave.* ☎ *989/754–2491* ⊕ *www.saginawartmuseum.org*), in nearby Saginaw, is a hidden gem.

Eat & Drink: Tucked into the former city hall, **Old City Hall Restaurant** (✉ *814 Saginaw St.* ☎ *989/892–4140* ⊕ *www.oldcityhallrestaurant.com*) flaunts an incredible wine list and 23 beers on tap, many from Michigan.

Stay: The **Historic Webster House** (✉ *900 5th St.* ☎ *989/441-0579* ⊕ *www.historicwebsterhouse.com*) is a Victorian-era B&B featuring stone walls, fireplaces, and Jacuzzi tubs. Each night there's a free wine-and-cheese reception for guests.

Breakfast: Although the brunch menu at **Harless + Hugh** (✉ *1003 Washington Ave.* ☎ *989/385–1657* ⊕ *www.harlessandhugh.com*) is tiny, it's done well. Choose from items like avocado toast, house waffles, and breakfast burritos with roasted tomato chutney. Mimosas, pour-over coffee, and cappuccinos are also served.

Day 6: Bay City, MI, to Traverse City, MI

146 miles (2 hours, 25 minutes without traffic and stops)

I-75 north to Route 72 west takes you to Traverse City, passing through a series of small towns along the way.

ALONG THE WAY

Nature: The 314-acre Seven Bridges Nature Area in Kalkaska offers easy hiking trails within a wetlands area, plus the remains of an 1882 sawmill.

Eat & Drink: Just before you reach Traverse City, **The Cottage** (✉ *472 Munson Ave.* ☎ *231/947–9261* ⊕ *www.cottagecafetc.com*) offers the ultimate in comfort food: all-you-can-eat fried perch.

TRAVERSE CITY

Do: If you love wine, Traverse City is your jam, as it's the state's most developed (and revered) wine region with two AVAs (American Viticultural Areas): Old Mission Peninsula AVA and Leelanau Peninsula AVA. The town of 16,000 residents also hugs Lake Michigan along the shores of

There are no cars allowed on peaceful Mackinac Island (you'll have to park your car overnight at a lot by the ferry dock).

Grand Traverse Bay. Tasting rooms are akin to Napa and Sonoma with food-pairing packages, vineyards on-site, and grand tasting rooms. **Green Bird Organic Cellars** (✉ *9825 E. Engles Rd.* ☎ *231/386–5636* ⊕ *www.greenbirdcellars.com*) is a cute winery stop; it's on a 67-acre organic farm and the owners produce both estate wines and hard ciders.

Eat & Drink: This town offers a lot of diverse dining but you shouldn't drive away without sampling locally grown cherries, woven into dinner entrées and desserts alike. Do a taste-around at **The Little Fleet** (✉ *448 E. Front St.* ☎ *231/943–1116* ⊕ *www. thelittlefleet.com*), a food-truck yard. Or opt for a water view at **Harrington's By the Bay** (✉ *13890 S.W. Bay Shore Dr.* ☎ *231/421–9393* ⊕ *www.harringtonsbythebay.com*) or the **Boathouse Restaurant** (✉ *14039 Peninsula Dr.* ☎ *231/223–4030* ⊕ *www. boathouseonwestbay.com*) for an upscale dinner, paired with local wine. And don't leave without sampling cherry pie at either of the two cafés run by **Grand Traverse Pie Company** (⊕ *www.gtpie.com*).

Stay: Switch things up on your trip by bunking at a winery's guesthouse, like the **Inn at Chateau Grand Traverse** (✉ *12301 Center Rd.* ☎ *231/938–6120* ⊕ *www. cgtwines.com*), located at a winery dating back to 1974.

Breakfast: Tucked into a former state hospital that's now a cool spot to shop and eat, **Red Spire Brunch House** (✉ *800 Cottageview Dr.* ☎ *231/252-4648* ⊕ *www. redspirebrunchhouse.com*) features items like red velvet pancakes and a loaded spud omelet.

Day 7: Traverse City, MI, to Mackinac Island, MI

117 miles (2 hours without traffic and stops)

Leaving Traverse City, travel north on I–75 or U.S. 31 to Mackinaw City, driving through the Gaylord State Forest Area. You'll hop on the Star Line Mackinac Island Ferry to car-free Mackinac Island.

The ferry trip takes 18 minutes and parking is available near the ferry's departure point.

ALONG THE WAY

Eat & Drink: Gaylord is an outdoorsy community with many restaurants as well as **Big Buck Brewery** (✉ 550 S. Wisconsin Ave. ☎ 989/448–7072 ⊕ www.bigbuck-brewery.com) with its robust menu of salads, burgers, and pizza.

Roadside Attraction: Just outside downtown Traverse City is "the world's largest cherry pie pan." Find it at the **Sara Lee Bakery Group** (✉ 3424 Cass Rd.).

MACKINAC ISLAND

Do: Even if you aren't staying at **Grand Hotel** (✉ 286 Grand Ave. ☎ 800/334–7263 ⊕ www.grandhotel.com), pop over for a self-guided tour of the 1887 grand estate, one of Mackinac Island's most photographed buildings. Two lighthouses are on the island: McGulpin Point Lighthouse and Old Mackinac Point Lighthouse. A horse-drawn carriage tour is a fun way to explore the island in less than a day. Fudge crafted on the island is a favorite souvenir.

Eat & Drink: Frequent island visitors love **Millie's on Main** (✉ 7294 Main St. ☎ 906/847–9901 ⊕ www.milliesonmain.com) for pub fare and drinks at **Pink Pony Bar** (✉ 7221 Main St. ☎ 906/847–3341 ⊕ www.pinkpony-mackinac.com), perched above the water and with cute pink umbrellas outdoors. Pink Pony serves also breakfast, lunch, and dinner.

Stay: The **Inn on Mackinac** (✉ 6896 Main St. ☎ 855/784–3846 ⊕ www.innonmackinac.com) is a vibrantly colored Victorian inn in the historic Marina District.

Breakfast: Lucky Bean (✉ 7383 Market St. ⊕ www.luckybeanmi.com) is a sleek and modern coffeehouse serving not only coffee and espresso drinks, but also bagels, pastries, and oatmeal to start your day off right.

Day 8: Mackinac Island, MI, to Marquette, MI

162 miles (2 hours, 50 minutes without traffic and stops)

Today you'll cross into Michigan's UP (Upper Peninsula) and drive through Seney National Wildlife Refuge on Route 77 north.

ALONG THE WAY

Nature: Pictured Rocks National Lakeshore (✉ N8391 Sand Point Rd. ☎ 906/387–3700 ⊕ www.nps.gov/piro)—named for the mineral stains on its sandstone cliffs—in Munising hugs the South Shore of Lake Superior.

Eat & Drink: Smoked fish is a delicacy in these parts. Try for yourself at **Cap'n Ron's Smoked Fish** (✉ 1336 Commercial St. ☎ 906/202–0960 ⊕ capn-rons.square.site) in Munising, which sells smoked whitefish, smoked fish dip, and smoked fish "sausage" to go as well as pasties (another signature food of the UP).

MARQUETTE

Do: This college town along Lake Superior (across the water from Thunder Bay, Ontario) has a vibrant downtown lined with a natural foods co-op and vintage stores. It's also surrounded by protected forests—including **Hiawatha National Forest** (☎ 906/428–5800 ⊕ www.fs.usda.gov) and Presque Isle Park—for easy day hikes. Stroll to the end of downtown for a neat glimpse at the mouth of Lake Superior.

Eat & Drink: Tucked into a former movie theater in downtown Marquette, **Delft Bistro** (✉ 139 W. Washington St. ☎ 906/273–2455 ⊕ www.thedelftbistro.com) is a chic, fun lunch and dinner spot while **Lagniappe** (✉ 145 Jackson Cut Alley ☎ 906/226–8200 ⊕ marquettecajun.com) offers a taste of Cajun cuisine. There's even a Voodoo Bar, pouring 20 Michigan craft beers.

Stay: Most of Marquette's lodging choices are chains, but the **Landmark Inn** (✉ *230 N. Front St.* ☎ *906/228–2580* ⊕ *www.thelandmarkinn.com*) is a good nonchain option. The inn also has a restaurant/pub and frames views of Lake Superior.

Breakfast: Café Bodega (✉ *517 N. 3rd St.* ☎ *906/226–7009* ⊕ *www.bodegamqt.com*) serves all-day breakfast every day of the week with a special focus on vegan/vegetarian cuisine and locally sourced ingredients.

Day 9: Marquette, MI, to Sturgeon Bay, WI

217 miles (3 hours, 45 minutes without traffic and stops)

U.S. 41 south traces the western shoreline of Green Bay through Wisconsin until you hit the city of Green Bay, before curling northeast to Sturgeon Bay. This is the largest city in Door County, a resort community popular with Chicagoans and Milwaukeeans, located on its southern portion between Green Bay and Lake Michigan.

ALONG THE WAY

Eat & Drink: Pick up Mexican lunch at **Blue Bike Burrito** (✉ *2020 Hall Ave.* ☎ *715/735–9889* ⊕ *www.bluebikeburrito.com*) in Marinette, Wisconsin, and find a spot along the waterfront to dine.

STURGEON BAY

Do: Learn more about the region's shipbuilding industry and Swedish heritage with a visit to **Door County Maritime Museum** (✉ *120 N. Madison Ave.* ☎ *920/743–5958* ⊕ *www.dcmm.org*). Door County is also home to five state parks with easy hikes and stunning water views. Closest to Sturgeon Bay are **Whitefish Dunes State Park** (✉ *3275 Clarks Lake Rd.* ☎ *920/823–2400* ⊕ *dnr.wisconsin.gov*), on the Lake Michigan side, and **Potawatomi State Park** (☎ *920/746–2890* ⊕ *dnr.wisconsin.gov/topic/parks/potawatomi*), on the Green Bay side.

Eat & Drink: The to-go sandwiches at **Door County Creamery** (✉ *10653 N. Bay Shore Dr.* ☎ *920/854–3388* ⊕ *www.doorcountycreamery.com*) are heavenly and you can enjoy them right next door at Sister Bay Beach, along Green Bay's shoreline in Sister Bay. Fish boils are a local tradition: try one out at **Old Post Office Restaurant** (✉ *10040 N. Water St.* ☎ *920/854–4034* ⊕ *www.oldpostoffice-doorcounty.com*) in Fish Creek for dinner. Numerous farm stands sell fresh or frozen cherries, depending on the season, along with cherry pies and other desserts.

Stay: Sturgeon Bay is loaded with cute inns and B&Bs, including **Holiday Music Motel** (✉ *30 N. 1st Ave.* ☎ *920/743–5571* ⊕ *www.holidaymusicmotel.com*), a laid-back music-themed motel with its own radio station, and **White Lace Inn** (✉ *16 N. 5th Ave.* ☎ *920/743–1105* ⊕ *www.whitelaceinn.com*), a romantic B&B walking distance to downtown.

Breakfast: It's worth the half-hour drive north of Sturgeon Bay to view goats grazing on the grass roof at **Al Johnson's** (✉ *10698 N. Bay Shore Dr.* ☎ *920/854–2626* ⊕ *www.aljohnsons.com*) in Sister Bay. You might even have time to stay for the Swedish pancakes. Across the street is Green Bay (the water, not the city).

Day 10: Sturgeon Bay, WI, to Chicago, IL

245 miles (4 hours without traffic and stops)

I–43 south takes you straight to Chicago (merging with I–94 just south of downtown Milwaukee), but for a route that rims Lake Michigan, take Route 42 south through the towns of Kewaunee and Two Rivers, before switching to I–43 south in Manitowoc.

ALONG THE WAY

Town: In Milwaukee, Lincoln Memorial Drive is where you can soak up Lake Michigan at its glory as you dodge dog-walkers, bicyclists, and runners along its paved paths. You'll also get a view of the Santiago Calatrava–designed **Milwaukee Art Museum** (✉ *700 N. Art Museum Dr.* ☎ *414/224–3200* ⊕ *www.mam.org*).

Eat & Drink: Stop by the **Milwaukee Public Market** (✉ *400 N. Water St.* ☎ *414/336–1111* ⊕ *www.milwaukeepublicmarket. org*), where a variety of vendors serve an eclectic mix of food and beverages.

Roadside Attraction: You can't miss the castle-motif **Mars Cheese Castle** (✉ *2800 W. Frontage Rd.* ☎ *855/352–6277* ⊕ *www.marscheese.com*) in Kenosha County, right on I–94 south at exit 340. About 400 varieties of Wisconsin cheese are sold here.

CHICAGO

Do: As the biggest city ringing the Great Lakes, Chicago has an incredible amount of sights and culture. Take a boat tour down the Chicago River and then a stroll along Lakefront Trail and Lake Michigan, which leads to the **Field Museum** (✉ *1400 S. Lake Shore Dr.* ☎ *312/922–9410* ⊕ *www.fieldmuseum.org*) and **Shedd Aquarium** (✉ *1200 S. Lake Shore Dr.* ☎ *312/939–2438* ⊕ *www.sheddaquarium.org*). The **Art Institute of Chicago** (✉ *111 S. Michigan Ave.* ☎ *312/443–3600* ⊕ *www.artic.edu*) is another must-see.

Eat & Drink: You can't leave Chicago without trying deep-dish pizza. **Lou Malnati's** (✉ *805 S. State St.* ☎ *312/786–1000* ⊕ *www.loumalnatis.com*) is a local institution. Afterwards, head north to the hip Lincoln Park neighborhood and its collection of bars, like dive bar **Delilah's** (✉ *2771 N. Lincoln Ave.* ☎ *773/472–2771* ⊕ *www.delilahschicago.com*) or blues music institution **Buddy Guy's Legends** (✉ *700 S. Wabash Ave.* ☎ *312/427–1190* ⊕ *www.buddyguy.com*).

Stay: On the city's Gold Coast, understated luxury abounds at the **Park Hyatt Chicago** (✉ *800 N. Michigan Ave.* ☎ *312/335–1234* ⊕ *www.hyatt.com*), which dominates the skyline high above the old Water Tower. The views are spectacular from many of its oversized rooms.

Breakfast: Old-school **Eleven City Diner** (✉ *1112 S. Wabash Ave.* ☎ *312/212–1112* ⊕ *www.elevencitydiner.com*) attracts locals looking for all-day breakfast and deli staples.

A Frank Lloyd Wright Tour

Written by Kristine Hansen

One of the world's most famous architects, Frank Lloyd Wright's masterful buildings are scattered all across the country (38 states hold at least one of his designs), but the best of the best lie between Chicago and Philadelphia. This trip will take you through small towns, major metropolises, and pastoral paradises, including the Mayan-inspired Unity Temple in Oak Park, Illinois; Fallingwater in rural Pennsylvania; and the recently restored Martin House in Buffalo, New York.

The godfather of Prairie School organic-style architecture may have been born in Wisconsin (in 1867), but Wright's adult years were spent in Oak Park, a Chicago suburb that today is home to the world's largest concentration of Wright-designed projects, including his home and studio. Wright enthusiastically took on residential and commercial commissions (from churches to cottages) during his 70-year career until his death at the age of 92 (in 1959). Buckle up and get ready for this highly immersive study into why Wright garnered a cult following worldwide.

At a Glance

Start: Chicago, IL

End: Philadelphia, PA

Miles Traveled: 1,245 miles

Suggested Duration: 7 days

States Visited: Illinois, Indiana, Michigan, New York, Pennsylvania

Key Sights: Beth Sholom Synagogue House; Fallingwater; Frank Lloyd Wright Home and Studio; Polymath Park; Unity Temple

Best Time to Go: Since some attractions are closed during the winter months, stick to spring and fall, which provide glimpses of flora and fauna, and fewer crowds.

Day 1: Chicago, IL, to Oak Park, IL

9 miles (20 minutes without traffic or stops)

The Chicago area is serviced by two major airports: O'Hare International Airport and Midway International Airport. Both are accessible to Oak Park and downtown Chicago via the "L" aboveground trains operated by the Chicago Transit Authority. You can also rent a car at each airport. Oak Park borders the city of Chicago on its west side, off I–290 (the Eisenhower Expressway), a 20-minute drive from downtown.

ALONG THE WAY

Town: Slow down your pace to properly take in the world's largest concentration of Wright projects in Oak Park's Frank Lloyd Wright–Prairie School of Architecture Historic District, on the National Register of Historic Places since 1973. Choose from a self-guided audio walking tour (sold in the home and studio's gift shop) or two-hour bicycle tour (weekends

between May and October). The houses are easy to find: look for hipped roofs, angular turrets, overhanging eaves, and disguised front doors.

Photo Op: Two blocks from Frank Lloyd Wright's home and studio is **Austin Gardens** (✉ *167 Forest Ave.* ☎ *708/524–2050* ⊕ *www.pdop.org*)—wrapped in an iron gate with a bronze bust of Wright at the south end of Forest Avenue.

OAK PARK

Do: Get a lesson in Wright's artistry (before he moved deeper into his boxy, Prairie-style design) via a 60-minute guided tour of the shingle-style **Frank Lloyd Wright Home and Studio** (✉ *951 Chicago Ave.* ☎ *312/994–4000* ⊕ *www.flwright. org*), in his namesake Historic District, home to dozens of residential commissions completed between 1896 and 1913. With UNESCO World Heritage site status, the modern, reinforced-concrete **Unity Temple** (✉ *875 Lake St.* ☎ *708/848–6225* ⊕ *www.unitytemple.org*) is a nod to Wright's Unitarian upbringing.

Eat & Drink: From Indiana rabbit to Maine lobster, all prepared by a chef whose culinary roots are in the Caribbean and Boston, **Hemmingway's Bistro** (✉ *211 N. Oak Park Ave.* ☎ *708/524–0806* ⊕ *www. hemmingwaysbistro.com*) is a nod to Oak Park's other famous former resident: author Ernest Hemingway. For a sweet treat, dip back a century at **Petersen's Ice Cream** (✉ *1100 Chicago Ave.* ☎ *708/386–6131*), in business at the same Oak Park address since 1919.

Stay: Immerse yourself more fully in a Wright design by waking up in the 1915 **Emil Bach House** (✉ *7415 N. Sheridan Rd.* ☎ *773/654–3959* ⊕ *www.emilbachhouse.com*) in Chicago's Rogers Park, with three bedrooms, two baths, and a full kitchen in the two-story home. Slivers of Lake Michigan are viewable from many rooms.

Breakfast: Ask any Emil Bach House docent where the best latte is and their

A Frank Lloyd Wright Tour

eyes will get all dreamy before mentioning **Charmers Café** (✉ *1500 W. Jarvis Ave.* ☎ *773/743–2233* ⊕ *www.charmerscafe.com*). The plant shop/café brews coffee and espresso drinks, plus the most indigo shade of lavender lemonade you've ever sipped, along with homemade "pop tarts" and the locally famous chimichurri egg sandwich.

Day 2: Oak Park, IL, to Chicago, IL

18 miles (35 miles without traffic and stops)

While your two sights today are both in Chicago, they are at opposite ends of the city: in Rogers Park just south of Evanston on the North Side and in Hyde Park on the South Side. Travel time between both is around 40 minutes. Taking Lake Shore Drive (U.S. 41 south) is the most scenic view, hugging Lake Michigan, with downtown Chicago on the final third of the route.

ALONG THE WAY

Photo Op: At **Chicago Cultural Center** (✉ *78 E. Washington St.* ☎ *312/744–6630* ⊕ *www.chicago.gov*), a handcrafted dome by Louis Comfort Tiffany—a staple in the Arts and Crafts movement, which informed Wright's styles—is a work of beauty. Fun fact: the Windy City contains the country's largest collection of Tiffany decorative-art glass.

Eat & Drink: You weren't planning to leave Chicago without a relish-and-mustard-coated hot dog tucked into a steamed poppy-seed bun, were you? Skip the cult-favorite chain Portillo's for an indie stand like **Fred and Jack's** (✉ *7600 S. Yale Ave.* ☎ *773/783–9700* ⊕ *www.orderfredandjacks.com*) on the South Side, one of Chicago's oldest, born out of a pushcart during the 1940s.

CHICAGO

Do: Start with a 45-minute guided tour of the Emil Bach House on the North Side. Its Cream City brick exterior was used abundantly in Milwaukee around the time of the home's 1915 construction, and the Frank Lloyd Wright Trust's restoration emulated nearly every furnishing and sconce from original drawings for a Japanese tea house. Next, head south to the 1909 **Frederick C. Robie House** (✉ *5757 S. Woodlawn Ave.* ☎ *312/994–4000* ⊕ *www.flwright.org*) on the University of Chicago campus in Hyde Park; three tours are available, and the in-depth, 90-minute one is perfect for serious Wright fans (Friday and weekends only). Tenets of Wright's designs, including embedded lamps in the dining table, were retained in the 2009 restoration. Crushed you didn't see Wright's Imperial Hotel in Tokyo before it was demolished in 1967? The hotel's signature chair is included in a permanent furniture exhibit in the house.

Eat & Drink: Sip a cocktail or enjoy oysters on the half shell at the beach-house-like **Cindy's Rooftop** (✉ *12 S. Michigan Ave.* ☎ *312/792–3502* ⊕ *www.cindysrooftop.com*) while viewing the Sir Anish Kapoor–designed *Cloud Gate* ("The Bean") sculpture in Millennium Park from above.

Stay: In Chicago's Fulton Market, where meatpackers once sizzled, **The Hoxton** (✉ *200 N. Green St.* ☎ *312/761–1700* ⊕ *www.thehoxton.com*) hosts *Top Chef* champion Stephanie Izard's rooftop Cabra Cevicheria.

Breakfast: Chicago diners are the real deal, like **Lou Mitchell's** (✉ *565 W. Jackson Blvd.* ☎ *312/939–3111* ⊕ *www.loumitchells.com*) in the Loop. Cram into a vinyl booth, close your eyes, and take a whiff of fluffy eggs, malted waffles, and silver-dollar pancakes—plus bottomless cups of coffee to fuel your ride.

Day 3: Chicago, IL, to Grand Rapids, MI

217 miles (3 hours, 25 minutes without traffic and stops)

Once you're out of Chicagoland (be prepared for traffic), it's a smooth, easy ride up to Michigan along I-94 east, often just a few miles inland from the Lake Michigan shoreline.

ALONG THE WAY

Photo Op: A quick drive-by of the 1939 **Andrew F. H. Armstrong House** (✉ *43 Cedar Trail*) in Ogden Dunes, Indiana, will remind you of Wright's talent of merging his buildings with the landscapes; the screened porch is nestled in a forested paradise.

Nature: With its new national park status, the 15,000-acre **Indiana Dunes National Park** (☎ *219/395–1882* ⊕ *www.nps.gov/indu*) in Porter, Indiana, flaunts 15 miles of shoreline on Lake Michigan's southern edge. Slip into hiking boots to explore its 50 miles of trails snaking through the namesake dunes along with wetlands, forests, and prairies.

Eat & Drink: These days the exit signs off I-94 tout wineries and CBD dispensaries, but locals know **Bit of Swiss** bakery (✉ *4333 Ridge Rd.* ☎ *269/429–1661* ⊕ *www.bitofswiss.com*) in Stevensville—pardon the pun—rises above with its grab-and-go mini cream cakes, fruit tortes, almond croissants, and cinnamon rolls. Outdoor café-style seating makes the cabin structure that much more charming.

Detour: While official tours do not take place, **The Acres** (✉ *Hawthorne Dr.*), a 70-acre subdivision in tiny Galesburg, just south of Grand Rapids, boasts four homes—plus a fifth built by Taliesin architect Francis "Will" Willsey a year after Wright's death—commissioned during the 1940s and 1950s by Upjohn

pharmaceutical scientists. In 2004, it landed on the National Register of Historic Places and is worth a drive through.

GRAND RAPIDS

Do: The 3,600-square-foot 1909 **Meyer May House** (✉ *450 Madison Ave. SE* ☎ *616/246–4821* ⊕ *www.meyermay-house.steelcase.com*) is an exquisite expression of Wright's Prairie style; it's owned by Steelcase, a local company contracted to make Wright's furnishings for the Johnson Wax Administration Building in Racine, Wisconsin. See George Mann Niedecken's signature chair "hoofs" and a mural unearthed during a late-1980s restoration. Because it's tucked into one of the country's largest historic districts (Heritage Hill), be sure to bring your walking shoes.

Eat & Drink: Along nearby Cherry Street are enough coffee shops, bars, and bakeries to get you wired or tanked. Book an, ahem, visitation at **Brewery Vivant** (✉ *925 Cherry St. SE* ☎ *616/719–1604* ⊕ *www.breweryvivant.com*), tucked into a converted funeral home's redbrick chapel and serving lunch and dinner items like poutine, duck nachos, and bratwurst (with house-brewed Belgian- and French-style beer, of course).

Stay: Seeing even just a small percentage of Heritage Hill's 1,300 homes—representing nearly every architectural style from 1844 on—might seem impossible, but staying overnight puts a serious dent in the effort. The **Leonard at Logan House** (✉ *440 Logan St. SE* ☎ *616/308–6585* ⊕ *www.leonardatlogan.com*), with just eight rooms, puts you in the thick of the action, serving a full breakfast in its 1914 storybook-like interiors. Otherwise, count yourself lucky if you snag a reservation at the Wright-designed, Usonian-style Samuel and Dorothy Eppstein House in Galesburg (available on Airbnb).

Breakfast: Despite its name, **Wealthy Street Bakery** (✉ *610 Wealthy St. SE* ☎ *616/301–2950* ⊕ *www.*

wealthystreetbakery.com) is not at all snooty. Heavy on pastries and loaded with gluten-free offerings, the bakery-café's menu includes seven breakfast sandwiches served on homemade ciabatta.

Day 4: Grand Rapids, MI, to Buffalo, NY

389 miles (6 hours without traffic and stops)

The fastest way to get to Buffalo is on I–69 east to Route 402 through Canada's southern Ontario province (bonus: Niagara Falls pit-stop!), crossing over the border on the Blue Water Bridge that links Port Huron, Michigan, with Sarnia, Ontario.

ALONG THE WAY

Nature: Straddling the U.S.-Canada border is **Niagara Falls State Park** (✉ *332 Prospect St., Niagara Falls* ☎ *716/278–1794* ⊕ *www.niagarafallsstatepark. com*), the country's oldest state park. Even if you only have time for a brief visit, the Observation Tower and four clearly marked Niagara Gorge hiking trails (stretch those legs!) are suitable orientations to this natural wonder.

Eat & Drink: At **Flip Burger** (✉ *305 Prospect St.* ☎ *716/278–1111* ⊕ *www.flipburger-inc.com*) in Niagara Falls, you can enjoy classic burgers and milkshakes on the seasonal patio.

BUFFALO

Do: When you reach Buffalo, buckle up for three off-beat, Wright-designed, posthumous landmarks based on his drawings. Modeled after the University of Wisconsin crew team's boathouse (which was never built), Wright apprentice Tony Putnam unveiled the Prairie-style **Fontana Boathouse** (✉ *1 Rotary Row* ☎ *716/362–3140* ⊕ *www.wrightsboathouse.org*) along the Niagara River in 2007. At home among dozens of antique cars in the

Buffalo Transportation Pierce-Arrow Museum, the 2014 Buffalo Filling Station (✉ *263 Michigan Ave.* ☎ *716/853–0084* ⊕ *www. pierce-arrow.com*) features a fireplace, deck, copper roof with twin totem poles, and salmon-hued concrete exterior. Finally, in Frederick Law Olmsted's Delaware Park (home to Forest Lawn Cemetery) lies the **Blue Sky Mausoleum** (✉ *972–990 W. Delavan Ave.* ⊕ *www.blueskymausoleum.com*), built in 2004.

In addition, Isabel and Darwin Martin's former 15,000-square-foot home (built between 1903 and 1905) at the **Martin House Complex** (✉ *125 Jewett Pkwy.* ☎ *716/856–3858* ⊕ *www. martinhouse.org*) saw one of the most extensive renovations of any Wright home (costing $52 million), right on down to the Tree of Life stained-glass windows.

Eat & Drink: Immigrant food vendors at the **West Side Bazaar** (✉ *1432 Niagara St.* ☎ *716/464–6389* ⊕ *www.wedibuffalo.org*) are partially funded by a local economic-development initiative, bringing their cuisine to this grab-and-go marketplace that also sells crafts. **Hutch's** (✉ *1375 Delaware Ave.* ☎ *716/885–0074* ⊕ *www.hutchsrestaurant.com*) whisks you to France with dinner delicacies like soft-shell crabs, prime rib, Faroe Island salmon, and Nova Scotia halibut.

Stay: The Richardson Hotel (✉ *444 Forest Ave.* ⊕ *www.therichardsonhotelbuffalo.com*), located within the historic

Richardson Olmsted Campus and once an insane asylum, shows off the prowess of one of America's most famed architects, H. H. Henry Richardson. **The Buffalo AKG Art Museum** (✉ *1285 Elmwood Ave.* ☎ *716/882–8700* ⊕ *www.buffaloakg. org*), home to works by artists like Willem de Kooning, Mark Rothko, Jackson Pollock, and Lee Krasner, is a quick stroll away.

Breakfast: The concentration of Wright projects in Buffalo is daunting and takes two days to explore—but you can check the memory of one off (the building perished in a 1950 fire) over eggs and bacon at **Swan Street Diner** (✉ *700 Swan St.* ☎ *16/768–1823* ⊕ *www.swanstreet- diner.com*), tucked into a fully restored, 1937 Sterling Company diner car and located across the street from the Larkin Administration Building.

Day 5: Buffalo, NY, to Pittsburgh, PA

275 miles (4 hours, 25 minutes without traffic and stops)

Taking I–90 west out of Buffalo, you'll travel southwest to Erie before connect- ing with I–79 south shortly after entering Pennsylvania. The landscape along I–79 south and I–76 east is gorgeous; picture lots of rolling green hills that likely inspired Wright's designs.

ALONG THE WAY

Attraction: The Martins' sprawling property just outside Buffalo in Derby— dubbed **Graycliff** (✉ *6472 Old Lake Shore Rd.* ☎ *716/947–9217* ⊕ *www.experi- encegraycliff.org*)—is perched above Lake Erie. The two-hour tour is a deeper immersion into the late 1920s estate designed by Wright.

Eat & Drink: East Aurora, New York, may be the location for many Hallmark holiday films, but the village's roots are in the **Roycroft Campus** (✉ *31 S. Grove St.* ☎ *716/655–0261* ⊕ *www.roycroftcam- puscorporation.com*), a utopian society founded by Elbert Hubbard in 1895, where craftspeople churned out Morris chairs and other Arts and Crafts designs within the guild. Tour the campus and enjoy lunch at the 1905 **Roycroft Inn** (✉ *40 S. Grove St.* ☎ *716/652–5552* ⊕ *www. roycroftinn.com*).

Detour: If you collect Fiestaware, you can easily spend an hour digging through selections in the **Fiesta Retail Outlet** (✉ *800 Fiesta Dr.* ☎ *304/387– 1300* ⊕ *www.fiestafactorydirect.com*) in Newell, West Virginia, where every color- ful crock and mug has been made since 1907. You'll likely have to cross the Wayne Six Toll Bridge to reach Newell, which does cost $1 each way (cash only). Three miles away in neighboring Chester, West Virginia, the **World's Largest Teapot** sits at the junction of Route 2 and U.S. 30. You're free to walk around the grounds to take pictures and read about the former concession stand's history. Fuel up at the gas station across the street before continuing on to Pittsburgh.

PITTSBURGH

Do: Pittsburgh itself doesn't have too many connections to Wright, but it's a good stopping point to prepare yourself for all the Pennsylvania-based Wright buildings you'll be seeing tomorrow. That doesn't mean the city itself is lacking in architecture. Just as it sounds, Pitts- burgh's "Millionaire's Row" (5th Avenue in Shadyside) is where steel barons in this Rust Belt city built their Victorian-era mansions. Between 1830 and 1930, Pittsburgh had more millionaires than any U.S. city.

Eat & Drink: Since 1933, **Primanti Bros.** (✉ *46 18th St.* ☎ *412/263–2142* ⊕ *www. primantibros.com*) has stuffed its sand- wiches with fries, and thankfully there are nine locations across Pittsburgh today. Head to the founding one in the Strip District, a neighborhood settled by Italian immigrants, and where the aroma

Fallingwater is on every architecture buff's bucket list.

of roasted garlic still reigns due to its many eateries and delis.

Stay: At the 8,000-square-foot 1870 **Parador Inn** (✉ *939 Western Ave.* ☎ *412/231–4800* ⊕ *www.theparadorinn.com*) in Pittsburgh's North Shore, breakfast is served with reggae music by owner Ed Menzer. At the **Calvary United Methodist Church** (✉ *971 Beech Ave.* ☎ *412/231–2007* ⊕ *www.calvarypgh.com*) across the street, a trio of Louis Comfort Tiffany glass windows are among the world's largest.

Breakfast: Offering all-day brunch every day of the week, **the Speckled Egg's** Southside location (✉ *428 S. 27th St.* ☎ *412/206–7793* ⊕ *www.thespeckledeggpgh.com*) serves everything from eggs in a basket to chia-seed pudding, along with staples with a twist like "quiche with a cause" (proceeds go to a local charity) or French toast with strawberry-cardamom jam.

Day 6: Pittsburgh, PA, to Mill Run, PA

67 miles (1 hour, 15 minutes without traffic and stops)

Today's quick route will take you to some of Wright's most famous designs. Conveniently, three of Wright's Pennsylvania projects (Kentuck Knob, Polymath Park, and Fallingwater) are within a tight radius: Kentuck Knob and Fallingwater are 7 miles apart while Polymath Park is about 45 minutes away. These are winding country roads, a nice change from the freeway.

ALONG THE WAY

Attraction: Tom and Heather Papinchak's **Polymath Park** (✉ *187 Evergreen La.* ☎ *877/833–7829* ⊕ *www.polymathpark.com*) in Acme relocates Wright homes from other parts of the country (yes, really) to this 130-acre subdivision. See interiors of Mäntylä (formerly in Minnesota) and Duncan (once in Lisle,

Illinois), plus Balter (designed by Wright apprentice Peter Berndtson) on the Wright House Collection tour. For an even more intimate experience, you can even stay the night at one of the homes.

Eat & Drink: Of course, you've had a McDonald's Big Mac at least once in your life, but you probably haven't ordered one at the **McDonald's** (✉ *575 Morgantown St.*) where it was first served, in Uniontown. That was in 1967 and a sign proves it. Otherwise you can pack a picnic to enjoy on the grounds of Polymath Park or Kentuck Knob—the latter has beautiful art sculptures.

Attraction: The Usonian-style **Kentuck Knob** (✉ *723 Kentuck Rd.* ☎ *724/329–1901* ⊕ *www.kentuckknob.com*) is located on 79 acres in Chalk Hill, Pennsylvania. Current owner Peter Palumbo overheard people talking about its need for a buyer while touring Fallingwater in 1985. He snapped up the elegant property but lives in another home nearby, leaving the house open for 90-minute in-depth and 45-minute standard tours.

Nature: Cucumber Falls in Ohiopyle State Park (✉ *124 Main St.* ☎ *724/329–8591* ⊕ *www.dcnr.state.pa.us*) in Ohiopyle is a popular day trip for Pittsburgh residents—you'll understand why once you spot the glorious 30-foot waterfall. It's only three minutes from Kentuck Knob. Park in the lot at the Cucumber Falls trailhead off Chalk Hill Road and climb down a few steps to the lookout point.

MILL RUN

Do: We've saved the best for last in this region. Even non-Wright fans will likely have heard of **Fallingwater** (✉ *1491 Mill Run Rd.* ☎ *724/329–8501* ⊕ *www.falling-water.org*), a weekend home in Mill Run designed in 1935 for Liliane and Edgar Kaufmann, owners of Kaufmann's Department Store in Pittsburgh. *Smithsonian Magazine* named the gorgeous home—perched on top of a waterfall—among 28 places to see before you die. There are daily self-guided and guided hour-long architectural tours, as well as three-hour brunches and sunset experiences.

Eat & Drink: Treetops Restaurant (✉ *187 Evergreen La.* ☎ *877/833–7829* ⊕ *www.treetopsrestaurant.net*) at Polymath Park is appropriately named for its treehouse-like location, an organic-architecture concept Wright would surely approve. Enjoy its vegan, vegetarian, and gluten-free meals (don't fret: there's also filet mignon).

Stay: The 2,220-acre **Nemacolin** (✉ *1001 Lafayette Dr.* ☎ *866/344–6957* ⊕ *www.nemacolin.com*) property holds three spectacular hotels: the Lodge, a Rockefeller's former hunting lodge; the Chateau, modeled after the Ritz Paris, and Falling Rock, a bucket-list item for any Wright fan. While there, go art-hopping at Reflection (a contemporary-art museum), wander through the Hardy family's 900-piece art collection, or observe the artist-in-residence's working studio.

Breakfast: Smoothies, breakfast sandwiches, and pastries at **Ohiopyle Bakery & Sandwich Shoppe** (✉ *85 Main St.* ☎ *724/329–2253*), just minutes from Fallingwater in the white-water-rafting mecca of Ohiopyle, are served by a farming family and paired with coffee.

Day 7: Mill Run, PA, to Philadelphia, PA

270 miles (4 hours without traffic and stops)

I–76 east is a great way to see nearly all of Pennsylvania's southern half, as you drive from the southwest part to the southeast tip. Philadelphia is serviced by Philadelphia International Airport, where rental cars can easily be returned.

ALONG THE WAY

Eat & Drink: It's one thing to pull over for ice cream. But **Igloo Soft Freeze** (✉ 462 E. Main St. ☎ 814/652–2442 ⊕ www. theiglooicecream.com) in Everett is literally inside an ice-cream-cone-shaped building.

Detour: At the **Allentown Art Museum** (✉ 31 N. 5th St. ☎ 610/432–4333 ⊕ www. allentownartmuseum.org), in Allentown, is the Francis Little House II, a reconstruction of the Wright-designed library that was demolished in 1971 along Lake Minnetonka in Minnesota. The library's two other sections are in the Metropolitan Museum of Art in New York City and the Minneapolis Institute of Art.

PHILADELPHIA

Do: Wright was 87 years old in 1954 when he designed the **Beth Sholom Synagogue** (✉ 8231 Old York Rd. ☎ 215/887–1342 ⊕ www.bethsholomcongregation. org), a Mayan revival synagogue in Elkins Park (just 9 miles and 40 minutes north of Philly). It opened five months after his 1959 death. See the modern marvel—including a 40-foot concrete monolith, a riff on Moses's stone tablets—on an hour-long Guided Architectural Building Tour. For a quick drive-by, check out the only other Wright-designed project near Philly: the **Suntop Homes** (✉ 152–154 Sutton Rd.). Built in 1939 in nearby Ardmore as a Usonian twist on row homes, the houses were designed to coax city people to the suburbs. Although two dwellings were destroyed in two separate fires, the last two remain.

Eat & Drink: One of the country's first food halls, **Reading Terminal Market** (✉ 51 N. 12th St. ☎ 215/922–2317 ⊕ www. readingterminalmarket.org) has continuously operated since 1893 in downtown Philly's Historic Landmark building. Even Pennsylvania Dutch cuisine is represented (by three vendors, including Hatville Deli, known for its Lebanon bologna and smoked-cheddar sandwich on Amish bread).

Shop: When you visit one of the country's oldest cities, the antiques shopping is bound to be epic. At **Architectural Antiques** (✉ 721 N. 2nd St. ☎ 215/922–3669 ⊕ www.architecturalantiques.com) in the Northern Liberties neighborhood, you might score anything from vintage pub decor to a newel post for your next home-remodeling project.

Stay: The **Lokal Hotel Old City** (✉ 139 N. 3rd St. ☎ 267/702–4345 ⊕ www. staylokal.com), in Old City, is a cute, modern refresh on a historic building, featuring six apartment-style rooms. For a step further back in history, book a room at the **Morris House Hotel** (✉ 225 S. 8th St. ☎ 215/922–2446 ⊕ www. morrishousehotel.com), a 1787 building within Philadelphia's Historic District where rates include breakfast and afternoon tea. Both are a short walk from the Liberty Bell and Independence Hall.

Breakfast: The **Bourse Food Hall** (✉ 111 S. Independence Mall E ☎ 215/625–0300 ⊕ www.theboursephilly.com), located inside the Victorian-era Bourse Building, is where Menagerie Coffee grinds Dogwood coffee beans daily. Grab a breakfast sandwich or yogurt and granola parfait, too.

Chapter 7

THE SOUTHEAST AND FLORIDA

Updated by
Brandon Schultz

WELCOME TO
THE SOUTHEAST AND FLORIDA

TOP REASONS TO GO

★ **Asheville:** A highlight of any Carolinas visit, Asheville wows with its arts, crafts, food, beer, and music scenes.

★ **Great Smoky Mountains National Park:** Even as the country's most visited national park, there is still more than enough beauty and deserted woodland for everyone to enjoy a peaceful communion with nature.

★ **Kentucky's Bourbon Trail:** Thirty-seven distilleries, including some of the world's best, make up the famed Kentucky Bourbon Trail.

★ **Martin Luther King Jr. National Historic Park:** As the home of MLK, Atlanta was a hub of the civil rights movement, and you can retrace his life by visiting this historic park along with his childhood home and burial place.

★ **Everglades National Park:** More than 1.5 million acres of South Florida's 4.3 million acres of subtropical, watery wilderness are part of Everglades National Park, one of the country's largest national parks.

1 The Blue Ridge Parkway. This famous drive takes you through scenic parts of North Carolina and Virginia.

2 The Best of the Carolinas. History, food, and gorgeous landscapes are everywhere in North and South Carolina.

3 National Parks of the Southeast. Experience the beauty of four national parks, including Great Smoky Mountains.

4 The Great American Whiskey Tour. Visit distilleries along Kentucky's Bourbon Trail and beyond.

5 The Civil Rights Tour. Retrace the civil rights movement through key sites in the South.

6 The Great American Music Road Trip. From New Orleans to Nashville, see how the history of American music mirrors the history of America.

7 The Best of Northern and Central Florida. The Atlantic and Gulf coasts of the Sunshine State offer beaches, history, and good eats.

8 The Best of Southern Florida. From Miami to Key West, you can see some of the most unique and stunning landscapes in the country.

From the southern reaches of the Appalachian Mountains to the swamplands spanning the country's southeastern coast, this part of the United States is filled with beautiful landscapes, happening cities, booming food scenes, and important, if often tragic, history. A road trip is the perfect way to truly appreciate this diversity, whether it's by taking the twists and turns of the Blue Ridge Parkway or visiting spots along the Civil Rights Trail.

The Blue Ridge Parkway

Written by Barbara Noe Kennedy

Snaking through the southern Appalachians, this classic parkway forces you to slow down. Luckily that just makes it easier to take in the majestic beauty of wild forests, splashing waterfalls, and misty mountains, with plenty of hiking, camping, and picnicking along the way. Started in 1935 for the express purpose of showcasing the mountains, the parkway winds 469 miles between Shenandoah National Park at Rockfish Gap, Virginia, in the north and Great Smoky Mountains National Park at Cherokee, North Carolina, in the south. Safe from development, it's a bucolic respite where black bears, deer, and other animals roam, and lavish flora changes with the season. There are some facilities along the way, including three lodges, six restaurants, several visitor centers, and multiple picnic areas.

While the parkway has provided decades of family fun and road-trip memories, it's important to remember that its creation displaced many residents, including the Eastern Band of Cherokee Indians, who fought against giving up the right-of-way through their lands at Qualla Boundary, the parkway's final 15 miles near Cherokee.

At a Glance

Start: Charlotte, NC

End: Richmond, VA

Miles Traveled: 767 miles

Suggested Duration: 6 days

The Blue Ridge Parkway

States Visited: West Virginia, Virginia, Kentucky, Tennessee, North Carolina, South Carolina, Georgia

---

States Visited: North Carolina, Virginia

Key Sights: Biltmore House and Estate; Blowing Rock; Brevard waterfalls; Great Smoky Mountains National Park; Museum of the Cherokee Indian

Best Time to Go: Springtime is glorious with blooming flowers while summer's wildflowers and autumn's multihued leaves are always gorgeous. Keep in mind the parkway is not maintained in winter and may close due to inclement weather year-round, particularly in the late fall through early spring.

Day 1: Charlotte, NC, to Bryson City, NC

180 miles (3 hours, 30 minutes without traffic and stops)

The trip begins in big-city Charlotte, which is quite a ways away from the Blue Ridge Parkway, but is a good starting point for anyone who needs to fly in and pick up a rental car. On your first day, you'll travel mostly fast highways—I–85, U.S. 321, and I–40—getting ever closer to the mountains. At Clyde, hop onto U.S. 74 for the final scenic push into Bryson City.

Hurricane Helene

In September 2024, Hurricane Helene hit the southeastern United States, bringing with it unprecedented levels of flooding in western North Carolina, resulting in over 228 deaths (including 115 deaths in North Carolina). This included the North Carolina section of the Blue Ridge Parkway; Asheville, North Carolina; and several roads and trails within Great Smoky Mountains National Park.

As of this writing, a significant part of the Blue Ridge Parkway located in North Carolina is closed to all traffic (the Virginia part of the parkway is fully reopened for the most part) with no exact timeline for reopening. Damage has been significant in some areas, and plans to rebuild may take months, or even years.

Currently, Day 2 (the part of the trip north of Cherokee), all of Day 3, and Day 4 (the area of the parkway between Bamboo, North Carolina, and and Fancy Gap, Virginia) of our Blue Ridge Parkway road trip as well as Day 2 of our Best of the Carolinas road trip are affected.

With tourism such an essential part of the economic recovery of these areas, we have kept the Blue Ridge Parkway road trip in its entirety, in the hopes that readers will be able to enjoy the full parkway once this book publishes. But before you travel on the parkway, please be sure to confirm which roads are reopened and which are still closed by visiting ⊕ www.nps.gov/blri/planyourvisit/roadclosures.htm. All the spots we mention are accessible via other highways and roads, and the National Park Service website currently has a helpful map with recommended detours around the closed parts of the highway.

ALONG THE WAY

Eat & Drink: Cauliflower fritters, shrimp-and-grits cakes, and burgers with smoked Gouda and fried onions are the sort of delicious dishes you'll find at **Olde Hickory Station** (✉ 232 Government Ave. SW ☎ 828/322–2356 ⊕ www.oldehickorystation.com), which occupies an old train station in the heart of Hickory, where U.S. 321 and I–40 meet.

Town: Take exit 119 off I–40 at Hildebran and follow Henry River Road south to **Henry River Mill Village** (⊕ www.henryrivermillvillage.com), an old milling village that *Hunger Games* fans will recognize. You can tour the abandoned village, including the buildings used as the Everdeens' house and Peeta's Bakery in the movies, and learn about the state's textile history. Future plans for the village include a restaurant, museum, and restored homes as vacation rentals.

Town: Just off I–40 at exit 103, Morganton's historic downtown, centered on a neoclassical courthouse, buzzes with funky shops, galleries, restaurants, cafés, and the popular **Brown Mountain Bottleworks** (✉ 115 E. Union St., Suite 3447 ☎ 828/367–0395 ⊕ www.brownmountainbottleworks.com). Here you'll find a dozen brews on tap along with more than 300 additional bottles and snacks from all over the state. There's a busy calendar of frequent live events, too.

BRYSON CITY

Do: This walkable, outdoorsy town on the edge of **Great Smoky Mountains National Park** (☎ 865/436–1200 ⊕ www.nps.gov/grsm) offers a relaxing vibe along the Tuckasegee River. Check out the petite downtown, and find outfitters that will help you fish, kayak, and/or paddleboard. The national park is within a hiking boot's distance, with plenty of trails to head out and explore, including the 4-mile Deep Creek Loop, which takes in two pretty waterfalls.

Eat & Drink: The Bistro at the **Everett Hotel** (✉ 16 Everett St. ☎ 828/488–1976 ⊕ www.theeveretthotel.com) is hands-down the nicest place in town. It's small but packs a lot of punch with a fresh, eclectic menu and daily specials: for example, bacon-draped meat loaf, or pan-seared Carolina mountain trout with a cornmeal crust. Don't miss the handcrafted cocktails (the mint for the mint juleps is grown locally). A more casual choice is **Jimmy Mac's** (✉ 121 Main St. ☎ 828/488–4700 ⊕ www.facebook.com/jimmymacsrestaurant), an all-American grill on Main Street featuring hand-cut steaks, fresh seafood, pasta, and a cavalcade of TVs.

Stay: Good choices include the **McKinley Edwards Inn** (✉ 208 Arlington Ave. ☎ 828/488–9626 ⊕ www.mckinleyedwardsinn.com), an upscale retreat in a landmark building; the **Folkestone Inn** (✉ 101 Folkestone Rd. ☎ 828/488–2730 ⊕ www.folkestoneinn.com), originally a 1920s mountain farmhouse; and **Lakeview at Fontana** (✉ 171 Lakeview Lodge Dr. ☎ 800/742–6492 ⊕ www.lakeviewatfontana.com), a spa retreat with basic rooms tucked into a gorgeous mountainscape.

Breakfast: Grab a coffee, bagels with signature spreads, and light fare at **La Dolce Vita** (✉ 191 Everett St. ☎ 828/488–5888 ⊕ www.dolcebryson.com).

Essential Listening

Old Crow Medicine Show's *Volunteer* album is a folksy, spirited ode to Americana bluegrass, the perfect companion as you make your way through the hills and dales of Appalachia.

Day 2: Bryson City, NC, to Asheville, NC

97 miles (2 hours, 40 minutes without traffic and stops)

Wind through the mountain landscapes via U.S. 19 and U.S. 441 south to Cherokee, where, just north, you'll finally jump onto the Blue Ridge Parkway at its southernmost terminus.

ALONG THE WAY

Nature: Drag yourself out of bed early to arrive just after sunrise at the **Oconaluftee Visitor Center** (✉ 1194 Newfound Gap Rd. ☎ 828/497–1904 ⊕ www.nps.gov/grsm) in Cherokee, near the Blue Ridge Parkway's southern terminus, where elk calmly graze in the meadows. You'll also find the **Mountain Farm Museum** (☎ 828/497–1904 ⊕ www.nps.gov/grsm), an authentic Smokies log homestead. And you can't miss the **Museum of the Cherokee People** (✉ 589 Tsali Blvd. ☎ 828/497–3481 ⊕ motcp.org), which takes a deep dive into Cherokee culture and history.

Photo Op: Be sure to spend some time in **Great Smoky Mountains National Park** (☎ 865/436–1200 ⊕ www.nps.gov/grsm) before striking out on the parkway. If nothing else, drive to the top of Clingmans Dome, the park's loftiest peak at 6,643 feet. Hike a half mile to the observation tower and gulp in the refreshing mountain air as you take in the 360-degree views of blue-hued peaks marching off into the distance.

Town: Drop off the parkway at Balsam Gap (mile marker 443.1), where U.S. 23/74 leads to the town of Sylva. The all-American Main Street has one-of-a-kind eats, activity outfitters, multiple bookstores, and four breweries (to stock up for later, of course). You could stay for an hour, enjoying coffee and homemade pie at the **Coffee Shop** (⊠ *385 W. Main St.* ☎ *828/586–2013*), or remain all day, enjoying the area's outdoorsy offerings. Go fly-fishing on the **WNC Fly Fishing Trail** (☎ *800/962–1911* ⊕ *www.flyfishingtrail. com*), with local outfitters available to take you out to the best fishing holes, or hike on the rugged 7-mile **Pinnacle Park Trail** (⊕ *www.discoverjacksonnc.com/out-doors/trails/pinnacle-park-trail*), offering supreme mountain panoramas.

Detour: Located about 15 miles south of Wagon Road Gap (mile marker 402) via U.S. 276, Brevard is not only a cute town, with retail favorites like the **White Squirrel Shoppe** (⊠ *6 W. Main St.* ☎ *828/877–3530* ⊕ *www.whitesquirrelshoppe.com*), but it's at the heart of North Carolina's "land of waterfalls." There are 250-plus cascades nearby, some small, some large, some famous (a couple were featured in *The Hunger Games* and *The Last of the Mohicans*), some not so much, but all beautiful.

Eat & Drink: Pisgah Inn (⊠ *408 Blue Ridge Pkwy.* ☎ *828/235–8228* ⊕ *www.pisga-hinn.com*), at mile marker 408 in Canton, sits 5,000 feet above the surrounding rugged terrain, providing spectacular mountain views to accompany your rainbow trout, fried chicken, and baked chicken pot pie.

ASHEVILLE

Do: Browse the art galleries, Appalachian craft shops, indie coffee shops, bookstores, and breweries (there are over 50 of them) in this funky, laid-back, music-and-beer-filled mountain town. The town's most famous site is the **Biltmore House and Estate** (⊠ *1 Lodge St.* ☎ *800/411–3812* ⊕ *www.biltmore. com*), George Vanderbilt's 250-room Gilded Age mansion, which remains the nation's largest private house and is open with a variety of tours.

Eat & Drink: It's hard to pick out just one or two places to dine in this hub of foodie creativity; stroll the downtown streets and it's guaranteed you'll find something to your liking. **Smoky Park Supper Club** (⊠ *350 Riverside Dr.* ☎ *828/350–0315* ⊕ *www. smokypark.com*) offers wood-fired pork chops, trout, New York strip, and more along the French Broad River while **The Montford** (⊠ *199 Haywood St.* ☎ *828/505–8750* ⊕ *www.themontford.com*) has small bites and craft cocktails (not to mention spectacular mountain sunsets from its rooftop perch). With 50 breweries and counting, don't forget to sample some beers in this epicenter of craft brewing; among the voluminous offerings are **Turgua Brewing Co.** (⊠ *3131 Cane Creek Rd.* ☎ *828/338–0218* ⊕ *www.turguabrew-ing.com*), a small farmhouse brewery on a 5-acre farm in Fairview, and **Whistle Hop** (⊠ *1288 Charlotte Hwy.* ☎ *828/338–9447* ⊕ *www.whistlehop.com*), with its train-caboose taprooms.

Stay: The classic parkway experience demands something retro. Try **June-Bug Retro Resort** (⊠ *355 Clarks Chapel Rd.* ☎ *828/208–1979* ⊕ *www.junebugret-roresort.com*), a 50-acre property sprin-kled with restored 1950s campers, or **Log Cabin Motor Court** (⊠ *330 Weaverville Rd.* ☎ *828/645–6546* ⊕ *www.theashevil-lecabins.com*), where rustic revival-style cabins celebrate the golden age of the American road trip.

Breakfast: Early Girl Eatery (⊠ *8 Wall St.* ☎ *828/259–9292* ⊕ *www.earlygirleat-ery.com*) is the place to go for southern comfort food created from fresh local ingredients, with locations in downtown, South Asheville, and West Asheville.

Day 3: Asheville, NC, to Blowing Rock, NC

89 miles (2 hours, 30 minutes without traffic or stops)

Today you'll follow the Blue Ridge Parkway's sinuous turns to Blowing Rock.

ALONG THE WAY

Eat & Drink: The homey **Switzerland Café** (✉ *9440 Rte. 226A* ☎ *828/765–5289* ⊕ *www.switzerlandcafe.com*) in Little Switzerland is a favorite stop on the North Carolina Barbecue Society Historic Barbecue Trail, though there are plenty of homemade nonbarbecue options as well. The tomato basil soup is a specialty.

Nature: The 1.75-mile (round-trip) **Linville Falls Plunge Basin Trail** (⊕ *www.nps.gov/blri/planyourvisit/linville-falls-trails.htm*), starting at the Linville Falls Visitor Center, is a gorgeous waterfall hike along Linville Gorge.

Detour: At 3,739 feet above sea level, Banner Elk is a historic alpine town near Grandfather Mountain, about 15 minutes off the parkway via Route 105 and Route 184. Visit the **Banner House Museum** (✉ *7990 Hickory Nut Gap Rd.* ☎ *828/783–8506* ⊕ *www.bannerhousemuseum.org*), showcasing 19th-century Blue Ridge life; wine-taste at **Banner Elk Winery** (✉ *60 Deer Run* ☎ *828/898–9090* ⊕ *www.bannerelkwinery.com*); sample local brews at the spectacularly situated **Beech Mountain Brewing Co.** (✉ *1007 Beech Mountain Pkwy.* ☎ *828/387–2011* ⊕ *www.beechmountainbrewingco.com*), or simply stretch your legs and poke into the shops and galleries in the downtown.

BLOWING ROCK

Do: In this cute, nature-loving town, you'll find upscale shops, galleries, cafés, and the **Blowing Rock Art & History Museum** (✉ *159 Ginny Stevens La.* ☎ *828/295–9099* ⊕ *www.blowingrockmuseum.org*), perfect for hanging out after a day of driving. You'll also find plenty of opportunities for hiking, fishing, and communing with nature in the surrounding wildlands.

Eat & Drink: The Speckled Trout (✉ *922 Main St.* ☎ *828/295–9819* ⊕ *www.thespeckledtrout.com*) offers a fresh take on Appalachian standards, with innovatively prepared North Carolina trout and more. The Devilish Eggs, with house-smoked trout and roasted red pepper sauce, are, well, devilishly good. The adjacent bottle shop has a breathtaking selection of local brews.

Stay: The Green Park Inn (✉ *9239 Valley Blvd.* ☎ *828/414–9230* ⊕ *www.greenparkinn.com*) is a Victorian dream, with live music in the lobby on Friday and Saturday nights and a made-to-order breakfast every morning. Another option, right on Main Street, is **Mountainaire Inn and Log Cabins** (✉ *827 Main St.* ☎ *828/295–7991* ⊕ *www.mountainaireinn.com*), with standard but clean rooms—splurge for a cabin.

Breakfast: The Penny Path (✉ *278 Shoppes on the Parkway Rd., Suite 35* ☎ *828/372–7020* ⊕ *www.facebook.com/thepennypathbr*) offers savory and sweet crepes in an upbeat, cozy space.

Day 4: Blowing Rock, NC, to Roanoke, VA

173 miles (4 hours without traffic or stops)

Today you'll stay on the Blue Ridge Parkway the entire way.

ALONG THE WAY

Nature: An easy, half-mile interpretive loop trail from mile marker 272.5 leads to the magnificent Cascade Falls.

Detour: Jump off the parkway at mile marker 260 to take a twisty, 30-mile loop via Route 163, U.S. 221, and Route 16 to West Jefferson and Glendale Springs, enjoying some spectacular natural beauty along the way. In both hamlets, you'll find tiny chapels adorned with Italian-style frescoes, the 20th-century masterpieces of Ben Long, who studied in Florence.

Eat & Drink: Since opening in 1949, the **Bluffs Restaurant** (✉ *45338 Blue Ridge Pkwy.* ☎ *336/372–7875* ⊕ *www.bluffsrestaurant.org*) in Laurel Springs has been legendary for its southern menu, notably its ham biscuits, fried chicken, and berry cobbler. This favorite is *the* place to savor sweet-potato pancakes in a booth overlooking the parkway.

Photo Op: It's hard to imagine a more picturesque mill than Mabry Mill with its reflective pond and surrounding forest that's downright stunning, especially in autumn. You'll find it at mile marker 176.

ROANOKE

Do: The largest city along the parkway has the culture, fine eats, and lodgings that go with urban living, but here the mountains always loom in the distance. Check out the neon **Roanoke Star** (✉ *2000 J. B. Fishburn Pkwy. SE* ☎ *540/853–2000* ⊕ *www.playroanoke.com*) atop Mill Mountain (and hike the Star Trail); find treasures at **Black Dog Salvage** (✉ *902 13th St. SW* ☎ *540/343–6200* ⊕ *www. blackdogsalvage.com*), home of the TV show *Salvage Dawgs*; and browse the historic **Roanoke City Market** (✉ *Market Sq. SE* ☎ *540/342–2028* ⊕ *www. downtownroanoke.org*), in operation since 1862. **Center in the Square** (✉ *1 Market Sq. SE* ☎ *540/342–5700* ⊕ *www. centerinthesquare.org*) is home to the city's art, science, and history museums, along with live theater, dance, and opera. **Explore Park** (✉ *56 Roanoke River Pkwy. Rd.* ☎ *540/427–1800* ⊕ *www.explorepark.org*), right off the parkway, is another must-stop, with a museum, ziplines, hiking and biking trails, and more.

Eat & Drink: In the city market, **Caribbica Soul** (✉ *215 Market St. SE* ☎ *540/330–2345* ⊕ *www.caribbicasoul.com*) has fragrant, smoky jerk chicken, while the extensive menu at **Martin's Downtown Bar & Grill** (✉ *413 1st St. SW* ☎ *540/985–6278* ⊕ *www.martinsdowntown.com*) features ribs, tacos, salads, wraps, and more—Monday night is half-price-hamburger night.

Stay: The luxe **Hotel Roanoke** (✉ *110 Shenandoah Ave. NE* ☎ *540/985–5900* ⊕ *www.hotelroanoke.com*), dating from 1882, has hosted presidents, rock stars, and celebrities, while **Roanoke Boutique Hotel** (✉ *539 Day Ave.* ☎ *540/420–4455* ⊕ *www.roanokeboutiquehotel.com*) occupies an 1890 Italianate home in Roanoke's historic district, with nature-loving hosts who can point you to the best of the area's outdoor activities.

Breakfast: Our Daily Bread (✉ *3334 Brambleton Ave.* ☎ *540/772–2200* ⊕ *www.odbb.com*) has omelets, hashes, and mouthwatering bakery selections from croissants to macarons.

Day 5: Roanoke, VA, to Staunton, VA

120 miles (3 hours, 30 minutes without traffic or stops)

The drive continues along the Blue Ridge Parkway to its northernmost terminus at Rockfish Gap. From here, hop onto I–81 for an hour and 20 minutes to Staunton, a bucolic drive through the Shenandoah Valley (even though it's all interstate highway).

ALONG THE WAY

Nature: The spectacular Peaks of Otter area at mile marker 85.6, with its tree-covered peaks towering above bucolic Abbott Lake, is worth a stop for several hours of exploring or even to stay overnight. Several hikes lead up the peaks and to a waterfall, and the **Peaks of Otter Lodge** (✉ *85554 Blue Ridge Pkwy.* ☎ *866/387–9905* ⊕ *www.peaksofotter.com*) has a restaurant famed for its fried chicken.

Fall is one of the best times to experience the Blue Ridge Parkway.

Town: Located 10 miles east of the parkway at mile marker 86, Bedford is a little town that's home to the **National D-Day Memorial** (✉ *3 Overlord Circle* ☎ *540/586–3329* ⊕ *www.dday.org*). The town lost 19 men on that fateful day in 1944. In addition, the 470-acre **Claytor Nature Study Center** (✉ *1844 Woods Rd.* ☎ *434/544–8360* ⊕ *claytor.lynchburg.edu*) is a bird-filled, trail-laced oasis.

Eat & Drink: Jump off the parkway at Indian Gap, at mile marker 47, for a 5-mile detour to **JJ's Meat Shak** (✉ *1607 Magnolia Ave.* ☎ *540/261–1489* ⊕ *www.jjsmeatshak.com*), a family-owned barbecue joint that started in a 20-foot trailer.

STAUNTON

Do: In this quintessential Shenandoah Valley small town, you can take an architectural walking tour of one of six historic districts filled with a panoply of buildings by esteemed architect T. J. Collins. Visit the **Woodrow Wilson Birthplace and Library** (✉ *20 N. Coalter St.* ☎ *540/885–0897* ⊕ *www.woodrowwilson.org*), attend a Shakespeare play at the **Blackfriars Playhouse** (✉ *10 S. Market St.* ☎ *877/682–4236* ⊕ *www.americanshakespearecenter.com*), the world's only re-creation of Shakespeare's indoor theater that was destroyed in the 1666 Great Fire of London, or go wine and beer tasting.

Eat & Drink: In this foodie town, try the always-packed **Shack** (✉ *105 S. Coalter St.* ☎ *540/490–1961* ⊕ *www.theshackva.com*) or **Zynodoa** (✉ *115 E. Beverly St.* ☎ *540/885–7775* ⊕ *www.zynodoa.com*), with its inspired southern cuisine.

Stay: Hotel 24 South (✉ *24 S. Market St.* ☎ *540/885–4848* ⊕ *www.hotel-24south.com*) opened its gracious doors in 1924 and remains a stylish retreat. Other interesting options include **Gibson's Warehouse** (✉ *19–21 Middlebrook Ave.* ☎ *540/324–5050* ⊕ *www.gibsonswarehouse.com*), a beautifully renovated 1905 warehouse-turned-apartment-rental designed by T. J. Collins, and the **Blackburn Inn** (✉ *301 Greenville Ave.* ☎ *540/712–0601* ⊕ *www.*

blackburn-inn.com), which occupies a former mental hospital dating from 1828.

Breakfast: Cranberry's Grocery & Eatery (✉ 7 S. New St. ☎ 540/885–4755 ⊕ www. gocranberrys.com) serves breakfast all day, with dishes created using local ingredients.

Day 6: Staunton, VA, to Richmond, VA

108 miles (1 hour, 40 minutes without traffic or stops)

You've left the Blue Ridge Parkway behind, so your last day consists of a leisurely drive east toward Richmond, home to the closest major airport in the area.

ALONG THE WAY

Town: Charlottesville is Thomas Jefferson's town, home to his breathtaking residence of **Monticello** (✉ 1050 Monticello Loop ☎ 434/984–9800 ⊕ www.monticello.org). But even without Jefferson, the city is a standout destination with lauded regional cuisine, a noteworthy music scene, and local vineyards that range among Virginia's best. Make a visit to Monticello or stroll the grounds of Jefferson's neoclassical masterpiece, the University of Virginia.

Eat & Drink: Take a seat at one of the outdoor tables at **Birdhouse** (✉ 711 Henry Ave. ☎ 434/443–0696 ⊕ www.birdhouse-charlottesville.com), where various helpings of rotisserie chickens are complemented by scrumptious southern sides. Don't forget a cup of green posole with chicken, a local favorite.

RICHMOND

Do: Virginia's capital city is also one of the oldest cities in America, making it the perfect place to soak up history and culture. Its museum scene is excellent—don't miss the **Virginia Museum of Fine Arts** (✉ 200 N. Arthur Ashe Blvd. ☎ 804/340–1400 ⊕ www.vmfa.museum) and the **Black History Museum and Cultural Center of Virginia** (✉ 122 W. Leigh St. ☎ 804/780–9093 ⊕ www.blackhistorymuseum.org); if you have time, visit the **Edgar Allan Poe Museum** (✉ 1914 E. Main St. ☎ 804/648–5523 ⊕ www.poemuseum.org). And don't forget to take a walk past **St. John's Church** (✉ 2401 E. Broad St. ☎ 804/648–5015 ⊕ www.historicstjohnschurch.org), the spot where Patrick Henry famously said, "Give me liberty or give me death."

Eat & Drink: If you want to splurge, book a table at **Lemaire** (✉ 101 W. Franklin St. ☎ 804/649–4629 ⊕ www.lemairerestaurant.com), named after Etienne Lemaire, maître d'hôtel to Thomas Jefferson from 1794 until the end of his presidency. The farm-to-table menu serves regional southern cuisine with small plates and entrées that feature local produce and regional meats and fishes. For something more low-key, **Lunch Supper** (✉ 1215 Summit Ave. ☎ 804/353–0111 ⊕ www.lunchorsupper.com) serves elevated southern pub food in a hip space.

Stay: A 70-foot-high ceiling with a stained-glass skylight and 10 of the original Louis Comfort Tiffany stained-glass windows, rich tapestries, and replicas of traditional Victorian furniture make the **Jefferson Hotel** (✉ 101 W. Franklin St. ☎ 804/649–4750 ⊕ www.jeffersonhotel.com) the most elegant hotel in Richmond.

Breakfast: Be prepared to wait in line to check out Richmond's favorite diner, **Millie's Diner** (✉ 2603 E. Main St. ☎ 804/643–5512 ⊕ www.milliesdiner.com). This is the place for brunch, serving everything from huevos rancheros to the signature Devil's Mess kitchen-sink omelet.

The Best of the Carolinas

Written by Stratton Lawrence

In a single day of exploring the Carolinas, you can stand at the highest point east of the Mississippi River and paddle through the Lowcountry, where the horizon across the flat coastal plains feels infinite. Few regions possess both the geographic and cultural diversity of the Carolinas. Appalachian culture and dialects persist in Blue Ridge hamlets, worlds away from the fishing- and water-sports-based lifestyle of the Outer Banks or the rich architectural history and food culture of Charleston.

A drive through North and South Carolina is a microcosm of America, from sleepy, centuries-old port towns like Beaufort to the forward-thinking, tech-focused Triangle cities of Durham, Chapel Hill, and Raleigh. On this road trip, you'll scale soaring peaks, stand at the edge of the continental shelf on Ocracoke Island, and dine on some of the country's finest seafood in downtown Charleston.

At a Glance

Start: Charlotte, NC

End: Charlotte, NC

Miles Traveled: 1,238 miles

Suggested Duration: 10 days

States Visited: North Carolina, South Carolina

Key Sights: Biltmore Estate; Congaree National Park; Fort Sumter Military Park; Jockey's Ridge State Park; Mt. Mitchell

Best Time to Go: During spring and fall, you'll avoid icy roads in the mountains, bitter cold winds at the beach, and summer's sweltering heat in the midlands. There's also the added bonus of fall colors and the spring bloom.

Day 1: Charlotte, NC, to Asheville, NC

130 miles (2 hours without traffic and stops)

Charlotte/Douglas International Airport (CLT) is the biggest airport in the Carolinas, where you're able to rent a car and head to the mountains without navigating through Charlotte traffic. Follow I–85 south to Kings Mountain, North Carolina, where you'll veer onto U.S. 74 until it meets I–26 in Columbus, taking you the final 30 miles to Asheville.

ALONG THE WAY

Nature: Hundreds of waterfalls cascade through western North Carolina, and one of the prettiest—and most accessible—is Little Bradley Falls, just five minutes off I–26 at Saluda. The 2.4-mile out-and-back hike gains only 150 feet in elevation and takes about 40 minutes each way, leading you to a magical triple cascade with an inviting swimming hole at the base.

Town: It takes about 60 seconds to walk across downtown Saluda, but every step is charming, from the train tracks that parallel Main Street to the **Purple Onion** café (✉ *16 E. Main St.* ☎ *828/749–1179* ⊕ *purpleonionsaluda.com*).

Eat & Drink: Since 1979, **Piggy's Ice Cream** (✉ *102 Duncan Hill Rd.* ☎ *828/692–1995* ⊕ *www.harrysandpiggys.com*) in Hendersonville has drawn in visitors with the herd of concrete animals on its roof. It's a perfect place to sit back in a rocking chair and wolf down a Hot Fudge Bonanza sundae.

ASHEVILLE

Do: Asheville's crown jewel is the **Biltmore Estate** (✉ *1 Approach Rd.* ☎ *800/411–3812* ⊕ *www.biltmore.com*), George Vanderbilt's 250-room palace in the Blue Ridge Mountains. If you're in the mood to splurge, you can stay at the estate's inn, but either way, spend an afternoon

The Best of the Carolinas

strolling the grounds and garden, including a tour of the mansion or on-site winery.

Eat & Drink: The brewery scene in Asheville is among the nation's best—there's a reason that big-time brewers like Sierra Nevada and New Belgium set up their East Coast operations in this area. For a taste of the city's best local suds, visit **Wedge Brewing Co.** (✉ *1 Page Ave.* ☎ *828/419–1740* ⊕ *www.wedge-brewing.com*) in downtown Asheville. Afterwards, scoot to your reservation at **The Admiral** (✉ *400 Haywood Rd.* ☎ *828/252–2541* ⊕ *www.theadmiral-asheville.com*), where the weekly menu draws from the best of the local harvest.

Stay: In the heart of downtown, walkable to Asheville nightlife and shops, **The Windsor** (✉ *36 Broadway St.* ☎ *844/494–6376* ⊕ *www.windsorasheville.com*) lets you enjoy modern luxury in a restored early-20th-century hotel.

Breakfast: Get to **Sunny Point Café** (✉ *626 Haywood Rd.* ☎ *828/252–0055* ⊕ *www.sunnypointcafe.com*) by 9 am to grab a table without a wait. This healthy breakfast mainstay is the city's favorite spot for creative morning entrées like carrot hot cakes and huevos rancheros with black bean cakes and cilantro crema.

Day 2: Asheville, NC, to Boone, NC

90 miles (2 hours without traffic and stops)

Today is all about the scenic drive, much of it along the Blue Ridge Parkway. After summiting Mt. Mitchell, continue on the parkway to Linville, where you'll take Route 105 the last 20 miles to Boone.

ALONG THE WAY

Detour: At 6,684 feet, Mt. Mitchell is the highest mountain in eastern North America, and the road to its summit—including

Essential Listening

About an hour into your first day's drive, you'll start to pick up WNCW 88.7, an FM station out of Isothermal Community College that serves as the cultural glue of western North Carolina. The station plays a diverse, bluegrass-heavy rotation that features new releases and live performances by North Carolina artists.

the approach along the Blue Ridge Parkway—is one of the country's most scenic drives. After winding to the apex, walk the quarter-mile paved trail to the observation deck to take in the astounding views in every direction. Bring a picnic for lunch when you reach the top.

Town: Perched on a ridge along the Blue Ridge Parkway, Little Switzerland charms with its Alpine architecture, sweeping views of the valley below, and celebratory square dancing on summer Saturday evenings at Geneva Hall.

Photo Op: In the shadow of Grandfather Mountain, the 228-foot **Mile-High Swinging Bridge** (✉ *2050 Blowing Rock Hwy.* ☎ *800/468–7325* ⊕ *www.grandfather.com*) stretches over a lush valley, offering visitors the chance to step out into the void.

BOONE

Do: In this mountain town, **Tweetsie Railroad** (✉ *300 Tweetsie Railroad La.* ☎ *800/526–5740* ⊕ *www.tweetsie.com*) is pure kitsch and pure fun. Ride the 3-mile circuit, pulled by a historic steam locomotive. There are also live shows, an amusement park for kids, and a petting zoo.

Eat & Drink: For a true taste of mountain flavors like local boar, venison, and trout

Hip Asheville is filled with trendy bars and restaurants.

cooked over fire, **Gamekeeper** (✉ *3005 Shulls Mill Rd.* ☎ *828/963–7400* ⊕ *www. gamekeeper-nc.com*) specializes in preparations of less common meats, including emu and antelope.

Stay: An early-20th-century car dealership and department store is now **The Horton Hotel** (✉ *611 W. King St.* ☎ *828/832–8060* ⊕ *www.thehorton.com*), a worthwhile property that's in walking distance of the Appalachian State University campus, and next door to a Mast General Store.

Breakfast: On the way out of town, grab a croissant and a cup of joe from **Hatchet Coffee Roasters** (✉ *150A Den Mac Dr.* ☎ *828/278–7505* ⊕ *www.hatchetcoffee.com*).

Day 3: Boone, NC, to Winston-Salem, NC

90 miles (1 hour, 30 minutes without traffic and stops)

You're headed due east on U.S. 421 today, descending from the Appalachian highlands into the foothills.

ALONG THE WAY

Town: The twin downtowns of Wilkesboro and North Wilkesboro straddle the Yadkin River, creating two walkable strips of shops and restaurants. This is the hometown of bluegrass great Doc Watson (and the festival he founded, MerleFest); a mural featuring the blind flatpicker graces a wall downtown.

Eat & Drink: Glenn's (✉ *800 River St.* ☎ *336/838–2541* ⊕ *www.facebook. com/GlennsRestaurantWilkesboroNC*) isn't fancy—this cash-only Wilkesboro diner has been dishing out burgers and dogs to musical legends in town for concerts, including Dolly Parton, for half a century. But you're here for one thing: livermush. This regional sausage-like specialty is made from ground pig liver, offal, and cornmeal. Put a slice or two in a buttermilk biscuit for a savory taste of the North Carolina foothills.

Roadside Attraction: Love Valley is like no other town in the Carolinas, partly because cars are not allowed; this is cowboy country, built by a couple in the 1950s to emulate the Wild West. Park just outside the small downtown and step into the western-inspired stores while watching cowpokes tie up their steeds to the hitching post. Saturday nights get a little rowdy here, so unless you're ready to join the party, visit during daylight hours.

WINSTON-SALEM

Do: Before Winston-Salem was the home of Camel cigarettes, the original town of Salem was a Moravian settlement, and the streets of the **Old Salem Museums & Gardens** (✉ 900 Old Salem Rd. ☎ 336/721–7350 ⊕ www.oldsalem. org) today are reminiscent of Williamsburg, Virginia, but not nearly as heavily trafficked. Walking the brick sidewalks of this incredibly well-preserved, living village takes you back in time.

Eat & Drink: Twisted Pine (✉ 527 N. Liberty St. ☎ 336/893–7069 ⊕ www.andrews-restaurantsws.com) offers solid taco and smash-burger menus along with excellent margaritas and one signature dessert: a hot fudge brownie à la mode.

Stay: The 55-acre **Graylyn Estate** (✉ 1900 Reynolda Rd. ☎ 336/758–2425 ⊕ www. graylyn.com) is worthy of a leisurely multiday stay. Rooms in the castle-like stone mansion are beautifully furnished. In the evenings, read in the stately library or play pool in the billiards room—it's like staying in a real-life game of Clue, minus the murder mystery.

Breakfast: You may stop in to **Krankies** (✉ 211 E. 3rd St. ☎ 336/955–5993 ⊕ www.krankiescoffee.com) for their delicious iced coffees, flavored with homemade syrup, but you can't leave without indulging in a chicken biscuit doused in honey and hot sauce.

Day 4: Winston-Salem, NC, to Durham, NC

80 miles (1 hour, 30 minutes without traffic and stops)

You're heading due east on I-40 for most of the drive today—a nearly straight shot.

ALONG THE WAY

Roadside Attraction: If you swing through High Point on your way out of Winston-Salem, the **World's Largest Chest of Drawers** (✉ 508 N. Hamilton St.) is a fascinating piece of the town's furniture-industry lore.

Town: Spend a few hours in Chapel Hill, walking Franklin Street and the campus of the University of North Carolina at Chapel Hill. Stroll through the **Coker Arboretum** (✉ 399 E. Cameron Ave. ☎ 919/962–0522 ⊕ www.ncbg.unc. edu) before visiting the **Carolina Basketball Museum** (✉ 450 Skipper Bowles Dr. ☎ 919/962–6000 ⊕ www.goheels. com), featuring jerseys and mementos from all-time greats who wore the Carolina Blue, including Michael Jordan and Vince Carter.

Eat & Drink: Grab a rooftop table at **Top of the Hill** (✉ 100 E. Franklin St. ☎ 919/929–8676 ⊕ www.thetopofthehill.com) in Chapel Hill, a brewery and restaurant at the center of town, overlooking Franklin Street.

Photo Op: Chapel Hill's **Old Well** (✉ E. Cameron Ave.) is a simple blue-domed rotunda with a water fountain, but it's one of the most photographed and recognizable landmarks in the state.

DURHAM

Do: During baseball season, the Durham Bulls are the hottest ticket in town. They may be the nation's most well-loved minor league team, and the downtown **Durham Bulls Athletic Park** (⊠ *409 Blackwell St.* ☎ *919/687–6500* ⊕ *www. milb.com/durham*) helps keep them a vital part of the city. If it's not a game day, stroll through the **American Tobacco Campus** (⊠ *300 Blackwell St.* ☎ *919/433– 1566* ⊕ *www.americantobaccocampus. com*) next door, a former cigarette company warehouse district that's been revitalized with shops, restaurants, and the headquarters of Burt's Bees.

Eat & Drink: In an elegant but relaxed dining room downtown, **Mothers & Sons** (⊠ *107 W. Chapel Hill St.* ☎ *919/294– 8247* ⊕ *www.mothersandsonsnc.com*) serves some of the South's best Italian fare. Choose from the bruschetta selection, then move on to the divine eggplant Parm. Save room for ice cream, around the corner at the **Parlour** (⊠ *117 Market St.* ☎ *919/564–7999* ⊕ *www.theparlour. co*).

Stay: Downtown's coolest spot to lay your head is **Unscripted Durham** (⊠ *202 Corcoran St.* ☎ *984/329–9500* ⊕ *www. unscriptedhotels.com*), a once-decrepit motor lodge that's been refurbished into a hip motel that features a pool and bar overlooking the city center. **The Durham Hotel** (⊠ *315 E. Chapel Hill St.* ☎ *919/768– 8830* ⊕ *www.thedurham.com*), just around the corner, is equally trendy, with its own rooftop bar pouring craft cocktails and local beers.

Breakfast: Monuts (⊠ *1002 9th St.* ☎ *919/286–2642* ⊕ *www.monutsdo- nuts.com*) makes Durham's best doughnuts, but their stellar menu ranges from hefty breakfast burritos to the "Guac Dirty to Me" biscuit.

Extend Your Trip

From Asheville or Charlotte: The Blue Ridge Parkway *(Ch. 7)*

From the Outer Banks: The East Coast's Best Beaches *(Ch. 2)*

From Charleston: The Civil Rights Trail *(Ch. 7)*; Civil War History and Battlefields *(Ch. 2)*

From Columbia: National Parks of the Southeast *(Ch. 7)*

Day 5: Durham, NC, to Nags Head, NC

220 miles (3 hours, 30 minutes without traffic and stops)

Head down I–40 to Raleigh, where you'll pick up U.S. 64, taking you 200 miles to the Outer Banks.

ALONG THE WAY

Nature: Lake Phelps, accessible via Pettigrew State Park (⊠ *2252 Lake Shore Rd., Creswell* ☎ *252/797–4475* ⊕ *www. ncparks.gov*), stands out among large lakes in the Carolinas because it's not man-made. Alligators and black bears abound in this region, and tall cypress trees line the banks. It's a glimpse of a primordial ecosystem that still persists in sparsely populated eastern North Carolina.

Town: Start your drive in the morning, allowing for several hours to explore the town of Manteo on Roanoke Island, where the "Lost Colony" settlers disappeared after establishing a settlement in 1587. Their (imagined) story is told via a live drama in an **outdoor theater** (⊕ *www. thelostcolony.org*) fronting Albemarle Sound (Andy Griffith got his start here, playing the role of Sir Walter Raleigh).

While touring the site of the colony, visit the ornate Elizabethan Gardens, a walled garden built in honor of the queen.

Eat & Drink: After the morning drive, recharge with a rockfish wrap or turkey Reuben from **Poor Richard's Sandwich Shop** (✉ 303 Queen Elizabeth St. ☎ 252/473–3333 ⊕ www.poorrichardsmanteo.com). Order it to go and eat by the waterfront in Manteo.

NAG'S HEAD

Do: At sunset, hike up the towering dunes (the tallest on the East Coast) at **Jockey's Ridge State Park** (✉ 300 W. Carolista Dr. ☎ 252/441–7132 ⊕ www.ncparks.gov), a barren expanse of sand that feels like trekking across the desert, and affords stunning views of the ocean and the sound from its ridge.

Eat & Drink: In the Outer Banks, you often choose between the view and the quality of your meal. Spend the sunset outside before dipping into the strip mall confines of **Blue Moon Beach Grill** (✉ 102 E. Dove St. ☎ 252/261–2583 ⊕ www.bluemoonbeachgrill.com), where the humble environs belie the care put into the fish tacos and seafood bucatini.

Stay: The most impressive thing about **First Colony Inn** (✉ 6715 S. Croatan Hwy. ☎ 855/207–2262 ⊕ www.firstcolonyinn.com) is its lawn; spread across a full acre, staying here feels like crashing at a friend's private estate. The second is that this massive wooden building was moved to this location, salvaging the structure after hurricanes and real estate prices forced it off the beachfront. First Colony mixes little luxuries with rustic authenticity, and the sea breezes and rocking chairs on the full-length porches don't hurt.

Breakfast: Grab a waterfront picnic table and breathe in the salt air while you enjoy a smoothie and multigrain banana pancakes at **Freshfit Café** (✉ 7531 S. Virginia Dare Trail ☎ 252/715–6444 ⊕ www.obxfreshfitcafe.com).

Day 6: Nags Head, NC, to Ocracoke, NC

90 miles (2 hours, 30 minutes without traffic and stops)

The drive down Route 12, through several oceanfront towns and a national seashore, is one of the country's greatest drives. Take your time, but keep in mind that the drive ends with a ferry to Ocracoke, which leaves every 15-to-30 minutes; depending on time of year, traffic can back up, forcing you to wait through several cycles to board.

ALONG THE WAY

Town: The drive through the Outer Banks alternates between undeveloped wildlife refuge and national seashore and the small towns pocketed between them. Rodanthe stands out for its **Chicamacomico Life-Saving Station** historic site (✉ 23645 Rte. 12 ☎ 252/987–1552 ⊕ www.chicamacomico.org), a small village of buildings from the days before the U.S. Coast Guard, when the U.S. Life-Saving Service remained at the ready to aid shipwrecked boats on the shoals off the Outer Banks.

Eat & Drink: In Rodanthe, **Taqueria Las Ahumaderas** (✉ 24594 Rte. 12 ☎ 252/548–9145) serves a surprisingly large variety of seafood-based Mexican fare from a waterfront food truck. Eat your enchiladas while watching the kitesurfers soar through the air along the sound.

Photo Op: You'll pass two lighthouses on today's drive, and each is worth a visit. The **Bodie Island Light Station** (✉ 8210 Bodie Island Lighthouse, Nags Head ☎ 252/441–5711 ⊕ www.nps.gov/caha) is clearly visible from Route 12, and known by mariners for its black-and-white-striped pattern. Even more famous is the spiral pattern of the **Cape Hatteras Lighthouse** (✉ 46379 Lighthouse Rd., Buxton ☎ 252/473–2111 ⊕ www.nps.gov/

caha), which reaches 210 feet and can be climbed during the summer.

OCRACOKE

Do: The island of Ocracoke feels trapped in time, and one of its charms is a slow pace of life that lets you do nothing but lie in a hammock, take a walk on the isolated beach, or browse the quaint craftsman shops that circle Silver Lake, the harbor that anchors the village. But if you have time, the 20-minute private ferry to Portsmouth Village is an amazing, eye-opening experience. Portsmouth's last residents moved away in 1971, leaving this once-bustling port abandoned. It's a true coastal ghost town, reachable only by boat, with buildings like the Methodist church and life-saving station maintained by the National Park Service and open for tours.

Eat & Drink: 1718 Brewing not only produces the best beer in the Outer Banks (try the Coffee Kölsch or Mexican Chocolate), but their **Plum Pointe Kitchen** (✉ *1129 Irvin Garrish Hwy.* ☎ *252/928–7586*) cranks out specialties like a crab-stuffed pretzel that elevates sunsets on its rooftop deck.

Stay: Ocracoke offers several upscale inns and bed-and-breakfast options, including the lovely **Ocracoke Harbor Inn** (✉ *144 Silver Lake Dr.* ☎ *252/928–5731* ⊕ *www. ocracokeharborinn.com*). For a real taste of Ocracoke culture and history, get a room at **Blackbeard's Lodge** (✉ *111 Back Rd.* ☎ *252/928–3421* ⊕ *www.blackbeardslodge.com*), a rustic but compelling inn spread over several buildings, interconnected by winding walkways and rooftop passageways.

Breakfast: Order from the window in the side of the house at **Magic Bean Coffee Bazaar** (✉ *35 School Rd.* ☎ *252/588–2440* ⊕ *www.facebook.com/MagicBeanOcracoke*), then relax in a lawn chair while sipping on a butterbeer coffee or a satisfying smoothie.

Day 7: Ocracoke, NC, to Wilmington, NC

160 miles (5 hours, 30 minutes without traffic and stops)

It's only 160 miles to Wilmington, but the trip today takes over five hours because it begins with a ferry ride. During the middle of the open-water trip, land is not visible in any direction. You're deposited at Cedar Island and then you drive on U.S. 70 through the "Down East" island communities of this isolated region, taking in sweeping vistas across the marsh for the first hour. After passing through Beaufort, take Route 24 along the coast to U.S. 17 in Jacksonville, for the final push back to civilization in Wilmington.

ALONG THE WAY

Town: The waterfront homes in Beaufort each have a plaque with the year they were constructed, and all are part of a self-guided walking tour offered by the **Beaufort Historic Site** (⊕ *beauforthistoricsite.org*). Tour on foot or via a double-decker red English bus.

Eat & Drink: Set on (and over) the water in Beaufort, **Moonrakers** (✉ *326 Front St.* ☎ *252/838–0083* ⊕ *www.moonrakersbeaufort.com*) cooks the local catch to perfection in its wood-fired grill. The first floor is casual, while upstairs is a bit fancier, with slightly better views. But head straight for the roof, where the smaller menu is worth the sacrifice for the clear vista at the Sky Deck bar.

Detour: It's only slightly out of the way to cruise across the bridge to Atlantic Beach, where **Fort Macon** (✉ *2303 E. Fort Macon Rd.* ☎ *252/726–3775* ⊕ *www.ncparks.gov*) has guarded the approach to Beaufort since the 1830s. The brick fortification, an important Civil War site, is built into a giant dune, and from its cannons, the views toward Shackleford Banks and Cape Lookout make it clear why this point was such strategic land to hold.

WILMINGTON

Do: Downtown Wilmington invites long walks, both through its shops and restaurant district on Water Street, fronting the Cape Fear River, and along Third Avenue, where historic mansions line the road for several blocks. Stroll through the gardens at the **Burgwin-Wright House** museum (⊠ *224 Market St.* ☎ *910/762–0570* ⊕ *www.burgwinwrighthouse.com*), and if you're a train aficionado, leave an hour to take in the **Wilmington Railroad Museum** (⊠ *505 Nutt St.* ☎ *910/763–2634* ⊕ *www.wrrm.org*), which holds the world record for the longest model train ever assembled.

Eat & Drink: Wilmington's dining scene has three all-stars: **Manna** (⊠ *123 Princess St.* ☎ *910/763–5252* ⊕ *www.mannaavenue.com*), **PinPoint** (⊠ *114 Market St.* ☎ *910/769–2972* ⊕ *www.pinpointrestaurant.com*), and **Seabird** (⊠ *1 S. Front St.* ☎ *910/769–5996* ⊕ *www.seabirdnc.com*), each taking pride in locally sourced seafood. Consider a progressive dinner, with raw oysters and cocktails at Seabird, lobster bruschetta at PinPoint, and speckled trout at Manna.

Stay: Along the river, **Hotel Ballast** (⊠ *301 N. Water St.* ☎ *910/763–5900* ⊕ *www.hotelballast.com*) has an imposing presence in Wilmington, but that also means spectacular views of the river and city from its modern, comfortable rooms.

Breakfast: Bespoke Coffee (⊠ *202 Princess St.* ☎ *910/769–4088* ⊕ *www.bespokecoffeenc.com*) serves the city's best cup of joe, but if you're hankering for substantial grub, visit **The Basics** (⊠ *319 N. Front St.* ☎ *910/343–1050* ⊕ *www.thebasicswilmington.com*) for the impressive build-your-own biscuit menu.

Day 8: Wilmington, NC, to Charleston, SC

180 miles (3 hours, 30 minutes without traffic and stops)

There are no turns on today's drive: just stick to U.S. 17 all the way down the coast to the "Holy City."

ALONG THE WAY

Eat & Drink: Restaurants along the entire Carolina coast advertise Calabash seafood, and today you'll pass through the real border town of Calabash, North Carolina. If you want to shamelessly indulge in a generous platter of fried seafood, do it at the **Boundary House** (⊠ *1045 River Rd.* ☎ *910/579–8888* ⊕ *www.boundaryhouserestaurant.com*).

Photo Op: North Myrtle Beach is where the shag, South Carolina's state dance, originated, and its clubs still fill up on Saturday nights with couples, old and young, sliding across the dance floor. Step into **Fat Harold's Beach Club** (⊠ *212 Main St.* ☎ *843/249–5779* ⊕ *www.fatharolds.com*), take in the historic room and black-and-white photos on the wall, and then take a few turns on the legendary dance floor yourself.

Town: You'll spend over an hour of today's drive passing the pancake houses and putt-putt courses of Myrtle Beach, South Carolina. The entire Grand Strand is tourist-driven, but there are a few hidden gems. It's worth stopping along the way for a round of minigolf—where else can you putt from the top of a 50-foot volcano or down the deck of a pirate ship?

CHARLESTON

Do: Charleston's unique peninsular geography is best appreciated from the water, and the best way to get onto Charleston Harbor is via a ferry to **Fort Sumter**

(☎ 843/883–2123 ⊕ www.nps.gov/fosu). Tour the fort—perhaps the most important coastal fortification during the Civil War—before returning to the Battery for a leisurely walk through the South of Broad neighborhood, home to countless historic mansions and the photogenic Rainbow Row. Finish the evening with a walk through the City Market, which stays open at night on summer weekends and during the holidays.

Eat & Drink: Charleston is a city where you can eat a five-star meal three times a day for weeks on end and never retrace your steps. For the pinnacle of the local catch, splurge on the seafood tower at **The Ordinary** (⊠ 544 King St. ☎ 843/414–7060 ⊕ www.eattheordinary.com). Other options include stopping into the **Bar at Husk** (⊠ 76 Queen St. ☎ 843/577–2500 ⊕ www.huskrestaurant.com) for their famous cheeseburger, or scarfing down the addictive okonomiyaki at **Xiao Bao Biscuit** (⊠ 224 Rutledge Ave. ⊕ www.xiaobaobiscuit.com).

Stay: Just far enough off the City Market to feel relaxed but still close to the action, **Emeline** (⊠ 181 Church St. ☎ 843/577–2644 ⊕ www.hotelemeline.com) combines the best of a big hotel (terrific restaurants and thoughtful amenities like filtered sparkling water) with the charm and creative perks of a boutique hotel (classic vinyl and an in-room record player).

Breakfast: Local miller Greg Johnsman knows how to stir up the perfect pot of grits, a skill he puts to use at **Millers All Day** (⊠ 120 King St. ☎ 843/501–7342 ⊕ www.millersallday.com), a King Street breakfast café with a throwback-soda-fountain feel.

Day 9: Charleston, SC, to Columbia, SC

115 miles (2 hours without traffic and stops)

Take I–26 west from Charleston to Columbia, and you'll steadily see hills start to form as you gently leave the Lowcountry behind.

ALONG THE WAY
Eat & Drink: Fill up your plate with pulled pork, mac and cheese, and collard greens at one of the three rustic buildings, all adorned with decades of memorabilia, at **Lone Star BBQ & Mercantile** (⊠ 2212 State Park Rd. ☎ 803/854–2000 ⊕ www.destination-bbq.com) in Santee.

COLUMBIA
Do: Many of the world's oldest and largest cypress trees stand deep in the swamp at South Carolina's only national park, **Congaree National Park** (☎ 803/776–4396 ⊕ www.nps.gov.cong), just 20 minutes from Columbia. A 2-mile boardwalk loop delivers you into woods and is accessible at all but the highest flood stages. When the Congaree River overflows its banks, this park can be almost entirely underwater, but when waters recede, hiking trails allow access deep into a primitive, wild ecosystem where deer, owls, and wild boar are a regular sight.

Eat & Drink: Set in a former auto-parts warehouse, **Motor Supply Company Bistro** (⊠ 920 Gervais St. ☎ 803/256–6687 ⊕ www.motorsupplycobistro.com) was ahead of its time when it opened in 1989, and it continues to set trends with its butcher program, local farmer sourcing, and approach to detail in everything from its infused cocktails to hand-mixed salad dressings.

Stay: Local beer on tap at check-in is just the first perk at **Hotel Trundle** (⊠ 1224 Taylor St. ☎ 803/722–5000 ⊕ www.

hoteltrundle.com), a trendy, bohemian downtown boutique that puts you in walking distance of the statehouse and the University of South Carolina campus.

Breakfast: Just outside the capitol building, **Immaculate Consumption** (✉ *933 Main St.* ☎ *803/799–9053* ⊕ *www.immaculate-consumption.com*) fuels legislative sessions with macchiatos, pastries, and a menu of sandwiches suitable for packing a picnic to go.

Day 10: Columbia, SC, to Charlotte, NC

90 miles (1 hour, 30 minutes without traffic and stops)

On your last day of driving, head due north on I–77, direct to the "Queen City."

ALONG THE WAY

Town: If you're up for taking back roads, detour to Camden, South Carolina, where the historic neighborhood of mansions and estates remains unpaved to allow for a gentler tread on horses' feet. This is thoroughbred country, and it's also an important Revolutionary War site and early colonial settlement.

Roadside Attraction: At the state border, you'll pass one of the Southeast's biggest theme parks, **Carowinds** (✉ *14523 Carowinds Blvd.* ☎ *704/588–2600* ⊕ *www.carowinds.com*). This is a roller coaster lover's dream park—among the dozen high-speed coasters is Fury 325, which soars 325 feet in the air and reaches 95 miles per hour.

CHARLOTTE

Do: At the **U.S. National Whitewater Center** (✉ *5000 Whitewater Center Pkwy.* ☎ *704/391–3900* ⊕ *www.whitewater.org*), you can paddle a kayak or raft through intense rapids, free-climb high in the air over a pool, soar through the air on a massive zipline, or mountain bike

through central North Carolina's most challenging trails.

Eat & Drink: In a restored church in the hip Plaza Midwood neighborhood, **Supperland** (✉ *1212 The Plaza* ☎ *704/817–7514* ⊕ *www.supper.land*) encourages leisurely, shared meals with its menu of steaks, pot roast, and rich southern sides. Or opt for the crowd-pleasing options at **Optimist Hall** (✉ *1115 N. Brevard St.* ☎ *980/701–0040* ⊕ *www.optimisthall.com*), a sprawling food hall with plenty of international flair.

Stay: For your last night in the Carolinas, enjoy true southern luxury at the **Duke Mansion** (✉ *400 Hermitage Rd.* ☎ *704/714–4400* ⊕ *www.dukemansion.com*), where the grounds and gardens are as thoughtfully maintained as the comfortable rooms.

Breakfast: Amelie's (✉ *136 E. 36th St.* ☎ *704/376–1781* ⊕ *www.ameliesfrenchbakery.com*), a French bakery with locations around Charlotte, is a local staple for coffee and breakfast sandwich croissants.

National Parks of the Southeast

Written by Stefanie Waldek

The American West might lay claim to some of the country's most famous national parks, but the Southeast has four of its own that are well deserving of a visit. Best of all, you can visit them in a single weeklong road trip. This adventure takes you to the stunning Skyline Drive of Shenandoah National Park in Virginia, the dramatic cliffs of New River Gorge National Park in West Virginia, the waterfalls of Great Smoky Mountains National Park (the most visited national park in America) in Tennessee and North Carolina, and the swamps of Congaree National Park in South Carolina. Along

National Parks of the Southeast

the way, you'll discover quirky roadside attractions, historic homes and hotels, and impressively good food.

At a Glance

Start: Charlotte, NC

End: Charlotte, NC

Miles Traveled: 1,120 miles

Suggested Duration: 7 days

States Visited: North Carolina, South Carolina, Tennessee, Virginia, West Virginia

Key Sights: Congaree National Park; Great Smoky Mountains National Park; Luray Caverns; New River Gorge National Park; Shenandoah National Park

Best Time to Go: While all the parks are open year-round, some facilities are seasonal, so it's best to take this road trip in the spring, summer, or fall.

Day 1: Charlotte, NC, to Meadows of Dan, VA

130 miles (2 hours, 30 minutes without traffic and stops)

Your journey begins at Charlotte Douglas International Airport—fly in, grab a rental car, and hit the road. It's a pretty short drive from Charlotte to Meadows of Dan as you head north via I–85 and U.S. 52, a route that brings you through Winston-Salem and past Pilot Mountain.

ALONG THE WAY

Eat & Drink: Stop for lunch in Winston-Salem, where you'll have plenty of options to satisfy even the pickiest eaters. Try **Sweet Potatoes** (✉ 607 N. Trade St. ☎ 336/727–4844 ⊕ www.sweet-potatoes.ws) for southern food or the **Katharine Brasserie + Bar** (✉ 401 N. Main St. ☎ 336/761–0203 ⊕ www.katharine-brasserie.com) for French cuisine.

Photo Op: As you leave Winston-Salem and drive north on U.S. 52, you'll spot an unusual rocky "knob" atop a hill—this is Pilot Mountain, a geologic icon in North Carolina. You can drive to the summit to snap photos of the panoramic views.

Town: The historic town of Mount Airy is a must-visit for Andy Griffith fans, where there's a museum dedicated to the actor. Griffith was born and raised here, and he likely used the location as inspiration for the fictional setting of Mayberry, from his eponymous show.

MEADOWS OF DAN

Do: Meadows of Dan isn't so much of a destination in itself, but its **Primland Resort** (✉ 2000 Busted Rock Rd. ☎ 855/876–6593 ⊕ www.aubergeresorts.com) certainly is. Book an overnight stay so you can spend the afternoon riding horses, going shooting, or driving RTVs across the 12,000-acre grounds; there's an outdoor adventure for everyone. At night, visit the resort's observatory for a stargazing session.

Eat & Drink: There are two dinner options at Primland: the fine-dining **Elements Restaurant** and the casual **19th Pub** (☎ 276/222–6966 ⊕ aubergeresorts.com/primland/dine).

Stay: Accommodations at Primland range from hotel-style rooms in the main lodge with classic wilderness-resort vibes to luxe private houses scattered across the property.

Breakfast: Breakfast is served at the resort, but if you'd like to eat on the road, drop by **Mabry Mill Restaurant & Gift Shop** (✉ 266 Mabry Mill Rd. SE ☎ 276/952–2947 ⊕ www.mabrymillrestaurant.com) just off the property for its signature oatmeal pancakes.

Shenandoah National Parks offers superb sunrises over the Blue Ridge Mountains.

Day 2: Meadows of Dan, VA, to Shenandoah, VA

170 miles (3 hours without traffic and stops)

The directions are simple today: drive north on I–81, then east on I–64 to get to the southern entrance of Shenandoah National Park.

ALONG THE WAY

Town: Stretch your legs in Roanoke, where you can grab a bite to eat or do a little sightseeing. Make a pit stop at the **Roanoke Pinball Museum** (✉ *1 Market Sq. SE* ☎ *540/342–5746* ⊕ *www.roanokepinball.org*) or browse the antiques shop **Black Dog Salvage** (✉ *902 13th St. SW* ☎ *540/343–6200* ⊕ *www.blackdogsalvage.com*), made famous by the TV show *Salvage Dawgs.*

Eat & Drink: You can take a trip to Germany without ever leaving Virginia by stopping for lunch at **Edelweiss German Restaurant** (✉ *19 Edelweiss La.* ☎ *540/337–1203* ⊕ *www.edelweissvirginia.com*) in Staunton, a favorite of locals and road-trippers alike.

Detour: History buffs might want to take a side trip to Charlottesville to tour Thomas Jefferson's **Monticello** (✉ *931 Thomas Jefferson Pkwy.* ☎ *434/984–9800* ⊕ *www.monticello.org*) and James Monroe's **Highland** (✉ *2050 James Monroe Pkwy.* ☎ *434/293–8000* ⊕ *www.highland.org*). The town is about a 45-minute drive past Shenandoah National Park.

SHENANDOAH NATIONAL PARK

Do: Cruise the winding Skyline Drive, which runs 105 miles through the length of **Shenandoah National Park** (☎ *540/999–3500* ⊕ *www.nps.gov/shen*). It'll take at least three hours to make the full trip one-way, and that doesn't include stops at the scenic overlooks. Don't forget to make time for a few hikes, too, like Blackrock Summit, an hour-long, 1-mile loop hike that hugs the mountain following along the Appalachian Trail.

Eat & Drink: Dine in the park at the **Pollock Dining Room** at Skyland (✉ *400 Skyland Upper Loop, mile 42* ☎ *877/847–1919* ⊕ *www.goshenandoah.com*), then follow with drinks at the Mountain Taproom in the same location. Just keep in mind that they're both open only seasonally. Head to Circa '31 at the **Mimslyn Inn** (✉ *401 W. Main St.* ☎ *540/743–5105* ⊕ *www.mimslyninn.com*) in Luray, Virginia, for dining all year long (and be sure to grab a cocktail at the speakeasy).

Stay: There are two seasonal hotels within the park's borders, **Skyland** (✉ *Mile 41.7–42.5, Skyline Dr.*) and **Big Meadows Lodge** (✉ *Mile 51, Skyline Dr.* ☎ *977/847–1919* ⊕ *www.goshenandoah.com*), as well as multiple cabins and campsites. For year-round stays, try the boutique **Hotel Laurance** (✉ *2 S. Court St.* ☎ *540/742–7060* ⊕ *www.hotellaurance.com*) in Luray.

Breakfast: Grab a coffee and a pastry at **Gathering Grounds Pâtisserie & Café** (✉ *24 E. Main St.* ☎ *540/743–1121* ⊕ *www.ggrounds.com*) in Luray to start your day.

Day 3: Shenandoah, VA, to New River Gorge, WV

210 miles (4 hours without traffic and stops)

You'll do a little backtracking south along I–81 before heading west on I–64.

ALONG THE WAY

Nature: The largest cave system in the eastern United States—that we know of, anyway—is **Luray Caverns** (✉ *101 Cave Hill Rd.* ☎ *540/743–6551* ⊕ *www.luraycaverns.com*), located just outside Shenandoah National Park. Impressively, the caverns are step-free, making the site completely accessible.

Town: Your drive today will bring you through White Sulphur Springs, West Virginia, home of famous resort **The Greenbrier** (✉ *101 W. Main St.* ☎ *844/837–2466* ⊕ *www.greenbrier.com*), noted for its bold decor by interior designer Dorothy Draper. The destination has been frequented for its therapeutic natural pools since the 18th century, but the Greenbrier has since turned it into a dining, shopping, and gambling hot spot. Oh, and there's a massive Cold War–era bunker beneath the hotel that you can tour, too—it was designed to house all members of Congress in the event of a catastrophe.

Eat & Drink: Fancy a not-so-fancy bite? Embrace a road-trip classic: a burger at **Jim's Drive In** (✉ *479 Washington St.* ☎ *304/645–2590* ⊕ *www.facebook.com/jimsdrivein*) in Lewisburg, West Virginia, which has been fueling motorists since the 1950s.

NEW RIVER GORGE NATIONAL PARK

Do: Established in 2020, **New River Gorge National Park** (☎ *304/465–0508* ⊕ *www.nps.gov/neri*) is best known for its adventure activities—namely white-water rafting on the New River and rock climbing the steep cliff faces of the gorge. For more low-key fun, drive across the 876-foot-tall New River Gorge Bridge or visit the coal-mining ghost town of Thurmond, where the former train depot now serves as a visitor center and museum for the national park.

Eat & Drink: There are no dining facilities within the park. Instead, enjoy a casual dinner of pizza and beer at **Pies and Pints** (✉ *219 W. Maple Ave.* ☎ *304/574–2200* ⊕ *www.piesandpints.net*) in Fayetteville.

Stay: Camping is permitted in the park, but for a more comfortable stay, there's the **Historic Morris Harvey House Bed-and-Breakfast** (✉ *201 W. Maple Ave.* ☎ *304/646–7561* ⊕ *www.morrisharveyhouse.com*) in Fayetteville, which has five cozy rooms.

Breakfast: Enjoy the all-day breakfast at **Cathedral Café** (✉ *134 S. Court St.* ☎ *304/574–0202* ⊕ *www.thecathedralcafe.com*), which is housed in—you guessed it—an old church. It's also a bookstore, so you can pick up a new read for the road.

Day 4: New River Gorge, WV, to Gatlinburg, TN

275 miles (4 hours, 30 minutes without traffic and stops)

Buckle up for a long drive today. You'll start off traveling south on I–77, then once you reach Wytheville, Virginia, you'll head west on I–81. Finally, you'll take U.S. 441 south to Gatlinburg, Tennessee.

ALONG THE WAY

Roadside Attraction: Before you start driving south, take a quick 15-minute detour north on Route 17 to the kitschy **Mystery Hole** (✉ *16724 Midland Trail* ☎ *304/658–9101* ⊕ *www.mysteryhole.com*) in Ansted, West Virginia. Started in the 1970s by a man claiming the area contains a mysterious force that bends the laws of gravity, the spot is now the ultimate in roadside silliness, leaning into its sideshow-esque reputation.

Eat & Drink: On New Year's Day in 1953, country crooner Hank Williams died in his Cadillac, reportedly in the parking lot of the Skyline Drive-In in Hilltop, West Virginia. Today that eatery is known as **Hank's Last Stop** (✉ *6329 Legends Hwy.* ☎ *304/469–1025*), and if you're hankering for a hot dog, this is the place to get one.

Town: Wytheville, Virginia, the hometown of first lady Edith Bolling Wilson, is the perfect place for a pit stop. You can visit **Mrs. Wilson's birthplace** (✉ *145 E. Main St.* ☎ *276/223–3484* ⊕ *www.edithbollingwilson.org*), which is not only a museum but also the home of Skeeter's World Famous Hot Dogs. Wytheville has plenty of local shops for you to peruse or you can head just outside of town to pet alpacas at **Cobb Hill Alpacas** (✉ *448 Turley Farm Rd.* ☎ *276/780–1690* ⊕ *www.cobbhillalpacas.com*).

Roadside Attraction: Interred at the Mountain View Cemetery in Rural Retreat, Virginia, is Dr. Charles Taylor Pepper, who is theorized to be the namesake of the soda that bears his name. (There's not much hard evidence to support this, but it's a big part of local lore.) If you really love Dr. Pepper, stop by to pay your respects.

GATLINBURG

Do: Gatlinburg is one of the gateways to Great Smoky Mountains National Park, and it's filled to the brim with entertainment. Ascend the **Gatlinburg Space Needle** (✉ *115 Historic Nature Trail* ☎ *865/436–4629* ⊕ *www.gatlinburgspaceneedle.com*), take in the views from the aerial tramway at the **Ober Gatlinburg Adventure Park and Ski Area** (✉ *1001 Parkway* ☎ *865/436–5423* ⊕ *www.obermountain.com*), or peruse the displays at the **Museum of Salt and Pepper Shakers** (✉ *461 Brookside Village Way* ☎ *865/430–5515* ⊕ *www.thesaltandpeppershakermuseum.com*).

Eat & Drink: After eating hot dogs all day, you might want a lighter dinner. Head to Pigeon Forge, and try one of **Local Goat's** (✉ *2167 Parkway* ☎ *865/366–3035* ⊕ *www.localgoatpf.com*) fresh salads or just give in and have a burger.

Stay: There are accommodations of all kinds (and all price points) in Gatlinburg, from the historic **Gatlinburg Inn** (✉ *755 Parkway* ☎ *865/436–5133* ⊕ *www.gatlinburginn.com*) to the tropical-themed **Margaritaville Resort** (✉ *539 Parkway* ☎ *865/430–4200* ⊕ *www.margaritavilleresortgatlinburg.com*). Many travelers also opt to rent self-service cabins.

Breakfast: Brave the crowds at the **Log Cabin Pancake House** (✉ *327 Airport Rd.* ☎ *865/436–7894* ⊕ *www.*

logcabinpancakehouse.com); you might have to wait a bit for a table, but it's worth every minute.

Day 5: Great Smoky Mountains National Park, NC and TN

As the most visited national park in the United States, Great Smoky Mountains National Park deserves a full day of your time. Today you have the entire day to explore the park from your base in Gatlinburg.

Do: Great Smoky Mountains (☎ *865/436–1200* ⊕ *www.nps.gov/grsm*) has more than 300 miles of scenic drives, so take the day to cruise them, including the 11-mile Cades Cove Loop Road (arguably the most scenic part of the Smoky Mountains) and the 14-mile Newfound Gap Road. And don't skip hiking—there are many waterfalls in the park, many of which are accessible by easy trails, like the 5-mile Abrams Falls Trail. If you don't need a full day in the park, you could backtrack to nearby Pigeon Forge, just 15 minutes north of Gatlinburg, which is home to **Dollywood** (✉ *2700 Dollywood Parks Blvd.* ☎ *800/365–5996* ⊕ *www. dollywood.com*), Dolly Parton's amusement park. If you head back to Gatlinburg early, make a visit to **Ripley's Aquarium of the Smokies** (✉ *88 River Rd.* ☎ *865/430–8808* ⊕ *www.ripleysaquariums.com*) or the shops of the **Great Smoky Arts & Crafts Community** (✉ *668 Glades Rd.* ☎ *865/412–1012* ⊕ *www.gatlinburgcrafts.com*).

Eat & Drink: Dining options are limited inside the park, so either bring your own picnic or take a break from the outdoors for lunch at the **Wild Plum Tea Room** (✉ *555 Buckhorn Rd.* ☎ *865/436–3808* ⊕ *www.wildplumtearoom.com*) in Gatlinburg; it has limited operating hours, so be sure to plan ahead. The eclectic lunch spot serves seasonal

fare made with local ingredients. For dinner, splurge on a meal at the **Peddler Steakhouse** (✉ *820 River Rd.* ☎ *865/436–5794* ⊕ *www.peddlergatlinburg.com*), a perfect spot for a romantic date in Gatlinburg.

Stay: Stay put at your hotel or vacation rental from last night.

Breakfast: Tennessee Jed's (✉ *631 Parkway* ☎ *865/412–1131* ⊕ *www.tennesseejeds.net*) is quick, easy, and delicious. Order a hearty breakfast sandwich, then finish your meal with the brown butter minicake. Who says you can't have dessert in the morning?

Day 6: Great Smoky Mountains, NC and TN, to Congaree, SC

240 miles (4 hours without traffic and stops)

Take U.S. 321 east to I–40, then connect to I–26 near Asheville, North Carolina, and head south.

ALONG THE WAY

Town: Though today's route technically skirts by Asheville, North Carolina, it's worth making a brief detour to visit this funky mountain town. Visit the impressive **Biltmore Estate** (✉ *1 Approach Rd.* ☎ *800/411–3812* ⊕ *www.biltmore. com*), peruse the city's many art galleries and studios, or pick up some honey at the **Asheville Bee Charmer** gift shop (✉ *32 Broadway St.* ☎ *828/505–7736* ⊕ *www. ashevillebeecharmer.com*).

Eat & Drink: The original **Willy Taco** (✉ *930 E. Main St.* ☎ *864/327–8228* ⊕ *www. willytaco.com*) is located in Spartanburg, South Carolina, where you might order an Angus cheeseburger taco, brisket egg rolls, or sweet corn fritters in queso fresco.

Roadside Attraction: Stop for a quick photo with the world's largest fire hydrant in Columbia, South Carolina, a 40-foot-tall, 675,000-pound behemoth known as **Busted Plug Plaza** (✉ *1404 Taylor St.*).

CONGAREE NATIONAL PARK

Do: The swampy **Congaree National Park** (☎ *803/776–4396* ⊕ *www.nps.gov/cong*) is known for its meandering boardwalk trails and its old-growth forest with some of the tallest trees east of the Mississippi. If you're seeking a little more adventure, rent a canoe and hit the water. Just be sure to pack plenty of bug spray. And speaking of bugs, one of the most spectacular sights in Congaree is the annual synchronous fireflies festival, during which thousands (maybe millions!) of the luminescent critters synchronize their flash patterns in one of nature's most mysterious shows. The event takes place between mid-May and mid-June, and tickets are awarded via a lottery system.

Eat & Drink: There are no dining options within the park, so pack a picnic for lunch, and then enjoy dinner and drinks at **929 Kitchen & Bar** (✉ *929 Gervais St.* ☎ *803/764–3825* ⊕ *www.929kitchen.com*) in nearby Columbia, where the menu features "upscale modern" Korean fare.

Stay: South Carolina's capital, Columbia, is the place to stay near Congaree; you can stay at boutique hotels like **Graduate Columbia** (✉ *1619 Pendleton St.* ☎ *803/779–7779* ⊕ *www.graduatehotels.com*) or **Hotel Trundle** (✉ *1224 Taylor St.* ☎ *803/722–5000* ⊕ *www.hoteltrundle.com*).

Breakfast: As a college town, Columbia is home to some stellar breakfast establishments serving greasy hangover cures. **Cafe Strudel** (✉ *300 State St.* ☎ *803/794–6634* ⊕ *www.cafestrudel.com*) is no exception—order its famous Hangover Hash Browns.

Day 7: Congaree, SC, to Charlotte, NC

90 miles (1 hour, 30 minutes without traffic and stops)

The final leg of your journey is an easy one—straight north on I-77 to catch your flight home.

ALONG THE WAY

Detour: To be perfectly honest, this is a pretty quiet stretch of the road trip, which is why you should make a little detour to Winnsboro, South Carolina, located about 10 miles off I-77. It's home to the **South Carolina Railroad Museum** (✉ *110 Industrial Park Rd.* ☎ *803/635–9893* ⊕ *www.scrm.org*), a historic town clock that's been running for more than a century, and a quaint Main Street with restaurants and shops.

Eat & Drink: Stop in Rock Hill, South Carolina, for a quick lunch at **Amélie's French Bakery & Café** (✉ *157 E. Main St.* ☎ *803/403–9409* ⊕ *www.ameliesfrenchbakery.com*), where you can enjoy light bites like sandwiches and soups. Be sure to grab a few pastries or macarons to go as a snack on your flight home.

The Great American Whiskey Tour

Written by Brandon Schultz

Bourbon doesn't always come from Kentucky, but it does originate in the United States and is the country's only federally legislated spirit, making it one of the most beloved whiskies in America and the centerpiece of any whiskey trail trip. Louisville is, and probably always will be, the heart of Bourbon Country so it's the perfect place to begin and end your eight-day, six-state whirlwind road trip. On this epic adventure, you will sample not just Kentucky bourbon (traveling along

The Great American Whiskey Tour

the famed Bourbon Trail) and Tennessee whiskey, but spirits from Virginia, Ohio, Indiana, and more, as whiskey distilling booms across all 50 states.

It goes without saying, but we'll say it anyway: it's especially important to drink responsibly throughout this itinerary and never drink and drive. There's plenty of time built into this trip to linger at each distillery, and remember that these are tastings, not ragers, so sip and savor thoughtfully.

At a Glance

Start: Louisville, KY

End: Louisville, KY

Miles Traveled: 2,040 miles

Suggested Duration: 8 days

States Visited: Indiana, Kentucky, Maryland, Ohio, Tennessee, Virginia, West Virginia

Key Sights: Jack Daniels Distillery; Jim Beam American Stillhouse; Keeneland Race Course; Maker's Mark Distillery; Mammoth Cave National Park

Best Time to Go: Spring and fall offer ideal temperatures for this journey, and mid-to-late fall brings the added bonus of fewer visitors at the distilleries.

Day 1: Louisville, KY, to Lexington, KY

85 miles (1 hour, 40 minutes without traffic and stops)

Today's drive is a simple start and the shortest leg of the trip, traveling an easy 80 miles eastward. Don't get too late of a start, though; you'll want plenty of time at the three distilleries along the way.

ALONG THE WAY

Town: Stop in Shelbyville, about 45 minutes from Louisville, and check out the **Bulleit Distilling Co. Visitor Experience** (⌧ *3464 Benson Pike* ☎ *502/647–5799* ⊕ *www.bulleit.com*). Here, where sustainability and technology are driving forces behind the production of the brand's traditional rye recipe, you'll find one of the more modern facilities on your journey and catch a shiny glimmer of the future of American whiskey. The tour and tasting will take about an hour.

Town: A half hour from Shelbyville is Versailles, where you'll want to stop to explore **Woodford Reserve Distillery** (⌧ *7785 McCracken Pike* ☎ *859/879–1812* ⊕ *www.woodfordreserve.com*) for a far more traditional approach to whiskey making. Bourbon was first made on this property in 1812, and you'll feel (and taste) the history everywhere. The tour and tasting will take an hour or so.

Eat & Drink: Snag lunch at **Glenn's Creek Café** (⊕ *www.woodfordreserve.com/our-distillery/glenns-creek-cafe-menu*) at the Woodford Reserve Distillery, where the chef in residence whips up distillery-inspired favorites, like Bourbon Trail Chili (made-from-scratch cornbread included) or the slow-cooked Bourbon Barbecue Pulled-Pork Sammich.

LEXINGTON

Do: Visit the **Old Pepper Distillery** (⌧ *1228 Manchester St.* ☎ *859/309–3230* ⊕ *www.jamesepepper.com*), where James E. Pepper is once again being distilled after the lot sat abandoned for more than 50 years. Now revitalized, it's the centerpiece of the Lexington Distillery District, featuring 25 acres of shops, eateries, and plenty of spots to stop for additional sips. Don't venture off without touring the distillery's small yet fascinating history museum, where you'll learn that the old-fashioned cocktail was allegedly invented for Colonel Pepper himself during a visit to New York City's Waldorf Astoria Hotel. Naturally, it's the only cocktail served here today. With more than 400 horse farms in the city, Lexington is the "horse capital of the world," so you may want to check out a stately site like **Keeneland Race Course** (✉ *4201 Versailles Rd.* ☎ *859/254–3412* ⊕ *www.keeneland.com*) to enjoy the beautiful grounds, scope some stellar horses, or catch a thoroughbred race. It's open daily to the public.

Eat & Drink: Grab a few slices of New York–style pizza at **Goodfellas Pizzeria** (✉ *1228 Manchester St.* ☎ *859/523–5280* ⊕ *www.goodfellaspizzeria.com*) in the Distillery District, just a few steps from Old Pepper Distillery. There's plenty of outdoor seating (and a bocce ball court), but be sure to poke around the industrial interior for a bit. Save room for dessert around the corner at **Crank & Boom Ice Cream Lounge** (✉ *1210 Manchester St.* ☎ *859/288–2176* ⊕ *www.crankandboom.com*), where local ingredients are churned into small-batch flavors like Kentucky blackberry and buttermilk, and bourbon and honey. Feel free to upgrade to a "spiked scoop."

Stay: Spend the night at **Origin Lexington** (✉ *4174 Rowan* ☎ *859/245–0400* ⊕ *www.originhotel.com*), where stylish rooms feature accents of moss green, soft gray, and leathery brown below alluring black ceilings. If you can't make it to the 24-hour fitness center, have a free yoga kit (mat, block, and strap) sent to your room.

Breakfast: Get ready for Day 2 with breakfast at **Josie's** (✉ *821 Chevy Chase Pl.* ☎ *859/523–8328* ⊕ *www.josies-ky.com*) in the Chevy Chase neighborhood of Lexington. This breakfast-all-day spot has lighter fare, like egg-white omelets and organic granola, for the health-conscious, and gluttonous, heavier fare, like sausage gravy and biscuits, for those setting a solid foundation for the day's whiskey consumption.

Essential Listening

Before entering Bardstown, listen to Stephen Foster's "My Old Kentucky Home, Good Night." This antislavery song was inspired in part by visits to Federal Hill, which you can visit when you arrive. The other assumed inspiration for this song was Harriet Beecher Stowe's groundbreaking antislavery novel, *Uncle Tom's Cabin*, which you might also listen to as an audiobook, but that one will take about 20 hours.

Day 2: Lexington, KY, to Bardstown, KY

120 miles (2 hours, 45 minutes without traffic and stops)

Today's goal is only about 60 miles southwest of Lexington, but it's smack between two classic distilleries you won't want to miss, so you'll need to shun the straight line and embrace a somewhat circuitous route just this once.

ALONG THE WAY

Town: Just over a half hour from Lexington, Lawrenceburg is home to **Wild Turkey Distillery** (✉ *1417 Versailles Rd.* ☎ *502/839–2182* ⊕ *www.wildturkeybourbon.com*), where the world's longest-tenured master distiller continues to oversee whiskey traditions that predate Prohibition. You'll also find Matthew McConaughey's favorite bourbon, Longbranch, here (he created it). The tour and tasting will take about one hour.

Photo Op: Just outside the entrance of Wild Turkey is a giant mural of, well, a wild turkey (you'll recognize it from the bottle). It's a perfect spot for an amusing pose to commemorate your wild whiskey wanderlust.

Eat & Drink: Have lunch at Star Hill Provisions at **Maker's Mark Distillery** (✉ *3350 Burks Spring Rd.* ☎ *270/865–2099* ⊕ *www.makersmark.com*). The chef in residence prepares seasonal menus of local Kentucky ingredients with hearty sandwiches and flavorful salads. The star of the menu is the Maker's and Ale-8-One Slushie, ideal for dessert.

Town: Stop in Clermont to tour the home of the world's best-selling whiskey at **James B. Beam Distilling Co.** (✉ *568 Happy Hollow Rd.* ☎ *502/543–9877* ⊕ *www.beamdistilling.com*). Jim Beam is aged twice as long as the legal requirement for bourbon, and the tour lasts a little longer than your typical distillery walk-through, too, so you may have time to safely snag an extra sip at the Jim Beam Bourbon Bar and linger a little at your last stop of the day. The tour and tasting take around 90 minutes.

BARDSTOWN

Do: Bardstown is more than a place to crash for the night. Depending on how early you get started today, you should be able to visit at least one or two of its main attractions, including the **Oscar Getz Museum of Whiskey History** (✉ *114 N. 5th St.* ☎ *502/348–2999* ⊕ *www.oscargetzwhiskeymuseum.com*), **Women's Civil War Museum** (✉ *204 E. Broadway St.* ☎ *502/349–0291* ⊕ *www.civil-war-museum.org*), and **My Old Kentucky Home** mansion (✉ *501 E. Stephen Foster Ave.* ☎ *502/348–3502* ⊕ *www.visitmyoldkyhome.com*). There are even a couple distilleries in town if you're up for more tasting (you're done driving for the day, so go for it).

Eat & Drink: Embrace Kentucky cuisine with dinner at **The Rickhouse** (✉ *112 Xavier Dr.* ☎ *502/348–2832* ⊕ *www.therickhouse-bardstown.com*), located just below the whiskey museum. Try the hot brown, a smothered Kentucky classic, or pair a premium steak with choices from the 150-bottle bourbon library.

Stay: Book a room in **The Talbott Inn** (✉ *101 W. Stephen Foster Ave.* ☎ *502/348–3494* ⊕ *www.talbotttavern.com/talbott-inn*) for a convenient stay in the center of downtown Bardstown, steps from the quaint town's restaurants and shops. You'll find modern rooms in a historic 1913 building and you can't beat the price or location. If you're up for some potential spook factor, you could check into the neighboring **Talbott Tavern** (✉ *107 W. Stephen Foster Ave.* ☎ *502/348–3494* ⊕ *www.talbotttavern.com*), a B&B built in 1779. Here you'll also find the world's oldest bourbon bar.

Breakfast: Day 3 comes with considerably more driving time, so pop into **Fresh** (✉ *114 N. 3rd St.* ☎ *502/331–6345* ⊕ *www.freshcoffeebardstown.com*) for a to-go breakfast. Grab some Good Folks coffee and a big ole pastry or two from this zero-waste kitchen with a locally sourced menu that changes weekly (and sometimes daily).

Day 3: Bardstown, KY, to Nashville, TN

300 miles (5 hours without traffic and stops)

Start fairly early today as the first leg of this journey takes you three and a half hours south to your first stop before about-facing northward toward Nashville.

ALONG THE WAY

Nature: If you can pull yourself out of bed even earlier, a slight detour of about 15 minutes in each direction will bring you to **Mammoth Cave National Park** (☎ *270/758–2180* ⊕ *www.nps.gov/maca*), home of the world's longest known cave system, just over an hour from Bardstown. The visitor center opens at 8 am, but if you want to spend the recommended three

Did You Know?

Now one of America's most popular names in bourbon, the Beam family first began producing whiskey in 1795. James Beam rebuilt the distillery after it closed during Prohibition, opening the Clermont space that officially became Jim Beam in 1935.

hours exploring the park, you may need to cut a distillery from your day.

Attraction: Leave Kentucky bourbon behind (for now) and move on to Tennessee whiskey today with a tour of **Jack Daniel's Distillery** (✉ *133 Lynchburg Hwy.* ☎ *931/759–6357* ⊕ *www.jackdaniels.com*) in Lynchburg, Tennessee. Theme tours range from 70 to 90 minutes for more traditional experiences and three hours for a filling tour that culminates in a country meal.

Eat & Drink: Have lunch in Lynchburg at **Miss Mary Bobo's** (✉ *295 Main St.* ☎ *931/759–7394* ⊕ *www.missmarybobos.com*), where southern hospitality has been the hallmark of every hearty meal since Miss Mary Bobo opened her kitchen in 1908 and ran it for more than 60 years. Now owned by the Jack Daniel's Distillery, the family-style restaurant has expanded to nine dining rooms serving more than 200 hungry patrons daily so you'll want to make reservations for this one.

Attraction: Relearn your whiskey history with a visit to **Nearest Green Distillery** (✉ *3125 U.S. 231 N* ☎ *931/773–3070* ⊕ *www.unclenearest.com*) in Shelbyville, Tennessee, where Uncle Nearest Premium Whiskey is produced. Uncle Nearest was the world's first African American master distiller and the man who taught a young Jack Daniel to filter his whiskey through sugar maple charcoal. The tour takes 90 minutes.

NASHVILLE

Do: You'll trip over things to do in Nashville, but make sure one of them is a visit to **Nelson's Green Brier Distillery** (✉ *1414 Clinton St.* ☎ *615/913–8800* ⊕ *www.greenbrierdistillery.com*). With a dramatic history including shipwreck and lost family fortune on the way to seeking the American dream, Charles Nelson went from soapmaker to grocer to distiller, becoming one of the pioneers of whiskey bottling before Prohibition closed the business. Generations later, his descendants rediscovered the distillery and relaunched the brand exactly 100 years after it had closed. The tour and tasting will take about 45 minutes.

Eat & Drink: Stay on theme with a visit to **Gertie's Bar** (✉ *507 12th Ave. S* ☎ *615/251–1404* ⊕ *www.gertieswhiskeybar.com*), which has one of the city's largest and most diverse whiskey collections, meaning you can branch out and try plenty of international options today. The full dinner menu from 404 Kitchen is available at the bar, so order some grub to balance your sips.

Stay: Slip into Nashville's urban style with a stay at **Waymore's Guest House** (✉ *811 Main St.* ☎ *615/650–9075* ⊕ *www.waymoresnashville.com*) in the city's artsy East Nashville neighborhood. Uniquely designed accommodations range from traditional and deluxe rooms and suites to legitimately cool bunk bed combos, and the rooftop bar boasts some pretty cool skyline views.

Breakfast: Try something new this morning by heading to **Yeast Nashville** (✉ *805 Woodland St.* ☎ *615/330–7521* ⊕ *www.yeastnashville.com*) and ordering a tongue-twisting Tex-Czech kolache with your morning tea. Traditional Czech kolaches are like thick Danishes of brioche-y dough filled with fruit, poppy seed, or cheese, but a Tex-Czech version embraces the tradition of the 19th-century Texas Czechs who started stuffing them with meat.

Day 4: Nashville, TN, to Bloomington, IN

275 miles (4 hours, 40 minutes without traffic and stops)

Head north on I–65 through Kentucky and into Indiana. It's a long drive, but a fairly direct route today.

ALONG THE WAY

Detour: Just under two hours into your drive, American history buffs will want to hop off I-65 in Kentucky for a 20-minute detour to **Abraham Lincoln Birthplace National Historic Park** (✉ 2995 Lincoln Farm Rd. ☎ 270/358–3137 ⊕ www.nps. gov/abli). The first memorial to Lincoln, 56 steps lead up the knoll to where he was born to commemorate his 56 years of life, and a humble replica of his one-room cabin can be found within the stately memorial at the top.

Detour: Pay a visit to **Starlight Distillery** (✉ 19816 Huber Rd. ☎ 812/923–9463 ⊕ www.starlightdistillery.com) at Huber's Orchard, Winery & Vineyards in Borden, Indiana, about an hour from the Abe Lincoln detour or three hours direct from Nashville. While originally launched to distill brandies from the vineyards' grapes, Starlight also produces a few single-barrel bourbons and ryes, and even a blackberry whiskey worth a taste. The distillery tour and tasting will take just 30 minutes, so you may want to tack on the 30-minute wine tour and tasting, too, for a broader understanding of the whole operation.

Eat & Drink: While road-tripping through small-town USA, have an all-American lunch of a burger and fries at **Norma Jean's Ice Cream** (✉ 302 E. Water St. ☎ 812/967–2663 ⊕ www.facebook. com/normajeansicecream) during your stop in Borden. Order from the window and chow down at the creekside picnic tables. You should finish this meal with some scoops of ice cream, and are encouraged to venture into flavors like Fat Elvis, Zanzibar chocolate, and orange pineapple.

BLOOMINGTON

Do: Just an hour south of Indianapolis, Bloomington is a quaint city near Lake Monroe with equal helpings of nature and culture. Downtown has plenty of shops and galleries, like the popular Fountain Square shop collective and the **I Fell** (✉ 415 W. 4th St. ☎ 812/361–6719 ⊕ www.ifellbloomington.wordpress.com) community art center with studios, shops, and a bakery. Check out the **Eskenazi Museum of Art** (✉ 1133 E. 7th St. ☎ 812/855–5445 ⊕ www.artmuseum.indiana.edu) and the **Wylie House Museum** (✉ 307 E. 2nd St. ☎ 812/855–6224 ⊕ www.libraries.indiana.edu) for indoor activities, or head to **McCormick's Creek State Park** (✉ 250 McCormick Creek Park Rd. ☎ 812/829–2235 ⊕ www. in.gov) or **Hoosier National Forest** (✉ 811 Constitution Ave., Bedford ☎ 812/275–5987 ⊕ www.fs.usda.gov) for outdoor time.

Eat & Drink: Visit Bloomington's first craft distillery, **Cardinal Spirits** (✉ 922 S. Morton St. ☎ 812/202–6789 ⊕ www.cardinalspirits.com), for dinner, drinks, and a tour. You're halfway through your whirlwind whiskey odyssey now, so take a break to appreciate sips of Cardinal's vodka, gin, or rum—these are the specialties here. For dinner, try the truffle chicken with mashed potatoes or the "salmon breeze" with broccolini and maitake mushrooms.

Stay: Check in to the **Showers Inn Bed & Breakfast** (✉ 430 N. Washington St. ☎ 812/334–9000 ⊕ www.showersinn. com) for a cozy stay in the center of town. The historic Showers-Graham house is outfitted with modern conveniences and upscale amenities at reasonable rates with complimentary parking.

Breakfast: Take advantage of the included breakfast buffet at the Showers Inn. In addition to the standards like fruit, yogurt, and cereal, you'll find homemade specialties like corned beef hash and poached eggs, spinach and Gruyère strata, and lemon poppy-seed pound cake.

Day 5: Bloomington, IN, to Columbus, OH

230 miles (3 hours, 50 minutes without traffic and stops)

Head north to Indianapolis before venturing east along I–70 for the majority of today's shorter drive. A stop in Indianapolis will keep the second leg just over two and a half hours, and there are no other major stops along the way, so feel free to take a later start and aim to be in Indy for lunch.

ALONG THE WAY

Town: Indianapolis is your sole stop before Columbus, so you'll have plenty of time to explore Indiana's capital city. If you can't wait until the evening for today's dose of whiskey, stop by **Westfork Whiskey Co.** (✉ *1660 Bellefontaine St.* ☎ *317/672–7468* ⊕ *www.westfork-whiskey.com*) for smooth sips of distilled Indiana grains in the tasting room. Other options include checking out the **Eiteljorg Museum** (✉ *500 W. Washington St.* ☎ *317/636–9378* ⊕ *www.eiteljorg.org*) for Native American and western art, the **Kurt Vonnegut Museum and Library** (✉ *543 Indiana Ave.* ☎ *317/423–0391* ⊕ *www.vonnegutlibrary.org*), and, of course, the **Indianapolis Motor Speedway** (✉ *4790 W. 16th St.* ☎ *317/492–8500* ⊕ *www.indianapolismotorspeedway.com*).

Eat & Drink: The Garage Food Hall (✉ *906 Carrollton Ave.* ☎ *317/556–1252* ⊕ *www.garageindy.com*) occupies the former garages of a Coca-Cola bottling plant (and later the city's school buses), offering a cavernous space filled with the outposts of the best local bites. Choose from *poke*, arepas, burgers, soul food, and so much more, or just stop in for a pint and a cup of killer ice cream.

COLUMBUS

Do: If you've had enough of museums from earlier today, check out outdoor Columbus by toddling around German Village, taking pics in **Topiary Park** (✉ *480 E. Town St.* ☎ *614/645–0197* ⊕ *www.columbus.gov*) or the **Columbus Park of Roses** (✉ *3901 N. High St.* ☎ *614/645–3391* ⊕ *www.parkofroses.org*), or admiring nature at **Hayden Falls Park** (✉ *4326 Hayden Run Rd.* ☎ *614/645–3300* ⊕ *www.columbus.gov*). Toward the end of your exploration, tour **Middle West Spirits** (✉ *1230 Courtland Ave.* ☎ *614/947–1231* ⊕ *www.middlewestspirits.com*), where it's all about appreciating the good life, as one cofounder describes a sip here as an "everyday special occasion." Try the ryes, including dark pumpernickel, and remember that bourbon doesn't have to be made in Kentucky—it's just a myth—so give it a go, perhaps in a cocktail at Service Bar on-site.

Eat & Drink: Service Bar (✉ *1230 Courtland Ave.* ☎ *614/947–1231* ⊕ *www.servicebar-columbus.com*) is the spot to stay for dinner, whether you went for that bourbon cocktail after your tour or not. Expect serious upgrades of familiar plates, like crispy ribs with fried broccoli in a hibiscus Commander Tso's sauce or roasted potato gnocchi with oxtail, kabocha squash, and truffle. Go overboard with not tres but cinco leches cake for dessert.

Stay: Although **The Blackwell** (✉ *2110 Tuttle Park Pl.* ☎ *614/247–4000* ⊕ *www.theblackwell.com*) caters to more of a business crowd and the austere exterior may not spark much joy, you'll love the four-star accommodations and service that come with this surprisingly affordable reservation.

Breakfast: Take one last bite of Columbus's German heritage with breakfast at **Valters at the Maennerchor** (✉ *976 S. High St.* ☎ *614/444–3531* ⊕ *www.valtersatthemaennerchor.com*), founded more than 150 years ago by a dozen German immigrants. Here you'll find skillets loaded with hearty helpings (including bratwurst, of course); you can even grab a traditional soft pretzel for the road on your way out.

Catoctin Creek Distilling Company produces Virginia's most award-winning whiskey.

Day 6: Columbus, OH, to Purcellville, VA

350 miles (6 hours, 40 minutes without traffic and stops)

Today's drive is the longest of the trip clocking in at just over six and a half hours traveling west into northeast Virginia. If you want to shave a little time off, you can buy back a half hour by skipping today's stops and taking a slightly more streamlined route.

ALONG THE WAY

Roadside Attraction: If six straight days of whiskey is turning you into something of a basket case, you'll want to stop for a photo with the World's Largest Basket on Main Street in the little town of Dresden, Ohio. It's 48 feet wide, 11 feet long, and 23 feet high, making it larger than some houses.

Eat & Drink: Since you'll want to get to Purcellville early enough to explore, you can stop at any service station along the route for lunch, but if you prefer something a little quainter, pop into **The Casselman** (✉ 113 Main St. ☎ 301/895–5055 ⊕ www.thecasselman.com) in Grantsville, Maryland, four hours into your drive. You'll find simple, country food with Pennsylvania Dutch and Amish influences, especially in the bakery downstairs, where there's also an antiques shop.

PURCELLVILLE

Do: You may be surprised to learn that Virginia is the birthplace of American whiskey. Visit **Catoctin Creek Distilling Company** (✉ 120 W. Main St. ☎ 540/751–8404 ⊕ www.catoctincreekdistilling.com) to tour the facility, try a whiskey flight, and snag a bottle of Virginia's most awarded whiskey, Roundstone Rye, to take home. A tour-and-tasting combo here will take about an hour. You're clearly in town for Catoctin Creek, but this is wine country, so you may want to check out one or two of the many surrounding wineries, too. For a less alcohol-induced activity, there aren't many spots more picturesque than **Blooming Hill Lavender Farm** (✉ *19929 Telegraph Springs Rd.* ☎ *703/431–0779* ⊕ *www.bloominghillva.com*), open to the public for strolling and shopping.

Eat & Drink: Don't be fooled by the barn location: **Magnolia at the Mill** (✉ *198 N. 21st St.* ☎ *540/338–9800* ⊕ *www.magnoliasmill.com*) is the best spot in town for a chic dinner on the more comfortable side of upscale. You'll find filet mignon, seared salmon with lump crab, and shrimp and grits served on white-linen cloths, but you're also in luck if you're looking for hickory-grilled burgers or brick-oven pizzas.

Stay: Springdale Village Inn (✉ *18348 Lincoln Rd.* ☎ *540/751–8686* ⊕ *www.springdalevillageinn.com*) is the B&B for you in Purcellville. Colonial cottage–decorated rooms provide cozy accommodations in the Federal-style estate house believed to be one of the last stops on the Underground Railroad, just 14 miles from the border to freedom. The five acres of bucolic bliss are well worth wandering, too.

Breakfast: Sit down early to Springdale Village Inn's daily farm-to-table breakfast and load up properly for the two-distillery day with a considerable drive between.

Day 7: Purcellville, VA, to Maxwelton, WV

320 miles (5 hours, 20 minutes without traffic and stops)

Head a bit farther east today before looping back westward toward Kentucky. You'll make it just about halfway, stopping in West Virginia for a little more whiskey and a good night's sleep.

ALONG THE WAY

Town: Your first whiskey stop today may be a surprising one. An hour east of Purcellville, stop at **George Washington's**

Distillery (✉ *5514 Mount Vernon Memorial Hwy.* ☎ *703/780–3383* ⊕ *www.mountvernon.org*) at Mount Vernon in Alexandria to tour a re-creation of one of the nation's earliest large-scale whiskey distilleries, and one of the most profitable ventures on Washington's estate. Washington's recipe is once again being produced, in very limited batches, since the distillery's reopening in 2007.

Town: Sample one last taste of Virginia whiskey at **KO Distilling** (✉ *10381 Central Park Dr.* ☎ *571/292–1115* ⊕ *www.kodistilling.com*) in Manassas, about 45 minutes west of Alexandria. Try a flight of Bare Knuckle whiskeys, including straight bourbon, wheat, and rye, from this relative newcomer to the craft distilling scene. A tour before your tasting will take about 30 minutes.

Eat & Drink: Have lunch in Manassas before the final 3½-hour haul to Maxwelton. At **The Bone BBQ** (✉ *9420 Battle St.* ☎ *703/330–3820* ⊕ *www.thebonebbq.com*), you'll find pulled pork, hickory-smoked chicken, smoked turkey, brisket, and more, served with sweet potato fries, mac and cheese, and baked potato on a menu that also includes specialty sandwiches like a brisket-and-pulled-pork po' boy and a few juicy burgers.

MAXWELTON

Do: Get a taste of Appalachian whiskey at **Smooth Ambler Spirits** (✉ *745 Industrial Park Rd.* ☎ *304/497–3123* ⊕ *www.smoothambler.com*) in the West Virginia mountains, where they believe their clean water, crisp air, and ideal climate produce some of the country's top spirits. Smooth Ambler specializes in bourbon whiskies, so be sure to take some comparison sips before returning to limestone-laced Kentucky tomorrow.

Eat & Drink: Most of the area action is in Lewisburg, five minutes from Maxwelton, and it's here that you'll find **Food & Friends** (✉ *878 Washington St. W* ☎ *304/645–4548* ⊕ *www.*

foodandfriendslewisburg.com), a neighborhood favorite for a good meal and equally good atmosphere. Check out the chargrilled menu for brisket, pecan-crusted chicken, baby back ribs, or bourbon-glazed salmon.

Stay: Maxwelton/Lewisburg isn't exactly a tourism area, so you won't be staying in town. Luckily, there's a sweet little hotel in nearby White Sulphur Springs, about 15 minutes away, and you'll spend a comfortable night here at **Howard's Creek Inn** (✉ 50 E. Main St. ☎ 304/667–9863 ⊕ www.howardscreekinn.com).

Breakfast: Back in Lewisburg, hit up **The Wild Bean** (✉ 1056 E. Washington St. ☎ 304/645–3738 ⊕ www.thewild-brew.com) for a dependable breakfast of huevos rancheros or the Papas Plato of home fries, fajita veggies, and avocado topped with buttermilk crema and salsa. You can also try the scrambled eggs menu, with plenty of add-ins like black beans, jalapeños, spinach, or sautéed peppers and onions.

Day 8: Maxwelton, WV, to Louisville, KY

360 miles (5 hours, 30 minutes without traffic and stops)

Your last day on the road is as easy as it gets—just hop on I–64 W and take it back to Louisville.

ALONG THE WAY

Town: Stop in West Virginia's capital city of Charleston to stretch your legs. Take a walk along the Kanawha River and check out Haddad Riverfront Park before strolling down Capitol Street in town. Make your way to **Capitol Market** (✉ 800 Smith St. ☎ 304/344–1905 ⊕ www.capitolmar-ket.net) on Smith Street to peruse the vibrant indoor-outdoor market and grab lunch before hitting the road again.

Eat & Drink: It's been a fairly meat-forward trip, as you'd expect from this barbecue-loving region, so step back from the pit for the afternoon and try some Cajun pasta with shrimp or good old-fashioned spaghetti and meatballs in spicy puttanesca sauce at **Soho's Capitol Market** (✉ 800 Smith St. ☎ 304/720–7646 ⊕ www.sohoscrw.com).

LOUISVILLE

Do: There is a ton of whiskey and bourbon to be had here. The great news is you can walk to many of the distilleries (or their outposts) in town, so you can taste a little more enthusiastically than when you were driving. Three spots you must hit are **Old Forester Distilling Co.** (✉ 119 W. Main St. ☎ 502/779–2222 ⊕ www.oldforester.com), home of America's first bottled bourbon; **Angel's Envy Distillery** (✉ 500 E. Main St. ☎ 502/890–6300 ⊕ www.angelsenvy.com), finished in port wine casks; and **Rabbit Hole Distillery** (✉ 711 E. Jefferson St. ☎ 502/561–2000 ⊕ www.rabbitholedistillery.com), a hypermodern outfit with an art collection as covetable as its spirits.

Eat & Drink: Have one last carnivorous feast at **Steak & Bourbon** (✉ 1321 Herr La. ☎ 502/708–2196 ⊕ www.steak-bourbon.com) where, as you'd guess, large slabs of beef and an even larger bourbon collection (about 70 varieties) are the specialties. Potatoes are particularly prized here, too, with their own section on the menu.

Stay: The Louisville hotel scene is small but surprisingly strong. End your trip on a cultural note with a stay at **21c Museum Hotel** (✉ 700 W Main St. ☎ 502/217–6300 ⊕ www.21cmuseumhotels.com/louisville), an eye-popping boutique that's also an art museum, complete with both permanent pieces and temporary exhibits. You'll recognize it by the golden *David* statue outside or the vibrant penguins that roam the halls (feel free to move them yourself and even take them to your room).

The Civil Rights Trail

Breakfast: For your final meal of the journey, head to **Highland Morning** (✉ *1416 Bardstown Rd.* ☎ *502/365–3900* ⊕ *www.highlandmorning.org*) for big portions of biscuits and gravy, crab cake Benedict, or a bacon-and-fried-egg sandwich on an English muffin. If you want to treat yourself, indulge in the sinful pancake menu, where Dreamsicle, Key West Key Lime, and Strawberry Shortcake are just a few of the tempting varieties available.

The Civil Rights Trail

Written by Chanté LaGon

Spanning over 100 locations across 15 states, the U.S. Civil Rights Trail retraces the fight for Black American civil rights during the pivotal civil rights movement of the 1950s and 1960s. On this road trip,

you'll see a selection of these essential sights as you travel through the American South's wow-inducing mountains and Spanish moss–covered public squares. From the hustle of Atlanta, "the city too busy to hate," to the old-world charm of Charleston, you'll find everything from monuments honoring Martin Luther King Jr. and other heroes of the movement to glimpses and remnants of African culture from long ago.

At a Glance

Start: Atlanta, GA

End: Atlanta, GA

Miles Traveled: 1,660 miles

Suggested Duration: 7 days

States Visited: Alabama, Georgia, Mississippi, South Carolina, Tennessee

Key Sights: Edmund Pettus Bridge; Martin Luther King Jr. National Historic Park; National Center for Civil and Human Rights; National Civil Rights Museum at Lorraine Motel; Rosa Parks Museum

Best Time to Go: This southern road trip offers pleasant driving weather year-round, but expect bonus activities—and bigger crowds—around the time of the Martin Luther King Jr. national holiday (the third Monday in January) or during Black History Month in February.

Day 1: Atlanta, GA, to Nashville, TN

250 miles (3 hours, 45 minutes without traffic and stops)

Hartsfield-Jackson Atlanta International Airport is home to Delta Air Lines so finding a convenient flight is quite easy. The world's busiest airport offers an expansive selection of car rental options, too, but there are outposts throughout the convention-hosting metro area if you're not flying in. Once you hit the road, motor up I–75 past Atlanta's heavy downtown traffic and about 30 minutes north, get a preview of the roadside mountains to come. You'll know you're more than halfway there when the highway winds through the Appalachian Mountains and over the Tennessee River in Chattanooga, along with some tight lanes that you'll have to share with big rigs pumping their breaks during the descent.

ALONG THE WAY

Photo Op: Before you hit the road, head to **State Farm Arena** (✉ *1 State Farm Dr.*) and take a picture near Centennial Olympic Park Drive. With the building's big "Atlanta" sign in the background, you'll feel as if you've officially stepped into one of the city's infamous reality TV shows.

Eat & Drink: The site of militia training during the Civil War, **Marietta Square** (✉ *99 S. Park Sq. NE* ⊕ *www.mariettaga.gov*) in Marietta, Georgia, is now home to quaint shops and a variety of restaurants, from Australian meat pies and barbecue to hot dogs and Mexican.

Roadside Attraction: Marietta's **The Big Chicken** (✉ *12 Cobb Pkwy. SE*) is just what it sounds like. Built in 1963 as part of a KFC, the drive-thru is optional, but a drive-by of the landmark (complete with moving beak and eyes) is a must.

Town: Before Atlanta's Georgia Aquarium became a must-see, the **Tennessee Aquarium** (✉ *1 Broad St.* ☎ *800/262–0695* ⊕ *www.tnaqua.org*) in Chattanooga drew visitors from throughout the region, and remains impressive with its two buildings and an IMAX 3-D theater. The **Chattanooga Zoo** (✉ *301 N. Holtzclaw Ave.* ☎ *423/697–1322* ⊕ *www.chattzoo.org*) and its more than 500 animals welcome visitors who prefer their exhibits on dry land. Rest your feet and view the city from above on the mile-long and 72%-steep-grade **Lookout Mountain Incline Railway** (✉ *3917 St. Elmo Ave.* ☎ *423/821–4224* ⊕ *www.ridetheincline.com*), in operation for more than 125 years.

NASHVILLE

Do: To best appreciate the city's civil rights history, center your visit in the downtown area, with easy access to the **National Museum of African American Music** (✉ *510 Broadway* ☎ *615/301–8724* ⊕ *www.nmaam.org*) and the **Davidson County Courthouse** (✉ *1 Public Sq.*). The Public Works Administration's modern courthouse is grand enough to take in on its own, but be sure to stroll through its plaza and to the nearby **Witness Walls** (⊕ *www.metroartsnashville.com/witness-walls*), commemorating protests led by civil rights leaders C. T. Vivian and Diane Nash in response to the bombing of a civil rights attorney's home in 1960. After the bombing, Nashville's laws segregating lunch counters began to loosen; make a visit to **Woolworth on 5th** (✉ *221 5th Ave. N* ☎ *615/891–1361* ⊕ *www.woolworthonfifth.com*), designated as a historic landmark in honor of the sit-ins that kicked off the city's civil rights movement.

Eat & Drink: For a taste of the spicy specialty born here, head to **Hattie B's Hot Chicken** (✉ *112 19th Ave. S* ☎ *615/678–4794* ⊕ *www.hattieb.com*). Music City lives up to its name, with storefront after storefront on Broadway piping music out its doors. Duck into any of the bars for a nightcap or to get the night started.

Stay: What's better than fine art, fine meals, and comfortable, modern rooms? **The Bankers Alley Hotel Nashville** (✉ *221 2nd Ave. N* ☎ *615/610–6400* ⊕ *www.hilton.com*) has all three. You'll feel as if you've stepped back in time at the **Fairlane Hotel** (✉ *401 Union St.* ☎ *615/988–8511* ⊕ *www.fairlanehotel.com*), but the service and amenities will match your present-day expectations.

Breakfast: At **417 Union** (✉ *417 Union St.* ☎ *615/401–7241* ⊕ *www.417union.com*), the service is attentive and friendly, with delicious breakfast basics such as shrimp and grits and chicken and waffles served in a lively spot filled with military memorabilia. Plus, there's a full bar for noteworthy Bloody Marys.

Day 2: Nashville, TN, to Memphis, TN

212 miles (3 hours without traffic and stops)

It's all "Music Highway" heading southwest to Memphis, the bluesy sister to Nashville's country and pop heritage. You'll cross the Tennessee River once more, and see more woodlands along the way, including a cut through the Hatchie National Wildlife Refuge.

Extend Your Trip

From Nashville or Memphis: The Great American Music Road Trip *(Ch. 7)*

From Memphis: Along the Mississippi *(Ch. 2)*

From Charleston or Atlanta: Civil War Battlefields and History *(Ch. 2)*

ALONG THE WAY

Nature: Natchez Trace State Park's (✉ *24845 Natchez Trace Rd.* ☎ *731/968–3742* ⊕ *www.tnstateparks.com*) 48,000 acres of public lands and lakes offer hiking, fishing, and pontoon cruises.

Town: Hit the halfway mark at Lexington, Tennessee, for a stretch and brief rest from the road. Explore the Civil War battleground at nearby **Parkers Crossroads** (☎ *731/968–1191* ⊕ *www.parkerscrossroads.org*), which is convenient for its self-guided driving tour.

Eat & Drink: A top-secret rub is just one reason **Bozo's Hot-Pit Bar-B-Q** (✉ *342 U.S. 70 W* ☎ *901/294–3400* ⊕ *www.bozoshotpitbar-b-q.com*) in Mason has been around for nearly 100 years. Make sure to get a piece of the homemade pie-of-the-day to go, and hope it's the unbeatable pecan pie.

MEMPHIS

Do: Start your stay on a high note along Beale Street. The area started as a commercial and entertainment hub for the area's African Americans around the time of the Civil War, and was reborn half a century later as the incubator for the Memphis blues sound, courtesy of Muddy Waters and B. B. King. The **Mason Temple** (✉ *930 Mason St.* ☎ *901/947–9319* ⊕ *www.cogic.org*), home base for the Church of God in Christ denomination, was where Martin

Luther King Jr. gave his "I've been to the mountaintop" speech in 1968, foreshadowing his untimely death. Just one day after his speech, he was assassinated at the Lorraine Motel; today it's one of the buildings that make up the must-see **National Civil Rights Museum** (✉ *450 Mulberry St.* ☎ *901/521–9699* ⊕ *www.civilrightsmuseum.org*).

Eat & Drink: Memphis is a barbecue town. You can't go wrong with the ribs or the chopped-pork sandwich at **Interstate Barbecue** (✉ *2265 S. 3rd St.* ☎ *901/775–2304* ⊕ *www.interstatebarbecue.com*). The shop's barbecue spaghetti may seem out of place, but it's a pasta-and-pork showstopper.

Stay: The **Guesthouse at Graceland** (✉ *3600 Elvis Presley Blvd.* ☎ *800/238–2000* ⊕ *www.guesthousegraceland.com*) is a destination hotel, complete with a music venue, so there's plenty to do and see on-site. But if you're an Elvis fan, the biggest perk is being within steps of the Graceland Mansion where The King lived.

Breakfast: From fancy lemon ricotta pancakes to basic buttermilk, **Staks** (✉ *4615 Poplar Ave.* ☎ *901/509–2367* ⊕ *www.stakspancakes.com*) makes them all. Or you can griddle them yourself, with a "Pour Your Own" option.

Day 3: Memphis, TN, to Jackson, MS

209 miles (3 hours without traffic and stops)

Head south into the Magnolia State from Tennessee, pausing for authentic southern food and to explore the Natchez Trace Parkway and the Ross Barnett Reservoir Overlook.

ALONG THE WAY

Detour: Add about an extra half hour to your travel time today to visit the small town of Sumner, Mississippi, home to the **Emmett Till Interpretive Center** (✉ *158 N. Court St.* ☎ *662/351–3791* ⊕ *www.emmett-till.org*). In 1955, 14-year-old Till was brutally murdered by two white men in the town of Money, 30 miles south of Sumner. The two men were eventually acquitted of his murder, which became a symbol of the horrific treatment of Black people in the American South.

Town: The scenic Natchez Trace Parkway runs through Ridgeland, Mississippi, about 15 minutes north of Jackson. You may catch sight of an alligator at Ross Barnett Reservoir, with views of the 33,000-acre lake at the overlook.

Eat & Drink: The fried catfish at **Cock of the Walk** (✉ *141 Madison Landing Circle* ☎ *601/856–5500* ⊕ *www.cockofthewalkrestaurant.com*) in Ridgeland is lauded by locals and offers a view of Ross Barnett Lake to boot.

JACKSON

Do: Center your visit to Jackson around a tour of the **home of Medgar Evers** (✉ *2332 Margaret W. Alexander Dr.* ☎ *601/345–7211* ⊕ *www.nps.gov/memy*), Mississippi's first NAACP field secretary and a civil rights activist who was assassinated in front of his home in 1963. **Tougaloo College** (✉ *500 W. County Line Rd.* ☎ *601/977–7700* ⊕ *www.tougaloo.edu*), a historically black college and university (HBCU) that served as a stopping place for the Freedom Riders, is also worth a visit. The campus was instrumental as a gathering place for the burgeoning civil rights movement. If you have time, make a visit to the **Mississippi Civil Rights Museum** (✉ *222 North St.* ☎ *601/576–6800* ⊕ *www.mscivilrightsmuseum.com*) to learn more about the Mississippi activists who made the movement possible.

Eat & Drink: Sit down to a hearty dish of angel hair pasta with lump crabmeat or the smoked salmon pizza at **Bravo!** (✉ *4500 I-55 N* ☎ *601/982–8111* ⊕ *www.bravobuzz.com*). The award-winning

Italian restaurant has been around for more than 20 years, likely due to its generous portions and lively but comfortable environment.

Stay: You'll do fine in any one of the city's major hotel chains, but for something different, the historic **Old Capitol Inn** (✉ 226 N. State St. ☎ 601/359–9000 ⊕ www.old-capitolinn.com) is the city's sole boutique hotel, with uniquely decorated rooms and a rooftop bar to unwind in after a day on the road.

Breakfast: The pies may take center stage here, but for a rotating menu of freshly baked scones, muffins, and sausage rolls you can grab and take to go, head over to **Urban Foxes** (✉ 826 North St. ☎ 769/572–5505 ⊕ www.urbanfoxesjxn.com).

Day 4: Jackson, MS, to Montgomery, AL

247 miles (4 hours without traffic and stops)

Pay homage as you travel between these two anchors of the civil rights movement, with the small but mighty Selma along the way.

ALONG THE WAY

Town: Selma is home to the **Edmund Pettus Bridge** (☎ 800/457–3562), where the late Senator John Lewis and others were brutally attacked on "Bloody Sunday" in early March 1965 for pushing to secure the right to vote. The **National Voting Rights Museum and Institute** (✉ 6 U.S. 80 E ☎ 334/526–4340 ⊕ www.nvrmi.com) captures the effort from the start, with photos and stories of the foot soldiers who took part in the marches and exhibits of what a jail cell and voting booth looked like at the time.

Eat & Drink: The wood-cabin environment of **Tally-Ho** (✉ 509 Mangum Ave. ☎ 334/872–1390 ⊕ www.facebook.com/tallyhoselma) in Selma is as much a draw as the steaks. **Lannie's Bar-B-Q Spot** (✉ 2115 Minter Ave. ☎ 334/874–4478) is far from fancy, but the pulled-pork sandwich and fried okra are local favorites. Both restaurants are under 10 minutes from the Edmund Pettus Bridge.

MONTGOMERY

Do: You may have a hard time choosing among the wealth of civil rights movement exhibits here. No matter what, be sure to visit the **Rosa Parks Museum** (✉ 252 Montgomery St. ☎ 334/241–8615 ⊕ www.troy.edu)—situated where the icon was arrested for refusing to sit in the back of a bus—and the **Civil Rights Memorial Center** (✉ 400 Washington Ave. ☎ 334/956–8439 ⊕ www.splcenter.org). Both offer unique and deeply moving perspectives that encourage self-reflection. If you have time, other spots include the **Freedom Riders Museum** (✉ 400 N. Court St. ☎ 334/414–8647 ⊕ www.ahc.alabama.gov), the **Legacy Museum** (✉ 115 Coosa St. ☎ 334/386–9100 ⊕ legacysites.eji.org/about/museum), and the **National Memorial for Peace and Justice** (✉ 417 Caroline St.).

Eat & Drink: Treat yourself to **Vintage Year** (✉ 405 Cloverdale Rd. ☎ 334/819–7215 ⊕ www.vymgm.com), and make sure to order from the thoughtful wine list; the restaurant started as the city's only wine shop. Here you'll find everything from expertly cooked steaks to crab cakes and pasta dishes.

Stay: Trilogy Hotel Montgomery (✉ 116 Coosa St. ☎ 334/440–3550 ⊕ www.trilogyhotelmontgomery.com) is a larger boutique hotel in the city's historic district, within blocks of many important sites, including the Alabama State Capitol building.

Breakfast: Stop by **Cahawba House** (✉ 31 S. Court St. ☎ 334/356–1877 ⊕ www.cahawbahouse.com) for cinnamon beignets and biscuits, served with locally sourced honey and jams. Top your biscuit with Conecuh sausage, an Alabama staple.

Day 5: Montgomery, AL, to Savannah, GA

334 miles (5 hours, 30 minutes without traffic and stops)

Head into Georgia's first city by way of college towns important to the civil rights movement, like Tuskegee, Alabama.

ALONG THE WAY

Town: You won't get too far into today's drive before reaching **Tuskegee University** (✉ *1200 W. Montgomery Rd., Tuskegee* ☎ *334/727–8011* ⊕ *www.tuskegee.edu*), the HBCU that hosted training for the Tuskegee Airmen and can claim Booker T. Washington, George Washington Carver, and the first African American National Book Award winner, Ralph Ellison, among its alumni. Take a few hours to tour the campus—the only one to have a National Historic Site designation—including a museum and grounds dedicated to its graduates.

Roadside Attraction: Get in touch with your inner schoolkid at the **Lunch Box Museum** (✉ *3218 Hamilton Rd.* ☎ *706/653–6240* ⊕ *www.columbuscollectivemuseums.com*) in Columbus, Georgia. If you'd rather stay in the car, the **Museum of Wonder: Drive-Thru** (✉ *970 Rte. 169, Seale* ⊕ *www.museumofwonder.com*) about 15 minutes south of Columbus, offers a 24/7 opportunity to get a glimpse of hundreds of oddities and art, some spooky and some kooky.

Eat & Drink: Hefty sandwiches served in an old train depot make the **Railroad Café** (✉ *117 Lowe St.* ☎ *478/827–5252* ⊕ *www.rrcafe.biz*) in Fort Valley, Georgia, a worthwhile stop. After lunch, get a proper welcome to the Peach State at **Lane Southern Orchards** (✉ *50 Lane Rd.* ☎ *800/277–3224* ⊕ *www.lanesouthernorchards.com*). You can't go wrong with the peach ice cream or a peach cobbler.

SAVANNAH

Do: While Savannah isn't huge on civil rights history, it makes a nice stopping point before Charleston. As one of the United States's first planned cities, you'll find plenty of history here, including its connected squares and famed **Forsyth Park** (✉ *2 W. Gaston St.* ☎ *912/351–3841* ⊕ *www.savannah-ga.gov*). Get the lay of the land with a trolley tour, hopping on and off to explore historic sites such as the **First African Baptist Church** (✉ *23 Montgomery St.* ☎ *912/233–6597* ⊕ *www.firstafrican-bc.com*), the **Owens-Thomas House & Slave Quarters** (✉ *124 Abercorn St.* ☎ *912/790–8800* ⊕ *www.telfair.org*), and the **Cathedral of St. John the Baptist** (✉ *222 E. Harris St.* ☎ *912/233–4709* ⊕ *www.savannah-cathedral.org*), one of the nation's largest Catholic churches in the South. The shops along River Street make for easy souvenir hunting. The area can get lively at night as visitors take advantage of the historic district's open-container laws.

Eat & Drink: For dinner, make reservations at the James Beard Award–winning **Grey** (✉ *109 Martin Luther King Jr. Blvd.* ☎ *912/662–5999* ⊕ *www.thegreyrestaurant.com*). Later, walk to the Perry Hotel for a delicious rooftop cocktail at the **Peregrin** (✉ *256 E. Perry St.* ☎ *912/559–8333* ⊕ *www.peregrinsavannah.com*). For something less sceney but with more of a party vibe, any bar along Bay Street, River Street, or at the city market will do.

Stay: The **Hyatt Regency Savannah** (✉ *2 W. Bay St.* ☎ *912/238–1234* ⊕ *www.hyatt.com*) and the **Westin Savannah Harbor Golf Resort & Spa** (✉ *1 Resort Dr.* ☎ *912/201–2000* ⊕ *www.marriott.com*) offer relaxing views of the Savannah River, and are perfectly situated for walking around downtown and River Street. Gorgeous Airbnb rentals in historic homes abound here, too.

The Eternal Flame at the Martin Luther King Jr. National Historic Site symbolizes the continuing efforts to realize Dr. King's dreams of equality.

Breakfast: Enjoy fresh pastries, a perfect cappuccino, and dreamy macarons at **Café M** (✉ *128 E. Bay St.* ☎ *912/712–3342* ⊕ *www.cafemsavannah.com*), an authentic Parisian bistro.

Day 6: Savannah, GA, to Charleston, SC

107 miles (2 hours without traffic and stops)

These cities may look familiar in landscape, with cobblestone streets and Spanish moss hanging from the trees, but Charleston's got a Lowcountry flavor all its own, distinguished by shrimp and grits, she-crab soup, and Frogmore stew.

ALONG THE WAY

Eat & Drink: Beaufort's **Dockside** (✉ *71 Sea Island Pkwy.* ☎ *843/379–3288* ⊕ *www. docksidebeaufort.com*) overlooks the water and serves just about any kind of seafood you may want. While their version of Frogmore stew is called by its more common name, Lowcountry boil, the key ingredients are all there: big shrimp, smoked sausage, corn on the cob, and potatoes. Paired with their hush puppies, it's a delicious combination.

Detour: The **Gullah Geechee Cultural Heritage Corridor** (⊕ *www.gullahgeecheecorridor.org*) is a 12,000-square-mile stretch that acknowledges the culture, language, and history of the West African descendants who were enslaved across the coastlands of South Carolina, North Carolina, Georgia, and Florida. You'd be remiss not to visit at least one of the history centers or museums dedicated to the centuries-old culture while you're in the area. Hilton Head Island, Johns Island, James Island, or Beaufort are stops that won't take you too far out of your way.

CHARLESTON

Do: You may be tempted to just stroll the city's historic downtown—and by all means do—but be sure to make a trip to the **Charleston City Market** (✉ *188 Meeting St.* ☎ *843/937–0920* ⊕ *www.*

thecharlestoncitymarket.com) for a handwoven basket while you're here. Pay tribute to the nine parishioners who lost their lives as a result of a shocking hate crime in 2015 at **Emanuel African Methodist Episcopal** (✉ 110 Calhoun St. ☎ 843/722–2561 ⊕ www.motheremanuel.com), the oldest AME church in the South.

Eat & Drink: If you can get a dinner reservation at **Husk** (✉ 76 Queen St. ☎ 843/577–2500 ⊕ www.huskrestaurant.com), you'll be wowed with its foodie-worthy elevations of common South Carolina staples—think Carolina rice, catfish, cornbread, and locally sourced vegetables.

Stay: There's an abundance of boutique hotels and historic-building accommodations in Charleston, so you have plenty of options. The most luxurious of the set, like the **French Quarter Inn** (✉ 166 Church St. ☎ 843/812–1900 ⊕ www.fqicharleston.com), can set you back more than $500 a night. If it's more about the sights than it is the stay, you may find that an Airbnb in one of the historic homes is your best bet.

Breakfast: Hit **The Daily** (✉ 652-B King St. ☎ 843/628–7049 ⊕ www.shopthedaily.com) for creative coffee creations, squeezed-on-the-spot juices, and a rotating cast of freshly baked pastries and take-out options.

Day 7: Charleston, SC, to Atlanta, GA

300 miles (5 hours without traffic and stops)

It's not the most scenic route, but as you head north, look for the lush golf greens of Augusta and get ready for the multilane metropolis where speedy driving belies any reputation about the "slow" South.

Essential Listening

Atlanta has become a mainstay in hip-hop culture, so just search for "classic Atlanta hip-hop" on your favorite music streaming service and bounce your way into the metro area with Ludacris, Lil Jon, Gucci Mane, and Outkast.

ALONG THE WAY

Town: Augusta boasts more than just the Masters Tournament. It sits on the banks of the Savannah River, so a stroll along the riverwalk is a low-key way to get a view of the town. Swamp life abounds at the **Phinizy Center** (✉ 1858 Lock and Dam Rd. ☎ 706/828–2109 ⊕ www.phinizycenter.org); kids will get a kick out of river otter and turtle sightings.

Eat & Drink: Abel Brown (✉ 491 Highland Ave. ☎ 706/738–6491 ⊕ www.abelbrownaugusta.com) in Augusta is where to go for oysters. The Johnny cake served with pimento cheese is a slice of savory southern charm.

ATLANTA

Do: The **National Center for Civil and Human Rights** (✉ 100 Ivan Allen Jr. Blvd. ☎ 678/999–8990 ⊕ www.civilandhumanrights.org) is a three-level, 43,000-square-foot, interactive, multi-sensory immersion into both the U.S. civil rights movement and global human rights efforts, complete with handwritten journals and personal items from Martin Luther King Jr. Speaking of King, stop by the Sweet Auburn district for a visit to **MLK's childhood home** (✉ 501 Auburn Ave. NE), the **King National Historic Park** (✉ 450 Auburn Ave. NE ☎ 404/331–5190 ⊕ www.nps.gov/malu), the **Ebenezer Baptist Church** (✉ 101 Jackson St. NE ☎ 404/688–7300 ⊕ www.ebenezeratl.org), and the **King Center** (✉ 449 Auburn

Ave. NE ☎ 404/526–8900 ⊕ www.thek-ingcenter.org), which is where Dr. King and Coretta Scott King are buried.

Eat & Drink: Get a delicious meal and a craft beer or cocktail, then work it all off with a few games at **Ponce City Market** (✉ 675 Ponce De Leon Ave. NE ☎ 404/900–7900 ⊕ www.poncecitymarket.com). The massive food court has something for everyone, whether it's Hop's Chicken, the award-winning H&F Burger, or a handy slice at Pizza Jeans. The rooftop midway is the perfect blend of adult amusement with classics like Skee-Ball and minigolf and a full bar.

Stay: Hotel Clermont (✉ 789 Ponce De Leon Ave. NE ☎ 470/485–0485 ⊕ www.hotelclermont.com) is within walking distance of Ponce City Market, and as a former "motor hotel," it only makes sense to book a night or two to close out your road trip. You'll fancy the mid-century modern decor and boho-chic vibe of the lobby. The French brasserie–style Tiny Lou's is worth a visit for dinner, too, but if you're still full from the PCM food court, make sure to at least get a nightcap on the hotel's rooftop or Lobby Bar.

Breakfast: "Relax, It's Just Eggs," reads one of the signs at **Thumbs Up Diner** (✉ 573 Edgewood Ave. SE ☎ 404/223–0690 ⊕ www.thumbsupdiner.com). And the vibe here is indeed a good kind of laidback. Don't get antsy while you wait for a table: if the bar is available, go for it. The potato-packed skillets, fish and grits, and generous omelets make it all worthwhile.

The Great American Music Road Trip

Written by Katherine Chou

From Motown to hip-hop to grunge, American music is a cultural institution, spanning time periods and genres, reflecting the nation's social concerns,

fashions, and current events. Every region in the country seems to have its own musical influence, but when you focus on what truly makes American music what it is, it all comes down to its southern roots. Namely, every American genre has its foundation in at least one of three roots: blues, jazz, and Appalachian music.

This road trip is a journey through that family tree of American music. You'll explore the three root genres and their origin stories, visiting New Orleans for jazz, the Mississippi Delta for blues, and Appalachia for its eponymous tunes. Then you'll trace some of their descendants, including rockabilly and soul in Memphis and country in Nashville, while also visiting other areas with an important musical legacy, including northern Alabama and eastern Kentucky.

But this trip isn't just about the dusty past. Music arose in these centers because of their culture and creative energy, which continue to inspire musicians today. This itinerary has live music almost nightly, so you'll see not only a glimpse of what American music was but also where it's heading.

At a Glance

Start: New Orleans, LA

End: Nashville, TN

Miles Traveled: 1,882 miles

Suggested Duration: 11 days

States Visited: Alabama, Arkansas, Kentucky, Louisiana, Mississippi, Tennessee, Virginia

Key Sights: Dollywood; Graceland; the Grand Ole Opry; Muscle Shoals Recording Studios; Preservation Hall

Best Time to Go: This trip is doable year-round, but beware that summers are sweltering in New Orleans and Mississippi, and hurricane season in New Orleans

The Great American Music Road Trip

stretches from June to November. Overall, spring balances the pros and cons best.

Day 1: New Orleans, LA

The trip starts with a focus on jazz, in the city often considered its birthplace. New Orleans has a lot to experience, so spend an extra day or two here if you can. Louis Armstrong New Orleans International Airport is located 11 miles west of downtown. Rental cars are available at the airport, but parking around town is a hassle and tickets are common. Rent a car when you're ready to hit the road instead.

At the turn of the 20th century, jazz first gained popularity in the city, with elements adopted from different groups, like layered rhythms, a call-and-response format, and expressive voicing from West African enslaved people; chords, the piano, and brass instruments from Europeans; and the *tresillo* rhythm (used in second-line funeral music) from Cubans. Brass bands were already popular in the late 19th century nationwide, then came ragtime, and a new sound evolved to combine the two, with the addition of improvisation. When Louis Armstrong and Jelly Roll Morton added "swing" notes (which sounds like a note swinging into the next), jazz was born.

By the 1920s, most of the city's jazz players left for Chicago and other cities, so the genre continued to evolve outside of New Orleans. Most notably, Louis Armstrong pioneered the shift from collective improvising to solo improvising. With this new emphasis on individual style, jazz broke off into many subgenres, including swing, bebop, cool jazz, fusion, and jazz rock.

Do: Start at the **New Orleans Jazz Historical Park Visitor Center** (✉ 916 N. Peters St. ☎ 504/589–4841 ⊕ www.nps.gov/jazz), where jazz musicians who double as park rangers give lively demos and performances that shed insight into the city's musical heritage. The Old U.S. Mint location houses the **New Orleans Jazz Museum** (✉ 400 Esplanade Ave. ☎ 504/568–6993 ⊕ www.nolajazzmuseum.org), which features rotating exhibits, plus one permanent display at the end, which is—spoiler alert—Louis Armstrong's first cornet. Be sure to spend some time wandering the French Quarter, stopping at Jackson Square to watch musicians perform on the pedestrian mall and in front of St. Louis Cathedral.

The adjacent Tremé neighborhood, where Louis Armstrong's childhood home and Black Storyville once stood, is the cradle of jazz. **Louis Armstrong Park** (✉ 701 N. Rampart St. ☎ 504/658–3200 ⊕ www.nola.gov) celebrates the city's musical heritage, and its most important landmark is Congo Square, the ancestral birthplace of New Orleans music. Most enslaved people spent their one day off each week here, drumming, dancing, singing, and chanting together, their polyrhythms laying the groundwork for jazz. These days, drummers can be found jamming in the square most Sunday afternoons. Perseverance Hall No. 4 is another landmark within the park; it was a society dance hall where jazz musicians played.

Other must-see musical sights in the city include the **Backstreet Cultural Museum** (✉ 1534 St. Philip St. ☎ 504/657–6700 ⊕ www.backstreetmuseum.org), whose spotlights on the city's African American culture and traditions tie into jazz; **Jelly Roll Morton's home** (✉ 1443 Frenchmen St.) in the Seventh Ward; **Fats Domino's home** (✉ 1208 Caffin Ave.) in the Ninth Ward; and **Music Box Village** (✉ 4557 N. Rampart St. ⊕ www.

musicboxvillage.com) in the Bywater, a playground of sonic exploration where houses and their interiors are the instruments and which embodies New Orleans's experimental spirit today.

Finally, if you see a marching band trailed by dancing revelers, it's a "second line" and you should join. While other groups also paraded to commemorate the dead, African Americans turned these into joyous celebrations, which also influenced jazz. Second lines most commonly occur for weddings now. Sunday afternoons in the French Quarter and Tremé are your best bet for catching one.

Shop: Louisiana Music Factory (✉ 421 Frenchmen St. ☎ 504/586–1094 ⊕ www.louisianamusicfactory.com) stocks rare records from regional artists that only a local shop would have. It's hailed as the best record store in town.

Eat & Drink: For lunch, **Parkway Tavern** (✉ 538 Hagan Ave. ☎ 504/482–3047 ⊕ www.parkwaypoorboys.com) in Mid-City created New Orleans's famed po' boy sandwich and remains a top spot to sample one. For dinner, **Gumbo Shop** (✉ 630 St. Peter St. ☎ 504/525–1486 ⊕ www.gumboshop.com) in the French Quarter serves traditional Creole dishes, including a Best of New Orleans–poll gumbo. Afterward, live music is an absolute must, and **Preservation Hall** (✉ 726 St. Peter St. ⊕ www.preservationhall.com) should be at the top of your list. Opened in 1961 to preserve traditional jazz, it's among the world's top music landmarks. If you can't get a ticket, other spots dedicated to jazz are **Fritzel's Jazz Club** (✉ 733 Bourbon St. ☎ 504/586–4800 ⊕ www.fritzelsjazz.com), the city's oldest club, and the legendary **Tipitina's** (✉ 501 Napoleon Ave. ☎ 504/895–8477 ⊕ www.tipitinas.com).

Stay: The **Soniat House** (✉ 1133 Chartres St. ☎ 504/522–0570 ⊕ www.soniathouse.com) in the French Quarter is a perennial favorite with old-world elegance and antiques throughout. On the other end of the design spectrum, the **Old No. 77 Hotel & Chandlery** (✉ *535 Tchoupitoulas St.* ☎ *504/527–5271* ⊕ *www.old77hotel. com*) in the Central Business District (CBD) has a chic, contemporary look punctuated by industrial accents from the building's warehouse past.

Breakfast: A beignet and chicory café au lait at **Café du Monde** (✉ *800 Decatur St.* ☎ *504/525–4544* ⊕ *www.cafedu-monde.com*) are musts, for breakfast or otherwise. They're open 24 hours, so you have no excuses. If you have more time, indulge in a jazz brunch like one at the ritzy **Commander's Palace** (✉ *1403 Washington Ave.* ☎ *504/899–8221* ⊕ *www.commanderspalace.com*) in the Garden District.

Day 2: New Orleans, LA, to Clarksdale, MS

347 miles (5 hours, 40 minutes without traffic and stops)

It's all about the blues today. After a stint on I–55, you'll reach the Mississippi Delta and U.S. 61, aka the Blues Highway. It's a full day with a nearly five-hour haul to the first major stop, so be prepared.

The Delta blues is like the bass line of American popular music—you don't always notice it, but it's there, laying the foundation. It was born in the cotton fields along U.S. 61, with the music of enslaved people at its core: spirituals (European hymns that enslaved people adapted to reflect their lives) and work songs and field hollers (group and individual vocalizations and songs in a call-and-response pattern, mirroring the rhythms of their labor). Facing similar struggles despite their eventual freedom, the descendants of these enslaved people continued to use music as an emotional outlet, but in modern ways. Now equipped with guitars, they modified the

call and response to a lone singer calling and their guitar responding, its sound distorted by sliding a bottleneck to mimic the human voice. Once the blues left the Delta, it combined with other music to spawn just about every modern genre we know.

ALONG THE WAY

Eat & Drink: Pop in to local favorite **Chuck's Dairy Bar** (✉ *20668 U.S. 61* ☎ *662/873–4021*) in Rolling Fork, Mississippi, for a Chuckburger—starring the dynamic duo of chili and slaw—and a chocolate shake.

Town: Stop in Leland, Mississippi, for the small **Highway 61 Museum** (✉ *307 N. Broad St.* ☎ *662/686–7646* ⊕ *www.highway61blues.com*), which spotlights area stars like Son Thomas. Then visit the nearby **Birthplace of Kermit the Frog Museum** (✉ *415 S. Deer Creek Dr. E* ☎ *662/686–7383* ⊕ *www.birthplaceofthefrog.com*). No, it's not music related, although Kermit does play a mean banjo in "Rainbow Connection." Jim Henson grew up in Leland, and the frogs at nearby Deer Creek allegedly inspired him to create Kermit. An original Kermit puppet lives in the exhibit, banjo in hands.

Town: Indianola's stellar **B. B. King Museum** (✉ *400 2nd St.* ☎ *662/887–9539* ⊕ *www.bbkingmuseum.org*) honors the hometown legend. Check out rare artifacts, play with high-tech exhibits, and meet a bunch of Lucilles (King's guitars).

Attraction: Seven miles east of Cleveland, Mississippi, is **Dockery Farms** (✉ *229 Rte. 8* ☎ *662/719–1048* ⊕ *www.dockeryfarms.com*), which many consider the birthplace of the blues because so many early greats lived and played here, including father of the Delta blues Charley Patton, Son House, Howlin' Wolf, and Robert Johnson.

Town: In the college town of Cleveland, the modern and interactive **GRAMMY Museum Mississippi** (✉ *800 W. Sunflower Rd.* ☎ *662/441–0100* ⊕ *www.grammymuseumms.org*) isn't specifically about the

Essential Listening

This is one road trip where a premade playlist is a necessity. Here are some must-plays.

"West End Blues" by Louis Armstrong

"Sweet Sixteen" by B. B. King

"Cross Road Blues" by Robert Johnson

"Try a Little Tenderness" by Otis Redding

"Hound Dog" and "Suspicious Minds" by Elvis Presley

"Hey Jude" by Wilson Pickett

"Next Girl" by The Black Keys

"Nobody Knows You When You're Down and Out" by Bessie Smith

"I Will Always Love You" and "Jolene" by Dolly Parton

"Can the Circle Be Unbroken" by the Carter Family

"Coal Miner's Daughter" by Loretta Lynn

"Uncle Pen" by Bill Monroe and His Blue Grass Boys

"Highwayman" by The Highwaymen (Johnny Cash, Waylon Jennings, Kris Kristofferson, Willie Nelson)

blues, but it does have a section where Keb' Mo' teaches you to write a song with him, which you can then mix and save.

Photo Op: Juke joints arose as unofficial drinking/gambling/blues dens during the Jim Crow era. **Po' Monkey's Lounge** (✉ 99 Po Monkey Rd.) in Merigold was one of the Delta's last rural ones and unlike any other, thanks to its colorful owner Willie "Po' Monkey" Seaberry. It shut down after Seaberry's death in 2016, but the shack is still standing, at least for now.

CLARKSDALE

Do: You'll arrive late, so visit Clarksdale's sights the next morning. The **Delta Blues Museum** (✉ 1 Blues Alley La. ☎ 662/627–6820 ⊕ www.deltabluesmuseum.org) houses a critical marker on the blues timeline: Muddy Waters's cabin. Two seminal Library of Congress recordings were made here in 1941–42 and, after hearing just how good he sounded, spurred Waters to move to Chicago, changing the trajectory of music forever. **The Blues Crossroads** (✉ 599 N. State St.), marked by three guitars, is the Delta blues photo. Robert Johnson was the most influential bluesman of all time, but

legend has it that he sold his soul to the devil for his mind-blowing guitar skills, right at these very crossroads.

Shop: In Clarksdale, pick up records, art prints, souvenirs, and insider information on everything Clarksdale and the blues at the eclectic **Cat Head Delta Blues & Folk Art** shop (✉ 252 Delta Ave. ☎ 662/624–5992 ⊕ www.cathead.biz).

Eat & Drink: Kill two birds with one stone and chow down at **Ground Zero** (✉ 387 Delta Ave. ☎ 662/621–9009 ⊕ www.groundzerobluesclub.com) while enjoying live blues. Try the fried catfish, a Delta staple, or fried chicken.

Stay: Fancy it's not, but the **Shack Up Inn** (✉ 001 Commissary Circle ☎ 662/624–8329 ⊕ www.shackupinn.com) is the closest you'll get to the Delta blues in your sleep. The converted sharecropper cabins, corrugated tin roof and all, also contain some welcome anachronisms like air-conditioning. In the town center, the **Travelers Hotel** (✉ 212 3rd St. ☎ 662/483–0693 ⊕ www.stayattravelers.com) is a modern option with an artsy vibe.

Breakfast: Head to **Our GrandMa's House of Pancakes** (✉ *115 3rd St.* ☎ *662/592–5290*) for a classic breakfast, delivered with a smile.

Day 3: Clarksdale, MS, to Memphis, TN

101 miles (2 hours without traffic and stops)

It's more blues today, plus a little bit of soul. It's a short and straightforward drive along U.S. 61 with a detour to Arkansas, a stop in Tunica, and then on to Memphis.

ALONG THE WAY

Detour: Sixteen miles south of Clarksdale on U.S. 49 are the Tutwiler Murals. They depict the pivotal moment when composer W. C. Handy first heard the blues, performed by a man who sang about a dog and played guitar with a knife. Confused? So was Handy. But he was intrigued enough to later adapt and compose the first commercially successful blues song ("Memphis Blues"). The murals also pay tribute to Tutwiler's Sonny Boy Williamson and to Delta landscapes.

Town: Take a 30-minute-return trip off U.S. 61 to Helena, Arkansas, to watch the renowned *King Biscuit Time* radio show broadcast at the Delta Cultural Center. They've aired live performances by the top blues artists since 1941, making it the oldest daily show in America. It runs from 12:15 pm to 12:45 pm on weekdays. The **Delta Cultural Center** (✉ *141 Cherry St.* ☎ *870/338–4350* ⊕ *www.deltaculturalcenter.com*) also has a worthwhile interactive exhibit on the region's blues, gospel, and country history.

Eat & Drink: Follow the blues legends of yore and the locals of today into the **Blue & White Restaurant** (✉ *1355 U.S. 61 N* ☎ *662/363–1371* ⊕ *www.*

blueandwhiterestaurant.com) in Tunica to try their Delta fried green tomatoes.

Town: The Gateway to the Blues Museum in Tunica Resorts (✉ *13625 U.S. 61* ⊕ *www.tunicatravel.com*) is housed in a photogenic rustic train depot from 1895. The well-designed museum tells stories about the blues pioneers and also connects their impact to later musicians from different genres, including the British Invasion bands. You can even assess the Delta blues' impact on you by recording your own blues song here.

MEMPHIS

Do: The **Stax Museum of American Soul Music** (✉ *926 E. McLemore Ave.* ☎ *901/261–6338* ⊕ *www.staxmuseum.com*) is easiest to reach by car. After Motown, Stax was the second-biggest soul music studio and was instrumental in the "Memphis sound" of stars like Otis Redding and Booker T & the MGs. Be sure to cut loose on the museum's disco floor and gawk at Isaac Hayes's 1972 Cadillac Eldorado with 24K gold accents and shag-fur carpeting. Downtown, the **National Civil Rights Museum** (✉ *450 Mulberry St.* ☎ *901/521–9699* ⊕ *www.civilrightsmuseum.org*) is located at the Lorraine Motel, where Martin Luther King Jr. was assassinated. While it's a must-see for obvious reasons, it also traces the African American struggle for equality, giving context to the evolution of not just soul music, which was connected to the civil rights movement, but also the blues, gospel, and all other music rooted in the African American experience.

Shop: On Beale Street, the **A. Schwab general store** (✉ *163 Beale St.* ☎ *901/523–9782* ⊕ *www.a-schwab.com*) is the last original Beale Street business standing (ca. 1876). An old-school soda fountain upstairs adds to the nostalgia, and a museum shows the area's history. Downstairs is packed with souvenirs and odd novelty items.

B.B. King, Ike Turner, and Elvis Presley all recorded songs at Sun Studio in Memphis.

Eat & Drink: Barbecue in Memphis is a serious business. Local opinions can be divided, but two excellent choices are Charlie Vergos's **Rendezvous** (✉ 52 S. 2nd St. ☎ 901/523–2746 ⊕ www.hogsfly. com) for dry-rubbed ribs and **Central BBQ** (✉ 147 E. Butler Ave. ☎ 901/672–7760 ⊕ www.eatcbq.com) for pulled pork. Barbecue nachos at the latter are also popular. For live music, head to Beale Street, the home of the blues. After the Civil War, the street became a southern hub for Black entertainment, attracting musicians from all over. B. B. King led the Memphis blues sound, so it's fitting that his eponymous club, **BB King's Blues Club** (✉ 143 Beale St. ☎ 901/524–5464 ⊕ www.bbkings. com) remains a top destination for live music here.

Stay: The boutique **Hu. Hotel** (✉ 79 Madison Ave. ☎ 901/333–1200 ⊕ www.huhotelmemphis.com) has a sleek mid-century modern look and a trendy vibe (that period in their name is not a typo). The rooftop bar is also perfect for watching sunsets and the Mighty Lights show on the Hernando De Soto Bridge. For upscale history, the **Peabody Hotel** (✉ 149 Union Ave. ☎ 01/529–4000 ⊕ www. peabodymemphis.com) has welcomed the fanciest of folks since 1869, and also the fanciest of ducks since the 1930s. The daily Peabody Duck March is worth a look. They waddle out to spend the day splashing in the lobby fountain before retreating for the evening to their $200,000 penthouse.

Breakfast: Sunrise Memphis (✉ 670 Jefferson Ave. ☎ 901/552–3168 ⊕ www. sunrise901.com) loves biscuit sandwiches and they load them up with creative southern goodness. The setting is equally fun, as are the beermosas (Miller Genuine Draft and orange juice).

Day 4: Memphis, TN

Memphis deserves a full day of your time, and today you'll explore its rockabilly and soul history. If you'd rather not drive today, a free shuttle (with entrance ticket) takes you between Sun Studio, Graceland, and the Rock 'n' Soul Museum.

For much of the 20th century, Memphis was a hotbed of musical innovation. Artists came from across the region, including B. B. King, Howlin' Wolf, Jerry Lee Lewis, Johnny Cash, Elvis Presley, Otis Redding, and Al Green. Their various musical styles mixed with Memphis's urban flavor in a massive melting pot and recombined into dynamic new genres.

Elvis Presley, who frequented Beale Street and Black gospel churches growing up, ignited a cultural revolution with his blend of blues and country that defined rockabilly. It was characterized by a driving beat, expressive vocals, guitar-break solos, and Sam Phillips's echo effect at Sun Studio. While it fizzled out by the end of the 1950s, it led directly to rock and roll, then punk, heavy metal, New Wave, and emo. Delta blues also transformed in Memphis, going electric with an upbeat tempo, jazz elements, and a band (sometimes with horns). B. B. King led the way with his expressive vibrato and note bending, which paved the way for rock's lead guitarists. Soul grew as a secular form of gospel, equally wrought with emotion that voiced the African American experience, but mixed with rhythm and blues (which, to oversimplify, combined blues and swing jazz). In Memphis, soul, led by Al Green, took on a purer, more gospel-leaning sound, often backed by radiant horns. By the 1970s, soul gave way to funk, disco, rap, hip-hop, neo soul, and contemporary R&B.

Do: Start at **Sun Studio** (✉ *706 Union Ave.* ☎ *901/521–0664* ⊕ *www.sunstudio. com*), the birthplace of rock and roll. Outtakes from sessions and behind-the-scenes stories about the legends who got their big breaks here (including B. B.

King, Ike Turner, and the "Million Dollar Quartet" rockabilly artists) keep the tour captivating. Plus you can stand on the X where a 19-year-old Elvis recorded his debut single, "That's All Right." Follow the King's footsteps to **Graceland** (✉ *Elvis Presley Blvd.* ☎ *901/332–3322* ⊕ *www. graceland.com*) next. This sprawling shrine to Elvis takes on average three to four hours to visit. Even if you're not an Elvis fan, don't be surprised if you become one by the end; in addition to the eye-popping design of the rooms, a wealth of personal artifacts and exhibits offer glimpses into the human side of the icon. Back on Beale Street, the Smithsonian's **Memphis Rock 'n' Soul Museum** (✉ *191 Beale St.* ☎ *901/205– 2533* ⊕ *www.memphisrocknsoul.org*) tracks the stories of these two influential genres. Well-stocked jukeboxes highlight each decade and tell the stories in song.

Eat & Drink: For lunch, **Coletta's Pizzeria** (✉ *1063 South Pkwy. E* ☎ *901/948– 7652* ⊕ *www.colettas.net*) is out by Stax; don't miss their barbecue pizza. For dinner, **Bar-B-Q-Shop** (✉ *1782 Madison Ave.* ☎ *901/272–1277* ⊕ *www.thebar- b-qshop.com*) near Overton Square has barbecue spaghetti, along with the usual barbecue favorites done their way. For live music with fewer tourists than Beale Street, **Wild Bill's** (✉ *1580 Vollintine Ave.* ☎ *901/409–0081* ⊕ *www.wildbills- memphis.com*) is a venerable juke joint in Midtown.

Breakfast: As the oldest diner in Memphis, the **Arcade** (✉ *540 S. Main St.* ☎ *901/526–5757* ⊕ *www.arcaderes- taurant.com*) is worth a visit whether you pick the Elvis booth or not. If you do sit there, you almost have to order the peanut butter and banana sandwich; if you resist, the sweet potato pancakes are a near-delicacy.

Day 5: Memphis, TN, to The Shoals, AL

203 miles (3 hours, 30 minutes without traffic and stops)

Today's drive gives you some more Elvis history, then takes you to northern Alabama, where two small studios in the middle of nowhere pumped out a distinct, genre-spanning sound. Take I–69 from Memphis via I–69 to I–269 north and I–22 east to Tupelo. From there, U.S. 45 connects you to the scenic Natchez Trace Parkway, which is a peaceful, forested drive through lands rich in Native American and American history.

FAME Studios in tiny Muscle Shoals pioneered the signature Muscle Shoals sound that defined southern soul in the 1960s. Often described as swampy, it's a mix of country, gospel, and rhythm and blues generated by the studio's session musicians. Artists like Aretha Franklin, Wilson Pickett, and Etta James recorded here initially, but as those records charted, artists across all genres came (and continue to come) seeking that special sauce. In 1969, FAME's rhythm-section session musicians broke off and opened Muscle Shoals Sound Studio in Sheffield, still with that calling-card sound. They, too, were successful, drawing the likes of the Rolling Stones ("Brown Sugar" and "Wild Horses" were recorded here), Bob Dylan, Willie Nelson, and many more.

ALONG THE WAY

Town: At the **Elvis Presley Birthplace** (✉ *306 Elvis Presley Dr.* ☎ *662/841–1245* ⊕ *www.elvispresleybirthplace. com*) in Tupelo, Mississippi, see a slice of Elvis's life long before the sideburns, gold lamé suits, and jungle room. You can peek inside the humble shotgun house where he entered the world. **Tupelo Hardware Co.** (✉ *114 Main St.* ☎ *662/842–4637* ⊕ *www.tupelohardware.com*) is where Elvis bought his first guitar and the spot he stood to make the purchase is marked.

Eat & Drink: Johnnie's Drive-In (✉ *908 E. Main St.* ☎ *662/842–6748*) is Tupelo's oldest restaurant (1945) and a local favorite (of a teenaged Elvis, too). Get a dough burger, also known as a slug burger elsewhere in northern Mississippi. Johnnie's version has a combo of dough and secret ingredients mixed into the meat.

Nature: If you're missing nature, the Natchez Trace Parkway is studded with opportunities for a walk. In **Tishomingo State Park** (☎ *662/438–6914* ⊕ *www. mdwfp.com*), the 1.8-mile Bear Creek Nature Trail has views over the valley and includes a suspension-bridge crossing and scenic rock formations.

Roadside Attraction: Visiting the **Coon Dog Cemetery** (✉ *4945 Coondog Cemetery Rd.* ☎ *256/383–0783* ⊕ *www.coondog-cemetery.com*) requires a rerouting, but when else will you visit one? Never, because this is the only one. Beloved raccoon-hunting dogs rest here permanently, their spots marked by often hand-chiseled headstones. Turn off Natchez Trace Parkway at Maud Road to get here.

THE SHOALS

Do: Both **FAME Studios** (✉ *603 E. Avalon Ave.* ☎ *256/381–0801* ⊕ *famestudios. com*) and **Muscle Shoals Sound Studio** (✉ *3614 N. Jackson Hwy.* ☎ *256/978–5151* ⊕ *www.muscleshoalssoundstudio. org*) can be toured. The original Muscle Shoals Sound Studio has even been restored to its 1970s state. Other spots include the **Alabama Music Hall of Fame** (✉ *617 U.S. 72 W* ☎ *256/381–4417* ⊕ *www.alamhof.org*) and the **W. C. Handy Museum and Library** (✉ *620 W. College St.* ☎ *256/275–3128* ⊕ *www.wchandymuseum.org*), which dives into this Father of the Blues' successful career as a bandleader, composer, businessman, and groundbreaker.

Elvis Presley lived at Graceland from 1957 until his death in 1977.

Eat & Drink: The nearby town of Florence has a creative—some might say hipster—vibe. For upscale, farm-to-table southern dishes with international flair, try **Odette's** (✉ *120 N. Court St.* ☎ *256/349–5219* ⊕ *www.odettealabama.com*). For dessert, stop by old-school **Trowbridge's** (✉ *316 N. Court St.* ☎ *256/764–1503*) for their legendary orange-pineapple ice cream. For live music, just outside town, there's the novelty of **Tuscumbia's Rattlesnake Saloon** (✉ *1292 Mt. Mills Rd.* ☎ *256/370–7220* ⊕ *www.rattlesnakesaloon.net*), inside a large cave, which was also a former hog pen.

Stay: The industrial chic **GunRunner Boutique Hotel** (✉ *310 E. Tennessee St.* ☎ *855/269–4724* ⊕ *www.gunrunnerhotel.com*) in Florence features 10 luxury suites draped in local pride. Themed rooms include Muscle Shoals Sound, Sam Phillips, and Single Lock.

Breakfast: Staggs Grocery (✉ *1424 Huntsville Rd.* ☎ *256/764–7382*) is all about the basics—eggs, grits, sausage, bacon, biscuits, etc.—and they do it well. But if you're here on a Friday morning, snag the biscuit with chocolate gravy because it only appears then.

Day 6: The Shoals, AL, to Pigeon Forge, TN

338 miles (6 hours without traffic and stops)

Enjoy a mix of southern gospel, rock, and blues today. It's a long drive and you'll lose an hour with the time-zone change. Take U.S. 43 north to Lawrenceburg, then U.S. 64 and I–24 east to Chattanooga. I–75 north, I–40 east, and Route 66 south take you to Pigeon Forge.

Although they developed concurrently and influenced each other, the so-called southern gospel of white southerners was different from the gospel of Black southerners. Black gospel had far-reaching influences on popular music, from soul to rock, and was characterized by choirs and the shared experience, with emotive singing, improvisation, and a call-and-response format. White gospel also played a role in later genres, especially country, but it focused on the individual's search for salvation and featured male quartets singing in harmony. Some artists, like Elvis, were deeply influenced by both styles.

ALONG THE WAY

Town: The **James D. Vaughan Gospel Music Museum** (✉ 31 Public Sq. ☎ 931/762–8991) in Lawrenceburg, Tennessee, explores a father of southern gospel's contributions to the genre, which included popularizing it by sponsoring the first professional quartets and founding a record company. The small museum is inside the Chamber of Commerce. Ask at the second-floor office during business hours to gain entry.

Town: In Chattanooga, Tennessee, channel your inner rocker at the **Songbirds Experience** (✉ 206 W. Main St. ☎ 423/531–2473 ⊕ www.songbirds-foundation.org) to explore everything electric guitar. Hands-on exhibits invite you to, among other things, build a guitar, experiment with amps, and learn to play. Then head to the **Bessie Smith Cultural Center and Chattanooga African American Museum** (✉ 200 E. Martin Luther King Blvd. ☎ 423/266–8658 ⊕ www.bessie-smithcc.org) for a small exhibit on Bessie Smith. The Chattanooga native, often considered the greatest blues singer of all time, was a pioneer among the female blues singers who were all the rage in the 1920s.

Eat & Drink: Chattanooga's culinary scene focuses on the creative, fresh, and natural. The local favorite for gourmet burgers (also with veggie options) is **Urban Stack** (✉ 12 W. 13th St. ☎ 423/475–5350 ⊕ www.urbanstack.com). Try the fried green tomato burger.

Photo Op: Now's your chance to snag a photo with Dolly Parton, and she won't blink. Sevierville's beloved daughter is immortalized in a statue in front of the **Sevier County Courthouse** (✉ 125 Court Ave.).

PIGEON FORGE

Do: This Great Smoky Mountains town is famous for one thing: **Dollywood** (✉ 2700 Dollywood Parks Blvd. ☎ 800/365–5996 ⊕ www.dollywood.com), Dolly Parton's amusement park. Not only is Dollywood a shrine to one of country's (and the country's) greatest music icons, but it's also an homage to the Great Smoky Mountains of her childhood. While there are museums that showcase Dolly's personal items, her tour bus, and a replica of the cabin she grew up in, there are also opportunities to watch craftspeople forge iron, blow glass, and more, keeping the area's heritage alive. Since this is Dolly's park, there's plenty of live music, too, including Appalachian, southern gospel, pop, oldies, and even a musical that chronicles Dolly's life, with some of her family members performing. And don't miss the roller coasters either; the Lightning Rod launches you up the hill at 45 mph, before dropping you at a 73-degree angle at 73 mph. Depending on what time you arrive in Pigeon Forge, it might be best to save Dollywood for the next morning and afternoon.

Eat & Drink: Just so there are no surprises, Pigeon Forge is like kitsch on steroids. Most restaurants are chains or fast food, but if you roll into town on an empty stomach, **Local Goat** (✉ 2167 Parkway ☎ 865/366–3035 ⊕ www.localgoatpf.com) is a locally sourced, made-from-scratch New American restaurant with just enough oddball gourmet burgers to keep things interesting. They also have local craft beers on tap and craft cocktails.

Stay: Dollywood's own **DreamMore Resort** (✉ 2525 DreamMore Way ☎ 800/365–5996 ⊕ www.dollywood.com) is a comfortable and clean option. But the perks are the best part: free shuttle to the park or free parking, complimentary TimeSaver pass that lets you jump the line for most rides and get reserved seating at shows, discounted park tickets, and VIP treatment with a special entrance to the park.

Breakfast: Stick to the kitsch by visiting **Frizzle Chicken Farmhouse Café** (✉ *2785 Parkway* ☎ *865/774–7707* ⊕ *www.frizzlechickenfarmhousecafe.com*). The breakfast is southern-style and the place is filled with 100 animatronic singing chickens.

Day 7: Pigeon Forge, TN, to Floyd, VA

233 miles (3 hours, 40 minutes without traffic and stops)

It's all about Appalachian music on this leg of the drive. If it's a Friday (which is when Floyd's Friday Night Jamboree takes place), head straight for Floyd to maximize time. Festivities start at 6:30 pm. From Pigeon Forge, head out to I–40 east, then I–81 north and Route 8 south to get to Floyd.

Along with blues and jazz, the third root genre of American music is Appalachian music (also called old-time or mountain music), which is characterized by acoustic string instruments and vocal harmonies. It was a product of various immigrant musical traditions brewing together in the isolated mountains. The most prominent components came from Irish, English, and Scottish settlers, who brought storytelling ballads about everyday struggles, hymns, jig and reel dancing, and the fiddle. Carrying on traditions from their enslaved ancestors, African Americans contributed a call-and-response structure and a precursor to the banjo, a Muslim African instrument that enslaved people re-created with hollowed-out gourds. The distinctive combination of fiddle and banjo was the driving force of this new music, as was a strong element of community.

ALONG THE WAY

Eat & Drink: If you spend the first half of the day at Dollywood, be sure to eat there before hitting the road. Dollywood's food has won awards in the amusement park world, like best pork barbecue at **Hickory House BBQ** (✉ *Craftsman's Valley* ⊕ *www.dollywood.com*). Whatever you do, don't skip the park's legendary cinnamon bread, whose flour comes from Dollywood's own gristmill. Another treat is the banana pudding, made from Dolly's personal recipe.

Town: Stop at the **Blue Ridge Music Center** (✉ *700 Foothills Rd.* ☎ *276/236–5309* ⊕ *www.blueridgemusiccenter.org*) in Galax, Virginia, to explore the evolution of Appalachian music. Fun, interactive exhibits let you mix mountain music and write lyrics.

FLOYD

Do: Floyd is a delightful small town where music, art, and farming live happily ever after. Join the community at the Friday Night Jamboree for the age-old Appalachian tradition of gathering for music and dance. **Floyd Country Store** (✉ *206 S. Locust St.* ☎ *540/745–4563* ⊕ *www.floydcountrystore.com*) has hosted this version since the 1980s. The lineup is southern gospel for the first hour, followed up with two rollicking sets by traditional string bands. The music isn't just on the stage, though—performances spill onto the streets. If you can't work a Friday evening in Floyd into your itinerary, the Floyd Country Store also hosts Americana Afternoons on Saturday at noon, which is acoustic roots music ranging from blues to jazz to bluegrass. Then the Sunday Music Jam runs practically all afternoon, with old-time music at 1:30 pm and bluegrass at 4 pm.

Eat & Drink: If you're attending the jamboree, grab a quick bite at the Floyd Country Store. They serve American classics, both old and new, and source from local farms as much as possible. For live music on non-jamboree days, both **Dogtown Roadhouse** (⌧ *302 S. Locust St.* ☎ *540/745–6836* ⊕ *www. dogtownroadhouse.com*) and **Buffalo Mountain Brewery** (⌧ *332 Webbs Mill Rd. N* ☎ *540/745–2491* ⊕ *www.buffalomountainbrewery.com*) host performances on weekend nights.

Stay: In the town center, **Floyd Hotel** (⌧ *300 Rick Lewis Way* ☎ *540/745–6080* ⊕ *www.hotelfloyd.com*) is eco-friendly and artsy with small-town charm. For something different, **Floyd Yurt Lodging** (⌧ *379 Parkway La. S* ☎ *540/505–4586* ⊕ *www.floydyurtlodging.com*) has one 30-foot yurt, complete with an indoor bathroom and a skylight view of the stars.

Breakfast: Many of the town's lodgings include breakfast, but if not, the **Pharmhouse Pharmacy & Café** (⌧ *311 E. Main St.* ☎ *540/745–3333* ⊕ *www.thepharmhouserx.com*) serves the regulars, along with breakfast tacos in creative combinations.

Day 8: Floyd, VA, to Bristol, TN

164 miles (3 hours without traffic and stops)

From Floyd, take U.S. 221 south to Galax, Virginia. Then connect to I–77 north and I–81 south to get to Bristol, which is in both Tennessee and Virginia.

Country music emerged in 1927 at the Bristol recording sessions, dubbed the Big Bang of Country Music. With compelling artists and new audio technology producing better sound, records and radio beamed this new music far beyond the local communities. The biggest stars to emerge from the sessions were the Carter Family and Jimmie Rodgers, respectively known as the First Family

and Father of Country Music. The Carter Family's music was rooted in traditional Appalachian ballads, but it was also progressive, particularly Maybelle Carter's guitar style. Known as the Carter scratch, Maybelle simultaneously played bass, rhythm, and melody, which was revolutionary at the time and continues to be emulated today. Mississippi-born Rodgers was also an innovator. His music incorporated different styles that he was exposed to as a traveling railroad worker, including blues and Swiss yodeling.

ALONG THE WAY

Eat & Drink: In downtown Galax, **Dairy Bar** (⌧ *609 S. Main St.* ☎ *276/236–9833*) is a good ole country burger-and-ice-cream joint with tasty food, great prices, and outdoor deck seating.

Detour: If it's a Saturday, the **Carter Family Fold** (⌧ *3449 A. P. Carter Hwy.* ☎ *276/594–0676* ⊕ *www.carterfamilyfold.org*) in Hiltons, Virginia, hosts a weekly evening concert and dance party (Appalachian-style, of course, with flatfooting and clogging). On-site and open for viewing before the concert are A. P. Carter's original general store, which houses a museum about the family, and the cabin that A. P. was born in, which was relocated here.

BRISTOL

Do: Visit the well-designed, Smithsonian-affiliated **Birthplace of Country Music Museum** (⌧ *101 Country Music Way* ☎ *423/573–1927* ⊕ *www.birthplaceofcountrymusic.org*) to learn about the Bristol sessions and their continued impact. Among the engaging exhibits, many of which are interactive, are curious facts about early audio technology, an audio appearance by Nirvana, and opportunities to sing along and dance. A good photo op is the Bristol Sessions murals, depicting many of the sessions' artists. It's on the Tennessee side of State Street (which is also the Virginia–Tennessee border).

Eat & Drink: Southern Craft BBQ in the **Sessions Hotel complex** (✉ *833 State St.* ☎ *276/285–5040* ⊕ *www.sessionshotel.com*) does gourmet takes on southern favorites, plus tacos with a barbecue treatment. There isn't much live music in town on a regular basis, but **LUMAC** (✉ *115 Country Music Way* ☎ *276/696–3535* ⊕ *www.bristolhotelva.com*) hosts live music every Tuesday at its rooftop bar and restaurant. For straight-up drinking, Bristol has several craft breweries, including **MWB Bristol Two Time Brewery and Taproom** (✉ *285 Moore St.* ☎ *276/821–3020* ⊕ *www.mwb-bristol.com*).

Stay: The Sessions Hotel, set in a complex of revitalized factories, features creative, industrial chic rooms that nod to the city's musical heritage. If the hard miles on the road have gotten to you, they also have an on-site spa and a relaxing rooftop bar.

Breakfast: Blackbird Bakery (✉ *188 Piedmont Ave.* ☎ *276/645–5754* ⊕ *www.blackbirdbakerybristol.com*) is a local favorite for their array of made-from-scratch doughnuts, pastries (including jalapeño-bacon kolaches), pies, baklava, brownies, bread, and more.

Day 9: Bristol, TN, to Lexington, KY

271 miles (5 hours, 10 minutes without traffic and stops)

Today the focus is on country and bluegrass. From I–81 north, head to U.S. 23 north, the Country Music Highway. This National Scenic Byway snakes through the green mountains of eastern Kentucky, a region that has produced more country hitmakers per capita than any other. Homegrown stars include, from south to north, Patty Loveless, Loretta Lynn, Chris Stapleton, Billy Ray Cyrus, and the Judds. Keep an eye out for road signs announcing whose hometown is coming up. This itinerary leaves U.S. 23 after Staffordsville (Chris Stapleton), so if you're looking for signs of Billy Ray or the Judds, detour to go farther north. After U.S. 23, head west for Lexington.

Bluegrass descended from Appalachian music, but with elements of blues and especially jazz mixed in. The whole genre boils down to one man: Bill Monroe, from western Kentucky. He started out playing mandolin in traditional string bands, but as his career progressed, he experimented with different sounds and musicians until he found a combination that became (and remains) the standard for bluegrass. The name for this new genre was even taken from his band, which was called the Blue Grass Boys. The instruments were upright bass, guitar, mandolin, banjo, and fiddle. The key components—and main differences from Appalachian music—were a lightning-fast tempo, a distinctive three-pick banjo style innovated by Earl Scruggs (now known as the Scruggs style), improvisation and soloing (jazz influences), and the characteristic "high, lonesome sound."

ALONG THE WAY

Eat & Drink: Some eastern Kentucky staples to look out for as you travel U.S. 23 are soup beans (pork-stewed pinto beans) with cornbread, salmon patties, and country ham. **Music Highway Grill** (✉ *419 Jenny Wiley Dr.* ☎ *606/889–1790* ⊕ *www.parks.ky.gov*) at Jenny Wiley State Resort Park in Prestonsburg has all three, plus other Kentucky favorites.

Town: In Paintsville, the **U.S. 23 Country Music Highway Museum** (✉ *100 Stave Branch Rd.* ☎ *606/297–7823* ⊕ *www.paintsvilletourism.com*) showcases the stars that hail from this region, with a memorabilia-filled display for each. It's small, but a nice homage to local heroes.

Nature: Stretch your legs with a short walk to 65-foot-high and 78-foot-long

Natural Bridge (✉ 2135 Natural Bridge Rd., Slade ☎ 606/663–2214 ⊕ www.parks. ky.gov). The shortest trail is 0.75 miles and you can walk to the top of bridge (be careful up there).

LEXINGTON

Do: Although Lexington isn't specifically a bluegrass hub, there's live bluegrass nearly every night somewhere in town, either formally or in a jam. Among these are two radio broadcasts you can attend. *Woodsongs Old-Time Radio Hour* broadcasts around the world from the historic **Lyric Theater** (✉ 300 E. 3rd St. ☎ 859/280–2201 ⊕ www.lexingtonlyric.com) on Monday nights while Red Barn Radio spotlights artists inspired by Appalachian Americana music; they broadcast on Wednesday night from **ArtsPlace** (✉ 161 N. Mill St. ☎ 859/255–2951 ⊕ www.lex-arts.org). Both shows include live music and chats with the artists.

Eat & Drink: Blue Door Smokehouse (✉ 819 National Ave. ☎ 859/252–4227 ⊕ www. bluedoorsmokehouse.com) has such good barbecued brisket and other meaty favorites that they often sell out, so go early. Just note they're only open in the (early) evening on weekends; otherwise they close in the midafternoon.

Stay: Staying at the sleek **21c Museum Hotel** (✉ 167 W. Main St. ☎ 859/899–6800 ⊕ www.21cmuseumhotels.com/lexington) is like spending the night at the MoMA, but legal. With four contemporary art galleries and art in every room and in the public spaces, there's always something that'll catch your eye.

Breakfast: Organic and locally sourced when possible, **Doodles** (✉ 262 N. Limestone ☎ 859/317–8507 ⊕ www. doodleslex.com) is both fresh and creative. Try the "pigs and puffs" or the dirty shrimp and grits. The Kentucky hot brown quesadilla gets an honorable mention for its morning twist on a Louisville creation.

Day 10: Lexington, KY, to Nashville, TN

225 miles (3 hours, 45 minutes without traffic and stops)

On today's drive, you'll go from bluegrass back to country. The route is straightforward with the Bluegrass Parkway taking you to Bardstown, then I–65 runs south all the way to Nashville, with a short detour in the suburbs of Hendersonville.

ALONG THE WAY

Town: With a downtown that looks like the classic American main street, Bardstown, Kentucky, has been hailed the Most Beautiful Small Town in America. If you're looking for a break, it's a nice place for a stroll.

Eat & Drink: Mammy's Kitchen (✉ 116 W. Stephen Foster Ave. ☎ 502/350–1097 ⊕ www.facebook.com/btownmammys) in Bardstown has a devoted local following, a space with personality, and home-cooked country food. You're in bourbon country, so try the bourbon Cinnabon flapjacks or the bourbon burger.

Detour: Bourbon tends to pop up in country songs a lot and you have to visit at least one distillery while in Bourbon Country. **Maker's Mark** (✉ 3350 Burks Spring Rd. ☎ 270/865–2099 ⊕ www. makersmark.com) in Loretto has an old-timey setting with preserved mid-19th-century distilling techniques. This detour adds less than 30 minutes to the day's drive.

Town: Around 20 miles outside Nashville, Hendersonville will always be home to Johnny and June Carter Cash. You can pay your respects to country's royal couple at **Hendersonville Memory Gardens** (✉ 353 Johnny Cash Pkwy. ☎ 615/824–3855), where they're buried.

NASHVILLE

Do: If you're not planning to attend a show at the **Grand Ole Opry** (✉ *600 Opry Mills Dr.* ☎ *800/733–6779* ⊕ *www.opry. com*), stop in for the daytime backstage tour on your way into town. Sometimes they'll let you stand in the performers' spot onstage—in the famed wooden circle that was cut from the Ryman Auditorium stage. Downtown, the **Johnny Cash Museum** (✉ *119 3rd Ave. S* ☎ *615/256–1777* ⊕ *www.johnny-cashmuseum.com*) houses an extensive collection of both public and private artifact offering different perspectives on his life. Upstairs, but under a separate ticket, is the **Patsy Cline Museum** (✉ *119 3rd Ave. S* ☎ *615/454–4722* ⊕ *www. patsymuseum.com*). Vignettes of her life are presented, along with artifacts. It's a relatively small exhibit, but provides a good look into her life.

Eat & Drink: Near downtown, family-owned **Peg Leg Porker's** (✉ *903 Gleaves St.* ☎ *615/829–6023* ⊕ *www.pegleg-porker.com*) hickory-smoked dry-rubbed ribs are a favorite, as are the pulled-pork platter and fried pie. A night out at Lower Broadway's honky-tonks is a must, preferably with boots on, which you can actually buy at one of the honky-tonks. Stop in at **Tootsie's Orchid Lounge** (✉ *422 Broadway* ⊕ *www.tootsies.net*) to soak up some history. It's across the alley from Ryman, so Opry stars used to sneak out the back after their set to wind down (or up?) at Tootsie's. **Robert's Western World** (✉ *416-B Broadway* ☎ *615/244–9552* ⊕ *www.robertswesternworld.com*) is the aforementioned boot seller, and also the honky-tonk that locals tend to recommend most. **Nudie's Honky Tonk** (✉ *409 Broadway* ⊕ *www.nudieshonky-tonk.com*) is another gem—Nudie was the rhinestone-tailor extraordinaire to music's biggest stars. His bold creations line the walls, including Elvis's famous gold lamé suit. Finally, for hardcore line dancing with plenty of space to free-style, **Wildhorse Saloon** (✉ *120 2nd Ave.*

N ☎ *615/902–8200* ⊕ *www.wildhorsesa-loon.com*) awaits.

Stay: For a historical experience, sleep in the former Nashville train station, which is now the **Union Station Hotel** (✉ *1001 Broadway* ☎ *615/726–1001* ⊕ *www. unionstationhotelnashville.com*). The 120-year-old building exudes old-world glamour with a 65-foot barrel-vaulted lobby ceiling, stained glass windows, and crystal chandeliers, but the recently renovated rooms have a sophisticated mid-century modern style.

Breakfast: Start your day at **Biscuit Love** (✉ *316 11th Ave. S* ☎ *615/490–9584* ⊕ *www.biscuitlove.com*) in the Gulch with a simple bonut (a biscuit doughnut dressed up with much more) or go all in with a decadent biscuit pairing that runs the gamut from hot chicken to bananas Foster.

Day 11: Nashville, TN

Your final day is all about country. Nashville International Airport is 8 miles east of downtown. Around town, parking can be expensive or difficult to find. Unless you're leaving right away, consider returning the car when you arrive and taking the shuttle bus or taxi to the airport.

After the Bristol Sessions, radio broadcasts like the Grand Ole Opry spread the new country music, catalyzing transformations, especially out west, where the "western" of "country and western" began to develop. These western forms were particularly influenced by Jimmie Rodgers, with his bluesy sound and yodeling. Gene Autry introduced the singing cowboy genre while Texan Bob Wills fronted the dance-hall western swing genre. But the most significant development spun off western swing after World War II, led by Ernest Tubb. It featured just a core rhythm section with a steel guitar and fiddle out front, a slower beat, twangy vocals, and glum, personal lyrics about heartbreak, adultery, and drinking. This new genre was honky-tonk, with Hank Williams at the forefront, becoming the foundation of all country music.

Honky-tonk became so popular that rockabilly combined it with the blues to dominate American culture. Nashville countered rockabilly's rise and honky-tonk's demise with the antithesis of honky-tonk—a pop- and jazz-infused sound with smooth vocals, backup singers, and a string orchestra without a single fiddle or steel guitar. Patsy Cline was a flagbearer of this Nashville sound. By the late 1960s and 1970s, traditionalists rebelled against this mainstream style, with Merle Haggard leading the Bakersfield sound, a western swing–rock hybrid, and Willie Nelson and Waylon Jennings leading outlaw country, which revived honky-tonk and merged it with blues, rockabilly, and rock. Since then, country has continued to swing back and forth between old-school honky-tonk and crossover pop.

Do: Start at the **Country Music Hall of Fame and Museum** (⊠ *222 Rep. John Lewis Way S* ☎ *615/416–2001* ⊕ *www. countrymusichalloffame.org*) for a primer on the genre's legacy. Rotating exhibits elevate this museum far beyond just a (fascinating) directory of country stars, so budget at least a couple of hours. Also, get your ticket to the perennial favorite **RCA Studio B** (⊠ *1611 Roy Acuff Pl.* ☎ *615/416–2001* ⊕ *www.studiob.org*) tour here, and book early. Inside RCA Studio B, you'll magically turn up in the 1950s, when the studio was cranking out the slick Nashville sound. Inside-scoop stories about icons who recorded there, including Elvis and Dolly Parton, bring the studio to life.

Back downtown, **Ryman Auditorium** (⊠ *116 5th Ave. N* ☎ *800/733–6779* ⊕ *www. ryman.com*) was built as a bona fide

tabernacle. Then once the Grand Ole Opry rolled in, it became known as the Mother Church of Country Music. But this building isn't just for country fans; the biggest stars across all genres, and even some cows, have stood on that hallowed stage. And if you're able to snag a ticket for a show here, any show, do it. Finally, the **National Museum of African American Music** (⊠ *510 Broadway* ☎ *615/301–8724* ⊕ *www.nmaam. org*) is an expansive exploration of the African American impact on American culture through music. While you've explored pieces of that story on this road trip, this museum lays all the pieces out to form a comprehensive picture.

Eat & Drink: Prince's Hot Chicken, a legendary purveyor of a legendary Nashville dish (hot chicken), now has a food truck downtown for lunch (⊠ *423 6th Ave. S* ⊕ *www.princeshotchicken. com*). Have a light (in volume) dinner at the **Grilled Cheeserie** (⊠ *2003 Belcourt Ave.* ☎ *615/203–0351* ⊕ *www.grilled-cheeserie.com*). With their ingenious concoctions, you'll never be tempted to order a grilled cheese from a kid's menu again. After dinner, the **Bluebird Café** (⊠ *4104 Hillsboro Pike* ☎ *615/383–1461* ⊕ *www.bluebirdcafe.com*) is a visit … if you can get in. Singer-songwriters, ranging from not-yet-known artists to megastars, perform and tell stories about the songs in this intimate showcase. Buy tickets online in advance or try your luck with the walk-up line.

Breakfast: While the **Pancake Pantry** (⊠ *1796 21st Ave. S* ☎ *615/383–9333* ⊕ *www.thepancakepantry.com*) in Hillsboro isn't only about pancakes, with 19 different varieties, they're still very much about pancakes. These range from workhorse silver dollars to the pancake with three sausage links tucked inside ("Pigs in a Blanket").

The Best of North and Central Florida

The Best of North and Central Florida

Written by Mark Sullivan

Orlando is usually a visitor's first (and often only) introduction to Florida, but for anyone who wants to expand their horizons beyond the theme parks, the city makes a great starting point to explore the rest of the state. Drive for an hour or two in any direction and you'll encounter a different Florida, one that's quite rich in historical sites and natural wonders.

This itinerary starts in Orlando, then travels up the Atlantic Seaboard, across the center of the state, and down the Gulf Coast. Along the way it passes through some of Florida's most fascinating destinations: windswept beaches, unique geological formations, and crystal-clear springs teeming with wildlife.

At a Glance

Start: Orlando, FL

End: Orlando, FL

Miles Traveled: 675 miles

Suggested Duration: 8 days

States Visited: Florida

Key Sights: Cocoa Beach; Daytona Beach; Disney Springs; Kennedy Space Center; St. Augustine

Best Time to Go: The Sunshine State is an all-season destination. School breaks and holidays tend to be the most crowded (especially Orlando) while summer sees the least amount of crowds.

Day 1: Orlando, FL, to Cape Canaveral, FL

55 miles (50 minutes without traffic and stops)

Land in Orlando, where you can pick up a rental car from the airport and ignore the urge to make a quick visit to Disney World. Once you take Route 408 east from Orlando, you'll notice a lot less congestion. Route 50 passes through protected lands, including the St. Johns National Wildlife Refuge. Route 405 across the Indian River takes you directly to Kennedy Space Center.

ALONG THE WAY

Nature: If you want to stretch your legs a bit, a section of the Florida Trail, the wildest of the 11 national scenic trails across the United States, can be accessed near the community of Christmas.

CAPE CANAVERAL

Do: One of Florida's most enduring attractions (it's been around longer than Walt Disney World or any of the other area theme parks) is the Kennedy Space Center. Explore its history at the **Kennedy Space Center Visitor Center Complex** (✉ *Space Commerce Way, Merritt Island* ☎ *855/433–4210* ⊕ *www.kennedyspacecenter.com*), where you can pay tribute to the men and women who've gone into space at the *Heroes & Legends* exhibit. If you can't wait to get some sun, Cocoa Beach is one of the prettiest stretches of sand in the area. Beachfront **Alan Shepard Park** (✉ *299 E. Cocoa Beach Causeway* ☎ *321/868–3258* ⊕ *www.cityofcocoabeach.com*) is named after an astronaut and is a favorite spot for watching rocket launches.

Eat & Drink: There are plenty of dining options in and around Cape Canaveral, but the food doesn't get any fresher than at **Seafood Atlantic** (✉ *520 Glen Cheek Dr.* ☎ *321/784–1963* ⊕ *www.seafoodatlantic.org*), a fish market with an alfresco dining room.

Stay: An oceanfront hotel, the **Inn at Cocoa Beach** (✉ *4300 Ocean Beach Blvd.* ☎ *321/799–3460* ⊕ *www.theinnatcocoabeach.com*) has a laid-back vibe and spectacular views.

Breakfast: As you're driving up the coast, stop in Titusville at **Le Crave** (✉ *2520 S. Washington Ave.* ☎ *321/292–7373* ⊕ *www.lecravecafe.com*), known for its delicious crepes and other savory and sweet breakfast treats.

Day 2: Cape Canaveral, FL, to St. Augustine, FL

128 miles (2 hours, 30 minutes without traffic and stops)

Today you'll head north up Florida's beautiful Atlantic coast. I–95 to Route 207 is the quickest way up the coast, getting you to St. Augustine in just under two hours. But since this is a road trip, you should cut over to the more scenic, two-lane coastal Route A1A north of Daytona Beach.

ALONG THE WAY

Eat & Drink: With an unbeatable location right on the pier, Daytona Beach's outpost of **Joe's Crab Shack** (✉ *1200 Main St.* ☎ *386/238–4050* ⊕ *www.joescrabshack.com*) is a local favorite. Grab a seat on the rooftop terrace and enjoy king crab legs (the specialty) served with potatoes and corn.

Photo Op: Billed as the "World's Most Famous Beach," Daytona Beach is one of the few in the country where you can drive your car right onto the sand, meaning there are a lot of tailgate parties in progress. (Alcohol is officially prohibited, but no one is actually checking.) It's 23 miles long, so the farther you get from the "Strip" near International Speedway Boulevard, the sparser the crowds.

The Rocket Garden is one of the Kennedy Space Center's most popular attractions.

ST. AUGUSTINE

Do: Straddling the sparkling Matanzas River is St. Augustine, the nation's oldest city. The gargantuan **Castillo de San Marcos National Monument** (✉ *1 S. Castillo Dr.* ☎ *904/829–6506* ⊕ *www.nps.gov/casa*), a fort built by the Spanish in 1695, proved surprisingly strong against British cannonballs. More petite is **Fort Matanzas National Monument** (✉ *8635 Rte. A1A S* ✉ *904/471–0116* ⊕ *www.nps.gov/foma*), which defended the city's southern borders beginning in 1742. That makes the colonial-style **Cathedral Basilica of St. Augustine** (✉ *38 Cathedral Pl.* ☎ *904/824–2806* ⊕ *www.thefirstparish.org*), built in 1795, a relatively recent addition to the city.

Eat & Drink: Located in the Historic District, **Collage** (✉ *60 Hypolita St.* ☎ *904/829–0055* ⊕ *collagestaug.com*) has a menu that's completely dependent on what the fishermen bring in that day. **The Floridian** (✉ *72 Spanish St.* ☎ *904/829–0655* ⊕ *www.thefloridianstaug.com*) is known for its vegetarian fare, but its menu of farm-to-table dishes satisfies even devoted meat eaters.

Stay: A stone's throw from the water, the luxe **Bayfront Marin House Historic Inn** (✉ *142 Avenida Menendez* ☎ *904/824–4301* ⊕ *www.bayfrontmarinhouse.com*) lets you gaze out at the playful dolphins in the Intracoastal Waterway.

Breakfast: Actually located on Cordova Street in the Historic District, the **Maple Street Biscuit Company** (✉ *39 Cordova St.* ☎ *904/217–7814* ⊕ *www.maplestreetbiscuits.com*) serves tasty breakfast sandwiches and other early-morning fare.

Day 3: St. Augustine, FL, to Amelia Island, FL

70 miles (1 hour, 20 minutes without traffic and stops)

Head to Amelia Island in the northeastern corner of Florida. As usual there's the fast way—U.S. 1 to I–295 to I–95 to Route 200—and the much more scenic route along the coast that detours onto Route A1A.

ALONG THE WAY

Town: Jacksonville may not be a tourist destination, but it has its charms. One of its highlights is **MOCA Jacksonville** (✉ 333 N. Laura St. ☎ 904/366–6911 ⊕ moca-jacksonville.unf.edu), housed in a stately downtown building that was once the headquarters of the Western Union Telegraph Company. The loftlike space is filled with modern art that's smart yet accessible. Even if you think you're not a zoo person, the **Jacksonville Zoo and Gardens** (✉ 370 Zoo Pkwy. ☎ 904/757–4463 ⊕ www.jacksonvillezoo.org) may win you over with large-scale exhibits of tigers, penguins, and venomous snakes. Don't miss Wild Florida, which showcases the state's surprisingly varied wildlife.

Eat & Drink: The sophisticated **Bistro Aix** (✉ 1440 San Marco Blvd. ☎ 904/398–1949 ⊕ www.bistrox.com), south of downtown on San Marco Boulevard, has classic French dishes like onion soup and steak frites, as well as homemade pastries.

AMELIA ISLAND

Do: Amelia Island is one of Florida's gems, with a beautiful coastline lined with massive sand dunes. There are seven parks that make up **Talbot Island State Parks** (✉ Rte. A1A N ☎ 904/251–2320 ⊕ www.floridastateparks.org), and three of them have beautiful beaches. Big Talbot, with its Boneyard Beach of wind-twisted trees, is a photographer's paradise, and Little Talbot is popular for swimming and beachcombing, while Amelia Island State Park is popular for its beachfront horseback riding. There are several must-see sights, including **Fort Clinch State Park** (✉ 2601 Atlantic Ave. ☎ 904/277–7274 ⊕ www.flori-dastateparks.org), home to one of the most perfectly preserved 19th-century brick forts in the country. It was built to dissuade the English from invading after the War of 1812.

Eat & Drink: In the historic town of Fernandina Beach, **Sliders Seaside Grill** (✉ 1998 S. Fletcher Ave. ☎ 904/277–6652 ⊕ www.slidersseaside.com) lives up to its name. The relaxed restaurant overlooks a surf break, so watching locals ride the waves is part of the fun. So is the menu, filled with dishes that pile on the seafood, like the crab-topped flounder.

Stay: Located on more than 1,300 acres of shoreline, the **Omni Amelia Island Resort** (✉ 39 Beach Lagoon Rd. ☎ 904/261–6161 ⊕ www.omnihotels.com) couldn't have a better location. The palm-shaded pool is the best place to take in the unobstructed ocean views. The last word in luxury, the **Ritz Carlton Amelia Island** (✉ 4750 Amelia Island Pkwy. ☎ 904/277–1100 ⊕ www.ritzcarlton.com) has indulgent rooms, superb service, and top-flight amenities like the Surrender Spa. Don't miss a meal at its top-rated restaurant, simply called Salt.

Breakfast: The garden bagel at **Amelia Island Coffee** in Fernandina Beach (✉ 207 Centre St. ☎ 904/321–2111 ⊕ www.ame-liaislandcoffee.com) won't win over New Yorkers, but the combo of cream cheese, hummus, avocado, tomato, and onion is undeniably tasty.

Day 4: Amelia Island, FL, to Gainesville, FL

97 miles (1 hour, 50 minutes without traffic and stops)

U.S. 301 takes you most of the way to Gainesville. Take a slight right at Waldo, and Route 24 takes you the last few miles.

ALONG THE WAY

Nature: If you need a break to stretch your legs, the 1.4-mile **Cary Trailwalker Trail** (✉ 7400 Pavilion Rd. ⊕ www.alltrails.com) is a loop through some unspoiled terrain.

The trailhead is near the town of Bryce on U.S. 301.

GAINESVILLE

Do: Gainesville is the home of the University of Florida, but there's more to do in and around this college town than cheer on the home team, including plenty of natural wonders. Scientists believe the sinkhole at the center of **Devil's Millhopper Geological State Park** (✉ *4732 Millhopper Rd.* ☎ *352/955–2008* ⊕ *www.floridastateparks.org*) formed thousands of years ago. After you descend past several waterfalls, you reach a subtropical paradise 12 stories below the surface. The **Prairie Paynes Preserve State Park** (✉ *100 Savannah Blvd., Micanopy* ☎ *352/466–3397* ⊕ *www.floridastateparks.org*), about 10 miles south of the city, is home to herds of wild horses. If that's not unusual enough, it also has free-roaming bison. Take it all in from the 50-foot-high observation tower.

Eat & Drink: The dining room at the storefront **Paramount Grill** (✉ *12 S.W. 1st Ave.* ☎ *352/378–3398* ⊕ *www.paramountgrill.com*) is surprisingly simple, letting the artistry of the food take center stage. All the dishes take advantage of the best local produce of the area.

Stay: Painted a sunny shade of yellow, the **Laurel Oak Inn Bed & Breakfast** (✉ *221 S.E. 7th St.* ☎ *352/519–3994* ⊕ *www.laureloakinn.com*) is an exquisitely restored Queen Anne–style Victorian showplace. Breakfast is a home-cooked meal, which becomes an extravaganza on the weekends with "Sweetness on Sunday."

Breakfast: As the name suggests, **Uppercrust** (✉ *4118 N.W. 16th Blvd.* ☎ *352/376–7187* ⊕ *www.uppercrustgnv.com*) is a bakery focusing on croissants and other perfectly executed pastries. It's located just outside the university area.

Day 5: Gainesville, FL, to Crystal River, FL

62 miles (1 hour, 25 minutes without traffic or stops)

Take Route 121 south to Williston, then U.S. 41 south past Rainbow Springs. Route 491 delivers you to Crystal River.

ALONG THE WAY

Nature: Humans first visited **Rainbow Springs** (✉ *19158 S.W. 81st Pl. Rd., Dunnellon* ☎ *352/465–8555* ⊕ *www.floridastateparks.org*) more than 10,000 years ago. Stone tools made by the Timucua people reveal the area's rich history. Today people head to the springs for a dip in the remarkably clean waters. There are three beautiful waterfalls—a rarity in Florida. They're all man-made, remnants from when this was a tourist attraction.

CRYSTAL RIVER

Do: Crystal River isn't undiscovered by any means, but it still remains a bit off the typical tourist trail. The six Native American burial mounds at **Crystal River Archaeological State Park** (✉ *3400 N. Museum Point* ☎ *352/795–3817* ⊕ *www.floridastateparks.com*) make this one of the longest continually occupied regions of the state. Head to the top of the Temple Mound for sweeping views of the nearby marshes. At **Crystal River National Wildlife Refuge** (✉ *1502 S.E. Kings Bay Dr.* ☎ *352/563–2088* ⊕ *www.fws.gov*), manatees congregate in large numbers from November to March. Make your way to Three Sisters Springs, part of the refuge, where you can spot dozens of the gentle giants in the remarkably clear water.

Eat & Drink: There's nothing fancy at the **Crab Plant** (✉ *201 N.W. 5th St.* ☎ *352/795–4700* ⊕ *www.crabplant.com*), a fish market on 5th Street in Crystal River. But the dining room has two big pluses: the freshest seafood you'll find in these parts and a view of the waters of King Bay. Stone crab, the specialty here, comes right off the owner's boat. Local shrimp is also caught right at the dock outside.

Stay: On the shore of Kings Bay, the **Plantation on Crystal River** (✉ *9301 W. Fort Island Trail* ☏ *352/795–4211* ⊕ *www.plantationoncrystalriver.com*) is an eco-friendly resort located on 232 acres near all of the area's nature preserves. The resort's on-site dive shop has daily snorkeling excursions.

Breakfast: The name doesn't do this place justice. Sure, but **Breakfast Station #9** (✉ *1676 S.E. U.S. 19* ☏ *352/228– 4077* ⊕ *www.breakfaststationcentral. com*) serves stick-to-your-ribs morning meals, and it's an equally good lunch stop if you get a late start.

Day 6: Crystal River, FL, to St. Petersburg, FL

91 miles (1 hour, 45 minutes without traffic and stops)

Head south on U.S. 98, then merge onto U.S. 19 for the rest of the drive to St. Petersburg.

ALONG THE WAY

Nature: There are many stretches of sand in this area that are worth an hour or two of your time, but these two state parks—both of which require a bit of effort to get to— are something special. A ferry from Honeymoon Island takes you to **Caladesi Island State Park** (✉ *Offshore Island* ☏ *727/469– 5918* ⊕ *www.floridastateparks.org*), the perfect place to kayak along a 3-mile route among the mangroves. Even more remote is Anclote Key State Park, three miles offshore from the town of **Tarpon Springs** (☏ *727/638–4447* ⊕ *www.floridastateparks.org*). After the ferry ride, hike to the lighthouse dating back to 1887 or find a remote spot on the sand all to yourself.

ST. PETERSBURG

Do: Enjoy your time in St. Petersburg, where the swaying palm trees and gentle bay breezes might get you to stay a little longer than you planned. The big attraction in this arts colony is **The Dalí** (✉ *1 Dali Blvd.* ☏ *727/823–3767* ⊕ *www.thedali. org*), an homage to famed Spanish painter Salvador Dalí. It has a surprising number of his works, including some from earlier in his career when he was still finding his signature surrealist style. One of Florida's old-school tourist attractions, **Sunken Gardens** (✉ *1825 4th St. N* ☏ *727/551–3102* ⊕ *www.sunkengardens.org*) is today a cool oasis in St. Petersburg's concrete jungle.

Eat & Drink: In the stunning 1920s Birchwood Hotel, **Birch & Vine** (✉ *340 Beach Dr. NE* ☏ *727/896–1080* ⊕ *www.thebirchwood.com*) is the see-and-be-seen spot in St. Petersburg, whether you're sitting in a banquette in the elegant dining room or outside on the patio. It ups the ante on all of its dishes, adding creative flourishes to local seafood.

Stay: Dating from 1933, the **Hollander Hotel** (✉ *421 4th Ave. N* ☏ *727/873– 7900* ⊕ *www.hollanderhotel.com*) has a distinctive Old Florida vibe. Rooms have lots of historic touches, and the pretty pool and the surrounding patio are party central on the weekends.

Breakfast: Often called the best breakfast in St. Petersburg by locals and tourists alike, the **Wooden Rooster** (✉ *104 2nd Ave. NE* ☏ *727/822–7373* ⊕ *www.thewoodenrooster.com*) has a hip vibe and serves a smooth cup of coffee.

Day 7: St. Petersburg, FL, to Sarasota, FL

37 miles (45 minutes without traffic or stops)

From St. Petersburg, I–275 sweeps you across the wide expanse of Tampa Bay. U.S. 19 and U.S. 301 then take you south to downtown Sarasota. Even nicer is the coastal Route 289 through Longboat Key.

ALONG THE WAY

Town: The **De Soto National Memorial** (✉ *8300 Desoto Memorial Hwy.* ☎ *941/792–0458* ⊕ *www.nps.gov/deso*) remembers the story of Spanish Conquistador Hernando de Soto, who came ashore with his men and a team of horses near what is now the town of Bradenton in 1539. The memorial also includes much about the Native people who were living here at the time.

Eat & Drink: Bradenton's **Beach Bistro** (✉ *6600 Gulf Dr.* ☎ *941/778–6444* ⊕ *www.beachbistro.com*) lives up to its name as a seaside spot with gorgeous views, especially at sunset. The award-winning cuisine includes creative fare like "lobster-cargots," large chunks of buttery lobster.

SARASOTA

Do: There is a string of barrier islands just west of Sarasota just waiting to be explored. Siesta Key is home to Siesta Beach, a gorgeous stretch of sand fronting 40 acres of nature trails. Also on Siesta Key is Turtle Beach, which is a little more secluded than most nearby spots. But Sarasota isn't just about the beaches. Built by John Ringling (of Ringling Brothers Circus fame), the **John and Mabel Ringling Museum of Art** (✉ *5401 Bay Shore Rd.* ☎ *941/359–5700* ⊕ *www.ringling.org*) is set within an Italian Renaissance-style palazzo. It originally housed Ringling's own encyclopedic collection of art, and now includes everything from Old Master paintings to modernist masterpieces. Also located on the museum grounds is Ringling's home, Ca' d'Zan, built to resemble the Doge's Palace in Venice.

Eat & Drink: In St. Armands Circle, a beautiful ring of elegant restaurants and other upscale businesses on St. Armands Key, you'll find **Café L'Europe** (✉ *431 St. Armands Circle* ☎ *941/388–4415* ⊕ *www.*

cafeleurope.net). It's elegant in a slightly old-fashioned way, as are the dishes; think sole meunière, potato-crusted grouper, and chateaubriand. North of St. Armands Key is Longboat Key, home to **Euphemia Haye** (✉ *5540 Gulf of Mexico Dr.* ☎ *941/383–3633* ⊕ *www.euphemia-haye.com*), a tucked-away cottage whose menu focuses on beef and lamb.

Stay: On Lido Key, the upscale **Lido Beach Resort** (✉ *700 Benjamin Franklin Dr.* ☎ *941/388–2161* ⊕ *www.lidobeachresort.com*) has two free-form pools, three hot tubs, and a perfectly manicured beach with perfectly spaced lounge chairs. Many of the elegant rooms have their own full kitchens, making them great for longer stays.

Breakfast: On Main Street in Sarasota, **First Watch** (✉ *1395 Main St.* ☎ *941/954–1395* ⊕ *www.firstwatch.com*) is close to the causeway that leads to St. Armands Key. It's focused on breakfast, brunch, and lunch with savory dishes like a carnitas omelet.

Day 8: Sarasota, FL, to Orlando, FL

131 miles (2 hours without traffic or stops)

On your last day, an easy drive on I–75 and I–4 take you back to Orlando, where you'll have some time to explore before your flight home the next day.

ALONG THE WAY

Roadside Attraction: Stop in Lake Wales to stroll around the grounds of **Bok Tower Gardens** (✉ *1151 Tower Blvd.* ☎ *863/676–1408* ⊕ *www.boktowergardens.org*). At its center is an art deco carillon set on 50 acres crisscrossed with paths and dotted with benches. It's old-timey Florida, and it's wonderful.

ORLANDO

Do: When locals spend the day at Disney, it's most often at **Disney Springs** (✉ *1486 E. Buena Vista Dr., Lake Buena Vista* ☎ *407/939–5277* ⊕ *www.disneysprings.com*) a massive shopping, dining, and entertainment complex. The attractions are endless, from floating above the waterfront in a hot-air balloon to speeding across the waves in a boat that looks like a vintage automobile. The best views are from a Mississippi River–style paddle wheeler.

Eat & Drink: There are a lot of dining options at Disney Springs—perhaps the most fun is **The Edison** (✉ *1570 E. Buena Vista Dr., Lake Buena Vista* ☎ *407/560–9288* ⊕ *www.theedisonfla.com*), a 1920s-style speakeasy. (It's Disney, so it's the kind of speakeasy where you can bring the kids.) This isn't a theme park grab-and-go meal, so expect entrées like pan-seared salmon, blackened mahimahi, and a delectable queen-cut prime rib. Be sure to reserve ahead of time here and at all of the Disney Springs sit-down eateries.

Stay: Disney's Saratoga Springs Resort and Spa (✉ *1960 Broadway, Lake Buena Vista* ☎ *407/827–1100* ⊕ *disneyworld.disney.go.com/resorts/saratoga-springs-resort-and-spa*) has it all, including a splendid spa where you can soak your troubles away. This lodging transports you to Upstate New York, where for more than a century people have enjoyed "taking the waters" at the natural hot springs.

Breakfast: Southern-style cooking at its most extravagant, **Chef Art Smith's Homecomin'** (✉ *1602 E. Buena Vista Dr., Lake Buena Vista* ☎ *407/560–0100* ⊕ *www.homecominkitchen.com*) takes your usual offerings and adds something unexpected. Why have run-of-the-mill eggs Benedict when you could have it with hush puppy cakes and grilled chicken tenders?

Extend Your Trip

For either Florida itinerary, connect Cocoa Beach with Miami to combine the two trips to create an ultimate Best of Florida experience.

The Best of Southern Florida

Written by Jessica Poitevien

Flat Florida may not be top of mind when it comes to road trips, but what it lacks in topography, it makes up for in abundant wildlife, vibrant cities, and a uniquely diverse mixture of cultures. South Florida, in particular, is a relatively small area—the longest you'll drive in one day is only four hours—but it's brimming with adventures of all kinds from its glamorous nightlife and ever-growing art scene to its natural beauty and foodie hot spots. On this six-day itinerary, you'll find out why Miami is known as Magic City before diving into Florida's wild side with visits to three national parks, including the only place on Earth where both alligators and crocodiles coexist. Throughout the week, you'll walk in Ernest Hemingway's shoes, share the sidewalk with a rooster or two, get a taste of slow-paced living, and much more.

People say Florida is strange, and perhaps it is, but this road trip will leave you with an appreciation for what makes the Sunshine State that perfect kind of weird.

At a Glance

Start: Miami, FL

End: Miami, FL

Miles Traveled: 430 miles

The Best of
South Florida

Suggested Duration: 7 days

States Visited: Florida

Key Sights: Biscayne National Park; Dry Tortugas National Park; Everglades National Park; Southernmost Point of the Continental United States; Wynwood Art District

Best Time to Go: With year-round sunshine and consistently warm temperatures, a visit to South Florida is always a good idea. But for optimal conditions, plan your visit for winter or early spring (December through April). That's when humidity is low, rainy days are sparse, and those pesky mosquitoes have mostly retreated.

Day 1: Miami (South Beach and Downtown Miami), FL

Miami aka Magic City aka the Capital of Latin America has enough to keep you entertained for a week or even more, but if you're short on time, there's plenty you can accomplish in two days. Pick up a rental car at Miami International Airport, then head north on I–95 to the infamous South Beach. That'll be your home base as you discover the many neighborhoods that make up Miami.

Do: The miles of beach are the main draw at South Beach, but this tourist favorite is also a hub for shopping, decadent dining, buzzing nightlife, and even a bit of art. Be sure to stroll down Lincoln Road for a taste of it all. Before nightfall, admire the distinct 1930s architecture of the Art Deco District before it transforms into party central. Although downtown Miami isn't the most popular place to hang out, museum lovers will find plenty to do here. For an overview of South Florida history, there's the **HistoryMiami Museum** (✉ 101 W. Flagler St. ☎ 305/375–1492 ⊕ www.history-miami.org), while admirers of art flock to the **Pérez Art Museum Miami** (✉ 1103 Biscayne Blvd. ☎ 305/375–3000 ⊕ www.

pamm.org), and science buffs should make their way to the **Phillip and Patricia Frost Museum of Science** (✉ 1101 Biscayne Blvd. ☎ 305/434–9600 ⊕ www.frostscience.org). To take in the skyline views, you can meander around **Bayfront Park** (✉ 301 Biscayne Blvd. ☎ 305/358–7550 ⊕ www.bayfrontparkmiami.com), shop 'til you drop at **Bayside Marketplace** (✉ 401 Biscayne Blvd. ☎ 305/577–3344 ⊕ www.baysidemarketplace.com), or go for a whirl on the **Skyviews Miami Observation Wheel** (✉ 401 Biscayne Blvd. ⊕ www.skyviewsobservation-wheels.com/skyviews-miami).

Eat & Drink: In South Beach, treat yourself to casual Italian fare at the chic but cozy **Di Mauro's** (✉ 1464 Washington Ave. ☎ 305/673–5774 ⊕ www.dimauromiami.com) or take your taste buds on a world tour at **Juvia** (✉ 1111 Lincoln Rd. ☎ 305/763–8272 ⊕ www.juviamiami.com), which combines French, Japanese, and Peruvian cooking styles. For several dining options in one area, head to the waterfront **Sunset Harbour** (✉ 1900 Bay Rd.).

Photo Op: Was that photo taken in Miami or Spain? Your friends will never know the difference when you snap a pic at Española Way in South Beach, a quaint, pedestrian-only street paved with cobblestones and lined with restaurants on both sides.

Stay: There are plenty of luxury getaways in Miami, but the **W South Beach** (✉ 2201 Collins Ave. ☎ 305/938–3000 ⊕ www.marriott.com) is an icon for many reasons, including its guest rooms that guarantee an ocean view. If you'd rather stay in the heart of all the action, the **Stiles Hotel** (✉ 1120 Collins Ave. ☎ 305/674–7800 ⊕ www.thestileshotel.com) is a great choice.

Breakfast: Quick but tasty breakfast sandwiches are par for the course at **A Simple Eggstaurant** (✉ 1516 Washington Ave. ☎ 305/497–9082 ⊕ www.eggstaurant.com), but for a healthy morning pick-me-up, **The Smoothie Shop** (✉ *1229 Washington Ave.* ☎ *305/532–4440* ⊕ *www.orderthesmoothieshop.com*) offers smoothies, acai bowls, and more.

Day 2: Miami (Wynwood Art District and Little Havana), FL

Your second day in Miami leaves the chaos of South Beach and heads to two less hopping, but just as essential, Miami neighborhoods.

Do: There are over 50 blocks of murals lining the streets of Wynwood, so take your time roaming around and admiring your favorites. **The Wynwood Walls** (✉ *2516 N.W. 2nd Ave.* ☎ *305/576–3334* ⊕ *www.thewynwoodwalls.com*) enclosure is the epicenter of all the street art, but don't forget to stop by a few of the galleries nestled between boutiques, bars, and restaurants. There's no doubt that the Cuban population has helped shape Miami into what it is today, so take a guided walking tour of Little Havana to learn about the neighborhood's history. A stop at **Domino Park** (✉ *1444 S.W. 8th Ave.* ☎ *305/859–2717* ⊕ *www.miamigov.com*) is also a must to see the *viejitos* (old men) playing the park's namesake game. If you're lucky, you might even get to join in. Meanwhile, art aficionados will appreciate a visit to **Cubaocho Museum & Performing Arts Center** (✉ *1465 S.W. 8th St.* ☎ *305/285–5880* ⊕ *www.cubaocho.com*) thanks to its collection of 19th- and 20th-century Cuban art.

Eat & Drink: For a sweet snack while in Wynwood, head to **The Salty** (✉ *50 N.W. 24th St.* ☎ *305/639–8501* ⊕ *www.saltydonut.com*) for doughnuts and coffee or **Fireman Derek's Bake Shop** (✉ *2545 N. Miami Ave., Bay 1* ☎ *786/703–3623* ⊕ *www.firemandereks.com*) for rich cakes, cookies, and pies, but your main meals of the day

should be reserved for Little Havana. When it comes to Cuban food, **Versailles** (✉ *3555 S.W. 8th St.* ☎ *305/444–0240* ⊕ *www.versaillesrestaurant.com*) is a restaurant that never disappoints. A sweet finish is not too far away at **Azucar Ice Cream Company** (✉ *1503 S.W. 8th St.* ☎ *305/381–0369* ⊕ *www.azucaricecream.com*), with its Cuban-inspired flavors like sweet plantain and caramel flan. Next, sip on mojitos and Cuba libres while dancing to—or at least admiring—some live salsa music at **Ball & Chain** (✉ *1513 S.W. 8th St.* ☎ *305/643–7820* ⊕ *www.ballandchainmiami.com*), which has been a Little Havana staple since it first opened in 1935.

Stay: It's best to stay put at wherever you spent your first night in Miami.

Breakfast: You'll find an Anthony Bourdain–approved, southern-style breakfast at **Yardbird Southern** (✉ *1600 Lenox Ave.* ☎ *305/538–5220* ⊕ *www.runchickenrun.com*).

Day 3: Miami, FL, to Everglades National Park, FL, to Coral Gables, FL

80 miles (1 hour, 45 minutes without traffic and stops)

Today's adventures are all about getting a glimpse of what South Florida looked like before developers created the cities we know today. You'll drive out west on U.S. 41, surrounded by flat marshes and canals, to visit Everglades National Park, then head back east to Coral Gables, a good jumping-off point for tomorrow's activities.

ALONG THE WAY

Nature: Everglades National Park (☎ *305/242–7700* ⊕ *www.nps.gov.ever*) is huge, so keep your trip focused around the **Shark Valley Visitor Center** (✉ *36000 S.W. 8th St., Miami*). Once you're in the park, keep your eyes peeled for alligators, herons, egrets,

An airboat tour is one of the most popular ways to see Everglades National Park.

deer, turtles, and more as you hike, bike (rentals are available), or take the tram tour around the 15-mile loop trail. At the halfway point, you'll find the 45-foot-tall Shark Valley Observation Tower with panoramic views that stretch as far as 20 miles.

Detour: Although you'll have to drive a bit past the Everglades National Park entrance to reach the **Miccosukee Indian Village** (⊕ www.miccosukee.com), this stop enriches the overall experience by giving more context to the Native people who have lived in the area for centuries. This replica village showcases the tribe's traditional way of life and features a museum with interactive exhibits, a gift shop, and an alligator demonstration area where you can expect to see brave Miccosukee men sticking their heads inside the mouth of a gator.

Roadside Attraction: A trip to the Everglades wouldn't be complete without hopping on an airboat ride to get a different perspective on this unique ecosystem. For smaller group experiences, opt for one of the four airboat companies within

the Miccosukee Indian Reservation. In particular, guides with **Tigertail Airboat Tours** (☎ 305/439–2745 ⊕ www.tigertailairboattours.com) share their knowledge not only of the landscape and wildlife, but also of the Miccosukee tribal history.

Eat & Drink: Only light snacks and beverage vending machines are available at the Shark Valley Visitor Center. Be sure to pack some food or eat before entering the park. You can also head to one of the Miccosukee restaurants near the park entrance. Just keep an eye out for signs pointing the way to fry bread, and you can't go wrong.

CORAL GABLES

Do: You'll probably arrive in Coral Gables exhausted from a day out in the Florida sun, but a post-nap, leisurely stroll down Miracle Mile is well worth it for some window shopping at the boutiques, as well as grabbing dinner and drinks. Literature lovers should swing by **Books & Books** (✉ 265 Aragon Ave. ☎ 305/442–4408 ⊕ www.booksandbooks.com), a locally owned, indie bookstore with a café that also offers flavorful meals.

Eat & Drink: Serving South Florida's carnivore community since 1962, **Graziano's** (✉ *2301 Galiano St.* ☎ *305/460–0001* ⊕ *www.grazianosgroup.com*) whips up Argentinian-style meals that are all about succulent cuts of beef, chorizo, and of course, perfectly paired wines.

Stay: There's a different kind of luxury that comes with a stay in Coral Gables—one that's classy, subdued, timeless, and not at all flashy. No place exudes that feeling more than the **Biltmore Hotel** (✉ *1200 Anastasia Ave.* ☎ *855/311–6903* ⊕ *www.biltmorehotel.com*), which opened in 1926 and still features its Spanish, Italian, and Moorish-inspired architecture in a truly grand setting.

Breakfast: Head to **Threefold Cafe** (✉ *141 Giralda Ave.* ☎ *305/704–8007* ⊕ *www.threefoldcafe.com*) to check out the only Aussie restaurant in town and enjoy a hearty breakfast that puts a twist on your usual morning favorites, like fried French toast with Nutella.

Day 4: Coral Gables, FL, to Biscayne National Park, FL, to Key Largo, FL

84 miles (2 hours without traffic and stops)

Today deserves an early start, so you can fit in all the essential detours needed to truly experience this area. Once you leave the garden-meets-city vibes of Coral Gables, it's a fairly uneventful drive down the Ronald Reagan Turnpike to reach Biscayne National Park. Then a mostly two-lane drive awaits as you continue south to Key Largo, the first of the Florida Keys.

ALONG THE WAY

Detour: The European influences of Coral Gables continue at the **Vizcaya Museum & Gardens** (✉ *3251 S. Miami Ave.* ☎ *305/250–9133* ⊕ *www.vizcaya.org*) in Coconut Grove, backtracking a bit to Miami, where you'll find a stunning Mediterranean-style villa with an impressive collection of centuries-old art. Explore the rooms of this home, but be sure to save plenty of time for the perfectly manicured waterfront gardens, a favorite photo shoot spot for both professionals and smartphone-wielding amateurs.

Eat & Drink: There are only light snacks and premade cold sandwiches available at Biscayne's Dante Fascell Visitor Center so it's best to eat before you reach the park. For an early lunch, head to South Miami, where you'll find **Grown** (✉ *8211 S. Dixie Hwy.* ☎ *305/663–4769* ⊕ *www.grown.org*), which focuses on organic ingredients on its vegan-and-vegetarian-friendly menu.

Nature: Since 95% of **Biscayne National Park** (✉ *305/230–1144* ⊕ *www.nps.gov/bisc*) is covered in water, you'll need some help exploring. Luckily, Biscayne National Institute (the tour operator arm of the park) offers plenty of guided adventures so you can sail, snorkel, paddle, or kayak your way around. Customized private tours are also available. If you're a scuba diver, don't miss out on the park's Maritime Heritage Trail, which showcases six of the many shipwrecks in the area.

Detour: On the second half of today's journey, you can also take a detour to the other entrance of Everglades National Park, via the **Ernest F. Coe Visitor Center** (✉ *40001 Rte. 9336, Homestead*). Hiking enthusiasts may appreciate the more natural trails of this side of the Everglades. And a chance to see crocodiles in the only place where they coexist with alligators, head to the southernmost tip of the park near the **Flamingo Visitor Center** (✉ *1 Flamingo Lodge Hwy., Homestead*).

Roadside Attraction: After all these outdoorsy adventures, head to the **Robert Is Here Fruit Stand** (✉ *19200 S.W. 344th St., Homestead* ☎ *305/246–1592* ⊕ *www.robertishere.com*) for the perfect afternoon pick-me-up. It's a slight detour west, but absolutely worth it to try the milkshakes and smoothies made with not-so-typical fruits like guanabana, black sapote, mamey, and more.

KEY LARGO

Do: The gateway to the Florida Keys, Key Largo is all about getting out onto the water, with diving and snorkeling being its most popular activities. Nobody comes to Key Largo without visiting **John Pennekamp Coral Reef State Park** (✉ *102601 Overseas Hwy.* ☎ *305/451–6300* ⊕ *www.floridastateparks.org*), one of the jewels of the state park system. Water-sports enthusiasts head to the adjacent Key Largo National Marine Sanctuary, which encompasses about 190 square miles of coral reefs, seagrass beds, and mangrove estuaries. If you've never tried diving, Key Largo is the perfect place to learn. Dozens of companies will be more than happy to show you the ropes, like **Quiescence Diving Services** (✉ *103680 Overseas Hwy.* ☎ *305/451–2440* ⊕ *www.keylargodiving.com*).

Eat & Drink: The only thing more enticing than the cute and quirky environment of **Mrs. Mac's Kitchen** (✉ *99336 Overseas Hwy.* ☎ *305/451–3722* ⊕ *www.mrsmacskitchen.com*), the most popular restaurant in Key Largo, is its full menu of fresh seafood. If you make it in time to watch the sunset, then you'll want to dine or get a drink at **Sundowners** (✉ *103900 Overseas Hwy.* ☎ *305/451–4502* ⊕ *www.sundownerskeylargo.com*), which offers incredible views over Florida Bay as you munch on their menu of steak, hearty sandwiches, and local seafood.

Stay: Baker's Cay Resort (✉ *97000 Overseas Hwy.* ☎ *305/852–5553* ⊕ *www.hilton.com*) offers the ultimate in luxury stays with its serene waterfront location and optional all-inclusive packages that are customizable to your needs. **Kona Kai Resort & Gallery** (✉ *97802 Overseas Hwy.* ☎ *305/852–7200* ⊕ *www.konakairesort.com*) also welcomes guests to a waterfront location but in a more intimate, kids-free setting. Don't forget to enjoy a stroll around the resort's botanical garden and sophisticated art gallery.

Breakfast: Check out **Doc's Diner** (✉ *99696 Overseas Hwy.* ☎ *305/451–2895* ⊕ *www.docsdiner.com*) for all your American breakfast favorites, along with highly rated (and highly sweet) French toast, pancakes, and waffles.

Day 5: Key Largo, FL, to Key West, FL

97 miles (2 hours, 15 minutes without traffic and stops)

Today you'll figure out why the southernmost segment of U.S. 1 is nicknamed the Overseas Highway as you cross more than 40 bridges through the Florida Keys before reaching Key West. The one- (at times two-) lane road can be frustrating, but the beautiful views are distracting enough, especially after you pass Marathon Key and find yourself on the Seven Mile Bridge, the longest bridge in all the Florida Keys.

ALONG THE WAY

Town: Besides Key West, Islamorada is one of the most popular places to visit in the Florida Keys. When you see a giant statue of a lobster, be sure to pull over and go shopping at **Rain Barrel Village** (✉ *86700 Overseas Hwy.* ☎ *305/521–2043* ⊕ *www.rainbarrelvillage.com*), where the work of more than 500 artists is on display and you can buy a variety of souvenirs, handmade crafts, and more. Just down the road is the **History of Diving Museum** (✉ *82990 Overseas Hwy.* ☎ *305/664–9737* ⊕ *www.divingmuseum.org*), featuring one of the world's largest collections of diving helmets, armored suits, and scuba gear, plus tons of diving memorabilia.

Shop: While there's no shortage of places offering the region's most famous dessert (sweet-but-tart Key lime pie), the award-winning version from the **Blond Giraffe Key Lime Pie Factory** (✉ *92220 Overseas Hwy.* ☎ *305/922–2400* ⊕ *www.blondgiraffe.com*) in Tavernier is among the best of the best.

Eat & Drink: For a late lunch, stop in Stock Island—about 15 minutes from Key West—for a fresh seafood meal at **Hogfish Bar & Grill** (✉ *6810 Front St.* ☎ *305/293–4041* ⊕ *www.hogfishbar.com*). People flock here for the creamy lobster bisque, the many preparations of locally caught fish, and the famous piña colada bread pudding, which can only be made in limited quantities and often sells out.

KEY WEST

Do: Aimlessly wandering the streets of Key West is entertaining enough with its plethora of shops, art galleries, and bars, but you'll want to go in with a game plan to make the most of your time. Float through the bright and airy greenhouse of the **Key West Butterfly and Nature Conservatory** (✉ *1316 Duval St.* ☎ *305/296–2988* ⊕ *www.keywestbutterfly.com*), where you'll find yourself totally surrounded by hundreds of birds and butterflies who aren't shy about landing on your shoulder. Less than a half mile away, the **Ernest Hemingway Home and Museum** (✉ *907 Whitehead St.* ☎ *305/294–1136* ⊕ *www.hemingwayhome.com*) tells the story of the prolific writer's time in the area, with some Key West history sprinkled in. As the sun begins to set, don't miss out on the biggest party in Key West at **Mallory Square** (✉ *400 Wall St.* ☎ *305/809–3700* ⊕ *www.mallorysquare.com*), where everyone gathers to watch the sunset alongside musicians, food vendors, and street performers.

Photo Op: Between the rogue roosters roaming the roads and the picture-perfect homes with wraparound verandas, Key West is chock-full of photo ops, but there are two in particular that you can't leave

the Keys without: the monument at the southernmost point of the continental United States, **Southernmost Point Buoy** (✉ *Whitehead St. and South St.*) and the mile marker 0 sign, signaling the start of the Overseas Highway.

Eat & Drink: Grab a bite at **Pepe's Cafe Key West** (✉ *806 Caroline St.* ☎ *305/294–7192* ⊕ *www.pepeskeywest.com*), which is believed to be the oldest eatery in the area and where steak and seafood are the specialties. No matter where you have dinner, end the night with a sweet treat at **Better Than Sex** (✉ *926 Simonton St.* ☎ *305/296–8102* ⊕ *www.betterthansexdesserts.com*), a dessert restaurant, followed by barhopping on Duval Street.

Stay: Teleport to the olden days of Key West with a stay at the **Curry Mansion Inn** (✉ *511 Caroline St.* ☎ *305/294–3265* ⊕ *www.currymansion.com*), a historic home turned B&B that's the perfect combination of cozy accommodations and central location. For a really unique stay, check out Airbnb's floating boat homes known as the Tiki Suites.

Breakfast: Fill up on seafood eggs Benedict, homemade banana bread, and more with the most "heavenly" breakfast in Key West, served at **Blue Heaven** (✉ *729 Thomas St.* ☎ *305/296–8666* ⊕ *www.blueheavenkw.com*).

Day 6: Dry Tortugas National Park, FL

Don't expect to drive much today because there are only two ways to get to Dry Tortugas National Park: via a flight with **Seaplane Adventures** (✉ *3471 S. Roosevelt Blvd.* ☎ *305/293–9300* ⊕ *www.keywestseaplanecharters.com*), the only company that flies to the park, or via a boat on the *Yankee Freedom III* ferry (✉ *100 Grinnell St.* ☎ *305/294–7009* ⊕ *www.drytortugas.com*).

Do: No matter how you arrive at **Dry Tortugas National Park** (☎ 305/242–7700 ⊕ www.nps.gov/drto), you must explore Fort Jefferson, whether on a guided tour or on your own. Then you'll have plenty of time to lounge on the beach, enjoy some world-class snorkeling fit for both beginners and experts, and go birding to spot the nearly 300 species that have been recorded in the area. Those who come on the ferry will have a fully narrated 45-minute tour of Fort Jefferson included in the price of their ticket, while seaplane guests have access to complimentary snorkeling gear.

Eat & Drink: There are no opportunities to purchase food while at Dry Tortugas National Park, so plan accordingly. If you choose to go on a day-trip aboard the *Yankee Freedom III* ferry, a breakfast snack and box lunch are included, but you still might want to bring some extra snacks. Seaplane Adventures provides their guest with water and soft drinks, but no food. If you head back to Key West at the end of the day, enjoy dinner at **Half Shell Raw Bar** (✉ 231 Margaret St. ☎ 305/294–7496 ⊕ www.halfshellrawbar.com), known for its conch ceviche and other fresh seafood.

Stay: If you're feeling adventurous, there are campsites available for overnight stays at Dry Tortugas National Park. Otherwise, head back to the comfort of your Key West home base.

Breakfast: Tasty bites in a eclectic surroundings are offered by the **Koffie House** (✉ 602 Greene St. ☎ 305/741–7647 ⊕ www.koffiehouse.com), while those in need of a quick breakfast with a side of photo ops can head to **Cuban Coffee Queen** (✉ 284 Margaret St. ☎ 305/292–4747 ⊕ www.cubancoffeequeen.com), where a small *Greetings from Key West* mural can be found on the side of the building.

Day 7: Key West, FL, to Miami, FL

164 miles (3 hours, 10 minutes without traffic and stops)

Today's drive will be the longest one of the trip as you make your way back to Miami to return your rental and say goodbye to the Sunshine State. As on the way down, you'll spend most of your time on the narrow Overseas Highway (U.S. 1) before crossing into the bigger cities of South Florida. Today's pit stops will be all about checking out the things you didn't see on your way to Key West.

ALONG THE WAY

Town: Every key in the Florida Keys chain has something different to offer, and Marathon is no exception. Stop here to spend time at the **Turtle Hospital** (✉ 2396 Overseas Hwy. ☎ 305/743–2552 ⊕ www.turtlehospital.org), where daily educational tours show guests how they rehabilitate and release turtles back into the wild. The **Dolphin Research Center** (✉ 58901 Overseas Hwy. ☎ 305/289–1121 ⊕ www.dolphins.org) is also nearby, offering visitors the chance to learn about these adorable mammals with an educational tour and even swim with them.

Roadside Attraction: Robbie's (✉ 77522 Overseas Hwy. ☎ 305/664–8070 ⊕ www.robbies.com) in Islamorada is a full-service marina with kayaking tours, parasailing adventures, sunset cruises, and more, but it's the tarpon feedings that made this place famous. For a few dollars, you'll get a bucket of fish that you can feed to the giant tarpon fish (also known as silver kings) who hang out by the dock. With a fish in hand, lower yourself toward the water and wait for them to jump up and grab the bait with their mouths wide open. Just watch out for the nearby pelicans also waiting to steal your fish. Robbie's also has a few shops with handcrafts, antiques, souvenirs, and more. It's also a great place to stop for lunch or even just coffee and ice cream.

Chapter 8

THE NORTHEAST

Updated by
Andrew Collins

WELCOME TO THE NORTHEAST

TOP REASONS TO GO

★ **Niagara Falls:** The three magnificent waterfalls that make up Niagara Falls have been attracting visitors for centuries.

★ **Harriet Tubman Byway:** This 125-mile route takes you through Maryland's eastern shore to more than 30 key spots in the legendary abolitionist's life.

★ **Cape May:** The crowning jewel of New Jersey's famously festive shoreline, Cape May is a charming throwback to Victorian resort towns.

★ **The White Mountains:** Offering spectacular hiking and skiing, these dramatic peaks and notches are unforgettable.

★ **Acadia National Park:** The Northeast's only national park, Acadia's 49,000 acres of protected forests, beaches, mountains, and rocky coastline can't be missed.

★ **Cape Cod National Seashore:** Thirty miles of beaches, sand dunes, swamps, marshes, wetlands, and pitch-pine and scrub-oak forest make up one of Cape Cod's most defining areas.

1 The Best of the Chesapeake Bay. Explore the coasts of Maryland and Virginia while experiencing one of America's most unique ecosystems.

2 The Best of New York State. The Empire State is filled with mountain landscapes, cool cities, historic spots, and scenic wineries galore.

3 The Best of Long Island and the Jersey Shore. Escape NYC by retreating to its underrated neighbors to the east and south, and their beaches, wineries, and museums.

4 The Best of New England. Visit all six states that make up this region in one trip packed with culture, history, and New England charm.

5 New England's Great Outdoors. Experience the best of New England's lakes, mountains, and national and state parks.

6 Coastal New England. Embrace the area's seafaring history by hitting up its best beach towns.

From the deep woods of New England to the lively beaches of the Mid-Atlantic (and the big cities of Boston, New York City, and Baltimore in between), the northeastern corner of the United States is rife with road trip opportunities and lessons in history, geology, and fine dining.

The Best of the Chesapeake Bay

Written by Barbara Noe Kennedy

As the world's largest estuary, the Chesapeake Bay is a salty realm of waterfront villages, historic lighthouses, migrating birds, refined inns, and bayside restaurants serving the region's impressive seafood bounty. First reconnoitered by Captain John Smith some 350 years ago, the historic domain of the watermen and women who still harvest its waters retains a bygone, peaceful vibe ideal for exploration and relaxation. This loop begins at the top of the bay in Baltimore, a historic city with a surprising number of cultural offerings, and makes its way south on country byways along the bay's western edge before curving back north along its eastern side. Along the way you'll discover Maryland's first colonial capital; trail-laced Westmoreland State Park; George Washington's birthplace; the refined waterside villages of Irvington and St. Michaels; and the nearly forgotten Smith Island.

The drive's latter portion through Maryland's Eastern Shore unveils several sites related to freedom fighter Harriet Tubman,

particularly along the Harriet Tubman Underground Railroad Byway. Tubman was born near Cambridge and used her knowledge of the Chesapeake's marshes, fields, and rivers in her quest to lead people north to freedom. In addition to historic sites, the area is filled with bed-and-breakfasts in genteel historic buildings, crab shacks, open-air seafood restaurants, and idyllic sunset-watching spots.

At a Glance

Start: Baltimore, MD

End: Baltimore, MD

Miles Traveled: 647 miles

Suggested Duration: 5 days

States Visited: Maryland, Virginia

Key Sights: American Revolution Museum; Annapolis Naval Academy; Baltimore Museum of Art; Harriet Tubman Underground Railroad National Historic Site; Historic St. Mary's City

Best Time to Go: Summer is prime beach time (although be prepared to deal with crowds), while spring and fall bring bird migration and gorgeous foliage (and fewer people). Oyster season is October through March, while blue crabs are harvested April through mid-December.

Day 1: Baltimore, MD, to Annapolis, MD

32 miles (40 minutes without traffic or stops)

Your first day is a perfunctory highway drive via I–97 and U.S. 50 southeast to Annapolis.

ALONG THE WAY

Nature: The paved Baltimore and Annapolis (B&A) Trail rumbles along an old railroad track for 13 miles between Glen Burnie and Annapolis, and it is beloved by walkers and bikers alike. A ranger station in Severna Park occupies an 1889 general store and has a small museum.

Detour: Sandy Point State Park (✉ *1100 E. College Pkwy.* ⊕ *www.dnr.maryland.gov*), 10 miles east of Annapolis via U.S. 50, gives you your first gorgeous glimpse of the Chesapeake Bay. The sandy beach is good for swimming, and you can also fish, crab, picnic, soak in some rays, and take in views of the stunning Chesapeake Bay Bridge.

ANNAPOLIS

Do: Maryland's capital is a leafy, walkable, boat-loving town filled with historic buildings that house boutiques, galleries, restaurants, inns, and museums. At the top of town sits the state capitol, the nation's oldest continuously working statehouse. From there, stroll down adorable Main Street toward Ego Alley at the harbor with its bougie yachts. The nearby grounds of the **Annapolis Naval Academy** (✉ *121 Blake Rd.* ☎ *410/293–1000* ⊕ *www.usna.edu*) are another tree-shaded place to stroll (don't miss the tomb of Revolutionary War naval commander John Paul Jones). You can also tour the **Thomas Shoal Point Lighthouse** (☎ *415/362–7255* ⊕ *www.*

thomaspointlighthouse.org), the bay's only active screwpile lighthouse, accessible by boat.

Eat & Drink: Take a water taxi from City Dock (or walk across Spa Creek Bridge) to Eastport, Annapolis's lively maritime neighborhood, where several local restaurants comprise Restaurant Row. Divine choices include **Boatyard Bar & Grill** (✉ *400 4th St.* ☎ *410/216–6206* ⊕ *www.boatyardbarandgrill.com*), a nautical-theme place to go for oysters on the half shell and Maryland's official state dessert, Smith Island cake; **Carrol's Creek Café** (✉ *410 Severn Ave.* ☎ *410/263–8102* ⊕ *www.carrolscreek.com*), serving local seafood overlooking Spa Creek; and **Galway Bay** (✉ *63 Maryland Ave.* ☎ *410/263–8333* ⊕ *www.galwaybaymd.com*), a fun Irish pub. **Chick & Ruth's Delly** (✉ *165 Main St.* ☎ *410/269–6737* ⊕ *www.chickandruths.com*), on Main Street, serves down-home breakfast, lunch, and dinner—it's a favorite spot to spy politicians.

Stay: You'll have your pick of wonderful inns and B&Bs here. The **Inn at Horn Point** (✉ *534 Burnside St.* ☎ *410/268–1126* ⊕ *www.innathornpoint.com*) in the historic maritime district has water views; **Annapolis Inn** (✉ *144 Prince George St.* ☎ *410/295–5200* ⊕ *www.annapolisinn.com*) conveys sumptuous living from bygone days; and the **Historic Inns of Annapolis** (✉ *58 State Circle* ☎ *410/263–2641* ⊕ *www.historicinnsofannapolis.com*) offers three boutique inns in meticulously restored historic buildings near the statehouse.

Breakfast: Miss Shirley's Café (✉ *1 Park Pl.* ☎ *410/268–5171* ⊕ *www.missshirleys.com*) is a popular southern-inspired breakfast spot, while **Iron Rooster** (✉ *12 Market Space* ☎ *410/990–1600* ⊕ *iron-rooster.com*) has homemade pop tarts and all-day breakfast.

The Best of Chesapeake Bay

Day 2: Annapolis, MD, to St. Mary's City, MD

70 miles (1 hour, 40 mins without traffic or stops)

Follow winding, tree-shaded Route 2 and Route 4 south to California, Maryland. From there, hop on Route 237 and Route 5 for the last scenic stretch into St. Mary's City.

ALONG THE WAY

Nature: A 4-mile out-and-back hike through **Calvert Cliffs State Park** (✉ *10540 H. G. Trueman Rd.* ☎ *443/975–4360* ⊕ *www.dnr.maryland.gov*) leads to the Chesapeake Bay, where you can hunt for fossilized shark's teeth.

Eat & Drink: Attached to the mainland via a bridge, Solomons Island is a humming boat-centric village with several waterfront restaurants, including the **Island Hideaway** (✉ *14556 Solomons Island Rd. S* ☎ *410/449–6382* ⊕ *theislandhide-awaysolomons.com*) and **Charles Street Brasserie** (✉ *120 Charles St.* ☎ *410/404–5332* ⊕ *www.charlesstreetbrass.com*).

ST. MARY'S CITY

Do: Maryland's first settlers arrived from England in 1634 and built a now long-vanished city along the St. Mary's River near the Chesapeake Bay. Today an outdoor living history museum and archaeological site, **St. Mary's** (✉ *18751 Hogaboom La.* ☎ *301/994–4370* ⊕ *www.hsmcdigshistory.org*) showcases the (rebuilt) town center with a stocked mercantile, a tobacco plantation, a Woodland Indian hamlet, and a replica of the *Dove*, the English merchant ship that brought the original colonists.

Eat & Drink: For fresh seafood, head to **Ruddy Duck Seafood and Alehouse** (✉ *16800 Piney Point Rd.* ☎ *301/994–9944* ⊕ *www.ruddyduckseafood.com*) in Piney Point, overlooking the Potomac River and St. George Creek.

Stay: Good options in the area include the **Quarters at Pier 450** (✉ *48342 Wynne Rd.* ☎ *301/679–3900* ⊕ *www.pier450. com*), a restored 1940s fishing camp, and the welcoming **Swanendele Inn at St. Mary's** (✉ *49946 Airedele Rd.* ☎ *301/576–9910* ⊕ *www.swanendeleinn.com*). And if you're a group, consider the **Cove Point Lighthouse** (✉ *3500 Lighthouse Blvd.* ☎ *410/326–2042* ⊕ *www.calvert-marinemuseum.com*) in Lusby, a historic lighthouse keeper's quarters with two rental units.

Breakfast: Good spots for homestyle favorites include **Linda's Cafe** (✉ *22608 Three Notch Rd.* ⊕ *www.facebook.com/ lindascafelpcity*) in Lexington Park and **Ye Olde Towne Cafe** (✉ *22685 Washington St.* ☎ *301/475–5151* ⊕ *www.facebook. com/yeoldetownecafe*) in Leonardtown.

Day 3: St. Mary's City, MD, to Irvington, VA

120 miles (2 hours, 30 minutes without traffic or stops)

Take a leisurely drive on Route 5 and Route 234 to U.S. 301. From there, amble south on two-lane country roads to Irvington through Virginia's Northern Neck.

ALONG THE WAY

Attraction: George Washington was born in 1732 at what's now the **George Washington Birthplace National Monument** (✉ *1732 Popes Creek Rd.* ☎ *804/224–1732* ⊕ *www.nps.gov/gewa*), just off Route 3 near Colonial Beach, Virginia. The house where Mary Ball gave birth burned down long ago, but within the 538 peaceful acres, you'll find a typical 18th-century home that conveys the mood of rural colonial life.

Nature: Oak- and maple-shaded trails lace **Westmoreland State Park** (✉ *145 Cliff Rd.* ☎ *804/493–8821* ⊕ *www.dcr.virginia. gov*), a hidden gem off Route 3 near

Montross. Look for bald eagles along the path down to Fossil Beach.

IRVINGTON

Do: A laid-back Tidewater town, Irvington is ideal for strolling, browsing unique boutiques, and slurping oysters. You can peek into the past at the **Steamboat Era Museum** (✉ *156 King Carter Dr.* ☎ *804/438–6888* ⊕ *www.steamboateramuseum.org*) and **Historic Christ Church** (✉ *420 Christ Church Rd.* ☎ *804/438–6855* ⊕ *www.christchurch1735.org*), dating from 1735. Other activities include fishing, golfing, or sailing.

Eat & Drink: Options for trying oysters including **Fish Hawk Oyster Bar** (✉ *480 King Carter Dr.* ☎ *804/438–4711* ⊕ *www.tidesinn.com*), or if you're up for a short drive, **Rappahannock Oyster Co.** (✉ *784 Locklies Creek Rd.* ☎ *804/204–1709* ⊕ *www.rroysters.com*) in nearby Topping, a working oyster farm with a riverfront restaurant, Merroir Tasting Room. The **Dog and Oyster Micro-Vineyard** (✉ *65 Tavern Rd.* ☎ *804/438–9463* ⊕ *www.hopeandglory.com*), located at the Hope and Glory Inn, produces wines that pair delectably with the local oysters they serve on the premises.

Stay: The **Tides Inn** (✉ *480 King Carter Dr.* ☎ *804/438–5000* ⊕ *www.tidesinn.com*) is a classic retreat with gorgeous bay views at every turn and even has its own Virginia Oyster Academy, where you can harvest and cook oysters (plenty of other activities include sailing, paddleboarding, wine-and-cheese sunset cruises, and an excellent spa).

Breakfast: The Local (✉ *4337 Irvington Rd.* ☎ *804/438-9356* ⊕ *www.facebook.com/thelocalirvington*), a community-based coffee shop, offers a tempting menu that includes breakfast sandwiches, acai bowls, and crab muffins.

Day 4: Irvington, VA, to St. Michaels, MD

265 miles (5 hours without traffic or stops)

Wander through Northern Neck country on Route 3 east to I–64, which shuttles across the York River and James River at the southernmost end of Chesapeake Bay. From Virginia Beach, follow U.S. 13 north, which sweeps you above (and beneath) the Chesapeake Bay via the 20-mile Chesapeake Bay Bridge-Tunnel. On the other side, follow U.S. 50 north to Route 33, which brings you into St. Michaels.

ALONG THE WAY

Attraction: The United States won the American Revolution in 1781 at Yorktown, where today you can visit the historic battlefield. Don't miss the state-of-the-art **American Revolution Museum** (✉ *200 Water St.* ☎ *757/253–4838* ⊕ *www.jyfmuseums.org*) with living-history experiences that include a re-created Continental Army encampment and a Revolution-era farm. You'll also find here the **Watermen's Museum** (✉ *309 Water St.* ☎ *757/887–2641* ⊕ *www.watermens.org*), celebrating the hardworking men and women who make a living off the Chesapeake's waters.

Eat & Drink: The Museum of the American Revolution has a café with colonial-inspired dishes, or you can try **Water Street Grille** (✉ *323 Water St.* ☎ *757/369–5644* ⊕ *www.waterstreetgrilles.net*), which serves seafood, pasta, and tapas with a York River view.

Detour: One of the Chesapeake's low-lying isles, **Smith Island** (⊕ *smithisland.org*) is accessible via a 50-minute passenger-ferry ride from Crisfield, Maryland. The island lives on the age-old ways of its watermen and waterwomen, who still make a living harvesting oysters and crabs from the bay's watery depths.

Explore the three villages, bird-watch, sample Smith Island cake, and listen for the Elizabethan accents left over from the original English colonists.

Nature: Migrating birds flock to **Blackwater National Wildlife Refuge** (✉ *2145 Key Wallace Dr.* ☎ *410/228–2677* ⊕ *www. friendsofblackwater.org*), a marshy sanctuary with hiking, kayaking, and the largest breeding population of bald eagles on the East Coast north of Florida. In addition, archaeologists have discovered a historic homestead within the refuge that was owned by Ben Ross, Harriet Tubman's father; Tubman likely spent time here as a child and lived here as a teenager.

Attraction: Harriet Tubman's famous escapes north started in the Cambridge area, where she spent her childhood. Her story is told in depth at the 17-acre **Harriet Tubman Underground Railroad National Historical Site** (✉ *4068 Golden Hill Rd.* ☎ *410/221–2290* ⊕ *www.nps. gov/hatu*). The 125-mile Harriet Tubman Underground Railroad Byway, linking historic sites related to Tubman's life, starts here. For even more insight into Tubman's life, a bit farther north in Cambridge you'll find the **Harriet Tubman Museum and Educational Center** (✉ *424 Race St.* ☎ *410/228–0401* ⊕ *www.harriettubmanmuseumcenter.org*).

ST. MICHAELS

Do: Once a thriving colonial seaport, this quintessential Chesapeake village is built for casual ambling, with one-of-a-kind shops, galleries, and restaurants along Talbot Street and open-air seafood restaurants and inns snuggling its harbor. It's also home to the esteemed **Chesapeake Bay Maritime Museum** (✉ *213 N. Talbot St.* ☎ *410/745–2916* ⊕ *www. cbmm.org*), a working 18-acre shipyard with generational shipbuilders, hands-on activities, and the 1879 Hooper Strait Lighthouse. Be sure to get on the water at some point; *Selina II* (✉ *101 N. Harbor Rd.* ☎ *410/726–9400* ⊕ *www.sailselina.*

com), a luxury sailing yacht, and **Patriot Cruises** (☎ *410/745–3100* ⊕ *www.patriotcruises.com*), with its narrated river cruises, are two possibilities.

Eat & Drink: The Chesapeake's bounty is served boiled, steamed, and grilled at **St. Michaels Crab & Steak House** (✉ *305 Mulberry St.* ☎ *410/745–3737* ⊕ *www. stmichaelscrabhouse.com*), in the historic harbor area. For something fancier but still local, try **Stars Restaurant** (✉ *308 Watkins La.* ☎ *443/258–2228* ⊕ *www. innatperrycabin.com*) within the Inn at Perry Cabin on the town's western edge.

Stay: St. Michaels has tons of options for upscale B&Bs and inns. The **Victoriana Inn** (✉ *205 Cherry St.* ☎ *410/443–9555* ⊕ *www.victorianainn.com*) overlooks the harbor; the **Parsonage Inn** (✉ *210 N. Talbot St.* ☎ *410/745–8383* ⊕ *www.parsonage-inn.com*), in a splendid Victorian, dates from 1883; and the **Inn at Perry Cabin** (✉ *308 Watkins La.* ☎ *410/745–2200* ⊕ *www.innatperrycabin.com*) is an elegant splurge.

Breakfast: The **Blue Crab** (✉ *102 S. Fremont St.* ☎ *410/745–4155* ⊕ *www. bluecrabcoffee.com*) serves delicious omelets, egg tostadas, apple fritters, and espresso drinks.

Day 5: St. Michaels, MD, to Baltimore, MD

160 miles (3 hours, 30 minutes without traffic or stops)

Take country roads east to Preston and north to Denton, along the Harriet Tubman Underground Railroad Byway (for those interested in exploring the byway further, a self-guided driving tour can be downloaded online). Then head north to I–95 via Route 404 and Route 213. From there, it's a straight shot back to Baltimore via I–95, which gives you time to explore one of America's most underrated cities.

The lively city of Baltimore even has its own Washington Monument.

ALONG THE WAY

Attraction: Hop on the Harriet Tubman Underground Railroad Byway between Preston and Denton, which showcases a total of 36 Tubman-related sites, including **Linchester Mill** (✉ 3390 Linchester Rd. ☎ 410/673–7929 ⊕ www.preston-maryland.us), a re-created 19th-century village in Preston offering a glimpse into life during Tubman's times; the restored, hand-hewn **James H. Webb Cabin** (✉ Grove Rd. ⊕ harriettubmanbyway.org/webb-cabin) in Preston, representing typical housing for most free African Americans in the 1800s; and **Tuckahoe Neck Friends Meeting House** (✉ 24820 Meeting House Rd. ⊕ www.carolinehistory.org) in Denton, one of five Quaker meeting houses whose members maintained a local Underground Railroad network.

Eat & Drink: Shore Gourmet (✉ 512 Franklin St. ☎ 410/479–2452 ⊕ www.caroline-culinaryarts.org) in Denton, housed in a century-old schoolhouse, is a fun place to stop for a healthy, fresh bite with ingredients form local farmers and producers.

Photo Op: Colonial buildings pack the historic village of Chestertown, with spectacular sunsets fanning out over its picture-perfect harbor.

Town: The graceful Chesapeake City Bridge offers a soaring view over the genteel village of Chesapeake City, a working canal town packed with restaurants and shops occupying 19th-century buildings.

Roadside Attraction: Duck decoys are an art form throughout the Chesapeake region, with the little town of Havre de Grace as the centerpiece. Decoy carvers have whittled away here for decades, a legacy celebrated at the **Havre de Grace Decoy Museum** (✉ 215 Giles St. ☎ 410/939–3739 ⊕ www.decoymuseum.com).

BALTIMORE

Do: In this thriving harborside metropolis, you'll find world-class museums, booming art scenes, historical sites, and excellent restaurants and bars. The free **Walters Art Museum** (✉ 600 N. Charles St. ☎ 410/547–9000 ⊕ www.thewalters.

org), the **Baltimore Museum of Art** (✉ 10 Art Museum Dr. ☎ 443/573–1700 ⊕ www.artbma.org), and the **American Visionary Art Museum** (✉ 800 Key Hwy. ☎ 410/244–1900 ⊕ www.avam.org) are gems for art lovers while the **National Aquarium** (✉ 501 E. Pratt St. ☎ 410/576–3800 ⊕ www.aqua.org) is considered one of the country's best. **Fort McHenry** (✉ 2400 E. Fort Ave. ☎ 410/962–4290 ⊕ www.nps.gov/fomc) commemorates Francis Scott Key's writing of the "Star-Spangled Banner." Or you can simply take in the waterfront scenes of historic Fell's Point and the Inner Harbor, both hopping with restaurants, shops, and galleries.

Eat & Drink: Peter's Inn in Fell's Point (✉ 504 S. Ann St. ☎ 410/675–7313 ⊕ www.petersinn.com), once a gritty biker bar, serves classy farm-to-market fare in a cozy space. For true Chesapeake flavor, try **Duda's Tavern** (✉ 1600 Thames St. ☎ 410/276–9719 ⊕ www.dudastavernfellspoint.com) in Fell's Point; **Faidley's Seafood** (✉ 119 N. Paca St. ☎ 410/727–4898 ⊕ www.faidleyscrabcakes.com) in the historic Lexington Market, famed for its jumbo lump crab cakes; or beachy **Nick's Fish House** (✉ 2600 Insulator Dr. ☎ 410/347–4123 ⊕ www.nicksfishhouse.com), with wooden decks overlooking the water.

Stay: Luxurious **Sagamore Pendry** (✉ 1715 Thames St. ☎ 443/552–1400 ⊕ www.pendry.com) in Fell's Point occupies the city's vintage Recreation Pier. The **Ivy Hotel** (✉ 205 E. Biddle St. ☎ 410/514–6500 ⊕ www.theivybaltimore.com) is another sumptuous option, in a historic mansion in the Mount Vernon neighborhood. The landmark **Lord Baltimore Hotel** (✉ 20 W. Baltimore St. ☎ 410/539–8400 ⊕ www.lordbaltimorehotel.com), built downtown in 1928, has an old world–style lobby.

Breakfast: Blue Moon Café (✉ 1621 Aliceanna St. ☎ 410/522–3940 ⊕ www.bluemoonbaltimore.com) in Fell's Point is bright and funky with hearty dishes like scrapple-and-egg sandwiches and crab-and-bacon Benedicts.

The Best of New York State

Written by Mark Sullivan

You'll be surprised how quickly the skyscrapers and apartment towers of Manhattan can give way to the countryside once you head upstate. Within a couple of hours you'll be traversing rolling hills and majestic stands of evergreen trees.

After leaving New York City, this trip takes you through some of the favored vacation destinations for city residents and out-of-towners alike. The Hudson Valley, the Catskills, the Adirondacks, and the Finger Lakes draw those who want to experience a slower pace of life and the state's spectacular scenery. There are plenty of alternate routes to choose, many taking you past waterfalls or through beautifully restored covered bridges.

At a Glance

Start: New York City, NY

End: New York City, NY

Miles Traveled: 1,162 miles

Suggested Duration: 9 days

States Visited: New York, Pennsylvania

Key Sights: Central Park; Finger Lakes wineries; Franklin D. Roosevelt National Historic Site; Niagara Falls; Storm King Arts Center

Best Time to Go: New York City shines no matter what season you visit. Unless you're in search of winter sports, Upstate New York is definitely more of a warm-weather destination. With so many outdoor activities, this itinerary is ideal to follow from late spring to fall.

The Best of New York State

Day 1: New York City, NY, to New Paltz, NY

92 miles (2 hours without traffic or stops)

Day one takes you north of the city into the heart of the Hudson Valley, heading up the scenic Palisades Parkway to the town of New Paltz.

ALONG THE WAY

Attraction: Perched on a picturesque spot overlooking the Hudson River, the **U.S. Military Academy at West Point** (✉ *2107 New S. Post Rd.* ☎ *845/938–2638* ⊕ *www.westpoint.edu*)—more commonly known as just West Point—is a short detour off U.S. 9W along Route 218. Stop by for a tour of the West Point Museum in one of the handsome stone buildings that make up the complex.

Fort Putnam, a key strategic point in the Revolutionary War, has been carefully restored.

Attraction: Spread out over 500 acres of fields and forests, **Storm King Arts Center** (✉ *1 Museum Rd., New Windsor* ☎ *845/534–3115* ⊕ *stormking.org*) is an impressive array of dozens of large-scale sculptures created by some of the best artists in the world, including David Smith, Alexander Calder, and Isamu Noguchi. A free shuttle takes you past the sculptures or you can walk through the grounds and find the perfect spot for a picnic lunch (and an art selfie).

Eat & Drink: Dating back to 1839 and claiming to be America's oldest winery, the stone buildings of **Brotherhood Winery** (✉ *100 Brotherhood Plaza Dr.* ☎ *845/496–3661* ⊕ *www.brotherhood-winery.com*) are a short drive west from Storm King in Washingtonville. After dining on country-style French fare at the restaurant, enjoy a tour and tasting.

NEW PALTZ

Do: The Shawangunk Mountains are the top destination in these parts, and 21,000 acres of this rocky terrain is in **Minnewaska State Park Preserve** (✉ *5281 Rte. 44/55, Kerhonkson* ☎ *845/255–0751* ⊕ *www.parks.ny.gov*). The jewel here is Lake Minnewaska itself, easily reachable from the Lake Minnewaska Visitor Center off Route 44.

Eat & Drink: It's no surprise that a university town like New Paltz would have such a diverse dining scene. One of the best eateries is **Ciao Bella** (✉ *5 Main St.* ☎ *845/256–9447* ⊕ *www.ciaobellanewpaltz.com*), a sophisticated northern Italian trattoria on Main Street.

Stay: Nothing can prepare you for the jumble of towers, turrets, and chimneys that make **Mohonk Mountain House** (✉ *1000 Mountain Rest Rd.* ☎ *845/795–3286* ⊕ *www.mohonk.com*) such an awe-inspiring sight. Even better is its location on a rocky outcropping over a crystal-blue mountain lake. To get here from New Paltz, take Mountain Rest Road west.

Breakfast: On Main Street, **Mudd Puddle** (✉ *Walter St. Market, 10 Main St.* ☎ *845/255–3436* ⊕ *www.muddpuddlecoffee.com*) is where locals congregate in the morning for coffee and conversation. The pastries are great, too.

Day 2: New Paltz, NY, to Hyde Park, NY

25 miles (47 minutes without traffic and stops)

Today take the Mid-Hudson Bridge to the eastern side of the Hudson Valley, exploring some of the region's most popular stops along the way. The day's final destination is Hyde Park, which was a relaxing retreat for the very presidential Roosevelt family. Both Theodore and Franklin spent time here, and Franklin's wife, Eleanor, turned it into a hub for her political organizing.

ALONG THE WAY

Town: The riverside community of Poughkeepsie is home to **Vassar College** (✉ *124 Raymond Ave.* ☎ *845/437–7000* ⊕ *www.vassar.edu*), founded in 1865 as a women's college. The 1,000-acre campus is well worth a stroll, especially if you duck into the striking Frances Lehman Loeb Art Center, designed by world-famous architect César Pelli.

Eat & Drink: On Poughkeepsie's Main Street, **Brasserie 292** (✉ *292 Main St.* ☎ *845/473–0292* ⊕ *www.brasserie292.com*) is a classic bistro down to its pressed-copper ceilings and red-leather banquettes.

Photo Op: The world's longest elevated pedestrian bridge, the 1¼-mile **Walkway Over the Hudson** (✉ *61 Parker Ave.* ☎ *845/834–2867* ⊕ *www.walkway.org*) runs from Highland in the west to Poughkeepsie in the east. It has some of the best views of New York's famous river.

HYDE PARK

Do: As it runs through Hyde Park, Route 9 becomes Albany Post Road. The thoroughfare is quite picturesque, lined with Dutch-colonial-style buildings made of golden fieldstone. Your first stop along the road should be the **Franklin D. Roosevelt National Historic Site** (✉ *4097 Albany Post Rd.* ☎ *845/229–5320* ⊕ *www.fdrlibrary.org*), the birthplace of the 32nd president. It's also home to his presidential library, the first such library to be constructed and designed by the president it honors. The only National Historic Site dedicated to a first lady, the **Eleanor Roosevelt National Historic Site** (✉ *54 Valkill Park Rd.* ☎ *845/229–9422* ⊕ *www.nps.gov/elro*) is at Val-Kill Cottage, the home she maintained about two miles from the family home. While the Roosevelt homes were family places, the **Vanderbilt Mansion** (✉ *119 Vanderbilt Park Rd.* ☎ *845/229–7770* ⊕ *www.nps.gov/vama*) was made for aristocratic living. It's considered one of the architectural treasures of the Northeast and can be explored by visitors today.

Eat & Drink: Just off Albany Post Road, the **Culinary Institute of America** (✉ *1946 Campus Dr.* ☎ *845/452–9600* ⊕ *www.ciachef.edu*) has an eye-popping location in a former Jesuit monastery. The most respected culinary school on the East Coast, it has five student-run restaurants. The best might be Bocuse, which serves classic French fare.

Stay: Across from the entrance to the Vanderbilt Mansion on Albany Post Road, the **Journey Inn** (✉ *1 Sherwood Pl.* ☎ *845/229–8972* ⊕ *www.journeyinn.com*) is a lovely B&B filled with treasures from the owner's travels. The lovely Vanderbilt Suite has two rooms done up in shades of ivory and gold.

Breakfast: On the grounds of the Culinary Institute of America, the **Apple Pie Bakery Café** (✉ *1946 Campus Dr.* ☎ *845/905-4500* ⊕ *www.applepiebakerycafe.com*) has soaring arched windows letting in lots of sunlight. The sweet and savory dishes are standouts.

Day 3: Hyde Park, NY, to Woodstock, NY

35 miles (55 minutes without traffic or stops)

Head north on Route 9G, crossing the Hudson once again on your way to the hippie (and, more and more these days, hipster) Catskills hangout of Woodstock.

ALONG THE WAY

Town: Often topping the list of the country's most charming small towns, Rhinebeck is bisected by Route 9, which is called Mill Street as it passes by the area's beautifully preserved century-old homes. Just outside town is **Wilderstein** (✉ *330 Morton Rd.* ☎ *845/876-4818* ⊕ *www.wilderstein.org*), a dazzling display of Victorian exuberance with a five-story-tall turret. Rhinebeck shines on summer weekends when there are air shows at the **Old Rhinebeck Aerodrome** (✉ *9 Norton Rd., Red Hook* ☎ *845/752–3200* ⊕ *www.oldrhinebeck.org*), which also offers exhilarating flightseeing rides over the Hudson Valley in restored antique biplanes. For a different vibe, head directly across the river to explore Kingston, a historic city (it was New York State's first capital) with an artistic bent.

Eat & Drink: You can't do better for lunch than **Terrapin** (✉ *6426 Montgomery St.* ☎ *845/876-3330* ⊕ *www.terrapin-restaurant.com*), just off Mill Street in Rhinebeck. Its location in an 1825 church makes it one of the region's most memorable restaurants. Or try **Top Taste** (✉ *446 Hasbrouck Ave.* ☎ *917/915–1310* ⊕ *www.instagram.com/toptastekingston*) in Kingston, a James Beard Award–nominated Jamaican restaurant serving up seriously flavorful pigeon peas with coconut rice, curried goat, and other island delights.

Detour: It's well worth a short detour up Route 9G to Annandale-on-Hudson, which is pretty much synonymous with the 540-acre campus of **Bard College** (✉ *30 Campus Rd.* ☎ *845/758–6822* ⊕ *www.bard.edu*). Its parklike surroundings make it one of the loveliest spots in the Hudson Valley, and the nearby village of Tivoli has a terrific little strip of cool eateries and indie shops.

Nature: One of the region's most rewarding hikes is at **Poet's Walk** (✉ *776 River Rd., Red Hook* ☎ *845/473–4440* ⊕ *www.scenichudson.org*), an easy 2.2-mile trail within a 120-acre park with sweeping views of the Hudson River in the foreground and the Catskill Mountains in the distance.

WOODSTOCK

Do: Although it might have a countercultural reputation thanks to a certain music festival, the town of Woodstock is actually pretty mellow. The Catskills Mountains community is perfect for an afternoon of window shopping, and you can't do better than duck into its boutiques, bookshops, and art galleries or stop for a cup of coffee at one of its numerous cafés. One standout cultural haven is the **Woodstock Artists Association and Museum** (✉ *28 Tinker St.* ☎ *845/679–2940* ⊕ *www.woodstockart.org*).

Eat & Drink: In a rambling farmhouse on Mill Hill Road, **Cucina** (✉ *109 Mill Hill Rd.* ☎ *845/679–9800* ⊕ *www.cucinawoodstock.com*) serves the area's best Italian fare. An art-filled bungalow with a romantic outdoor deck is home to **Silvia** (✉ *42 Mill Hill Rd.* ☎ *845/679–4242* ⊕ *www.silviawoodstockny.com*), which offers artfully presented modern American fare and inventive craft cocktails.

Stay: "Hippie chic" might be the best way to describe the **Hotel Dylan** (✉ *320 Maverick Rd.* ☎ *846/684–5422* ⊕ *www.thehoteldylan.com*), a boutique hotel with surprisingly sophisticated rooms. It's on Maverick Road, six minutes from downtown.

Breakfast: Longtime favorite **Oriole 9** (✉ *17 Tinker St.* ☎ *845/679–5763* ⊕ *www.oriole9.com*) is the breakfast spot people rave about, especially because most of the produce comes from the owner's organic farm (lunch is tasty, too). Or take a slight detour a bit west of Woodstock to sample the highly rated yet simple breakfasts at the **Phoenician Diner** (✉ *5681 Rte. 28, Phoenicia* ☎ *845/688–9957* ⊕ *www.phoeniciadiner.com*); specialties include corned beef hash and chicken and waffles.

Extend Your Trip

From Saratoga: Retracing the American Revolution *(Ch. 2)*

From Niagara Falls: All the Great Lakes *(Ch. 6)*; A Frank Lloyd Wright Tour *(Ch. 6)*

From New York City: The Best of Long Island and the Jersey Shore *(Ch. 8)*; Coastal New England *(Ch. 8)*

Day 4: Woodstock, NY, to Saratoga Springs, NY

99 miles (2 hours without traffic or stops)

Your destination today is Saratoga Springs, where people have gone to "take the waters" for hundreds of years. You can take I–87 most of the way there, passing into the Adirondack Mountains and their gentle hills and evergreen forests along the way.

ALONG THE WAY

Town: With its more than 100 antiques shops, hipster haven Hudson is the perfect place to pass an hour or two. About four miles south of town on Route 9G is **Olana State Historic Site** (✉ *5720 Rte. 9G* ☎ *518/751–0344* ⊕ *www.olana.org*), a 37-room Moorish-style castle built in the 1870s by Hudson River School artist Frederic Church. Looking like a temple crossed with a railroad station, it's unforgettable. Don't miss the property's sleek glass-walled Frederic Church Center for Art & Landscape.

Eat & Drink: In a fickle community that's always looking for the next big thing, Hudson's **Swoon Kitchenbar** (✉ *340 Warren St.* ☎ *518/822–8938* ⊕ *www.swoonkitchenbar.com*) has stood the test of time. It's farm-to-table fare that stands up to the hype.

Town: The tiny village of Kinderhook has two outsized attractions. On Old Post Road is the **Martin Van Buren National Historic Site** (✉ *1013 Old Post Rd.* ☎ *518/764–1041* ⊕ *www.nps.gov. mava*), a Federal-style mansion owned by the country's eighth president. And of the best surviving examples of 18th-century Dutch-colonial style is the handsome **Luykas Van Alen House** (✉ *2589 Rte. 9H* ☎ *518/758–9265* ⊕ *www.cchsny.org*).

SARATOGA SPRINGS

Do: On the National Register of Historic Places, 2,200-acre **Saratoga Spa State Park** (✉ *19 Roosevelt Dr.* ☎ *518/584– 2535* ⊕ *www.parks.ny.gov*) is a year-round draw, with walking trails in warmer weather and cross-country skiing in winter. This is also where you'll find the Roosevelt Baths and Spa. On the grounds of Saratoga Raceway, the **Saratoga Harness Racing Museum and Hall of Fame** (✉ *342 Jefferson St.* ☎ *518/587–4210*) is a celebration of the region's Thoroughbred horse racing tradition. Yaddo is a highly regarded artists' colony, and it's a treat to wander through the formal gardens.

Eat & Drink: In an intimate storefront on Phila Street, **Bocage Champagne Bar** (✉ *10 Phila St.* ☎ *518/450–1115* ⊕ *www.bocage-champagnebar.com*) offers an impressive selection of fine French bubbly and still wines along with caviar, tinned fish, and cheese and charcuterie plates. If you're looking for a more substantial meal, your best choice is the elegant **15 Church** (✉ *15 Church St.* ☎ *518/587–1515* ⊕ *www.15churchrestaurant.com*).

Stay: For a taste of what visitors a century ago experienced when they came to Saratoga Springs for a relaxing retreat, book a stay at the **Gideon Putnam Resort and Spa** (✉ *24 Gideon Putnam Rd.* ☎ *866/890–1171* ⊕ *www.gideonputnam.com*). It has a perfect spot inside the borders of Saratoga Spa State Park.

Breakfast: It bills itself as a bakery, but **Mrs. London's** (✉ *464 Broadway* ☎ *518/581–8100* ⊕ *www.mrslondonbakery.com*) is also the perfect spot for a cup of coffee and an oven-fresh pastry.

Day 5: Saratoga Springs, NY, to Lake Placid, NY

125 miles (2 hours, 40 minutes without traffic or stops)

It's a pretty simple route—I-87 to Route 9N to Route 73—that leads directly to Lake Placid, a wintertime destination that might just be even more beautiful in the summer. Veer off onto Route 9N to take in beautiful Lake George and Lake Champlain along the way.

ALONG THE WAY

Photo Op: New York's Route 9N runs alongside the western shores of Lake George and Lake Champlain, making it one of the most scenic drives in the region.

Eat & Drink: On Main Street in the lakeside community of Bolton Landing, family-run **Cate's Italian Garden** (✉ *4952 Lake Shore Dr.* ☎ *518/644–2041* ⊕ *www.catesitaliangarden.com*) offers a wide range of classic dishes.

Attraction: Originally named Fort Carillon, this structure built by the French in 1755 was captured by the British in 1759 and renamed **Fort Ticonderoga** (✉ *102 Fort Ti Rd.* ☎ *518/585–2821* ⊕ *www. fortticonderoga.org*). It fell into the hands of colonists in 1775, but only until the British realized they could put cannons atop nearby Mt. Defiance.

LAKE PLACID

Do: Built for the 1932 Olympic Games, the **Olympic Center** (✉ *2634 Main St.* ☎ *518/523–1655* ⊕ *www.lakeplacidolympiccenter.com*) was home to the "Miracle on Ice," where the American men's ice hockey team took the gold medal away from the seemingly unbeatable Soviets. Feel the thrill of victory with bobsled and luge rides on the competition track.

Eat & Drink: Located within the Mirror Lake Inn, **The View** (✉ *77 Mirror Lake Dr.* ☎ *518/302–3000* ⊕ *www.mirrorlakeinn.com*) lives up to its name with floor-to-ceiling windows overlooking the sparkling waters below and the tallest peaks of the Adirondacks in the distance.

Stay: The region's only waterfront resort, the posh **Lake Placid Lodge** (✉ *144 Lodge Way* ☎ *518/523–2700* ⊕ *www.lakeplacidlodge.com*) makes the most of its location with stunning views from almost everywhere, including your room. Expect extras like crackling fireplaces and hand-hewn furnishings.

Breakfast: Fluffy flapjacks topped with locally made maple syrups are the specialty at the **Farmhouse Café** (✉ *2726 Main St.* ☎ *518/523–3139*) on Main Street.

Day 6: Lake Placid, NY, to Alexandria Bay, NY

132 miles (2 hours, 45 minutes without traffic and stops)

Due west from Lake Placid, mostly along Route 3 and Route 26, is Alexandria Bay. This stretch of shoreline along the St. Lawrence River is known for its "castles" built by wealthy New Yorkers as weekend retreats.

ALONG THE WAY

Eat & Drink: A great place to refuel is the **Pine Grove** (✉ *166 Main St.* ☎ *518/359–3669*), where comfort foods take pride of place in the menu. It's on Main Street in Tupper Lake.

Roadside Attraction: In Tupper Lake, the **Wild Center** (✉ *45 Museum Dr.* ☎ *518/359–7800* ⊕ *www.wildcenter.org*) lets you stroll above the treetops on a series of wooden walkways.

ALEXANDRIA BAY

Do: The Thousand Islands region, which spans the U.S.-Canadian border, has attracted wealthy vacationers for more than a century. George C. Boldt, proprietor of the Waldorf Astoria hotel in New York, began building the 120-room **Boldt Castle** (✉ *1 Heart Island* ☎ *315/482–9724* ⊕ *www.boldtcastle.com*) in 1900. It remained unfinished for more than 70 years, when it was finally completed in spectacular fashion. Modest in comparison is the 28-room **Singer Castle** (✉ *1136 Rte. 6* ☎ *315/324–3275* ⊕ *www.singercastle.com*), built in 1905 as a summer home for Frederick C. Bourne, president of Singer Co. Ltd. of sewing machines fame. Take a boat tour to either castle from Alexandria Bay.

Eat & Drink: There are plenty of convivial waterfront eateries in the area, with **Riley's by the River** (✉ *48 James St.* ☎ *315/482–7777* ⊕ *www.rileysbytheriver.com*) standing out for its eclectic pub fare and St. Lawrence Seaway views.

Stay: Just 10 miles southwest of Alexandria Bay in Clayton, the **1000 Islands Harbor Hotel** (✉ *200 Riverside Dr.* ☎ *315/686–1100* ⊕ *www.1000islandsharborhotel.com*) sits right on the edge of the St. Lawrence River and has lovely views from its guest rooms.

Breakfast: Locals rave about the quiches at **Coffee Pot Cathy's** (✉ *3 James St.* ☎ *315/482–0818*), a favorite in Alexandria Bay.

Day 7: Alexandria Bay, NY, to Geneva, NY

145 miles (2 hours, 20 minutes without traffic or stops)

On day six, you're headed to the Finger Lakes, New York's top wine region. I–81 takes you down to Syracuse, and then I–90 skirts across the northern tips of the long, slender lakes that give the region its name.

ALONG THE WAY

Town: A collegiate city, Syracuse is filled with institutes of higher learning. But the **Erie Canal Museum** (✉ *318 Erie Blvd. E* ☎ *315/471–0593* ⊕ *www.eriecanalmuseum.org*) just feels like fun, with a replica of a canal boat in a handsome 1850s building that once served as a weigh station.

Eat & Drink: Once a darling of the biker crowd, Syracuse's **Dinosaur Bar-B-Que** (✉ *246 W. Willow St.* ☎ *315/476–4937* ⊕ *www.dinosaurbarbque.com*) is now known throughout the state for its barbecued ribs and salt potatoes.

Town: Just before you reach Geneva, you'll pass by the town of Seneca Falls, famous as the location for the first women's rights convention in the United States in 1848, considered the beginning of the suffrage movement. Today you can visit the **Women's Rights National Historical Park** (✉ *136 Fall St.* ☎ *315/568–0024* ⊕ *www.nps.gov/wori*) and the **National Women's Hall of Fame** (✉ *1 Canal St.* ☎ *315/568–8060* ⊕ *www.womenofthehall.org*).

GENEVA

Do: New York's best-known wine region, the Finger Lakes encompasses 11 extremely long, narrow bodies of water created 10,000 years ago when the glaciers receded. There's not really a main town of the Finger Lakes, but Geneva, on the northern tip of Seneca Lake, has a bustling downtown and lots of cultural activities. The main activity, though, is visiting wineries. A longtime favorite is **Fox Run Vineyards** (✉ *670 Rte. 14, Penn Yan* ☎ *315/536–4616* ⊕ *www. foxrunvineyards.com*), on Route 14 south of Geneva. It's housed in a converted Civil War–era dairy barn. On Route 76 near the town of Hammondsport is **Heron Hill Winery** (✉ *9301 Rte. 76* ☎ *607/868–4241* ⊕ *www.heronhill.com*), known for its beautiful views of Keuka Lake. Also on Keuka Lake is **Dr. Konstantin Frank Vinifera Wine Cellars** (✉ *9749 Middle Rd.* ☎ *800/320–0735* ⊕ *www.drfrankwines.com*), founded by a Ukrainian immigrant who is considered the father of viniculture in the region. Be sure to drive responsibly as you visit the wineries, or sign up for a winery tour that does the driving for you.

Eat & Drink: In the town of Dundee, halfway between Geneva and Watkins Glen, is **FLX Wienery** (✉ *5090 Rte. 14* ☎ *607/243–7100* ⊕ *www. flxwienery.com*), where you'll find homemade brats, chorizo, and other types of sausage. Dundee's Glenora Wine Cellars is home to the farm-to-table favorite **Veraisons** (✉ *5435 Rte. 14* ☎ *800/243–5513* ⊕ *www.glenora. com*), which is inspired by produce from local purveyors. In a space that was once a convenience store on Geneva's West Lake Road, **Ports Café** (✉ *4432 W. Lake Rd.* ☎ *315/789–2020* ⊕ *www. portscafe.com*) is now a chic eatery with a globe-trotting menu. On Route 414 in Hector, the beloved **Stonecat Café** (✉ *5315 Rte. 414* ☎ *607/546–5000*) is a wonderful place to stop for dinner or weekend brunch. Ingredients come from local farms like Lively Run Goat Dairy.

Stay: Built in 1889, the massive **Belhurst Castle and Winery** (✉ *4069 W. Lake Rd.* ☎ *315/781–0201* ⊕ *www.bellhurst. com*) is on the National Register of Historic Places. It sits outside the town of Geneva on the northwestern shore of Seneca Lake, providing sweeping views from many of its rooms. An understated elegance imbues **Mirbeau Inn & Spa** (✉ *851 W. Genesee Street Rd.* ☎ *877/647–2328* ⊕ *www.mirbeau. com*), on Genesee Street Rd. in the town of Skaneateles.

Breakfast: In downtown Geneva, the friendly coffeehouse **Grounded** (✉ *68 Castle St.* ☎ *315/325–4063* ⊕ *www. groundedgeneva.com*) serves expertly prepared lattes and hearty chicken and waffles and breakfast burritos.

Niagara Falls is made up of American Falls and Bridal Veil Falls in New York and Horseshoe Falls in Canada.

Day 8: Geneva, NY, to Niagara Falls, NY

121 miles (2 hours without traffic and stops)

Today I–90 will take you to New York's northwest corner, which holds the city of Buffalo and the treasured American icon that is Niagara Falls.

ALONG THE WAY

Attraction: A few miles west of Geneva is **Sonnenberg Mansion and Gardens** (⊠ 250 Gibson St. ☏ 585/394–4922 ⊕ www.sonnenberg.org) in the town of Canandaigua. The 52-acre grounds are a magnificent example of late-Victorian garden design.

Eat & Drink: In downtown Canandaigua, the storefront **Patty's Place** (⊠ 33 N. Main St. ☏ 585/396–9470 ⊕ www.pattysplacediner.com) is an ideal place to fuel up for the morning's drive. The breakfast pizza, piled with sausage, bacon, mozzarella, and cheddar, is a crowd-pleaser.

NIAGARA FALLS

Do: Once you arrive in the city of Buffalo, you're going to want to visit the metro area's most famous feature. Misty mornings are perhaps the best time to visit Niagara Falls—made up of American Falls and Bridal Veil Falls in New York and Horseshoe Falls across the border in Ontario, Canada—but there's not really a bad time to visit. Take it all in from **Niagara Falls State Park** (⊠ 332 Prospect St. ☏ 716/278–1794 ⊕ www.niagarafallsstatepark.com), established in 1885 to protect the public's access to the falls.

Eat & Drink: On Buffalo's Rhode Island Street, the **Left Bank** (⊠ 511 Rhode Island St. ☏ 716/882–3509 ⊕ www.leftbankrestaurant.com) is a dimly lit bistro with a friendly bar and a relaxed back garden. A far-reaching wine list doesn't overlook the best New York vintages at **Wine on Third** (⊠ 501 3rd St. ☏ 716/589–9463 ⊕ www.wineonthird.com), a long, narrow eatery that's not far from the falls, but away from the crowds.

Stay: The classic choice is the **Red Coach Inn** (✉ *2 Buffalo Ave.* ☎ *716/282–1459* ⊕ *www.redcoach.com*), on Buffalo Street in Niagara Falls. Rooms are individually decorated in English country house style.

Breakfast: You'll rub elbows with plenty of locals at **Betty's in Buffalo** (✉ *370 Virginia St.* ☎ *716/362–0633* ⊕ *www.bettysbuffalo.com*), a modern take on the classic diner. Try the Scrambled Mess, which is a pile of fresh vegetables and asiago cheese over eggs, accompanied by home fries.

Day 9: Niagara Falls, NY, to New York City, NY

388 miles (6 hours, 30 minutes without traffic and stops)

The last day of the trip is the most driving-heavy as you head back through the Finger Lakes toward New York City. The long journey is still quite scenic, with its views of New York's farming communities. Depending on if you make stops, you might only have one night in NYC to take in what the city has to offer, so consider expanding your trip. Another option is adding on a night in the southern Finger Lakes region, either in Watkins Glen or Ithaca, to break up the journey.

ALONG THE WAY

Town: Billing itself as "America's Most Fun Small Town," Corning is a southern Finger Lakes town that's home to the unique **Corning Museum of Glass** (✉ *1 Museum Way* ☎ *607/937–5371* ⊕ *www.cmog.org*), the world's largest museum of glass and glass artifacts. Corning's past and present is steeped in glassmaking, which you can see from the many art galleries, boutiques, and studios lining its streets.

Eat & Drink: Carey's Brewhouse (✉ *58 Bridge St.* ☎ *607/377–5651* ⊕ *www.careysbrewhouse.com*) in Corning serves a collection of local and international brews as well as your standard pub grub.

NEW YORK CITY

Do: It's a bit insane to recommend only one day in what is considered by many to be the most exciting city in the world, but it is possible to see the highlights in a day. Don't miss wandering around **Central Park** (☎ *212/310–6600* ⊕ *www.centralparknyc.org*) and a visit to one of the major museums; both the **Metropolitan Museum of Art** (✉ *1000 5th Ave.* ☎ *212/353–7710* ⊕ *www.metmuseum.org*) and the **American Museum of Natural History** (✉ *200 Central Park W* ☎ *212/769–5100* ⊕ *www.amnh.org*) are right next to Central Park, albeit on opposite sides. Afterward, wander south to the Theater District to catch a Broadway show.

Eat & Drink: New Yorkers will never agree on where to get the best slice of pizza in New York City, but luckily you have plenty of options to choose from. Take the subway downtown to the West Village for a pie (no slices) at **John's of Bleecker St.** (✉ *278 Bleecker St.* ☎ *212/243–1680* ⊕ *www.johnsofbleecker.com*) or try a slice at **Patsy's Pizzeria** (✉ *61 W. 74th St.* ☎ *212/579–3000* ⊕ *www.patsyspizzeria.us*) on the Upper West Side near the Museum of Natural History. If you went downtown, end your night with some bar-hopping through the Village; don't miss a cocktail at **Employees Only** (✉ *510 Hudson St.* ☎ *212/242–3021* ⊕ *www.employeesonlynyc.com*). If you decide to stick with uptown, try a cookie at **Levain Bakery** (✉ *351 Amsterdam Ave.* ☎ *917/464–3782* ⊕ *www.levainbakery.com*).

Stay: Midtown is filled with overpriced and teeny-tiny hotels, but the elegant suites at the **Luxury Collection Hotel Manhattan Midtown** (✉ *151 W. 54th St.* ☎ *917/590–5400* ⊕ *www.marriott.com*) are spacious and worth the money. Or head to NoMad to spend the night at the hip **Made Hotel** (✉ *44 W. 29th St.* ☎ *212/213–4429* ⊕ *www.madehotels.com*). The rooftop bar has excellent city views.

Breakfast: The best bagel in the city is another hotly contested disagreement among New Yorkers. Take your pick between **Russ & Daughters** (✉ 179 E. Houston St. ☎ 212/475–4880 ⊕ www.russanddaughters.com) on the Lower East Side or **Tal Bagels** (✉ 357 1st Ave. ☎ 212/387–8100 ⊕ www.instagram.com/talbagels), which has several locations across Manhattan.

The Best of Long Island and the Jersey Shore

Written by Stefanie Waldek

Sure, it's easy to fill a New York City vacation with plenty of activities—after all, it's one of the greatest cities in the world. But if you've already checked most of the boxes on your to-do list there, it's time to consider what else to see in the region. Whether you're an out-of-towner extending your trip or a local looking for a getaway, this itinerary brings you to the best of Long Island and New Jersey, from quintessential summer hot spot the Hamptons and the wineries of the North Fork, to the megaresorts of Atlantic City and Victorian-era Cape May.

At a Glance

Start: New York, NY

End: Jersey City, NJ

Miles Traveled: 600 miles

Suggested Duration: 6 days

States Visited: New Jersey, New York

Key Sights: Atlantic City Boardwalk; Cape May Lighthouse; Montauk Point Lighthouse; Shelter Island; The Stone Pony

Best Time to Go: Beaches abound in this itinerary, so traveling in summer is a no-brainer. That said, summer does mean larger crowds, and hotels often book up far in advance. The shoulder seasons offers great deals, and winters at the beach can be magical in their own right.

Day 1: New York City, NY, to Montauk, NY

120 miles (2 hours, 30 minutes without traffic and stops)

New York City has plenty of spots to pick up rental cars, including at its two major airports, JFK and LaGuardia. As you head east out of the city into Long Island, you'll want to consult your traffic apps. There are multiple highways that traverse Long Island—take whichever one has the least traffic.

ALONG THE WAY

Town: There's a lot to see and do at the far eastern end of Long Island, so try making it all the way to Southampton before stopping. Stretch your legs by strolling through the village (where you can stop at the various boutiques and restaurants), and visit the **Parrish Art Museum** (✉ 279 Montauk Hwy., Water Mill ☎ 631/283–2118 ⊕ www.parrishart.org).

Eat & Drink: In East Hampton, stop for lunch at the **Hampton Chutney Co.** (✉ 107 Newtown La. ☎ 631/267–3131 ⊕ www.hamptonchutney.com), which serves dosas (crepe-like wraps) stuffed with South Indian and American fillings, from masala potatoes to smoked turkey.

Nature: Prefer a more natural stop for a driving break? Take a short hike in Montauk's **Hither Hills State Park** (✉ 164 Old Montauk Hwy. ☎ 631/668–2554 ⊕ www.parks.ny.gov), where you can climb the Walking Dunes, 80-foot-tall sand dunes that "move" through the woods and swallow everything in their path—incredibly slowly, of course.

The Best of
Long Island and
the Jersey Shore

MONTAUK

Do: Montauk is a go-to summer hot spot for well-to-do New Yorkers, with a slightly more laid-back vibe than its glitzier neighbors in the Hamptons. The beach beckons here, but be sure to carve time out from your sunbathing and surfing sessions to visit **Montauk Point Lighthouse** (✉ 2000 Montauk Hwy. ☎ 631/668–2544 ⊕ www.montauklighthouse.com), hike through a former World War II military base at **Camp Hero State Park** (✉ 1898 Montauk Hwy. ☎ 631/668–3781 ⊕ www.parks.ny.gov), and stop for a beer at **Montauk Brewing Co.** (✉ 62 S. Erie Ave. ☎ 631/668–8471 ⊕ www.montaukbrewingco.com).

Eat & Drink: The **Surf Lodge** (✉ 183 Edgemere St. ☎ 631/483–5045 ⊕ www.thesurflodge.com) is the life of the party in Montauk—it's the place to eat, drink, and listen to music from the afternoon until the early hours of the morning.

Stay: As Montauk's popularity has grown, so have its hotel options. You still can't go wrong with the classics: book a stay at Montauk icon **Gurney's** (✉ 290 Old Montauk Hwy. ☎ 631/668–2345 ⊕ www.gurneysresorts.com/montauk), lauded for its spa. But if you want to try a more contemporary option, luxurious **Marram** (✉ 21 Oceanview Terr. ☎ 631/668–2050 ⊕ www.marrammontauk.com) is a great choice.

Breakfast: Start your day with a wholesome breakfast from health café **Naturally Good** (✉ 779 Montauk Hwy. ☎ 631/668–9030 ⊕ www.naturallygoodcafe.com).

Day 2: Montauk, NY, to Greenport, NY

30 miles (1 hour, 30 minutes without traffic and stops)

Backtrack down Route 27 west before turning north on Route 114 as you make your way to the heart of Long Island wine

Extend Your Trip

From Cape May: The East Coast's Best Beaches *(Ch. 2)*

From New York City: The Best of New York *(Ch. 8)*; Coastal New England *(Ch. 8)*

country. Although you can keep heading west on Route 27 and then north on Route 48 to reach Greenport, the more fun route is to take a ferry to spend some time on idyllic Shelter Island. A second ferry on the other side of the island will take you right to Greenport. Both ferries allow cars.

ALONG THE WAY

Detour: If you have time for a detour, make a stop at the **Pollock-Krasner House** (✉ 830 Springs Fireplace Rd., East Hampton ☎ 631/324–4929 ⊕ www.pkhouse.org), the home and studio of famed American artists Jackson Pollock and Lee Krasner. Located in the village of Springs, the farmhouse is by reservation only and about 10 minutes out of your way.

Town: Before you hop on the South Ferry to Shelter Island, explore the village of Sag Harbor. Pick up coffee and a snack at **Grindstone Coffee & Donuts** (✉ 7 Main St. ☎ 631/808–3370 ⊕ www.grindstonedonuts.com), peruse the exhibits at the **Sag Harbor Whaling & Historical Museum** (✉ 200 Main St. ☎ 631/725–0770 ⊕ www.sagharborwhalingmuseum.org), and browse the many antiques shops in town.

Eat & Drink: When you make it over to Shelter Island, stop for lunch at **Salt Waterfront Bar & Grill** (✉ 63 Menantic Rd. ☎ 631/749–5535 ⊕ www.saltshelterisland.com) for fresh catches.

Nature: One of Long Island's best natural gems is the **Mashomack Preserve** (✉ 79

S. Ferry Rd. ☎ *631/749–1001* ⊕ *www.
nature.org*) on Shelter Island, covering
2,039 acres of forests, marshes, and
beaches. Take a quick hike or bring your
binoculars to go birding.

GREENPORT

Do: Use Greenport as your base camp
for touring the wineries and breweries
of the North Fork. Some of the area's
best include **Bedell Cellars** (⊠ *36225
Main Rd., Cutchogue* ☎ *631/734–
7537* ⊕ *www.bedellcellars.com*),
Borghese Vineyard (⊠ *17150 Middle Rd.,
Cutchogue* ☎ *631/734–5111* ⊕ *www.
borghesevineyard.com*), and **Greenport
Harbor Brewery** (⊠ *42155 Main Rd.,
Peconic* ☎ *631/477–1100* ⊕ *www.
greenportbrew.com*). When you've had
your fill, head to the beach for a leisurely
afternoon, kayak at **Orient Beach State
Park** (⊠ *40000 Main Rd.* ☎ *631/323–
2440* ⊕ *www.parks.ny.gov*), or go shopping in town.

Eat & Drink: Claudio's (⊠ *111 Main
St.* ☎ *631/477–0627* ⊕ *www.claudios.
com*) is a Greenport legend, serving
seafood since 1870—the institution has
since branched out to open several other
local eateries and bars, including a pizza
spot.

Stay: Book a stay at the 16-room boutique hotel **The Menhaden** (⊠ *207 Front
St.* ☎ *631/333–2777* ⊕ *www.themenha-
den.com*), which blends modern design
with traditional coastal elegance. Be sure
to have a cocktail at the rooftop bar to
enjoy views of the harbor.

Breakfast: Family-owned diner **Crazy Beans**
(⊠ *2 Front St.* ☎ *631/333–2436* ⊕ *www.
crazybeansrestaurant.com*) opened in the
2010s, but it has plenty of 1950s flair.

Day 3: Greenport, NY, to Asbury Park, NJ

*160 miles (2 hours, 45 minutes without
traffic and stops)*

Again, let the traffic apps pick your route
across Long Island. But as you approach
New York City, take the Cross Island
Parkway over the Throgs Neck Bridge,
then I–95 across the George Washington
Bridge into New Jersey. Eventually, you'll
head south on the Garden State Parkway
and over to one of the hippest towns on
the famed Jersey Shore.

ALONG THE WAY

Roadside Attraction: Fort Totten (⊠ *100
Totten Ave.* ☎ *718/352–4793* ⊕ *www.
nycgovparks.org*) in Queens is home to
an interesting Civil War–era fortress. If
you have the time, take a ranger-guided
tour to learn about the site's history.

Detour: Did you know you can get a taste
of New England–seaside charm right in
New York City? The Bronx's City Island
feels a world apart from the bustle of
Manhattan. Stop by for a seafood lunch
at **City Island Lobster House** (⊠ *691 Bridge
St.* ⊕ *718/885–1459* ⊕ *www.cilolobster-
house.com*) or **Sammy's Fish Box** (⊠ *41
City Island Ave.* ☎ *718/885–0920* ⊕ *www.
sammysfishbox.com*).

Eat & Drink: If you'd prefer to hold out for
lunch, head to **Evan's Restaurant** (⊠ *8 Cliff-
wood Ave. W* ☎ *732/566–9122* ⊕ *www.
evansrestaurant.com*) in Matawan, New
Jersey, a classic family-owned Greek
diner.

ASBURY PARK

Do: Asbury Park has a long and storied
history as a Jersey Shore resort town.
Although it went through some hard
times at the end of the 20th century,
it has since come roaring back as a
hip weekend getaway. It's perhaps
best known for the legendary concert hall **The Stone Pony** (⊠ *913 Ocean*

Ave. ☎ 732/502–0600 ⊕ www.stone-ponyonline.com), where Jersey icons Bruce Springsteen and Jon Bon Jovi both got their start. But at its heart, Asbury Park is a beach getaway, so be sure to spend some time at Asbury Park Beach and its historic boardwalk, now lined with buzzy restaurants and bars.

Eat & Drink: Drop by the **Wonder Bar** (✉ 1213 Ocean Ave. ☎ 732/455–3767 ⊕ www.wonderbarasburypark.com) for Yappy Hour, a dog-friendly happy hour, then stay for dinner and a concert. Or head to the trendy **Barrio Costero** (✉ 610 Bangs Ave. ☎ 732/455–5544 ⊕ www.barriocostero.com) for modern Mexican fare and creative cocktails.

Stay: Boutique hotels abound in Asbury Park. Favorites include the retro-chic **Asbury Hotel** (✉ 210 5th Ave. ☎ 732/774–7100 ⊕ www.theasburyhotel.com) in a former Salvation Army building and the luxurious **Asbury Ocean Club** (✉ 1101 Ocean Ave. ☎ 732/481–0706 ⊕ www.asburyoceanclub.com).

Breakfast: New Jersey is renowned for its diners, and in Asbury Park, **Toast** (✉ 516 Cookman Ave. ☎ 732/776–5900 ⊕ www.toastcitydiner.com) is the go-to for breakfast.

Day 4: Asbury Park, NJ, to Atlantic City, NJ

80 miles (1 hour, 30 minutes without traffic and stops)

Today's route is pretty simple: just continue south on the Garden State Parkway. If you're traveling in the summer, be ready for some serious beach traffic, especially on Saturday (when most of the weekly summer rentals change owners).

ALONG THE WAY

Roadside Attraction: Even if you know nothing about the Jersey Shore, you've probably heard of the eponymous hit MTV show that brought worldwide fame (or maybe infamy) to the region. **The house where the party happened** (✉ 1209 Ocean Terr. ⊕ www.shorestore.com) is still there, Italian flag on the garage and all. (You can even rent it out.) Make a stop in Seaside Heights to snap a photo and take a stroll on the nearby, equally as famous, boardwalk.

Eat & Drink: A gas station chain for lunch? Look, Wawa isn't just any old roadside fuel-up spot—stopping for lunch here is practically a rite of passage on the Jersey Shore. You'll find plenty along today's route, but the **Wawa Barnegat** (✉ 945 W. Bay Ave.) is right off the parkway and just before your Long Beach Island detour. Order a hoagie, make a milkshake, and grab a few snacks for the road.

Detour: Let's be honest—you're not going to Atlantic City for the beach. So if you want an afternoon in the sun, take a quick detour to low-key Long Beach Island, better known as LBI.

Photo Op: If you've made the LBI detour, make a quick stop at **Barnegat Light** (✉ 208 Broadway ☎ 609/494–2016 ⊕ www.state.nj.us) to photograph the picturesque lighthouse.

ATLANTIC CITY

Do: Despite its interesting history (it inspired the board game Monopoly and had quite the role in the Prohibition era), today Atlantic City is known for one thing, and one thing only: gambling. But if hitting the slots is not your thing, you can also roam the boardwalk (which is the oldest and longest in the United States), catch one of the big headliner shows, or go shopping at the **Tanger Outlets** (✉ 2014 Baltic Ave. ☎ 609/344–0095 ⊕ www.tangeroutlet.com).

Eat & Drink: Celebrity chef restaurants go hand in hand with big casinos, but it's the local spots that really showcase AC's charm. **Chef Vola's** (✉ 111 S. Albion Pl. ☎ 609/345–2022 ⊕ www.chefvolas.com) is a traditional BYOB Italian spot, while **Dock's Oyster House** (✉ *2405 Atlantic Ave.* ☎ *609/345–0092* ⊕ *www.docksoysterhouse.com*) offers seafood galore.

Stay: If you're going the casino route, the **Borgata** (✉ *1 Borgata Way* ☎ *609/317–1000* ⊕ *www.theborgata.com*) is one of the city's best, though it is located off the boardwalk. For something totally different, stay at the **Chelsea Inn** (✉ *8 S. Morris Ave.* ☎ *609/345–4700* ⊕ *www.thechelseainn.com*), a Victorian-era B&B established in 1880.

Breakfast: Bagels are a must when in New Jersey. In Atlantic City, grab one for the road from **Hot Bagels and More** (✉ *212 Pacific Ave.* ☎ *609/541–3488* ⊕ *www.hotbagelsandmore.com*).

Day 5: Atlantic City, NJ, to Cape May, NJ

50 miles (1 hour without traffic and stops)

It's back on the parkway again, as you take it all the way down to exit 0 and the end of the Jersey Shore (and to one of the best beach destinations on the East Coast).

ALONG THE WAY

Roadside Attraction: Take the scenic route back to the parkway (drive south along Atlantic Avenue to Margate City) to see **Lucy the Elephant** (✉ *9200 Atlantic Ave.* ⊕ *www.lucytheelephant.org*), a 65-foot-tall landmark built in 1881. According to *The New York Times*, Lucy is "the oldest surviving example of zoomorphic architecture on Earth."

Eat & Drink: Stop for lunch at Ocean City's **Bakeria 1010** (✉ *955 Asbury Ave.* ☎ *609/600–7023* ⊕ *www.bakeria1010ocnj.com*), a pizzeria-bakery combo known for its incredible bread.

Town: It's a fairly short drive today, so right before you reach Cape May, make a pit stop in Wildwood to explore its

famous 38-block-long boardwalk (plus three amusement park piers). The town is also a hub for mid-century architecture, particularly the Doo Wop style. Visit the **Doo Wop Experience Museum** (✉ *4500 Ocean Ave.* ☎ *609/551–2289*) to learn more.

CAPE MAY

Do: Dotted with Victorian mansions and lined with a family-friendly boardwalk, Cape May is the southernmost point on the shore and one of the country's oldest seaside resorts. Go shopping at the Washington Street Mall (a pedestrian-only strip in the center of town), climb the **Cape May Lighthouse** (✉ *215 Light House Ave.* ☎ *609/224–6066* ⊕ *www.capemaymac.org*), or simply hit the beach. At night, take a ghost tour by lantern light—the historic town has quite a few spooky legends.

Eat & Drink: Start with dinner at the harborfront **Lobster House** (✉ *906 Schellengers Landing Rd.* ☎ *609/884–8296* ⊕ *www.thelobsterhouse.com*), then move on to beers at the **Rusty Nail** (✉ *205 Beach Ave.* ☎ *609/884–0017* ⊕ *www.caperesorts.com*). For cocktails, try the Prohibition-style Brown Room at Congress Hall.

Stay: Dive into Cape May's Victorian past at one of the many B&Bs or book a room at historic **Congress Hall** (✉ *200 Congress Pl.* ☎ *888/944–1816* ⊕ *www.caperesorts.com*), originally opened in 1816. For something more contemporary, there's **Lokal** (✉ *5 Stockton Pl.* ☎ *609/536–9157* ⊕ *www.staylokal.com*), a boutique "micro-resort" with eight stylish rooms.

Breakfast: Uncle Bill's Pancake House (✉ *261 Beach Ave.* ☎ *609/884–7199* ⊕ *www.unclebillspancakehouse.com*) is a Cape May institution that satisfies diners with warm, fluffy stacks of pancakes and other breakfast items.

Cape May is filled with grand Victorian mansions.

Day 6: Cape May, NJ, to Jersey City, NJ

154 miles (2 hours, 30 minutes without traffic and stops)

Retrace your steps north on the parkway, then take I–278 into the New York metro area. But before ending your trip, spend your last night in Jersey City, NYC's underrated neighbor across the Hudson. You can still easily take a flight back from JFK or LGA, or the even-closer Newark International Airport.

ALONG THE WAY

Nature: You might've heard of New Jersey's Pine Barrens, a 1.1 million-acre ecosystem that's the reported home of the Jersey Devil. Take a hike through them at **Double Trouble State Park** (⊠ *581 Pinewald Keswick Rd., Bayville* ☎ *732/341–4098* ⊕ *www.state.nj.us*). Jersey Devil sightings not guaranteed.

Eat & Drink: Stop for a quirky diner lunch at **Shut Up and Eat** (⊠ *804 Main St.* ☎ *732/349–4544* ⊕ *www.shutupandeat-tr.com*) in Toms River, where the waitstaff famously don pajamas instead of a uniform.

Town: Get your last fill of New Jersey's boardwalks in Point Pleasant Beach— **Jenkinson's Boardwalk** (⊠ *300 Ocean Ave. N* ☎ *732/892–0600* ⊕ *www.jenkinsons. com*) has an aquarium, rides, an arcade, and minigolf. If you're still hungry, stop for a bite at the original Jersey Mike's Subs while you're here.

JERSEY CITY

Do: Located right across the Hudson River from NYC, Jersey City has long been relegated to bridge-and-tunnel status, but as the most diverse city in all of America, it more than deserves your love. Explore **Liberty State Park** (⊠ *1 Audrey Zapp Dr.* ☎ *201/915–3400* ⊕ *www.nj.gov/dep/parksandforests/parks/libertystatepark. html*) and visit **Liberty Science Center** (⊠ *222 Jersey City Blvd.* ☎ *201/200–1000* ⊕ *www.lsc.org*); you can even take a ferry to Liberty Island and the Statue of Liberty (which any Jersey local will tell you is actually in New Jersey). Or just take a stroll on the 18½-mile Hudson River Waterfront Walkway, which gives you perhaps the best views of New York City you'll find anywhere.

Eat & Drink: You might have heard some choice food critics declare that the best New York pizza is actually in New Jersey. See what the fuss is about at **Razza** (✉ 275 Grove St. ☎ 201/356–9348 ⊕ www.razzanj.com), which serves wood-fired pies that regularly top best-pizza lists. Or head to India Square, home to the highest concentration of Indian Americans in the Western Hemisphere. You have plenty of incredible Indian restaurants to choose from here, but **Rasoi** (✉ 810 Newark Ave. ☎ 201/222–8850 ⊕ www.rasoi123.com) is one of the best. Afterwards, grab a drink at **dullboy** (✉ 364 Grove St. ☎ 201/795–1628 ⊕ www.dullboybar.com), a vaguely literary-themed cocktail bar with some serious speakeasy vibes.

Stay: Spend your last night at the **Canopy by Hilton Jersey City Arts District** (✉ 159 Morgan St. ☎ 201/241–4664 ⊕ www.canopy3.hilton.com), which has smartly designed rooms, free use of bicycles, and a cool restaurant and bar.

Breakfast: Head 10 minutes north to Hoboken (Frank Sinatra's hometown) to grab a Taylor ham-egg-and-cheese bagel sandwich (another Jersey must-eat) at **Bagels on the Hudson** (✉ 802 Washington St. ☎ 201/798–2221 ⊕ www.bagelsonthehudson.com).

The Best of New England

Written by Jen Rose Smith

From high peaks and beach breaks to swimming holes and art museums, this New England adventure loops through the best of the region in eight packed days. Luckily for any traveler, the Northeast offers epic road-tripping on a miniature scale: a few hours behind the wheel can take you from sea level to the highest point in the northeastern United States.

Along the way, duck into picture-postcard towns for clam shacks, craft beer, and maple syrup shots. Take plenty of covered-bridge and lighthouse selfies to shore up your Yankee cred. And it's not all small-town life—in Portland, Providence, and Boston, soak up the history and culture that keep New England a creative hotbed.

At a Glance

Start: Boston, MA

End: Boston, MA

Miles Traveled: 695 miles

Suggested Duration: 8 days

States Visited: Connecticut, Maine, Massachusetts, New Hampshire, Rhode Island, Vermont

Key Sights: The Breakers Mansion; The Freedom Trail; Mark Twain House; Massachusetts Museum of Contemporary Arts; Mt. Washington

Best Time to Go: Razzle-dazzle foliage displays make autumn a spectacular time to travel through this region, and sunny weather can easily stretch through mid-October. But if you want to maximize beach time and swimming hole stops, join the summer crowds that flock to the shore and mountains in July and August.

Day 1: Boston, MA, to Portland, ME

112 miles (1 hour, 45 minutes without traffic and stops)

Hop between two maritime heavyweights on your way from Boston to Portland, pausing to explore historic houses,

The Best of New England

---

waterside seafood joints, and islands with a spine-chilling history.

ALONG THE WAY

Town: In Portsmouth, you can stroll the brick-lined downtown to the edge of the Piscataqua River, where restaurant decks jut out over the bustling waterway. You could spend a morning among the historic houses at the **Strawbery Banke Museum** (⊠ *14 Hancock St.* ☎ *603/433–1100* ⊕ *www.strawberybanke.org*), and this neighborhood is also the starting point for boat trips to the storied Isles of Shoals (a history of piracy, murder, and ghosts suffuses these small islands, long populated by an independent lot who, according to many, hadn't the sense to winter on the mainland).

Photo Op: Pretty in white, red, and black, picture-perfect **Nubble Light** (⊠ *Sohier Park Rd.* ☎ *207/363–1040* ⊕ *www.nubblelight.org*) in York, Maine, is among the most photographed lighthouses in the world.

Nature: Just north of the tony Kennebunks is the 3-mile-long **Goose Rocks Beach** (⊠ *Dyke Rd.* ☎ *207/967–3465* ⊕ *www.kporttrust.org/goose-rocks-beach*), among the prettiest stretches of sand in southern Maine.

Eat & Drink: Just before you arrive in Portland, duck off the road for classic Maine lobster rolls or fried clams at **The Lobster Shack at Two Lights** (⊠ *225 Two Lights Rd.* ☎ *207/799–1677* ⊕ *www.lobstershacktwolights.com*) in Cape Elizabeth. Outdoor picnic tables here have views of the nearby lighthouse.

PORTLAND

Do: Wander the I. M. Pei–designed **Portland Museum of Art** (✉ *7 Congress St.* ☎ *207/775–6148* ⊕ *www.portland-museum.org*), home to many works by Maine artist Winslow Homer, then hop on a schooner for a sunset cruise of Casco Bay. Craft breweries are big here, but there are also chic cocktail bars and ultrabrowsable Old Port boutiques.

Eat & Drink: Seafood gets center stage at **Eventide Oyster Co.** (✉ *86 Middle St.* ☎ *207/774–8538* ⊕ *www.eventideoysterco.com*), where Maine oysters are displayed on a mammoth, ice-field chunk of granite just inside the door. The brown-butter lobster roll, served in a steamed bun, is a New England legend. After dinner, head to the funky basement bar **Maps** (✉ *64 Market St.* ⊕ *www.instagram.com/maps_bar_portland*), which is just a few blocks away.

Stay: Budget hotels are scarce in Portland, and it's worth staying in a central location to enjoy the city at night. Splurge for a room at **The Press Hotel** (✉ *119 Exchange St.* ☎ *207/808–8800* ⊕ *www.thepresshotel.com*), where you'll spend the night in the former home of the *Portland Press Herald* newspaper, with typewriter art on the walls to prove it.

Breakfast: The justifiably famous **Standard Baking Co.** (✉ *75 Commercial St.* ☎ *207/773–2112* ⊕ *www.standardbakingco.com*) is the place to go for buttery morning buns, fluffy scones, and top-quality joe using beans from Portland's Coffee by Design.

Day 2: Portland, ME, to Conway, NH

61 miles (1 hour, 30 minutes without traffic and stops)

Go from Portland's salty air to the heart of New Hampshire's White Mountains,

Extend Your Trip

From Portland: New England Great Outdoors *(Ch. 8)*

From Boston: Retracing the American Revolution *(Ch. 2)*

passing thick forests broken by glassy lakes.

ALONG THE WAY

Town: Stretch your legs while exploring the lakeshore of Casco, Maine's **Sebago Lake State Park** (✉ *11 Park Access Rd.* ☎ *207/693–6231* ⊕ *www.maine.gov*), where you'll find locals fishing from the boat launch, a tangle of hiking trails, and excellent swimming right off the beach.

Eat & Drink: Keep driving past Conway to have lunch at the grand **Omni Mount Washington Resort** (✉ *310 Mt. Washington Hotel Rd.* ☎ *603/278–1000* ⊕ *www.omnihotels.com*) in Bretton Woods, New Hampshire, which has gorgeous sunset views of Mt. Washington. Cocktails on the shady back porch—or scones in the old-fashioned tearoom—will make the 45-minute side trip worth your while.

CONWAY

Do: A base camp for year-round adventures in the White Mountains, Conway leads to steep hiking trails and wild scenery. From here you can drive to the top of Mt. Washington, ride the historic cog railway, or pick one of many nearby trailheads for a long walk through the woods.

Eat & Drink: Irish pub food at **May Kelly's Cottage** (✉ *3002 White Mountain Hwy.* ☎ *603/356–7005* ⊕ *www.maykellys.com*) is ideal as hearty post-trail fare, with live-music sessions on some weekend nights.

Stay: You'll find plenty of creature comforts at the **Red Elephant Inn Bed and Breakfast** (✉ 28 Locust La. ☎ 603/356–3548 ⊕ www.redelephantinn.com), with its eight cozy rooms and friendly hosts. North of Conway at the foot of Mt. Washington, the **Glen House** (✉ 979 Rte. 16 ☎ 603/466–3420 ⊕ theglenhouse. com) offers rustic-chic accommodations in a stylish contemporary lodge with a terrific restaurant.

Breakfast: Upstairs tables at the **Stairway Café** (✉ 2649 White Mountain Hwy. ☎ 603/356–5200 ⊕ www.facebook. com/stairwaycafe) make for prime people-watching in downtown Conway, and all-day breakfasts include fat stacks of pancakes, homemade hash, and venison sausage.

Day 3: Conway, NH, to Woodstock, VT

111 miles (2 hours, 30 minutes without traffic and stops)

Watch the peaks close in as you follow the famously scenic Kancamagus Highway across White Mountain National Forest. Follow the lush Connecticut River Valley right into Vermont to discover Woodstock's picture-perfect, miniature town center.

ALONG THE WAY

Nature: Located near the 7-mile marker on the Kancamagus Highway, **Lower Falls** (✉ Kancamagus Hwy. ☎ 603/536–6100 ⊕ www.fs.usda.gov) is a broad, beautiful swimming hole in the Swift River that's ideal for cooling off on hot days.

Town: Just across the river from Dartmouth College, Norwich was founded in 1765, making this one of Vermont's oldest European communities. It's home to the excellent **Montshire Museum of Science** (✉ 1 Montshire Rd. ☎ 802/649–2200 ⊕ www.montshire.org) and the flagship location of **King Arthur Flour**

(✉ 135 U.S. 5 S ☎ 802/649–3361 ⊕ www. kingarthurflour.com).

Eat & Drink: Contemporary, locally sourced American fare is the draw at casually sophisticated **Elixir** (✉ 188 S. Main St. ☎ 802/281–7009 ⊕ www. elixirrestaurantwrjct.com) in White River Junction, Vermont. Just up the street, **Tuckerbox** (✉ 1 S. Main St. ☎ 802/359–4041 ⊕ www.tuckerboxvermont.com) serves flavorful Turkish food along with specialty teas and coffees.

Photo Op: Just before you get to Woodstock, duck into tiny Quechee to snap a photo of **Simon Pearce** (✉ 1760 Quechee Main St. ☎ 802/295–1470 ⊕ www. simonpearce.com), a glass-blowing studio in a restored woolen mill by the Ottauquechee River. Just downriver is a pretty covered bridge, built after the historic original was shattered by tropical storm Irene.

WOODSTOCK

Do: Wander Woodstock's pretty town center, then meet a dairy herd of Jersey cows at **Billings Farm and Museum** (✉ 69 Old River Rd. ☎ 802/457–2355 ⊕ www. billingsfarm.org). Even if it's not the springtime maple season, it's worth a visit to **Sugarbush Farm** (✉ 591 Sugarbush Farm Rd. ☎ 802/457–1757 ⊕ www.sugarbushfarm.com), where you can sample syrup made from sap collected in the surrounding forest.

Eat & Drink: At casual pub **Worthy Kitchen** (✉ 442 Woodstock Rd. ☎ 802/457–7281 ⊕ www.worthyvermont.com), an immense drinks menu featuring local craft beers is scrawled onto the wall. The hearty plates of fried chicken, burgers, and salads are sourced from Vermont farms.

Stay: Friendly staff and updated rooms elevate the basic, 1960s-style **Sleep Woodstock Motel** (✉ 4324 W. Woodstock Rd. ☎ 802/332–6336 ⊕ www. sleepwoodstock.com), easily the best budget option in a town known for

Riding the cog railway to the top of Mt. Washington rewards you with stunning vistas.

high-end accommodations. Upgrade to the historic **Jackson House Inn** (✉ *43 Senior La.* ☎ *802/457–2065* ⊕ *www. jacksonhouse.com*) for a huge farmhouse breakfast, and ultracomfy rooms in a restored building.

Breakfast: Excellent cappuccinos arrive alongside breakfast burritos, avocado bagels, and maple syrup–drenched pancakes at **Mon Vert Café** (✉ *28 Central St.* ☎ *802/457–7143* ⊕ *www.monvert-cafe.com*), a local hangout in the town center.

Day 4: Woodstock, VT, to North Adams, MA

97 miles (2 hours, 15 minutes without traffic and stops)

Follow scenic Route 100 through a lineup of verdant valleys, then duck into historic Manchester on your way to arty North Adams.

ALONG THE WAY

Town: New Englanders have vacationed in Manchester, Vermont, since before the Civil War, in grand mansions that are now gently faded. Before moving on, visit the **American Museum of Fly Fishing** (✉ *4070 Main St.* ☎ *802/362–3300* ⊕ *www.amff. org*) or check out **Hildene** (✉ *1005 Hildene Rd.* ☎ *802/362–1788* ⊕ *www.hildene. org*), the former home of Robert Todd Lincoln.

Eat & Drink: At **Depot 62 Café** (✉ *515 Depot St.* ☎ *802/366–8181* ⊕ *www.depot62. com*) in Manchester, who can resist a lunch of pizza and Mediterranean food served in the back of a furniture store?

Roadside Attraction: Tucked behind the staid-looking Wilburton Inn in Manchester is the **Museum of the Creative Process** (✉ *Wilburton Dr.* ☎ *802/445–5280* ⊕ *www.museumofthecreative-process.com*), an eccentric museum dedicated to the unconscious, conflict resolution, and the creative process. In practice, that means lots of giant sculptures.

Shop: Bennington Potters (✉ *324 County St.* ☎ *800/205–8033* ⊕ *www.bennnigtonpotters.com*) in—you guessed it—Bennington, Vermont, has been making heavy, glazed stoneware dishes for more than 70 years.

Detour: Drive to **Mt. Greylock** (✉ *30 Rockwell Rd., Lanesborough* ☎ *413/499–4262* ⊕ *www.mass.gov*), the highest point in Massachusetts, adding an extra 18 miles to your day's road time. Up at the top of the mountain, enjoy big views across the Berkshires and pause for a drink at the historic **Bascom Lodge** (✉ *3 Summit Rd.* ☎ *413/743–1591* ⊕ *www. bascomlodge.net*). It's also a great place to stay after visiting North Adams.

NORTH ADAMS

Do: In the heart of the Berkshires, the city of North Adams is a haven for artists and art lovers. Visit the vast **Massachusetts Museum of Contemporary Arts** (✉ *1040 Mass MoCa Way* ☎ *413/662–2111* ⊕ *www.massmoca.org*) to see one of the finest art collections in the Northeast.

Eat & Drink: Seriously nothing-fancy **Jack's Hot Dog Stand** (✉ *12 Eagle St.* ☎ *413/664–9006* ⊕ *www.jackshotdogstand.com*) has the feel of a gritty, small-town classic. (Not actually a stand, it's a hole-in-the-wall restaurant.) For more contemporary tastes, head to **Public Eat + Drink** (✉ *34 Holden St.* ☎ *413/664–4444* ⊕ *www. publiceatanddrink.com*), then check out the microbrews at **Bright Ideas Brewing** (✉ *111 Mass MoCA Way* ☎ *413/346–4460* ⊕ *www.brightideasbrewing.com*).

Stay: Perched on the summit of nearby Mt. Greylock is the Arts and Crafts–style **Bascom Lodge** (✉ *3 Summit Rd.* ☎ *413/743–1591* ⊕ *www. bascomlodge.net*), which has very basic rooms and spectacular views. Right by Mass MoCa is the utterly stylish **Porches Inn** (✉ *231 River St.* ☎ *413/664–0400* ⊕ *www.porches.com*), where

rooms are stocked with vintage finds and art you can buy.

Breakfast: In Mass MoCA itself is **Tunnel City Coffee** (✉ *87 Marshall St.* ☎ *413/398–5304* ⊕ *www.tunnelcitycoffee.com*), with house-roasted beans and a lineup of delicious pastries.

Day 5: North Adams, MA, to Litchfield, CT

76 miles (1 hour, 50 minutes without traffic and stops)

Follow scenic U.S. 7 all the way through the Berkshires, then slip into the green hills of northwestern Connecticut.

ALONG THE WAY

Town: It's easy to see why Norman Rockwell decided to live and paint in the picture-perfect historic town of Stockbridge, Massachusetts. Take a break to stroll the Main Street shops, check out the **Norman Rockwell Museum** (✉ *9 Glendale Rd. [Rte. 183]* ☎ *413/298–4100* ⊕ *www.nrm. org*), or explore the beautiful house-museum **Chesterwood** (✉ *4 Williamsville Rd.* ☎ *413/298–3579* ⊕ *www.chesterwood.org*). Afterward, head to Great Barrington, Massachusetts, where an old church has been converted into the **Guthrie Center** (✉ *2 Van Deusenville Rd.* ☎ *413/528–1955* ⊕ *www. guthriecenter.org*), a shrine to Arlo Guthrie's career that holds regular jam sessions.

Eat & Drink: Rubiner's Cheesemongers and Grocers (✉ *264 Main St.* ☎ *413/528–0488* ⊕ *www.rubiners.com*) in Great Barrington is a cheese lovers' paradise that combines a fantastic cheese shop with a small café specializing in grilled-cheese sandwiches. If you'd rather picnic, grab a cheese wedge to go with a fresh whole-grain loaf from **Berkshire Mountain Bakery** (✉ *367 Park St.* ☎ *413/274–1313* ⊕ *www. berkshiremountainbakery.com*) in Housatonic.

Shop: Antiques are business in the Berkshires, and the section of U.S. 7 from Great Barrington to Sheffield is called "Antiques Alley."

LITCHFIELD

Do: Quiet and upscale Litchfield is one of the country's finest examples of a late-18th-century New England town. Promenade around the gracious Litchfield Green, where you'll find a classic white-steepled church and the **Litchfield Historical Society** (✉ 7 South St. ☎ 860/567–4501 ⊕ www.litchfieldhistoricalsociety.org), which organizes tours of the nearby **Tapping Reeve House** (✉ 82 South St. ☎ 860/567–4501 ⊕ www.litchfieldhistoricalsociety.org).

Eat & Drink: Sip small-batch spirits from **Litchfield Distillery** (✉ 569 Bantam Rd. ☎ 860/361–6503 ⊕ www.litchfielddistillery.com), then head to **West Street Grill** (✉ 43 West St. ☎ 860/567–3885 ⊕ www.weststreetgrill.com) for refined takes on American bistro fare.

Stay: Accommodations are pricey around these parts. The **Litchfield Inn** (✉ 432 Bantam Rd. ☎ 860/567–4503 ⊕ www.litchfieldinnct.com) is a comfortable favorite, with updated rooms and an impressive breakfast spread. If you're ready to splash out and want something with more personality, snag the 780-square-foot treehouse at high-end **Winvian Farm** (✉ 155 Alain White Rd., Morris ☎ 860/567–9600 ⊕ www.winvian.com).

Breakfast: Drive 7 minutes west of town for coffee, pastries, or a breakfast sandwich at **Arethusa a Mano** (✉ 833 Bantam Rd., Bantam ☎ 860/567–5722 ⊕ www.arethusafarm.com), set on beautiful Arethusa Farm.

Day 6: Litchfield, CT, to Providence, RI

104 miles (2 hour, 30 minutes without traffic and stops)

Wind through the quietest corners of Connecticut and past state capital Hartford, then touch down in Rhode Island's creative, gritty, quirky capital.

ALONG THE WAY

Eat & Drink: Just before Hartford, you'll pass through the attractive and historic suburb of West Hartford, which has a bounty of excellent restaurants, including the Spanish tapas eatery **Boqueria** (✉ 46 S. Main St. ☎ 860/222–9922 ⊕ www.boqueriarestaurant.com).

Town: The capital of Connecticut, Hartford is worth a stop to discover the homes of **Harriet Beecher Stowe** (✉ 77 Forest St. ☎ 860/522–9258 ⊕ www.harrietbeecherstowecenter.org) and **Mark Twain** (✉ 385 Farmington Ave. ☎ 860/247–0998 ⊕ www.marktwainhouse.org), which are right next to each other. And art lovers could spend hours in the **Wadsworth Atheneum** (✉ 600 Main St. ☎ 860/278–2670 ⊕ www.thewadsworth.org), the oldest art museum in America.

Shop: The "Quiet Corner" of northeast Connecticut is overflowing with antiques shops. The **Antiques Marketplace** (✉ 109 Main St. ☎ 860/928–0442 ⊕ www.facebook.com/antiquesmarketplace) in Putnam draws the finest goods from hundreds of vendors; nearby **Jeremiah's Antiques Shops** (✉ 26 Front St. ☎ 860/928–0666 ⊕ www.facebook.com/jeremiahsantiques) is another favorite.

PROVIDENCE

Do: As Rhode Island's capital, Providence proves itself as a quirky city with lots of history, good eats, and a strong arts scene. Browse from ancient to contemporary works at the **Rhode Island School of Design Museum of Art** (✉ *20 N. Main St.* ☎ *401/454–6500* ⊕ *www.risdmuseum.org*), then check out the plethora of galleries and shops downtown. Duck into the Greek revival **Providence Athenaeum** (✉ *251 Benefit St.* ☎ *401/421–6970* ⊕ *www.providenceathenaeum.org*) and say hello to the bust of local horror writer H. P. Lovecraft.

Eat & Drink: Among the highly acclaimed restaurants in this outstanding food city, the **Slow Rhode** (✉ *425 W. Fountain St.* ⊕ *www.facebook.com/theslowrhode*) presents a menu of creative modern southern dishes infused with locally sourced ingredients. For a taste of Italian American heritage in Providence, head to tiny **Bonanno Vinicola** (✉ *256 Atwells Ave.* ☎ *401/575–6047* ⊕ *bonannopvd.com*) and eat tinned fish, bruschetta, and charcuterie with fabulous wine pairings. Afterwards, walk through a lingerie shop to enter the speakeasy-style bar **Justine's** (✉ *11 Olneyville Sq.* ☎ *401/454–4440* ⊕ *www.instagram.com/justinesolneyville*).

Stay: In a city that loves design, the most stylish option is **The Dean** (✉ *122 Fountain St.* ☎ *401/455–3326* ⊕ *www.thedeanhotel.com*), which combines a modern aesthetic with vintage furnishings. Meet other budget-minded travelers at **Esperanto Providence Hostel & Guesthouse** (✉ *62 Nolan St.* ☎ *401/216–8807* ⊕ *www.providencehostel.com*), with clean, cozy shared rooms that are a 15-minute walk from downtown.

Breakfast: Enjoy a savory breakfast using whole-grain bread from the famed **Seven Stars Bakery** (✉ *820 Hope St.* ☎ *401/521–2200* ⊕ *www.sevenstarsbakery.com*); they also have a full line of pastries that are among the best in New England.

Essential Listening

The podcast *Crimetown* is a fascinating tale of mob corruption at the height of the bad old days in Providence.

Day 7: Providence, RI, to Newport, RI

33 miles (45 minutes without traffic and stops)

A quick drive to Newport leaves more time for beach lounging, mansion exploring, and taking in the vibe of a town that's all about seaside vacations.

ALONG THE WAY

Shop: Before you leave Providence, duck into **Lovecraft Arts & Sciences** (✉ *65 Weybosset St.* ☎ *401/264–0838* ⊕ *www.weirdprovidence.org*), a shop dedicated to weird fiction, horror, and all things H. P. Lovecraft.

Eat & Drink: There are outlets of **Del's Lemonade** (✉ *6525 Post Rd.* ☎ *401/885–2225* ⊕ *www.facebook.com/delsnorthkingstown*), a frozen-lemonade joint, all around the state, but it just feels right to pick up a frosty, green-and-yellow cup in North Kingstown to enjoy as you roll over the bridge into Newport.

Town: Blink and you'll miss the island of Jamestown, which is located between the mainland and Newport itself. Duck off the main road, though, and you can climb the tower at the **Beavertail Lighthouse Museum** (✉ *Beavertail Rd.* ☎ *401/423–3270* ⊕ *www.beavertaillight.org*), with gorgeous views into Block Island Sound.

NEWPORT

Do: Grand, historic mansions like **The Breakers** (✉ *44 Ochre Point Ave.* ☎ *401/847–6544* ⊕ *www.new-portmansions.org*) are glimpses of the Gilded Age excess that made Newport a prime vacation destination for the rich in the early-20th century; walking the beautiful **Cliff Walk** (✉ *119 Memorial Blvd.* ☎ *401/845–5544* ⊕ *www.cliffwalk.com*) lets you peer into their backyards. Another highlight is the austere and beautiful **Touro Synagogue** (✉ *85 Touro St.* ☎ *401/847–4794* ⊕ *www.tourosyn-agogue.org*), the oldest in the United States. Don't let all that history keep you from the beach, where there's surfing, sunbathing, and a total scene.

Eat & Drink: Chowder at **The Black Pearl** (✉ *30 Bannister's Wharf* ☎ *401/846–5264* ⊕ *www.blackpearlnewport.com*) is something of a Newport tradition, or you can head to **Flo's Clam Shack** (✉ *4 Wave Ave.* ☎ *401/847–8141* ⊕ *www.flosclam-shacks.com*) in nearby Middleton for Rhode Island–style clam cakes. Dessert is an Awful Awful ice-cream shake (that stands for "awful big, awful good") at Middletown's **Newport Creamery** (✉ *208 W. Main Rd.* ☎ *401/846–2767* ⊕ *www.newportcreamery.com*). At night, head down to the waterfront, where you'll find bustling pubs on Bannister's Wharf.

Stay: With a close-to-the-water location and shockingly low prices, the **Seamen's Church Institute** (✉ *18 Market Sq.* ☎ *401/847–4260* ⊕ *www.seamens-newport.org*) is the town's best bargain (they used to cater to passing sailors). Prices skyrocket from there, but if you can afford it, the **Castle Hill Inn** (✉ *590 Ocean Dr.* ☎ *888/466–1355* ⊕ *www.castlehillinn.com*) on Ocean Drive is a waterfront stunner.

Breakfast: An old-school down-home breakfast spot set in a historic downtown storefront, **Franklin Spa** (✉ *229 Spring St.* ☎ *401/847–3540* ⊕ *www.franklin-spari.com*) is a longtime favorite for its raisin-bread French toast, eggs Benedict, and the like.

Day 8: Newport, RI, to Boston, MA

101 miles (2 hours without traffic and stops)

Return to the mainland on your way back to Boston via the historic seaside towns of New Bedford and Plymouth.

ALONG THE WAY

Town: Discover why Herman Melville set his epic novel *Moby-Dick* in New Bedford at the **New Bedford Whaling Museum** (✉ *18 Johnny Cake Hill* ☎ *508/997–0046* ⊕ *www.whalingmuseum.org*), and wander the shops in the restored historic district.

Eat & Drink: Sip maritime-themed ales and lagers on the sunny patio at **Moby Dick Brewing Co.** (✉ *16 S. Water St.* ☎ *774/202–6961* ⊕ *www.mobydick-brewing.com*) in New Bedford while enjoying lunch from a menu of pub favorites. Or make a final seafood fueling stop at laid-back **Wood's Seafood** (✉ *15 Town Wharf* ☎ *508/746–0261* ⊕ *www.woodsseafoods.com*) in Plymouth, which is located right on the town wharf.

Town: Plymouth is where the *Mayflower* passengers finally disembarked, a history on display at the excellent **Plimoth Patuxet Museums** (✉ *137 Warren Ave.* ☎ *508/746–1622* ⊕ *www.plimoth.org*). While some sights in town glorify pilgrim history at the expense of the people who lived here before they arrived, Plimoth Patuxet is all about engaging with both colonial and Wampanoag history.

BOSTON

Do: New England's biggest city has plenty to keep visitors occupied, including a pair of fascinating historic walks. Stroll the 2½-mile **Freedom Trail** (☎ *617/357–8300* ⊕ *www.thefreedomtrail.org*) all the way from Boston Common to Charlestown, then hop the ferry back to downtown. Next, set out on the engaging Black Heritage Trail, a highlight of which is the **Museum of African American History** (✉ 46 Joy St. ☎ 617/725–0022 ⊕ www.maah.org).

Eat & Drink: Eat your way through the Italian American North End, choosing from enormous subs at **Monica's Mercato** (✉ 130 Salem St. ☎ 617/742–4101), brick-oven-baked pies at **Regina Pizzeria** (✉ 11½ Thacher St. ☎ 617/227–0765 ⊕ www.pizzeriaregina.com), or updated seafood classics at **Neptune Oyster** (✉ 63 Salem St. ☎ 617/742–3474 ⊕ www.neptuneoyster.com). For dessert, try the cannoli at two rival bakeries: **Mike's Pastry** (✉ 300 Hanover St. ☎ 617/742–3050 ⊕ www.mikespastry.com) and **Modern Pastry** (✉ 257 Hanover St. ☎ 617/523–3783 ⊕ www.modernpastry.com). Nightlife is wildly varied, with options that range from jazz at **Wally's Café** (✉ 427 Massachusetts Ave. ☎ 617/828–1764 ⊕ www.wallyscafe.com) to the colonial-era **Warren Tavern** (✉ 2 Pleasant St., Charlestown ☎ 617/241–8142 ⊕ www.warrentavern.com).

Stay: Channel salty-sailor energy with a berth on the houseboats or yachts at **Green Turtle Floating Bed & Breakfast** (✉ 1 Pier 8, 13th St., Charlestown ☎ 617/337–0202 ⊕ www.greenturtlebb.com) in the Charlestown Navy Yard. A rock-and-roll vibe at **The Verb** (✉ 1271 Boylston St. ☎ 617/566–4500 ⊕ www.theverbhotel.com) makes the Fenway-area hotel a standout, and there always seems to be a party down by the pool.

Breakfast: Sticky buns, lemon tarts, and brioche from **Flour Bakery** (✉ 131 Clarendon St. ☎ 617/437–7700 ⊕ www.flourbakery.com) are worth the hype. For something heartier, try the cafeteria-style brunch at **The Paramount** (✉ 44 Charles St. ☎ 617/720–1152 ⊕ www.paramount-boston.com) in Beacon Hill, but be prepared to line up for this popular spot.

New England's Great Outdoors

Written by Jen Rose Smith

Pack your hiking boots to experience the wild side of a region where scenic beauty waits around every turn. This nature-seeking, seven-day adventure passes through New England's national parks, mountain peaks, scenic lakes, and river valleys.

In between stops to follow hiking trails and animal tracks, duck into outdoorsy communities dedicated to active adventures. This route begins and ends on the coast, but you'll take in some of America's most captivating mountain ranges, from New Hampshire's White Mountains to the low-lying Taconics of Vermont. Get ready for fresh air and freedom.

At a Glance

Start: Portland, ME

End: Portland, ME

Miles Traveled: 1,000 miles

Suggested Duration: 8 days

States Visited: Maine, New Hampshire, Vermont

Key Sights: Acadia National Park; Ben & Jerry's Factory; Lake Winnipesaukee; Mt. Katahdin; Smuggler's Notch

Best Time to Go: Peak travel destinations hum with crowds and energy in the summer months, when there's ideal weather for swimming in lakes and rivers. But if hiking, scenery, and wildlife-watching are your main goals, consider traveling in the fall. Late September though early October you can view colorful foliage at high elevations and have a good chance for sunny, warm days at sea level.

Day 1: Portland, ME, to Bar Harbor, ME

164 miles (3 hours, 20 minutes without traffic and stops)

Travel scenic U.S. 1 (most locals just call it "Route 1") and take in views across quiet coves, hidden beaches, and patches of deeply shaded evergreen forests. In between, bustling tourist towns serve lobster rolls and a good-timing, vacationland spirit. You'll eventually reach Mount Desert Island, a gorgeous hideaway that's home to the laid-back but sophisticated town of Bar Harbor and Acadia National Park, the only national park in the Northeast.

ALONG THE WAY

Nature: Stroll a curve of sandy beach at **Birch Point Beach State Park** (✉ *459 S. Shore Dr., Owls Head* ☎ *207/941– 4014* ⊕ *www.maine.gov*) to find views of the Mussel Ridge Islands that dot Mussel Ridge Channel in Penobscot Bay.

Town: A fishing town turned artistic hub, Rockland brings together old and new Maine. Find paintings by Maine legend Andrew Wyeth at the **Farnsworth Art Museum** (✉ *16 Museum St.* ☎ *207/596– 6457* ⊕ *www.farnsworthmuseum.org*) or walk the 1-mile Rockland Breakwater to a sturdy brick lighthouse that guides in passing schooners. This is also home to the Audubon Society's **Project Puffin Visitor Center** (✉ *311 Main St.* ☎ *207/596– 5566* ⊕ *seabirdinstitute.audubon.org*), which offers boat tours to see the comeback puffin colony at Eastern Egg Rock.

Eat & Drink: Tiny Rockport is home to the sunlight-filled restaurant **Nina June** (✉ *24 Central St.* ☎ *207/236–8880* ⊕ *www. ninajunerestaurant.com*), where chef Sara Jenkins has won accolades for her boldly flavored Mediterranean fare using local ingredients.

Photo Op: Traditional sailboats called windjammers spend summers tied up in the beautiful Camden harbor, so pause to snap a photo of their wooden masts bobbing in the current.

BAR HARBOR

Do: Hop a free shuttle bus from Bar Harbor into **Acadia National Park** (☎ *207/288–3338* ⊕ *www.nps.gov/ acad*), where the partially one-way Park Loop Road offers access to a series of scenic viewpoints and hiking trails. This 47,000-acre wonderland of seaside cliffs, forested mountains, and pristine beaches is one of the East Coast's most jaw-droppingly scenic spots. For an easy stroll, follow a path along Jordan Pond; a more challenging trek is the rocky climb up the Beehive, using ladder rungs sunk right into the granite. At low tide, a path leads right from Bar Harbor to Bar Island, but timing is key: the sand spit linking the town and the island is only exposed for a few hours each day.

Eat & Drink: Oversized popovers at **Jordan Pond House** (✉ *2928 Park Loop Rd., Seal Harbor* ☎ *207/276–3781* ⊕ *www.jordan- pondhouse.com*) are a Mount Desert Island tradition, best eaten on the lawn with a generous side of strawberry jam and sweet butter. For dinner, though, a lobster dinner is essential. With picnic tables overlooking the water, **Stewman's Lobster Pound** (✉ *35 West St.* ☎ *207/288– 0346* ⊕ *www.stewmanlobsterpound. com*) serves old-school feasts.

Stay: A rooftop infinity pool sets the chic **West Street Hotel** (✉ *50 West St.* ☎ *207/288–0825* ⊕ *www.thewest- streethotel.com*) apart in a town that leans toward old-fashioned style; the water views over Frenchman's Bay means you can catch a fabulous sunrise without getting dressed. Ten minutes outside Bar Harbor is rustic **Emery's Cottages on the Shore** (✉ *181 Sand Point Rd.* ☎ *207/288–3432* ⊕ *www.emeryscot- tages.com*), where cozy, stand-alone cottages are a short walk from the beach.

New England's
Great Outdoors

Acadia National Park has plenty of hiking options.

Breakfast: Stacks of blueberry pancakes with Maine maple syrup give you a reason to linger at **2 Cats Restaurant** (✉ *130 Cottage St.* ☎ *207/288–2808* ⊕ *www.twocatsbarharbor.com*), but the lobster Benedict is memorable, too.

Day 2: Bar Harbor, ME, to Millinocket, ME

121 miles (2 hours, 15 minutes without traffic and stops)

Leave the coast behind as you head north toward Maine's highest summit: Mt. Katahdin. *Katahdin* means "Greatest Mountain" in the Penobscot language, and anyone who sees the awe-inspiring sight will immediately understand the name.

ALONG THE WAY

Town: Lined in stolid brick and brimming with history, Bangor is a former lumber hub with a slightly haunted, frontier feel. Get in the spirit by taking a ghost-themed walking tour or just stroll by the novelist Stephen King's house—the front gates are decorated, fittingly, with spiders and bats.

Eat & Drink: The homey **Harvest Moon Deli** (✉ *72 Columbia St.* ☎ *207/947–3354* ⊕ *www.harvestmoondeli.com*) is a local favorite for sandwiches and salads. Eat in the small dining room or get a take-out meal you can eat at the nearby Bangor waterfront.

Roadside Attraction: A plaque mounted on Bangor's 31-foot **Paul Bunyan statue** (✉ *519 Main St.* ⊕ *www.bangormaine.gov*) hedges its bets by declaring itself "reputed to be the largest statue of Paul Bunyan in the world." Competition aside, this is a famous Maine landmark that's not to be missed.

MILLINOCKET

Do: Mt. Katahdin is the centerpiece of **Baxter State Park** (✉ *64 Balsam Dr.* ☎ *207/723–9500* ⊕ *www.baxterstatepark.org*), whose Togue Pond Gate entrance is 25 minutes beyond downtown Millinocket. Climbing the mountain itself requires a high level of physical fitness and a full day of hiking, but there's plenty of ways to experience the park if you're only spending a day here. Spot bog plants on the stroll from the Togue Pond Gatehouse to Cranberry Pond or rent a canoe on-site for a paddle around Togue Pond itself. Designated a national monument by President Barack Obama, nearby **Katahdin Woods and Waters** (✉ *Swift Brook Rd. at Rte. 11* ☎ *207/456–6001* ⊕ *www.nps.gov/kaww*) is far less well-known than Baxter. While the facilities are still rustic here, there's a handful of great hiking and biking trails that depart from the monument's Katahdin Loop Road.

Eat & Drink: Rub shoulders with through-hikers at the **Appalachian Trail Cafe** (✉ *210 Penobscot Ave.* ☎ *207/723–6720* ⊕ *www.facebook.com/appalachiantrailcafe*)—hundreds of AT "finishers" have autographed the ceiling here. The big burritos, burgers, and sandwiches are perfect trail-recovery fare.

Stay: A wooden sauna and guest canoes make the **New England Outdoor Center** (✉ *200 Katahdin View Dr.* ☎ *207/723–5438* ⊕ *www.neoc.com*) a great place to relax after a day on the trail (or on the road). Camping, cabins, and lodge accommodations are comfortable and friendly, with hearty, American-style meals available on-site at the River Driver's Restaurant.

Breakfast: Millinocket is a small town that doesn't have too many food options, so Appalachian Trail Cafe is a good bet for breakfast too, with plates weighed down under piles of home fries and scrambled eggs.

Day 3: Millinocket, ME, to Franconia, NH

278 miles (5 hours, 10 minutes without traffic and stops)

The woods turn deeper and darker as you cross the vastness of western Maine before the White Mountain peaks erupt into jagged-rock summits. If you don't mind the extra driving time, an alternative route to the interstate follows quieter U.S. 2 through a series of mill and logging towns past their heyday.

ALONG THE WAY

Town: Augusta, Maine's quiet capital city, lines up on both sides of the Kennebec River, and the British-era **Old Fort Western** (✉ *16 Cony St.* ☎ *207/626–2385* ⊕ *www.oldfortwestern.org*) is preserved right at the edge of the water. Guided tours of the grounds tell stories of the 18th-century French and Indian War, and some spaces are filled with period furniture and artifacts.

Eat & Drink: Just before you reach the New Hampshire border, little Bethel is the place to stop for pub fare and microbrews at the **Sunday River Brewing Company** (✉ *29 Sunday River Rd.* ☎ *207/824–4253* ⊕ *www.sundayriverbrewingcompany.com*). Start with homemade pretzels dunked in beer sauce, then tuck into sandwiches, burgers, or the house-specialty gourmet mac and cheese.

FRANCONIA

Do: Gorge walls climb high above the pathway at **Flume Gorge** (✉ *852 Daniel Webster Hwy.* ☎ *603/745–8391* ⊕ *www.nhstateparks.org*), where kids (and grown-ups) can dart over and around a jumble of boulders. Get a more expansive view of things from the **Cannon Mountain Aerial Tramway** (✉ *260 Tramway Dr.* ☎ *603/823–8800* ⊕ *www.cannonmt.com*) that leads to an observation deck atop the peak. There's a short trail on the summit, or you could hike up via the 3.8-mile Kinsman Ridge Trail and hop the tram back down.

Eat & Drink: A short drive from Franconia is the genteel dining room at **Sugar Hill Inn** (✉ *116 Rte. 117* ☎ *603/823–5621* ⊕ *www.sugarhillinn.com*), where evenings are lit with candles and, if it's cold, a roaring fire. The European-influenced, regional sourced dishes are worth the splurge.

Stay: Rooms at the Sugar Hill Inn are delightful, especially when drifting off after a rich dinner. Or if you're unable to stay for longer than one night (there's a two-night minimum), consider driving 10 minutes west to **Rustic Log Cabins** (✉ *1450 Sugar Hill Rd.* ☎ *603/838–6731* ⊕ *www.rusticlogcabins.com*) in Lisbon, where seven buildings set along Salmon Hole Brook are equipped with kitchens, wood-burning fireplaces, and outdoor fire pits.

Breakfast: Polly's Pancake Parlor (✉ *672 Sugar Hill Rd.* ☎ *603/823–5575* ⊕ *www.pollyspancakeparlor.com*) is famed for—you guessed it—fat stacks of flapjacks. At this James Beard Award–winning joint, they come in oatmeal buttermilk, buckwheat, and whole wheat, add-ins are generous, and each meal comes with a sugar coma–inducing tray of maple syrup, maple spread, and maple sugar.

Day 4: Franconia, NH, to Stowe, VT

74 miles (1 hour, 30 minutes without traffic and stops)

After a gentle dive into the Connecticut River valley, climb back into the rolling terrain of Vermont's Green Mountains. It's all two-lane roads and small towns as you meander across the rural state on the way to a historic resort community.

ALONG THE WAY

Town: Grand old houses with peeling paint hint that St. Johnsbury's glory days are in the past, but you still can explore remnants of the era when St. J was flying high. The remarkable **St. Johnsbury Athenaeum** is an essential stop (✉ *1171 Main St.* ☎ *802/748–8291* ⊕ *www.stjathenaeum.org*); it's a library-cum-art-gallery with canvases by notable Hudson River School artists. Just down the street is the **Fairbanks Museum & Planetarium** (✉ *1302 Main St.* ☎ *802/748–2372* ⊕ *www.fairbanksmuseum.org*), a natural-history museum with such treasures as a mosaics made from beetles, 19th-century dioramas, and plentiful taxidermy.

Eat & Drink: In Vermont, soft-serve ice creams are called creemees, and the finest creemees are made with maple syrup. **Tootsie's Ice Cream** (✉ *5847 Rte. 15* ☎ *802/563–2152*) in Danville is a contender for the most beloved maple creemee around.

Roadside Attraction: The **American Society of Dowsers** (✉ *184 Brainerd St.* ☎ *802/684–3417* ⊕ *www.dowsers. org*)—the folks who use sticks to find water—is based in Danville. Stop by their bookstore to browse titles such as *A Pocket Guide to Spirit Animals* and *Energy Medicine: The Essential Techniques*.

Shop: Continue a few more miles to the **Hastings Store** (✉ *2748 U.S. 2* ☎ *802/684–3398*) in West Danville. It's a classic country store, the kind that sells both candy bars and farm equipment, and it's also the place to bet on next spring's "ice-out." That's when the ice on nearby Joe's Pond finally breaks up—for a dollar a pop, fill out a ticket with the date and time you think it will happen. The proceeds are split between the winner and the teeny town's general fund, so it's for a good cause. (And if you need some pointers before committing, there's a list of past ice-outs at the cash register.)

STOWE

Do: Stop to wander the cute shops in Stowe village, then rent a bike for a leisurely ride along the 5.3-mile Stowe Rec Path. In between river crossings and meadows, it wanders past great refreshment spots, such as **Idletyme Brewing Company** (✉ *1859 Mountain Rd.* ☎ *802/253–4765* ⊕ *www.idletyme-brewing.com*). To get views of Mt. Mansfield, Vermont's highest peak, take Route 108 until it narrows to a ribbon of road winding between boulders and cliffs. The narrow pass is called Smuggler's Notch, popular with climbers and hikers who follow trails into the surrounding forest.

Eat & Drink: The bartenders at **Doc Pond's** (✉ *294 Mountain Rd.* ☎ *802/760–6066* ⊕ *www.docponds.com*) spin vintage vinyl to a laid-back crew in this gourmet pub, where the patio and fire pit are a favorite hangout on summer evenings. Tucked onto the sprawling property of the Von Trapp family (yes, the very one from *The Sound of Music*), you'll find the **Von Trapp Brewery and Bierhall** (✉ *1333 Luce Hill Rd.* ☎ *802/253–5750* ⊕ *www.vontrappbrewing.com*), a cavernous space with homemade Austrian-style beers, sausages, pretzels, and very respectable burgers.

Stay: A mid-century modern design is mixed with summer camp–inspired flourishes at **Field Guide Lodge** (✉ *433 Mountain Rd.* ☎ *802/253–8088* ⊕ *www.fieldguidestowe.com*), with its outdoor pool and hot tub that are blissful after a day of driving. Mountain bikers will rejoice because the Cady Hill Forest trails pass right through the property's backyard.

Breakfast: Find the best espresso in town at **Black Cap Coffee & Bakery** (✉ *144 Main St.* ☎ *802/253–2123* ⊕ *blackcapvermont.com*) along with smoothies, breakfast sandwiches, and fresh-baked pastries.

Day 5: Stowe, VT, to Burlington, VT

48 miles (1 hour without traffic and stops)

The landscape flattens as you descend into the Champlain Valley. At the end of the last glacial period, this was the bottom of the great, inland Champlain Sea. Perched on the edge of lovely Lake Champlain is the artsy, outdoorsy college town of Burlington, a perfect starting point for getting out on the water.

ALONG THE WAY

Town: Stop for fresh doughnuts and apple cider at **Cold Hollow Cider Mill** (✉ *3600 Waterbury Stowe Rd.* ☎ *802/244–8771* ⊕ *www.coldhollow.com*) in Waterbury on your way to Waterbury Reservoir, where you can rent a canoe for a paddle along the forested shoreline. Watch for loons at dawn and dusk, but keep your distance, as mating pairs are sensitive to disturbance.

Eat & Drink: A stop at the **Ben & Jerry's ice cream factory** (✉ *1281 Waterbury-Stowe Rd.* ☎ *802/337–1201* ⊕ *www.benjerry.com*) in Waterbury is all but obligatory. Grab a cone, snap a selfie with the original ice cream van, and don't forget to visit the Flavor Graveyard, where headstones honor dearly departed ice-cream varieties.

Detour: A quick jaunt south takes you to genteel Shelburne, where the grand Vanderbilt-Webb estate is now open to the public as **Shelburne Farms** (✉ *1611 Harbor Rd.* ☎ *802/985–8686* ⊕ *www.shelburnefarms.org*). A 2-mile stroll takes you from the visitor center past grazing sheep and cows to the lakefront. Next, visit the eclectic Shelburne Museum to find everything from fine art to a full-size paddle-wheel boat on the rambling, indoor-outdoor grounds.

BURLINGTON

Do: Browse the shops and galleries along pedestrian-only Church Street, then head down to the Burlington Waterfront for views of the Adirondack Mountains across the water. From there, a bike path extends along the shoreline—the 10.9-mile trail continues north through neighborhoods and forests, then continues for four miles on a narrow causeway raised up above the water that's part of the Island Line Rail Trail. On summer weekends, you can go even farther, as a tiny bicycle ferry links the causeway with the island of South Hero.

Eat & Drink: A tempting array of creative, locally sourced dishes at **Hen of the Wood** (✉ 55 Cherry St. ☎ 802/540–0534 ⊕ www.henofthewood.com) make this a favorite place for special dinners—the inventive cocktails are also a highlight of dining here. Or stroll south past City Hall Park to **Pizzeria Verità** (✉ 156 St. Paul St. ☎ 802/489–5644 ⊕ www.pizzeriaverita.com), whose blistered, Neapolitan pies are best followed by a bitter, Italian digestif from the restaurant's extensive amaro menu. Craft beverages are huge in Burlington, too, so end your night with a visit to **Citizen Cider** (✉ 316 Pine St. ☎ 802/497–1987 ⊕ www.citizencider.com) to sample their crisp hard ciders (several of which are hard to find in stores).

Stay: Walking distance from the waterfront and downtown landmarks, **Hotel Vermont** (✉ 41 Cherry St. ☎ 802/651–0080 ⊕ www.hotelvt.com) has a great location and a fresh take on all things Vermont. Simple yet stylish rooms are stocked with locally made wool blankets and Vermont art, and the downstairs Juniper Bar carries every single Vermont-made spirit.

Breakfast: Friendly and with a sidewalk patio, **Cafe Saint Paul** (✉ 196 St. Paul St. ☎ 802/239–1774 ⊕ www.cafesaintpaulvt.com) is known for its hearty breakfasts both sweet and savory. If the

buttermilk pancakes don't hit the spot, the avocado toast surely will. Or you can grab a bagel sandwich at popular **Myer's Wood Fires** (✉ 408 Shelburne Rd. ☎ 802/863–5013 ⊕ www.myersbagels.com), which bakes dense and chewy Montreal-style bagels.

Day 6: Burlington, VT, to Manchester, VT

100 miles (2 hours, 20 minutes without traffic and stops)

Wind between orchards and low mountains in one of Vermont's most scenic and uncrowded regions, as you make your way to a historic town that's been a fresh-air escape for hikers, anglers, and artists since the Civil War.

ALONG THE WAY

Eat & Drink: In little Vergennes, **lu•lu ice cream** (✉ 185 Main St. ☎ 802/777–3933 ⊕ www.luluvt.com) dishes out delightful scoops of "farm-to-spoon" ice cream, with a rotating lineup of flavors that range from classic cookies-and-cream to vegan dragonfruit sorbet. If you're arriving later in the day, **Bar Antidote** (✉ 35 Green St. ☎ 802/877–2555 ⊕ www.barantidote.com) has pub food with appealing vegetarian options and beers provided by on-site Hired Hand Brewing Co.

Town: A rambling spread of carefully tended farmland, **Shoreham's** valley-floor location is prime for growing. Sample the goods at **Champlain Orchards** (✉ 3597 Rte. 74 ☎ 802/897–2777 ⊕ www.champlainorchards.com), whose farm store has apples by the peck, apple pies, apple cider, cider syrup, and well, you get the idea. The orchard's more than 140 varieties of apples go from Japanese Akane to the Minnesota-bred Zestar!, with opportunities to pick your own during harvest season.

MANCHESTER

Do: The Battenkill River has long drawn anglers to this community, where there's fine—if challenging—trout fishing up and down the valley. It's also, a little surprisingly, a major hub for fishing gear; tour the Orvis rod factory and you'll get an up close look at a process that's both high-tech and artistic. Just next door is the small but fascinating **American Museum of Fly Fishing** (✉ 4070 Main St. ☎ 802/362–3300 ⊕ www.amff.org). There's also an Orvis fly-fishing school if you want to give it a try. Or you can try out one of the many hikes through the surrounding forest. The 2-mile walk to **Lye Brook Falls** is a favorite, or you can take the steep, 5.8-mile round-trip trek to the summit of **Equinox Mountain,** the highest peak in the Taconic mountain range (you can also drive to the top of this dramatic summit).

Eat & Drink: Drop by Vermont's first Burmese restaurant, **Moonwink** (✉ 4479 Main St. ☎ 802/768–8671 ⊕ www.facebook.com/moonwinkvt), with dishes including green-mango salad, curries, and noodles swimming in rich, fishy broths. If you can snag a reservation and you're in the mood for something special, the six-table **Silver Fork** (✉ 48 West Rd. ☎ 802/768–8444 ⊕ www.the-silverforkvt.com) is a delight for nuanced but unfussy food with Caribbean and European influences.

Stay: The old-fashioned and welcoming **Wilburton Inn** (✉ 257 Wilburton Dr. ☎ 802/362–2500 ⊕ www.wilburton-inn.com) is perched on a hilltop spot with excellent views. Rooms are comfortable, if a little dated, and there's an outdoor pool for lolling about in the afternoon sunshine. The on-site Museum of the Creative Process is scattered across the lawn, with odd, towering statues and musings from the émigré intellectual who founded the family-owned inn.

Breakfast: With a cute coffee-pot sign to mark the spot, homey café **Up for Breakfast** (✉ 4935 Main St. ☎ 802/362–4204) is the place to pile on eggs, home fries, and French toast before hitting the road.

Day 7: Manchester, VT, to Meredith, NH

132 miles (2 hours, 50 minutes without traffic and stops)

Head once more across the Green Mountains, then drive north along the Connecticut River back into New Hampshire via scenic Route 104. The road takes you to the state's central Lakes Region, where the largest, Lake Winnipesaukee, has 180 miles of coastline.

ALONG THE WAY

Photo Op: Small town Cornish, New Hampshire, is best known for its covered bridges and for having been the home of the late reclusive author J. D. Salinger. Don't miss a postcard-worthy photo of the Cornish-Windsor Bridge, the 460-foot bridge that connects New Hampshire to Vermont across the Connecticut River. Erected in 1866, it is the longest covered wooden bridge in the United States.

Eat & Drink: Home to Dartmouth College, Hanover has one of the more eclectic restaurant scenes in the area. Stop for lunch at **Murphy's on the Green** (✉ 11 S. Main St. ☎ 603/643–4075 ⊕ www.murphysonthegreen.com), a popular pub with walls lined with shelves of old books. The varied menu features everything from burgers and salads to pad Thai and house-smoked tofu street tacos.

MEREDITH

Do: For many years a workaday mill town with relatively little tourism appeal, Meredith has become a popular summer getaway thanks largely to the transformation in recent years of several historic downtown buildings into Mill Falls, now a cluster of hotels, restaurants, and shops overlooking Lake Winnipesaukee. Your time here will be all about exploring Lake Winnipesaukee, so at **Ekal Activities Center** (⊠ *285 Daniel Webster Hwy.* ☎ *603/677–8646* ⊕ *www.millfalls. com*), rent stand-up paddleboards, kayaks, canoes, Aqua-Cycles, and bicycles.

Eat & Drink: Just up the road in Center Harbor, the boathouse-inspired bistro **Canoe** (⊠ *232 Whittier Hwy.* ☎ *603/253–4762* ⊕ *www.canoecenterhabor.com*) sits high above Lake Winnipesaukee. It's known for seafood, including wood-fired, bacon-wrapped scallops and a creamy, entrée-size haddock chowder topped with herbs and crushed Ritz crackers.

Stay: Choose from four lodgings at **Mill Falls at the Lake** (⊠ *281 Daniel Webster Hwy.* ☎ *844/745–2931* ⊕ *www.millfalls. com*): relaxing Church Landing and Bay Point are both on the shore of Lake Winnipesaukee while the convivial Inn at Mill Falls—with a pool—and Chase House are across the street, next to a 19th-century mill that houses shops and restaurants.

Breakfast: With big windows overlooking the lake and timber posts and ceiling beams, **Lakehouse Grille** (⊠ *Church Landing at Mill Falls at the Lake* ☎ *603/279–5221* ⊕ *www.millfalls.com*) captures the rusticity of an old-fashioned camp dining room. Feast on classic American favorites with interesting twists, such as eggs Benedict topped with Maine lobster.

Day 8: Meredith, NH, to Portland, ME

82 miles (2 hours without traffic and stops)

On your last day, travel along the northern reaches of the Lakes Region into a low-key but still lovely part of Maine that takes you to its biggest city.

ALONG THE WAY

Town: With Squam Lake to the west, Lake Winnipesaukee to the south, and the Sandwich Mountains to the north, Center Sandwich offers one of the prettiest environments in the Lakes Region. At Moultonborough's 200-acre **Loon Center** (⊠ *183 Lees Mill Rd.* ☎ *603/476–5666* ⊕ *www.loon. org*), you can learn about the progress made in helping restore the state's loon population; vantage points on the Loon Nest Trail overlook the spot resident loons sometimes occupy in late spring and summer. If you're visiting in the fall, a hike up nearby Red Hill is a must. The 2,030-foot mountain really does turn red in autumn. At the top of the moderately steep 1.7-mile Fire Tower Trail, you can climb a fire tower for 360-degree views of Lake Winnipesaukee and Squam Lake, as well as the White Mountains beyond.

Eat & Drink: In a converted barn adorned with paintings by local artists, rustic **Corner House Inn** (⊠ *22 Main St.* ☎ *603/284–6219* ⊕ *www.nhcornerhouse.com*) is in an 1840s building in Center Sandwich village, serving classic American fare.

PORTLAND

Do: When the weather's good, everyone in Portland heads outside, whether for boating on the water, lounging on a beach, or walking and biking the promenades. Of the city's two promenades, the Eastern Promenade, often overlooked by tourists, has by far the best view. Gracious Victorian homes, many now converted to condos and apartments, border one side of the street. On the other is 68 acres of hillside parkland that includes Fort Allen Park and, at the base of the hill, the Eastern Prom Trail and tiny East End Beach and boat launch.

Eat & Drink: Small, hip **Duck Fat** (⊠ *43 Middle St.* ☎ *207/774–8080* ⊕ *www. duckfat.com*) is always packed, even in midafternoon. The focus here is everyday farm-to-table fare: the signature Belgian fries are made with Maine potatoes cooked, yes, in duck fat and served in paper cones, and the milkshakes are legendary. Afterward, find your way into no-fuss, basement speakeasy **Lincolns** (✉ *36 Market St. ⊕ www.facebook.com/ lincolnsportlandmaine*) where all drinks cost only $5 (here's your only hint on finding the location: enter through the red doors at 36 Market St. and head downstairs).

Stay: In the beautifully restored Mellen E. Bolster House, **The Francis** (✉ *747 Congress St. ☎ 207/772–7485 ⊕ www. thefrancismaine.com*) is a boutique hotel with a mid-century modern vibe that seamlessly compliments the building's immaculately preserved historical design elements.

Breakfast: Don't pass up a chance to try the sweet and savory, all-natural, Maine potato-based doughnuts at **Holy Donut** (✉ *194 Park Ave. ☎ 207/874– 7774 ⊕ www.theholydonut.com*). Standards are glazed in flavors such as dark chocolate–sea salt, maple, pomegranate, triple berry, and chai, or stuffed with delicious fillings like bacon and cheddar, or ricotta. There are always new inventions, too, such as salted chocolate caramel and Key lime pie.

The New England Coast

Written by Jen Rose Smith

Soak up salt air and sea views on a coast-hugging route through New England's finest beach towns. Wandering between clam shacks and surf breaks, you'll hit peak vacation mode in classic Yankee style, with plenty of time to stretch out on your own patch of sand.

In between beach stops, soak up the region's fascinating culture at museums and historic sites, then catch postcard-worthy sunsets while perched at dockside cafés. This nine-day route goes from blue-blood New England to

an LGBTQIA+ nightlife mecca, then on to the home stretch of the south-facing coast, finding seafaring communities where harpooneers once strolled the cobblestones and schooners ruled the waves.

At a Glance

Start: Portland, ME

End: New York City, NY

Miles Traveled: 561 miles

Suggested Duration: 8 days

States Visited: Connecticut, Maine, Massachusetts, New Hampshire, New York, Rhode Island

Key Sights: Cape Cod National Seashore; Coney Island; Mystic Seaport Museum; Salem Witch Trials Memorial; Yale University

Best Time to Go: Vacationing crowds energize the peak summer months of July and August, when joining the throng is all part of the fun. But just keep in mind that means there will be crowds (and traffic) and often lodging in these areas books up far in advance (and many rentals only rent in one-week increments). Plan your trip for June or September to balance warm weather with lower prices and uncrowded beaches. And if you prefer ocean views under moody autumn skies, an October trip is perfect for blustery seaside strolls.

Day 1: Portland, ME, to Kennebunkport, ME

29 miles (40 minutes without traffic and stops)

A short day between Portland and Kennebunkport leaves plenty of time for exploring Maine's coastal havens, which range from nautical kitsch to preppy chic.

The New England Coast

ALONG THE WAY

Photo Op: If you think Maine's oldest lighthouse looks familiar, it's because Cape Elizabeth's **Portland Head Light** (✉ *12 Captain Strout Circle* ☎ *207/799–2661* ⊕ *www.portlandheadlight.com*) stars on calendars and postcards in every souvenir shop. Snap that essential photo from nearby rocks, then take the time to stroll around surrounding Fort Williams Park, which includes disused gun batteries built between 1896 and 1906.

Town: A seven-mile beach fronts the summer town of Old Orchard Beach, but it's the classic pier and boardwalk that make it an essential detour. Give in to the neighboring amusement park and you could while away the day here.

Eat & Drink: Take quiet Route 9 from Old Orchard Beach to Kennebunkport, and you'll hit tiny Cape Porpoise just before arriving. There overlooking the sea-fishing nets and buoys is **Casa Seventy Seven** (✉ *77 Pier Rd.* ☎ *207/987–2001* ⊕ *www. seventyseven.casa*). The beachy menu's lobster rolls and steamed mussels earn raves from locals.

KENNEBUNKPORT

Do: The Kennebunks—especially Kennebunkport—provide the complete Maine Coast experience: white-clapboard houses, rocky shorelines, sandy beaches, quaint downtowns, lobster boat–packed harbors, and seafood restaurants of every type. Browse the tony souvenir shops flanking Dock Square, then continue along Ocean Avenue, which parallels the Kennebunk River. From June through September, **First Chance Whale Watch** (✉ *4 Western Ave.* ☎ *207/967–5507* ⊕ *www. firstchancewhalewatch.com*) shuttles visitors to summer feeding grounds that attract finbacks, humpbacks, minkes, and the occasional blue whale.

Eat & Drink: Sunset drinks and seafood on the dock at **Arundel Wharf** (✉ *43 Ocean Ave.* ☎ *207/967–3444* ⊕ *www.the-arundel-wharf.com*) are a Kennebunkport

Extend Your Trip

From New York City: Best of Long Island and the Jersey Shore *(Ch. 8)*; Best of New York State *(Ch. 8)*

tradition; you'll get a front-row seat for watching boats nose along the Kennebunkport River. Follow it up with sweet treats at **Rococo Artisan Ice Cream** (✉ *8 Western Ave.* ☎ *207/835–1049* ⊕ *www. rococoicecream.com*), specializing in quirky flavors including goat cheese–blackberry and spicy rocky road.

Stay: Well-appointed glamping tents at **Sandy Pines Campground** (✉ *277 Mills Rd.* ☎ *207/967–2483* ⊕ *sandypines-camping.com*) are full of breezy style, and family-friendly amenities include a playground and saltwater pool (there are regular tent sites, RV sites, and cottages too). And while it's a bit time-worn, the budget-friendly **Seaside Inn** (✉ *80 Beach Ave.* ☎ *207/967–4461* ⊕ *www.kennebunkbeachmaine.com*) has an unbeatable location on Gooch's Beach, reached via a private, sandy path.

Breakfast: Walking distance from Dock Square, **Mornings in Paris** (✉ *21 Western Ave.* ☎ *207/204–0032* ⊕ *www.morningsinparis.com*) is ideal for picking up a fresh-baked chocolate croissant or melty croque monsieur sandwich before hitting the road.

Day 2: Kennebunkport, ME, to Hampton, NH

41 miles (50 minutes without traffic and stops)

Cross the Piscataqua River on your way to New Hampshire's pint-sized seacoast, where you'll find a lineup of clam shacks, arcades, and partiers flanking the state's only big sandy beach.

ALONG THE WAY

Town: Just past the historic merchant town of Portsmouth is tiny Rye, New Hampshire, where the **Seacoast Science Center** (✉ 570 Ocean Blvd. ☎ 603/436–8043 ⊕ www.seacoastsciencecenter.org) has aquariums and kid-pleasing touch tanks. Stretch your legs exploring the surrounding Odiorne Point State Park, a patchwork of salt marshes, rocky shores, and green space.

Eat & Drink: Old-timey lunch wagon **Gilley's Diner** (✉ 175 Fleet St. ☎ 603/431–6343 ⊕ www.gilleysdiner.com), in Portsmouth, New Hampshire, offers nostalgia, steamed hot dogs, and unpretentious fast food in a converted 1940s trolley car.

HAMPTON BEACH

Do: Much of the fun in Hampton is just soaking up the sun-and-sand crowd along the sandy-beach waterfront, where gaggles stroll between fried-dough stands and open-air bars. Pinball and Skee-Ball enthusiasts should make a pilgrimage to **Funarama** (✉ 169 Ocean Blvd. ☎ 603/926–2381 ⊕ www.hamptonbeachcasinoh.com) and **Playland Arcade** (✉ 211 Ocean Blvd. ☎ 603/926–3831 ⊕ www.hamptonbeach.org), located 500 feet apart on Ocean Boulevard.

Eat & Drink: Enormous slabs of fried dough the length of your arm, usually topped with cinnamon sugar or powdered sugar, are a meal unto themselves and a Hampton Beach tradition—there are shops everywhere, but **Blink's Fry Doe** (✉ 191 Ocean Blvd. ☎ 603/926–8933 ⊕ www.facebook.com/blinksfrydoe) is a perennial favorite. Or join the all-day crowds on the decks at **Sea Ketch Restaurant** (✉ 127 Ocean Blvd. ☎ 603/926–0324 ⊕ www.seaketch.com), a favorite for hurricane-glass drinks and sunset views.

Nature: It's not just cruising and cocktails in Hampton Beach. Just north of town

is the wonderful Hampton Salt Marsh Conservation Area, an estuary with very fine bird-watching opportunities.

Stay: A little removed from the noise along the strip, **Atlantic Breeze Suites** (✉ 429 Ocean Blvd. ☎ 603/967–4781 ⊕ www.atlanticbreezesuites.com) outshines the rather shabby alternatives in the more crowded core. All rooms have kitchenettes, and many have balconies that overlook the ocean or salt marsh.

Breakfast: Sip coffee under a fleet of model airplanes in the **Airfield Cafe** (✉ 9A Lafayette Rd. ☎ 603/964–1654 ⊕ www.theairfieldcafe.com), a North Hampton diner located at the edge of Hampton Airfield. Even better, snag an outdoor picnic table and enjoy house-specialty crab cake Benedict with views of the small planes coming in for a landing.

Day 3: Hampton, NH, to Gloucester, MA

33 miles (1 hour without traffic and stops)

Go from the wild beach-party scene to a working harbor town as you follow a gently curving coast toward the rocky outline of Cape Ann.

ALONG THE WAY

Eat & Drink: Among Massachusetts fried-clam aficionados, the **Clam Box of Ipswich** (✉ 246 High St. ☎ 978/356–9707 ⊕ www.clamboxipswich.com) earns some of the region's highest marks. Pay more for the "native clams," which are whole-bellied alternatives to the more processed strips.

Town: Quiet today, Essex, Massachusetts, was once a 17th-century ship-building powerhouse, a history that's on display at the small **Essex Shipbuilding Museum** (✉ 66 Main St. ☎ 978/768–7541 ⊕ www.essexshipbuilding.

org). After that, stretch your legs on the 4-mile-long **Crane Beach** (✉ Ipswich ⊕ www.thetrustees.org), flanked by pristine dunes and a maritime pitch-pine forest. This pretty spot is one of the world's most important nesting places for piping plovers.

Detour: A 10-minute drive beyond Gloucester is pretty Rockport, an artists' colony overflowing with souvenir shops and art galleries. Don't miss snapping a photo of the bright-red replica fishing shack called Motif No. 1; once you see the rebuilt 1840 landmark, you'll find it everywhere, from paintings to calendars to postcards.

GLOUCESTER

Do: While Cape Cod gets all the fame, Massachusetts's northern beaches are quite pretty, and Gloucester comes with a particularly interesting maritime history. Browse a tangle of working fishing boats in the harbor on your way to the **Maritime Gloucester** (✉ 23 Harbor Loop ☎ 978/281–0470 ⊕ www.maritimegloucester.org), a museum and aquarium where you'll see wooden boats being restored and displays on the town's seafaring past.

Eat & Drink: Octopus salad and Portuguese soup at the beloved **Azorean Restaurant & Bar** (✉ 133 Washington St. ☎ 978/283–5500 ⊕ www.azorean-restaurant.com) are reminders that many Gloucester fishermen have Portuguese roots by way of the Azores. For great burgers and corner-bar energy, **Stone's Pub and Eatery** (✉ 242 Main St. ☎ 978/515–7366 ⊕ www.stonespubandeatery.com) is a friendly option with a long list of beers on tap.

Stay: Basic rooms overlooking Smith's Cove are the draw at **Rocky Neck Accommodations** (✉ 43 Rocky Neck Ave. ☎ 978/381–9848 ⊕ www.rockyneckaccommodations.com), located within the historic Rocky Neck artists' colony. Each has access to a private or rooftop deck, and there are a handful of restaurants and attractions within walking distance.

Breakfast: Grab a seat at the counter of **Two Sisters Coffee Shop** (✉ 27 Washington St. ☎ 978/281–3378) for hearty breakfasts and homemade bread. Fluffy stacks of French toast are a favorite, or try fish cakes if your appetite for seafood is still going strong.

Day 4: Gloucester, MA, to Hyannis, MA

106 miles (1 hour, 55 minutes without traffic and stops)

Duck into witch-mad Salem on your way to Cape Cod, where the Massachusetts landscape curls into a tendril of historic towns, sandy beaches, and dunes.

ALONG THE WAY

Town: Famed for its history of persecuting so-called witches, Salem eventually turned tragedy into a bit of a sideshow, complete with a boatload of spooky legends and witchy souvenirs; today the town is filled with both kitschy and hip shops selling herbs, crystals, and fortunes (if you're going to get your Tarot cards read anywhere, do it here). The town's **Witch Trials Memorial** (✉ 24 Liberty St. ⊕ www.salemweb.com) is more sober, and located a short distance from the excellent **Peabody Essex Museum** (✉ 161 Essex St. ☎ 978/745–9500 ⊕ www.pem.org), with a fine, permanent exhibit of maritime art. After that, stroll to the 75 open-air murals that make up the **Punto Urban Art Museum** (✉ 91-1 Peabody St. ☎ 978/745–8071 ⊕ www.puntourbanartmuseum.org).

Eat & Drink: Pick up brittle and fudge at **Ye Olde Pepper Companie** (✉ 122 Derby St. ☎ 978/745–2744 ⊕ www.oldepeppercandy.com), which claims to be the oldest candy company in America, or stop by **Far from the Tree** (✉ 108 Jackson St. ☎ 978/224–2904 ⊕ www.

Cape Cod National Seashore is one of the most beautiful places on the New England coast.

farfromthetreecider.com) to sample homemade hard ciders made with local apples. If you're craving something more substantial, you can't beat the blistered-crust, wood-fired pizza pies from **Bambolina** (✉ *288 Derby St.* ☎ *978/594–8709* ⊕ *www.bambolinarestaurant.com*).

HYANNIS

Do: This bustling Cape Cod hub is a longtime base for the Kennedy family, and home to the thoughtfully curated **John F. Kennedy Hyannis Museum** (✉ *397 Main St.* ☎ *508/790–3077* ⊕ *www.jfkhyannismuseum.org*); stop there to take in period photos of the former president and Jackie O. In the evening, join a sunset sailing cruise on the harbor by Bay Spirit Tours, or—if your timing is right—catch a Hyannis Harbor Hawks game at **McKeon Park** (✉ *120 High School Rd.* ⊕ *www.harborhawks.org*). They're part of the Cape Cod Baseball League, where some of the country's most promising college athletes spend summers playing for intimate crowds.

Eat & Drink: The fried cauliflower and gourmet hot dogs are tempting, but the real draw at **Finn's Craft Beer Tap House** (✉ *16 Barnstable Rd.* ☎ *508/534–9756* ⊕ *www.finnscraftbeertaphouse.com*) is the truly impressive lineup of brews from across New England. On warm nights, try snagging a spot on the enclosed patio.

Stay: Meet fellow travelers in the **Hyannis Hostel** (✉ *111 Ocean St.* ☎ *508/775–7990* ⊕ *www.hiusa.org*), which offers a low-key environment, private rooms, and budget-friendly dorms. The hostel only operates from May through September, but the **Cape Cod Harbor House Inn** (✉ *119 Ocean St.* ☎ *508/771–1880* ⊕ *www.harborhouseinn.net*) is open year-round and offers simple but well-maintained rooms directly across the street from the town harbor.

Breakfast: Browse for novels to read at the beach while eating a breakfast sandwich or good old-fashioned peanut butter–and–banana toast at downtown's **Bread + Roses Bookshop and Cafe** (✉ *302 Main St.* ☎ *774/470–5125* ⊕ *www.brcapecod.com*).

Day 5: Hyannis, MA, to Provincetown, MA

48 miles (1 hour without traffic and stops)

Follow the Cape as it wraps back to what locals call "the end of the world"—a picturesque fishing village that's also one of the world's most famous LGBTQIA+ resort destinations, Provincetown. Pause as you make your way there for seaside villages, fresh oysters, and some of the finest beaches in New England.

ALONG THE WAY

Nature: The broad beaches at **Cape Cod National Seashore** (✉ *99 Marconi Site Rd., Wellfleet* ☎ *508/255–3421* ⊕ *www. nps.gov/caco*) seem nearly endless, inviting long walks between the water's edge and crumbling coastal cliffs. Find wild roses blooming in the dunes here, and spot seals, turtles, whales, and the occasional great white shark in the chilly Atlantic water. Start at the **Salt Pond Visitor Center** (✉ *50 Nauset Rd.* ☎ *508/255–3421* ⊕ *www.nps.gov/caco*) in Eastham, where you'll find schedules for ranger-led tours and talks.

Town: The tiny town of **Wellfleet** is famed for delicious oysters and an artsy community. Most shops carry free maps of the community's art galleries, which are mostly clustered in a walkable stretch of Commercial Street.

Eat & Drink: Sample oysters fresh from the sea at Wellfleet **Bookstore & Restaurant** (✉ *50 Kendrick Ave.* ☎ *508/349–3154* ⊕ *www.wellfleetoyster.com*); the family-run spot has its own oyster farm located just across the road. BYOB **Moby Dick's Restaurant** (✉ *3225 U.S. 6* ☎ *508/349–9795* ⊕ *www.mobys. com*) is a favorite in the New England snack-shack tradition, with great clams and chowder served amid fishing-themed flotsam and jetsam.

Roadside Attraction: Find quirky memorabilia at **Wellfleet Flea Market** (✉ *51 U.S. 6* ☎ *508/349-0541* ⊕ *www.wellfleetcinemas.com*), a weekend event that takes over the daytime hours of the Wellfleet Drive-In Theatre. Bring plenty of cash to trade for shell art, old clothes, and treasures unearthed from Cape Cod's many historic homes.

PROVINCETOWN

Do: Wander the galleries and score tickets to a drag show on Commercial Street, where you can soak up the castaway feel of a town that's a long way from anywhere. This is the first place the Pilgrims touched down in North America, an event marked at the **Pilgrim's Monument** (✉ *1 High Pole Hill Rd.* ☎ *508/487–1310* ⊕ *www.pilgrim-monument.org*), which has views across the end of the Cape. There's plenty of wild nature here, too, whether you're on a whale-watching boat tour to Stellwagen Bank or wandering trails that lead from the **Province Lands Visitor Center** (✉ *171 Race Point Rd.* ☎ *508/487–1256* ⊕ *www.nps.gov/caco*) into Cape Cod National Seashore.

Eat & Drink: Nostalgic grilled cheese meets classic takes on seafood at casual spot **The Canteen** (✉ *225 Commercial St.* ☎ *508/487–3800* ⊕ *www.thecanteenptown.com*), but their most popular item is an excellent rendition of fish-and-chips. Built into a former sea captain's home, **Strangers and Saints** (✉ *404 Commercial St.* ☎ *508/487–1449* ⊕ *www. strangersandsaints.com*) has a nautical theme and a menu that melds cuisines from every corner of the Mediterranean.

Stay: Within walking distance of the Commercial Street bars is the friendly (and historic) **Pilgrim House** (✉ *336 Commercial St.* ☎ *508/487–6424* ⊕ *www. pilgrimhouseptown.com*), which boasts Henry David Thoreau as a past guest. If you're up for staying out of town, the **HI Truro Hostel** (✉ *111 N. Pamet Rd., Truro* ☎ *508/349–3889* ⊕ *www.hiusa. org*) is a budget-friendly, seasonal option that's walking distance from a breezy Atlantic-facing beach.

Breakfast: Pick up fried-dough *malassadas* or caramelized egg tarts from **Provincetown Portuguese Bakery** (✉ *299 Commercial St.* ☎ *508/487–1803* ⊕ *www.provincetownportuguesebakery.com*), a particularly sweet part of the Cape's rich Portuguese heritage. The best espresso is from **Kōhi Coffee Company** (✉ *199 Commercial St.* ☎ *774/538–6467* ⊕ *www.kohicoffee.com*), conveniently located a 5-minute walk away.

Day 6: Provincetown, MA, to Narragansett, RI

134 miles (2 hours, 35 minutes without traffic and stops)

Hopscotch across the fractured southern coasts of Massachusetts and Rhode Island to reach a good-time surf town with matchless sunsets.

ALONG THE WAY

Town: Once a whaling capital, New Bedford sent hundreds of sailing ships around the world. Explore that history at the **New Bedford Whaling Museum** (✉ *18 Johnny Cake Hill* ☎ *508/997–0046* ⊕ *www.whalingmuseum.org*), then visit Seamen's Bethel, a church where a salty congregation once heard sermons ringing out from a pulpit shaped like the prow of a ship. Both are part of the **New Bedford Whaling National Historical Park** (✉ *33 William St.* ☎ *508/996–4095* ⊕ *www.nps.gov/nebe*), which curates downloadable, self-guided tours of the historic city.

Eat & Drink: Old-school Italian American favorites are the stars at New Bedford's **Ma Raffa's Italian Restaurant** (✉ *85 Rockdale Ave.* ☎ *508/992–8467* ⊕ *www.maraffas.com*), whose menu features spaghetti and meatballs, subs, thin-crust pizza, and all things red sauce.

Essential Listening

You're not going to make it through the whole book, but taking in the first chapter of the *Moby-Dick* audiobook will get you in the mood for whaling-town lore as you travel through Bedford.

NARRAGANSETT

Do: South-facing beaches attract some of Rhode Island's best surf waves, and Narragansett Town Beach is the place to be on sunny days. Rent a board in the parking lot and paddle into the lineup, or just spread out your towel and enjoy the show. To see a less-crowded side of this jigsaw coast, rent a boat or board from **Narrow River Kayaks** (✉ *94 Middlebridge Rd.* ☎ *401/829–7534* ⊕ *www.narrowriverkayaks.com*) to explore **John H. Chaffee National Wildlife Refuge** (✉ *43 Crest Ave.* ☎ *401/364–9124* ⊕ *www.fws.gov*) via the slow-moving Narrow River.

Eat & Drink: Enjoy panoramic ocean views from the deck at the **Coast Guard House** (✉ *40 Ocean Rd.* ☎ *401/789–0700* ⊕ *www.thecoastguardhouse.com*), a vintage standby for early-evening drinks; feel free to enjoy a can of Narragansett beer, but keep in mind the actual brewery is about 40 minutes north in Pawtucket. The food at Coast Guard House isn't great, so head over to the **Bike Stop Cafe** (✉ *148 Boon St.* ☎ *401/284–1414* ⊕ *www.facebook.com/thebikestopcafe*), a cycling-themed hangout with great pizza and tacos.

Stay: Boutique style in 16 rooms sets the **Break Hotel** (✉ *1208 Ocean Rd.* ☎ *401/363–9800* ⊕ *www.thebreakhotel.com*) apart from the crowd in Narragansett, where accommodations lean generic. A heated, outdoor saltwater pool is flanked by comfy loungers, where you can order from the hotel restaurant menu; breakfast is a lineup of sweet and savory small plates.

Breakfast: If you're skipping hotel fare, stop by **Tommy D's Diner** (✉ 120 Knowlesway Extension ☎ 401/789–1122 ⊕ www.tommydsmenu.com) for a classic American-style breakfast on your way to **Point Judith Lighthouse** (✉ 1470 Ocean Rd. ☎ 401/789–0444 ⊕ www.uscg.mil), where the morning light is ideal for photographs across Block Island Sound.

Day 7: Narragansett, RI, to Mystic, CT

36 miles (50 minutes without traffic and stops)

A short day's drive leaves time to wander sandy beaches, sip champagne cocktails, and step into the world of a 19th-century seafarer.

ALONG THE WAY

Town: The upscale enclave of Watch Hill has one of Rhode Island's finest beaches, **Napatree Point** (✉ Fort Rd. ☎ 401/315–5399 ⊕ www.thewatchhillconservancy.org); it's a curving, sandy spit with frilly dune grass and plenty of shorebirds. If you're traveling with kids in tow, this stop is a must for the 19th-century **Flying Horse Carousel** (✉ 151–153 Bay St. ⊕ www.merrygoroundbeach.com), an easy visit on your way to the **Watch Hill Lighthouse and Museum** (✉ 14 Lighthouse Rd. ⊕ www.watchhilllighthousekeepers.org).

Eat & Drink: Located within the famed Ocean House hotel, the **Secret Garden champagne bar** (✉ 1 Bluff Ave. ☎ 401/584–7000 ⊕ www.oceanhouseri.com) is the place to sip Veuve Clicquot cocktails and nibble an orange marmalade crepe. It's fancy but fun, and open from May through October. You can also find

something more substantial at **Ten Sandwiches** (✉ 98 Bay St. ☎ 401/315–2620 ⊕ www.tensandwiches.com), with its all-organic menu of sandwiches, salads, and espresso.

MYSTIC

Do: Sprawling along the Mystic River, the **Mystic Seaport Museum** (✉ 75 Greenmanville Ave. ☎ 860/572–0711 ⊕ www.mysticseaport.org) recreates life in a 19th-century seaport, complete with ringing blacksmiths' hammers, costumed interpreters, and real historic vessels. It's easy to get caught up in the old-time spirit, even if you're not a seafaring buff. This is the largest maritime museum in the United States, and it's easy to spend a whole day here. Nearby is the excellent **Mystic Aquarium** (✉ 55 Coogan Blvd. ☎ 860/572–5955 ⊕ www.mysticsquarium.org), home to beluga whales, sea lions, and penguins.

Eat & Drink: Yes, the classic 1988 Julia Roberts movie is based on a real-life eatery called **Mystic Pizza** (✉ 56 W. Main St. ☎ 860/536–3700 ⊕ www.mysticpizza.com), where locals and visitors slide into homey booths for pizza and fried pickles. Big, fresh salads and soups from **Mystic Salad Co.** (✉ 12 Cottrell St. ⊕ www.facebook.com/myssaladco) are perfect to-go lunches; find a spot by the nearby Mystic River to watch boat traffic drifting by.

Stay: A series of historic buildings are updated with nautical flair at **The Whaler's Inn** (✉ 20 E. Main St. ☎ 860/536–1506 ⊕ www.whalersinnmystic.com), whose convenient downtown location is ideal for walking to restaurants and bars.

Breakfast: Pick up classic French treats, including sweet and savory croissants, at **Sift Bake Shop** (✉ 5 Water St. ☎ 860/245–0541 ⊕ www.siftbakeshopmystic.com), and snag a sourdough baguette to munch in the car when you hit the road.

Day 8: Mystic, CT, to New York City, NY

134 miles (2 hours, 45 minutes without traffic and stops)

Watch the Connecticut coast rear up into America's most famous city, and where Coney Island is a people-pleasing taste of seaside nostalgia served NYC style.

ALONG THE WAY

Town: Tours of New Haven's **Yale University** (☎ 203/432–4771 ⊕ www.yale.edu) take in several libraries and the campus's gorgeous Gothic architecture. Save time for additional visits to the **Yale University Art Gallery** (✉ 1111 Chapel St. ☎ 203/432–0600 ⊕ artgallery.yale.edu), the **Morris Steinert Collection of Musical Instruments at Yale** (✉ 15 Hillhouse Ave. ☎ 203/432–0822 ⊕ collection.yale.edu), and **Yale Center for British Art** (✉ 1080 Chapel St. ☎ 203/432–2800 ⊕ britishart.yale. edu), each free to the public. Another highlight is the **Peabody Museum of Natural History** (✉ 170 Whitney Ave. ☎ 203/432–8987 ⊕ www.peabody.yale.edu), with a famed collection of dinosaur skeletons.

Eat & Drink: New Haven–style pizza is called "apizza," a pie that's whisper thin and crisped in coal-fired ovens. The two heavyweights for apizza are **Frank Pepe's Pizzeria Napoletana** (✉ 157 Wooster St. ☎ 203/865–5762 ⊕ www.pepespizzeria.com), famed for its white-clam pizza, and **Sally's Apizza** (✉ 237 Wooster St. ☎ 203/624–5271 ⊕ www.sallysapizza. com), a favorite for red-sauce versions; they're located on the same street only a few doors apart—go with whichever has the shorter wait.

NEW YORK CITY

Do: Close out a tour of seaside towns by exploring NYC's own beachy vacation spot: Coney Island. It's not hard to love the bustle of old-fashioned amusement park rides, hot dog stands, and other diversions along a long, sandy beach in Brooklyn. The area's wild history is on display at the **Coney Island Museum** (✉ 1208 Surf Ave. ⊕ www.coneyisland.com), whose starring attraction might be the warped collection of fun-house mirrors.

Eat & Drink: Nathan's Famous (✉ 1310 Surf Ave. ☎ 718/333–2202 ⊕ www.nathansfamous.com) hot dogs are a Coney Island icon, and the original is still humming at the corner of Surf and Stillwell Avenues. Ignore the other menu items and choose from a regular hot dog or chili cheese dog. As you eat, consider the astonishing fact that the record holder of the annual Nathan's Famous International Hot Dog Eating Contest (held each July 4 in Coney Island) downed 76 of these in 10 minutes.

Stay: Cross the Marine Parkway Bridge to spend the night at the **Rockaway Hotel** (✉ 108–10 Rockaway Beach Dr. ☎ 718/474–1216 ⊕ www.therockawayhotel.com), a stylish and modern landmark with great views back across Jamaica Bay.

Breakfast: Visit nearby **Last Stop Gourmet Shop** (✉ 222 Beach 116th St. ☎ 718/945–6450 ⊕ www.laststopgourmet.com) for stick-to-your-ribs diner fare, including hearty lox omelets.

Chapter 9

OUTSIDE THE LOWER 48

Updated by
Anna Weaver

WELCOME TO OUTSIDE THE LOWER 48

TOP REASONS TO GO

★ **Denali National Park:** The most accessible of Alaska's national parks and one of only three connected to the state's highway system, the 6-million-acre wilderness offers spectacular mountain views, a variety of wildlife, striking vegetation, and unforgettable landscapes.

★ **Haleakala National Park:** Some of the best hiking in Maui can be found in this park, along the Road to Hana.

★ **Oahu's North Shore:** As you head to the North Shore of Oahu, stop along the way at fruit stands, shrimp trucks, beaches, world-famous surfing spots, and scenic overlooks.

★ **El Yunque National Forest:** The only U.S. tropical rain forest is laced with hiking trails and full of flowing waterfalls, cool rivers, and beautiful mountain views.

1 **The Best of Alaska.** A road trip from Anchorage to Fairbanks is one of the best ways to see all the remarkable landscapes that Alaska has to offer.

2 **The Road to Hana.** One of the world's most famous drives, Maui's precarious road has more than 600 curves and crosses some 50 gulch-straddling bridges in just 52 coastline miles.

3 **The Best of Oahu.** Make a loop around the scenic coast of Hawaii's most popular island.

4 **The Best of Puerto Rico.** Explore beyond the typical tourist spots with a road trip through the mountains and beaches of Puerto Rico.

Once you leave the continental United States, taking a road trip might be a little more challenging, but it can still be the perfect way to explore Alaska, Hawaii, or any of the country's island territories.

The Best of Alaska

Written by Joey Besl

An Alaska road trip is unlike any other road trip you will take in the United States: no billboards, few gas stations, and just a handful of highways. That means you can worry less about directions—some days you'll only make one turn—and instead focus on the endless epic-ness unfolding outside your windshield.

This seven-day itinerary spotlights the best of Alaska's road system, including national parks, glacier hikes, fishing towns, and mountains in every direction. Time your trip for summer when the sky stays bright around the clock. You'll need those extra hours of daylight to soak in everything Alaska has to offer.

⇨ *Alaska Route 3 is also known as the George Parks Highway and Parks Highway. All three are used interchangeably in this chapter.*

At a Glance

Start: Anchorage, AK

End: Fairbanks, AK

Miles Traveled: 960 miles

Suggested Duration: 7 days

States Visited: Alaska

Key Sights: Alaska Native Heritage Center; Denali National Park; Kenai Fjords National Park; Museum of the North; Turnagain Arm

Best Time to Go: Cold weather makes this trip much more challenging, so you'll want to visit May through July.

Day 1: Anchorage, AK, to Homer, AK

221 miles (4 hours, 15 minutes without traffic and stops)

Pick up a rental car at the Anchorage airport and head south on the Seward Highway (aka Route 1). Your trip starts with one of the best drives in the country along Turnagain Arm and ends high above the coast on the Kenai Peninsula. The road splits about 90 miles south of Anchorage; follow the signs for Homer and the Sterling Highway.

ALONG THE WAY

Detour: Whittier is perhaps the most unique town in an already unique state. A former army base turned cruise port, its residents famously live in the same building (with a post office, market, and school attached so no one has to go outside). If you time it right, it's only an 11-mile, 25-minute drive off the Seward Highway, but this can't be a casual detour: Whittier is only accessed by a one-way tunnel through the mountains that stays open in each direction just 15

The Best of Alaska

0 — 50 miles
0 — 75 km

Map locations: Fairbanks **8**, North Pole, Nenana, Healy, Denali National Park **7**, Cantwell, Igloo City, Denali, Ke'sugi Ken Interpretive Center, Denali Hwy. (closed in winter), Trapper Creek, Talkeetna **6**, Paxson, Tok, Northway, Slana, Chistochina, Gakona, Glennallen, Richardson Hwy., Alaska Hwy., Willow, Hatcher Pass **5**, Hatcher Pass Rd., Glenn Hwy., Wasilla, Palmer, Bodenburg Butte, Eagle River, Copper Center, Wrangell–St. Elias National Park & Preserve, Anchorage **1**, Girdwood, Winner Creek Trail, Hope, Portage, Whittier, Valdez, Cordova, Lake Clark National Park & Preserve, Kenai, Soldotna, Sterling, Seward Hwy., Prince William Sound, Newhalen, Ninilchik, Sterling Hwy., Exit Glacier Nature Center, Seward **3**, Chenega Bay, Iliamna Lake, Anchor Point, Fox Island, Resurrection Bay, Cape St Elias, Homer **2**, Kenai Fjords National Park **4**, Seldovia, Kachemak Bay, KENAI PENINSULA, Gulf of Alaska, ALASKA RANGE, CHUGACH MOUNTAINS, Cook Inlet

minutes of each hour. There's not much to do in town, but the views are unbeatable. Surrounding peaks cradle alpine glaciers, and when the summer weather melts the huge winter snow load, you can catch glimpses of the brilliant blue ice underneath. You can often spot sea otters and harbor seals in the harbor.

Eat & Drink: Located right off the highway, **St. Elias Brewing Company** (⊠ *434 Sharkathmi Ave.* ☎ *907/260–7837* ⊕ *www. steliasbrewingco.com*) in Soldotna serves stone-fired pizzas alongside its menu of soups and salads. Or stock up on meat and cheese at **Lucy's Market** (⊠ *338 Homestead La.* ☎ *907/262–3232* ⊕ *www. lucysalaska.com*) for an upscale picnic on your drive.

Photo Op: Surrounded by wildflowers and overlooking the ocean, the small Russian Orthodox church in Ninilchik is well worth a visit. Take the marked turnoff at milepost 134.8 of the Sterling Highway.

HOMER

Do: Founded in the late 1800s as a gold-prospecting camp, today Homer is an eclectic community with an interesting mix of fishers, actors, artists, and writers. The Homer Spit is a unique landform jutting out into Kachemak Bay that houses many of the town's restaurants and hotels, along with a 360-degree view of the surrounding mountains. Step down to the docks to watch fishermen work and seagulls scavenge.

Eat & Drink: Enjoy some inventive seafood at **Fresh Catch Cafe** (⊠ *4025 Homer Spit Rd.* ☎ *907/756–3486*) then head to the **Salty Dawg Saloon** (⊠ *4380 Homer Spit Rd.* ☎ *907/235–6718* ⊕ *www.saltydawg-saloon.com*), a classic example of the textbook-Alaskan bar: dim, unfussy, dollar bills stapled all over the walls, and a bell at the bar (don't ring it unless you're buying a round for everyone).

Stay: Wake up with the waves (and possibly the whales) at **Land's End** (✉ 4786 Homer Spit Rd. ☎ 907/235–0400 ⊕ www.lands-end-resort.com), perched at the edge of Homer Spit.

Breakfast: Cozy up in the counter line at **Two Sisters Bakery** (✉ 233 E. Bunnell Ave. ☎ 907/235–2280 ⊕ www.two-sistersbakery.net). This popular spot with a wraparound porch and a kid-friendly backyard offers cakes, quiche, vegan muffins, and more.

Day 2: Homer, AK, to Seward, AK

168 miles (3 hours, 30 minutes without traffic and stops)

Take the Sterling Highway (Route 1) north to retrace yesterday's drive. Think of it as another chance to view the distant volcanoes rising over the water. Then turn right on the Seward Highway (Route 9) and head south to the seaside in Seward.

ALONG THE WAY

Eat & Drink: Odie's Deli (✉ 44315 Sterling Hwy. ☎ 907/260–9000 ⊕ www.odiesdeli.com) in Soldotna offers sandwiches, soups, and a generous menu of freshly baked cookies, or you can pick up some pub food at **Kenai River Brewing Co.** (✉ 308 Homestead La. ☎ 907/262–2337 ⊕ www.kenairiverbrewing.com).

Detour: Take the turnoff at mile 56.3 and drive 35 miles to Hope, where the gold rush crowds are long gone but their log cabins remain. Grab a snack at the rust-roofed **Historic Hope Cafe & Campground** (✉ 18416 B Ave. ☎ 907/782–3300 ⊕ www.historichopecafeandcampground.com) and wander the few dusty streets, clamber around the muddy tidal

flats, and relish the relaxed pace in this end-of-the-road town.

SEWARD

Do: Surrounded on all sides by Kenai Fjords National Park, Chugach National Forest, and Resurrection Bay, Seward offers all the quaint realities of a small railroad town with the bonus of some jaw-dropping scenery. Stroll through Waterfront Park and swap stories with the families and camper-van crowds staying the night at the beach. Take a short drive along the coast (and past a gushing waterfall) for a quieter beach walk at Lowell Point.

Eat & Drink: Seward's restaurants cluster all along Fourth Avenue. Both **Chinooks** (✉ 1404 4th Ave. ☎ 907/224–2207 ⊕ www.chinooksak.com) and **Ray's Waterfront** (✉ 1316 4th Ave. ☎ 907/224–5606 ⊕ www.rayswaterfrontak.com) offer seafood with harbor views. Pick up a pint at **Seward Brewing Company** (✉ 139 4th Ave. ☎ 907/422–0337 ⊕ www.sewardbrewery.com) or, for the full Alaska experience (think bright-orange ring buoys and bears in baseball hats on the wall), head to **Yukon Bar** (✉ 201 4th Ave. ☎ 907/224–3063 ⊕ www.facebook.com/yukon.bar).

Stay: Go big and take a 45-minute boat ride to Fox Island for a tranquil night at **Kenai Fjords Wilderness Lodge** (✉ Fox Island, Resurrection Bay ☎ 800/808–8068 ⊕ www.alaskacollection.com). Or check in at the **Van Gilder Hotel** (✉ 308

Essential Listening

Before your trip, listen to Pamyua. This self-described tribal soul band, with members that hail from Alaska and Greenland, combines Inuit drums with funk vocals.

Adams St. ☎ 907/224–5518 ⊕ www. vangilderseward.com) downtown, open since 1916 and listed on the National Register of Historic Places.

Breakfast: Housed in an old church and lined with local artwork, **Resurrect Art** (✉ 320 3rd Ave. ☎ 907/224–7161 ⊕ www. resurrectart.com) is a cozy coffee shop and gallery that's the perfect launch point for a day on the road. Lounge on the choir-loft couches and watch the town wake up through the massive church window, then refill your coffee on the way out the door.

Day 3: Kenai Fjords National Park, AK

12 miles (40 minutes without traffic and stops)

Take a day to explore Kenai Fjords National Park, located a quick boat ride from Seward. Glacier tours dock at the small-boat harbor on Fourth Avenue north of downtown. If you want to explore on foot, drive 3½ miles north on the Seward Highway (Route 9) and turn left on Herman Leirer Road (called Exit Glacier Road by locals). The road parallels Resurrection River and ends at Exit Glacier Nature Center.

This is spectacular coastal parkland incised with sheer, dark, slate cliffs rising from the sea, ribboned with white waterfalls, and tufted with deep-green spruce. Kenai Fjords offers a rare opportunity for an up-close view of blue tidewater glaciers as well as some remarkable ocean wildlife.

AFTERNOON
Nature: Hankering to hike? From the **Exit Glacier Nature Center** (✉ 24620 Herman Leirer Rd., Seward ☎ 907/422–0535 ⊕ www.nps.gov/kefj), it's a straightforward walk to experience views of Exit Glacier. You can also join a ranger for a 90-minute guided walk. More

adventurous types can tackle the Harding Icefield Trail, a strenuous 8.2-mile round-trip hike up the mountain that provides once-in-a-lifetime views of an endless spread of thick, ancient ice.

Photo Op: If you're on a glacier cruise, you don't need our recommendations. The entire ride will be a never-ending photo op as you cruise past calving glaciers and spot orcas, puffins, otters, harbor seals, porpoises, and sea lions.

EVENING
Do: Once you've finished exploring Kenai Fjords, head back to Seward for the night. If you can, make time for the **Alaska Sealife Center** (✉ 301 Railway Ave., Seward ☎ 888/379–2525 ⊕ www.alaska-sealife.org) and its charismatic crew of seals, sea lions, eiders, and octopi. The facility also offers backstage tours, allowing guests to feed puffins in the aviary or get up close with the otters.

Eat & Drink: Flamingo Lounge (✉ 208 4th Ave., Seward ☎ 907/224–3700 ⊕ www. flamingoalaska.com) is a surf-and-turf spot with a red-vinyl Rat Pack vibe. If nothing else, poke your head inside to see the wall-to-wall collection of ceramic decanters. After dinner, scoop up gelato at **Sweet Darling's** (✉ 205 4th Ave., Seward ☎ 907/224–3011 ⊕ www. sweetdarlings.com).

Stay: Get a spot on the water for your second night in Seward. **Harbor 360 Hotel** (✉ 1412 4th Ave. ☎ 907/224–2550 ⊕ www.harbor360hotel.com) is perched on the docks near downtown, while **Windsong Lodge** (✉ 31772 Herman Leirer Rd. ☎ 800/808–8068 ⊕ www. alaskacollection.com) is 2 miles from town along the Resurrection River.

Breakfast: Zudy's Café (✉ 501 Railway Ave., Seward ☎ 907/224–4710 ⊕ www. instagram.com/zudyscafe) sits right on the waterfront, inside Seward's former downtown train station.

A glacier cruise is one of the best ways to see Kenai Fjords National Park.

Day 4: Seward, AK, to Hatcher Pass, AK

182 miles (3 hours, 30 minutes without traffic and stops)

Today might sound a bit confusing, but it's really just two turns. Head north on the Seward Highway (Route 1) all the way back to Anchorage, the state's only big city. Turn right on Sixth Avenue near downtown and take the Glenn Highway (still Route 1) all the way past Palmer. Then turn left on Palmer Fishhook and wind your way into the mountains.

ALONG THE WAY

Town: Home to Alaska's premier ski resort, Girdwood offers outdoor adventures year-round. Stop at **Alyeska Resort** (✉ *1000 Arlberg Ave.* ☎ *907/754–2111* ⊕ *www.alyeskaresort.com*) and soak up some sun on the Adirondack chairs out back, or take the tram to the top of the mountain for a beer and a bite at **Bore Tide Deli & Bar** (✉ *1000 Arlberg Ave.* ☎ *907/754–2237* ⊕ *www.alyeskaresort.com*).

Eat & Drink: While in Girdwood, the **Double Musky Inn** (✉ *Mile 0.3, Crow Creek Rd.* ☎ *907/783–2822* ⊕ *www.doublemuskyinn.com*) offers Cajun seafood dishes and a Mardi Gras vibe. For lighter fare, grab soup and a sandwich at **The Bake Shop** (✉ *194 Olympic Mountain Loop* ☎ *907/783–2831* ⊕ *www.thebakeshop.com*) to enjoy on the picnic tables outside.

Nature: The wide, well-maintained Winner Creek Trail winds through the rain forest from Alyeska Resort to Glacier Creek.

Photo Op: Just one block off your route through Anchorage, the postcard-style *Greetings from Alaska* mural offers a quick stop for a fun photo on your way out of town.

Shop: This is a great time to explore a bit more of Anchorage. Stop by the **Anchorage Museum Store** (✉ *625 C St.* ☎ *907/929–9200* ⊕ *www.anchoragemuseum.org*) to pick up art, books, and jewelry that spotlight Indigenous and northern design. **Oomingmak** (✉ 604 H St. ☎ 907/272–9225 ⊕ www.qiviut.com) is cooperatively owned by hundreds of Alaska Native women across the state who sell their wool crafts in the tiny downtown shop. Housed in an original city building from 1915, **The Kobuk** (✉ 504 W. 5th Ave. ☎ 907/272–3626 ⊕ www. kobukcoffee.com) is a gift shop on Town Square Park with coffee and doughnuts in the back room.

Attraction: If you only have time for one sight in Anchorage, make it the **Alaska Native Heritage Center** (✉ 8800 Heritage Center Dr. ☎ 907/330–8000 ⊕ www. alaskanative.net), which provides an informative introduction to Alaska's Indigenous people, with village exhibits, demonstrations, dances, storytelling, and more.

HATCHER PASS

Do: Hatcher Pass is an all-season playground stocked with glacial lakes, jagged peaks, and alpine meadows to explore. Check out deep-blue Summit Lake just two miles down the gravel Hatcher Pass Road, where you can go late-summer-berry picking anywhere above the treeline and listen for whistling marmots. **Independence Mine State Historical Park** (✉ 23264 Gold Cord Rd., Palmer ⊕ www. dnr.alaska.gov) offers an interpretive trail through a handful of well-preserved buildings from Hatcher Pass's heyday as a gold rush hub.

Eat & Drink: Hatcher Pass Lodge (✉ Mile 17.5 and Fishhook Willow Rd., Gold Cord Rd., Palmer ☎ 907/745–1200 ⊕ www. hatcherpasslodge.com) has a small menu and a bar with incredible views in the main lodge. It's the only option up in the mountains, so consider stopping at the grocery stores along the highway in Palmer if you want something else.

Stay: The colorful A-frame cabins at Hatcher Pass Lodge are a perfect base camp for exploring the area. The

accommodations are certainly basic, but that's just more incentive to get out in the mountains.

Breakfast: Head back down the hill to **Vagabond Blues** (✉ 642 S. Alaska St. ☎ 907/745–2233), a sunny coffee shop and community hub in downtown Palmer.

Day 5: Hatcher Pass, AK, to Talkeetna, AK

91 miles (2 hours without traffic and stops)

If you (and your car) are feeling adventurous, take the 49-mile Hatcher Pass Road for a rugged gravel trek. The road opens after the snow melts, which might not happen until July. If you prefer pavement, drive back through Palmer and hop on the Parks Highway (Route 3) to Talkeetna.

ALONG THE WAY

Town: Start your day with a stroll through Palmer's small downtown, popping your head into the bookstores, galleries, and coffee shops on Alaska Street. The free Palmer Museum is located alongside the visitor center in a log cabin nearby.

Roadside Attraction: The nonprofit **Musk Ox Farm** (✉ 12850 E. Archie Rd. ☎ 907/745–4151) in Palmer houses several dozen musk oxen and collects their fur to make fine qiviut wool. Schedule a tour or pick up some wool at the gift shop.

Eat & Drink: Turkey Red (✉ *550 S. Alaska St.* ☎ *907/746-5544* ⊕ *www.turkeyredak. com*) is a bright café and bakery in Palmer where ingredients are sourced from local businesses and area farms. **Schwabenhof** (✉ *4115 E. Palmer-Wasilla Hwy.* ☎ *907/357–2739*) is an eight-sided log cabin near Wasilla serving beer, brats, and incredible mountain views on the patio.

Detour: Want to climb a mountain but are intimidated by, well, everything you see in all directions? The (relatively) little lump known as Bodenburg Butte, located south of Palmer, offers 360-degree views of the Mat-Su Valley from its 874-foot summit. You just need to pay a small parking fee at the base.

TALKEETNA

Do: At this funky little mountain town, outfitters offer everything from jet boats to zipline tours, though the most celebrated adventure is a flightseeing circuit of Denali. Scoop up snacks at **Nagley's Store** (✉ *13650 E. Main St.* ☎ *907/733–3663* ⊕ *www.nagleysstore.com*), the former home of Talkeetna's cat mayor Stubbs, who died in 2017. Cross the railroad bridge and explore the sandbars where the Talkeetna and Susitna Rivers meet.

Eat & Drink: The porch at **Mountain High Pizza Pie** (✉ *22165 C St.* ☎ *907/733–1234* ⊕ *www.facebook.com/Mountain-HighPizzaPie*) is a favorite for glacier pilots, rafting guides, and mountain climbers. Denali Brewing Company's beers are available at the **Denali Brewpub** (✉ *13605 E. Main St.* ☎ *907/733–2537* ⊕ *www.denalibrewpub.com*). End the night at the **Fairview Inn** (✉ *101 N. Main St.* ☎ *907/733–2423* ⊕ *www. fairviewtalkeetna.com*), a historic building and bar that hosts live bands through the summer.

Stay: One of the state's last operating roadhouses, the **Talkeetna Roadhouse** (✉ *13550 E. Main St.* ☎ *907/733–1351* ⊕ *www.talkeetnaroadhouse.com*) is a can't-miss slice of Alaskan history. Reserve a suite, a bunk, or the "lil cabin in the back." The Roadhouse also offers coin laundry and showers in case you've been car-camping.

Breakfast: Again, it has to be the Talkeetna Roadhouse. With family-style tables inside and rocking chairs on the porch, prepare to swap stories with your neighbors over breakfast scrambles, cinnamon rolls, and coffee.

Day 6: Talkeetna, AK, to Denali National Park, AK

154 miles (2 hours, 30 minutes without traffic and stops)

Drive back down the Talkeetna Spur Road and turn right onto the Parks Highway (Route 3). Get glimpses of Denali as the mighty mountain creeps closer on today's drive. Just outside the entrance to the park, in its northeast corner, you'll find a strip of hotels, restaurants, and shops; this is where you'll most likely stay for the night. You can also head 12 miles north to the town of Healy, which offers a similar collection of restaurants and hotels.

ALONG THE WAY

Nature: Ke'sugi Ken is a recently developed section of **Denali State Park** (☎ *907/745–8950* ⊕ *www.dnr.alaska.gov*) offering camping, cabins, and a pavilion for picnicking. There are also walking paths and the Curry Ridge trailhead, a beginner-friendly 7-mile out-and-back climb to a subalpine lake. Turn right at mile 135.4; Alaska State Parks charges a $5 daily parking fee.

Shop: Stocked with a few things you need and most things you don't, **Wal Mike's** (✉ *Mile 114.8, W. George Parks*

Hwy. ☎ 907/733–2637 ⊕ www.facebook.com/WalMikes), a junk emporium in Trapper Creek, is a worthy stop for Alaska knickknacks and roadside entertainment.

Roadside Attraction: Originally intended as a one-of-a-kind hotel, Igloo City is an abandoned four-story concrete igloo (with windows!) that never opened and now looms forever unfinished just off the highway past mile 188.

DENALI NATIONAL PARK

Do: Alaska's most visited attraction, **Denali National Park and Preserve** (☎ 907/683–9532 ⊕ www.nps.gov/dena) is a 6-million-acre wilderness that offers spectacular mountain views (including of Denali itself, the highest peak in North America), a variety of wildlife, striking vegetation, and unforgettable landscapes. You can drive your own car the first 15 miles of the Denali Park Road, or venture farther with a park bus. During the summer, the National Park Service offers narrated tour buses along with cheaper transit buses that let you hop on and off when you want to explore (just be aware that the Denali Park Road is closed at mile 43 due to a landslide and is not expected to open until summer 2026 at the earliest). You can also go rafting with **New Wave Adventures** (☎ 907/683–2040 ⊕ www.newwaveadventures.com); the last trips leave at 6 pm. Or check out **Cabin Nite Dinner Theatre** (✉ Mile 231, George Parks Hwy. ☎ 800/276–7234 ⊕ www.denaliparkvillage.com) just outside the park entrance for an all-you-can-eat family-style dinner bonanza where the servers are the singers.

Eat & Drink: Prospectors Pizzeria and Alehouse (✉ Mile 238.9, George Parks Hwy. ☎ 907/683–7437 ⊕ www.prospectorspizza.com) serves only-in-Alaska toppings like elk meatballs, reindeer sausage, and king crab. And for something different in this land of burgers and beer, stop by **Thai and Chinese Food To Go** (✉ Mile 238, George Parks Hwy. ☎ 907/306–3545) where the creativity lacking in the name can luckily be found on the menu.

Stay: You'll find plenty of timber-lined lodges popping up around the park gates. Claim a cabin at **Crow's Nest** (✉ Mile 238.5, George Parks Hwy. ☎ 907/683–2723 ⊕ www.denalicrowsnestcabins.com) or a room at **Denali Bluffs Hotel** (✉ Mile 238.4, George Parks Hwy. ☎ 907/683–7000 ⊕ www.denalibluffshotelalaska.com). For a quieter experience, **Tonglen Lake Lodge** (✉ Mile 230, George Parks Hwy. ☎ 907/683–2570 ⊕ www.tonglenlake.com) is a tucked-away bed-and-breakfast 10 miles south of the park.

Breakfast: Head 11 miles north to Healy to find **Rose's Café** (✉ Aurora Denali Lodge, Mile 249, George Parks Hwy. ☎ 907/683–7673). It's not much to look at from the road, but locals love the pancakes and omelets.

Day 7: Denali National Park, AK, to Fairbanks, AK

120 miles (2 hours without traffic and stops)

Spend your morning exploring more of Denali, and then take the Parks Highway (Route 3) north all the way to Fairbanks. Return your dusty, muddy rental car in the morning at Fairbanks International Airport.

ALONG THE WAY

Eat & Drink: 49th State Brewing Company (✉ Mile 248.4, George Parks Hwy. ☎ 907/683–2739 ⊕ www.49statebrewing.com) in Healy is home to a replica of the bus used in the movie Into the Wild (the actual bus where adventurer Christopher McCandless lived was airlifted from its longtime location in a remote corner of Denali in 2020 after several hikers died trying to reach it; its new home is the Museum of the North in Fairbanks). **Golden Eagle Saloon** (✉ 3630

Main St. ☎ *907/479–0809)* is a classic Alaskan dive bar just off the road in Ester, with a big front porch and burgers you grill on your own.

Town: Nenana is best known for its annual Ice Classic, a statewide split-the-pot where Alaskans try to guess the exact minute the Tanana River's melting icepack will lurch forward each spring. The whole thing is endearingly captured in the 2019 documentary *Classic.* Learn more at Nenana's log cabin visitor center.

Detour: Keep driving through Fairbanks for another 14 miles to reach North Pole. It's nothing much, but there's a year-round Christmas store, candy-cane-striped light poles, and a city council member named Santa Claus (of course).

FAIRBANKS

Do: When you arrive in Fairbanks, the main hub of northern Alaska, tour the **Museum of the North** (✉ *1962 Yukon Dr.* ☎ *907/474–7505* ⊕ *www.uaf.edu*) or meet the resident reindeer at the **Large Animal Research Station** (✉ *2220 Yankovich Rd.* ☎ *907/474–5724* ⊕ *www. uaf.edu/lars*); both are part of the University of Alaska–Fairbanks. Paddle through downtown with a two-hour boat rental from **Canoe Alaska** (✉ *1101 Peger Rd.* ☎ *907/457–2453* ⊕ *www.canoealaska.com*). Pick up a last-minute memory at the Alaska Geographic Bookstore, one of many draws at the **Morris Thompson Cultural and Visitors Center** (✉ *101 Dunkel St.* ☎ *907/459–3700* ⊕ *www.morristhompsoncenter.org*).

Eat & Drink: Fairbanks is known for its Thai food, and **Thai House** (✉ *412 5th Ave.* ☎ *907/452–6123* ⊕ *www.thaihousealaska.com*) downtown has been serving pads and satays since 1989. Stop by **HooDoo Brewing Co.** (✉ *1951 Fox Ave.* ☎ *907/459–2337* ⊕ *www.hoodoobrew.com*) to see what food truck is parked at the biergarten. Aviation-inspired **East Ramp Wood-Fired Pizza** (✉ *3788 S. University Ave.* ☎ *907/451–7492* ⊕ *www.*

Essential Listening

Dark Winter Nights is a hilarious, heartwarming, and strange podcast that features Fairbanks residents sharing their stories at live events each winter.

eastramppizza.com) has propellers on the walls and airplane seats in the lobby; pick up a pie and watch planes take off from the airport runway outside.

Stay: Wedgewood Resort (✉ *212 Wedge-wood Dr.* ☎ *800/528–4916* ⊕ *www. fountainheadhotels.com*) includes a wilderness sanctuary, waterfowl refuge, and an impressive antique-auto museum.

Breakfast: The local favorite is **The Cookie Jar** (✉ *1006 Cadillac Ct.* ☎ *907/479–8319* ⊕ *www.cookiejarfairbanks.com*), a breakfast-all-day restaurant with cinnamon rolls to go. Or stop by **Lulu's** (✉ *364 Old Chena Pump Rd.* ☎ *907/374–3804* ⊕ *www.lulusbagels.com*) for breads, spreads, bagels, and coffee.

The Road to Hana

Written by Lehia Apana

California has the Pacific Coast Highway, Italy has the Amalfi Coast, and Australia has the Great Ocean Road. Hawaii's answer? The spectacular Road to Hana on the island of Maui.

Also known as Hana Highway (Routes 36 and 360), this famed drive is a destination in itself: 52 miles of snaking roads, single-lane bridges, and enough blind turns to give you chicken skin. The reward is arriving at one of the last unspoiled Hawaiian frontiers, whose isolation has preserved its rustic beauty and endless charm. Getting there is where

Essential Tips

The Road to Hana is shared by visitors and local residents, so it's understandable that while some drivers are in cruise mode, others simply need to get on with their day. It's good etiquette to pull over if there's a car on your bumper, and to stop only at designated pull-outs. As tempting as it is to get closer to [insert any number of outrageously scenic possibilities here], be sure to respect private property and keep to designated paths.

Cell reception is spotty along the Road to Hana and some areas outside Hana

town, so it's not a bad idea to print or save maps/itineraries for offline use.

If you're prone to motion sickness, you'll want to bring a nausea remedy for the winding drive.

Bring cash, as some roadside vendors aren't set up for credit card transactions.

Grab snacks and/or a picnic lunch in Kahului to tide you over between the scattered food opportunities along the Road to Hana.

the fun starts. The route from central Maui to Hana may seem short—and those in a rush can make the drive within two to three hours—but if you do it right, it should take all day. Along the way you'll see waterfalls, tropical forests, eclectic roadside stands, and enough Pacific Ocean panoramas to fill your camera's memory card for a lifetime.

At a Glance

Start: Kahului Airport, HI

End: Hana, HI

Miles Traveled: 52 miles

Suggested Duration: 1 day

States Visited: Hawaii

Key Sights: Garden of Eden; Haleakala National Park; Twin Falls; Upper Waikani Falls; Waianapanapa State Park

Best Time to Go: This route is popular year-round. The best time of day to start your drive is early morning (from 6 to 7 am). You'll get ahead of the traffic and likely have many stops all to yourself.

Morning: Kahului to Hana

33 miles (1 hour, 15 minutes without traffic and stops)

This route starts near Kahului Airport, where there are plenty of options for renting a car if you haven't already done so. In general, you'll need a vehicle to truly explore Maui, and the Road to Hana is no exception. With so much to see in every direction—including skyward—now's the time to splurge on that convertible or pop-top Jeep.

ALONG THE WAY

Nature: Located near mile marker 2, **Twin Falls** (✉ *6300 Hana Hwy., Haiku* ☎ *808/463–1275* ⊕ *www.twinfalls-maui.net)* is what tropical dreams are made of, and if you time it right, you'll avoid the pesky crowds. Arrive when it opens at 7 am, follow an easy jungle trail to the falls, and enjoy having this natural wonder all to yourself. It's the first of several waterfalls you'll see along your journey.

Attraction: After mile marker 16, Hana Highway changes from Route 36 to Route 360 and the markers start over

The Road to Hana

again. Half a mile past the second 10-mile mark, you'll reach the **Garden of Eden arboretum** (✉ *10600 Hana Hwy., Haiku* ☎ *808/572–9899* ⊕ *www.mauigardenofeden.com*). It's worth a stop if you can spare at least an hour. You'll want enough time to visit the highlights of this 25-acre site, which include a vast collection of ti, one of the original "canoe plants" introduced to Hawaii by the early Polynesians.

Photo Op: Keanae is a tight-knit community known for cultivating the Hawaiian staple crop kalo, or taro, and many residents remain deeply connected to their culture. Marvel in the emerald-hued patchwork of kalo terraces and Pacific panoramas near the Keanae Overlook, near mile marker 17. Alternatively, take the turnoff to Keanae Peninsula located just before the lookout.

Roadside Attraction: Nicknamed "Three Bears," Upper Waikani Falls is a trio of waterfalls located past mile marker 19. They're visible from the roadside, or you can scramble down a short but steep trail to reach the water.

Eat & Drink: Head to the original **Coconut Glen 's** location (✉ *1200 Hana Hwy., Haiku* ☎ *808/248–4876* ⊕ *www.coconutglens.com*) at mile marker 27½ and scoop up some of the creamy coconut-based vegan ice cream in flavors like classic coconut, spicy chili, or *lilikoi* (passion fruit). **Nahiku Marketplace** (✉ *1546 Hana Hwy., Hana*) also has a number of small spots to grab a bite.

Afternoon: Hana to Kipahulu

13 miles (45 minutes without traffic and stops)

By now the serpentine road has straightened out and you've passed the "Welcome to Hana" sign. There's still plenty to experience on this stretch of pavement, including black-sand beaches and waterfalls.

ALONG THE WAY

Nature: Home to a black-sand beach and freshwater caves for adventurous swimmers, **Waianapanapa State Park** (☎ *808/248–4843* ⊕ *www.dlnr.hawaii. gov*) also includes a walkable 3-mile section of the ancient coastal trail known as the King's Highway, built for Maui's famed chief Piilani in the 1500s. The park is located near mile marker 32.

Nature: Turn off Hana Highway near mile marker 51 to arrive at Hamoa Beach, which also boasts black-sand shores, but is more spacious and great for swimming. If you're staying overnight in Hana, consider spending a few additional hours here tomorrow.

Nature: Venture toward Kipahulu on Hana Highway until you reach Oheo Gulch, a cascading series of freshwater pools that empty into the Pacific. Located within **Haleakala National Park** (☎ *808/572–4400* ⊕ *www.nps.gov/hale*), the $30-per-car entrance fee is good for three days and includes entry to Haleakala's Summit District. This is also the start of the 4-mile round-trip Pipiwai Trail, which passes through a bamboo forest and leads to a 400-foot waterfall. You'll find this by mile marker 42 (past Hana, mile markers count down).

Detour: Venture just a few miles past Kipahulu and you'll encounter the drive-by waterfall known as Wailua Falls. It's close enough to spot from the road, and

there's parking nearby for those who want a closer look. From here, backtrack toward Hana.

Evening: Kipahulu to Hana

9.7 miles (30 minutes without traffic and stops)

Hana is the pot of gold at the end of the rainbow. It's worth spending a night or two here so you can explore the town's natural beauty at a leisurely pace. Alternatively, remain in Kipahulu overnight and drive back toward Hana the following day.

ALONG THE WAY

Town: Kipahulu's drive-up camping site is located on a bluff above crashing surf, and includes tables, barbecue grills, and pit toilets. There are zero dining options nearby, so plan to cook under the stars tonight. The campground is within Haleakala National Park, and $8-per-night reservations are required for a campsite.

Eat & Drink: For those heading back to Hana for the night, be warned that few eateries remain open past sunset. **Hana Ranch Restaurant** (✉ *5031 Hana Hwy.* ☎ *808/270–5280* ⊕ *www.hyatt. com*) is an excellent choice that does and features locally sourced ingredients.

Stay: After a long day of exploring, **Hana-Maui Resort** (✉ *5021 Hana Hwy.* ☎ *808/400–1234* ⊕ *www.hyatt. com*) offers a comfy place to rest your head. This landmark hotel oozes island elegance, and its central location makes it a great base for exploring.

The Oahu Coast

Written by Anna Weaver

While road-tripping on an island doesn't seem like it would take too long, there's so much to see and do on Oahu, the busiest island in Hawaii, that you can easily stretch out your travels, seeing

The Road to Hana is filled with narrow, winding roads.

everything "The Gathering Place" has to offer. This six-day itinerary allows you to take in Oahu's beauty, sample its extraordinarily diverse cuisine, and learn more about its rich history and culture while staying at a different spot on the island each night.

If you would prefer not to change hotels every night, you could set up a home base in Waikiki and travel out to each day's destination, though you'd lose some time going back and forth.

At a Glance

Start: Waikiki, HI

End: Honolulu, HI

Miles Traveled: 155 miles

Suggested Duration: 6 days

States Visited: Hawaii

Key Sights: Diamond Head State Monument; Iolani Palace; Kaena Point State Park; Pearl Harbor National Memorial; Waikiki Beach

Best Time to Go: Hawaii can be visited year-round, though you may want to avoid the rainier season from around February through April, which also overlaps with spring break travel.

Day 1: Waikiki, HI

9 miles (20 minutes without traffic and stops)

Today's route is straightforward. Whether you arrive at Honolulu International Airport in the daytime or evening, you'll head straight to Waikiki to settle in for a night (or two) and get your bearings. Don't rent a car just yet so you can avoid pricey hotel parking fees—you can take a rideshare, cab, or TheBus from the airport to your hotel and you'll be able to explore most of Waikiki's shops, restaurants, and its famous beach on foot or via bus/rideshare/cab/trolley.

Do: Get your souvenir shopping out of the way, take a surf lesson at Waikiki Beach, relax with a mai tai by your hotel pool, and dive into Hawaii cuisine. Waikiki stays up late, so now is a good chance to try and break your jet lag while enjoying live music and drinks at the many clubs, bars, and music venues along the Waikiki strip.

Eat & Drink: Take in an oceanfront panorama at the breezy Waikiki location of **Monkeypod Kitchen** (✉ *2169 Kalia Rd.* ☎ *808/900–4226* ⊕ *www.monkeypodkitchen.com*), one of Hawaii restauranteur Peter Merriman's eateries, while sipping a lilikoi-foam mai tai or local beer and dining on casual fare that's often locally sourced. Long-standing beachside favorite **Duke's Waikiki** (✉ *2335 Kalakaua Ave.* ☎ *808/922–2268* ⊕ *www.dukeswaikiki.com*), named after famed Hawaiian surfer Duke Kahanamoku, is known for its tropical cocktails, hula pie, and American Hawaiian casual cuisine.

Stay: If you're okay with a larger, bustling resort, stay at the oceanfront **Sheraton Waikiki** (✉ *2255 Kalakaua Ave.* ☎ *808/922–4422* ⊕ *www.marriott.com*) with its infinity and family pools, cocktails, and light eats at Rumfire, along with plenty of other amenities. For a grander stay, pick the oldest hotel in Waikiki, the **Moana Surfrider** (✉ *2365 Kalakaua Ave.* ☎ *808/922–3111* ⊕ *www.marriott.com*), with both historic and modern rooms and an oceanfront veranda where you can enjoy the popular afternoon tea. For a mid-century-modern-meets-Hawaii vibe in a smaller space, choose the **Laylow** (✉ *2299 Kuhio Ave.* ☎ *808/922–6600* ⊕ *www.marriott.com*).

Breakfast: Before you head out from Waikiki, grab pastries and 100% Kona coffee at **Kona Coffee Purveyors** (✉ *2330 Kalakaua Ave.* ☎ *808/450–2364* ⊕ *www.konacoffeepurveyors.com*) in the International Marketplace. If you'd like a more leisurely breakfast on the way out of Waikiki, head north a bit into Manoa Valley for breakfast on the lanai at **Waioli Kitchen**

& Café (✉ *2950 Mānoa Rd.* ☎ *808/744–1619* ⊕ *www.waiolikitchen.com*). The eatery also serves as a vocational training site for people in recovery for substance abuse and the recently incarcerated.

Day 2: Waikiki, HI, to Kahala, HI

5 miles (20 minutes with no traffic or stops)

There are several car rental options in Waikiki. If you don't want to be spotted a mile away as a tourist, avoid renting a brightly colored convertible. It's a short route between Waikiki and Kahala, so there's plenty of time for stops along the way for hiking and eating; plan about five or six hours for all of today's adventures.

ALONG THE WAY

Nature: Diamond Head National Monument (☎ *808/587–0300* ⊕ *www.dlnr.hawaii.gov*) is where you can spend two hours (round-trip) hiking the extinct volcano's rim for a panoramic view of the south shore. Although it's not an overly arduous hike, you'll want to wear good shoes and have water, a hat, and sunscreen for this mostly unshaded trek. Advance reservations for entry and parking are required and can be made up to 30 days prior.

Eat & Drink: For lunch, head to Kaimuki, where many local foodies like to dine. Celebrity chef Lee Anne Wong runs brunch favorite **Koko Head Café** (✉ *1120 12th Ave.* ☎ *808/732–8920* ⊕ *www.kokoheadcafe.com*). You can also try kalua pig and barbecue at **Surfing Pig Hawaii** (✉ *3605 Waialae Ave.* ☎ *808/744–1992* ⊕ *www.thesurfingpighawaii.com*).

KAHALA

Do: Once you've arrived in upscale Kahala, you can settle in at your hotel and choose to swim with the dolphins at your resort's lagoon, do some shopping at **Kahala Mall** (✉ *4211 Waialae Ave.* ☎ *808/732–7736* ⊕ *www.*

The Oahu Coast

kahalamallcenter.com), or swim and watch the sunset at Kahala Beach. If you're a golfer, there's a neighboring course.

Eat & Drink: Hoku's (✉ *5000 Kahala Ave.* ☎ *808/739–8760* ⊕ *www.hokuskahala.com*) at the Kahala Hotel serves sophisticated island food. A good amount of the fusion menu at **Kapa Hale** (✉ *4614 Kilauea Ave.* ☎ *808/888–2060* ⊕ *www.kapahale.com*) focuses on fresh local produce.

Stay: The mid-century-styled **Kahala Hotel & Resort** (✉ *5000 Kahala Ave.* ☎ *808/739–8888* ⊕ *www.kahalaresort.com*) has excellent service, a small but nice beach and pool, a dolphin lagoon, and several good restaurants.

Breakfast: Grab a quick breakfast at the hotel's Plumeria Beach House or a nearby coffee shop and get on the road to make two morning stops.

Day 3: Kahala, HI, to Kailua, HI

22 miles (45 minutes without traffic and stops)

Today you'll have lots of options for sightseeing stops as you follow the southeastern shoreline and up the windward coast to the beachside community of Kailua. Be sure to pack some snacks to get you through to lunch in Kailua.

ALONG THE WAY

Nature: If you want to swim and snorkel in crystal-clear waters teeming with ocean life, stop at **Hanauma Bay State Park** (✉ *7455 Kalaniana'ole Hwy.* ⊕ *www.honolulu.gov*). The park is open Wednesday through Sunday starting at 6:45 am, and you'll want to be there first thing if you hope to get one of the limited, same-day spots. It's better to try and snag timed entry tickets when they go online two days in advance. This reservation system

Essential Listening

While you're driving in a good signal area, tune in to local radio channels 100.3 (Hawaiian contemporary), 98.5 (reggae), or 105.1 (classic Hawaiian) to get a sense of the wide range of island music.

keeps daily visitors at a manageable level for the bay's fragile ecosystem.

Nature: A lower-pressure morning stop that's still best done first thing to avoid the sun and heat is a hike up the paved **Makapuu Point Lighthouse Trail** (☎ *808/587–0300* ⊕ *www.dlnr.hawaii.gov*). It's especially wonderful during whale-watching season (December through early May), as you'll have a great chance of spotting whale spouts from the lookouts along the trail. Save about two hours for this stop.

Photo Op: You'll see several lookouts or pull-off spots great for photos along the coastline as you drive from Kahala through Hawaii Kai and head toward Waimanalo and Kailua.

KAILUA

Do: Once a quiet beachside town, tourism has found Kailua and its two stretches of beach (Kailua Beach proper and Lanikai, which is trickier to access parking-wise). There are many good places to eat and shop in town, but you'll want to spend most of your time here on the beach. You can also take an easy stroll or bike ride along the **Kawainui Marsh** (☎ *808/768–3003* ⊕ *www.dlnr.hawaii.gov*) trail around sundown to take in the beautiful wetlands and appreciate the way the sun hits the surrounding hillsides at the end of the day.

Oahu's North Shore is one of the most famous surfing destinations in the world.

Eat & Drink: For lunch, **Kalapawai Market** (⌗ 306 S. Kalaheo Ave. ☎ 808/262–4359 ⊕ www.kalapawaimarket.com) is a good grab-and-go spot near the beach. Its sit-down spinoff in Kailua town, **Kalapawai Café and Deli** (⌗ 750 Kailua Rd. ☎ 808/262–3354 ⊕ www.kalapawaimarket.com), has pizzas, burgers, sandwiches, and the like at lunchtime and more upscale fare at dinner (you'll also find another location in Waimanalo on your way to Kailua from Kahala). **Island Snow** (⌗ 130 Kailua Rd. ☎ 808/263–6339 ⊕ www.islandsnow. com) has two locations serving the shave ice that Barack Obama loves. For dinner, **Nico's Kailua** (⌗ 970 N. Kalaheo Ave. ☎ 808/263–3787 ⊕ www.nicoskailua. com) along the canal has delicious and fresh fish dishes and other island-inspired entrées, yummy cocktails, and live music most nights.

Shops: Kailua town is packed with boutiques that sell clothing, jewelry,

household items, swim attire, body products, and more. Bibliophiles will enjoy picking up a beach read or browsing the Hawaiiana and children's sections of the small, independent bookstore **Bookends** (⌗ 600 Kailua Rd. ☎ 808/261–1996 ⊕ www.bookendskailua.com).

Stay: Kailua has no hotels, so you'll want to find a legal B&B or short-term lodging like **Kailua Beach Properties** (☎ 808/261–1653 ⊕ www.patskailua.com). In neighboring Kaneohe, you can choose from cottages or suites at **Paradise Bay Resort** (⌗ 47-039 Lihikai Dr. ☎ 808/239–5711 ⊕ www.paradisebayresort.com).

Breakfast: Grab some local favorite *malassadas,* deep-fried sweet dough rolled in sugar, from the **Agnes' Bake Shop** (⌗ 5 Ho'olai St. ☎ 808/284–4963 ⊕ www. facebook.com/agnesbakeshop) food truck parked in the Manuhealii clothing store lot.

Day 4: Kailua, HI, to Turtle Bay, HI

34 miles (60 minutes without traffic and stops)

On this day, you'll follow what locals consider a classic road trip up the windward coast and ending on the North Shore. There are usually fruit-and-veggie stands and shrimp trucks along the roadsides between Kahaluu and up past Kahuku.

ALONG THE WAY

Detour: Take breakfast or a snack to eat at **Hoomaluhia Botanical Garden** (✉ *45-680 Luluku Rd.* ☎ *808/233–7323* ⊕ *www. honolulu.gov*) in Kaneohe, which is on the way up the coast to the North Shore. Loved by selfie seekers for its lush and photogenic location up against the Koolau Mountains, this sprawling botanical garden has easy walking paths, campsites, and a large man-made fish pond.

Eat & Drink: Next, grab a Hawaiian plate lunch at **Waiahole Poi Factory** (✉ *48-140 Kamehameha Hwy.* ☎ *808/239–2222* ⊕ *www.waiaholepoifactory.com*), where you can eat freshly pounded poi and try the Sweet Lady of Waiahole dessert. Another lunch option is to pick from one of several delicious shrimp trucks and have a garlic shrimp with rice plate lunch. Giovanni's and Romy's are often cited as rivals for the best shrimp truck on Oahu.

Roadside Attraction: At **Tropical Farms Macadamia Nuts** (✉ *49-227 Kamehameha Hwy.* ☎ *808/237–1960* ⊕ *www.macnutfarm.com*), you can browse the country store for souvenirs, coffee, and other foodstuffs, including, of course, macadamia nuts.

Detour: Another potential stop on your way up to the North Shore, **Kualoa Ranch** (✉ *49-560 Kamehameha Hwy.* ☎ *808/237–7321* ⊕ *www.kualoa. com*) is a great place for movie buffs who want to take the film tour highlighting movies and TV shows that have been shot on the ranch's 4,000 acres (*Jurassic Park* was a major one).

Photo Op: Laie Point is a quick off-the-highway stop at a beautiful ocean overlook and sea arch.

TURTLE BAY

Do: After your busy day, settle in at your hotel and enjoy a relaxing dinner.

Eat & Drink: The original **Seven Brothers-Kahuku "At the Mill"** (✉ *56-565 Kamehameha Hwy.* ☎ *808/852-0040* ⊕ *www.sevenbrothersburgers.com*) sells huge burgers, loaded fries, seasonal shakes, fresh salads, and seafood plates.

Stay: A large, oceanfront luxury hotel on the tip of the North Shore, the **Ritz-Carlton O'ahu Turtle Bay** (✉ *57-091 Kamehameha Hwy.* ☎ *808/293–6000* ⊕ *www.turtlebayresort.com*) offers rooms, suites, and bungalows. Its adult and *keiki* (kiddie) pools and beach access will win over the young and old alike.

Breakfast: Grab a coffee and a healthy papaya bowl at the original **Sunrise Shack** (✉ *59-158 Kamehameha Hwy.* ☎ *808/638–0506* ⊕ *www. sunriseshackhawaii.com*) on your way to your morning hike. Or spend a little more time with a sit-down breakfast at **Café Haleiwa** (✉ *66-460 Kamehameha Hwy.* ☎ *808/637–5516* ⊕ *www.cafehaleiwahawaiianislands.com*).

Day 5: Turtle Bay, HI, to Ko Olina, HI

60 miles (1 hour, 40 minutes without traffic and stops)

Today you'll head west from Turtle Bay to enjoy a morning walk out to Kaena Point. Stop at Haleiwa before continuing down the highway to the resort community of Ko Olina. The area you drive through from

Haleiwa to Ko Olina used to be mostly sugarcane and pineapple fields.

ALONG THE WAY

Nature: It can get hot out at **Kaena Point State Park** (⊕ www.dlnr.hawaii.gov), so make the 40-minute drive from Turtle Bay to the North Shore entrance of the gorgeous, wild, and rugged park in the morning. There's little shade so wear a hat and sunscreen and bring water. This nature preserve on the westernmost tip of Oahu is home to native birds, Hawaiian monk seals, and other endangered plants and animals.

Town: On your way back from Kaena Point, stop in Haleiwa for shopping and shave ice, and then drive along the North Shore for a look at its famous surfing beaches. If you're there in the winter, you'll likely catch sight of some big swells.

Eat & Drink: Dine on the lanai at **Haleiwa Beach House** (✉ 62-540 Kamehameha Hwy. ☎ 808/637–3435 ⊕ www.haleiwabeachhouse.com) or take your burgers, sandwiches, and shoestring fries to go from **Kua Aina** (✉ 66-160 Kamehameha Hwy. ☎ 808/637–6067 ⊕ www.kua-aina-hawaii.com) and eat them at the beach.

Detour: After refueling in Haleiwa, you could backtrack to **Waimea Valley** (✉ 59-864 Kamehameha Hwy. ☎ 808/638–7766 ⊕ www.waimeavalley.net) and take the tram or walk the 30 minutes to Waimea Falls. There are changing facilities for those who want to swim at the lifeguard-supervised natural swimming hole. Call ahead to see if the falls are open, as excessively dry or rainy conditions will prevent swimming. On certain days you'll also be able to learn traditional Hawaiian games and go on history and botany walks through the lush grounds.

Roadside Attraction: If you've got a hankering for pineapple Dole Whip, head to the **Dole Plantation** (✉ 64-1550 Kamehameha Hwy. ☎ 808/621–8408 ⊕ www.doleplantation.com), but skip the souvenir-stuffed store and pick-a-pearl vendors and walk around back to where the café is. Kids may like to try the pineapple maze and train ride through agriculture fields.

KO OLINA

Do: Ko Olina was transformed from agricultural land to a resort area in the early 1990s. Its four man-made lagoons and a few natural ones make this area perfect for swimming and snorkeling.

Eat & Drink: If you've been longing for a luau, **Paradise Cove** (✉ 92-1089 Ali'inui Dr. ☎ 808/842–5911 ⊕ www.paradisecove.com) has arguably the most entertaining one on the island. **Mina's Fish House** (✉ 92-1001 Olani St. ☎ 808/679–0079 ⊕ www.michaelmina.net) is an oceanfront fine-dining establishment where fish sommeliers will help you pick the perfect island fish dish.

Stay: If you're a Disney family, splurge on **Aulani** (✉ 92-1185 Ali'inui Dr. ☎ 866/443–4763 ⊕ www.disneyaulani.com), with its nicely appointed rooms and large complex of pools, slides, and other water features available for hotel guests only. **The Four Seasons Resort Oahu at Ko Olina** (✉ 92-1001 Olani St. ☎ 808/679–0079 ⊕ www.fourseasons.com) is your most upscale choice with great restaurants. **Marriott's Ko Olina Beach Club** (✉ 92-161 Waipahe Pl. ☎ 808/679–4700 ⊕ www.marriott.com) has villas and standard guest rooms along with some impressive pools.

Breakfast: On your way out of town, grab an acai bowl and coffee at **Island Vintage Coffee** (✉ 92-4450 Kapolei Pkwy. ☎ 808/312–1416 ⊕ www.islandvintagecoffee.com).

Day 6: Ko Olina, HI, to Honolulu, HI

25 miles (35 minutes without traffic and stops)

Today you'll wrap up your Oahu road trip by driving back to Honolulu, stopping on the way to tour Pearl Harbor, and ending in Chinatown and downtown Honolulu. You'll drop off your rental car and fly out of Honolulu International Airport the next day.

ALONG THE WAY

Detour: Not too far off your path between Ko Olina and Honolulu is **Pearl Harbor National Memorial** (✉ *1 Arizona Memorial Pl.* ☎ *808/422–3399* ⊕ *www.nps.gov/perl*), marking the spot of the attack that launched America into World War II. Reserve your tickets in advance to go out to the USS *Arizona* Memorial over the sunken battleship of the same name. World War II buffs may also want to visit the USS *Bowfin* Submarine Museum and Park, the Battleship *Missouri* Memorial, and the Pearl Harbor Aviation Museum.

Eat & Drink: Helena's Hawaiian Food (✉ *1240 N. School St.* ☎ *808/845–8044* ⊕ *www.helenashawaiianfood.com*) serves some of the best Hawaiian food on the island.

Detour: Bishop Museum (✉ *1525 Bernice St.* ☎ *808/847–3511* ⊕ *www.bishopmuseum.org*) will teach you much about Hawaiian and Pacific Islander history and culture, with special attention given to the Hawaiian monarchy.

HONOLULU

Do: Along with showing you how 19th-century Hawaiian royals lived, a tour of **Iolani Palace** (✉ *364 S. King St.* ☎ *808/522–0822* ⊕ *www.iolanipalace.org*) will teach you about the monarchy's tragic history and how the United States overthrew the Hawaiian Kingdom in 1893. Other historic buildings you can walk to are the state capitol building, the city and county headquarters at Honolulu Hale, the King Kamehameha statue outside Aliiolani Hale, and the former Armed Services YMCA building that is now the state art museum, Capitol Modern.

Eat & Drink: Many of Oahu's most innovative restaurants are in Chinatown. Among them is **The Pig and the Lady** (✉ *83 N. King St.* ☎ *808/585–8255* ⊕ *www.thepigandthelady.com*), serving modern Vietnamese cuisine, and award-winning **Senia** (✉ *75 N. King St.* ☎ *808/200–5412* ⊕ *www.restaurantsenia.com*), a small, upscale, and inventive restaurant. The once-industrial **Kakaako** (⊕ *www.ourkakaako.com*) neighborhood is now a lively, mural-strewn area known for its dining and shopping.

Shop: Chinatown is full of an eclectic mix of stores. You might want to walk through **Maunakea Marketplace** (✉ *1120 Maunakea St.*) and **Kekaulike Market** (✉ *1039 Kekaulike St.*) just to marvel at the diversity of foods and goods for sale. Consider taking a guided food or culture tour through the area, like the twice-weekly tours offered by the **Hawaii Heritage Center** (✉ *1040 Smith St.* ☎ *808/521–2749* ⊕ *www.hawaiiheritagecenter.org*). You can also stop by the sprawling **Ala Moana Shopping Center** (✉ *1450 Ala Moana Blvd.* ☎ *808/955–9517* ⊕ *www.alamoanacenter.com*) and **Ward Village's South Shore Market** (✉ *1170 Auahi St.* ☎ *808/591–8411* ⊕ *www.wardvillage.com*) for last-minute gifts for others or yourself.

Stay: Check in to the **Ala Moana Hotel** (✉ *410 Atkinson Dr.* ☎ *808/955–4811* ⊕ *www.alamoanahotelhonolulu.com*) for an affordable and centrally located Honolulu hotel on your last night in Hawaii.

Breakfast: If you have time before heading to the airport, grab a satisfying, local-style breakfast and delicious pastries at **Liliha Bakery**'s Macy's Ala Moana location

(✉ *1450 Ala Moana Blvd.* ☎ *808/944–4088* ⊕ *www.lilihabakery.com*). It's also a convenient last chance for some shopping after you eat.

The Best of Puerto Rico

Written by Jessica van Dop DeJesus

It's easy to have a typical Caribbean vacation in Puerto Rico, but this island offers much more than just sun and sand. By renting a car and exploring beyond the standard tourist areas of San Juan and its surrounding beaches, you'll get a deeper sense of the vibrant island, from its lush countryside and expansive mountain valleys to its booming culinary scene and fascinating history. But, of course, you'll still have time for some beach days over this seven-day adventure that takes you around the island's perimeter, with stops in legendary beach towns like Ponce and Rincon.

At a Glance

Start: San Juan, PR

End: San Juan, PR

Miles Traveled: 356 miles

Suggested Duration: 6 days

Territories Visited: Puerto Rico

Key Sights: Bosque Estatal de Guánica; El Yunque National Forest; Las Cavernas de Camuy; Luquillo Beach; Old San Juan

Best Time to Go: Puerto Rico is a great place to visit year-round. May through August is considered the low season with lower hotel rates and less crowds. Be mindful when traveling in September, October, and early November, as these are the prime months of hurricane season; sporadic rainy days are standard during this time of year.

Day 1: San Juan, PR, to Fajardo, PR

37 miles (45 minutes without traffic and stops)

When you arrive in Puerto Rico, pick up your rental car at the San Juan International Airport (SJU). There are plenty of rental car agencies in the terminal. Take Route 3 and cruise through San Juan and Carolina, the bustling city surrounding San Juan. Once you leave the San Juan metro area, you will start seeing the lush green mountains that encompass the El Yunque rain forest to your right and turquoise blue beaches to your left.

ALONG THE WAY

Detour: As you head out of San Juan, take a 20-minute detour to Piñones, where you can enjoy *coco frío* (cold coconut water) and snacks with a beachside view.

Nature: The northeast coast of Puerto Rico is known for the must-see **El Yunque National Forest** (☎ *787/888–1880* ⊕ *www.fs.usda.gov*). The only tropical forest in the U.S. Forest System, El Yunque is home to hundreds of endemic species of birds and plants.

Photo Op: Located a few miles from the El Yunque entrance, La Coca Falls is a stunning spot to take a photo.

Town: After a hike in El Yunque, head to Luquillo Beach in the upbeat, sunny town of Luquillo to take a dip in the crystal clear, calm waters. It's one of the most popular beaches on Puerto Rico's northeast coast. If you're into surfing, check out the swells at nearby La Pared Beach.

Eat & Drink: Grab a bite to eat at one of Luquillo Beach's kiosks; these small restaurants offer a variety of Puerto Rican fried snacks. One of the best is **Terruño Comida Artesanal** (☎ *787/889–8989*), which offers a casual yet elevated version of Puerto Rican beach classics like *bacalaitos* (fried cod), *mofongo*, and rice dishes.

The Best of Puerto Rico

FAJARDO

Do: A coastal city on the northeastern tip of Puerto Rico, Fajardo is home to several interesting attractions. Seven Seas is a stunning beach perfect for swimming, while Las Croabas is home to a marina with local fishermen and **Las Cabezas de San Juan** (☎ 787/722–5882), a nature reserve offering magnificent views (you can also take a kayak tour to explore the stunning bioluminescent bay).

Eat & Drink: One of the most beloved restaurants in the area is **La Estación** (✉ *Carr. 987, Km 4.20* ☎ *787/863–4481* ⊕ *www. laestacionpr.com*), which serves Nuyorican-style barbecue and other Puerto Rican fusion dishes. Enjoy the slow-cooked barbecued pork over ripe plantains or a whole fried red snapper. Or at **Rincón del Faro** (✉ *Carr. 987, Km 5.2* ☎ *787/863–0028* ⊕ *www.instagram. com/rincondelfarofajardo*), you can enjoy lighthouse views and a seafood-forward menu on an ample patio.

Stay: Book a vacation rental at **Las Casitas** (✉ *1000 El Conquistador Ave.* ☎ *787/863–1000* ⊕ *www.lascasitas-village.com*); adjacent to El Conquistador Resort, these colorful little houses come with amenities such as private pools and idyllic sea views.

Breakfast: Founded by a former engineer, **Aroma Cafe** (✉ *100 Calle Unión* ☎ *787/567–5173*) offers pastries and various drinks made with local coffee beans. Or cozy **Panadería Monte Brisas** (☎ *787/863–3363*) sells pastries, coffee, and delicious ham-egg-and-cheese sandwiches.

Day 2: Fajardo, PR, to Cayey, PR

58 miles (1 hour, 15 minutes without traffic and stops)

Driving from Fajardo to Cayey takes you through the winding roads of the Cordillera Central, the mountain range that traverses the entire island of Puerto Rico. Keep your eye out for plenty of greenery, colorful mountainside homes, and fantastic views.

ALONG THE WAY

Detour: As you leave Fajardo, take a quick 20-minute detour to Salto (Charco) El Hippie, a stunning freshwater swimming hole.

Town: Almost halfway through today's drive, you'll encounter the city of Humacao. This coastal town is home to a natural reserve and a fun boardwalk area with restaurants and bars.

Nature: Stop by the **Humacao Nature Reserve** (☎ *787/397–1900*), where you can rent bikes or kayaks to explore the unique mangrove vegetation surrounding the area.

Eat & Drink: The farm and restaurant known as **Bacoa** (✉ *Carr. 31, Km 22* ☎ *939/342–4691* ⊕ *www.bacoapr. com*) in the town of Juncos is the perfect stop for lunch (just note that it's closed Tuesday and Wednesday). The restaurant specializes in local ingredients cooked over an open flame.

Photo Op: Go for a stroll at La Plaza de Recreo in the town of Caguas. This cozy town square is lined with colonial architecture.

Nature: Carite State Park covers several municipalities leading to the town of Cayey. The dense green forest leads to one of the largest lakes in Puerto Rico.

CAYEY

Do: Nestled in the middle of the Cordillera Central, the mountain town of Cayey offers spectacular views of the island. In addition, it's home to the most *lechoneras* (restaurants specializing in roasted pork) in all of Puerto Rico.

Eat & Drink: A lechonera located in the mountains of Cayey, **El Cuñao** (✉ *Bo Pedro Avila Carr. 1, Km 65.5* ☎ *787/263–0511* ⊕ *www.lechoneraspr.com*) serves

The colorful streets of San Juan are filled with history.

excellent roasted pork with classic sides like *arroz con gandules* (rice and pigeon peas) and stewed tropical root vegetables such as yucca and taro root. **El Mesón de Melquiades** (✉ *Carr. 15, Ramal 741* ☎ *787/738–4083* ⊕ *www.elmesonde-melquiades.com*) is an upscale restaurant serving Puerto Rican classics like cod stew and pork chops.

Stay: El Pretexto (✉ *Carr. 715* ⊕ *www.elpretextopr.com*) is a stunning "culinary farm lodge" located in the mountains of Cayey. The property also hosts a series of renowned communal-table dinners that are open to outside guests. For something even more rustic, pack your camping gear for a night at **Cercadillo Camp Grounds** (⊕ *www.facebook.com/CercadilloCampGrounds*), which offers campsites, bathrooms, and other essential camping amenities.

Breakfast: Montellano Bakery (✉ *Carr. 14, Km 72.4* ☎ *787/301–0891*) is a mainstay in Cayey, selling coffee, pastries, and sandwiches.

Day 3: Cayey, PR, to Ponce, PR

45 miles (1 hour without traffic and stops)

As you drive from Cayey to Ponce, the largest city on the southern coast of Puerto Rico, you'll travel past several southern coastal towns. The easiest and fastest way to get to Ponce is Route 52.

ALONG THE WAY

Detour: On your way to Ponce, take a 30-minute detour to **Pozuelo,** a fishing area in Guayama, Puerto Rico. You can kayak through the mangroves or have lunch at one of the many small restaurants in the area.

Eat & Drink: Enjoy seafood on the beach at **Ladi's Place** (✉ *Calle A-86, Playa de Salinas* ☎ *787/824–1900* ⊕ *www.ladisrestaurant.com*), in the coastal town of Salinas. The restaurant's patio is pretty much right on the sandy beach; if you're there late enough, you can catch a stunning sunset.

Nature: Take a detour to the town of Coamo and relax for an hour or two in the **Coamo Hot Springs** (✉ *Río Coamo* ☎ *787/825–6668*).

Roadside Attraction: You can't miss the "Letras de Ponce" as you enter Ponce from Route 52. These gigantic red letters spell out the town's name, giving you a warm welcome.

PONCE

Do: Known as the "Pearl of the South", Ponce is a cultural hub for the island, with several well-known museums like the **Museo de Arte de Ponce** (✉ *2325 Av. Las Américas* ☎ *787/840–1510* ⊕ *www.museoarteponce.org*) and the **Museum of Puerto Rican Music** (✉ *42 Calle Reina Isabel*). No trip to Ponce is complete without a photo at the **Parque de Bombas,** the classic red-and-black fire station erected for the 1882 World's Fair. It was a working fire station until 1990, when it became a museum.

Eat & Drink: A quaint restaurant located in Ponce city center, **Chef's Creations** (✉ *100 Calle Reina Isabel* ☎ *787/848–8384* ⊕ *www.facebook.com/chefscreations*) specializes in open-fire dishes. You will most likely catch the lively owner, chef Jorge Rivera, chatting with the guests. Afterwards, sample craft cocktails alongside ocean views at **El Marlin** (✉ *Calle Atocha* ☎ *787/315–0334* ⊕ *www.facebook.com/william.collazo23*), a fun cocktail bar located within La Plaza de Mercado; don't leave without sampling a flaming tiki cocktail.

Shop: La Plaza de Mercado de Ponce is an indoor/outdoor market specializing in locally made artwork, local produce, and drinks.

Stay: The centrally located **Boutique Hotel Belgica** (✉ *122 Calle Villa* ☎ *787/844–3255* ⊕ *www.hotelbelgica.com*) is a quaint hotel in a beautiful colonial building in the heart of the city center.

Breakfast: Grab a toasted Mallorca bread and a cortado at **Melao Bakery** (✉ *Calle Union* ☎ *787/813–5050*) located in Ponce's town square.

Day 4: Ponce, PR, to Rincón, PR

60 miles (1 hour, 35 minutes without traffic and stops)

Take Route 2 along the southern coast of Puerto Rico and head north to the town of Rincón, which has plenty of beaches and attractions. One day might not be enough, so this is the perfect place to extend your trip for a day or two.

ALONG THE WAY

Nature: Did you know that Puerto Rico has a dry forest? The Bosque Estatal de Guánica is a subtropical dry forest located on the southwest coast of Puerto Rico. Plants such as cacti surround the forest, an interesting contrast from the rain forest on the northeast coast.

Roadside Attraction: The **Casas de Colores of Yauco** (✉ *29-37 Calle E. Sanchez Lopez*) are a colorful spectacle located in the city center of Yauco. Although the colorful homes are popular with tourists, locals still live in them.

Town: San Germán is one of the oldest towns in Puerto Rico and home to one of the first Catholic churches in the Americas, Porta Coeli, built in 1609. Situated in a valley, the city center is surrounded by mountains and lined with colonial architecture.

Detour: Cabo Rojo is a 30-minute detour, but you will find some of the most tranquil beaches in Puerto Rico here. One highlight is Combate Beach, a stunning beach straddling a nature reserve. And don't miss the Salinas de Cabo Rojo; its pink salt flats make a fantastic backdrop for a photo.

Eat & Drink: Annie's Place (✉ *101 Rte. 101* ☎ *787/254–2553* ⊕ *www.instagram. com/anniesplaces*), a fun, beachside restaurant in Cabo Rojo, makes a mean passion-fruit mojito. If you come for dinner, it also has one of the most beautiful sunsets on the island.

Photo Op: Head to Punta Guaniquilla Nature Reserve to take a photo with surreal rock formations over 11 million years old.

RINCÓN

Do: The lively town of Rincón is known for its surfing community. People come from all over the globe to catch the waves here, especially during the winter months when the swells are very high. The town and its surroundings are laid-back and ideal for relaxing by the beach.

Eat & Drink: Have a delicious dinner at cozy **Estela** (✉ *Carr. 115, Km 14* ☎ *787/823–1795* ⊕ *www.estelarest. com*), which mixes global flavors with local ingredients. Or you can treat yourself to fresh fish tacos made with the catch of the day at **La Cambija** (✉ *Calle Cambija* ☎ *787/823–1118* ⊕ *www.insta-gram.com/lacambija*), a popular beach spot. For something unique, **Gylro** (✉ *24 Calle Muñoz Rivera* ☎ *787/291–7410*) calls itself a "Greekrican" restaurant, specializing in gyros with a Puerto Rican twist; it's also known for its creative cocktails and live music on the weekends.

Shop: Every Thursday night, the Rincón city center hosts an art market with local artisans.

Stay: The private villas at the **Horned Dorset Primavera** (✉ *Carr. 429, Km 3* ☎ *787/823–4030* ⊕ *www.horneddorset.net*) are the epitome of luxury. The properties have private pools, unique decor, and stunning ocean views. With picture-perfect bohemian decor, the **English Rose** (✉ *Carr. 413, Km 2* ☎ *787/823–4032* ⊕ *www. theenglishroserincon.com*) in Rincón is a more affordable favorite. Perched on a

Essential Listening

Some must-haves for your playlist for your Puerto Rico road trip include: a classic salsa mix with Marc Anthony, Gran Combo de Puerto Rico, and Hector Lavoe; Plena Libre, a long-standing Puerto Rican band specializing in traditional *plena* music; the Afro-Puerto Rican sounds of *bomba* music that originated in the town of Ponce; and laid-back Puerto Rican reggae from Cultura Profetica.

hill, the property offers stunning views of the coastline.

Breakfast: A local chain originating in the neighboring town of Mayaguez, **Ricomini** (✉ *Rte. 115, Km 12* ☎ *787/823–5707*) is known for its pastries, especially its guava jelly roll.

Day 5: Rincón, PR, to Lares, PR

31 miles (1 hour without traffic or stops)

Head deep into the Cordillera Central as you travel from Rincón to Lares, a historic small town in the center of Puerto Rico. Route 111 provides a dazzling scenic route through the countryside with lush vegetation, rivers, and waterfalls.

ALONG THE WAY

Detour: Head to the town of Aguadilla to one of the best-known beaches in Puerto Rico, Crashboat Beach. The pier has survived multiple hurricanes and is the perfect place for an adventurous dive.

Town: San Sebastián is another well-known mountain town in Puerto Rico, with several coffee-producing farms.

Eat & Drink: A local farm in San Sebastián, **Hacienda la Fe** (✉ *Rte. 111, Km 18.7* ☎ *787/638–0656* ⊕ *www.facebook. com/haciendalafepr*) has an on-site restaurant with Puerto Rican favorites such as mofongo (mashed, fried green plantains topped with meat or seafood).

Photo Op: The area known as Gozalandia is home to Los Robles waterfall, and the family who owns the land also manages the parking lot and runs a small restaurant and bar. The waterfall is a short 20-minute hike from the parking lot.

LARES

Do: Lares is a small town (population 3,925), but you can use it as a base to explore the center of the island. For history buffs, Lares played an important role in Puerto Rico's independence from Spain; in 1868, it was the location of an armed uprising called El Grio de Lares. This was the first major revolt against Spanish colonial rule on the island.

Eat & Drink: Located in a scenic part of Lares, the small, locally owned **El Sartén de Fary** (✉ *Carr. 135, Km 5.1, Castan-er* ☎ *787/404–8846* ⊕ *www.instagram. com/el.sartende.fary*) serves breakfast, lunch, and dinner. And when you're in Lares, you have to go to **Heladería Lares** (✉ *10 Calle Vilella* ☎ *787/378–4288*) to sample their famous ice cream. The shop has been around for decades, and is known for unique flavors like rice-and-beans along with more standard flavors.

Stay: The **Hacienda El Jibarito** (✉ *Carr. 445m Km 6.5* ☎ *787/280–4040* ⊕ *www. haciendaeljibarito.com*), located in San Sebastián, makes for a lovely farm-stay experience. The farm grows its own coffee beans and provides tours of the property. Local and family-owned, **Adjuntas Riverside** (✉ *PR123 Km 36.6 Int PR522 Km 0.1* ☎ *787/829–1717* ⊕ *www. facebook.com/ParadorVillasSotomayor*) provides campgrounds available on their sprawling farm, with spectacular views of Adjuntas.

Breakfast: One of the best-known coffee makers in Puerto Rico, **Café Lareño** (✉ *Carr. 128, Km 5.7* ☎ *787/897–7762* ⊕ *www.cafelarenopr.com*) has a small café where you can grab a coffee and pastries. The coffee farm also offers tours.

Day 6: Lares, PR, to San Juan, PR

125 miles (2 hours, 45 minutes without traffic and stops)

This route will take you from the center of Puerto Rico to its northern coast and back to San Juan. You will go from the mountains to the Atlantic Ocean, lined with plenty of charming beaches.

ALONG THE WAY

Nature: Puerto Rico is home to the third most extensive underground cave system in the world, **Las Cavernas de Camuy** (✉ *Carr. 129, Km 18.9* ☎ *787/898–3136*). Take some time to explore its winding trails and massive sinkhole on a guided tour.

Town: Arecibo is a seaside town with several beaches, a marina, and a lighthouse. It's also home to **Cueva la Ventana** (✉ *Rte. 10, Km 75* ☎ *787/322–3554* ⊕ *cuevaventana.com*), a famed "window cave" that provides stunning views of the island's northwestern coast. Make sure to buy tickets online ahead of time to secure a spot.

Eat & Drink: Get your seafood fix at lively beachside **Salitre Mesón Costero** (✉ *Rte. 681, Km 3.8* ☎ *787/816–2020* ⊕ *www. salitre.com*) in Arecibo. The menu features locally caught fish like yellowfin tuna, red snapper, and wahoo.

SAN JUAN

Do: As the capital of Puerto Rico, San Juan is one of the island's most popular tourist destinations. Take some time to explore the cobblestone streets of Old

Did You Know?

San Juan's Condado Lagoon offers many water activities, including paddleboarding and canoeing. While on the water, you might see any number of endangered species that call the lagoon home, including the brown pelican, the magnificent frigatebird, and the North American manatee.

San Juan, one of the oldest cities in the Americas. Be sure to climb to the top of **El Castillo de San Felipe del Morro** (✉ *501 Calle Norzagaray* ☏ *787/729–6960* ⊕ *www.nps.gov/saju*), which was built in the 1400s to protect San Juan from pirates. Paddleboard along the Condado Lagoon, and you may spot a manatee or two.

Eat & Drink: At **Orujo** (✉ *906 Av. Juan Ponce de León* ☏ *939/282–3524* ⊕ *www.orujotaller.com*), the tasting menu is a favorite among local foodies; chef Carlos Portela focuses on local ingredients and classic techniques here, like ripe plantains topped with shredded short rib. Located in the heart of La Placita de Santurce (the city's hopping nightlife district), **Santaella** (✉ *219 Calle Canals* ☏ *787/722–7600* ⊕ *www.josesantaella.com*) is a beloved spot for locals and tourists alike, thanks to the inventive dishes like shredded green plantains topped with crab and Japanese seaweed salad. Afterward head to **Junglebird** (✉ *254 Calle Canals* ⊕ *www.instagram.com/junglebird-bar*), known for its clever cocktails and impressive bar menu from James Beard–nominated chef Paxx Caraballo.

Stay: Women-owned **La Botánica Hotel** (✉ *1808 Av. McLeary* ☏ *787/646–4012* ⊕ *www.labotanicahotel.com*) focuses on Ayurvedic techniques in its acclaimed spa, offering facials, massages, and other healing methods. Tucked into a small side street in Old San Juan, **Villa Herencia** (✉ *23 Caleta de las Monjas* ☏ *844/468–3577* ⊕ *www.facebook.com/VillaHerenciaHotel*) is a quaint small hotel with antique furniture and quirky art.

Breakfast: A longtime favorite, **Kasalta** (✉ *1966 Av. McLeary* ☏ *787/727–7340* ⊕ *www.kasalta.com*) has some of the best pastries in San Juan. Order a cortado with a *quesito* (a puff pastry filled with sweetened cream cheese).

Index

Photo Credits

Fodor's BEST ROAD TRIPS IN THE USA

Publisher: Stephen Horowitz, *General Manager*

Editorial: Douglas Stallings, *Editorial Director;* Jill Fergus, Amanda Sadlowski, *Senior Editors;* Brian Eschrich, Alexis Kelly, *Editors;* Angelique Kennedy-Chavannes, Yoojin Shin, *Associate Editors*

Design: Tina Malaney, *Director of Design and Production;* Jessica Gonzalez, *Senior Designer;* Jaimee Shaye, *Graphic Design Associate*

Production: Jennifer DePrima, *Editorial Production Manager;* Elyse Rozelle, *Senior Production Editor;* Monica White, *Production Editor*

Maps: Rebecca Baer, *Map Director;* Mark Stroud (Moon Street Cartography), *Cartographer*

Photography: Viviane Teles, *Director of Photography;* Namrata Aggarwal, Neha Gupta, Payal Gupta, Ashok Kumar, *Photo Editors;* Jade Rodgers, Shanelle Jacobs, *Photo Production Interns*

Business and Operations: Chuck Hoover, *Chief Marketing Officer;* Robert Ames, *Group General Manager*

Public Relations and Marketing: Joe Ewaskiw, *Senior Director of Communications and Public Relations*

Fodors.com: Jeremy Tarr, *Editorial Director;* Rachael Levitt, *Managing Editor*

Technology: Jon Atkinson, *Executive Director of Technology;* Rudresh Teotia, *Associate Director of Technology;* Alison Lieu, *Project Manager*

Writers: Kristy Alpert, Lehia Apana, Joey Besl, Margot Bigg, Cassandra Brooklyn, Katherine Chou, Andrew Collins, Amber Gibson, Kristine Hansen, Aimee Heckel, Barbara Noe Kennedy, Chanté LaGon, Stratton Lawrence, Shoshi Parks, Jessica Poitevien, Elise Riley, Brandon Schultz, Jen Rose Smith, Mark Sullivan, Jessica van Dop DeJesus, Stefanie Waldek, Anna Weaver

Editor: Amanda Sadlowski

Production Editor: Elyse Rozelle

2nd Edition

ISBN 978-1-64097-784-6

ISSN 2769-4909

SPECIAL SALES

This book is available at special discounts for bulk purchases for sales promotions or premiums. For more information, e-mail SpecialMarkets@fodors.com.

PRINTED IN TURKEY

10 9 8 7 6 5 4 3 2 1

About Our Writers

 Margot Bigg is a freelance travel writer and editor based in Portland, Oregon. She's lived and worked all over the world, most recently in India, where she worked at *Time Out Magazine* and contributed to the last three editions of *Fodor's Essential India*. Though now back in the States, she continues to contribute to a variety of Indian publications, including local editions of *Rolling Stone* and *National Geographic Traveler*, as well as U.S. publications ranging from *Sunset Magazine* to *VICE*. Margo updated the West Coast chapter for this edition.

 Former Fodor's staff editor **Andrew Collins** is based in Mexico City but spends a good bit of the year traveling throughout the United States, especially northern New Mexico, where he formerly resided. A longtime contributor to more than 200 Fodor's guidebooks, he's also a regular contributor to The Points Guy travel website. He's also written for dozens of mainstream and LGBTQ+ publications, and he teaches travel writing and food writing for New York City's Gotham Writers Workshop. You can find more of his work at ⊕ *AndrewsTraveling.com*, and follow him on Instagram at @TravelAndrew. He updated the Experience, Trips of a Lifetime, and Northeast chapters this edition.

Based in Milwaukee, Wisconsin, **Kristine Hansen** loves to hit the road to explore what's beyond her city and doesn't hesitate to pull over for a cute café or Frank Lloyd Wright–designed home. She's the author of *Wisconsin Cheese Cookbook: Creamy, Cheesy, Sweet, and Savory Recipes from the State's Best Creameries and Wisconsin Farms* and *Farmers Markets: Tours, Trails and Attractions*. She updated the Midwest and the Plains chapter this edition.

 Aimee Heckel is a Colorado native who has been working at Colorado newspapers for nearly two decades. She's the head writer for TravelBoulder. com, the Colorado travel expert for Tripsavvy, and a book editor. Heckel also freelances for the *Boulder Daily Camera* and has worked as a regular travel writer for *USA Today* ⊕ *10Best.com*. She updated the West and the Rockies chapter this edition.

Shoshi Parks is a freelance writer, outdoor adventurer, and avid road-tripper from San Jose, CA. As a Ph.D. in anthropology, her work focuses on travel, history, food, and heritage in the U.S. and around the globe. Her writing has appeared in Atlas Obscura, *Smithsonian Magazine*, *Afar*, NPR, *Bon Appetit*, and elsewhere. Find her at ⊕ *shoshiparks. net*. She updated the Southwest and Texas chapter this edition.

Brandon Schultz is a travel and lifestyle writer who loves experiencing the world and telling others about it. He enjoys everything from luxury resort getaways to road trips and couchsurfing adventures, and believes that where you travel is often less important than how you travel. He's the author of six books and lives in Brooklyn, New York. He updated the Southeast and Florida chapter this edition.

About Our Writers

Writer and multimedia journalist **Anna Weaver** is a sixth-generation *kamaaina,* born and raised in Kailua, O'ahu. She can never get enough Spam *musubi, malassadas,* or hiking time in her home state. Anna has written for *Slate, Simplemost,* and such Hawaii publications as the *Honolulu Advertiser* (now *Star-Advertiser*), *Honolulu Magazine,* and *Pacific Business News.* She updated the Outside the Lower 48 chapter this editon.

In addition, the road trips in this book were originally written by the following writers: **Kristy Alpert, Lehia Apana, J. Besl, Cassandra Brooklyn, Katherine Chou, Amber Gibson, Barbara Noe Kennedy, Stratton Lawrence, Chanté LaGon, Jessica Poitevien, Elise Riley, Jen Rose Smith, Mark Sullivan, Jessica van Dop DeJesus,** and **Stefanie Waldek**.